Resource Records of Pike/Walthall Counties Mississippi, 1798–1910

CONTAINING A COMPLETE REPRINT OF
PIKE COUNTY, MISSISSIPPI
1798–1876

Pioneer Families and Confederate Soldiers
Reconstruction and Redemption
by
Luke Ward Conerly

and

Miscellaneous Legal and Family Records Pertaining to the Areas of Pike and Walthall Counties, Mississippi
by
E. Russ Williams, Jr.

New Material Copyright 1978
By: The Silas Emmett Lucas, Jr.

All rights reserved. No part of this publication may be reproduced, stored in a retrieval system or transmitted in any form or by any means without the prior written permission of the publisher.

Please direct all correspondence and orders to:

SOUTHERN HISTORICAL PRESS, Inc.
PO BOX 1267
375 West Broad Street
Greenville, SC 29601
southernhistoricalpress@gmail.com

ISBN #0-89308-104-3

TABLE OF CONTENTS

PART I

	Page
PIKE COUNTY, MISSISSIPPI, 1798-1876, by Luke Ward Conerly	1-368

PART II

13TH REGIMENT, MISSISSIPPI MILITIA	1
ABSTRACTS OF PENSION RECORDS FOR VETERANS, WAR OF 1812	4
1816 CENSUS OF PIKE COUNTY, MISSISSIPPI	8
1820 CENSUS OF PIKE COUNTY, MISSISSIPPI	11
EARLY LISTS OF MEMBERS OF BOGUE CHITTO OR CRAIN'S CREEK BAPTIST CHURCH, PIKE COUNTY, MISSISSIPPI, 1824-1827 and 1834	16
SOME EARLY MEMBERS OF NEW ZION BAPTIST CHURCH, PIKE COUNTY, MISSISSIPPI, 1823-1830	16
SOME EARLY MEMBERS OF NEW ZION BAPTIST CHURCH ON A LIST PRIOR TO THE NOVEMBER MEETING, 1866	17
1825 TAX LIST FOR PIKE COUNTY, MISSISSIPPI	19
1835 TAX LIST FOR PIKE COUNTY, MISSISSIPPI	25
1843 TAX LIST FOR PIKE COUNTY, MISSISSIPPI	31
MARRIAGE AND DEATH NOTICES FROM THE MAGNOLIA GAZETTE	35
OBITUARIES FROM THE BOGUE CHITTO BAPTIST ASSOCIATION OF MISSISSIPPI, 1872-1910	42
MARRIAGES AND DEATHS (OBITUARIES) ABSTRACTED FROM THE NEW ORLEANS CHRISTIAN ADVOCATE, PIKE COUNTY, MISSISSIPPI, 1853-1910	65

FAMILY SKETCHES

Albritton	89	Holmes	131
Alford	92	Kemp	142
Allen/Allmand	99	Lee	145
Bacot	99	Newsom	148
Bickham	101	Pierce	150
Bullock	101	Pound/Pounds	150
Burkhalter	102	Regan	155
Carter	102	Rhodus	156
Conerly/Connerley	105	Tate	157
Coney	114	Tate	163
Crawford	116	Tyler	165
Dillon	117	Vaughan	166
Ellis	120	Morgan	167
McCarty	120	Sandifer	167
Johnson/Johnston	121	Varnado	168
Ellzey	122	Albritton Supplement	169
Felderen-Felder	124	Ellzey Supplement	170

COMPLETE NAME INDEX TO PART I	171
COMPLETE NAME INDEX TO PART II	179

PREFACE

Three-quarters of a century ago, Luke Ward Conerly commenced his study of the history of Pike County, Mississippi. Having descended from many of the old pioneer families who settled in Marion and Pike Counties, he set out to record a few facts about those who had turned the area from a primitive frontier into a civilized community. His work was not so perfect as its many users would have liked, but his end product was a pioneer in its own right. After all, he wrote and published one of the earliest county histories in the State of Mississippi. His book has been abstracted, re-published, and presented in more forms than perhaps any county history ever published. There is little doubt that it has been used more than any other.

About fifteen years ago while teaching music at Bogalusa Junior High School, the present editor-compiler, in conjunction with Miss May Davis, the former librarian in Bogalusa High School, and in an effort to get copies of Conerly's long out-of-print book for themselves, decided to issue a xerographic reproduction of this valuable work. The success of that effort was tremendous.

Now after having received so many requests for additional copies, and for more data on the Pike County pioneers, this editor is again presenting the Conerly work for the public. The original book is being presented in an unaltered format with a complete name index as prepared by Miss Davis. In addition, the reader will find an appendix added to the book which includes obituaries, census, tax lists, soldiers of the War of 1812, and numerous family sketches. On rare occasion a correction is added for some statement or family sketch as given by Conerly in his earlier work. In all, the reader will find about 6,000 names in the index to the appendix alone.

This editor-compiler has a vested interest in Pike County and its history. He had ancestors and an uncountable number of relatives who lived once in the area. Then he married in 1961 a girl with more roots in the county than he. Now with four children (Anne, Kemp, Melanie, and Evan) the interest in old Pike County has been increased. The four children named have as a heritage the county's entire political, religious, and social history as so many of their ancestors helped take the country from its primitive origins. They descend from such old founding families as Alford, Bickham, Magee, Holmes, Dillon, Smith, Kemp, Pounds, and others. It is hoped that this Conerly reprint and the appendix will give them an understanding of the area from which they get much of their heritage.

The editor-compiler's children are not alone in enjoying the great heritage which Pike and Walthall County offers. As all data in both sections of this work will illustrate, the number of descendants of the pioneer families of the region total in the thousands. Thus the objective of this book is for each and every one to have the opportunity to have this material at his disposal.

This work, as all such releases, cannot be guaranteed to be free from error. But it has been this compiler's hope that all will be as nearly perfect as humanly possible. Transcription of names and dates always leaves room for mistakes--and surely some mistakes have been made. So use this work, as any published record, with the same caution and the same understanding as if you yourself collected and presented the material.

Many who will browze the pages of this book will complain that it does not contain the data that they seek. But one must remember that all early official court records for Pike County were lost in 1882. Thus other sources--church records, newspapers, and private collections and compilations--have, by necessity, been used for assimilating this data. The task is unending. If this new edition of source records meets approval, and if the demand warrants, a second volume of Pike/Walthall County material will be attempted. This editor-compiler plans another such book in which he will present more obituaries, more tax lists, more census, and miscellaneous records found in neighboring court houses and state repositories.

A work of this type cannot be attempted and completed without the assistance of many interested people. My wife, Mary Beth Simmons Williams, has had to listen to all my speculations, grumblings, and other sentiments while the work was in progress. And, I could not have presented the work at all if she had not typed the manuscript. The credit for those who have contributed data for the family sketches has been noted within each presentation. As you use these family sketches in any way, please note the names of these persons and at least give them a silent thanks for their efforts and willingness to share what they had compiled. And above all, do not fail to remember Luke Ward Conerly, who was interested in his own heritage and the history of his home county long before others became so aware of such presentations, thereby making this entire effort possible.

                                                          E. Russ Williams, Jr.
                                                          Associate Professor of History
                                                          Northeast Louisiana University
                                                          Monroe, Louisiana 71203

PIKE COUNTY MISSISSIPPI

1798-1876

Pioneer Families and Confederate Soldiers
Reconstruction and Redemption

BY
LUKE WARD CONERLY

NASHVILLE, TENNESSEE
BRANDON PRINTING COMPANY
1909

Copyright, 1909, by Luke W. Conerly.

To the

Pioneer Ancestors

Patriotic and Devoted Women and Confederate Soldiers

of Pike County, Mississippi

This Work is Dedicated

by

The Author

Introduction

The object of writing this book was the preservation of the names of the Confederate soldiers of Pike County, Mississippi.

In presenting it to the public the author does so with the consciousness of having performed a sacred duty, purely and simply, and he believes that without his work much would have been lost of historical interest and importance to the future of Pike County and to the historian.

It was not a part of his plans to enter into details of the Civil War except such as related to Pike County and the gallant men whose names appear on the rolls of the companies incorporated in the work and remembrance of the women of that period; and, in connection with them, it seemed just and proper to go back to the early days of the pioneer settlement of the territory embraced in Pike County and give a record, as far as possible, of the brave men and women who left their homes in the older States to locate in the wilds and amid the dangers of a new territory; men and women who became the ancestors of a hardy, self-reliant race of unbending fortitude and heroic virtues. To his mind there is a glory enshrining their memory akin to that which belongs to and embelishes the Revolution of '76.

An examination of records in the Department of Archives and History in the State House disclosed to the writer that the muster rolls and records were incomplete, being those made out and filed in 1861, and not containing names of recruits that entered the Confederate service with these companies and served through the war, nor any final statements, thus leaving out of the records a large number of men who were engaged in the most eventful scenes of the great conflict, and some companies not appearing among the records at all. This made it necessary to obtain them otherwise, which has required many years and a most careful revision through the aid of survivors of the different companies The names of many who went into the service with other commands have been lost, but the author feels that so far as concerns the names of members of companies organized in and going out from Pike County his record is measurably correct, and trusts that his care and labor and great personal expense will prove useful, instructive and valuable, as well as interesting, and will be appreciated by those into whose hands it may come.

Illustrations

	PAGE
Alford Bridge over Bogue Chitto River	12
Barr, Thos. M	351
Bonney, Nelson P	288
Boyd, Capt. A. A	194
Brent, Col. Preston	197
Chisholm, Mrs. Eloise	349
Collins, Hon. Frederick W	264
Conerly, Mrs. A. L	74
Conerly, Buxton R	230
Conerly, Chauncey P	202
Conerly, Mrs. L. W	348
Conerly, Owen	73
Coney, Lieut. Van. C	350
Connally, Capt. Thos. J	190
Dick, Isaac C	51
Duncan, Lieut.-Col. James Henderson	236
Dunn, Miss Norma	353
Ellis, Ezekiel Park	62
Geo. Smith's Water Mill and Dam Over Kirkland's Creek	82
Harris, Gen. Nathaniel H	229
Hart, Dr. R. T	354
Hartwell, Charles E	354
Holmes, Capt. John	173
Hoover, Capt. Kit	207
Hoover, Martha L. J	345
Hoover Iron Bridge	224
Iron Bridge, Scene on Bogue Chitto River	36
Lamkin, Hon. J. T	202
Lamkin, Dr. Wm. J	176
Lamkin, Mrs. W. J	138
Lampton, Benjamin	257

ILLUSTRATIONS

	PAGE
Matthews, Capt. Samuel A	172
McGehee, W. Frank	350
McNair, Captain	196
Miller, Mrs. Joe	138
Peter Sandifer in Bear Fight Scene on McGee's Creek, 1820	64
Portrait of Author	Frontispiece
Prewitt, Ansel H	155
Root, Geo. W	352
Sparkman, Dr. A. P	297
The Bonnie Blue Flag	opp. 147
Travis, Lieut. John Q	187
Tyler, Wm. G	83
View on F. W. Collin's Farm	265

Contents

CHAPTER I.

	PAGE
A Veteran of 1812	23
Act Creating Territory	31
Bacot, Laban	32
Bogue Chitto River, The	15
Bones of Soldier of War of 1812 interred in Chalmette Cemetery	22
Carroll, General	16
Claiborne, Governor	26
Cleveland, David	24
Commissioners to Fix Seat of Justice	14
Convention, Constitutional	31
Constitutional Convention, 1832	32
County Officers, List of	27
Courts, Where Held	14
Dedication	5
Formation of Territorial Government, 1798	11
Gov. Winthrop Sargent	26
Harvey, Michael	12
Hernando DeSoto	10
Holmes, Governor	10
Holmes, Major Andrew Hunter	14
Holmesville Survey	15
Holmesville, Incorporation of	26
Home Life	32
Introduction	7
Marion County, December 9, 1811	11
Marion County, Division of, December 9, 1815	13
McNabb, J. Y.	25
M. DeSalle	10
Military Duty	31
Mississippi, Admission as State	26
New County, Law Creating	25
Origin of Mississippi	9
Pike County, Creation of, 1815	10
'Possum and Coon Hunters	34
Seat of Territorial Government	13
Warren, John	12
Williams, Governor	26

CONTENTS

CHAPTER II.

	PAGE
Alfred, Edwin	36
Bacot, Laban, Born	47
Bacot, Laban, Elected Sheriff 1817	47
Barnes, John	37
Barr, Joseph	41
Bogue Chitto Church, The	44
Burglary Statute	48
Catching, Joseph	52
Cothern, William	44
Crawford, Rev. Jesse	45
Early Settlers	35
Ellzey, John	39
Felder, Peter	37-41
First Born Son	38
First Sheriff's Office	47
Fortinberry, William	39
Gatlin, Colonel James	46
George III	54
Grist Mill, A	37
Little, Margaret	38
Magee, Jeremiah and Sire	49
Martin, Josiah	49
McCollough, Alexander	42
McCollough, William	35
McEwin, Mathew	42
McMorris Family	50
Otopasas, The	35
Pecan Tree, A	35
Quin, Daniel	37
Reeves, John	45
Reeves, Lazarus	44
Sandell, Daniel	36
Sartin, John	39
Sartin, Major	39
Simmons, William	41
Simmons, Willis	41
Smith, Jeremiah	36
Sparkman, Reddick T	56
Taylor, John	35
Thomas, Captain Westley	52
Turnipseed, Dr	44
Walker, John	42

CONTENTS

	PAGE
Warren, John	35
Washington, On the Death of	53
Whipping Post, The	48
"Widow Phillips"	48

CHAPTER III.

Andrews, James	92
Bearden, Jeremiah	79
Boon, William	66
Bracey, Harrison	68
Bullock, Joel	68
Burkhalter, Daniel	66
China Grove	58
Craft, James	78
Conerly, Owen and Luke	58
Connally, Thomas J.	72
Craft, John	78
Collins, Chauncey	84
Darbun Creek	67
Dillon, Richard	87
Ellis, Stephen	59
Ellis, Ezekiel Parke	61
First Postoffice	62
Fort Mims	60
Gartman, Bartholomew	75
Great Land Excitement	93
Grubbs, Gilbert	75
Hall, Armistead	87
Harvey, Michael	70
Holmes, Elisha	66
Jones, Benjamin	69
Lamkin, William	75
Lamptons, The	90
Lawrence, John	86
Lewis, Quincy	76
Ligon, Colonel William B	76
Martin, Wiley	86
May, Joseph	92
McAlpin, Dr.	76
O'Brian, Daniel	86
Owen, Jacob	81
Pacific-Atlantic Hurricane	63
Parker, Joseph	79

CONTENTS

	PAGE
Payne, Nelson	85
'Possum for Sally	72
Pushmataha, General	60
Ratliff, Richard	68
Ratliff, George, (slave)	79
Raiford, Needham B	88
Ravencraft, William	71
Sartins Church	59
Smith, Charles	80
Smith, George, Sr	87
Sneed, John	75
Stalling, John	81
Stovall, Ralph	58
Thompson, Parish	59
Tylertown	81
Tyler, William G	83
When the Stars Fell	91
Youngblood, Benjamin	90

CHAPTER IV.

Allen, Gabriel	100
Bain, Senaca McNeil	127
Balloon Incident	131
Bickham, Mrs. Elizabeth	117
Bond, Henry	99
Bonney, Henry S	128
Brumfield, John	105
Carr, Frank	121
Coney, William	129
Cothern, William	99
Ellzey, William	128
Finch's Dog	128
First Masonic Lodge	112
First Methodist Camp Meeting	106
Gray, Sherod	95
Hart, John	94
Hoover, Judge Christian	99
In the Forties	115
Johnson, William R	120
Kaigler, John	98
Lamkin, John T	120
Leake, Walter	107

CONTENTS

	PAGE
Leggett, William	105
Lewis, Judge Lemuel	129
Lichtensteins, The	116
McNair, E	110
Mitchell, Marmaduke	131
Must Take a Ducking	133
Nelson, Dr. James M	123
New Orleans, Jackson & Great Northern Railroad, The	124
Packwood, Dudley W	121
Pike's Legislators	107
Pound, Daniel W	106
Quin, Colonel Peter	100
Salem Baptist Church	107
Seat of Government at Columbia	107
Sibley Incident	102
Silver Creek Church	97
Sincerity Lodge, F. & A. M., No. 214	123
Stuart, Oscar James E	120
Still Creek	97
Stockdale, Professor	120
Stone, William A	111
Wingoes, The	118

CHAPTER V.

Abolition Emissaries	149
Bacot, Levi	136
Black Abolition Party	145
Banner Association	137
Banner Presentation, 1860	137-142
Beauregard, General, and Fort Sumter	158
Bonny Blue Flag, The	147
Brunette, Rene H	152
Buchanan, James	157
Burkhalter, Flem, Was Up to the Game	154
Cain, General William	145
Coffin, Levi, the Slave Thief	169
Coney, Miss Rachel E	137
Davis, Jefferson	158
Election of Lincoln and Hamlin	146
First Fandango, The	153
First Settlers of Summit	151, 153
Fall Election, 1860	146

CONTENTS

	PAGE
Forbade Importation of Slaves	144
Four Tickets in the Field	146
Garland, William H	153
Grading of the Railroad	155
Greeley, Horace	159
Hard to Escape History	162
Lincoln's Call for 75,000 Men	161
Maryland Invaded and Subjugated	159
Massachusetts the First to Legalize Slavery, in 1641	169
Miller, Captain Joseph H	157
Miss Coney's Address	141
New England Troops Furnished to Rob the South	170
New England the Fomenters of Secession	144, 163, 166
New York in 1859 and 1860	168
Political Excitement	143
Prewitt, Ansel H	155
Quitman Guards, 1859	137
Secession Convention	148
Secession of South Carolina	146
Secession of Mississippi	147
Slave Traders and Kidnapers	144
State of Maryland, The	158
Some Notes on Secession	163
Treachery of United States Government	159
Weathersby, Hugh Eugene	140, 142, 150
Wingo, Green, Hung	153
Year 1860, The	145

CHAPTER VI.

All of Pike's Men in the Field	221
Artisans of Pike County	214
Ball, Lieutenant Sampson	224
Banks Driven Across Potomac	216
Battle of Bull Run	175
Battle of Winchester, Virginia	216
Bogue Chitto Guards	190
Bain, Col. Seneca McNeil	178
Brent Rifles	197
Brown, Captain, Killed	216
Captain James Conerly's Company M. M.	211
Capture of Jefferson Davis	226

CONTENTS

	PAGE
Cold Harbor	216
Colonel Wingfield's Militia	210
Confederate Prisoners	225
Conover Conspiracy	227
Conquered Banner, The	237
Conscription Act	212
Cross Keys	186
Dahlgreen Rifles	191
Desperate Encounters	223
Dick, Ike C., Wounded	217
Dixie Guards	207
Enemy's Great Army	219
Fall of Fort Sumter	211
First Battle of Manassas	175
Fremont and Shields	216
General Lee's Army	217
Great Problem	214
Grierson's Raid	223
Homespun Dress	215
Holmesville Guards	201
Hoover, Capt. Kit	207
How Fort Gregg Was Defended	230
Jackson, Stonewall	213
Land of Desolation, A	225
Lincoln Assassinated	226
Lincoln's Perfidy	220
McNair Rifles	193
Nash's Company	200
President Davis' Call for Troops	172
Quin, Col. Wm. Monroe	201
Quitman Guards	172
Rhodes' Cavalry	209
Seeds of Grief	237
Shiloh	217
Sixteenth Mississippi Regiment	174
Southern Cross is Furled	237
Stockdale's Cavalry	203
Summit Rifles	183
Surratt, Mrs., Hung	226
Travis, John Quincy	181
Union Prisoners	226-228
Wirz, Captain, Hanged	227

CONTENTS

CHAPTER VII.

	PAGE
Alcorn, James L	256
Ames, General Adelbert	254
Burris Magee Trial	281
Cotton in 1865	241
Clinton Riots	266
Cold-blooded Sentiment, A	248
Collins, Fred W	262-266
Conditions of the South in 1865	242
Coushatta	269
Clark, Governor Charles	251
Danger That Threatened, The	246
DeCline, Colonel	268
Death Roll of Armies	272
Election in 1871	258
Fate of Mrs. Lecour and Daughter	268
Galloway, Bishop	273
Grant Parish, Louisiana	268
Head, Joseph	255
Hurst, D. W	284
Ku Klux Klan, The	248
Long-haired Goat, The	286
Miscegenation	246
Negro Outrage	267
Negro Troops at Holmesville	247
Newspapers	288
Otkin, Charles H	278
Peabody Public School	278
Quin, Judge H. M	280
Roane, W. H	258
Rowland, Hon. Dunbar	253
Sharkey, William L	252
State Expenditures	258
Terrible Vandalism	259
When the Armies Were Disbanded	247
Young, Charles B	254

CHAPTER VIII.

Ames Impeached	305
Bridges, Hugh Q	302
Buried the Hatchet	311
Collins, F. W	298

CONTENTS

	PAGE
Cordova Impeached	304
Davis, A. K., Removed	304
Death of William H. Roane	305
Election of 1875	294-298
Felder, R. H	298
Fired on by Negroes	303
Firing of Columbus	298
Garland, William H., Jr.	297
In Louisiana	291
Laying of Corner Stone of New Court House	307
Legislative Investigation	304
Letter from General Featherston	306
Magnolia Election	302
Magnolia Herald, The	299
Negro Camp Meetings	293
New Orleans Democrat	305
No Loud Crowing Cocks	300
Origin of "Bulldozer"	292, 294
Patton, Charles L	303
Redmond & Barrett	303
Removal of the Court House	295
Results of Election	299
Reunion of the Sixteenth Mississippi Regiment	306
Sparkman, Dr. A. P.	297
Stupidity of the Nineteenth Century	314
Travis, J. Q.	302
United States Cavalry at McComb	303
White League, The	292

CHAPTER IX.

Activity of White Leaguers and Bulldozers	329
Ames, ex-Governor Adelbert	317
Apprehension of the People	323
Barrett, Fred	322
Church, Rev. H. M.	322
County Convention	319
Congressional Convention	319
Debt of Mississippi	317
Gains & Swazey	324
Grant Must Call Off His Dogs	323
Grant Would Invade Arkansas	329
Haven, Bishop	322

CONTENTS

	PAGE
His Fraudulency	331
Hoover, Mrs. Martha L. J.	345
Jackson, Colonel Mose	324
Little Joe Lewis	339
Lynch, John R.	321
Magnolia Herald, The	322
Masonic Emblem	346
Nomination of Presidential Candidates	320
One Weber	324
Organization of Clubs	319-320
Outrage in Lawrence	326
Packwood, Bridges and Conerly	327
Population of Pike County	331
Rate of Taxation	318
Sequel to Quitman Guards Banner	350
Sheridan, Phil. A.	323
Stone, John M.	318
Torch Light Procession	328
Tylertown Club	325
Wild Jim Barnes	332

History of Pike County, Mississippi

CHAPTER I.

ORIGIN OF MISSISSIPPI.

The territory of Mississippi was owned and occupied by the Natchez, Choctaw, Chickasaw, Biloxi, Pascagoula, Chocchuma, Tunica and Yazoo Indians.

The Chickasaws and Choctaws were the most powerful and occupied the northern, central and southern parts of the territory.

The Natchez lived along the Mississippi River, the Biloxies and Pascagoulas on the Gulf coast, and the Tunicas and Yazoo tribes lived on the Yazoo River.

The Chocchumas lived in the eastern part of the territory.

Spain nominally possessed this territory until 1699, when the French under Pierre LeMoine d'Iberville made a settlement at Biloxi and called it Louisiana, with Biloxi the seat of government.

In 1763 Mississippi Territory became a province of England, known as West Florida, and a province of Spain in 1781, the Spanish seat of government being at Natchez.

In 1795 the Natchez district became a part of the United States, and the Mississippi Territory was formed by act of Congress in 1798.

While a territory of Georgia that portion lying east of the Mississippi River between latitude 31° and the mouth of the Yazoo River was called the county of Bourbon.

In 1795 Georgia sold to four companies about three millions of acres of this territory for two and one-half cents per acre.

The census of 1800 gave Mississippi Territory a population of 8,850 for the counties of Pickering, Adams and Washington, and the census of 1810 gave a population of 40,352 for the counties of Pickering, Adams, Washington, Baldwin, Amite, Claiborne, Franklin, Madison, Jefferson, Warren, Wayne and Wilkinson.

The District of Mobile, lying east of Pearl River, west of the Perdido and south of the 31st degree of latitude, was annexed to Mississippi in 1812.

Hernando DeSoto and his Spanish followers were the first white men mentioned in our histories to explore the territory now the State of Mississippi. They came in on the Black Warrior and Tombigbee Rivers in 1540.

In 1673 Pere Jacques and Louis Joliet came down the Mississippi River, probably as far as Natchez.

In 1683 LaSalle, a French explorer, passed down the Mississippi River to the Gulf of Mexico.

A colony was planted on the Bay of Biloxi in 1699 by Pierre LeMoine d'Iberville.

Fort Rosalie, where Natchez stands, was built in 1716 under direction of Bienville, Governor of Louisiana.

In 1721 a colony was started at Pascagoula. The Mississippi Territory became a part of Georgia in 1732.

In 1809, under the administration of Gov. David Holmes, the Indians began to give trouble and in August, 1812, Fort Mims was attacked by 1,000 Creek Indians and their British allies under Weatherford, McQueen and Francis, and 260 of the garrison massacred. The following year their holy city, Escanachaha, was destroyed by an expedition of Mississippians under General Claiborne.

PIKE COUNTY.

The territory of which the county of Pike is a part was originally occupied by the Chickasaw, Choctaw and Natchez Indians.

According to our histories, the first European who visited the region of country of which the State of Mississippi was then a part, was Hernando DeSoto, a Spaniard who, having projected the conquest of Florida, came from Cuba in 1539 with a considerable force and traversed the country to a great distance, and, in the spring of 1541, first discovered the Mississippi River, five or six hundred miles above its mouth.

In 1683 M. LaSalle visited the same region and gave it the name of Louisiana, in honor of Louis XIVth of France. We are told by early writers that over this undefined but vast extent of country the French claimed jurisdiction, and, in 1716, they began a settlement at Natchez on the Mississippi River, and erected a fort.

In 1763 they ceded the country east of the Mississippi River to the English, and the latter ceded it to Spain in 1783.

In 1798 the Spaniards abandoned it to the United States.

In 1798 the territory lying between the western boundary of Georgia and the Mississippi River, and which until now had been claimed by Georgia and called the Georgia Territory, was erected by Congress into a district territorial government by the name of the Mississippi Territory.

Under this government, with Winthrop Sargent at its head, the Territory was divided into two counties—the southern portion being called Adams County and the northern portion Pickering County.

Under acts of December 9, 1811, all that tract of country within the following boundaries, to-wit: "Beginning on the line of demarkation where the fourth range of townships east of Pearl River intersects the said line, thence west with said line of demarkation to the sixty mile post east of the Mississippi, being the first range of townships west of Tansopiho; thence north on said line of townships to the Choctaw boundary line; thence along the said Choctaw boundary line to the fourth range of townships east of Pearl River; thence with said range to the beginning, shall constitute a county which shall be called Marion" (named in honor of Gen. Francis Marion).

John Ford, George H. Nixon, William Whitehead, Stephen Noble and John Graves were appointed commissioners for Marion County with power to establish a seat of government, which was located on Pearl River at a place called Columbia.

At this period the country was comparatively an unbroken wilderness with but few inhabitants who had been lured by the thoughts of adventure to abandon their homes in the older States of Georgia, South Carolina, North Carolina and Tennessee, and with their families and transportable property, penetrated the depths of this wilderness as pioneers, to begin the foundation of new homes and a great State government.

John Applewhite and Jacob Ford, with others from North Carolina, with their families, embarked in flatboats on the Cumberland River, floated down to Natchez and moved across to Pearl River and settled, and Michael Harvey came in there from Georgia in 1808. As far back as 1798 immigrants began to come in and locate on the different

THE ALFORD BRIDGE OVER BOGUE CHITTO RIVER IN THE
NORTHERN PART OF PIKE COUNTY

streams threading the extensive territory embraced in Marion County, the Pearl and Bogue Chitto Rivers receiving the larger number and extending in groups along the Tansopiho, the Otopasas, Magees Creek and their numerious tributaries.

John Warren is said to have settled on the Otopasas about seven miles north of the town of Holmesville as early as 1799; and John Magee even earlier than this on Magees Creek, and Jacob Owens on Dry Creek about 1800. Between this time and 1816 they came in larger numbers, locating themselves more nearly to the beautiful clear-water streams and tributary branches.

The river and creek bottoms were covered with a dense growth of wild cane and the pine hill regions with a wild pea commonly known as partridge pea, beggar lice and other rich vegetation and grasses, affording magnificent pasturage for horses, cattle, sheep, goats and hogs; and the swamps with mast-producing trees, and the streams abounding with an inexhaustible supply of fish. Wild deer, turkeys, bear, wolves, panthers, cats, coons, opossums, beavers, otters, squirrels and the numerous feathered tribe for game were practically inexhaustible.

Reports going back from those who were first to venture into these regions to their friends and kindred in the States induced others hence, and during the intervening years prior to 1815 the population had increased so as to be numbered by the thousands instead of the few dozens, scattered over the 20,000 square miles of this county of the Mississippi Territory. Nearly, if not all, of the first settlers of Marion County embraced within the designated lines of Pike County squatted on public lands, built their homes and lived on them long before acquiring deeds from the government, and hence the map of the first entries cannot be relied upon as a guide to determine the date of settlement, and some of them not for nearly a half century afterwards.

While yet a territory the seat of government of Mississippi was located alternately at Washington and Natchez.

By an act of December 9, 1815, of the Territorial General Assembly, the county of Marion was divided in the following manner, which record was transcribed from the county records of Pike several years before the destruction of the courthouse in Magnolia, when the records of court were lost:

"Beginning on the line of demarkation at the southeast corner of Amite County, running from thence east along said line thirty miles; thence a line to run due north to its intersection with the summit of the dividing ridge between the waters of Bogue Chitto and Pearl Rivers, after the same shall cross the waters of Magees Creek; thence along the said ridge until it intersects the southern boundary of Laurence County; and all that tract of territory fromerly a part of Marion County, lying north and west of the lines thus described, shall form a new county to be named Pike" (in honor of General Zebulon Pike).

Until the commissioners appointed to fix the permanent seat of justice had designated the spot, the place of holding court in Pike County was at the residence of Gabriel Allen, who acquired ownership to the north half of section 28, township 3, range 9 east in January 17, 1815, and March 8, 1816, on the west side of the Bogue Chitto River, near the geographical center of the new county.

Benjamin Bagley, Peter Felder, Sr., Obid Kirkland, William Bullock and David McGraw, Sr., were appointed commissioners to fix on the site for public buildings, to be located at the most eligible place within three miles of the geographical center of the county of Pike, said place so fixed to remain as the permanent seat of justice. These commissioners were required to procure, by purchase on the best terms, or by donation, as much land as necessary for the seat of justice, provided the quantity was not less than forty acres nor more than one hundred and sixty acres, and to have an equal regard for eligibility of situation and the convenience of the inhabitants, so as to promote the best interests of the county. Said lands to be laid off in town lots, reserving a sufficient quantity for a public square, a courthouse, jail and church; the balance to be sold and the proceeds used for county purposes.

The commissioners having located the spot and procured the property as required by the law, an act was passed by the General Assembly, December 11, 1816, ratifying the action of the commissioners and giving it the name of Holmesville, in honor of Maj. Andrew Hunter Holmes.*

The commissioners, in selecting this spot for a seat of justice, acted with great wisdom, not only on account of its being near the geographical center of the county, but from a picturesque point of view,

---

*Major Andrew Hunter Holmes was an army officer: Captain, of the 24th Infantry, in 1812; he was major June 8th to September 4th, 1813; was major 32nd Infantry, April 18, 1814. He was killed August 4th, 1814, in an attack on Fort Mackinac, Michigan.

its sanitation and its availability as a business center and watering facilities.

The town was located on a sloping hummock, partly in section 28, acquired by Gabriel Allen, and partly in section 21, acquired by R. Hardly, at the base of a high range of pine hills gently circling its western and southern borders, spreading out fan-like northeastward, with the beautiful Bogue Chitto River forming its northeastern boundary.

This stream takes its rise from a multitude of springs and branches that come out north and west of Brookhaven, in Lincoln County, Bogue Chitto and Johnson stations, and flows in a southeasterly direction through Pike County and Washington Parish and empties into Pearl River in St. Tammany Parish, La. It is one of the most lovable and picturesque streams to be found anywhere in the South. Its waters, coming from pure limpid springs that supply its numerous tributaries, flow softly and sweetly over gravel beds from the northern boundary of the county till it passes away in its meanderings into Louisiana, mirrowing in its bright waters the grand scenery bordering either side of it for over a hundred miles. At intervals, and alternately, it is overlooked by high ridges covered with majestic pine, oak, beech, magnolia and a multitude of other valuable growth, that moan eternally as they are fanned by the ocean's breezes. Its waters, like all other inland streams, were full of fish, and its forests inhabited by wild game in great abundance, and the trapper and the hunter had all the employment desired.

Just at the foot of the hammock, on which the town of Holmesville was built, was a ravine or slough that reached from the river above, passing on down and emptying into it below, forming a small island between the base of the town and the river. Along this ravine was a network of fresh-water springs which were utilized for drinking and household purposes by the first settlers, but wells were afterwards dug and good water obtained at a depth of twenty feet and over.

The river for a long distance in front of Holmesville was deep and unfordable and had to be crossed on flatboats made for the purpose and used as public ferries. The first one of these was located above the town some distance near the home of widow Mulligan, known as Carroll's ferry, where General Carroll, commanding a small division of Tennessee troops, crossed on his route to New Orleans during the War of 1812 and 1815. This was afterward abandoned and another one was established below the island in front of the town and was worked by Solomon Quin, a negro slave who belonged to Mrs. Martha Quin, widow of Col. Peter Quin, one of the original settlers of the town. For many years after this Solomon was a noted ginger-cake and corn beer vendor at all the gatherings and occasions of public interest in the history of Holmesville.

General Carroll, above mentioned, marched through the country all the way from Tennessee to New Orleans and cut his trail, or path, through the forests as he traveled, for the purpose of reaching New Orleans in time to aid Gen. Andrew Jackson in defence of that city against the British invaders under General Packingham. His route through Pike County was nearly due north and south, crossing Bogue Chitto above the town of Holmesville at a point afterwards known as Carroll's ferry, and passing down on the west side of the river, keeping the main ridge route as nearly as practicable to Love's Creek, through the Brumfield, Forest, Leggett, Pound, Walker and Simmons neighborhood, and thence due south on through Washington Parish, La. After the battle of Chalmette, fought on the 8th of January, 1815, General Carroll returned with his Tennessee troops through Pike County the same route he had blazed out on his advance, and camped for awhile on Loves Creek.

There were a few pioneer settlers in this section at that time with family names as above mentioned. While camped here he lost one of his men and buried him in the woods beside the trail he had cut out and marked the grave with a slab hewed out of a tree cut from the woods. In this particular section this trail has since been kept well marked and the pioneer settlers, their children and grand children and great grand children have kept an eye on the grave of this gallant Tennessee soldier all along down the passing years.

While compiling notes and records for this work the writer had occasion to accept the hospitality of Henry S. Brumfield, who lived nearby, and who was born and raised in the neighborhood. Mr. Brumfield's ancestors and others had transmitted to him a knowledge of this grave and he made it a point to care for it in order that its identity might not be lost. He mentioned the circumstances to the writer and the following morning went with him and showed him the grave, a note of which was taken at the time.

In 1907 Congress passed an act making appropriation for the Chalmette Cemetery, records and monuments, or memorials, to the heroes of that battle. This fact coming to the knowledge of the writer, he addressed a letter to Hon. Luke Wright, Secretary of War, acquainting him with the traditions and history of Gen. Carroll's march through Pike County and the death and burial of this soldier in an isolated place in the woods of Love's Creek, suggesting that if the government would furnish a suitable, lasting slab or mark for the grave, Mr. Henry S. Brumfield and himself would put it up, both being ex-Confederate soldiers and feeling an interest in so doing; and, inasmuch as the government was going to make Chalmette a National Cemetery and mark the graves of soldiers who fell there, it seemed to him proper that the government should have a consideration for, and not overlook the remains of this one who had served in that memorable campaign, whose name had been lost by the decay of the wooden slab that bore its inscription, but the identity of whose last resting place was without a question of doubt in his mind. The result was that the matter was referred to the Quartermaster General of the army, and through correspondence between Captain P. W. Whitworth, Quartermaster U. S. A., Washington, D. C., and the writer, and Captains Louis F. Gerrard and Arthur Cranshon, Quartermasters U. S. A., and Major Arthur M. Edwards, Commissary, U. S. A., New Orleans, La,. arrangements were made and instructions given to Capt. Thomas O'Shea, Superintendent of the Chalmette Cemetery, to be accompanied by the writer from Gulfport, to proceed to Pike County, locate the grave and disinter the remains and convey them to New Orleans for reinterment in the Chalmette Cemetery. This was done October 9, 1908. Arriving at Magnolia on the night of the 5th, they proceeded the following day, being conveyed to the spot by Henry Brumfield, Jr., where they procured the assistance of Elisha Thornhill and son and Capt. Frank Grouche, formerly of Baton Rouge, ex-officer of the regular army of the Spanish War period, who assisted in the work of taking up the remains. Ninety-three years had passed since the event. The soldier was buried in his uniform without a coffin. The remains were flattened to a thickness of about one inch and the bones greatly crumbled. There was a thin, dark streak indicating the uniform, and some of the army brass buttons used at that time were recovered, and some of the teeth—altogether perhaps about fifteen or twenty pounds, which were placed in a zinc-lined box prepared for the purpose. On the 7th of October, the remains were conveyed to New Orleans and on the 8th reinterred at Chalmette. Mr. Elisha Thornhill, above mentioned, is a grandson of William Thornhill, one of the first pioneer settlers of the Tylertown district. He married Hettie Forest, a daughter of David W. Forest and Amelia Hall and granddaughter of Richard Forest and Mary ——————, from Alabama, who settled near Love's Creek, where he raised his large family of sons and daughters.

Capt. Frank Grouche is a son of Mr. Alex. Grouche, the noted hotel keeper in the city of Baton Rouge. He married Etta Mahier, daughter of Mrs. A. T. Mahier, both of the first French families of that city.

The following letters were received by the author from the War Department in reference to this incident:

WAR DEPARTMENT,

OFFICE OF THE QUARTERMASTER GENERAL.

(234,383)

Mr. Luke W. Conerly,   WASHINGTON, August 18, 1908.
Gulfport, Miss.

SIR:

I am directed by the Quartermaster General to acknowledge the receipt of your letter of July 18, 1908, addressed to the Secretary of War, reporting the finding of the grave of one of General Carroll's men in Pike County, Miss., who died while traveling with his command on the way to New Orleans in 1814–15; and in which you request that a suitable marker be furnished for his grave, which is now only temporarily marked with a slab hewed out of yellow pine, and is decaying very rapidly.

In reply you are informed that an effort has been made to obtain the name and service of this soldier from the records of the office of The Adjutant General of the Army, but I regret to state that such effort has proved fruitless. If, however, no objection be interposed, the necessary steps will be taken for the disinterment of these remains and shipment to the national cemetery at Chalmette, La., for reinterment. There the grave will be appropriately marked and perpetually cared for.   Respectfully,

P. WHITWORTH,
Captain and Quartermaster, U. S. A.

WAR DEPARTMENT,

OFFICE OF THE QUARTERMASTER,

416 HIBERNIA BANK BUILDING.

Mr. Luke W. Conerly,   NEW ORLEANS, LA., August 20, 1908.
Gulfport, Miss.

SIR:

The Quartermaster General of the Army has furnished this office with a copy of his communication to you dated August 18, 1908 (No. 234,383), relative to your report of the finding of the grave of one of General Carroll's men in

Pike County, Miss., who died while traveling with his command on the way to New Orleans, La., in 1814-15.

With a view of having the remains disinterred and removing same to the Chalmette, La., National Cemetery, near New Orleans, La., for reinterment, I have the honor to request that you please furnish this office with the following information, viz.:

1. The name, date of death, etc., of the deceased, and any other information which you might give bearing on the subject.
2. If practicable, the exact location of the grave, and the approximate distance to the nearest railroad leading to this city.
3. The approximate cost of making a pine box 10x10x26 inches, of one inch lumber.
4. Approximate cost of disinterring, boxing, and conveying the remains to the nearest railroad leading to this city.

It is thought that the information desired under items 3 and 4 could be obtained from some of the local undertakers in the vicinity.

Thanking you in advance for your courtesy, I am,

Very respectfully,

ARTHUR CRANSHON,

Captain and Quartermaster, U. S. Army.

P. S. A self-addressed envelope is enclosed for reply, which need not be stamped. C.

WAR DEPARTMENT,

OFFICE OF THE QUARTERMASTER,

416 HIBERNIA BANK BUILDING.

(1011.)

NEW ORLEANS, LA., September 21, 1908.

Mr. Luke w. Conerly,
 Griswold, Harrison County, Miss.

SIR:

Referring to your letter of September 1st, 1908, I have the honor to inform you that the Quartermaster General of the Army has approved the application of this office that you accompany the Superintendent of the Chalmette, La., National Cemetery to the grave of one of General Carroll's men buried in Pike County, Miss., as stated in your communication referred to above.

In this connection, you are further informed that this office will furnish the necessary transportation to cover the journey, and in addition you will be allowed not exceeding $3.00 *per diem* for your necessary expenses.

In order to facilitate matters in this respect, will you please inform this office at the earliest practicable date when it will be agreeable for you to take this trip, and in doing so please allow at least three (3) days' latitude in order that all arrangements can be perfected, and that no confusion may arise.

Also give full directions as to where you may be found, so that the superintendent will have no trouble in locating you.

Thanking you in advance for your courtesy.

Very respectfully,
LOUIS F. GARRARD, JR.,
Captain and Quartermaster, U. S. Army.

By ARTHUR M. EDWARDS,
Major, Commissary, U. S. Army,
In charge of office.

WAR DEPARTMENT,

OFFICE OF THE QUARTERMASTER,
416 HIBERNIA BANK BUILDING.

(1011.)

NEW ORLEANS, LA., September 30, 1908.

Mr. *Luke W. Conerly,*
Gulfport, Miss.

SIR:

In compliance with instructions contained in 2nd indorsement, office of the Quartermaster General of the Army, dated September 14, 1908 (234,383), you will please proceed at the earliest practicable date after receipt of this communication, to this city, reporting upon arrival to this office for instructions, and accompany the Superintendent, Chalmette, La., National Cemetery, to Pike County, Miss., for the purpose of positively locating the grave of one of General Carroll's men buried there, who died while traveling with his command on the way to New Orleans in 1814-15.

Upon completion of this duty you will return to your home, Gulfport, Miss., via New Orleans, La.

Actual expenses not exceeding $3.00 per day will be allowed, and whenever practicable receipts should be obtained for expenditures on account of meals and lodgings while traveling under these orders.

Transportation will be furnished by this office.

The travel directed is necessary in the public service.

Very respectfully,
LOUIS F. GARRARD, JR.,
Captain and Quartermaster, U. S. Army.

WAR DEPARTMENT,
OFFICE OF THE QUARTERMASTER,
416 HIBERNIA BANK BUILDING.
(1011.)

Mr. Luke W. Conerly,   NEW ORLEANS, LA., September 30, 1908.
   Rural Delivery, Route No. 3,
      Gulfport, Miss.

SIR:

Replying to your favor of 22nd instant, I have the honor to enclose herewith Transportation Request P-No. 8126, covering journey between Gulfport, Miss., and this city.

This request should be presented to the agent of the Louisville & Nashville Railroad at Gulfport, who will furnish you a regular ticket in exchange.

It is desired, if practicable, that you come to New Orleans on Monday morning, October 4th, on the train arriving here at 8:50 a. m., and on arrival call at the office, room 416, Hibernia Bank building, corner Carondelet and Gravier Streets, and meet the Superintendent of the National Cemetery, and both then can leave on the evening train for Magnolia, Miss.

Trusting this may be agreeable to you, I beg to remain

Very respectfully,
LOUIS F. GARRARD, JR.,
Captain and Quartermaster, U. S. Army.

WAR DEPARTMENT,
OFFICE OF THE QUARTERMASTER,
416 HIBERNIA BANK BUILDING.

Mr. Luke W. Conerly,   NEW ORLEANS, LA., October 8, 1908.
   Gulfport, Miss.

SIR:

Upon the receipt of a letter from you addressed to the Secretary of War, the Quartermaster General of the Army directed this office to take up the matter with a view to disintering the remains of one of General Carroll's men whose burial place was known to you, and have the remains given a lot in the Chalmette National Cemetery. This matter was taken up with you, and request was made of you to accompany the Superintendent of the Chalmette National Cemetery to this burial place in order that he might make the disinterment. This you did and the matter has been satisfactorily attended to, due to your assistance, and I have the honor to thank you for the services rendered.

Very respectfully,
LOUIS F. GARRARD, JR.,
Captain and Quartermaster, U. S. Army.

BONES OF SOLDIER OF WAR OF 1812 INTERRED IN CHALMETTE CEMETERY

Events of the stirring days at the close of the war of 1812 were recalled yesterday by an incident which took place at the Chalmette National Cemetery when the bones of a Tennessee soldier, a hero of the battle of Chalmette, who had died in Mississippi while returning to his home, found their last repose in the cemetery by order of the Secretary of War, Luke Wright. No ceremony attended the reinterment of what remained of the unidentified body of the soldier; simply the act of burial in the grave provided by the national government. No one was present but the Superintendent of the Chalmette Cemetery, Thomas O'Shea who saw that the soldier's bones were decently laid beneath the sod in a zinc-lined box provided for the purpose.

Behind the discovery of the body of the veteran buried ninety-three years ago is a pretty story, and that the bones were honored with interment in the national cemetery is due to the energy of a Confederate veteran, Sergeant Luke W. Conerly, of Gulfport. Six years ago Mr. Conerly, who was a native of Marion County, Miss., learned while making a search of the old records of Pike County, which was formerly a part of Marion, that there was the body of a soldier of 1812 buried in a grave near the banks of Love's Creek, about eleven miles from Magnolia, on the place of the Brumfield family. By making inquiries he learned the exact location of the grave, and began to make efforts to secure the removal of the body to the Chalmette Cemetery.

Last year there was an act passed by Congress authorizing the removal of the bodies of soldiers to national cemeteries at the government's expense, and Mr. Conerly corresponded with Secretary Taft. He said that the only person who had an exact knowledge of the location of the grave was Henry S. Brumfield, a grandson of the original owner of the Brumfield plantation, who is a man well advanced in years. This caused the department to act quickly, and last week Capt. Louis F. Garrard, Jr., United States Quartermaster here, received orders to have Mr. Conerly find the grave and exhume the remains.

The exhumation was made Wednesday. Mr. Conerly and Superintendent O'Shea of the Chalmette Cemetery being piloted to the grave by Mr. Brumfield and an aged negro servant. It was found that the pine slab which had marked the grave had rotted away until there was no part of the inscription left by which it could be identified. Mr. Brumfield said that the records in his family were that the soldier had been one of the brigade of Gen. Carroll, of Tennessee, who had lost a man while returning from the battle of Chalmette in 1815, when the Tennesseans had given valuable aid to Gen. Andrew Jackson. No trace of the unfortunate soldier's name could be found, except that the records said the name had been cut in a pine slab which had been placed to mark the grave.

Mr. Conerly said that the veteran must have been a man of about six feet in height, from the size of the grave, which had been dug in a porous clay that held the original shape in which it had been cut to form the grave. Only the teeth and a few of the larger bones were found in what was left of the soldier. He had evidently been buried uncoffined, but as evidence that a soldier had been buried there two tarnished and rust-eaten brass buttons were found by Mr. Conerly.

With them were fragments of a blue uniform. Mr. Conerly said that the total weight of the remains must have been about fifteen pounds.

The bones and other remnants were reverently placed in the box and taken to Magnolia, where they were shipped to New Orleans, arriving Wednesday night. Yesterday morning a report was made to Capt. Garrard, and the remains were interred in the national cemetery.

Mr. Conerly came to New Orleans with them. He said that he was engaged in writing a history of Pike County, and that the most gratifying result of his work had been the finding of the bones of this soldier.—New Orleans *Times-Democrat*, October 9, 1908.

A VETERAN OF 1812.

A survivor of the famous battle of New Orleans, fought on the 8th day of January, 1815, who has lain in a lonely grave for ninety-three years in Pike County, was disinterred by order of the United States War Department Wednesday, and the fragments of his bones taken to the national cemetery at Chalmette and re-buried there.

The story of the finding of this ancient veteran's grave by the War Department makes a chapter of interesting history.

In the war of 1812-15 with England, its most conspicuous battle was that fought between ten thousand of Wellington's trained soldiers under Gen. Pakenham, and less than five thousand pioneer frontiersmen under Gen. Andrew Jackson, on the field of Chalmette, near New Orleans. Although the Treaty of Ghent between young America and the mother country was signed on Christmas Eve of 1814, both Pakenham and Jackson were ignorant that peace had been declared, and when the British general came up the Mississippi River to capture New Orleans, "Old Hickory" was lying behind cotton bales with five thousand deadly rifles peering between them. Pakenham, himself a great military leader and strategist, disembarked his troops and formed them on the plain on the west shore of Lake Borgue. In solid phalanxes and with beautiful precision, the Wellington soldiers advanced upon that long line of cotton bales. When the enemy came within two hundred yards the pioneers fired, and the resulting slaughter was terrific. No less than twenty-five hundred Britons bit the dust, and the magnificent army was thrown into the utmost confusion. Jackson won the victory with practically no loss and saved the city of New Orleans from sack and pillage.

In that army of American pioneers was a band of men—how many is not known—who had marched from Tennessee under Gen. Carroll. Passing through Mississippi's great pine forests, they blazed a trail. That trail passes entirely through Pike County, and can be easily traced to this day. After the war was ended, and Gen. Jackson had disbanded his army, Gen. Carroll and his troops returned to Tennessee by the same trail. It is a matter of tradition that they camped for some time at a place ten miles east of Magnolia, and on what is now land belonging to Mr. H. S. Brumfield. While there, presumably recuperating, one of them died and was buried. His comrades laid him in a grave and marked the spot with a slab of yellow pine, hand-hewn and polished. During all these years, the grave has been carefully marked. Mr. Henry S. Brumfield, Sr., one of the best known citizens of this county, states that he himself has replaced the wooden slab several times, so that the identity of the grave can be established without question.

Last June, Mr. Luke Conerly was made acquainted with these facts, and, in company with Mr. H. S. Brumfield, visited the grave. He collected all the traditional data available with reference to the soldier's death and burial, and furnished the same to the War Department, requesting that the government provide a permanent mark for the grave and, if possible, ascertain the name of the soldier. The War Department satisfied itself as to correctness of the facts, and the investigation resulted in Capt. Thos. O'Shea, Superintendent of the National Cemetery at Chalmette, being directed to disinter the remains and re-bury them in Chalmette.

Last Wednesday morning, accompanied by Mr. Conerly, Capt. O'Shea came to Magnolia. They drove out to the grave and were met there by Mr. H. S. Brumfield, owner of the land, and Mr. E. T. Thornhill, of Walker's Bridge. On beginning the work of disinterment, it was found that the clay soil was packed as hard as though it had never been disturbed, but on reaching a depth of five feet it was soft and loamy. At this depth, the bones of the veteran were discovered. There was no sign of a coffin, and it is probable that none was available for his burial. The bones were loose and a great many of them had wholly disintegrated. Some fragments of the soldier's uniform were unearthed but these crumbled to dust as soon as touched. The most important discovery, however, and one which clinches the question of identity, was two brass buttons such as were used on military uniforms in the war of 1812. The buttons had retained their original form, but the lettering on them was undecipherable.

Capt. O'Shea carefully gathered every bone that could be found, and placing them in an ordinary wooden box, took them to New Orleans with him on the afternoon train. There they were placed in a casket and interred with military honors in the national cemetery. So far, it has been impossible to ascertain the name of the soldier, and hence upon his tomb will be engraved the simple but significant words:

"UNKNOWN SOLDIER
U. S. A.
WAR OF 1812." —*Magnolia Gazette.*

Closely clustered around Holmesville, who figured in its conception and its birth, were David McGraw, Gabriel Allen, C. Brent, R. Hardley, John Smith, Peter Quin, Sr., John Kaigler, Anthony Perryman, Benjamin Bagley, William Love, Henry Ragland, Hans Hamilton, Josiah Martin, David Morgan, James Y. McNabb, David Cleveland, Jeremiah Williams, Phillip and Joseph Catchings, J. Peck, Jonathan Catchings,

John Felder, David Winborne, John Magee, Solomon Causey, David Dixon, Dr. Wiley P. Harris and Joseph Thornhill.

In January, 1816, J. Y. McNabb was elected clerk of the Inferior and Superior Courts, and David Cleveland was elected sheriff, and they entered into bond on the 29th day of January, 1816. In August, 1817, Laban Bacot was sheriff, under the new State regime. In the fall election of 1818, Henry Quin was elected clerk and Laban Bacot sheriff.

James Y. McNabb issued the first marriage license in Pike County, February 13, 1816, to Jacob Keen and Keziah Gates. The ceremony was performed by Vincent Garner, justice of the peace.

The map of the survey of the town of Holmesville shows that a portion of the town is located on lands formerly owned by Gabriel Allen, in section 28, and a portion on lands formerly owned by R. Hardley, acquired by him in 1812, being the southwest quarter of section 21, township 3, range 9 east. At this time Peter Quin owned the northeast quarter of section 29, which corners with the southwest quarter of section 21 and the northwest quarter of section 28—the map indicating that Holmesville is located in sections 21 and 28.

There has been some speculation as to the original ownership of the public square in the old town of Holmesville, it being claimed that it was donated conditionally and was to be permanently the seat of justice, and that a removal of the seat of justice would work a reversion of the ownership to the heirs of the donors or vendors.

The law creating the new county and authorizing the appointment of the commissioners also empowered them to procure by purchase or donation, to the county, a tract of land for a permanent seat of justice, not specifying any conditions as to what should be done with it except as provided by this act. The act speaks for itself, and surely intended a fee simple title and the inalienable right to control and use or dispose of it as county property; because it says the commissioners must sell the land in town lots, reserving enough for a public square, a courthouse, jail and church. Then, if the public square should revert, why not all the other lands sold into town lots and reserved for a church also revert, in event the public interest demanded at some future time the removal of the seat of justice. The closest investigation by the writer of the records before their destruction by fire failed to disclose any reservations or conditions on the part of those dealing with the commissioners. This square of ground is a sacred and historical spot, and it should be held by the county of Pike in perpetua. Around it clusters some glorious memories, from the date of its fixture as a seat of justice to that when it ceased to be such, and to the present day. The history of Pike County is indissolubly interwoven with it for ninety years. From here heroes went and gave their life-blood for Mississippi's cause—the children and grandchildren of its pioneers, and here, it is claimed by many, that Pike County's monuments should be erected to commemorate the deeds of her heroic men and her matchless women.

In 1817 Mississippi was admitted into the Union as a State, and David Holmes, who had served as Governor since 1809, was elected Governor by the people.

The act of Congress passed March 1, 1817, authorizing a State government of the Mississippi Territory, defining its boundaries, reads as follows:

"Sec. 2. The said State shall consist of all the territory included within the following boundaries, to-wit: Beginning on the river Mississippi at the point where the southern boundary line of the State of Tennessee strikes the same, thence east along the said boundary line to the Tennessee River, thence up the same to the mouth of Bear Creek, thence by a direct line to the northwest corner of the county of Washington, thence due south to the Gulf of Mexico, thence westwardly, including all the islands within six leagues of the shore, to the most eastern junction of Pearl River with Lake Borgne, thence up said river to the 31st degree of north latitude, thence west along the said degree of latitude to the Mississippi River, thence up the same to the beginning."

Winthrop Sargent received his appointment as first Governor of Mississippi Territory by John Adams, President of the United States, in 1799. He was succeeded by W. C. C. Claiborne in 1801. Robert Williams was appointed Governor in 1805, and was succeeded by David Holmes in 1809.

In 1820 an act was passed by the General Assembly of Mississippi to incorporate the town of Holmesville. An election was held and

James C. Dickson, Peter Quin, Jr., I. Aiken, Wiley P. Harris and Major Lea were chosen trustees; Buckner Harris, assessor, collector and town constable, and William Orr, treasurer. Previous to this, in 1819, William Dickson, Peter Quin, Peter Felder and Matthew McEwen presided as justices of the orphan's court, which had jurisdiction in probate matters. In 1822 this system was changed by the Legislature.

Jeremiah Bearden and Reddick T. Sparkman constructed a hotel in Holmesville and operated it for many years; also Thomas Guinea.

Jack Summers owned and operated a tan yard at the upper part of town near the river and the present location of the bridge.

Following is a list of county civil officers after admission of the State in the Union:

PIKE COUNTY CIVIL OFFICERS.
1818.

Names.	Dates.	Commissioned.
James Y. McNabb	February 6	Chief Justice of the Quorum.
Richardson Bourman	February 6	Justice of the Quorum.
Peter Quin, Jr.	February 6	Justice of the Quorum.
Laban Bacot	February 6	Assessor and Collector.
Benj. Bagley	March 10	Chief Justice of the Quorum.
Ralph Stovall	April 10	Justice of Peace.
James Baggett	April 10	Justice of Peace.
William Carter	April 10	Justice of Peace.
Matthew McEwen	April 10	Justice of Peace.
Nathaniel Wills	April 10	Justice of Peace.
Nathan Sims	April 10	Justice of Peace.
Thomas Arthur	April 10	Justice of Peace.
Benj. Morris	April 10	Justice of Peace.
William Carter	April 10	Justice of Peace.
Henry Quin	April 10	Justice of Peace.
Josiah Martin	April 10	Justice of Peace (resigned.)
James Gorden	April 10	Constable.
Jessee Craft	April 10	Constable.
Am Verdaman	April 10	Constable.
Edward Bullock	April 10	Constable.
James Legett	April 10	Constable.
Henry Hale	April 10	Constable.
Nathaniel Gaugh	April 10	Constable.

Names.	Dates.	Commissioned.
Thomas Rouse	April 10	Constable.
Henry Goldman	April 10	Constable.
Joseph C. Smith	April 10	Constable.
Nathan Morris	April 12	Justice of Peace and Quorum.
Wiley P. Harris	May 1	Ranger.
James C. Dickson	May 1	County Surveyor.
David Dickson	May 1	Notary Public (resigned.)
Peter Quin	July 3	County Treasurer.

1819.

Names.	Dates.	Commissioned.
Laban Bacot	January 19	Assessor and Collector.
Jesse King	February 6	Justice of Peace.
Eleazer Bell	February 6	Justice of Peace.
William Dickson	February 20	Justice of Quorum.
Peter Felder, Sr.	February 20	Justice of Quorum.
Mathew McEwen	February 20	Justice of Quorum.
Eleazer Bell	February 20	Justice of Quorum.
Felix Allen	April 17	County Treasurer.
Leonard Varnado	April 17	Justice of Peace.
John Wilson	April 17	Justice of Peace.
William Donohoe	April 17	Constable.
Simon Osteen	April 17	Constable.
Henry Goleman	April 17	Constable.
Buckner Harris	April 17	Constable.
Nathaniel Goff	April 17	Constable.
William Norman	April 17	Constable.
James C. Dickson	July 16	Justice of Peace.
Jesse Harper	July 16	Justice of Peace.
Philemon Martin	July 16	Constable.
Floyd Williams	July 16	Constable.
Zaccheus Davis	July 16	Constable.
Laban Bacot	August 14	Sheriff.
Peter Quin, Sr.	August 14	Coroner.
Jesse Craft	November 15	Constable.
Thomas Harvey	November 15	Constable.
Abden Taylor	November 15	Constable.

1820.

Names.	Dates.	Commissioned.
Laban Bacot	February 3	Assessor and Collector.
Elbert Burton	February 25	Ranger.
Jacob I. Pernell	February 25	Constable.
Samuel Roberts	February 25	Constable.
Daniel Thomas	April 12	Justice of Peace.

Names.	Dates.	Commissioned.
Thomas Rule	April 12	Constable.
James C. Breland	April 12	Constable.
Abden Tyler	April 12	Constable.
Richard Quin	October 7	Justice of Peace.
Jesse Craft	October 7	Justice of Peace.
Elbert Hines	October 7	Justice of Peace.
Derril H. Martin	October 7	Constable.
William Carter	October 7	Constable.
Thompson Wallace	October 7	Constable.

1821.

Names.	Dates.	Commissioned.
Laban Bacot	January 3	Assessor and Collector.
James Y. McNabb	February 12	Justice of Quorum.
Samuel Higginbottom	May 30	Ranger.
James Bridges	May 30	Constable.
Thomas Gatland	May 30	Constable.
Laban Bacot	August 16	Sheriff.
Josiah B. Harris	August 16	Coroner.
Richardson Bowman	October 19	Justice of Peace.
William Prichard	October 19	Constable.
Richard Bowman	November 29	Judge of Probate.

1822.

Names.	Dates.	Commissioned.
Laban Bacot	January 14	Assessor and Collector.
James Willing	February 7	Constable.
Benjamin Thomas, Sr	February 7	Justice of Peace.
Henry Quin	February 7	Justice of Peace.
A. M. Perryman	February 7	County Treasurer.
Dorrel Young	February 7	Justice of Peace.
Daniel Felder	February 7	Constable.
Thomas Pleasant	April 26	Justice of Peace.
David Cleveland	April 26	Justice of Peace.
Nathaniel Wells	April 26	Justice of Peace.
Thomas Rule	April 26	Justice of Peace.
Jesse King	April 26	Justice of Peace.
Nelson Higginbottom	April 26	Justice of Peace.
Benjamin Morgan	April 26	Justice of Peace.
James Waddle	April 26	Justice of Peace.
Drury Chandler	April 26	Justice of Peace.
Malachi Thomas	April 26	Justice of Peace.
Edward Bullock	April 26	Constable.
David Cleveland	January 19	Judge of Probate.
James C. Dickson	August 1	Justice of Peace.

HISTORY OF PIKE COUNTY, MISSISSIPPI

Names.	Dates.	Commissioned.
Vincent Garner	June 29	Associate Justice.
Barnabas Allen	June 29	Associate Justice.
James Y. McNabb	September 19	Justice of Peace.
Jesse Harper	September 19	Justice of Peace.

1823.

Peter Quin, Jr.	January 4	Judge of Probate.
Laban Bacot	January 15	Assessor and Collector.
Robert Love	January 22	Associate Justice.
Gorden D. Boyd	March 20	County Surveyor.
Wiley P. Harris	March 20	Justice of Peace.
Thomas Hart	March 20	Justice of Peace.
Daniel Felder	March 20	Justice of Peace.
John Black	March 20	Ranger.
John Wilson	March 20	Justice of Peace.
Laban Bacot	August 25	Sheriff.
Josiah B. Harris	August 25	Coroner.
James Roberts	September 17	Justice of Peace.
Richard Quin	September 17	Justice of Peace.
Leroy Tatum	September 17	Justice of Peace.
Daniel Quin	September 17	Justice of Peace.
James Hope	September 17	Justice of Peace.

1824.

Laban Bacot	January 20	Assessor and Collector.
William W. Pearson	March 16	County Surveyor.
Henry Richardson	March 16	Justice of Peace.
David Bullock	March 16	Justice of Peace.
Robert Love	June 8	Judge of Probate.
Nathaniel Wells	June 8	Associate Justice.
Peter Quin, Jr.	June 23	Justice of Peace.
Jacob Coon	June 23	Justice of Peace.
Michael Prescott	June 23	Justice of Peace.

1825.

Robert Love	January 15	Judge of Probate.
William Wilson	January 15	Associate Justice.
Peter Quin	January 15	Ranger.
Laban Bacot	February 5	Assessor and Collector.
Richard Davidson	March 28	Justice of Peace.
Matthew McEwen	March 28	Justice of Peace.
Thomas Rule	July 8	Justice of Peace.
Jacob Owens	September 29	Justice of Peace.
James Y. McNabb	December 26	Justice of Peace.

1826.

Names.	Dates.	Commissioned.
Laban Bacot	January 30	Assessor and Collector.
Daniel Sistrunk	April 12	Justice of Peace.
Davis Barren	January 21	Justice of Peace.
John Felder	September 27	Justice of Peace.

1827.

Names.	Dates.	Commissioned.
Laban Bacot	February 4	Assessor and Collector.
William Dickson	February 8	Associate Justice.
Leroy H. Tatum	January 10	Justice of Peace.
Stephen Ellis	January 10	Justice of Peace.
Daniel Bullock	April 9	Justice of Peace.
James Chamberlain	April 9	Justice of Peace.
James Roberts	April 9	Justice of Peace.
Thomas Reaves	April 9	Justice of Peace.
William G. Martin	April 9	Justice of Peace.
Peter Quin	April 9	Justice of Peace.
Jacob Coon	April 9	Justice of Peace.
Jonathan Carter	April 9	Justice of Peace.
William Carter	April 9	Justice of Peace.
Peter McDonald	April 9	Justice of Peace.

The act of Congress providing for the formation of the Mississippi Territory into a State government was passed March 1, 1817, fixing the boundaries of said State and providing for a convention to be held by the people to frame a constitution which was to assemble in the town of Washington on the first Monday of July, 1817.

In this convention Pike County was represented by David Dickson, William J. Minton and James Y. McNabb.

The act of Congress passed April 7, 1798, establishing the territorial government of Mississippi provided that it should not be lawful for any person or persons to import or bring into said Territory, from any port or place, without the limits of the United States, any slave or slaves, under penalty of $300 fine and the freedom of every such slave or slaves thus brought in from foreign ports.

Under the laws established by the territorial government every free male person between the ages of sixteen and fifty years were subject to military duty, and every militiaman enrolled for service on foot was required to furnish himself with a musket and bayonet, cartridge box and thirty rounds of cartridges, or rifle and tomahawk, powder horn and bullet pouch, with one pound of powder and four pounds of bullets, six flints, priming wires, brushes and knapsacks. Each horseman was required to furnish himself with a sword, one pistol, twelve rounds of cartridges, three flints, a priming wire, small portmanteau, and such other arms and accoutrements as might be directed by the commander in chief.

In the constitutional convention of 1832 Pike County was represented by James Y. McNabb and Laban Bacot.

The constitution framed then changed the judiciary system, and gives to Mississippi the honor of being the leader in making the judiciary elective.

A high court of errors and appeals, to sit twice a year, consisting of three judges, elected from three districts; a circuit court held twice a year in each county, a superior court of chancery, a probate court and board of police for each county, all elected by the people and by ballot.

EARLY HOME LIFE.

Home life in Pike County in its early settlement and for a generation after was simple and natural. As time grew apace young people grew up, formed attachments and married, then selected a suitable tract of land and, with the help of neighbors and friends, constructed an humble pine-pole hut to begin life with. A little patch was cleared for a garden; a few chickens that the old folks gave them, a pair of pigs, a heifer or cow and calf, and perhaps a pony, constituted the bulk of personal property. The bedstead was of a home-made pattern, framed and held together by interlacing quarter-inch cotton cords, made by hand at the old home, which constituted the bed-spring, but more often it was framed to the walls in one corner of the cabin, and made of ordinary split timber. A three-legged griddle to cook corn hoe-cakes on, a saucepan, a common frying pan and a small oven to bake, sufficed for the kitchen outfit. A common wooden bench and a few three-legged stools would do to sit on until the head of the household could manage to do better. The lands upon which they settled were public property, but the right thus secured must not be disturbed. Wash basins, water buckets, milk piggins and well buckets were made by hand in the shops of those who manufactured the reels, spinning wheels and looms, which all who could must be provided with. There were no allurements beyond the environments of these simple homes to distract the minds of the beginners of farm life, and their thoughts and energies were concentrated on the development and strengthening of the resources acquired. Love in its primeval purity, strengthened by mutual confidence, with radiant hope and faith in the Divine Ruler, shone with resplendent beauty. The young husband, with his axe and his rifle on his shoulder, his clear sounding horn swung to his side, with his ever attendant faithful dog, went about his duties with self-confidence and a buoyant heart. The young wife, with rosy cheeks, a loving smile, a happy heart, made the little home an Eden of joy and gave strength to his soul in the battle of life. They drank from the sweetest and most sparkling fountains the inspirations that cement the marriage bonds. On Sunday, hand in hand, they could walk to church together to listen to the exhortations of a pious neighbor and sing:

> "Jesus my all to heaven is gone,
> He whom I fix my hopes upon."

The little pine-pole meeting-house was good enough for them. It may, however, seem very simple to the reader of the present day, who has known only the comfort and luxuries which wealth brings, but the reader of to-day, be he rich or poor, whose ancestors belong to America's past history, sprang from just such people as these, living under just such conditions.

The little boys that went 'possum hunting and were taught to swim and to ride a horse or ox and use the rifle and the shot gun were training for emergencies.

In all ages of the world men have sprung from the simplest conditions of life when stirring events called them into action and reached the acme of renown. The great schools might prepare some for high stations and scientific purposes, but there must be those, hardy and strong, who can clutch the cold steel with a fearless hand and dare death in any form when necesssity calls.

The 'possum and coon hunters, the bear trailers and trappers, the grapplers with the wolf and the tiger cat, who sprung from those hardy and brave men and women whose names adorn the pages of this work, are on the rolls, and they are there to tell to the world, along down through the ages, who it was that gave to the pages of their country's history a golden glitter.

From King's Mountain and Valley Forge, from Trenton and the Cowpens, from Bunker Hill and Ticonderoga, from Jamestown and the Talapoosa, the blood of patriotism was transmitted with the advancing years, and in the deep wilderness of the Territory of Mississippi it was made healthy and strong by the necessary activities and rustic life of its people. The great body of the pioneers of Pike came from revolutionary sires, schooled in the science of Indian fighting and the hardships and exposures incident to camp life, the hunt for wild game, and the labor of their farms. They had inherited the characteristics of their fathers and mothers, and they were properly qualified to undertake the mission of establishing new homes in these unbroken wilds and of laying the foundation of a great State government.

The young men from North and South Carolina, Georgia and elsewhere, offsprings of revolutionary patriots and colonial settlers, thought nothing of putting their young wives on horseback or taking it afoot with their few belongings, armed with combination flint and steel shotgun-rifles, and tramping it hundreds of miles through the wilderness to the Territory of Mississippi; and their heroic wives thought less of the dangers and hardships to be encountered. It is this sort of material from which Mississippians sprung, and it is this sort of blood that has brought lustre to her name. This book will tell you who some of them were, men and women, and where they settled in Pike County.

CHAPTER II.

In the foregoing chapter an outline of events leading down to the creation and political organization of Pike County has been given.

In the present chapter it is proposed to speak more directly of some of the families that immigrated here and the occupations engaged in in the early settlements on the different streams. It is not proposed to undertake this in detail. The absence of records, and even tradition, connected with many of the original settlers who have passed out of memory of the oldest living men and women in the county, makes it impossible.

In 1799 John Warren and his wife, Priscilla, settled on the Otopasas (now called Topisaw) below the junction of East Fork and on the west side of the stream. This property was acquired by Michael Brent in the early fifties or perhaps before 1850. He sold it to Owen Conerly, and from his widow it passed to and through other hands to William Garner. There he constructed a hewed log cabin of yellow pine and opened a little farm. Tradition tells us that there was a small opening here when Warren came, indicating that the land had been cultivated many years before, probably by Indians. The house built by him is on the place yet and in a fair state of preservation. A pecan tree, said to have been planted by him, which has been in bearing for over fifty years, is a monarch now, the oldest and largest known in Pike County, and is perhaps the first pecan tree planted in the county.

Just below and south of this place John Taylor settled, probably near the same time, now owned by S. Cicero Walker The original settlement was on the crest of a high pine ridge overlooking the valley of the Otopasas. Fifty years ago it had grown up into a wilderness again, but again opened and put in cultivation.

John Warren and Priscilla were the parents of Sally Warren, wife of William McCollough, who came to Pike County in 1814, at the age of fifteen. His father, Alexander McCollough, came from Ireland into Georgia. His wife was Miss Marshall from Scotland.

After William McCollough married Sally Warren they settled on Topisaw and became the parents of Winston, Jasper, Olive, Sarah and Melinda McCollough.

Edwin Alford was born in North Carolina in 1792, and after his birth his parents moved to Georgia, where he remained until 1807, when he came to the Territory. In 1818 he married Martha, a daughter of Jeremiah Smith, and settled a place on the Bogue Chitto in the southern portion of the county. They raised six sons and five daughters. Jeremiah Smith came from Lancaster District, South Carolina, in 1808. He moved in a cart, and settled on a place near Dillontown,

IRON BRIDGE
Scene on the Bogue Chitto River

where Edwin Alford married Martha. He was the father of Eli' Edwin and Wyatt Smith. He was one of the finest mechanics of his time. He died in 1843 at the age of sixty-one. When these people settled here they had to travel a distance of some twenty miles to a grist mill, located near where the town of Tangipahoa on the I. C. R. R. now stands, to get their corn ground into meal—near where Camp Moore was located during the Civil War.

Daniel Sandell was the son of Henry Sandell and Catherine Nobles, who lived in Orangeburg District, South Carolina, where he was born in 1792. In 1814 he was enlisted in Colonel Nixon's regiment of Mississippi infantry, which was ordered to Florida to reinforce the army engaged against the Seminole Indians He was married to Charity Elenor Corley, daughter of Jeremiah Corley, from Barnwell District, South Carolina, September 17, 1815, a short time before the creation of Pike County, and in 1816 he settled on the well-known Sandell place, west of Magnolia. He was the father of Gabriel, Walter, Rev. John Westley Sandell, Samuel Murray and Monroe, Mary Ann and Martha.

Peter Felder settled the Vaughn place, near Magnolia, in 1811. A Methodist Church was established in this neighborhood, and in 1810 the first Methodist camp meeting was held here. It was afterwards known as Felder's Church.

A grist mill was erected across Sweetwater, a small stream emptying in the Bogue Chitto near Walker's Bridge, on a farm settled by Daniel Quin, in 1810, and many people traveled thirty and forty miles to it to have their corn ground into meal for bread.

Daniel Quin was a son of Peter Quin, Sr., who came to Pike County in 1812. He married Kitty Deer. They were the parents of Rodney, William and Frank, and Emily, who married Jeremiah Coney.

In 1798 John Barnes, with his young wife and little daughter, Margaret, then only a few years of age, emigrated from Georgia. They took passage in a large dugout which he constructed out of a cypress tree, launching it on the Cumberland River and floating down the connecting waters into the Mississippi River and landed at Natchez. Barnes was an accomplished young mechanic, and he and his young wife had only one child, little Margaret, then only five or six years of age. They wanted to come to the far West, to the Mississippi Territory, of which he had heard so much, to settle down in life and build themselves a home. He cut down a big cypress tree, dug it out with his adz and fashioned it and launched it on the turbid waters, put all his belongings in it, and he and his young wife and little Margaret took passage for more than a thousand miles down unknown and perilous streams. With his trusty rifle, a brave heart, a loving, heroic wife, a sweet little child, he pushed off from Georgia's shore and paddled on down, stopping here and there to camp over night under the trees or to kill wild game to supply their needs. When he arrived at the head of Mussel Shoals, a very dangerous continuation of rapids for a long distance, he landed his dugout and was visited by an Indian, who advised him not to undertake to shoot the rapids with his wife and child in the boat, that there was a near cut by a pathway to the river below the rapids which they could take, and that he himself would accompany him and steer the boat safely through. It was already late in the evening, but Barnes wished to pass the rapids at once while he had the Indian to help him through. After the Indian had directed Mrs. Barnes how to go they pushed out to make the descent. Night had overtaken them, and when they arrived at the point where Barnes' wife was to meet them it was late and she was not there and failed to answer to his call or the sound of his horn. The Indian then explained that he forgot to tell her the path forked, and said she must have taken the wrong direction leading out into the deep, dark wilderness, which proved to be true. Leaving the Indian in care of his boat, Barnes, with his gun, his horn and a torch, went out in search of his lost wife and child. Beating back on the trail as directed until he reached the one the Indian surmised his wife had taken, he pursued that for a long distance until at length he found her sitting beneath the trees with her little child hugged up in her arms, patiently waiting for and trusting her husband to rescue them. When they returned to their dugout they found that the Indian had stolen much of their valuables and fled. In due course of time Barnes with his little family arrived safely at Natchez, and afterward worked his way out to Beaver Creek, in Amite County, where he remained for awhile, when he moved to Pike County and settled on Union Creek near where Union Church was subsequently erected. He built a grist mill over Union Creek in 1813, and a ginning and carding machine, to prepare rolls for the spinning wheel.

It is a curious fact, that 104 years after Barnes' novel departure from Georgia his romantic adventure should be recorded by this writer, as related to him in person by the first born son of little Margaret, at the age of ninety years, and within a few miles of where he was born.

In the State of Tennessee at this early time there lived a Widow Sartin, who had a little boy named John. She married a man named Lee, and they moved from Tennessee to Amite County in 1810. Here John Sartin met little Margaret Barnes. Their associations and friendship ripened into love, and when Margaret Barnes arrived at the age of seventeen she became the wife of young John Sartin. They settled in the woods and opened a little farm on Magees Creek, a few miles south of China Grove, which was afterward known as the Woodruff place. It was here that Major Sartin, their first son, was born, November 28, 1812. They were also the parents of William, Joseph, Alfred, John, Leander and James Sartin and Amanda, wife of Martin P. Roberts; Helen, wife of John Boone, and Emily, wife of Jackson Bearden.

William Fortinberry came from Lancaster District, South Carolina, and settled in the southeastern portion of the county in 1819. He died in 1840, leaving six sons and four daughters. One of his sons, W. J. Fortinberry, was a Baptist preacher and spent his life in that section of the county in the cause of the Church. Another son, G. C. Fortinberry, was a member of the 9th Mississippi Regiment of United States Militia, under Col. Peter Quin, in 1825 and 1827. Wyatt Smith married Eusaba Fortinberry.

John Ellzey came from Fairfield District, South Carolina, in 1817. He married Elizabeth Coney, daughter of Aquila Coney from Georgia, in 1823 They were the parents of Frank, James, William, and Daniel Ellzey. His second wife was Indiana Hall. John Ellzey and William Sibley assisted the contractor, Thomas Tompkins, to build the first jail erected in Holmesville. Shortly after the building was finished and received from the contractor, Tompkins, having committed some little trivial breach of the peace, was the first to be locked up in it.

Thomas Ellzey was the third son of Louis Ellzey, of South Carolina, and came to Mississippi in 1817. He married Mary, a daughter of Daniel Quin, on Sweetwater, near where it empties into Bogue Chitto, at Walker's Bridge, in 1825. He settled on Leatherwood, where he raised a large family. He contracted yellow fever in 1847 while on a business trip to Covington, La., during the prevalence of an epidemic, and died with it at the residence of Col. Jesse Thomas, on Leatherwood, before he could be conveyed home. He was a member of the board of police for many years. His father, Louis Ellzey, was a full-fledged Englishman of the noted Ellzey Cragg, a mountain point in England, and his mother was a full-blooded German. Her name was Eve Shafter. They met in South Carolina and married, then immigrated to Pike County and first settled on the Bogue Chitto River near what has been known as Stalling's Ferry. Thomas Ellzey and Mary Quin were the parents of Ross A., Rankin C., Wesley, Jackson, Mary, Harriet, Caroline Sarah, Josephine, Joan, Courtney and Thomas. The Ellzeys sprung from good fighting stock and were substantial citizens in the early history of the county. They were brave, hardy, industrious men and women, accumulators of wealth and could always be depended on in times of peril and emergencies. Ross A. Ellzey, the elder of the sons of Thomas Ellzey and Mary Quin, was born on the 20th of June, 1826, and received his education in the common neighborhood schools of the county. At the age of twenty-six he married Amanda Booker, a daughter of James and Mary Booker, of Clinton, La., and a graduate of the Silliman Institute of that place. In 1848 he was chosen as a delegate to represent Pike County in a railroad convention held in New Orleans, which was the beginning of the agitation of the question of the constitution of the New Orleans, Jackson & Great Northern Railroad. In the fall of 1853 he was elected to the Legislature of Mississippi and remained a member of that body until he was succeeded by Levi Bacot in 1856. He settled the old Deer place on Magees Creek and pursued, principally, the occupation of a farmer. He became one of the charter members of the Magees Creek Lodge, F. & A. M., No. 282, in 1866. He taught school in his young days and was for some years a member of the board of school directors, with Henry Badon, William Hoover and George W. Simmons. The other children of Thomas Ellzey and Mary Quin married as follows:

Rankin C. to Mary Thompson, daughter of Hugh Thompson; Wesley to Margaret Brumfield, daughter of Isaac Brumfield; Caroline to Dr. James H. Laney; Harriet to Morgan Coney; Sarah to Samuel McNulty; Josephine to Elisha C. Andrews; Joan to Simeon R. Ratliff;

Courtney to William Badon; Jackson to Mary Felder; Mary to Joseph O'Mara, deputy sheriff under Parham B. Williams in 1848. Thomas died early.

William Simmons came from Georgia and settled on Balachitto in 1809. He married Nancy Hope, daughter of James Hope, who settled there about the same time. From them came Solomon and Cyrus Simmons. He was captain of a militia company, and in 1846 was elected to the Legislature with Ephriam Rushing.

Willis Simmons came from Georgia with his wife, Jane Goslin, in 1810, and settled on Bogue Chitto below Walker's Bridge. Their children were Mason, William (Black Bill), Willis, Richard, George, Jackson, Narcissa and Holly. "Black Bill" Simmons married Nancy Rymes, daughter of William Rymes and Nancy Hogg, and they were the parents of Calvin Simmons.

Joseph Barr came from South Carolina in 1802. His wife was Eliza Mellard, daughter of Joseph Mellard, near Monticello in Laurence County. They settled on Magees Creek in the China Grove neighborhood. They were the parents of William A., Thaddeus H. S., James A., R. Wesley, Thomas M., and Annor, wife of Wm. B. Lignon, Jr., Caroline, wife of Wiley Elliott, and Amanda, wife of Dewitt Ellzey.

Peter Felder came from Barnwell District, South Carolina, in 1811, and settled what is known as the Vaughn place near Magnolia. As previously stated, he was one of the commissioners appointed by the Governor, under acts of December 9, 1815, to select, procure and fix the permanent seat of justice of Pike County. He filled the position of one of the justices of the Orphan's Court along with William Dickson, Peter Quin and Matthew McEwen, which had jurisdiction in probate matters. He was the father of John Felder, who was born in Barnwell District, South Carolina, in 1793, and married Elizabeth Sandell, near Felder's Church, October 15, 1812. They were the parents of Mary Catherine, who married Seaborn Alford, and Wyatt Westley, Elizabeth G. Gabriel Nally, Levi Darius, Robert Henry and Simeon Noble. John Felder was a leading member of the Methodist Church. In 1840 he settled a farm on Topsiaw and in company with Christian Hoover, Hardy Thompson, David Winborne, Matthew

McEwen, Samuel Whitworth, Archie McEwen and Silas Catchings, in 1843, established the Topisaw Camp Grounds. In 1846 he had a water-mill constructed over Topisaw—upright saw, grist and cotton gin, near the camp grounds, under the supervision of Luther Smith, assisted by his sons, Levi and Robert. He and his wife were deeply devoted to their religion, and to them the community owed much in the upbuilding of the Methodist denomination and maintenance of the church and camp meetings held there. Their sons and daughters were all Christian people of the same faith.

Alexander McCollough emigrated from Ireland to Georgia. His wife was a Miss Marshall from Scotland. They were the parents of William McCollough, who came to Pike County in 1814 at the age of fifteen, married Sally Warren and settled on Topisaw. From them sprung the McCollough family: Winston, Benjamin, Jasper, Olive, Melinda and Sarah.

Matthew and Archie McEwen came from Carolina in 1800 and settled on Topisaw. James, a son of Matthew, married Nancey Barnes, widow of John Barnes, who was once probate judge of Pike County. Nancey was a Bearden before she married John Barnes and was the mother of Pinkney and W. Clinton Barnes.

John Walker was a native of Virginia, born in 1785. He emigrated to Georgia and married Sarah Gates, who was born in 1790. They emigrated to the Mississippi Territory in 1814 and settled on Topisaw. They were the parents of Jeremiah, William, John E., David C., Augustus, Sarah, Elizabeth, Mary, Zebiah, Martha and Elisha Walker.

John E. Walker was born January 28, 1815, the year after his parents came from Georgia, and was the first child of the Walker family born in Pike. His brother, William, married Ruth Harvey, daughter of Michael Harvey, who settled on Pearl River in Marion County in 1808, where Daniel Harvey was born in 1812.

There was a William Walker who settled on Silver Creek in the southern portion of the county, who was a cabinet maker, not related to the Topisaw family. He came from Georgia and married Jane Duncan, a daughter of Cullen Duncan and Fanny Conerly, subsequently wife of Elijah Turnage. The following are the names of their children: Martha Ann, who first married her cousin, James Duncan, and becoming a widow married John Cothern; Sarah Jane, who remained single; Barbara, who married John Estess; Pollie died early; Annie, who married William Rushing; Levisa, who married Charlie Rainey; Margaret, who married Harper Garner, son of Calvin Garner and Ruhamie Ward of Laurence County, from South Carolina; Cornelius, who married Nannie Boone, daughter of Skinner Boone; Wesley,———.

This William Walker's elder daughters became expert in their father's trade, being his only help. Sarah Jane never married and gave her entire time to her father in the workshop, where they made spinning wheels, reels, looms, chairs and other articles of furniture by hand and with the use of a turning lathe run by water power, milk piggins, water buckets, churns, etc. Much of the furniture manufactured by them has been in use seventy-five years. A small armchair, with a rawhide bottom, made of white hickory, bought from them for the writer in 1846 is yet in use and well preserved.

Roda Walker married Nathaniel Wells, being his second wife. He was major of a regiment during the Florida War. His father, Thomas Wells, belonged to the colonial revolutionists, and was killed in the memorable battle of Kings Mountain, North Carolina, in 1780, where the English General Ferguson was defeated, killed, and his entire force captured after a most gallant and sanguinary conflict with the mountaineer forces under the gallant commands of Cols. Campbell, Shelby, Sevier, McDowell, Cleveland, Williams and Winston, which turned the tide of the revolutionary war in favor of the struggling Americans, of which Jefferson said: "It was the joyful enunciation of that turn in the tide of success that terminated the Revolutionary War with the seal of our independence." And Daniel Webster said: "When to be patriotic was to endanger business and homes and wives and children and to be ready also to pay for the reputation of patriotism by the sacrifice of blood and life."

It will be seen in future pages how these eloquent words spoken by these master minds connected with a government these illustrious southern patriots fought so hard and heroically to establish, will apply to their descendants eighty years after this glorious victory at Kings Mountain.

With Rhoda Walker, Wells had two sons, Eleazor and James, and two daughters, Rhoda and Elizabeth.

William Cothern married Nancey Gates, from Georgia, and settled the Turnipseed place on the east side of Topisaw, five miles north of Holmesville, in 1815. They were the parents of Elijah Cothern, who married Cathorine Dunaway, daughter of Johnathan Dunaway, and they were the parents of John, Joseph and William Cothern. One of the first grist mills run by water power built in Pike County was constructed across Carters Creek on the plantation owned by John Cothern, which was settled by John Carter, one of the earliest settlers, from whom this creek took its name.

Turnipseed, above mentioned, married Miss Brent, daughter of John Brent, sister of John A., William, Mike and Jacob. He was a large slave owner and worked them in the production of cotton. He was a man of fine intellectual qualities. His children with Miss Brent were Laura, who married Ben. Briley; Clifton, who married Miss Ada Marshal, whose father settled in Holmesville after the Civil War and was a lawyer; Harris, who became a dentist; Berkley, who married Mary Huffman.

Lazarus Reeves came from South Carolina and settled on Clear Creek in 1811. This little stream rises west of Summit, running in an eastern direction, emptying into Bogue Chitto near the plantation of Laban Bacot. Lazarus Reeves was the father of John Reeves, who settled on Clear Creek in 1812, and Alfred Reeves, who settled on Topisaw, and Zachariah Reeves, Baptist preacher.

The Bogue Chitto Baptist Church was constituted and located on a place subsequently owned by Alex. McMorris, on the Bogue Chitto River, on the 31st day of October, 1812, by Lazarus Reeves, Annis Dillon, Priscilla Warren, Sarah Norman, John Brent, Sr., William Denman, John Warren, Sarah Thompson, Sarah Denman and David McGraw. This church was afterwards moved to Carters Creek, and Zachariah Reeves was connected with it during his lifetime. He was a man who wielded a great influence over the followers of his faith. He was contemporaneous with Rev. Jesse Crawford of Silver Creek and Rev. Wm. J. Fortinberry at New Zion. They were not educated men. Their learning came from the common schools of the community, such as could be afforded by the pioneer fathers and by a faithful and sincere study of the holy scriptures and the inspiration that sprung from the rugged experiences of their time, and they were regarded by those who adhered to their faith and followed in the footsteps of their teachings as men of power—plain, homespun leaders and teachers of God's word, who could touch up their followers and bring them to the foot of the Cross in this interior wilderness and make them children of the Messiah. In those days their church houses were mostly built of round pine poles or hewn logs, and the people wore plain clothes. The women went to church in calico and homespun dresses, and wore their fly bonnets, and the old grandmothers their frilled caps and specks, and the young girls thought themselves lucky to be decked off on meeting days with a few red ribbons. There was no butterfly flutter nor makeup of the rouge and the kid glove. A little cinnamon sometimes, when it could be had, constituted the main article of perfumery, and they were often glad to get that, as an attractive feature. Their splendid beauty, in these healthful pine woods regions, was a gift of nature from nature's God. They inherited from their mothers and grandmothers all the attributes of fortitude, patience, industry and loving kindness; and they grew up as women worthy indeed to become the mothers of the young heroes who served under the Southern Cross, led by such men as commanded the Confederate forces in the great Civil War.

And it might be well for the present day generation of young men and women to profit by learning more of the early training and the chivalrous manhood and womanhood that stepped so proudly forth in the early sixties to bear the brunt of one of the most stupendous conflicts against overwhelming odds known in the annals of war. They got their early training, from an educational and religious point, in these little log cabin school houses and churches.

John Reeves was the father of Jesse, William E., Elijah and Warren, and Leah, wife of William Williams; Lenora, wife of Jasper

McCollough; Jane, wife of Pink Cole, and Mary, who lost her first husband, Ruben Williams, in the Confederate Army, subsequently wife of David Forest. At the compilation of these notes in 1902, Wm. E. Reeves, then eighty years of age, possessed and exhibited to the writer a photographic group of the above-named four brothers and sisters, all living.

Edward Gatlin settled a place on Clear Creek a short distance above its intersection with the Bogue Chitto River in 1815 and built a mill over it which was run by water power. The plantation is now occupied by John Thompson. The spot where the present residence stands is one of the most picturesque in that section of the county.

Col. James Gatlin was a son of Edward and Elizabeth Gatlin, who emigrated to Pike County in 1812 from South Carolina. He married Rosalba Wells, a daughter of Nathaniel Wells, one of the colonial soldiers of the Revolution, of Kings Mountain fame, and his wife, Elizabeth, also from South Carolina. They were married at the old Wells homestead, south of Johnston Station, in 1831. Their children were: Julia; Zebulon B. Gatlin, who married Martha Hoover; Elizabeth Gatlin, who married Dr. Germany; Mary Gatlin, who married Mr. Anderson; *John B. Gatlin, Lieut., who married Amanda H. Strickland. Ebenezer Gatlin commanded Summit Rifles, at Blood Angle, battle of Spottsylvania, Virginia, May 12, 1864, mortally wounded; Thomas Gatlin, died in Confederate war service; Nathaniel W. Gatlin; William Gatlin.

The following persons settled homes along Clear Creek and Bogue Chitto between 1810 and 1818:

William and David Bullock, in 1812; I. N. Simms, L. Leggett, B. Gatlin, Ezra Estiss, T. Gatlin, R. Williams, N. Williams, E. Johnson, W. McNulty, Michael McNulty, in 1816; J. McNulty, in 1811; David Cleveland, Vincent Garner, J. Andrews, W. Andrews, David McGraw and Robert Love, in 1811; A. King settled a part of the Hardy Thompson plantation in 1811; David Cleveland, on what is yet known as the Cleveland place, in 1811; J. Denman and R. Hamil-

---

*See Dixie Guards.

ton, in 1815; C. Ryals, 1817; Peter Quin, Sr., on section 22, in 1813; Peter Quin, Jr., in 1817.

The lives of these men and their descendants were closely associated with all that section of the county between Holmesville and the northern boundary of the county on both sides of the Bogue Chitto River and along Clear Creek. B. Jones settled on Clabber Creek. It is to be regretted that the writer, though using great efforts, has failed to obtain better information regarding their families. Many of them were prominent in political affairs of the county. Michael McNulty erected a mill across Clear Creek at the same spot where Stuart's mill now stands. He was the father of William and Sam McNulty, of whom more will be said further on in this work.

Laban Bacot was born April 23, 1776, in South Carolina, and married Mary Letman in 1797. They emigrated from South Carolina to the Mississippi Territory in 1807, coming down the Cumberland, Ohio and Mississippi Rivers to Natchez and settled on Beaver Creek, in Amite County. They subsequently settled on the Tansopiho, near where Chatawa now stands. He was the son of Samuel Bacot, who was born in 1745 and married Margaret Alston. To them were born Samuel, Susana, Elizabeth, Maria Louisa and Mary Lucinda. His wife, Mary, died in 1812, and he then married Margaret M. Love, April 23, 1822, and they became the parents of Lorinda, wife of Joe Tuff Martin; Robert, Levi, William, Adam Bacot and Julia; also Rachael, who died in infancy.

In 1817 Mississippi was admitted as a State in the Union, and David Holmes, who had served as Governor since 1809, was elected Governor by vote of the people. Laban Bacot was elected at this time Sheriff of Pike County, succeeding David Cleveland, who had held that position since the organization of the municipal government of the county. It has often been erroneously stated that Laban Bacot was the first sheriff of Pike County. Under the territorial government David Cleveland was selected and commissioned as sheriff upon the organization of Pike County and served as such until the State was admitted into the Union, in 1817, when there was a general election held and Laban Bacot was the first elected sheriff of the county after the State's admission into the Union. During his incumbency he lived on a little farm seven miles north of Holmesville, on one of the small tributaries of Clear Creek. There being no public office buildings in Holmesville, he constructed an office on his farm, of peeled yellow pine poles, notched together and hewed down on the sides, which he used as the sheriff's office, being the first one built for that purpose in the county. This little log cabin, the first sheriff's office erected in the county, is yet standing in the yard on the plantation he subsequently settled on Clear Creek above its junction with Bogue Chitto, owned by his son, Levi, and is in a good state of preservation. Laban Bacot was re-elected in 1821 and served continuously until 1826, when he was succeeded by T. Norman.

During Bacot's term the whipping-post law was in vogue, and it sometimes became his duty to execute the sentence imposed, and if the judge thought the case an aggravated one he would order the sheriff to "have it well laid on."

On one occasion while court was in session a disturbance occurred at a whisky shop (then called grocery) near-by, and the judge ordered the offender to be brought into court. He was materially intoxicated and incapable of self-locomotion, and the sheriff returned without him. The judge again ordered that he be brought into court. Bacot ordered Parish Thompson, a powerful man with a loud, coarse voice, to bring him in. Thompson shouldered the fellow, packed him into the courtroom and piled him over in front of his honor, at the same time saying, "Where will you have him, jedge?" There was a law in force at this time which read as follows: "Any person who shall break into any house in the night time with the intent to take, steal or carry away any property therein, shall be adjudged guilty of burglary, and upon conviction thereof shall suffer death."

There was a little oak tree standing near the southeast corner of the public square which was used by Sheriff Bacot in the discharge of his duties as a whipping-post. This tree acquired the name of "Widow Phillips," as a man by that name was the first to be tied to it and receive a dressing with the official cat-'o-nine tails, for the commission of some trivial offense.

"Widow Phillips" grew large and strong and got to be a giant oak, spreading its massive branches far out, affording a splendid shade in after years for those in attendance on court. It lived to be a hundred years old and then died, and in 1902 it lay prone upon the earth, cut down by the axman. Thus passed away the last relic of the whipping-post of Pike County.

Jeremiah and Sire Magee settled on Collins and Magees Creeks near the junction of the two streams in 1811. About this time, or perhaps earlier, Dickey Magee built a grist mill over Collins Creek a little above the ford where the Monticello and Covington road crosses it. Portions of the foundation of this mill can yet be seen at times. It has been observed that under certain actions of the water there is a deposit of earth which hides if trom view; then again, the deposit is removed and the foundation is visible. When a small boy the writer crossed this ford and saw the water pouring in limpid beauty off the old foundation. Fifty-two years later he visited this spot and saw portions of the foundation still preserved and uncovered by the earth though under water. Some years after this mill went to decay another one was constructed some distance above it at a more eligible place with higher and narrower banks. These old mill ponds have grown up with large trees and where the upper mill stood a hill has been formed by the accumulation of alluvial thrown up by frequent high floods of water coming down from the cultivated lands and hills above.

William Willis Magee, a brother of Sire and Jeremiah, was one of the first Baptist preachers coming to this country from South Carolina. Josiah Magee settled on Dry Creek opposite the town of Tylertown.

Josiah Martin and his wife, Elizabeth Glass, came from North Carolina and settled on Big Tonsopiho, where Joseph T. Martin (known as Joe Tuff) was born, April 13, 1812. He always claimed to be the first boy child born in Pike County. The fact is he was not born in Pike County, but in Marion County, because there was no such a county as Pike when Joe Tuff was born. Major Sartin was close after him, for he was born on Magees Creek November 28th, of the same year. It was about three years after these remarkable events, 1815, before Marion County had this valuable and historical territory plucked from her great body. At any rate, be it said to his honor, Joe Tuff was born in that portion of Marion County which became a part of Pike. There were three other brothers, sons of Josiah Martin and Elizabeth Glass: Wm. G. Martin, who married Sally Wicker; James B. Martin, who married Mary Pearson; Jack Martin, who lived and died a bachelor; and Eliza R. Martin, who married John McNabb, leaving no issue.

Joe Tuff married Lorinda Bacot, daughter of Laban Bacot, the sheriff, with whom he raised a large family of children. Joe settled down to farming, was a "hale fellow, well met," and often a conspicuous figure on public occasions; a good-hearted man and a prosperous farmer and citizen.

THE MC MORRIS FAMILY.

It has previously been stated in this chapter that the Bogue Chitto Baptist Church was constituted and located on Bogue Chitto on a plantation owned by Alexander McMorris. There were two by this name, Alexander, Sr., and Alexander, Jr.

The elder Alexander McMorris was from Scotland. His wife, Elizabeth Baxter, was also from Scotland. They emigrated to America and were married in Edgefield District, South Carolina, at the close of the Revolutionary War, where they lived until their children were nearly all grown, when they came to Mississippi and settled in Amite County. Alexander McMorris, Jr., was their son.

Joseph Herrington, of Irish descent, and Anne Brown, of English parentage, were married in Sumpter District, South Carolina, where all their children were born. They then moved to Tennessee, where both died, after which their children moved to Mississippi and also settled in Amite County. Among these children was Esther Herrington, who became the wife of Alexander McMorris, Jr., in 1842, and in 1843 he bought the place on Bogue Chitto, where the church was organized in 1812, and lived there until his death, in 1850.

Alexander McMorris, Jr., and Esther Herrington had two children: Richard H. McMorris, who married Maggie Jones, and Esther Ann McMorris, who married Isaac Charles Dick.

After the death of her husband, Mrs. Alexander McMorris married Wesley H. Thomas, and they were the parents of Mary M. Thomas, who married William Powell; Baxter Thomas, who married Ettie Norell, of Jackson, Miss., and Wesley A. Thomas, who married Miss Willie Smith, of Vicksburg, Miss.

Baxter Thomas was the first white child born in the town of Summit.

Alexander McMorris, Jr., had a sister named Nancy, wife of Hardy Thompson, who lived east of Bogue Chitto on the road leading to Holmesville, and was a large slave owner and cotton planter.

ISAAC C. DICK
of the Summit Rifles. 16th Mississippi Regiment, Color Bearer. Severely wounded in desperate charge at Cold Harbor. Subsequently member Washington Artillery

Isaac Charles Dick, who married Esther Ann McMorris, was a son of Jacob Dick, who was born in Switzerland and emigrated to France. His wife was Susanne Jonté of France. They were Huguenots. They and their families came over to New York, where Jacob Dick and Susanne Jonté were married, after which they moved to Louisville, Ky., where Isaac Charles Dick was born. He afterwards went to New Orleans, and when the railroad reached Summit he drifted there and subsequently married Esther Ann McMorris.

The following article has been copied from the *New Orleans Daily Delta:*

"We were shown by Mr. Isaac C. Dick, of 1914 Jackson Avenue, this city, a Bible printed in the year 1568. It is printed in double column, in Latin and French—one column being the translation of the other. In connection with this volume is the royal privilege of the king, which was absolutely necessary before a literary work could be issued. It is one of the oldest, if not the oldest, Bibles heard of in this country—being 330 years old. It has the original binding save the back and corners. Mr. Dick's grandparents became possessed of this old volume in France, it being left at their home by one of Napoleon Bonaparte's officers on the occasion of that emperor's march to Germany in 1806. It is in a remarkable state of preservation, and the print is very legible."

Capt. Westley Thomas, above mentioned, who married Widow McMorris, was a member of Jefferson Davis' 1st Mississippi Regiment in the war with Mexico and participated in all the fighting done by that command in Mexico.

Joseph Catching and his wife, Mary Holiday, moved from Georgia and settled on the Bogue Chitto, two miles below Holmesville in 1812. They had five children, as follows: Thomas Catching, who married Miss Clendenon, and lived in Hinds County, the parents of T. C. Catching, ex-Congressman, Mrs. Mary Baird and Mrs. Nannie Torry; Benjamin Catching, who married Miss Hickenbottom and resided in Copiah County; Silas Catching, who married Miss Ann Drake and lived in Pike County; Sally Catching married Robert Love; Seamore Catching married Sarah Smith, who came from North Carolina in 1812. They had two sons, Charles and Joseph, aged twenty and eighteen, killed in the battle of Shiloh, Tennessee. They had a son, Seamore, who married Miss Ada Marshall; Silas married Jennie Lilly, of Hazlehurst, and lived in Somerset County, Kentucky. John married Maggie Duffy, and also resided at Somerset, Ky.

Sally May Catching married Robert M. Carruth, of Amite County.

Florence married Frank Causey, of McComb City, and Wm. Love Catching married Miss Winnie Nall, of McComb.

In 1812 John Smith settled on the Bogue Chitto four miles below Holmesville. His wife was Elizabeth Love, and they were the parents of James (Wild Jim Smith), Narcissa, Margaret and Sarah.

Narcissa married Judge James B. Quin, Margaret, H. F. Bridges, and Sarah, Seamore Catching, the father of Sally May, Robert M. Carruth's wife. Mrs. Carruth has in her possession a copy of the *Ulster County Gazette*, Vol. II, published at Kingston, N. Y., under date of Saturday, January 4, 1800, ruled in mourning for the death of Gen. George Washington, who died December 14, 1799, aged sixty-eight, containing the proceedings of the United States Senate in reference to the death of this illustrious citizen, the Senate's address to the President and his reply from which the following is copied:

"Among all our original associates, in the Memorial League of the Continent, in 1774, which first expressed the sovereign will of a free nation in America, he was the only one remaining in the general government. Although with a constitution more enfeebled than his, at an age when he thought it necessary to prepare for retirement, I feel myself alone, bereaved of my last brother; yet I derive strong consolation from the unanimous disposition which appears in all ages and classes, to mingle their sorrows with me on this common calamity to the world.

"His example is now complete and it will teach wisdom and virtue to magistrates, citizens and men, not only in the present age, but in future generations as long as our history shall be read. If a Trajia found a Pliny, a Marcus Aurelius can never want biographers, eulogists or historians.
"JOHN ADAMS."
"United States, Dec. 22, 1799."

In memory of this event the *Ulster County Gazette* contains the following:

ON THE DEATH OF GENERAL WASHINGTON.
BY A YOUNG LADY.

What means that solemn dirge that strikes my ear?
What means those mournful sounds—why shines the tear?
Why toll the bells the awful knell of Fate?
Ah! why those sighs that do my fancy sate?
Where'er I turn the general gloom appears,
Those mourning badges fill my soul with fears;
Hark! yonder rueful noise—'tis done—'tis done!—
The silent tomb enshrines our Washington.
Must virtues exalted yield their breath?
Must bright perfection find relief in death?
Must mortal greatness fall? A glorious name!

What then is riches, honor and true fame?
The august chief, the father and the friend,
The generous patriot—let the muse commend!
Columbia's glory and Mount Vernon's pride
There lies enshrined with numbers at his side!
There let the sigh respondent from the breast,
Heave in rich numbers—let the growing reft
Of tears refulgent beam with grateful love;
And the sable mourning our affliction prove.
Weep, kindred mortals—weep—no more you'll find
A man so just, so pure, so firm in mind;
Rejoicing angels, hail the heavenly sage;
Celestial spirits the wonder of the age.

Mrs. Carruth also has the beautiful silk, gold fringed Master Mason's apron with the symbolic emblems of that ancient order, worn by her grandfather, Joseph Catching, who as well as being a pioneer of Pike was a member of Rising Brotherhood Lodge, No. 7, of Holmesville, and a certificate of membership of Joseph Catching, 15th of May, in the year of Masonry 5830 (1830) signed Thonly L. White, W. M.; Jimmerson Statham, J. W.; Arak Wilson, Sect. Also a certificate of membership of Joseph Catching from Holmesville Lodge, No. 69, dated January 1, 1847, A. L. 5847, signed George Nicholson, W. M.; James Kenna, S. W.; J. B. Statham, J. W.; Sam A. Matthews, Sect.

GEORGE III.

George III of England was born on the 4th of June, 1738. On tho 27th of May, 1759, he was married to Hannah Lightfoot. He died on the 29th of January, 1820. They had a son, Buxton Lawn, whe married Mary Dawson (or Dorson), a granddaughter of the Lord Mayor of London of the same name. Buxton Lawn and Mary Dawson were the parents of the following named children: Buxton, Robert, Henry, Mary, Betsy, Cathorine, Susan, William, Ann and Eliza. Of these, Robert, Mary, Eliza and Ann drifted to New Orleans, after coming over to New York in company with their mother, in search of the husband and father whom they missed on his return to England, and died there soon after.

Robert Lawn (changed to Layton) married Susan Gilchrist, first wife, and Margaret Newman Hewes, New Orleans, La.; Mary married Charles K. Porter, New Orleans, La.; Ann first married Mr. McKitrick, and then Samuel James Stephens. With McKitrick she had one daughter, Mary, who was the wife of Joe Kirkland. Eliza married William B. Ligon, Sr.

Ann Louisa Stephens, daughter of Ann Lawn (Widow McKitrick), was the wife of Owen Conerly, and mother of this writer.

Joe Kirkland had a son named Dud, who was a Mexican War veteran, lived and died in East Feliciana Parish, La.; also a son named Weston.

Ann Lawn Stephens was the mother of Cathorine, who married John C. Huey, New Orleans, La.; Cecelia, who was the wife of William Forshey, a sculptor and portrait painter, from Missouri, lived a while in Holmesville—had previously been a member of the Louisiana Legislature, and was Mayor of Brookhaven in the sixties.

It is a curious circumstance how the grandchildren of the King of England strayed away from there and became identified as they have been with Louisiana and Mississippi. Ann Louisa Stephens, Mrs. Huey and Mrs. Forshey and the children of William B. Ligon, Sr., with Eliza Lawn, being the great grand children of that monarch.

Samuel James Stephens, husband of Ann Lawn, was a native of Ireland, highly educated, an eminent physician and surgeon, and an attache of the staff of Napoleon Bonaparte. He possessed a miniature likeness of himself and Bonaparte taken together and set in gold, showing a strong resemblance between them and evidencing a close friendship. He was one of the volunteer exiles from France who came to Louisiana after the fall of his illustrious chief. He met and married Mrs. McKitrick and lived in Covington and New Orleans. Ann Louisa, his daughter, was well educated, spent some of her younger days with her brother-in-law, Joe Kirkland, and with her uncle and aunt, Col. William B. Ligon and wife, She taught school at China Grove, where she met young Owen Conerly and married him in 1838, in her twentieth year of age. She read and spoke French fluently. She was a woman of fine mental qualities, a great reader, historian and conversationalist, and was regarded as one of the brightest and most intellectual women of her time who lived in Pike County. She was a fluent writer and occasionally contributed to the local newspapers—in later years established in Holmesville. She was musical and poetical, an ardent Methodist in religion, and lived and died in the faith.

There is no language this writer can command which will enable him to pay a just tribute to his beautiful and gifted mother. Around the family fireside and in the sanctity of a home, in his childhood, youth and young manhood, he imbibed the inspirations of her soul. Whatever talents he may possess, manifested in a perusal of this book, he owes to her and a father who had an intellect as clear and bright as the waters that flow from the most beautiful' fountain.

The Laytons, descendants of Robert (Lawn) Layton and the Hewes connected with this branch; the Porters, the Hueys, Gilchrists and the Prestons of New Orleans are all connections of George III and Hannah Lightfoot; springing from Robert Lawn, Mrs. Eliza Ligon, Mrs. Mary Porter, and Mrs. Ann Stephens.

In Pike County, all the descendants of the children of Col. William B. Ligon and Eliza Lawn and those of Owen Conerly, Jr., and Ann Louisa Stephens, are direct descendants; also the children of Mrs. Cecelia R. Forshey, widow of Wm. Forshey, now of Texas. She had only two children, Cecelia and Florence, the latter being the wife of John W. Coffee.

Reddick Taylor Sparkman came from Bunkham County, North Carolina. His wife was Nancy Woodward Pearson, of Edgefield District, South Carolina. They were among the early settlers of Holmesville. Reddick Sparkman was a first-class mechanic and contractor and built many of the first fine residences of Holmesville. He was one of the builders and owners of the Holmesville Hotel, which subsequently fell into the hands of his son-in-law, William R. Johnson, who married his daughter Martha, the widow of —— Richmond. One of the residences built by him is still standing and is the home of Dr. Lucius M. Quin. In company with Thomas Arthur he constructed a water-mill over a small bayou below town through which the water was turned from the Bogue Chitto by the construction of a rock dam above. The machinery was run by means of a large undershot wheel. It was an upright saw and grist mill. He was major in the militia of the county and an active politician, being a democrat when the Whig party existed. He served as sheriff for several terms, the exact dates being given elsewhere in official lists.

Reddick Sparkman and Nancy Woodward Pearson, his wife, were the parents of the following children: Martha E., whose first husband was Mr. Richmond, the father of Dilla and Reddick Richmond; her second husband was William R. Johnson, the hotel keeper, and her third husband R. Y. Statham, who first married her sister Ann Maria and was left a widower.

Cynthia Adaline, who married James A. Ferguson.

Victoria, the wife of Frank M. Quin.

Alvira, the wife of Capt. John Holmes.

The names of their sons are Thomas Wiley, William L. and Achilles P. Sparkman. Thomas Wiley died in his youth. William L. was killed at the time of the breaking of Lee's lines at Petersburg, Va. He belonged to the Quitman Guards and was on the skirmish line when they (Harris' Mississippi Brigade) were ordered to assemble in Fort Gregg and hold it at all hazards. He fell before reaching the fort. Achilles P. Sparkman was severely wounded in the abdomen, penetrating the bladder, in the battle of Cross Keys, Va., during the celebrated Valley Campaign, when Stonewall Jackson and R. S. Ewell joined forces to drive N. P. Banks out of Winchester, which disabled him for life. Mention of him will be found in future pages of this work. He married Mary E. Vaught, the daughter of Maj. W. W. Vaught, who was a quartermaster in the Confederate Army.

CHAPTER III.

CHINA GROVE AND MAGEES CREEK.

China Grove was first settled and owned by Ralph Stovall, in 1815. He settled on land about one-quarter of a mile from where the China Grove schoolhouse and church have stood since established. At the foot of a steep elevation there is a splendid freestone, cold water spring, east of the church, that formed an ever-flowing branch which bubbled on down westward and emptied into Magees Creek. This spring and branch afforded ample water for domestic purposes and for stock. At this period of the first settlement of the community under the Stovall regime, the church erected here belonged to the Baptist denomination. There was a grove of China trees set out in the grounds around the schoolhouse, which was a little log building (the original church house), and the church yard, which gave it the name of China Grove. Ralph Stovall employed John Barnes, the grandfather of Major Sartin, and constructed a set of mills over Magees Creek, about a mile south or southwest direction from the church, and his residence, run by water power.

These mills consisted of an upright saw, a cotton gin and press, a rice pestle mill and fan, for cleaning, and a grist mill. It was built across the stream at the foot of a bluff, which afforded a good embankment on the east side. Drury and Henry Stovall, brothers of Ralph, settled a few miles north of China Grove at this same period. Richard Ratliff in 1817, Benjamin Youngblood in 1816, Ben Jones in 1818 and Joseph Thornhill in 1812.

In 1822 Owen Conerly and his brother, Rev. and Dr. Luke Conerly, emigrated from North Carolina, Duplin County. They were sons of Cullen Conerly and Letticia. They married sisters. Owen married Mary and Luke married Rebecca, daughters of William Wilkinson and Elizabeth. The latter left no issue. Owen and Mary were married January 14, 1808, in the town of Fayetteville, N. C., county of Cumberland. When they came to Mississippi, Owen Conerly purchased all of Ralph Stovall's property at China Grove. Rev. and Dr. Luke Conerly settled near by in Marion County, on the headwaters of the

Pushepatapa, in the vicinity of Waterholes Church. After this the church house property which had been used by the Baptists, being included in the act of sale, was turned into a Methodist Church. The children of Owen Conerly and Mary Wilkinson were Cullen, William W., John R., Eliza, Owen, Emily, Luke (died early), Rebecca (died early), Cathorine (died early), Mary Jane and James, Melissa and Susan (died early).

Some of the early settlers of Magees Creek, more or less identified with China Grove, were Parish Thompson, James Craft, Zachariah McGraw, Owen Elliott, John Merchant, school teacher and preacher; James Reed, James May, William Reed, Noah Day, chairmaker; Jacob Smith, Joseph May, William Boon, Stephen Ellis and Joseph Newsom.

In 1813 Sartin's Church was established by John Sartin, Joseph Newsom, James Reed, John May, Joseph May, Owen Elliott and Stephen Ellis.

Stephen Ellis was a school teacher and minister of the gospel, and was one of the prime movers for the establishment of a church here, as well as being a pillar of strength to pioneer Methodism in this section. The house constructed here was built of peeled pine logs and was used as a house of worship, a day school and a Sunday-school, with Stephen Ellis as the minister, teacher and superintendent. This man took such a conspicuous part in the spiritual, intellectual and social upbuilding of Magees Creek that he and his brother, Ezekiel Parke Ellis, afterward district judge of the Florida Parishes, La., deserve more than a passing notice in these reminiscences. They were the sons of John Ellis, born in Virginia, and connected with the Tucker and Randolph families, whose father was a man of great force of character, a planter and a Christian. Their mother was Sarah Johnson, born in Virginia also, and connected with the Kershaw and Lowry families of that State.

John and Sarah Ellis moved to Georgia and thence to Pike County, Mississippi, and afterwards to Louisiana, in the territorial period. The Ellis families of Copiah and adjoining counties are of the same stock. George, John, Reuben, Stephen and William Ellis were names of members of this branch.

William Millsaps, of Browns Wells; T. J. Millsaps, of Hazlehurst; Mrs. Sally Wadsworth, widow of Rev. Wm. Wadsworth, and Dr. George E. Ellis, of Utica, Miss., are among those recalled as offshoots of the Mississippi branch of the family.

When tidings of the massacre at Fort Mims reached South Mississippi Stephen Ellis, still in his teens, joined a company of mounted riflemen, raised in Pike, Marion and adjoining counties, and with this volunteer command served under General Coffee in the little army of Gen. Andrew Jackson, then operating in Alabama and Georgia against the hostile Indians and their British allies. He saw hard service under Coffee, who was Jackson's great cavalry chief, in that fearful wilderness campaign. He participated in the sanguinary battle of the Horse Shoe Bend on the Tallapoosa River, where defeat broke the power and spirit of the Creek Indians for all time, and he took part in other minor engagements, served faithfully until the close of the war and was honorably discharged. He was a fine reconteur and delighted in entertaining his hearers of recollections of Jackson and Coffee, Houston and Davy Crockett, and of the pompous bearing and self-importance of the Choctaw chief, General Pushmataha, one of Jackson's brigadiers.

Stephen Ellis married Mary Magee, sister of John, Hezekiah and William Magee. He moved from Pike County to near Franklinton, in Washington Parish, Louisiana; was a successful planter and man of considerable means. He was a man of deep religious convictions, a preacher of force and earnestness, logical and zealous, and his ministry resulted in lasting good. He was a great reader, strong thinker and writer. He delighted to teach the young and spent years of his life thus. He was for years superintendent of education and held other positions of trust. He possessed engaging manners, fine social qualities. He was handsome and happy hearted, content and true in friendship. His only living son is Stephen R. Ellis, of Acadia Parish, Louisiana. His daughters living are Mrs. Melissa Wiggins, of Sharon, Miss., widow of Rev. David M. Wiggins; Mary, widow of Rev. Benj. Impson; Gabriella, widow of Hugh Bateman, and Mrs. Ellen Babington, wife of Robert Babington, of Franklinton, La.

His descendants include the family names of Ellis, Burris, Wiggins, Simms, Impson, Bateman, Babington, Hartwell, Sykes, Lampton, Bickham, Maggee and others. One daughter, Sara Ellis, married Judge James M. Burris, another Rev. L. A. Simms, and another Jason Bateman. He died at his home near Franklinton about 1869 in the seventy-ninth year of his age, the triumphant death of a Christian, carrying along with him in the eternal hereafter the sweetest recollection of those who survived him.

There are many people yet living in Pike County and elsewhere who remember this good man, who were children then. His beautiful character, his love of children, his zeal in religion and the uplifting and upbuilding of the Methodist Church in Pike County and in Washington Parish are indelibly stamped upon their memories. Traditions of him have gently and sweetly floated down the stream of time—among the descendants of those who clustered about him, from the head waters of Magees Creek to where the earth has been made holy and sacred as his last resting place in Washington Parish, Louisiana.

Ezekiel Parke Ellis lived in Pike County on Magees Creek and taught school also in the early history of the county. He was twelve years younger than his brother Stephen, and therefore figured later on. He married the youngest daughter of Col. Thomas Cargill Warner, who served under Gen. Andrew Jackson at New Orleans in 1814 and 1815, and was judge of the probate court of Washington Parish, Louisiana, for many years.

Ezekiel Ellis became a lawyer and was judge of his district for many years, dying at Amite City in 1884 at the age of seventy-nine years. He, like his illustrious brother, was a man of splendid intellect, moral influence and force of character and transmitted his splendid virtues to his sons and daughters. His son, E. John Ellis, was a lawyer and brilliant orator, a man of great personal magnetism, a member of Congress from the Second Louisiana District from 1875 to 1885, dying in Washington City, D. C., in 1889. Stephen D. Ellis, a practicing lawyer at Amite City and Surveyor of the Customs of the Port of New Orleans under President Cleveland, and Thomas Cargill

Warner Ellis, senior judge of the civil district court of New Orleans, are living. The latter was closely associated with Gov. John McEnery during the celebrated dual government in Louisiana, of Wm. Pitt Kellogg and John McEnery, and took an active part in the overthrow of the disgraceful carpet-bag regime in that State in the reconstruction period. He has always been a man of fine intellect, clear views, legal acumen, an elegant and forceful writer, a true, noble-hearted, lasting friend, and while filling the ardent and responsible position of senior judge of the civil district court of New Orleans has also filled the chair of law lecturer at the Tulane Institute in that city.

EZEKIEL PARK ELLIS

One daughter of Ezekiel Ellis is the widow of Rev. John A. Ellis, of the Mississippi Conference, who was chaplain of the 29th Tennessee Regiment of the Confederate States Army. The above named sons all served honorably through the Civil War, in the Army of Tennessee. It is the splendid qualities possessed by such men as Stephen and Ezekiel Ellis and transmitted by them to their descendants that has thrown around the early history of Pike County a halo of romance, and gives to the writer of this epoch an inspiration and a labor of love.

During this early period of China Grove there were few postoffices, mostly located at the county seats of justice. There was none at China Grove until 1836, when the first postoffice was located through the efforts of Col. William B. Ligon at his plantation on Magees Creek, a few miles south of China Grove, and he made postmaster. It was given the name of China Grove postoffice through him. It was subsequently moved to Raiford's store, three miles nearer to the church, and afterwards, in the fifties, to Packwood's store, about three-quarters of a mile south of the church. China Grove is about equidistant from Holmesville and Columbia, and the residence of Owen Conerly being located at the crossing of the Monticello and Covington road and the Holmesville-Columbia road, made it a central and convenient stopping place for travelers. Owen Conerly and Mary Wilkinson raised five sons: John R. (Jackie), Cullen, William, Owen and James, and three daughters: Eliza, Emily and Mary Jane, and they all became settlers on Magees Creek or near it. Owen Conerly, Sr., kept his mill in operation attended by his son, Owen, Jr., until his death, about 1848, after which the property was sold at administrator's sale and fell in the hands of Needham B. Raiford, the Methodist minister, who at that time filled the pulpit at China Grove. Owen Conerly, Sr., and his brother, Luke, were among the organizers and principal supporters of the Methodist Church at this place up to the death of the former and the removal of the latter to Western Louisiana, in 1848.

After the sale of his father's China Grove property and the mill, Owen Conerly, Jr., having purchased a place higher up on Magees Creek, settled by John Gordon in 1817, erected a saw, grist mill and cotton gin. He sold a portion of this property to Thomas J. Connally, a blacksmith, who named these places " 'Possum Trot," from which the 'Possum Trot road leading from there to Tylertown derived its name.

In 1812 Peter Sandifer came from South Carolina on pack horses and first settled at "Thick Woods" near Baton Rouge, La., and from there he came to Magees Creek and settled a few miles below China Grove on the west side of the creek below Conerly's mills, through which lands the 'Possum Trot road runs. This was in 1820. During that year the noted Pacific-Atlantic hurricane, commencing on the Pacific Ocean, passed through the country to the Atlantic somewhere in North Carolina. It made a swipe through Pike County, striking in from Amite County along a little stream which derived its name, Hurricane Creek, from that circumstance. It struck in and swept over the old McCay settlement near Muddy Springs, where the Spinks

PETER SANDIFER IN BEAR FIGHT SCENE ON MAGEE'S CREEK, 1820.

brothers live, following a course a little south of Holmesville and through below China Grove where Peter Sandifer had settled. It was about one-half mile wide and did great damage outside of its central line by the side currents, destroying timber and other things as it passed. It wiped Sandifer's improvements off the face of the earth. Neighbors were far apart in those days, but it was customary to help each other in all cases of emergency, so the Magees and Thornhills, lower down on the creek, and others were summoned to his aid. On account of the abundance of bear and panthers, wolves and wild cats, it was unsafe to leave women and children unprotected. In this instance, as well as others, they took their wives and children, their guns and dogs, along with them. When they reached Sandifer's the men went to work to put up a new house, some cutting blocks and some pine poles and peeling them, and some riving boards, and the women to making preparations for their meals. There was a spring some distance away which afforded water, and the children were sent there for water. When they reached the spring a large black bear had possession of it. The children were greatly frightened upon meeting the bear so suddenly and their screams brought out the entire fighting force with their guns, knives and dogs. The bear, however, was undismayed and stood his ground against the big pack of trained dogs, and a genuine battle ensued. It was difficult to shoot the bear without endangering the lives of the valuable dogs engaged in the conflict, so the men let the fight go on until finally the bear picked up one of the most valuable of the dogs and proceeded to caress him vigorously while folded in his massive arms. The dog screamed for dear life, and this was too much for the owner and he and others rushed in with their big knives and the battle became one of exciting interest until bruin succumbed at last from loss of blood. This was a noted bear fight, but one among many of such incidents that happened in that section of the county. Magees Creek had a wide, flat bottom, which was in those days covered with a very thick undergrowth and wild cane, affording suitable hiding places for these wild animals. In this neighborhood Daniel Burkhalter and his wife, Mary Palmore, had settled on Varnal, which empties into Magees Creek just above Sandifer's. Their settlement was on the hill near the ford where the Holmesville and Columbia road crosses. They owned a negro slave woman who had some children. One was a child just sitting alone, and was left in the yard with the larger child to mind it, while the grown people were out at work. A large, fat coon came up in the yard and caught the little child by the cheek and held on to it. The screams of the children brought the mother to the house to learn the cause and the coon refused to let go. Then the master came and had to choke the coon to death to make it let go the child's cheek.

The wild animals and birds afforded great sport to the early settlers as well as meat in abundance for their families.

Daniel Burkhalter and Mary Palmore were the parents of Henry, William, John and James Burkhalter, and Eliza, who married Joseph Luter; Cynthia, who married Mike Jones; Mary, who married William Kaigler; Sarah Ann, who married Frank Leland; Louisa, who married Willis Magee, and subsequently Elbert Magee.

Indian Creek is one of the head streams of Magees Creek, and got its name from being the camping-grounds of the Choctaw Indians. It was first settled by William Boon and his sons later on and by the father of Wiley Elliott, who married Caroline Barr.

William Boon had four sons: John, Richard, Frederick and Skinner Boon. John married Helen M. Sartin.

Joseph Thornhill, who settled in this community in 1812, married Elizabeth Fitzpatrick in South Carolina. The following are the names of their children: Liddy, who married Claiborne Rushing, of lower Magees Creek; Polly, who married Jack Reddy, upper Magees Creek; Evan J., Lucella, John, Hiram, Joseph Patrick and William Thornhill, who was the father of Dr. Jo. M. Thornhill.

Elisha Holmes, Sr., came from Georgia with his wife, Sally Stovall, a sister of Drury, Ralph and Henry Stovall. They settled on Collins Creek in the early part of 1800, contemporaneously with the Magees. They were the original ancestors of the extensive Holmes family in Pike County. They were the parents of the following children: Coleman, who married Polly Ann Foil, sister of William Foil, from Georgia; Josiah, who married Agnes Sumrall; Benjamin, who married Mary Sumrall; William, who married Jane Foil, sister of Ann; Jesse, who married Nancy Sumrall; James, who married Nancy Shirley; Cynthia, who married David Brumfield; Betsey, who married Isaac Brumfield; Jennie, who married Willis Brumfield; Elisha, who married Mary Roberts, daughter of David Roberts, from Georgia, and Berry, who never married.

Elisha Holmes, Jr., settled on Varnal Creek and was the father of Thomas H. Holmes, who married Telitha Duncan, daughter of James Duncan and Winnie Carmon. His daughters were Polly, Ellen,

Emily, Harriet and Sarah, who married George Gartman, and Elizabeth (Betsey), who married Dave Gartman.*

Benjamin Holmes, the husband of Mary Sumrall, settled on the east side of Magees Creek some two miles north of China Grove. He was a farmer and bell manufacturer. He made them by hand in his shop and supplied the people with bells. He raised a large family of boys and girls and was the father of Dave and Capt. John Holmes, the last captain of the Quitman Guards, and Benny Holmes of the same company; James and Needham and Betsey, Mary Ann and Emily. All the Holmes whose names may be found in the rolls of the several military companies of Pike and incorporated in this book sprung from Elisha Holmes, Sr., and Sally Stovall, those glorious old Georgia ancestors, like the rest of them, who first planted themselves in the wilds of the Mississippi Territory, gave to the Confederacy its heroes and its heroines.

Darbun Creek, one of the head tributaries of Magees Creek, got its name from Colonel McGowan, an eccentric bachelor, who settled there with his brother, Elijah McGowan, in 1815, along with Drury and Henry Stovall, brothers of Ralph Stovall, the founder of the China Grove settlement, Richard Ratliff and Harrison Bracey. They were all slave owners and progressive and successful cotton planters.

Drury Stovall was born in Georgia in 1770, and his wife, Lucey Wright, was born in the same State in 1780. They were married in

---

*Isaac Duncan, a son of James Duncan and Winnie Carmon, was murdered by some negroes while plowing in his field. He had previously had a difficulty with negroes named Love and Pink Conerly. Subsequently Love was killed in his cabin by some one on the outside at night, his slayer shooting him through a crevice of the cabin. Isaac Duncan was supposed to be the one who did it, but there was no proof of it, and the grand jury failed to find any against him. This led to the murder of Duncan by negroes who slipped up to his fence and hid themselves and then shot him down at his plow. After disabling him and having him cut off from his own gun, they rushed in on him and, though begging for his life, they beat his brains out and left him. Ike Duncan assured this writer that he was innocent of the killing of Love and he has been informed by others in a position to know that he was not guilty of the crime. Ike Duncan was a mason and master of his lodge, and he was buried by that order, and had one of the largest funerals ever known in eastern Pike County. His murderers escaped punishment.

1803. From them came Charles Green, John Lewis, Thomas Peter, William J. and Felix Crawford Stovall. Charles Green Stovall remained in Georgia and the other brothers settled in the Darbun neighborhood and became the direct ancestors of the Stovall Confederate soldiers.

Harrison Bracey came from South Carolina in 1815 and married Elizabeth McGowan, a sister of Col. James and Elijah McGowan. They were the parents of Sarah, who married William Mellerd; Mary, who married Hugh Craft; Cynthia, who married Needham L. Ball; Rebecca, who married Calvin Ratliff, subsequently wife of Jackson Holmes; Margaret, who married Sherod Gray, and Lucy, who married Mike Pearson, and Washington and Harrison Bracey, Jr. The latter married Louisa Ball, daughter of Jesse Ball, Sr.

Harrison Bracey, Sr., was a nephew of President William Henry Harrison on the mother's side.

Richard Ratliff settled on Darbun in 1817. He married Mary Stovall (called Polly), daughter of Drury Stovall and Lucy Wright, from Georgia. Richard Ratliff and Mary Stovall were the parents of Franklin, Warren, Calvin, Green, Robert (died young) and Simeon R. Ratliff. Richard Ratliff was a large slave owner and acquired considerable means as cotton planter and by general farming.

Simeon R. Ratliff, one of the survivors of the Quitman Guard, is the only one of these sons living. He married Joan Ellzey, one of Pike County's most beautiful girls, at the close of the Civil War.

Joel Bullock came from North Carolina and settled in Marion County in 1818. His wife was Rhoda Davies, whom he married before coming to Mississippi. He was related to William and David Bullock, who settled on Clear Creek. They were the parents of Hugh, Quinney, Davies, Thomas, William, Lemuel and Samuel (twins), Richard, Simeon, Joseph, Rhoda, Delia, Eptha and Louisa, who married Mr. Ginn.

Lemuel T. Bullock, who resided on Varnal, married Joan, a daughter of Jerry Smith.

Jake Smith and his wife came from Germany, first to South Carolina or Georgia, and then to Mississippi, and settled on the west side of Magees Creek, a few miles north of Tylertown, where they lived and died and are buried. Five children were born to them: Daniel, Jacob, John, William and Salena.

Daniel married a Miss Magee. William married Angeline, daughter of John Magee. John married Miss Morgan. Jacob Jr., married ———, and Salena married Hugh Ginn. Sarah, a daughter of Jacob Smith, Jr., married Leander Sartin.

Benjamin Jones came from South Carolina in 1811, and acquired property on Magees Creek in 1818. He was a gunsmith, and married Polly Harvey, daughter of Michael Harvey. They were the parents of Mike Jones, who married Cynthia Burkhalter, daughter of Daniel Burkhalter and Mary Palmore.

Joel Bullock and Rhoda Davies were married in North Carolina, emigrated to Mississippi and settled in Marion County. Hosey Davies, a relative, and Newton Cowart, also came about the same time, also Stephen and John Regan. These people, with Luke Conerly, formed a group or settlement around Waterholes Church, just outside the line formed by the creation of Pike County.

Huey Bullock married Caroline Smith; Quinney married Liddy Graves; Richard, Miss Magee; Lemuel, Joan Smith; daughter of Gentleman Jake Smith; Simeon, Nancey L. Williamson; Joseph, Nancy Ann Davis.

William and Davis Bullock, who settled on Clear Creek in 1812, were a branch of this family.

Governor Bullock, of Georgia, brother of Capt. Theodore Roosevelt's wife, mother of Theodore Roosevelt, President of the United States, belonged to the same family. Another branch settled in Virginia. They were all Irish stock from England, and came to America prior to the Revolutionary War. There was a branch of the Davis (Davies) family who settled in Laurence County. These people were all known for their high integrity, honest purposes—substantial, law-abiding citizens, adhering to the Baptist faith in religion.

Thomas Bullock had two sons: William and John Thomas. John Thomas was a natural-born ventriloquist, which his schoolmates and play fellows learned of him in childhood, playing hide-and-seek. He was wild and daring even in his early years, and during the Civil War, by a ruse, he, with twelve young boys, captured 300 Yankee raiders in Laurence County while out on one of their expeditions from Natchez. He had thirteen Confederate flags, made by the women out of such stuff as they could hastily put together to represent the Confederate battle flag, and placed them in position so as to indicate the presence of so many regiments, and by a ruse drew them inside his lines, and when the proper time arrived the color-bearers exhibited their flags and the enemy discovered that they were surrounded without any hope of escape. Bullock rode out to meet them and asked what they proposed to do, surrender or be slaughtered? "It is a question for you to determine instantly or I will fire on you with my entire command." The officer in charge of the raiders saw the thirteen battle flags waving defiantly from the woods and he yielded at once. Bullock ordered them to line up and stack their arms, waved for a courier from his battle line, to whom he gave instructions to have General Bullock's ordnance officer to take care of these guns and to send a guard of twelve men to him at once, and with these he escorted the raiders into Confederate headquarters, where they learned to their mortification the trick played on them. His adventurous spirit knew no bounds, and at the close of the Civil War he joined the Texas Rangers and served with them for years and eventually died in the service of the United States Government as a detective.

It is related of him that he got to be such an expert rider and marksman that he could lean down beside his horse's neck, circle at full speed around a tree and girdle it, firing underneath his horse's neck. The writer was a childhood schoolmate with him and personally knew of his ventriloquism and reckless daring.

Michael Harvey came from Georgia. His wife was Mary Clowers. They first settled on Pearl River, in 1808, below Columbia, the same year that his son, Harris Harvey, was born. They afterwards settled near China Grove. Their sons were: Harris, Daniel, Evan, Thomas, Doc, Mike, Pearl, Sr., Jesse and Jack. There was a Pearl Harvey, Jr., son of Harris, who was a member of the Quitman Guards, 16th Mississippi Regiment, who died with the measles at Corinth in 1861.

The Harveys constitute a large family of descendants. Harris Harvey married Liddy Smith, daughter of Jerre Smith. Dan married Melovie, a sister of Liddy. Each of these brothers raised large families of sons and daughters identified with Magees Creek and its vicinity. Evan Harvey owned property near where McComb City was afterwards located, becoming one of the original pioneers and founders of East McComb. Ruth, a daughter of Michael Harvey, married William Walker, a son of John Walker and Mary Gates, who emigrated to Mississippi in 1814. It is claimed that Michael Harvey dug the first well in Pike County, located on the plantation of Irvin R. Quin, near McComb City. The descendants of these people will be spoken of in future pages of this work, with the same generation of others constituting the citizenship of Pike County in this interesting period.

William Ravencraft settled in the Territory in the early part of the century on a little stream forming one of the head tributaries of Magees Creek, which took the name of Ravencraft Creek. Like all other pioneer settlers who built grist mills at that period, he brought his millstones with him fixed on an axle like a cart and drawn by an ox or horse. All the millstones we have any record of brought to the Territory from South Carolina, of which water-mills were constructed in Pike, were transported this way. South Carolina and Georgia in those early days were fruitful of ingenious and skilled mechanics. William Ravencraft was one of this number. He was a fine cabinet-maker, made wagons, chairs, reels, spinning wheels, looms, shuttles, slays and fancy white hickory hamper baskets, some of which are in use to this day. There was a man here then from Copenhagen, Denmark, named Henry Mundalow, who made it a business to peddle the products of Ravencraft's shop and those of Wiley Rushing, living lower down on Magees Creek. Much of the furniture made by these skilled pioneers was transmitted to their descendants and are in use the present day, though worn by frequent scouring with sand to keep them white. The family in Pike without its spinning wheel, reel and loom, prior to the Civil War, was not considered up-to-date. The long distance to markets, the necessity of self-reliance and living on home products, gave the people, men, women and girls a schooling which, in after years, demanded of them the exercise of those heroic virtues that have made them famous throughout the world for sublime fortitude and unparalleled patriotism. William Ravencraft and Wiley Rushings on Magees Creek and the Walkers down on Silver Creek and the Bogue Chitto; John Warren, Jesse Day and John Stogner, Simpson Laurence and others, though poor in purse, are recalled as the mediums, the founders, the grandfathers of these splendid characteristics of the men and women of Pike County in the days and years that tried their souls. In his early childhood the writer visited many of these places of industry along on Magees Creek, and was familiar with their location over a half century ago. The mill that John Warren built for Ralph Stovall in 1817 below China Grove was the home of his infant years. Visiting this spot sixty years later he finds the foundations, and where his childhood feet toddled a veritable wilderness; and the stone that makes the name of William Ravencraft live in history imbedded in the little stream over which it clattered then.* William Ravencraft's property descended to his son Joe, who inherited the mechanical genius of his father and kept up the business assisted by his son George during his lifetime. In the meantime the waters of Ravencraft Creek began to fail and the little grist mill being very small and running so slowly, it took a whole night to grind a hopper full (about a bushel) of corn.

Thomas J. Connally, the blacksmith, afterward known as "Tallaboly," who married Sally McNabb and was living at " 'Possum Trot," told the story on Ravencraft's mill in his shop one day: That being belated one night on business in that section on account of the absence of roads and darkness he got turned round and didn't know which route to pursue. After awhile he heard a dog baying and concluded to go to it, consoling himself that he would probably get a big fat " 'possum" for dinner for Sally and the children. It was only at intervals the dog would bay, boo, woo! boo woo! Coming nearer he heard a clattering noise and the splashing of water, and now and then, boo woo! His heart leaped with joy over the prospect of that

*Since recovered by Elisha Thornhill on Love's Creek, residing on the old Forest homestead.

fat 'possum. He knew Sally and the children would be fed. He could well afford to lay in the woods all night and sleep soundly too with the assurance that Sally would be provided for. When he reached the baying dog he was struck with astonishment. It was Ravencraft's mill doing its nightly work grinding corn into meal, and the dog in the box eating it as it came out of the chute. He would lick it up and then raise his head and eyes heavenward and boo woo for some more meal. Said he, "I wound my way out of the wilderness that night a wiser but sad and disappointed man. No 'possum for Sally."

The sons of Owen Conerly, Sr., settled around him in the vicinity of China Grove, except Cullen, who married Levisa Lewis. He bought the Thornhill place in the fork of Magees Creek and Dry Creek. He erected a set of mills, saw, gin and grist, over Dry Creek above its junction with Magees Creek, bought out a store from Garland Hart, and established a postoffice which was called Conerly's postoffice. Owen Conerly, Jr., who

OWEN CONERLY
The Author's Father

after the death of his father in 1848, bought the Gordon place two miles north of China Grove, and in 1852 and 1853 built a mill over Magees Creek there, sold it to his brother James; then it passed to Joseph Luter, and is now owned by Mr. Rushing. William and John R. (Jackie) emigrated to Western Louisiana, the former subsequently returning to Pike.

Maj. Owen Conerly, a nephew of Owen, Sr., was a son of John Conerly in North Carolina. He married Susan Tynes and settled near the Marion and Pike County line, east of China Grove. He was a wheelwright, carriage maker and farmer, and was noted for keeping a large flock of goats. He raised a large family of children, sons and daughters who have always been identified with that section of Pike. One of the brothers of Maj. O. William Conerly settled on Pearl River. The children of Owen Conerly, Sr., married as follows: Cullen married Levisa Lewis, a daughter of Martin Lewis, of Marion County.

Mrs. A. L. Conerly
Wife of Owen Conerly

Owen, Jr., married Ann Louisa Stephens, of New Orleans, a daughter of Samuel James Stephens, an eminent Irish linguist and surgeon, an attache of the staff of Napoleon Bonaparte, and Ann Lawn, daughter of Buxton Lawn and Mary Dawson, or Dorson, of London, England. She was a school teacher, and came out in this region to Joe Kirkland's, who had married an elder sister, and settled on Kirklands Creek. She was a niece of Col. William B. Ligon's wife, Eliza Lawn.

John R. Conerly married Elizabeth Tines. William married Caroline Starns, with whom he raised James, Jr., and Mark. Two other sons, John and William, who died young. He subsequently married Margaret Connally, daughter of Price Connally, from Georgia, sister to "Tallyboly" and to William Tyler's wife and to George, Crosby, Jack and Rebecca. They had one daughter, Lulu. James Conerly married Mary Lamkin, daughter of Sampson L. Lamkin, the surveyor. Eliza married Jesse Ball, giving him three sons and a daughter—William, Newton and Needham and Rebecca. Lived on Magees Creek. Emily married Daniel Ball, Marion County. Mary Jane first married Jabez Lewis, brother to Cullen's wife, and raised one child, Mira, who married Monroe Smith. She afterward, as widow by death, married Benjamin Lampton, son of William Lampton, a brick mason from Kentucky, who made his beginning on a little farm north of Tylertown, formerly Conerly's postoffice.

Gilbert Grubbs came from Georgia. He married Elizabeth Sandifer. She was a daughter of Peter Sandifer, Sr., who settled on Magees Creek in 1820, the year of the great Pacific-Atlantic hurricane, and a sister of William, Jackson, Peter, Jr., and Robert. Gilbert settled on Union Creek in the same period with John Warren. He was the father of Benjamin Grubbs, Peter and Gilbert, Jr. Benjamin was the father of Henry Grubbs. His wife was Ellen Gartman, a daughter of Bartholemew Gartman, from Germany. Bartholemew Gartman's wife was a daughter of Daniel O'Quin, Nellie, from North Carolina. Her brothers were Daniel, Ezekiel and Jehu O'Quin. Bartholemew Gartman and Nellie O'Quin were the parents of George, David, Josiah, John and Perry Gartman and Cynthia, who married Joe Deer; Katie, who married Charles Carter in Louisiana; Mary, who married Elias Smith; Caroline, who married William Grubbs, and Ellen, who married Benjamin Grubbs.

George Gartman married Sarah Holmes, daughter of Elisha Holmes, Jr.

Henry Grubbs married Lenoir Angeline Ellzey, daughter of Louis Ellzey and Mary Ann Holmes.

Henry Grubbs owns the plantation on Magees Creek settled by a man named Toney about 1798, who sold it to Robert Sandifer, who built the hewed-log house on it now occupied by its present owner. It passed into the hands of his brother John, who sold it to Sampson L. Lamkin, a son of William Lamkin.

John Snead married Mary Gooch in Georgia. They were the parents of Keziah Snead, who was the wife of William Lamkin, the father of Sampson L. Lamkin the surveyor, and John T. Lamkin, the eminent lawyer of Pike County. The tombstones marking the graves of William Lamkin and Mary Gooch Snead can be seen on this place carefully preserved by Henry Grubbs and his wife.

Dr. McAlpin married Cathorine Wilkinson in North Carolina. She was a sister of Mary and Rebecca, wives of Owen, Sr., and Luke Conerly. With Dr. McAlpin she had two sons, Patrick and Mark. Dr. McAlpin dying early, these two boys were raised and educated by Luke Conerly. Cathorine afterwards married Calvin Magee, a Baptist minister, who emigrated to Sabine Parish, Louisiana. Patrick became a school teacher and taught in the little old log schoolhouse at China Grove. It was here that this writer sat upon his knees and learned to know what A and B were, at the point of his little ivory handled penknife. Fanny Conerly, a sister to Owen, Sr., and Luke, married Cullen Duncan, and becoming a widow she married Elijah Turnage. She was the mother of James Duncan. Polly Conerly, another sister, married —— Guy, the father of William Guy, ancestors of the Guys in Amite and Pike Counties.

Chelly married a Blunt in Covington County, and another sister married Isaac Newton in Laurence, and they are the ancestors of the Blunts and Newtons in that section of South Mississippi.

Quinney Lewis was a brother of Martin Lewis and Judge Lemuel (Lammy) Lewis, of Marion County. He and his wife, Patsey (Uncle Quinney and Aunt Patty), were contemporaneous with the Conerlys. They were, like them, devout Methodists. Their home was on Magees Creek some four or five miles below China Grove. They were great pillars of the Church here along with the Woodruffs, the Youngbloods, the Conerlys and the Sartins. Quinney Lewis and his devoted wife furnished two able ministers to the Mississippi Conference, Henry P. and William Bryant Lewis, and a number of their descendants belong to the ministry. They were the parents of Barney Lewis, one of the pioneer newspaper men of Pike County, located at Holmesville with Robert Ligon. Barney Lewis married Keziah, daughter of Sampson L. Lamkin and Narcissa Sessions.

In 1836 Col. Wm. B. Ligon obtained a large tract of land from the Government about five miles south of China Grove and settled there. Colonel Ligon had lived in Covington and owned a line of schooners working through the lakes and plying between Covington, New Orleans and Pensacola. He had taken an active part with Gen. Andrew

Jackson in 1814 and 1815. He had participated with the American colonists of Texas in their struggle for independence from Mexico, and was wounded in one of the battles. He was a man of considerable means when he settled here, and engaged in merchandise, farming and keeping the postoffice, which he had named China Grove. He was a native of Virginia, emigrated to South Carolina, thence to New Orleans, and married Eliza Lawn, daughter of Buxton Lawn, of London, England, and Mary Dawson, or Dorson. He had a brother who lived at Rienza in Tishomingo County. The names of his children are Robert, William B., Jr., John, Buxton, Lemuel T. and Charles A., and his daughters were Mary, Elizabeth Ann, Susan and Martha.

Robert married Angeline Bearden; William B., Jr., married Annor Barr and Mary Stovall, second wife; John, Sally J. Moseby, of Jackson, Hinds County; Buxton, Miss Barrett, of Hinds County; Lemuel Thomas, Mellie Muse, of Louisiana; Charles died a bachelor; Elizabeth Ann married Lemuel Jackson Quin—their children are as follows: Irvin Alonzo, who married Lizzie Luter; Martha Eliza, died early; Mary Arvazena, wife of Elisha C. Andrews; Lucy Marcella, wife of William Huey; Alice Cornelia, first husband Sam Stuart, second husband Dr. Cole; Laura Virginia, died young; George Nicholson Quin, who married Sarah Brumfield; John Ligon Quin, who married Ida, daughter of Giles Lewis; Lemuel Gracey Quin, who married Alice, daughter of Giles Lewis; Nancey Bridges, wife of Luther Burns; Josephus Murray Quin, who married Minnie Shontell; Sarah Elizabeth, wife of David Burns; Susan, John Shilling and Martha, Dave Ford.

On account of the part taken by him in the independence of Texas, Colonel Ligon was allotted a large tract of land in Texas by the Republic, but he never thought enough of it to prove and claim it. Land at that time being so cheap in Texas it was not considered worth the expense and trouble to acquire the deed. While engaged in the schooner trade between Covington and Pensacola he owned a negro slave who was one of his trusty sailors, but who was subject to trance spells which sometimes lasted for several days. On one trip he employed two new sailors as helpers on the schooner run by the negro, and they being ignorant of the nature of these spells thought him dead and threw him overboard, to the great sorrow of his master. He was a Methodist and pillar in the Church, but not demonstrative in religion. He was a man of high character, honorable purposes, a soldier of worth, and as such and a citizen of Pike County has left an untarnished record to be proudly remembered by his descendants.

In these early years of the settlement of Magees Creek we have no record of any doctors except those of the Thomsonian practice. Owen and Luke Conerly and their wives, "Aunt Polly" and "Aunt Becca," as they were called, were usually relied on in all extreme cases except surgery. Dr. Wiley P. Harris was at Holmesville, fifteen and twenty miles distant. Later on Dr. McQueen came from Washington Parish, and eventually Drs. Booth, May and Payne. Composition tea and lobelia was a favorite prescription for fevers, measles, etc., and a great medicine made by the settlers was called "Black Medicine," concocted from the star grass roots, and given as a spring tonic.

John Sartin, Jr., son of John Sartin, Sr., and Margaret Barnes, married Seleta Craft, daughter of John Craft, from Tennessee, and lived on what is known as the old Salty place, originally settled by Owen Elliott, on Canada Branch, one of the head tributaries of Magees Creek. He established a tannery on Tilton Creek in Marion County, which was used in the interest of the Confederacy during the Civil War. Their son, William Sartin, served in Pierce's cavalry company from Marion under Colonel Peyton and General Woods.

John Craft, Sr., had two brothers, James and Major. James married Ebiline Thompson, a sister of Parham, Sr., and Parish, Sr.

Major Craft married Nancey Hamilton, sister to John Craft's wife, and Mrs. Bearden. Major Craft was the father of Dr. Sidney M. Craft, who lived in Hinds County, near or at Jackson.

James had two sons, Hugh and Jack, and five daughters.

James M. Buckley married "Nug," the mother of Gov. A. H. Longino's wife. Hugh Craft killed Quince Cooper, who was pursuing him with a drawn knife around a house, and Hugh shot him to death with a Colt's repeater. It was clearly a justifiable homicide, and nothing was done about it.

Melie Manning and Nancey Deer were married in South Carolina and came to Pike in 1839 and settled on Ravencraft Creek. Their son John married Elizabeth Sandifer, and they were the parents of Joseph M., John W., Moses Moak and Westly J. Manning.

Joseph Parker and his wife, Mila Deer, came from Barnwell District, South Carolina, and settled on Varnal. Their children were William, Sarah and Nancey.

Jeremiah Bearden came from Tennessee and married Rachael Hamilton. He was one of the original settlers of Holmesville, and, in company with Reddick Sparkman, built the first hotel there. It was subsequently known as the Johnson Hotel, kept by William Johnson, who married widow Richmond, a daughter of Reddick Sparkman. The children of Jeremiah Bearden and Rachael Hamilton were Jack, and Nancey who married John Barnes, father of Pink and Clinton C. Barnes, and afterward married Matthew McEwen; Delilah, wife of Judge H. M. Quin, and Angeline, wife of Robert Ligon. These girls were twins. Jeremiah Bearden subsequently settled on Topisaw and died there. His wife lived to be very old and died in 1870.

George Ratliff, a slave of Richard Ratliff, purchased his freedom from the Ratliff estate. He was a fine mechanic and hired his time from his master. He was a mulatto, a good man and was well thought of by the whites. He married a slave woman of his own race and was honored with a splendid dinner given by the white people of Magees Creek. He settled a farm on Darbun and was the founder of Georgetown, located on the head of Darbun in the northeast corner of the county.

Other noted slaves on Magees Creek were Austin Bracey, Daniel and Griffin Ratliff, Prime Ball, Mose Conerly, Rans Lewis, Harry and Ike Conerly. The latter was a preacher, a teamster, and managed the log-cart for his master's mill. He sang his songs and preached to his oxen and prayed for them and his people. To him life as a slave was sweeter and happier than it was when emancipation endowed him with citizenship, and forced upon him the responsibility of providing for himself and family. And old Aunt Becca, his master's cook. The writer remembers when in his tender childhood he went to grandpa's and Aunt "Becca" took him upon her knees in the kitchen and caressed him and gave him the best there was in the pot and fed him with the little "niggers" under the massive shade trees with buttermilk and potlicker and bread.

Harriet Beecher Stowe and other Northern writers have given to the world the darkest picture of an institution for which the Southern people were not responsible, but brought to them by the slave speculators of the New England States.

Charles Smith and his wife, Nelly Hickenbottom, came from South Carolina in 1811 and settled on Magees Creek, west side, below China Grove, near Peter Sandifer. Their children were Elias, who married Mary Gartman; Zachariah, Pharo, Joseph and Charles.

Bill Finny settled on Kirklands Creek in the neighborhood of the Magees. According to tradition nearly all new settlements have had their Bill Finny. Whether this is a myth or whether the story of Pike's Bill Finny went abroad is not known. It is a fact, however, according to tradition from the original settlers of Magees Creek, that there was a William Finny who settled on Kirklands Creek. It is related of this man that he had an aversion to work and failed to produce corn to bread his family, and his neighbors got tired of providing it for him, and held a meeting to determine what should be done with him without violating the statutes. It wouldn't do to hang him or shoot him or knock him on the head with a pine knot. After long parleying it was determined to bury him alive. There was no law "agin" that. So they made a box and put it in a cart and went after Bill. They found him stretched out on the gallery as usual. They informed him of the decision of the court and he offered no objection nor made any resistance, and they picked him up and laid him in the box in the cart and proceeded to a distant burying ground. On the way they met a neighbor who enquired what was the matter. "Nothing, we are only going to bury Bill Finny."

"What! Is Bill dead?"

"No; we are going to bury him alive."

"For what?"

"Because he has no corn to make bread for his family, wont raise any and we are tired of furnishing it."

"Don't do that, men; I'll let him have some corn."

Bill lazily turned his eyes in the direction of his sympathetic friend and asked:

"Is it shelled?"

"No, it is not; you will have to shell it."

"Then drive on the cart," said Bill.

And they drove it on and dumped him out in the graveyard and left him there.

John Stalling settled near the confluence of Kirklands and Magees Creeks. He came from South Carolina. His wife was Nancey Dillon. When he settled there no salt could be had nearer than Natchez, a distance of a hundred miles. He walked to Natchez by such paths as he could find, did little jobs of work to pay for it and packed it home on his shoulder. They had one daughter, who married John Williams. Their son, James Stalling, married Sally Pearson, and they were the parents of Winnie, who married Eli Brock; Jane, who married Calvin Simmons; Eliza, who married James Simmons; Margaret, who married E. C. Holmes; Nancy, who married W. J. Holmes. Their other sons were John, Jeff and Willie.

Jacob Owen was born in South Carolina in 1780 and his wife, Mary Googe, in 1784. They settled on Dry Creek between 1800 and 1805. They moved from South Carolina on horseback. He built a small grist mill on Dry Creek, but on account of scarcity of water he afterwards went lower down and built another mill, which subsequently fell into the hands of Boardman and Tyler.

Tylertown was first known as the Magee Settlement. Cullen Conerly went there in 1850 and became the owner of the quarter section lying due north of the Thornhill tract, and bought out the Garland Hart store and established a postoffice which was called Conerly's postoffice, and the place bore that name for many years. He erected a mill about a half mile below the Owens or Tyler mill and farmed on his plantation. This he sold to Ephriam Rushing, and his mercantile interest was sold to Benjamin Lampton, who had married his sister, Mary J. Conerly, the widow of Jabez Lewis, and here Benjamin Lampton laid the foundation of the mercantile business of Tylertown, and which, through the business tact of his sons, has grown to such large proportions and become famous in Pike County and in Laurence and Marion.

GEORGE SMITH'S WATER MILL AND DAM OVER KIRKLANDS CREEK, SOUTHEAST PIKE COUNTY
Mr. Smith is standing on the framework of the dam, and members of his family are in the mill building. Mr. Smith is a Confederate Veteran of Co. E, 16th Miss., Harris' Brigade, A. N. V.

Clarkston Dillon settled on Bogue Chitto. Clara Dillon married George Smith, Sr. She and Willis, Theopholis and Laurence were children of Richard Dillon.

Tylertown has always been considered a part of Magees Creek, though the village as now located is on Dry Creek, which empties into Magees Creek a short distance below. Its first settlement dates back to the emigration of the Magees and Thornhills. William Thornhill and his wife, Liddy Breland, came from South Carolina and settled here. They had a son, Elisha, who was born in South Carolina in 1799. His wife was Mary Carr. Their children were William B., Hillary B., Elizabeth, Isham, John M., Brian, Mary Ann, James W., Millie Ann and Susan Ann.

Tylertown is located on a tract of land originally acquired by J. Thornhill September 20, 1816.

By custom the place got to be called Tylertown, and the postoffice was changed to that name in honor of W. G. Tyler.

William G. Tyler came from Boston, Mass., and was an artillery soldier under Gen. Andrew Jackson in the War of 1812 and 1815 against the hostile Creeks and their British allies, and participated in the battle of New Orleans (Chalmette) in 1815, which settled the fate of the English arms in America. He was a cannoneer and delighted in artillery practice. He was a splendid blacksmith, and moulded the small mortars used to fire salutes on public occasions. His wife was Mary Connally, daughter of Price Connally, a blacksmith from Georgia, and Mary Corker, whom he married in St. Helena Parish, Louisiana. They raised five children, William Thaddeus Tyler, who married Mollie Quin, daughter of Judge James B. Quin and Narcissa Smith; Lizzie, who married Newton Ball; Safrona, who married Mark R. Conerly; Fanny, who married Frank McLain; Sarah, who married John Alford.

WM. G. TYLER
Tylertown

Cullen Conerly and his wife, Levisa Lewis, were the parents of Owen, Jr., No. 2, who married Teletha Warner. Owen was color-bearer of the 33d Mississippi Regiment of Featherstone's Brigade, and was killed in the desperate assault on the enemies' works at the battle of Franklin, Tenn. John M., William M., Mary Ann (Polly), Rebecca, Eliza, Cathorine and Martha. John M. Conerly's first wife was Jane Lampton, daughter of William Lampton, of Kentucky, and sister to Benjamin, James and Frank. William M. Conerly married Sarah, daughter of Harris Harvey. Polly married John Colquhoun; Rebecca married Loftlin Colquhoun; Cathorine (Kitty), W. H. H. Brumfield, and Martha, Needham Holmes.

Chauncey Collins was from Salisberry, Conn.; born in 1810, he came to Mississippi in 1840 and married Amelia, daughter of Elias Woodruff and Ailsey Collins, of Columbia, Marion County, in 1842. He settled on a little stream emptying into Magees Creek southeast of Tylertown and a little below the junction of Dry Creek with that stream. It acquired the name of Collins Creek from him. Here he established a tannery and shoe shop, and lived the rest of his life. He had been a clock merchant for some years. He kept his hides in tan vats for two years and made the most lasting shoe to be had. Everybody almost in the country patronized him when they could obtain his goods. He was a highly intelligent man, a fine historian and conversationalist. His wife had two brothers—William, who went to Florida, and Seth Woodruft, who went to DeSoto Parish, Louisiana. His children were Caroline Victoria, who married Daniel Tate; Julia E., who married J. A. Morris; Frederick W., Warren N., Seth W., George H., Chauncey and Wesley.

Elias Woodruff was from Newark, N. J., whose father, Seth Woodruff, was one of three brothers who came from England to New Jersey. Seth Woodruff removed to New Albany, Ind. He was a Baptist preacher and probate judge, and baptized the first person ever baptised in the Ohio River up to that time and at that point.

The Woodruffs of New York State and New Jersey are descendants of the above-mentioned three brothers.

Elias Woodruff wandered from New Jersey and came to the newly constituted Mississippi Territory. For many years he was considered by his people as a lost member of the family, as they could not hear from him. At length means were provided and a brother was sent to search for him. After long months of overland travel, without a single clue, except that Elias had gone to the Mississippi Territory, working his way through the deep forests, by ways and paths, his brother found him in Pike on his little pine-woods farm where he had settled below China Grove, on Magees Creek, with his wife, Ailsey Collins, and one little daughter, Mary.

After long persuasion, he induced them to return with him to Newark, N. J., where little Mary died, after which, becoming dissatisfied they returned to their old home in Pike and raised a large family of sons and daughters, among them Amelia, the wife of Chauncey Collins, and Lucetta (who married W. G. Evans, Sr.), the mother of Hon. W. G. Evans, of Gulfport, ex-State Senator. Lucetta died while this son was an infant, and like many other Southern children in the past, owed much of the care given him to a good old black mammy; and W. G. Evans has worked his way up to a high and honorable position among his fellowmen. Ailsey Collins, his maternal grandmother, the wife of Elias Woodruff, was a pious, good woman, a member of the Methodist Church at China Grove in the days when the magnificent eloquence and influence of Stephen Ellis united the early settlers of that section of Magees Creek, in the establishment of a church that has been kept up for eighty years, and the influence of which has been sown broadcast over the land.

Elias Woodruff was a soldier in Jackson's army, serving in the battle of Chalmette, New Orleans, La., in 1815, and his widow drew a pension from the government up to the time of her death.

Mrs. Mary Woodruff, surviving widow of Seth Woodruff, of Louisiana, is a native of Charlotte, North Carolina. Her maiden name was Mary S. Ritch and she is a lineal descendant of John Ford, one of the signers of the Mecklenburg Declaration of Independence. Her brother, Thomas L. Ritch, of Charlotte, N. C., served during the civil war on the staff of Gen. J. E. B. Stuart, the famous Confederate cavalry general of the Army of Northern Virginia, under Gen. R. E. Lee.

Western Williams, son of Moses Williams and Eliza Woodruff Williams, of Mansfield, La., was a Confederate soldier and was in the siege of Vicksburg. After the war he emigrated to Texas and married Miss Maggie Houston, daughter of General Sam Houston, of Texas. Their daughter, Miss Madge Williams, the granddaughter of Sam Houston, by popular selection, christened the United States battle-ship Texas, when it was placed in commission some years ago.

Nelson Payne ran away from his parents in Tennessee and followed General Carroll's command in their long march to New Orleans, and was with them in the battle of Chalmette. He was too young to be enlisted, but remained with the command until its return through Pike County, where he stopped and made it his home. He subsequently married a daughter of Benjamin Morgan, with whom he had the following children: Wm. Mac, Thomas W., Nelson R., Wm. Lafayette, Ann and S. C. Payne, who married John Kirby, who was the father of John H. Kirby, now known as the saw-mill king of Texas; also Mary A. C., the wife of Jack Craft.

Nelson Payne, being left a widower, he subsequently married Jemima Owens, with whom he had the following children: Albert G. C., Louis J. and J. B. Payne and L. C., who married Ben Morgan; Morgana, who married Westley Sartin; Laura J., who married Marion Branton; Alice, who married Jesse Harvey, and R. E., who married Tom Harvey.

Price Connally and Mary Corker were the parents of Thomas J. Connally (Tallyboly), who married Sally McNabb; George, Crosby, Jackson and Rebecca.

Wiley Martin married Laura Quin, daughter of William Quin, who was murdered while asleep in camp on a trip to Covington with William Catching, in Washington Parish, by a negro who was hung for the crime in Franklinton, La., in the early fifties.

Matthew Brown married Mary, daughter of William Sandifer.

John Laurence, who lived on Union Creek, married Polly Bardwell.

In 1846 Owen Conerly, son of Owen Conerly, Sr., of China Grove, raised a military company of the young men of Magees Creek and surrounding communities for service in the Mexican War, then being prosecuted by the United States Government. He was chosen its captain and tendered its services to the Government, but before the company could reach the army the war closed and the volunteers disbanded. Their names have not been preserved as they should have been. Simeon Bullock for one is known to have been a member of this company.

J. Daniel O'Brien was a native of Ireland and came to Canada with his parents when a boy. He served in the Mexican War with Virginia troops and afterwards went to North Carolina and married Mary

Conklinton, and then emigrated to Pike County and settled on Magees Creek below Tylertown in the early fifties. Sally Dillon married Wm. Thomas O'Brien, Katie Rushing married James S. O'Brien, and after her death he married her sister, Eveline Dillon.

Armistead Hall and his wife, Rachael O'Quin, came from South Carolina in 1816 and located in the Jake Owens' neighborhood on Dry Creek. Their children were Ezekiel Hall, who married Bertha Sandifer; John, who married Martha Prewett; Armistead, Nancy B., Thomas David Forest's first wife; Gracia, who married Abraham Lazar; Jane and Harriet, twins, who married James Thornhill and Leroy Breland respectively; William Hall, brother to Ezekiel Hall, married a daughter of Jake Owens; Patsey Hall married David O'Quin, and Barsheba, Daniel O'Quin.

Richard Dillon was born in Ireland and came to South Carolina prior to the Revolutionary War and joined the colonists in the war with Great Britain. He was captured and made a prisoner of war, taken back to England and compelled to work in a copper shop until the close of the war when he was liberated and returned to South Carolina, and with his wife came to Mississippi and settled on Bogue Chitto, at what is known as Dillon's Bridge, or Dillontown. They were the parents of Clarkson, Laurence, Willie and Theopolis.

George Smith, Sr., and his wife, Clara Dillon, settled near Dillon's Bridge on the Bogue Chitto in 1817. Their son, Dort Smith, married Lucretia Dykes, whose father came from Georgia and settled on the Tangipahoa. George Smith, Sr., had a negro slave woman named Rebecca, who recently died at the age of ninety-five. She was a mother at fifteen and nursed Dort Smith at his infancy. A ferry-boat was used at Dillontown for many years. In 1873 the citizens in the community built a bridge, and they rebuilt it after it was washed down by a flood in the river.

G. L. Barnes, a great grandson of John Barnes, who came from Georgia in 1798, lives near this place. His father and his grandfather were named William.

Jasper Smith, son of George Smith, Sr., and Clara Dillon, married Mary Holmes, daughter of William Holmes.

Dr. N. C. Smith married Daniel Smith's daughter, Melissa.

Densmore Smith married Nancy and Eliza Smith respectively, and Pernissa, Jeremiah Smith.

Dort Smith built his mill over Magees Creek in 1860.

Jeremiah Smith, brother of George, moved from South Carolina before the others came, bringing his little belongings in a cart.

Richard Dillon married Henry Magees' widow, daughter of Ephriam Rushing.

Henry and Fleet Magee were brothers.

Richard Magee, a faithful negro slave of Henry Magees', was born on Pushepatapa eighty-nine years ago, and was living when these notes were taken in 1902.

William G. Tyler owned a faithful negro slave named Dick who was noted for his great strength and obedience to his master. Dick was a powerful man and worked at the mill and cut logs. He could cut more logs in a day than any two negroes in the country. It is related of him that some years after emancipation, and he became separated from his master by force of circumstances, he was discharged by an employer because he made $15.00 in one week cutting stock logs with an axe at 10 cents a log. It was too much money for a negro to earn in six days cutting stock logs, was the reason given for his discharge.

Needham Raiford came from North Carolina. His first wife belonged to the Penn family of Louisiana. He was a Methodist minister and filled the pulpit during his lifetime at China Grove. He acquired considerable wealth as a cotton planter, in land, slaves and stock, and employed Joseph Barr, who was an experienced farmer and manager. His plantation is located a short distance south of China Grove Church. He became the owner of the entire landed estate of Owen Conerly, Sr., about 1850, at administrator's sale, including the plantation and Ralph Stovall mill property. He was fond of hunting, and on one of his trips to North Carolina he procured some long-eared blue speckled deer hounds. They were slow trailers, but whenever they got a smell at a deer's track it was almost certain to become somebody's venison. They stuck to their game for days, and even weeks. On one occasion they started a deer on Magees Creek, chased it up the Darbun, around by the Waterholes Church in Marion and back, and then out on Pearl River in the neighborhood of the Lenoir's, above Columbia, then back to its former lair on Magees Creek and was captured. In his young boyhood the writer helped to capture several of these animals after they had been chased for days by Raiford's hounds, run into creeks by fresh dogs entering the chase.

N. B. Raiford's first wife brought him no issue, and during the early sixties, having been left a widower, he married Miss Emma Summers, of Smith County. With her a son was born. The father died, and then the child, and the mother became possessed of the bulk of the estate. She afterwards became the wife of A. S. Bishop. She was a lady of the sweetest and most charming manners; a lovely hostess at the splendid plantation mansion on Magees Creek. She belonged to that class of young women in the early sixties possessing those virtues which commanded the chivalrous attentions of Mississippi's best young men.

Owen Conerly's mill on the Gordon place was erected in 1852-53. Jeremiah Fields, Thomas and James Barnett, John Colquhoun and Lane Wreatherford were the millwrights employed. This mill was sold to his brother James and his farm was traded to James A. Ferguson for mercantile and town property in Holmesville. While owning this mill one of his little boys, Robert, six years old, was killed by a stock log rolling over him and crushing him to death while out in the woods with the negro driver of the log-cart (Harry). The log was lying on the side of a steep hill, supported by a small hickory grub, and it was supposed the little fellow got on the log, and rocking, gave it a start.

The children raised by Owen Conerly and Ann Louisa Stephens were Chauncey Porter (Dr.), Luke W., Mary Ann, Buxton R., Owen F., Thomas B., Samuel L. and Edward S. Conerly. There were others that died early, Lula and Cecelia.

When Ralph Stovall owned the mill he built over Magees Creek below China Grove he hauled lumber to Covington, La., a distance of sixty-five miles, on wagons to supply customers there.

Schools have been maintained at China Grove and at Sartins almost continuously since the settlement of that section. Among the teachers who served in the community were Joseph Smith, Patrick McAlpin, Charles and Joseph Bancroft. These were pay schools supported by parents of the children. There was no public school system in the State. All the schools were supported by tuition fees given the teachers. There was a public school fund which the law provided should be distributed in proportion to attendance of each child, which was paid to the parents of the pupils, but so small as to count but little.

THE LAMPTONS.

In 1740, Samuel and William Lampton came to Virginia from England. They were there when the revolution began and were ardent colonial patriots. In the meantime the Earl of Durham died, and their younger brother remained in England. Samuel Lampton, who died in Virginia, should have succeeded to the earldom. William Lampton moved to Kentucky. One of his descendants, William Lampton, came to Mississippi and settled in Marion County near China Grove. He was the father of Benjamin Lampton, James and Frank Lampton, and the first wife of John M. Conerly, Elizabeth, Sarah and Lucy. Samuel L. Clemens (Mark Twain), President Jefferson Davis, Henry Watterson, of the *Courier-Journal*, and other distinguished men can trace their lineage back to Samuel Lampton, who ought to have been Earl of Durham. It is said there was an estate of over $75,000,000 due the heirs of the Earl after his death. Benjamin Lampton and his wife, Mary Jane Conerly, were the parents of Walter M., Lucius L., Thadeus B., Iddo W., Edward, Mollie and Cora.

Benjamin Youngblood, in company with Maj. Benjamin Bickham and John Brumfield, came from South Carolina in 1811. The latter went to Washington Parish. He and wife were detained in Marion County by the birth of his son, Joe, and remained there until their death at the age, respectively, of ninety years.

Quinney Lewis and his wife, Martha, came from North Carolina about 1820 and settled on the east side of Pearl River, fifteen miles south of Columbia. They remained here for some twenty-three years and associated themselves with the Methodist Episcopal Church, and were devout Christians. In 1843 they moved to Pike County and settled on Magees Creek five miles south of China Grove, and pursued the occupation of farming for twelve or fourteen years and then moved to Holmesville. They were known as Uncle Quinney and Aunty Patty. He was born May 28, 1794, and died on his place near Holmesville in 1881. She was born in 1800 and died in 1875.

They raised six sons, viz.: Barney, the founder and editor of the *Holmesville Southron;* Martin, Lemuel, Henry P., William Bryant and James W. Lewis.

Their daughters were Celia Ann who married Warren Alford; Mary Jane, who married Chestine Allen, Abigail married Ralph Regan in 1845; Elizabeth married Hyram Ware, first husband, killed during the Civil War, and John D. Warner, second husband.

Quinney Lewis, with such help as he could get, constructed the old Pine Grove Church, west of Magees Creek, about 1844. He and his wife were ardent workers in the cause of Christianity during their entire lifetime, after their conversion while residing in Marion County. There was not a married couple in Pike County who were manifestly more devoted to each other and to their religion than they were. They took life easy, were always happy and could always find time to go to church; to Sunday-school and to prayer-meeting, and their doors were open for the entertainment of friends on all occasions.

About 1856 two of their sons, Henry P. and William Bryant, were converted to religion and became associated with the Methodist Church. Great spiritual revivals were held at Pine Grove and at China Grove, and it was at the latter place that William Bryant delivered his first exhortation when not more than sixteen years of age, and after this the two brothers became permanently associated with the Mississippi Conference.

WHEN THE STARS FELL.

In 1833 a great meteoric display occurred. There are a few people living in Pike County yet, white and black, who have a vivid recollection of this wonderful phenomena. It was on a dark night, and the shower was so great and brilliant as apparently to set the whole heavens ablaze. The ignorant and superstitious were frightened and thought it portended the destruction of the earth, and they resorted to prayer. The event has been handed down and spoken of by those who were living then as "When the stars fell," and many old negroes of the present day date their birth back to that period.

In 1849 and 1850 a temperance organization, known as the Sons of Temperance, was organized and maintained at Holmesville and at China Grove. This organization excluded women as members.

In 1859 and 1860 another temperance organization, known as the Social Circle, sprung into life, taking in boys and girls from fifteen up and men and women.

Martin Lewis, a brother of Quinney Lewis, came from North Carolina in 1820. His wife's name was Nancy. They first settled on Ten Mile Creek near Waterholes Church, in Marion County, near the dividing line of Pike. He afterwards moved to Stovall Springs, above Columbia, where he died in 1857. He and his wife had several sons; Samuel, Josiah, Henry, Barney, Jabes and Silas. Josiah married a Miss Smith; Henry's wife was Eliza Faulk.

Joseph May came from South Carolina in the latter part of 1700. He was the father of Joseph May, Jr., who married Clarisa Daughtery from Tennessee, and they settled on the head of Magees Creek on the old homestead yet known as the Jo May place. Their children were Joda, who married Annie Maxwell, of Laurence County; Obed, who married Mary Lenoir, a daughter of Hope Lenoir, of Marion County; Dr. William M. May, whose first wife was Mary Wilson, of New Orleans, La., and second wife Margaret Badon; Jared B. May, bachelor, Co. E., 16th Miss. Regt., A. N. V.; Robert, who married Narcissa Cooper, daughter of Fleet Cooper, of Laurence County; Satina, who married Robert Bacot; Madaline, who first married Wm. G. Ellzey (Dutch Bill), and being left a widow, married Henry Badon after the Civil War; E. D. May married Rachel Ginn.

James Andrews, who came from Georgia, married Miss McGraw in Pike County. Their children were Thompson, William, Burrell and Felix and Minerva, who married Garner Gates and lived in Holmes County.

James Andrews' second wife was Rachel Gullage, and they were the parents of Jack Andrews.

Thompson Andrews married Lizzie Pearson; Burrell married Mary Walker, daughter of John Walker. They were the parents of Elisha C., Thomas J., Wm. Pinkney, John Warren, Zebulon P., James Berkley, Sarah Jane, Rhoda Elizabeth and Charlie Lee.

James Andrews settled on Bogue Chitto in early 1800.

Thompson Andrews and Lizzie Pearson were the parents of Martha, who married Thomas Brent; James, Mac and Felix.

Felix Andrews, Sr., married Widow Thigpen, of Holmes County, and were the parents of Warren and Wilkes Andrews.

GREAT LAND EXCITEMENT.

In the early fifties a great excitement was started in Pike County by John King. An order had been issued by the Interior Department under statutory provisions authorizing the entry of lands at twelve and one-half cents an acre, giving to all free persons of lawful age the right to purchase 160 acres and as many more acres as he might wish at $1.25 an acre.

A large number of people had squatted on lands under the territorial government and under the early State government, and had failed to secure patents. John King suddenly pounced on a few farms and began the work of ousting or trying to remove the original settlers. This procedure not only obtained in Pike, but throughout the State, and the people became aroused. The example of John King was followed by others, and no man who had failed to apply for a patent on the lands he had settled was safe, or did not feel so, even from his near neighbors. The very fact that anyone of lawful age should secure 160 acres under the "bit law" and thousands of acres more at $1.25, brought about the condition of peril for the homes they had spent so many years in building and placed them at the mercy of land grabbers, who were rushing to the State land office for speculative purposes. The land office was located at Washington, near Natchez, in Adams

County, to which the people flocked from all parts of the State to enter land and to try to save their homes from the clutches of the speculators and grabbers, who had no regard for squatter sovereignty or rights of first settlement. There never was such an excitement known in the history of the land office. Accommodations could not be had for the large numbers in Natchez and Washington and the vicinities, and the people camped out until they could get a turn at the register. It was a long, slow, tedious siege. Mr. Wm. Whitehurst, the receiver, was severely taxed in labor as well as patience. An incident occurred at the land office during this eventful period which has been transmitted as relating to Pike County. Rev. J. H. Harris, a Methodist minister, who was well known in Pike County, was one of the seekers for real estate from some other portion of the State, and so was Michael Jones, from the head of Varnal Creek in Pike County. Jones got in the line of "take your turn" ahead of Harris, and when his turn came he occupied the attention of the receiver in trying to properly locate his claims to such a length as to wear the patience of those behind, and particularly Harris, who was extermely anxious to get in. Harris composed the following lines and pinned them over the door for the amusement of all the others in line:

> Accursed the owl that ate the fowl,
> And left the bones for Michael Jones;
> No mortal man hath seen the like
> Of such a monster, here from Pike.

CHAPTER IV.

John Hart came from England and settled at Newborn in North Carolina. His wife was a Miss Bryant. They raised a son named John Bryant Hart and a daughter named Sally. From Newborn John Bryant Hart went to South Carolina, joined the Colonial Army and engaged in the Revolutionary War against Great Britain with South Carolina troops. He married a Miss Gill and came to Mississippi Territory in 1800 and settled on the Bogue Chitto River about a mile from Bogue Chitto station. He and his wife raised four sons, James, John, Joseph and Isaiah, who preceded him and settled in the same locality on the Bogue Chitto. Joseph Hart belonged to Andrew Jackson's command in the Florida War against the Seminole Indians. In May, 1861, at the age of seventy years, he joined the Bogue Chitto Guards under command of Capt. R. S. Carter, and was elected second lieutenant and served with distinction through the war.

John Hart married Martha Meredith from Fairfield District, South Carolina. Her father was killed while moving to Mississippi by an Indian at the Chattahoochie River, who threw a chunk at another man, striking him and killing him, which resulted in an Indian killing. The Harts were descendants of Pocahontas stock. John Hart and Martha Meredith were the parents of Dr. R. T. Hart, who married Selena, daughter of Peter A. Quin and Tamentha Gray.

Sherod Gray came from Richmond, Va., about 1820 and married Mary Hamilton, sister of Dr. Hans Hamilton, who was born and raised near Holmesville, where he taught school. He procured land near where Walkers Bridge now stands across Bogue Chitto and built a mill over Loves Creek. He employed a man named Beasley to build his residence, a fine two-story building, on a plan almost identical to those of N. B. Raiford, Owen and Luke Conerly, Christian Hoover, Richard Quin, Gilbert Gibson, Wright B. Leggett, James B. Quin, Henry Quin and others along the Bogue Chitto. They were large two-story buildings with shed roofs on either side dropping below the upper story, sash and blind windows, with rooms on front and back, giving half-front and half-back gallery, usually brick chimney at each end and fireplaces down and upstairs. The upstairs were sometimes divided into one large and two small rooms and sometimes a wing was extended from one end of the residence for a dining-room, the kitchen being set back away from it. Some of these old residences are standing yet, notably those of N. B. Raiford, on Magees Creek, and Christian Hoover, east of Bogue Chitto; a number of them were destroyed by fire. The old home of Christian Hoover has one of the finest front-yard gates perhaps ever constructed in Pike County.

Such houses as these were not constructed by the first settlers. The first were usually made of peeled pine poles, notched in at the corners, for immediate use, then added to. The next grade being double penned, hewed log houses, open entry, front gallery and back and shed rooms. The floors were first made of split punchings or boards, and the roofs were covered with boards weighted down with poles cleated to make them secure.

The children of Sherod Gray and Mary Hamilton were as follows: Margiman, who married Rachel Andrews; Thaddeus, who married Selena Burris; Cicero, who married Isopline Butler; Lemuel, who married Ellen Guinn; Sherod, who married Margaret Bracey; Isaiah, who married Sally Gardner; Cathorine, who married John H. Magee; Eviline, who married Ray Harvey and Ben Crawford, second husband; Sophia, who married Reel Thompson and John Hucabee; Selena, who married Hatton Weathersby; Margaret, who married William Jones; Tamentha, who married Peter A. Quin.

Near Sherod Gray's plantation, or on a part of it, was a muck swamp which was a noted resort for dangerous wild animals, such as wild cats, panthers and bear. In the fifties the Gray boys killed a large Bengal tiger in this swamp. While a boy visiting there at this time the writer saw the hide of this animal stretched and tacked on the wall of a building, and it was here that he was afflicted with one of the most violent attacks of the "buck-ague" a mortal ever had, while on a deer drive with Cicero and Sherod Gray and John Colquhoun. They had fixed it so as to drive the deer to his stand. After awhile the dogs started yelping faintly, but louder grew.

> "And faintly farther distant borne,
> Was heard the clanging hoof and horn."

The cold chills flashed through the youngster's physical organism. He shuddered. There was a sense of congestion approaching, a smothering and gasping for breath. Presently the deer was seen standing in the open road, within thirty feet of him, mildly looking at him. He became struck with a semi-blindness. He reeled, staggered, threw his gun down and it fired somewhere in the direction of where this innocent little animal stood looking at him. It was the trying ordeal of his life. He must have drawn blood, but there was no actual proof of it. It is true the dogs set up a more animated yelp, but that was all. The horn sounded a recall, and—

"Back limped, with slow and crippled pace,
The sturdy leaders of the chase."

The boys came in to find the would-be hero of the occasion crestfallen and sick.

Silver Creek Church (Baptist) was constituted on Silver Creek, near Louisiana line, in 1814, by Thomas Batson, William Iles, William Busby, Silas Bullock, Joshua Stockstill, Loflin Fairchild, William Bond, Henry Bond, John Thompson, Frederick Craft, David Hines, Walter Jacobs and Willis Simmons. Rev. Nathan Morris was called to supply this church as minister July 15, 1816, and was succeeded by Jesse Crawford in 1835.

Still Creek, a small stream forming one of the head tributaries of Tangipahoa, was first settled by William Bagley Like many other sections in Pike at that time it was a wild, outlandish country, a wilderness of wild cane, full of bear, wolves and other dangerous animals. The bear were so bad at times that they would come into the yards at night and attack the hogs in the lots and pens, where they could get at them easier than chasing them through the cane. The men never went out day or night without their guns and knives and dogs. Bagley owned a whisky still and learned the bear's fondness for sweetened whisky, which enabled him to trap many of them. He made peach brandy and corn juice, as the settlers called it. It is related that there was an old lady in the neighborhood whose people had emigrated and brought her from a wheat-growing country and she had a dislike to cornbread. She used to say that she never did like corn in any shape or fashion until Bill Bagley got to making that corn juice; she could manage to worry down a little of it then. Still Creek thus got its name.

William Bagley settled the Powell place, between Still Creek and the Tangipahoa. Bagley acquired considerable wealth here raising hogs, cattle and horses, and making corn juice. He sold out his interests in Pike years after his coming and went to Covington, La., to engage in other business, and there died of yellow fever.

John Kaigler came from South Carolina prior to 1810 and settled on that tract of land east of Holmesville, lying between Bogue Chitto and Otopasas, erecting his residence on the latter stream above its junction with Bogue Chitto near to where the bridge now stands. His wife was Rebecca Wells. She rode horseback part of the time, and he walked, carrying his noted double-barreled shotgun-rifle. They brought all their belongings with them, and had a rough, adventurous trip. At this place is where Andrew Kaigler was born in 1811, according to the best obtainable evidence which was transmitted from father to son and other members of the family. If this be true it "knocks the honors" off of Joe Tuff Martin's and Wild Bill Smith's claims that they were the first boy children born in Pike County. There were many disputes between them as to which was entitled to the honor on occasions in Holmesville when they would meet around the festive board.

John Kaigler was a hard-working man and careful manager, and the beautiful South Carolina girl who elected to share his perils in the long wilderness tramp from South Carolina to Mississippi was a strong support in laying the foundation and building up their home and fortune.

John Brent, Sr., and William Cothern, Sr., were contemporaneous with John Kaigler and his wife.

Andrew Kaigler married Mary Levisa Noland, born and raised near Woodville in Wilkinson County, where his father had moved, leaving Adam, a trusty negro slave, in charge of his Topisaw plantation. Andrew subsequently returned to the original home, where he remained in after life. Their sons were George, Frank, Phillip and Willie, and their daughters Jane and Julia.

A sister of Andrew Kaigler, Rebecca, married John A. Brent, son of John Brent, with whom she had two children, William E. and Fanny Brent, wife of Col. Preston Brent.

William Cothern settled the Turnipseed place on Topisaw prior to 1815. His wife was Nancy Gates, and they were the parents of Elijah Cothern, whose wife was Cathorine Dunaway, daughter of Jonathan Dunaway, and they were the parents of John, Joseph and William Cothern.

Carters Creek derived its name from John Carter, who settled John Cothern's place and built a mill over that stream above its junction with the Topisaw.

John Brent, Sr., Hezekiah Williams, Thomas Guinea and one of the Newman family were early settlers along on the Topisaw.

Isaac Saddler came to the Mississippi Territory with the Walker family in 1814 and settled on a tract of land which afterward became a part of the Hoover plantation.

Judge Christian Hoover settled his place in 1823. His wife was Mary Newland Nails, and he lived on this place until his death. He served as probate judge of Pike County for several years, and was a Representative and Senator in the General Assembly. He acquired considerable wealth as a cotton planter and owned over a hundred negroes. His sons were William, Thomas and Christian. William was a minister and Chaplain of the 33d Mississippi Regiment, C. S. A. He married Martha S. J. Thompson, near Greensburg, La. Thomas was a lawyer and died young. Christian became a doctor and married Miss Barnes, of Marion County.

One of Judge Hoover's daughters, Mary, married Benjamin C. Hartwell, from the State of Maine, who came to Jackson in 1836 and settled in Pike County in 1850.

Julia Hoover married Dudley May, from Kentucky, disabled at the battle of Shiloh. Eliza (Dump) Hoover married George K. Spencer, of Columbus, Ga. Nancy Hoover married George Wells, of Amite County. They were the parents of Nannie Wells, left an orphan. Sarah Hoover married Thaddeus C. S. Barr.

Henry Bond and his wife, Miss Muse, came from Georgia and settled on the Balachitto, on what is known as the William Allen place. Their children, Preston, married Annie Muse; Thomas, a Baptist preacher, Rebecca Felder; Henry, Samentha Dickerson; Rebecca, Louis Ballard; Liddie, Willis Mullins; Betsy, Jesse Barron; Milton Napoleon married Mary C. Wilson and settled in Amite County.

Gabriel Allen was one of the first settlers near Holmesville. He was the father of Felix Allen and was from Tennessee.

Felix Allen was the father of Chestine Allen, who married Jane Lewis, daughter of Quinnie Lewis, and Cathorine, the wife of Westley Kline, the grocery keeper of Holmesville, with his first wife, Cathorine Williams, who died in Tennessee, he came to Mississippi in 1814 and settled on Bogue Chitto below Silver Creek Church. He had twin daughters, Cathorine and Olivia, born in Tennessee with his first wife. In 1828 he married Olivia M. McGehee, of Amite County.

Wm. M. Allen married Julia McGehee. His second wife was Louisa J. Bickham, daughter of Thomas Carroll Bickham, of Washington Parish.

Mrs. Nancy Bridges, who was the mother of Frank and Linus Bridges, and lived on Leatherwood, was a daughter of Peter Quin, Sr., who came to Pike (then Marion) in 1812, and settled on Topisaw, and sister to Daniel, Peter, Jr., Henry, Richard and Rev. and Dr. Hugh Quin.

Col. Peter Quin, Jr., came to Pike in 1815 and settled at Holmesville. He married Martha Cathorine Moore in North Carolina. Her mother was a Miss Murray, sister of the author of Murray's Grammar. Their children were Hugh Murray, Peter C., Irvin Moore, Josephus R., Lemuel J., Selena, wife of Dr. George Nicholson; Cynthia, wife of Dr. Leland; Courtney, wife of Dr. Jesse Wallace, and Dewitt Clinton.

Daniel Quin, son of Peter, Sr., married Kitty Deer, and they were the parents of Rodney, William, Frank and Emily, wife of Jeremiah Coney.

Henry Quin married Elizabeth Graham, and their children were Peter G. Quin, Arthur and Henry G. and Minerva, wife of General Cain; Amanda, wife of James Garner, Amite County; Mary, wife of Thomas Garner, Amite County; Elizabeth Hugh, wife of Dr. Vincent Jones Wroten.

The following are the children of Dr. Wroten and Elizabeth Hugh Quin: Margaret Elizabeth; William Monroe, who married Eleanor

Lombard, adopted daughter of Robert Lea, of St. Helena Parish, Louisiana; Dewitt Henry, who married Eliza Sprich; Kate Minerva, wife of Charles E. Davis, of St. Helena Parish, Louisiana; Mary Eloise.

Dr. Vincent J. Wroten was a son of Wiley H. Wroten and Margaret Jones, early pioneers from South Carolina, who settled on Topisaw, where he was born the 2d of May, 1818. He was educated in the common schools of the country, and in his early manhood read medicine. He was graduated from the Kentucky Medical College and held a high rank among the members of his profession. He was married to Elizabeth Hugh Quin in 1844, after which he settled on a farm on the Big Tangipahoa River, in the western portion of Pike County, and pursued the practice of medicine in connection with his agricultural interests. He was a member of the Methodist Episcopal Church, South. He was an ardent temperance leader in the latter forties and early fifties, when the Sons of Temperance sprung into existence and the Social Circle temperance organization was established. He settled in Magnolia in 1872 and represented Pike County in the Legislature that year and in 1873, and was regarded as one of its ablest members. Dr. Wroten was a natural-born gentleman in the true acceptation of the term; polished by education and Christianity. He was a peacemaker among men and was sought in counsel by those in trouble. He loved the Church and its fellowship. He sprung from the throng of true nobility that swelled the ever-filling ranks of the new Territory and State of Mississippi in its pioneer days. He left the imprint of his sublime nature behind him and transmitted it to his descendants. He knew no word that would crush another's heart. He was so refined and gentle, so sympathetic, that his great heart melted in the presence of distress or suffering, and the angel of mercy gave to him the sublime attribute of peaceful pleasure in giving relief and comfort to the helpless and distressed. And he has left to his family and friends a name and reputation without blemish.

His son, Dr. William Monroe Wroten, was a member of Stockdale's cavalry, under General Bedford Forest of the Confederate Army, and his name appears on the roll of that company. He succeeded his distinguished father in the practice of medicine at Magnolia, where he still resides, and acknowledged to be one of the leading physicians of the county.

Richard Quin, also son of Peter, Sr., married Mary Graham, sister to Henry Quin's wife, and they were the parents of James B. Quin, Peter A., William Monroe, Hillary and Richie.

Col. Peter Quin was a man of broad views, strong character and moral influence. In 1819 he presided as superior justice of the Orphans (probate) Court. He was one of the trustees of the town of Holmesville, under an incorporating act of 1820, and when the Orphans Court system was abolished in 1822 Peter Quin was elected probate judge, being succeeded by Robert Love in 1824. During his incumbency as superior justice a circumstance known as the Sibley Incident occurred, which has been handed down as part of the judicial proceedings had in the pioneer establishment of law and justice in the new county.

Westley Kline, a son-in-law of Felix Allen, kept a small whisky shop in Holmesville, the first we have any record of in the county. The building was constructed of pine poles, peeled and notched up at the corners. The floor was made of split punching. The roof was also made of poles notched together so as to give it the proper incline. This was covered by long clapboards and weighted down with poles cleated so as to hold them fast. This was the customary way of building houses in the absence of saw mills and nails. The door and window hinges were made of seasoned oak or hickory, and the locks were wooden slide bolts that worked in sockets fastened to the inside of the door and a wire key shaped to suit. Jesse King was a justice of the peace. On one occasion there was a large gathering in Holmesville, and Kline's establishment was a popular resort. When night came on Kline was compelled to close, as the law required him to keep an orderly house, and a row had taken place in which Wm. Sibley was concerned. He had left his coat and hat in the grocery, but he succumbed to force of circumstances and took a long snooze under the shadows of the "Widow Phillips," the noted whipping-post (oak tree), that stood on the public square. When he woke up he thought of his hat and coat being locked up in Kline's grocery. He climbed to the roof, removed the boards and brought them out, placing the boards in position as he found them. Kline knew he had left them there and wondered how he got them out. Sibley acknowledged how he had taken them out and he was reported on his own confession to Justice King and tried for burglary under the statute already given, convicted and sentenced by King to be hung on a certain day. Sibley complained at the severity of the sentence, as he had taken nothing but his own hat and coat. The justice of the peace was inflexible. He had sworn to support the constitution and enforce the laws of the land. Sibley had violated a law which provided against the breaking and entering in the night time the house of another, which also forbid the taking and carrying away anything whatever. Sibley had taken and carried away his own hat and coat. He had violated the law and must hang on the day ordered by the court. He begged to be allowed an opportunity to fix up his business affairs in order to be ready to meet his doom. He was paroled on his own recognizance with the distinct promise that he would return for the execution of the sentence. He was pursuaded and went to work and got up a petition signed by nearly all the men in the county and by the justice himself to the Governor for pardon. This was a great task, as the people were scattered over a large territory and took up so much of the valuable time of the petitioner that it would be a close run for him to reach the Governor at Washington in Adams County and return, in case his pardon was refused, in time to comply with his word of honor with the honorable court that had passed the sentence of death upon him.

One cold, drizzling morning Sibley rode into Holmesville and hailed at the gate of Judge Peter Quin.

"Hello, Billy, come in," said Quin, "come into the fire; what are you doing scouting around such a morning as this?"

"Going to Washington to see the Governor to try to get my pardon, and come in to get you to sign my petition."

"Petition for what?" asked Quin.

"Well, you know King had me tried for burglary for going into

Kline's grocery through the roof that night, and taking out my hat and coat which I had left in there when he shut up and went away; and he sentenced me to be hung according to law on a certain day, and I haven't got much time to lose now and get back on time, and I want you to sign it."

"Let me see it," said Quin.

Peter Quin took good time and read all the names, and then called Patsey, his wife, and told her to have some breakfast fixed for him and Billy. "You mustn't go without your breakfast, Billy."

After examining the petition thoroughly he looked at Billy and crumpled the document up in his hands and threw it in the fire, to the bewonderment of the man whose life was in the scales suspended by the thread of Justice King's decree and who had ridden hundreds of miles to procure the signatures to this petition. It was a cold, heartless act. A personal friend, and yet he would thus doom him by the wanton destruction of his only hope for life.

With all his sense of honor, Billy was a fighter; Peter Quin was too, but he was a born commander—could control himself and others also. Billy Sibley got furious; he rose from his chair with tiger eyes gleaming at Peter Quin, and invited him out of his yard for settlement. Quin called Patsey and told her to hurry up breakfast, that Billy was in a hurry. "Don't go till you get your breakfast; come, be seated and get quiet, and wait till after breakfast." Billy yielded finally, but with a sad and desolate heart. It was a crucial moment. The gallows was being constructed already; men were practicing the formation of the hangman's knot with the rope that was to break his neck. The yellow clay that lay in piles on either side of the chasm that was to be the receptacle of his last remains floated before his vision. His appetite waned and breakfast was a "forceful conclusion."

When breakfast was over Peter Quin sat himself in front of Billy Sibley, and said:

"Billy, King may know something about the Bible, as I believe he is a member of your church and one of its deacons, but he don't know much about law. I have a right to set aside his decree, which he had no legal right to enter in his court. Go home and attend to your business and to your family affairs, and if King attempts to interfere with you, send him to me." And this was Sibley's pardon and a circumstance he delighted to relate in after years. He was a man of the highest integrity and honor. His word was his bond, and he would have returned to King's court and suffered himself to be swung from the gallows rather than violate his promise, but for the circumstance above related.

John Brumfield and his wife, Margaret Kelly, came from York District, South Carolina, and settled in Washington Parish, Louisiana, in 1813. Their children were Jesse, Willis, David, James, Charles, Isaac, Nathaniel, Alexander and Lucy.

Jesse Brumfield married Hannah Youngblood, of Washington Parish, and first settled on Union Creek in Pike County, which place was subsequently owned by Harris Harvey. The names of their children are Benjamin, Henry S., Mary L., Jesse A., Joseph W., James Monroe, Susan Lucinda (Lucy), John R. and Leah E.

Jesse Brumfield afterwards settled a plantation on or near Bogue Chitto, south of Holmesville, formerly settled by William Love in 1809. He was elected sheriff in 1843 and served four years. In 1848 he was elected to the Legislature and served one term. He was for many years a member of the board of supervisors.

David Brumfield married Cynthia Holmes, daughter of Elisha Holmes, Sr., from Georgia; Isaac Brumfield married Elizabeth Holmes, her sister, and they were the parents of Nathaniel, Jr., Jesse K., Harrison and Lucy Jane, who married Green B. May; Sarah Margaret was the wife of Wesley J. Ellzey; Mary married Edwin May; Angeline, Jabe Conerly.

William Leggett and his wife, Jemima Goff, came from Georgia and settled on Bogue Chitto near the Louisiana-Mississippi line, about 1807. Their children were Benjamin Wright and William Pinkney.

Benjamin Wright Leggett married Elizabeth Kennedy McGehee, daughter of William McGehee, of Amite County. Their children were John G., Jane Olivia and Virginia Ann.

B. W. Leggett settled on a place formerly settled by a man named White, on Loves Creek. His son, John G. Leggett, married Mary

Simmons; Jane Olivia, Daniel M. Pound; Virginia Ann, David C. Walker.

Daniel Walker Pound and his wife, Julia Ann Clayton, emigrated from Tennessee about 1830 and stopped on the Homochitto and subsequently came into Pike and settled on Hominy Creek in the northwestern portion of the county, and afterward moved near Magnolia. Besides their son, D. M. Pound, they had two daughters, Virginia Ann, who married a German named J. F. Shoup, and Rachael F., who married Joseph M. Lewis.

Thomas W. Pound, son of Daniel W., with his first wife in Tennessee, married Lucinda Hall, of Amite County; Eliza Jane was a daughter by his second wife.

Daniel W. Pound was surveyor of Pike County for eighteen years, and succeeded George Cato, who succeeded Sampson L. Lamkin. He was supervisor for a number of years, taught school in his young manhood, and was a lifelong member of the Baptist Church.

John Black and William Cage were among the first lawyers to locate in Holmesville. The former was elected United States Senator.

Harmon Runnels represented the two counties of Marion and Hancock in the General Assembly of the Territory; in 1814, previous to the erection of Pike County and after the creation of Laurence County, the three counties were represented by John Bond, Jr., in 1816, and after the creation of Pike he was succeeded by Elbert Burton as the Representative of the district.

In 1810 the first Methodist camp-meeting was held near Magnolia, under the supervision of the Felders and Sandells, and in their neighborhood.

At the October election in 1819 Vincent Garner, David Cleveland and William Dickson were elected to represent Pike County in the Legislature.

Charles Stovall represented the counties of Marion, Laurence, Pike and Hancock in the Senate from 1817 to 1821.

In 1820 John P. Hamilton was Judge of the Superior Court of Pike.

Anthony Perryman was the first man to establish a mercantile business in Holmesville after it was made the seat of justice.

HISTORY OF PIKE COUNTY, MISSISSIPPI 107

In 1822 Pike County was represented in the Legislature by Wiley P. Harris, William Dickson and James Y. McNabb, with David Dickson as Senator for Pike and Marion. At this time Walter Leake, who succeeded George Poindexter, was Governor and the seat of government was located at Columbia, in Marion County, where Governor Leake was inaugurated. This same year the capital of the State was fixed at Jackson, located near Pearl River in Hinds County, being nearer the center of the State.

In 1823 Richard Davis and David Cleveland were Representatives, and the following December Davis was dropped and William Dickson and Wiley P. Harris were elected. In 1825 Harris was Senator for Pike and Marion and remained until 1830.

In 1823 James Y. McNabb was elected clerk in place of J. C. Dixon, and remained until 1833, when he was succeeded by George McNabb, who served as clerk until 1839.

In 1826 the Salem Baptist Church was constituted, near the spot where the town of Magnolia is located. The founders of this church were Rev. Charles Felder, Rev. Asa Mercer and Rev. Shadrack Coker.

The organization of this church under its original name was kept up until 1873, when its name was changed to Magnolia Baptist Church.

In 1824 Nathaniel Wells, Col. Peter Quin and David Cleveland were Representatives, and in 1826 Cleveland, with William Dickson and Vincent Garner, were elected. This year David Holmes was re-elected Governor, but was succeeded by Gerard C. Brandon in 1827, who served until 1833.

In 1827 R. T. Sparkman was elected sheriff and served until 1838.

PIKE'S LEGISLATORS.

A complete list of the men who have represented Pike County in the Senate and House of Representatives of the State Legislature since 1817:

SENATORS.

1817 David Dickson
1818 David Dickson
1819 David Dickson
1820 David Dickson
1821 David Dickson
1822 William Spencer
1823 William Spencer
1824 William Spencer

SENATORS—CONTINUED.

1825	Wiley P. Harris	1866	W. F. Cain
1826	Wiley P. Harris	1867	W. F. Cain
1827	Wiley P. Harris	1868	W. F. Cain
1828	Wiley P. Harris	1869	W. F. Cain
1829	Wiley P. Harris	1870	John Gartman
1830	Wiley P. Harris	1871	John Gartman
1831	William C. Gage	1872	Hiram Cassedy, Jr.
1832	William C. Gage	1873	Hiram Cassedy, Jr.
1833	Franklin Love	1874	J. F. Sessions
1834	David Cleveland.	1875	J. F. Sessions
1835	Jesse Harper	1876	R. H. Thompson
1836	James Y. McNabb	1877	R. H. Thompson
1837	James Y. McNabb	1878	R. H. Thompson
1838	Cornelius Trawick	1879	R. H. Thompson
1839	Cornelius Trawick	1880	A. H. Longino
1840	Franklin Love	1881	A. H. Longino
1841	Franklin Love	1882	A. H. Longino
1842	Christian Hoover	1883	A. H. Longino
1843	James B. Quin	1884	S. E. Packwood
1844	James B. Quin	1885	S. E. Packwood
1845	James B. Quin	1886	S. E. Packwood
1846	George Nicholson	1887	S. E. Packwood
1847	George Nicholson	1888	Thos. B. Ford
1848	Davis E. McCoy	1889	Thos. B. Ford
1849	Davis E. McCoy	1890	T. B. Ford
1850	Davis E. McCoy	1891	T. B. Ford
1851	Davis E. McCoy	1892	J. H. McGehee
1852	J. M. Nelson	1893	J. H. McGehee
1853	J. M. Nelson	1894	J. H. McGehee
1854	J. M. Nelson	1895	J. H. McGehee
1855	J. M. Nelson	1896	W. B. Mixon
1856	Franklin Love	1897	W. B. Mixon
1857	Franklin Love	1898	W. B. Mixon
1858	Franklin Love	1899	W. B. Mixon
1859	J. B. Chrisman	1900	J. H. McGehee
1860	J. B. Chrisman	1901	J. H. McGehee
1861	J. B. Chrisman	1902	J. H. McGehee
1862	J. B. Chrisman	1904	Clem V. Ratcliff
1863	J. B. Chrisman	1905	Clem V. Ratcliff
1864	P. C. Quin	1906	Clem V. Ratcliff
1865	W. F. Cain		

REPRESENTATIVES

1817	Elbert Burton	1843	Hiram Terrell
1818	Elbert Burton		J. A. Bradford
1819	Vincent Garner	1844	E. Millsaps
	David Cleveland	1845	E. Millsaps
1820	Vincent Garner	1846	B. W. Leggett
	David Cleveland		E. Rushing
1821	William Dickson		William Simmons
	James Robinson	1847	B. W. Leggett
1822	Wiley P. Harris		E. Rushing
1823	R. Davidson		William Simmons
1824	R. Davidson	1848	Jesse Brumfield
1825	Peter Quin	1849	Jesse Brumfield
	N. Wells	1850	S. A. Matthews
1826	Peter Quin	1851	S. A. Matthews
	N. Wells	1852	J. G. H. Sasser
1827	Peter Quin	1853	J. G. H. Sasser
1828	Peter Quin	1854	R. A. Ellzey
1829	R. Davidson	1855	R. A. Ellzey
1830	S. Sharp	1856	Levi Bacot
	A. Cunningham	1857	Levi Bacot
1831	Franklin Love	1858	D. C. Quin
	John Given	1859	H. E. Weathersby
1832	Franklin Love	1860	H. E. Weathersby
	John Given	1861	H. E. Weathersby
1833	Jesse Harper		J. O. Magee
	W. G. Martin	1862	J. O. Magee
1834	Jesse Harper	1863	J. R. G. McGehee
	W. G. Martin	1864	J. R. G. McGehee
1835	Franklin Love	1865	J. W. Huffman
	W. G. Martin	1866	J. W. Huffman
1836	Franklin Love	1867	J. W. Huffman
	A. Cunningham	1868	J. W. Huffman
1837	Hardy Carter	1869	J. W. Huffman
	A. Cunningham	1870	W. H. Roane
1838	W. A. Stone	1871	W. H. Roane
	Thomas Denman	1872	V. J. Wroten
1839	W. A. Stone	1873	V. J. Wroten
	Thomas Denman	1874	S. E. Packwood
1840	Jesse Harper	1875	S. E. Packwood
	James Cunningham	1876	James M. Causey
1841	B. W. Leggett	1877	James M. Causey
	J. A. Bradford	1878	James M. Causey
1842	Hiram Terrell	1879	James M. Causey
	J. A. Bradford	1880	James C. Lamkin

REPRESENTATIVES—CONTINUED.

1881	James C. Lamkin	1895	S. E. Packwood
1882	W. F. Simmons		James M. Tate
1883	W. F. Simmons	1896	W. W. Pope
1884	James C. Lamkin		J. B. Webb
	George M. Govan	1897	W. W. Pope
1885	James C. Lamkin		J. B. Webb
	George M. Govan	1898	W. W. Pope
1886	T. F. Causey		J. B. Webb
	James A. Bates	1899	W. W. Pope
1887	T. F. Causey		J. B. Webb
	James A. Bates	1900	P. E. Quin
1888	J. H. Crawford		J. M. Tate
	S. M. Simmons	1901	P. E. Quin
1889	J. H. Crawford		J. M. Tate
	S. M. Simmons	1902	P. E. Quin
1890	J. G. Leggett		John A. Walker
	Theo. McKnight	1903	P. E. Quin
1891	J. G. Leggett		John A. Walker
	Theo. McKnight	1904	W. B. Mixon
1892	S. E. Packwood		W. W. Pope
	James M. Tate	1905	W. B. Mixon
1893	S. E. Packwood		W. W. Pope
	James M. Tate	1906	W. B. Mixon
1894	S. E. Packwood		W. W. Pope
	James M. Tate		

The members of the Constitutional Convention of 1890 were S. E. Packwood and Frank A. McLain.

E. McNair was Judge of the Circuit Court of Pike County from 1853 to 1866.

Charles Bancroft held over as probate clerk until 1867 and was succeeded by William M. Conerly. Sampson L. Lamkin succeeded S. A. Matthews as circuit clerk in 1861, and served until 1870, when he was succeeded by Fred W. Collins, appointed by Governor Alcorn.

Fred W. Collins was elected to the same office in 1871, re-elected in 1873 and held until January, 1876, when he was succeeded by Dr. A. P. Sparkman by election in the fall of 1875.

Robert H. Felder succeeded Louis C. Bickham as sheriff, and held until after the close of the war in 1865.

Levi D. Felder was appointed in his stead under the provisional government of Governor Sharkey. Robert H. Felder filled the term as deputy sheriff, as he could not take the "iron-clad" oath required under the reconstruction acts of Congress. Levi D. Felder held the office until Charles B. Young was appointed by Governor Ames. Young disappeared.

Ansell H. Prewitt was appointed by Governor Alcorn.

Prewett was assassinated on the cars while conveying the famous prisoner, Jas. W. Head, to Jackson. Head was charged with the killing of Abraham Hiller, of Magnolia. His confederates, said to be a portion of the noted Quantrell partisans of the Trans-Mississippi Department, stopped the train near Bogue Chitto station, killed Sheriff Prewett and wounded his son Elisha and Deputy W. L. Coney, and all made their escape.

In 1838 W. H. Gibson succeeded R. T. Sparkman as sheriff, served until 1840, when he was succeeded by Lemuel J. Quin.

In 1843 Jesse Brumfield succeeded Quin and served until 1846, when Parham B. Williams was elected, followed by Robert Bacot in 1850, and in 1861 Louis C. Bickham was elected.

William A. Stone, so long a resident of Pike, acting a conspicuous part in her early history, was born in the District of Maine March 12, 1804, in the town of Livermore, Oxford County, where his father, Col. Jesse Stone, resided. He was a graduate of Bendoin College of the class of 1825. At this time forty-four entered the Freshman Class, among them Longfellow, Abbott, Bradbury and Sawtelle, who became distinguished men. Wm. A. Stone studied law under Peleg Sprague, for many years District United States Judge. He was admitted to the bar in 1828 and settled in the town of Prospect, but shortly removed to Mississippi and settled in Pike, and was one of the conferees of Buckner Harris, Judge Hagan and Dillingham. He served in the Legislature, and in 1839 he sold his interests in Holmesville to John T. Lamkin, a young lawyer who had emigrated from Georgia.

While in Pike County he was appointed by Governor McNutt to fill the unexpired term of Judge Walker, who had resigned.

Robert Love served as probate judge until 1836. Judge Hoover served until 1840, was succeeded by William Coney, but re-elected in 1842, and served until 1848, when James B. Quin was elected, followed by J. W. McEwen in 1849, and he succeeded in 1852 by Dr. George Nicholson. In 1859 Nicholson was succeeded by Hugh Murray Quin.

T. B. Paddleford was probate clerk in 1839, served until 1845, when Leonard Magee was elected. Magee resigned after serving one year, and was succeeded by H. M. Quin, who served until 1853, when Samuel A. Matthews was elected.

In 1855 Matthews was elected circuit clerk and served until 1861; Wiley A. Young, probate clerk in 1855, and re-elected in 1857 and 1859, and was succeeded by Charles Bancroft in 1861, who served until 1866.

The first Masonic lodge established in Pike County was Rising Virtue Lodge, No. 7, and was located near Holmesville. In 1846 it was succeeded by and merged into the Holmesville Lodge, No. 69, with George Nicholson, Master.

In the course of time the town of Holmesville had acquired a population of about four hundred souls, and good schools were maintained here as well as other sections of the county. Samuel T. Gard, Professor Vincent, Mrs. A. L. Conerly, Joseph Smith, Thomas R. Stockdale, S. McNeil Bain, Charles Bancroft, Mrs. Cecelia R. Forshey, Mary Graves, Ann Strickland, John D. Warner, all figured as teachers here.

As the settlement of the county increased and the agricultural interests became enlarged, there was an impetus given to all classes of industry and the professions, excepting the manufacture of mercantile goods. The resources of the people were agricultural. The increase in the production of cotton induced an increase of slave laborers, purchased from traders coming from Kentucky, Tennessee and Virginia, and as the farmers became able many of them invested largely of their farm earnings in negroes. The markets for their cotton were Covington, New Orleans, Baton Rouge and Natchez, transported to each of these places, except New Orleans, by ox-wagons, under the care of trusty negro drivers. Looms, spinning-wheels, cards and reels were kept in motion on the farms and plantations in order to provide the coarser fabrics for family use and clothing for the slaves. It must not be understood that all the citizens of Pike County were slave owners. Perhaps a large majority of them were not. The institution, under careful management and control, produced wealth, and through its distribution an elevating and prosperous condition was manifested. The self-sustaining characteristics of the population engendered a feeling of independence and patriotism. The laws provided that all voters should be enrolled in militia companies and attend the muster drills, which were usually held in Holmesville or near there. Fourth of July celebrations were kept up in different sections of the county. Horse races, foot races and wrestling matches and other athletic sports were encouraged. At the schools these and townball constituted sources of amusement, and the large number of water courses in the county enabled the boys and many of the girls to learn to swim. The shotgun and the rifle were early placed in the hands of the boys, to become expert in their use. Their fathers and their grandfathers had to rely on them for defense of their families against wild animals that infested the country, and hostile Indians. Horseback riding prevailed altogether until at least three decades from the early settlement of the county. Buggies and carriages at $250 and $500 could only be afforded by men of large means. Those who owned them in Pike County prior to 1850 could be numbered on the fingers of the hand. Judge Christian Hoover is said to have been the first man in Pike County to own a buggy, a veritable curiosity in the sight of the masses. Later on they came out with finer turn-outs—closed carriages and handsome spans, but these were few and far between. The great body of cotton planters, though able, stuck to the noble horse and saddle. The girls were all taught to ride horseback, and this is the way they went to church, the celebrations and to the fandangoes. The roads would be lined up with long columns of pairs on horseback.

At the Fourth of July celebrations great dinners were provided, with the finest barbecued meats and all the good things the county could afford. Everybody contributed. Holmesville was noted for these splendid occasions. Orators were provided, from whose lips gems of beautiful thoughts flashed and electrified the masses and made brighter the dreams of aspiring youth. The grounds were smoothed off, or platforms erected, music provided, and the resplendent beauty of our country girls mingled in the mazes of the dance with the gallant and chivalric young men. The banks of old Bogue Chitto were decked with gayest attire. On what was once the island at the foot of the bridge in the beech grove was a favorite place for these events. The dawn was broke by the thunder of an improvised cannon, which was kept up through the day. Old Glory waved proudly from a staff a hundred feet high. The music of the fife and drum and the parading of volunteer companies, under officers with attractive uniforms and brass buttons, stirred their patriotic ardor.

At Tylertown, when the people of that section overflowed with love for their country, they got up a Fourth of July barbecue there. Cullen Conerly, as orator of the day, instilled their minds with the sentiments of '76, and William G. Tyler, one of Jackson's old artillery boys of Chalmette fame, made the indelible impress with the boom of his own manufactured mortars, over there across Magees Creek, where Mike Roark taught school, and limbered up obstreperous youths with hickory poles. From Pike to Pinder Ridge, in Washington Parish, Flem Berkhalter with his noted violin, chased the midnight demons away and lit the halls where smiles and beauty beamed, with an inspiration that in memory floats adown the channel of time like an enchanting dream.

Holmesville got to be a great resort, and through the summer months was often crowded with people seeking rest and relief from the unhealthful atmosphere of New Orleans and the dangers of cholera and yellow fever which often prevailed there. Its healthfulness, picturesque scenery, pure water, facilities for outdoor sports and quiet pleasures, made it a desirable place for a summer vacation. It was a trip across Lake Ponchartrain and a carriage ride for sixty-five miles from Covington, but it was a mecca of country hog and hominy, pure milk and butter, solid clabber and cream, fat 'possum and sweet potatoes, eggs and chicken pie. The beautiful river with its crystal waters flowing past its doors afforded recreation in boating, bathing and fishing. How many angelic forms have been mirrored in its classic waters? Campbell, with his multiplied inspiring genius has not given mankind a touch of the picture Bogue Chitto offered then to the master poets and painters of the world. Its verdant banks, its cool retreats, its climbing vines, the perfume of its wild flowers, the trilling notes of woodland songsters, the thrill of the soul that beauty and loveliness bring.

In the forties Robert Ligon got possession of the Bearden-Sparkman Hotel. He had married Bearden's beautiful daughter, Angeline, a young woman of most pleasing manners, and being a man of fine address and social qualities, his house was crowded with guests. Barney Louis came in afterward, and in company with Robert Ligon, began the publication of the *Southron*, a newspaper very much needed, which acquired a large circulation and became a medium of great interest to the people. Later on, in 1853, this paper fell into the hands of Henry S. Bonney, who clung to its helm all through this eventful decade.

A few of the abler classes of citizens began to bring in pianos. The violin, the guitar, banjo and flute had come in with the march of the fife and drum and quills. In the moonlight nights around the hotel would cluster old and young to listen to the strains of music and soft sweet voices of charming girls and women. All over the county beautiful plantation homes were coming to the front. Up and down the Bogue Chitto, from Judge Hoover's, on either side, to Dillontown; out on the Tangipahoa, the Topisaw, Sweetwater, Silver Creek, Magees Creek and the Bahala, the charm of rural life was exemplified with an industrious hum and prosperous conditions. Peace and plenty, happiness and contentment, prevailed everywhere.

Early in the forties John D. Jacobowsky came in from Prussia, settled in Holmesville and opened a mercantile business, being associated with Joseph Hart, who married his sister, Susan, and later on with Jake Hart, his nephew, who married Pauline Hilborn, sister to Ben. Hilborn.

Pincus Morris, Mike, Mary, Sarah, Hannah, and Bertha were children of Joe Hart and Susan Jacobowsky.

Hyman, Meyer, Isaac and Simon Lichenstein were residents of Holmesville and occupied a store on the corner opposite that of Jacobowsky and Hart, the latter being on the same block and connected with the hotel building. Across the street from Jacobowsky and Hart was the store of Dr. George Nicholson, who owned that block, upon which his residence stood, since occupied by Robert Bridges.

From the little log hut occupied by Kline as a grocery the California House sprung into life, which was constructed into a first-class barroom, owned by Lemuel J. Quin.

Parham B. Williams, who married Miss Brent, a sister of John A. Brent, and who was elected sheriff in 1848, lived in a pretty two-story house in the upper part of town called Sandy Hook. Across the street from him was the residence of Mr. McCarley, who married a sister to Williams' wife, the mother of John and George McCarley.

On the place settled by Thomas Ellzey in Holmesville, afterwards owned by Dr. James M. Nelson, and latterly by Twist, opposite the old Peter Quin place, a well was dug thirty feet below the surface and a large cypress log was reached. It was discovered that on this log a fire had been built, which was indicated by the charred remains on top of it and the fragments of wood used in building the fire. The log was cut through and the well completed. This circumstance indicated that ages ago the charming hammock upon which the town of Holmesville was built was once a cypress swamp or lagoon.

Below town at a point where a slough made out on the western side of the river, a rock dam was constructed to raise the height of the water in this slough. Just above the junction with its river below a mill was built over it by Sparkman and Arthur, which was run by a large undershot wheel. Rev. Bryant Louis became the owner of this mill. He subsequently took Owen Conerly as a partner, who afterwards became sole owner, and constructed a framed dam across the main river opposite the mill in 1857 or 1858, the foundation of which is there yet. This writer, as a boy, pulled the trigger of the battering ram that sent the piling of that dam down through the gravel, an inch a lick. It was a long, tedious job, but it was a lasting one. This mill was purchased by William Guy, and subsequently went to decay, but the frame foundation across the river is still preserved.

William Zeigler, who married Miss McClendon, sister of Stephen McClendon, was one of the older settlers of Pike and lived in Holmesville on the block north of the home of Dr. George Nicholson. Due east of Zeigler was the home of the Lichensteins; on the same block was the home of R. H. Miskell (Captain Dick), the postmaster.

E. H. Pezant kept a grocery store in a building adjoining the California House; then came John T. Lamkin's law office and Dr. Wallace's drug deparment.

South of the Lichensteins was the home of the Widow Sparkman, wife of Reddick, the hotel builder. East of her was Josh Bishop and his father, who owned Nancy, a faithful negro woman, who was his housekeeper and who after the death of the old man and Josh kept the home and raised and educated Josh Bishop's only two children, "Sis" and her brother John. She earned a support for herself and these two helpless orphans by taking in washing. She was well respected, and sent Sissie and her brother to Sunday-school and church and the very best social gatherings. She was childless herself and devoted her life to the support and education of these two white children of her young master Her grave and her last resting place may be forgotten, but in after time if these lines should chance to fall beneath the eyes of the descendants of Johnnie and Sissie Bishop, a responsive voice will echo back to the little cabin in Holmesville where lived and died this good-hearted black mammy. "God bless Nancy Bishop."

Mrs. Elizabeth Bickham, widow of Thomas Bickham, of Washington Parish, lived in the southern part of town. She was the mother of Dr. Benjamin Bickham, of Hinds County, and of Louis C. Bickham, who was elected sheriff in 1859, former deputy under Robert Bacot; also Benton and Alexander Mouton Bickham and Mary, who married Dr. Hillory Quin; Sarah, who married Dr. Germany, and Hannah, who married Richie Quin. Louis Bickham, the sheriff, married Margaret Lindsey, daughter of B. B. Lindsey, a millwright.

William Monroe Quin, who owned a large cotton plantation about eight miles west of town, once known as Quin Station, owned a residence and lived across the street from Mrs. Bickham, now owned and occupied by Dr. Lucius M. Quin. This residence was built by Reddick Sparkman. Next to him, on same block, was the home of Jacobowsky and Hart, afterward Wm. A. Barr. East of this, on Carroll Srteet, was the old home of Tom Guinea, then James A. Ferguson and Owen Conerly. At the foot of the ridge, on the west and south of the old Liberty road, was the residence of John S. Lamkin, lawyer, who married Bella Tunison, of Monticello. On the other side was the Baptist Church, and further north the residence of S. A. Matthews, a native of Ohio, who married Caroline, daughter of William Ellzey. Next to him, and facing the courthouse square, was the home of John T. Lamkin, the lawyer from Georgia, who bought it from Wm. A. Stone in 1839. His wife was Thurza A. Kilgore. Crossing Leatherwood while on his way to Holmesville he met with an accident and lost all the money he had, $100 in gold, in the creek, which was never recovered. At his time the movement for volunteer reinforcements for the army in Mexico was commenced, and he was one of the number.

At the foot of Main Street, near the river, two men from Virginia, Horatio and Asa Wingo, club-footed twins, lived, built a hotel, barroom and tenpin alley. Horatio married Miss Brent and Asa Mrs. Guinea. They were rough men and great fighters, and they were always in it side by side together. Their deformed feet necessitating perfectly round shoes, and their weight thrown on the ankles made it difficult to stand still, and in walking they had to be supported by sticks, good-sized hickory clubs, which they used in their personal encounters.

The Finches came to Pike County from Georgia in the early fifties. There were four brothers of them, James A., John, William and Milus. They settled on Varnal at the old Burkhalter place, where the Holmesville and Columbia road crosses. William and Milus joined the Quitman Guards and both of them died in the Confederate service. James and John subsequently settled at Holmesville. John Finch was the father of James, Jr., Joseph and Thomas. Being left a widower, he married Sally Sandifer, daughter of Jackson Sandifer of Magees Creek, and sister of Joe and Wallace.

A peculiar circumstance happened shortly after the Civil War which caused young James Finch to be sent to the penitentiary on a charge of assault and battery with a dangerous weapon with intent to kill, of which he was not guilty. He got into an altercation with an ex-slave named Prime Ball during which Ball was stabbed in the jaw with a pocket-knife. After serving awhile in the State penitentiary Finch made his escape and came home, but eluded arrest. There was a man named Doan, who had come in from Arkansas and married Widow Ballew, formerly Miss Brent. Doan was present at the altercation between Finch and the negro, Ball and while Finch was eluding arrest he was taken sick and on his death-bed confessed under oath, in the presence of legal officers, that he himself had stabbed Ball in the jaw, reaching over Finch's shoulder during the altercation. He was a friend to Finch and promised when the trial came that he would clear Finch of the charge, but failed to do so With Doan's confession and a petition signed by all the prominent men of the county, Finch walked into the Governor's office at Jackson and stated his case. The Governor requested him to call again at 4 P. M., which he did, received his pardon and returned home.

The knife-blade run into Prime Ball's jaw was broken off in it and remained in the jaw for two years, causing an enlargement of the jaw and a running sore, which demanded the skill of a surgeon when the blade was discovered.

It must be remembered by the reader that this period of which I write Holmesville was the only town in the county. No other had been thought of. The circuit courts were held in the spring and fall every six months, and lasted two weeks, for the trial of civil and criminal cases. The petit jurors, the grand jurors and the witnesses, litigants, curiosity seekers, sportsmen and lawyers from adjoining counties brought great crowds of people to the courthouse. The hotels and boarding houses were unable to accommodate the crowds, and hundreds returned home at night or scattered out among friends in the vicinity.

Wm. R. Johnson had married Martha Sparkman, widow of Mr. Richmond, who succeeded Robert Ligon in the hotel, and these occasions were a boom for it—the California House, where Bob Wade did the mixing, the Wingo Hotel, bar and tenpin alley. Court times were lively occasions for Holmesville, and the term never ended without a general entertainment, of a delighted public, with wrestling, foot racing and fist fights. Without these, court weeks were not considered first-class occasions. Carroll Newman served as bailiff for many years, and his voice could be heard a mile. The juror who failed to answer his call was docketed five dollars.

During the fifties, when Judge McNair held the bench, the Holmesville bar was composed of John T. Lamkin, Oscar J. E. Stuart, Hugh Murray Quin, William J. Bain, John S. Lamkin, Thomas Hoover, H. E. Weathersby and Thomas R. Stockdale; and the visiting lawyers were David W. Hurst, Hyram Cassidy, H. F. Johnson, District Attorney McMillan and Judge Vannison of Monticello and Bentonville Taylor of Covington. Thomas R. Stockdale entered the practice after two years' teaching of school in Holmesville. He was a native of Philadelphia, Pa., and a graduate of a Pennsylvania college.

At this time John T. Lamkin was the great criminal lawyer of South Mississippi. He knew every man in the county and was a friend to them all. Pike County jurors were usually men of moral excellence—crime was inexcusable. The killing of a human being must not be tolerated under any circumstances. This was the fiat of the people. The law of God said "Thou shalt not kill," "He who sheds man's blood by man his blood shall be shed." This was a principle that lived in Pike County; criminals knew it and they knew it would require a Napoleon to save them. Lamkin was a man of superior moral and magnetic influence, fine physical build, large, protruding eyes, eloquent, argumentative, forceful, convincing. He knew his jurors and he knew the power he must bring to bear upon them. When he failed to acquit one charged with murder or manslaughter the hangman's noose and the walls of the penitentiary were the visions that floated before the eyes of the culprits.

In 1854 Frank Carr was charged with the murder of his father, who lived on the head of Leatherwood. There was an old-fashioned muzzle-loading squirrel rifle in the rack over the door of the house. Old man Carr had been away from home and came back at night intoxicated, and began abusing and whipping his wife, Frank's mother; Frank interceded. The old man reached for the rifle. No one knew it was loaded. Frank seized the gun and in the scuffle for the possession of it the piece fired and killed Frank's father. These are about the facts. Every effort was made in a legal way to save his life. He was condemned by a jury and was hung on a gallows erected at the one-mile post on the old Liberty road west of Holmesville in the presence of a large gathering of people from the surrounding country, in 1856, while Robert Bacot was sheriff. The writer, then a fifteen-year-old boy, witnessed the execution. He did not then, nor does he now, believe that Frank Carr was criminal in the unfortunate killing of his father.

At the same time Bill Catchings, a negro, was hung on the same gallows with Carr for the murder of his master, Silas M. Catchings.

During Robert Bacot's term a man named Robertson was hung at the jail on the public square for the murder of "Calico" Williams. Williams' wife was indicted and convicted with Robertson and given a life sentence in the penitentiary.

At the hanging of Robertson he pleaded so hard that his life be spared the sheriff submitted it to a vote of the people present, but the majority with members of the police jury said that the law must be enforced. The sheriff then declined to spring the trap, and turned it over to his deputy, Louis C. Bickham, to perform the duty as ordered by the court.

In 1850 Dudley W. Packwood came to Pike County and settled at China Grove, on the old Ralph Stovall property, subsequently the home of Owen Conerly, Sr. He was born in New London, Conn., in 1792, and came to New Orleans in 1810, and was in Jackson's army at the battle of New Orleans. He subsequently removed to Covington, La., and lived in Alabama, where his two sons, Samuel E. and Joseph H., were born.

Dudley W. Packwood's father, Joseph Packwood, was a sea captain during the Revolutionary War and served in the interest of the colonies against Great Britain. In a naval engagement he lost one of his eyes. His wife was Demise Wright.

Dudley W. Packwood's wife was Cathorine Elliott, born in 1803, eastern shore of Maryland, and daughter of Samuel Elliott. She sprung from the Waggaman family, mother's side, of the eastern shore. She and her husband were married in Covington, La., in 1817. Her parents died when she was very young. Dudley W. Packwood was a farmer and lived at China Grove until his death, aged seventy-six. His wife died in 1872.

Their elder son, Joseph H. Packwood, was a farmer and merchant and spent his life from 1850 to his death in 1900 at China Grove. He married Mary, daughter of Joseph Youngblood and Eliza Bickham.

Samuel E. Packwood graduated at Centenary College in 1857, graduated at law in New Orleans in 1858, and began the practive in St. Francisville, La., and was living there at the outbreak of the Civil War. As he was not a member of any of the companies that went out from Pike County it would be proper to state here that he was a member of the 13th Mississippi of Barksdale's Brigade, Army Northern Virginia, which served with great distinction in the numerous conflicts in Virginia, and participated in the battle of Gettysburg, Pa.

At the close of the war he resumed the practice of law in Holmesville, and after removal of the seat of justice to Magnolia made that place his home. He was a member of the State House of Representatives, 1874–1876, 1892–1894, and of the Senate 1884 and 1886.

Ballard and William Raiford, nephews of N. B. Raiford, also came to Magees Creek about 1850 and engaged in merchandising at China Grove. Ballard Raiford married Nancy, daughter of Henry B. Lewis, who lived in the Darbun neighborhood. William Raiford went to Amite County, married there and became identified with that county.

Dr. Booth, a young Englishman, came in about this time, married Sarah Magee and settled on Magees Creek in the Jesse Ball neighborhood, and he and Dr. William May became the physicians of upper Magees Creek.

Dr. James M. Nelson, from Tennessee, was one of the conferees of Drs. Jesse Wallace and Hillory Quin and Nicholson at Holmesville.

In 1850 a cold wave passed over the country destroying the crops in the month of May. The previous year, 1849, was the great desrtuctive flood year. In 1855 a great drouth occurred, and the following year was the first time in the history of the county up to then that grain had to be imported for farm use.

Christian Fisher operated a shoe shop at the foot of Main Street in Holmesville and employed a force of Dutch shoemakers.

Henry Lotterhos kept a bakery and sold ginger cakes and beer. Afterwards moved to Summit.

William C. Alford operated a wagon shop on Main Street; George Brumfield a saddler's shop.

Henry Frances was a carriage maker and had his shop near the foot of the old bridge, and Tom Donahoe was one of his workmen.

Joe Page was a carpenter, and lived at the foot of the hill near the Masonic lodge. He married the widow of Henry Francis, who was a sister of the wife of H. S. Bonney.

In 1849 and 1850 a tempreance organization, known as the Sons of Temperance, was kept in a flourishing condition at China Grove.

In 1856 Sincerity Lodge of Free and Accepted Masons, No. 214, was organized, with the following members: James H. Laney, Samuel F. Gard, John G. Leggett, Oscar J. E. Stewart, Owen Conerly, Cullen Conerly, William C. Alford, Benjamin Wright Leggett, Barney Lewis, William Hinson, Felix S. Campbell and P. Ballard Raiford; James H. Laney, Master; Samuel F. Gard, Senior Warden; John G. Leggett, Junior Warden.

Shortly after its organization under the charter, John T. Lamkin, John S. Lamkin, William A. Barr and William McCusker became members.

THE NEW ORLEANS, JACKSON & GREAT NORTHERN RAILROAD.

In 1848 a railroad convention was held in the city of New Orleans, La., to consider the construction of a steam railway to penetrate Mississippi and to connect with other systems then in operation. William Ellzey and Ross A. Ellzey were sent as delegates from Pike County to the convention.

The question had been agitated for a number of years, but no definite route had been determined upon. There were three parties in the convention, favoring different routes. That party, led by Tom Marshall, then president of the Jackson & Vicksburg Railroad, was in favor of the route that the Yazoo & Mississippi Valley road now runs. One party was in favor of crossing the Lake Ponchartrain at Madisonville and from thence to Jackson, pursuing a course which would bring it to the town of Holmesville, which would offer a location and facilities for one of the finest cities in the State.

After two weeks of discussion it was finally agreed to pursue a route passing the western shore of Ponchartrain and crossing the Pass Manchac.

James Robb was one of the zealous advocates of this great enterprise.

The articles of the charter of the company were formed in accordance with the provisions of a general law of the State of Louisiana, approved March 11, 1850. This law was framed in conformity with the 123d article of the constitution of 1844, which limited the duration of corporations to twenty-five years.

A convention of the State assembled in 1852 to frame a new constitution, abolished this restriction and delegated to the Legislature the power of granting special charters.

An act was passed and approved April 22, 1853, fixing the capital at eight millions of dollars, with exemption from taxation, and giving perpetual existence, besides other important and liberal privileges.

James Robb, L. Matthews, Wm. H. Garland, Peter Conway, Jr., Judah P. Benjamin, H. C. Carmack, George Clarke, Isaac T. Preston, J. P. Harrison, Wm. S. Campbell, Glendy Burke, R. W. Montgomery,

H. S. Buckner, A. D. Kelly and E. W. Moise were appointed commissioners for the purpose of receiving subscriptions to the stock of the corporation. James Robb was elected president of the company. The subscription books were opened in New Orleans in April, 1851, and $300,000 conditionally subscribed.

Subscriptions to the amount of $3,250,000 were received on the line of the railroad.

Louisiana took shares to the amount of $1,600,000, which added to the previous subscriptions increased the total stock to $4,850,000. A corps of engineers was organized under the direction of Col. W. S. Campbell, in June, 1851, and commenced an examination and survey of the country between New Orleans and the State line, near Osyka, which, on account of the Ponchartrain swamps and unbroken forest, consumed nearly a year.

In 1852 James Clarke entered on his duties as chief engineer of the southern division.

A law granting privileges to the company in Mississippi was passed soon after the organization of the company.

The first eleven miles of the road were put under contract in September, 1852, and twenty-five and a half miles to the south Pass Manchac in October.

Early in December the road to the State line was let, making in all eighty-seven and one-third miles under contract and in process of construction.

The route in Louisiana begins at Claiborne Street, following the center of Calliope to Canal Avenue, then deflects to the west by a curve of 11,460 feet radius, and continues straight to the estate of Minor Kenner; crosses Bayou La Branch about a half-mile from Lake Ponchartrain, and continuing nearly parallel with its western shore to the thirtieth mile, crosses South Pass Manchac at the foot of Lake Maurepas, on the thirty-seventh mile, reaching the pine woods at forty-six miles from New Orleans, and enters Mississippi at a place which belonged to a Mr. Stephenson and John H. Moore at the time of completion to that point in 1854.

Jesse Redmond, who settled in this county in 1812, was the original owner and settler on the land upon which the town of Osyka was built. He was engaged in the battle of New Orleans in 1815.

Louis H. Varnado kept the first hotel; William H. Jones the first school; James Lea the first store; Jacob Ott the first steam sawmill, all in 1854. Isham E. Varnado furnished nearly all the shingles to build the town. The churches were built in the following order: Presbyterian, Episcopalian, Catholic and Baptist. Oyska was the terminus of the road for about two years. It built up rapidly, many stores were added to the town and it became the focus of a large country trade which had previously been centered at Holmesville or was going to Covington, Baton Rouge and Natchez.

During 1854 and 1855 the work on the railroad progressed slowly. The financial affairs of England and this country were of such a nature that the company was not able to convert the securities into cash at anything short of an unwarrantable sacrifice, and apart from their securities they had little or nothing with which to carry on the work. Five miles of track was laid and crossties for ten miles more were furnished. The iron for the road was purchased in England and had to be transported across the Atlantic on sailing vessels.

By April, 1857, the road was completed through Pike County, and depots established at Magnolia and Summit.

Oscar J. E. Stewart owned a negro blacksmith named Ned, who was the inventor of a double-geared turning-plow and cotton scraper, formed so as to off bar and scrape both sides of the cotton row at once. Stewart applied in Ned's name, or for him, to the patent office department for a patent. The department refused to grant the patent in Ned's name on the ground that he was a slave and not recognized as a man or citizen, to whom patents should issue. It will be seen later on what a different construction the government authorities placed upon the constitution in reference to the relations of the negro with that sacred instrument. During the fifties sectional and political feeling ran high.

It is not intended in this work to enter into a discussion of the vexed problems and political upheavals that excited the entire country from 1850 to 1861, but to show by a recital of facts the part Pike County took in events of that period.

In 1853-54 the building for the Holmesville Lodge, F. & A. M., No. 69, was contracted for by John Arthur. John Laurence and John Davidson were employed on the building. The lumber was contracted for with Owen Conerly at the new mill he had constructed on Magees Creek, fifteen miles distant. It was a time contract, stipulating that the lumber should be delivered by a certain time, and had to be hauled on ox-wagons. Owen Conerly had a proviso agreed upon and inserted in the contract, that his mill, being a water-mill, in case of long drouth and water became scarce, and he was thus disabled from coming strictly to time, he was to have further indulgence. This condition happened, and Arthur sued him for damages in the circuit court. Conerly managed and pled his own side of the case and won it before the jury.

This Masonic building was a two-story house and was erected north of the residence of John T. Lamkin, next to the Methodist Church, in Sandy Hook. The lower story was divided into two rooms, which were used for school purposes. It was here that Thomas R. Stockdale, in 1856-7 and 1857-58, maintained one of the finest schools ever had in Holmesville, assisted by two excellent young ladies, Miss Mary Graves, who afterwards became the wife of Dr. John Huffman, a dentist, and Miss Ann Strickland. It was a mixed school of young men, boys and girls. They were about equally divided in numbers, and the classes were graded and mixed in recitations, but separate in rooms, and the girls were taught the higher branches the same as the boys, and in classes with them. In closing the school term in 1858, Prof. Stockdale gave one of the grandest school examinations and exhibitions ever held in the town or county. It was held in the Methodist Church. After the close of this school Stockdale took up the study of law and soon graduated.

S. McNeil Bain and wife; William J. Bain. a young lawyer, and Miss Orrie Gillis, from Illinois, then came to Holmesville, and the school was taken by McNeil Bain and Orrie Gillis, and taught by them the next two years.

At one of the meetings of Holmesville Lodge James Finch, who was a member, had a dog to follow him, which got into the ante-room and went to sleep. The lodge closed and left the dog locked up in the building. The building was not otherwise in use, and when the lodge met again the next moon there they found Finch's lost dog, still alive.

Josephus R. Quin constructed a handsome residence opposite the Methodist Church. His wife was Miss Murphy, of Kentucky, sister of Captain Murphy, of the Summit Rifles. They had two little girls, Mollie and Katy. Their residence was subsequently occupied by Dr. Coates and then by William A. Barr.

Henry S. Bonney, the editor and proprietor of the *Independent*, consrtucted a residence and lived at the foot of the ridge on the southern border of the town. Dr. James M. Nelson, on the corner opposite the southwest corner of the public square.

William Guy married Telitha Turnage, widow of Rev. Bryant Lewis, and lived in the two-story residence opposite J. D. Jacobowsky.

Col. James Roberts, from Washington Parish, constructed a residence in Sandy Hook near that of Sheriff Parham P. Williams and Benjamin C. Hartwell, son-in-law of Judge Christian Hoover, between him and the Methodist Church.

William Ellzey, who lived some five miles south of Holmesville, was a brother of Thomas Ellzey, of South Carolina. He married Esther Sibley, of Amite County. He was a large cotton planter and slave owner. He had a son William (known as Dutch Bill) who married a daughter of Joseph B. May, on Magees Creek, afterwards wife of Henry Badon, Jr. Another son, Dewitt, married Amanda Barr. His daughter, Caroline, married S. A. Matthews, and Nancy married Dr. D. H. Quin, second wife. His daughter Angeline married John Keegan, of Monticello.

William Ellzey emigrated to Natchitoches Parish, Louisiana, in the latter part of the fifties, where he and his wife and an unmarried daughter, Emma, spent the remainder of their lives.

While William Ellzey was a member of the railroad convention in New Orleans in 1848 he was one of the advocates of crossing the

Ponchartrain at Madisonville and pursuing as nearly as practicable the old military route followed by General Carroll from Jackson, by way of Covington, keeping west of the Bogue Chitto to Holmesville.

William Coney and his wife, Rachel, came from Georgia early in 1800 during the territorial government. Their sons were Jeremiah, Jackson, William and Louis.

Jeremiah Coney's wife was Emily Quin, and they were the parents of Franklin, William, Van C., Luke J., Joel R., Mary E., Sarah K., Caroline A., Jane and Jerzine.

Jackson Coney married Emiline Morgan, and their children were Jasper, Loraine, Charles J., Rachel and Josephine and Wm. L. Coney.

William Coney's wife was Eliza Morgan, and they were the parents of Morgan, Green, Dariel, Ann, Eva and Rosa.

Louis Coney's wife was Isabell Kaigler, and they had four sons, Aquila, William and John (twins) and Louis. John and William, the twins, were so nearly alike that it was difficult at times to tell which was John and which was William. The latter had a small dimple in one cheek, by which means alone persons could distinguish them.

A man of great prominence in eastern Pike and western Marion in a manner identified with both counties was Judge Lemuel Lewis. He was a son of Benjamin Lewis and Celia ———, and was born in Rebecca County, North Carolina, in 1804, and married Mary Williams, a daughter of Giles and Sallie Williams, in 1824, and settled in Marion County in 1831. They were the parents of twelve children, as follows: Cecelia, who married Joseph Smith, the school teacher; Sarah, who married Patrick W. R. McAlpin, school teacher; Martha, who married A. J. Brumfield; Giles W., who married Rebecca Yarborough; Cathorine, who married Thomas Bickham; Susan, who married Jabez Yarborough; Margaret, who married Benjamin Graves; Alexander; Benjamin, who married Margaret Sumrall; John, who married Mary J. Sumrall; Rosa, who married E. Pigot; Joseph, who married Ellen Bass; Malinda, who married Ella Pigot.

Judge Lewis was a most exemplary man and citizen. He was strictly upright and honest, religious and devoted to the cause of religion and justice; and all of his children were Christian people.

He was a guiding star in all that constituted the best citizenship in the settlement and upbuilding of a new country. To him the people looked for advice and counsel. He was a strong pillar of the Methodist Church, and he and his children (most of whom were citizens of Pike) were so nearly identified with Pike County that he was always claimed as one of her own.

Judge Lemuel Lewis was Judge of the county court of Marion for twenty-three years, and filled the position with eminent satisfaction to his people. Being a widower, in 1865 he married Mary Winborne, a daughter of David Winborne, on Topisaw, and moved to that place in 1867, where he afterwards lived and died.

The writer knew him from his earliest recollection, and can give testimony to his pure and unblemished character, in addition to which it is related of him by others that he was one of the best men that ever lived. But he lived in a community of western Marion and eastern Pike, composed largely of men of noble attributes of character, among them Stephen Regan, Hosey Davies, Dr. Cowart, Luke Conerly, Owen Conerly, Sr., Needham Raiford, William B. Ligon, Quinney Lewis—all pioneers and Christian people.

In 1854 there was a cotton-picking race on Magees Creek between John Holmes, son of Benjamin Holmes, and Pearl Harvey, son of Harris Harvey, that excited great interest in the community. The picking took place on Benjamin Holmes' place, by draw, and John Holmes came out the winner with 500 pounds of seed cotton in one day's work. This was a feat that few if anyone had eve performed befo e.

In 1854 George Stuart emigrated from Scotland, marri d Mary V. Magee, daughter of Judge T. A. Magee, of Franklin County. He procured the property on Clear Creek and the mill buil. by Michael McNulty in 1846.

After the railroad reached Magnolia W. W. Vaught settled in the pine woods east of the town and erected a steam circular sawmill, one of the first of the kind put in operation in the county. Previous to this time all the sawmills in the county were run by water power and were upright mills. The machinery of the Vaught mill was brought up from New Orleans on the cars to Osyka in 1855, and was hauled from there to its location east of Magnolia on the old Holmesville road. David Ulmer was connected with this mill.

Abraham Hillier was from Alsace, Germany, and married Caroline Openheimer of the same country in Jackson, Miss., and came to Pike County in 1855, and settled in Magnolia, where he engaged in the business of merchandising, and whose children became permanently identified with town. Their children are Jonas, Ellie, Annie and Albert.

Marmaduke Mitchell married Mary Bradley Tupple, of Tennessee, born and raised in North Carolina. He emigrated to the Territory of Mississippi and first settled near Camden, and came to Pike County in in 1860. He was the father of Algenon Mitchell, who married Elizabeth Tilman, sister to Mary and Lucy Tilman. He was the father of Algenon, a member of the Summit Rifles, who had been detailed with a force of marines and was killed at Balls Bluff on the James River in Virginia, in a skirmish with the enemy, three or four days after the surrender of Lee at Appomattox.

Algenon Mitchell, Sr., built a steam sawmill about one mile west of Summit and subsequently took J. J. White as a partner.

John Tilman married Rachel Martin and moved from South Carolina to Tennessee.

Rachel Martin was the daughter of Matthew Marshall Martin, of South Carolina, one of the brothers engaged in the Revolutionary War.

In 1858 two balloonists, a man and a woman, ascended in a balloon in New Orleans with the intention of sailing to Jackson, Miss. They went up late in the afternoon, sailed over Lake Ponchartrain, progressing finely until they passed the dividing line of Washington Parish and Pike County, near the home of Dr. McQueen. The balloon came down nearer to the earth than they supposed and became entangled in the top of a tree, some fifty feet above the ground. In this deplorable condition the occupants had to remain until daylight, when the man arranged some lines and let himself down, then went to the house of McQueen, who got the assistance of Chauncey Collins and secured the safe release of the woman from her perilous situation, and saved the balloon. The circumstance created a great sensation in this section of the county. There were many who had never heard of a balloon.

It was announced by the balloonists that a lecture would be given at Conerly's postoffice (Tylertown), and an exhibition showing the philosophy of air navigation for which a small fee would be charged to enable them to pursue their journey overland to Jackson. This brought out nearly all the people for miles around, who were well entertained by the woman's lecture and the ascension of large paper balloons inflated with hot air. The same was done at Holmesville, and the peculiar accident of the aerial navigators proved a source of profit. Some very large paper balloons were sent up at Holmesville and floated off in a southern direction. Ghost stories were numerous then. Mysterious manifestations were frequently spoken of. The old Cleveland house on the Bogue Chitto was a noted abandoned residence where no family could live on account of the restless and ever-demonsratable antics of its unseen occupants. The fame of this old house had spread far and wide, not only among the naturally superstitious negroes, but among the whites as well; and these paper balloons cut a dash that overturned the equilibrium of human reason for a few days in some neighborhoods, until an inquest could be held to establish the fact that they were really earthly.

It was a dark night, and one of these balloons floated off and dropped in the pathway of Wm. M. Conerly, who had witnessed the exhibition and who lived two miles below town. On his return home he encountered the ghost standing erect in his path, which led through a dark, thick skirt of timber. At first he said he was shocked at the sudden appearance of the apparition. All the hobgoblin stories he had ever heard of flashed upon his memory. He stood in speechless amazement and looked at it for a moment, then thought of the big paper balloons which he had seen sent up and floated off in this direction.

One of the great secrets conducive to the successful management of the negro race in slavery times was the cultivation of a cheerful and happy disposition, and in their leisure hours the enjoyment of music and the dance. Those who had a talent for instrumental music were provided with the violin, the banjo, the tambourine or other instruments. Many of them arranged cane quills with all the notes accompanied with stringed instruments and the tambourine, and they learned from their young masters and mistresses all the negro dialect songs of the period—"Old Kentucky Home," "Nelly Gray," " 'Way Down on the Suwanee River," "Jump, Jim Crow," "Old Folks at Home" and "Hog Eye."

They never had any thoughts or cares for the future. Their masters provided everything. They lived in good comfortable cabins with as many rooms as necessary for the health and comfort of the families, with yards for their own chickens, and garden patches, usually cultivated by the wife and mother of the family. On the small farms the master and mistress attended the sick in person, and where a doctor was necessary he was provided with the same promptness as for the members of the white family. On the larger plantations comfortable hospital buildings were kept in constant readiness under the care of a salaried physician. As a slave the great mass of negroes in the South were a contented and happy people. Discipline and work were necessary for his support and well being. He did not have to worry over the question of how he was to get his rations or to feed his wife and children. To do the will of his master as directed was the routine of his life; and he could lie down and sleep without any thought for to-morrow. "Sufficient unto the day is the evil thereof." Come day, go day, with a full stomach, gave him contentment. He was allowed the enjoyment of holiday seasons, a half-holiday on Saturday, to go to town or to the stores to do his little trading, have his fandangoes, or go to meeting on Sunday in the country where the white folks worshipped, or have a minister to preach to them separately.

MUST TAKE A DUCKING.

In nearly all the large schools in Pike County it got to be customary for all male students who entered after the first week's organization to be subjected to different kinds of hazing, and when the school was located near a stream they must be ducked. Not only the boys were to be ducked, but on occasions of public holiday, if the teacher refused to give the students the privilege the same penalty was put upon him, and they never allowed the schools to proceed after the holiday until this work was accomplished, or a compromise agreed upon. It was an annual species of fun practiced in the schools of Michael Roark. He never would grant the vacation on the 4th of July, and he always got his "ducking," because he would face the music and try to outwit the boys and have school on the 4th or any other holiday.

Roark was an Irishman, and while he was one of the strictest disciplinarians as a teacher he was a jolly-natured man, and he put himself in the position to be acted upon.

This was also a noted practice with the Holmesville schools. As a rule the teachers would yield to the wishes of the students, but occasionally one would come along who would refuse the application of the school for the accustomed event.

In 1855–56 Edward Carruth taught school in Holmesville. He had a large school and a number of young men; among them were Frank and Tom Roberts, Plummer Johnson, Benton Bickham, Walter Bridges, and a good platoon of lesser lights. Inquiries were quietly made several days previous whether Mr. Carruth was going to give us 4th of July. No answer could be obtained until the close of the day's school on the 3d, when one of the scholars arose from his seat and asked him if he was going to give us 4th of July. Carruth spitefully answered "no," and ordered him to take his seat. This was regarded as a challenge to battle, and the boys accepted it. The following morning the school house was barricaded and no one allowed to enter it. At the usual hour Carruth came walking up and was met face to face by the entire school of youngsters. A note was handed him which read:

"Sir: Unless you consent to give the usual 4th of July holiday you will not be permitted to open school again this week."

Signed, "THE WHOLE SCHOOL."

Carruth turned pale, gritted his teeth and compressed his lips, stepped back with one foot and ran his hand under the breast of his coat, as if to say, like Rhoderic Dhu:

> "Come one, come all, this rock shall fly
> From its firm base as soon as I."

"Gentlemen, stand back; I am armed!" "Shoot and be d-d-ducked," some one said. "You'll be d-d-ducked in that river!" The boys moved up, Carruth commenced backing, the boys crowded on. "Duck him! Duck him!" They chorused it. The teacher wheeled about face—a good run better than a bad stand! and made for his boarding-house, closely pursued by the boys, yelling like tigers. The whole town turned out. It was a gala day for the boys. Carruth was imprisoned in his room. They couldn't enter his premises, but they guarded them day and night, and the schoolhouse too. They kept it up all the week and would have prolonged the siege indefinitely had not the patrons interceded and persuaded the young men and boys to let the school open again the following week. The larger boys were expelled from school by the teacher and the younger chaps given a severe lecture, and more especially the "kid" that had the audacity to hand him that note—the one who records this incident. But it was the turning point for the usefulness of Carruth's school. From that day until the close of the term it waned. He was disliked by his scholars and his influence with them was gone forever.

CHAPTER V.

Levi Bacot was elected a member of the State Legislature for the sessions of 1856 and 1857. His father, Laban Bacot, one of the early pioneers and sheriff of Pike County after Mississippi had been constituted a State, was a member of the constitutional convention in 1832, noted for taking the advance step in making the judiciary elective.

About this time Levi Bacot was married, in the town of Holmesville, to Miss Ann Roberts, daughter of Col. James Roberts, of Washington Parish, Louisiana. At this time Robert Bacot was sheriff of the county.

In 1857 the railroad track was laid to Summit, a depot established there and Lemuel J. Quin employed as agent. George T. Gracey ran the first engine into Summit, and succeeded Lemuel J. Quin as agent.

A flag-station was located at Chatawa between Osyka and Magnolia, and another one on the plantation of William Monroe Quin, between Magnolia and Summit, and called Quin Station.

The Sincerity Lodge of Free and Accepted Masons, No. 214 organized at Holmesville by dispensation from the Grand Lodge was removed to Magnolia, about two years after its organization in 1856.

Much of the large trade which has been concentrated at Osyka was turned to Magnolia, and after the establishment of depot facilities at Summit the trade was cut up between these towns.

The construction of the railroad through the county, nine miles distant from the seat of justice, and scattering of an immense trade that once centered there to these new railroad towns springing up, foretold the decline and partial extinction of the once beautiful and romantic town of Holmesville. If the visions that sprung into the fertile imaginations of William and Ross A. Ellzey, at the railroad convention in New Orleans in 1848, could have been realized by the adoption of the route they advocated, not a town or city in the State could have surpassed it in beauty, loveliness and desirability for a home; its unequalled water facilities for the promotion of all kinds of industries, and its unsurpassed healthfulness.

The little town struggled hard for existence against its young and growing rivals.

J. D. Jacobowsky and Jacob Hart and the Lichensteins removed to Summit. William A. Barr and John Holmes set up in the corner occupied by Jacobowsky & Hart. Conerly & Felder and Dr. George Nicholson kept going, and the seat of justice still maintained there. Holmesville was spared the mortification of a premature death and ultimate extinction from the map of towns.

In 1859 a military company was organized in Holmesville by Preston Brent, recently a graduate of Drennon Springs Military Institute of the State of Kentucky, with twenty or thirty members from the town and vicinity. Their uniforms were of the United States regulation blue, with brass buttons, and caps with the old style artillery cockade plume. They were provided with fife and drums, and the old style Harpers Ferry muskets, and had their monthly drills. Preston Brent was elected captain and devoted himself to the task of bringing the young men up to the proficiency taught in the schools, and was patient, kind and earnest in his endeavors and gradually added strength to the ranks. The name chosen for this organization was Quitman Guards, in honor of Gen. John A. Quitman, who had become conspicuous in the military history of the country and added lustre to its fame.

Some time in the early part of 1860 Miss Rachel E. Coney, the seventeen-year-old daughter of Jackson Coney and Emiline Morgan, conceived the idea of presenting a handsome banner to Captain Brent's company, and, assisted by Miss Nannie Ellzey, daughter of William Ellzey, began the work of enlisting the ladies of Pike County in the effort to accomplish this object, and an association was organized in Holmesville, known as the Quitman Guards Banner Association, composed of the following ladies: Madams John T. Lamkin, Samuel A. Matthews, Dr. Jesse Wallace, John S. Lamkin, Henry S. Bonney, J. Cy. Williams, Dr. George Nicholson, Hugh Murray Quin, Louis C. Bickham, Wm. Guy, Dr. D. H. Quin, H. F. Bridges, Richie Quin, Christian Hoover, Hardy Thompson, Benjamin C. Hartwell, Mrs. Eliza Bickham, Mmes. Owen Conerly, William A. Barr, John A. Brent,

Preston Brent, Jackson Coney, Widow Turnipseed, Mmes. Andrew Kaigler, James A. Ferguson, Wm. Johnson, Wm. Monroe Quin, William Ellzey, Jeremiah Coney, Cullen Conerly, R. Y. Statham, James Conerly, Wm. M. Conerly, Joseph Page, Parham B. Williams, Mrs. Elizabeth Ware, and the following young ladies: Misses Rachel E. Coney, Nannie Ellzey, Fanny Wicker, Emma Ellzey, Laura Turnipseed, Fanny A Lamkin, Elizabeth and

Mrs. Joe Miller, nee Rachel E. Coney, Who presented the Banner to the Quitman Guards, of Pike County, in 1860, on the part of the ladies of the county, and was received on the part of the company by Hugh Eugene Weathersby July 4th, 1860.

Frances Lamkin, Mary A. Conerly, Mrs. Jennie McClendon, Lucy Brumfield, Victoria Williams, Louvenia Williams, Sarah K. Coney, Mary E. Hartwell, Eliza Hoover, Nannie Wells, Julia Hoover, Mollie Quin, Alice Quin, Alvira Sparkman, Bettie Miskell, Eliza Thompson, Elizabeth Thompson, Cathorine Conerly, Eliza Conerly, Mollie Magee, Mary E. Vaught, Julia Bacot, Maggie Martin, Martha Jane Sibley, Julia Kaigler, Louisa, Mary and Levisa Newman, Eliza and Ellen Guy, and the following chosen as flower

Mrs. W. J. Lamkin

girls: Misses C. Augusta Lamkin, Julia Wallace, Ida Wallace, Ida Matthews, Sissie Johnson, Sissie Bishop, Nannie Quin, Alice Bickham, Mollie Bickham, Flora Bonney, Rachel McClendon and Mollie Barr.

The 4th of July, 1860, an occasion always celebrated by the people with barbecues, public speeches and other patriotic demonstrations, was the occasion selected to make the presentation of the banner to the Quitman Guards.

Colonel Eshelman, of the Washington Artillery of New Orleans, was delegated to superintend the making of the banner. The flag was made of heavy white silk, double fold, with gold fringe borders and a representation of a large American eagle interwoven in the center presenting the coat of arms of the United States. On one side it bore the inscription:

"PRESENTED TO THE QUITMAN GUARDS
BY
THE LADIES OF PIKE COUNTY"

On the everse side:

"OUR COUNTRY AND OUR HOMES"

The price paid for it was $250, which amount was contributed in small sums ranging from 50 cents to $5.

It was received at Holmesville by Samuel A. Matthews, a resident of the town who had been selected as its custodian.

A public meeting was held in the Baptist Church by the ladies for the purpose of selecting one of their number, with two assistants, to present the banner to the Quitman Guards on the 4th of July, 1860, the day of the celebration of American Independence. Two names were presented for the honor: Miss Rachel E. Coney and Miss Mary Ann Conerly, but the latter, on account of the recent death of her father, Owen Conerly, declined; and Miss Coney was selected, and she appointed as maids of honor Misses Emma Ellzey and Fanny Wicker.

All the necessary preparations having been made, when the day arrived this event and the great barbecue, and an oration to be delivered by Hugh Eugene Weathersby, a brilliant young lawyer and Representative of the State Legislature, brought to the town of Holmesville one of the largest gatherings of people that ever assembled there.

A platform was erected on the public square in front of the residence of Dr. George Nicholson, near the courthouse, by Samuel A. Matthews and Chauncey P. Conerly, as committee appointed by the Quitman Guards.

Benton Bickham, one of the handsomest young men of the town and of the Quitman Guards, was selected as the standard bearer of the company.

Thomas R. Stockdale was selected as attendant to the young ladies in the ceremony of introduction. When the time arrived Benton Bickham, meeting the girls at the residence of Mr. Matthews, and bearing the banner, escorted them to the platform.

The Quitman Guards, clothed in their full uniform, with their burnished muskets, were drawn up in line in front and facing the platform when the ceremonies of the presentation were commenced, by the following address, delivered by Miss Fanny Wicker, who was introduced by Thomas R. Stockdale:

"Ladies and Gentlemen: We have assembled here to-day to evince in some degree the high esteem in which we hold and the great admiration with which we regard those who are willing to undergo the severe labor of military discipline for their country's good—those who, in the hour of peril, are the maintainers of her rights, the protectors of our firesides and our homes.

"To you, gentlemen of the Quitman Guards, the ladies of Pike County this day address themselves, with a token of their appreciation of your generous chivalry, in thus taking upon yourselves the armor of your country; for it is a badge of honor which they are proud to recognize. They have selected this, the most glorious day in all the calendar of time, that its sacred memories may throw around the scene a deeper and more lively interest. For, upon this day, every patriot's heart must swell with emotions of thanksgiving for the inestimable blessings which American independence has showered upon this, the happiest of all lands. The ladies of Pike County have deemed this national emblem, around which clusters the memory of so many glorious deeds, the most appropriate expression of their confidence in the valor of our citizen soldiery

"Permit me now to introduce Miss Coney, who in their behalf, bears this flag."

MISS RACHEL E. CONEY'S ADDRESS.

"Soldiers of the Quitman Guards: In behalf of the ladies of Pike County, we are happy to greet you in the noblest attitude that freemen can occupy—soldiers of their native land. For love of country, that of great instinct of the soul, that pervades every clime and nation, and which prompts alike 'the shuddering tenant of the frozen zone' and the swarthy inhabitant of the tropics, to deem his own the pride of every land, is a principle which, indeed, ennobles humanity. But without that noble spirit which prompts him to step between danger and his country—a patriotism of an ignoble cast—and the difference between him and a soldier is the difference between a slave and a freeman. There is no nobler principle of the soul than patriotism, so full and free that it embraces one's whole country—but when we search for its origin, one finds that its vitality emanates from a single spot, the dearest in his native land—the spot to which the warrior's heart ever turns, whether marching on the plains of the far off land or riding upon the ocean's wave,

"In every clime the magnet of the soul,
"Touched by remembrance, trembles to the pole.

"Speaking for our sex, it is the nucleus around which clusters all our hopes, and the fount from which emanate all our joys—the place whose atmosphere floats so brightly around us that even life's sorrows fail to darken its halo—the halo of our homes.

"He was a patriot who wrote, and surely there is music in the soul of him who sung:

' 'Mid pleasures and palaces tho' we may roam,
Be it ever so humble, there's no place like home.'

"And you will allow us to add, there is no place like America for a home and our country is dear because it protects our home. Thus it is not strange that we should regard with jealous eye what is light or darkness, and more than life or death to us; and that we should greet, with grateful hearts, those who would intervene a shield between our country and danger, however remote. For well do we know, and it would be ungrateful not to acknowledge it, that on all the green earth, there is no country in which woman occupies so truly an exalted position as in the land of the gallant and brave. With great deference to the opinions of those who deem all military displays useless demonstrations in times of peace, we would say there is no ray of light shines into the future except as it is reflected by the past; and we see all along the world's history startling examples which press upon every great and prosperous nation the necessity of well armed soldiery.

"When the proud Anglo-Saxon stepped, as from the ocean, upon the shores of this untamed land, and the wilderness had fled from before his face, and the mountains looked proudly down upon the valleys where civilization loomed up in peaceful glory, then did Oriental misrule reach forth to enslave his fair daughter of the Land of 'the Setting Sun.' But in that hour of peril, she called to her citizen soldiery, and brave hearts responded from hills and valleys, who stayed the giant arm and loosened the iron grasp of the oppressor. Once, since then, has her liberty been maintained, and once her honor defended by the same mighty power.

"And now, although peace has long spread her white wings over the land, and the clouds have continued to drop their bounty down into the lap of the earth, and prosperity has taken her abode here, there may be a cloud in the horizon 'of the size of a man's hand' which may yet gather and darken the whole heavens, and, looking down with wrathful brow, threaten terrible destruction. And as the miser looks kindly upon the strong bars that secure his cherished treasures, we rejoice to see between our homes and the storm *a battlement which no flood has ever borne down.*

"We present you this flag as a memento of our appreciation of your gallantry in enlisting in the service of the greatest country the earth has ever turned to the sun. We have inscribed among the stars the motto nearest our hearts, in token of our confidence in the brave spirits who shall unfurl it to the breeze.

"In memory of the land we love above all others, we have placed upon it the insignia of our native State, whose colors have been borne always in triumph on many a fearful field, through many a fierce struggle, by the gallant old man whose honored name you bear.

"We present you this flag upon its own birthday, with no desire to encourage a spirit of aggressive warfare, or to kindle within your breasts the fires of ambition, for every true woman's heart revolts at the thought of a catalogue of the slain, which might bear the name of her dearest friend; but if such a dire calamity should come, which may the God of nations avert, that the land of our birth should be disgraced, our country dishonored or our homes invaded, whether it be threatened by an alien enemy or a fratricidal hand, we ask you to take this flag and beat back the foe.

"The history of the past warrants the assertion that no true American, and we are sure that no brave son of the gallant State of Mississippi, where we are proud to claim our homes, would purchase ease or escape danger at the cost of independence; and every woman of noble soul, though sad the thought, would deem it a dearer joy, whether he be father, brother or lover, to spend a life of solitude in strewing flowers upon a hero's grave than in peace to share a vassal's home.

"To you we commit our country and our homes, with the confident hope that upon each Independence Day, for generations to come, brave soldiers will tread the soil of America to the sound of martial music."

At the conclusion of Miss Coney's address she presented the banner, which was received by H. E. Weathersby, on the part of the Quitman Guards in a few well-chosen remarks, in which he stated that "where duty calls the Quitman Guards will go;" and thus the young ladies were considered as adopted members of that company.

At the conclusion of these ceremonies the people repaired to the beech grove at the foot of the bridge over the Bogue Chitto River, where the barbecue was held and where Eugene Weathersby delivered the oration of the occasion; Colonel Eshelman and others of the Washington Artillery being present, specially invited guests of the occasion.

Political excitement and sectional feeling between the Northern and Southern States had become greatly intensified by questions pertaining to the new territory acquired from France by purchase from Napoleon Bonaparte, the admission of Texas and other new States, the right of property in slaves, the extension of slavery in the new territory and the sovereignty of States. The Constitution of the United States recognized the right of property in slaves and threw around it its protecting arm and upheld it by decisions of its highest tribunals, and the owners claimed the right to remove to any of the public domain with this species of property. This privilege was contested by those at the North who were opposed to allowing any owner of slaves to enter the new territory. A noted suit was instituted in Missouri as a test case, known as the Dred Scott case, to determine the question whether a negro slave taken into territory claimed by abolitionists to be non-slavery territory, by his owner, should remain a slave or be liberated. Dred Scott was taken into this disputed territory by his owner, an army officer, who died leaving him in the territory, and the question was sprung as to what disposition should be made of him. None of his owner's heirs wanted him, yet he was property, and the courts were resorted to. It was greedily seized upon by abolition political agitators at the North and a great effort made to secure a verdict against the slave owners of the South, but the Supreme Court of the United States held that the removal of the slave with his owner into non-slave holding territory did not change the status of the slave as property and decreed that he be delivered to the nearest heir at law of the deceased owner. This was done, and the negro was liberated or emancipated by the owner. This judgment of the highest tribunal of the United States Government created an intense furore throughout the North among the abolitionists. There had been many years of wrangling over this question which brought about the extension of Mason's and Dixon's line, and for forty years the country was more or less agitated over matters pertaining to the rights of the States. The Southern States as such were not responsible for the institution of slavery nor its establishment within their borders When Virginia was a colony under Great Britain, in 1620, the first load of negro slaves were landed at Jamestown from a Dutch vessel. It was fostered and nursed by the English crown up to 1807 and by people in the Eastern States. New England men, New England money, New England vessels, New England inhumanity, in coalition with the English crown and Dutch navigators, are the parents of the trade in slavery and its establishment in this country, and Massachusetts the first slave State. It proved unprofitable to the North on account of the long winters, but profitable to the South under good management, and after the slave trade was forbidden by act of Parliament in 1807, and the Southern States passed laws forbidding any further importation of slaves from foreign countries, and it ceased to be a source of wealth to the avaricious Yankee, then schemes were concocted to bring about its abolition in the South by those who were jealous of Southern prosperity.

Long before the admission of Mississippi as a Territory the South was so apprehensive of future troubles growing out of the accumulation of negroes that they passed laws prohibiting the landing of African negroes on their shores and the organic act creating the Territory of Mississippi forbade it; but the slave speculators and kidnappers of New England with hundreds of vessels continued to ply their avocation and smuggled them through from the North and unfrequented lakes and rivers unguarded by government and where communication to legal authority was difficult. Virginia put a stop to it as soon as it was in her power to do so, and it was one of the express stipulations constituting Oglethorpe's charter for the establishment of his Moravian Colony in Georgia. Any attempts of Northern haters of the South to fix the blame of the institution on the people of the South, or their secession from the Union for the purpose of perpetuating it, is disproved by all the facts connected with its history.

General William Cain had been appointed general of the militia organizations of South Mississippi counties, and in 1860 he ordered a review to take place in the town of Magnolia. The Quitman Guards were ordered out and responded, the whole company going to Magnolia, clothed in their military uniforms, to participate in the grand review. General Cain was handsomely uniformed and mounted on a splendid iron-gray charger, accompanied by a numerous staff of elegantly uniformed officers. It was a gala day in Magnolia, but the Quitman Guards had possession, from a military point of view, of the entire field, under direction of the commanding general. No other troops presented themselves for review, and the history of the occasion becomes deficient by the absence of the mass of South Mississippi forces. Nevertheless this was a historical occasion. It was a niche in events to follow. It was duty performed.

The year 1860 was a stormy period in the political history of the country. The Southern States clung tenaciously to the constitution and combatted every infringement of its provisions assailed by its enemies. So many things had been done and threatened that endangered their peace and happiness that they were seriously considering the question of a dissolution of the Union, by passing ordinances of secession, and forming a separate government, with which there could be some unity of feeling, friendship and mutual benefits. The student of political history must turn to other works to learn all the causes which plunged the country into a great fratricidal conflict after this time. Pike County is only a drop in the bucket that overflowed, a grain of sand on the shore lashed by the sea of human blood.

On May 16, 1860, a Republican convention, a purely sectional body of men, was held in the city of Chicago, Ill., for the purpose of nominating candidates for President and Vice-President of the United States. This party at the time was commonly known as the "Black Abolition Party," and was composed of delegates of the abolition faith. Not a single Southern State was represented in it. At this convention

Abraham Lincoln, a lawyer and politician, was nominated for President, and Mr. Hamlin of Maine was nominated for Vice-President.

Abraham Lincoln had proclaimed that the Union "could not permanently endure half slave and half free." This of itself was a declaration on his part, endorsed by this purely sectional convention, that the institution of slavery was to be attacked and should be abolished if possible. A society of abolitionists had been formed in England long before the abolition of slavery and the slave trade by the English Parliament, and another one in the city of Philadelphia in the early thirties.

At the convention of Democrats, which met in Charleston, S. C., there was a division which resulted in the nomination of two sets of candidates. Stephen A. Douglas, of Illinois, being selected for President, and Herschel V. Johnson, of Georgia, for Vice-President, by one faction, and John C. Breckenridge, of Kentucky, for President, and Joseph Lane, of Oregon, for Vive-President, by the other faction.

Another convention assembled in the city of Baltimore, Md., and nominated John Bell, of Tennessee, for President, and Edward Everett, of Massachusetts, for Vice-President.

Thus there were four tickets in the field. At the election in November following, there were 4,676,853 votes polled. Of this number Lincoln and Hamlin received 1,866,352, and of the 303 votes cast in the electoral college they received 180 and were declared elected. It was clearly sectional in its results. Lincoln and Hamlin received a little over one-third of the popular votes and over one-half of the electoral vote. Their party leaders had declared against the institution of slavery and that it could not exist "only by virtue of municipal law," "no law for it in the territories." This was an open declaration of lynching the Constitution of the United States and setting aside the decision of its Supreme Court. The South saw its perils. Her institutions had been assailed and her constitutional rights tramped upon for forty years, and her people thought it was time to seek relief by separation.

After the announcement of the election of Lincoln and Hamlin, South Carolina, acting in her sovereign capacity as a State, in December, 1860, passed the ordinance of secession, severing her relations with the general government. Mississippi followed on the 9th of January, 1861, Dr. James M. Nelson, of Holmesville, being the delegate from Pike County.

The convention which passed the ordinance of secession adopted the Bonnie Blue Flag as the State flag. The main field of which was white with a red fringe around its borders and a square blue field occupying about one-fourth of the flag in the upper corner attached to the staff. In this blue field a single white star. In the white field of the flag was the imprint of a green tree. The adoption of this flag inspired the writing of the song of the "Bonnie Blue Flag" by Harry McCarthy.

SONG OF THE BONNIE BLUE FLAG.

BY HARRY M'CARTHY.

We are a band of brothers, and native to the soil,
Fighting for our liberty, with treasure blood and toil;
And when our rights were threatened, the cry rose near and far,
Hurrah for the Bonny Blue Flag that bears a single star!

CHORUS.

Hurrah! Hurrah! for Southern rights, Hurrah!
Hurrah for the Bonny Blue Flag that bears a single star.

First, gallant South Carolina nobly made the stand;
Then came Alabama, who took her by the hand;
Next, quickly, Mississippi, Georgia and Florida,
All raised on high the Bonny Blue Flag that bears the single star.

Ye men of valor, gather round the banner of the Right,
Texas and fair Louisiana, join us in the fight!
Davis, our loved President, and Stephens, statesman rare,
Now rally round the Bonny Blue Flag that bears the single star!

And here's to brave Virginia, the Old Dominion State,
With the young Confederacy at length has linked her fate,
Impelled by her example, now other States prepare
To hoist on high the Bonny Blue Flag that bears a single star!

THE SECESSION CONVENTION.

In the Mississippi Official and Statistical Register of 1904, compiled and edited by Dunbar Rowland, Director Department of Archives and History, the following account of the Secession Convention is given:

"It was a notable assemblage that met in the Hall of Representatives on the morning of January 7, 1861, and one girt for action. The time for argument, concession, compromise had passed. The supreme act remained to be done. The convention set about its business in a spirit of seriousness, as aware of the tremendous responsibility pressing upon it, but with an unfaltering look toward the one fixed goal. The one hundred delegates, representing the flower of the State, soon organized themselves in a business-like manner by the selection of W. S. Barry of Lowndes to preside. A committee of fifteen was speedily appointed to draft an ordinance of secession. Mr. Lamar was chairman. The overwhelming sentiment of the convention in favor of immediate secession, as opposed to any form of 'co-operation with other States,' had already declared itself unmistakably.

"On the third day of the committee's deliberations the ordinance was reported by Mr. Lamar as chairman. The man who, later in life, was to reach out across the chasm between the North and South was the central figure in the drama of secession. Efforts to retard its passage or change its complexion were in vain. The roll call on the main question began amid a breathless silence. The name of J. L. Alcorn, an ardent co-operationist, was first called. 'The Rubicon is crossed,' he said, 'I follow the army that leads to Rome.' Others yielded to the dominant sentiment, and the ordinance passed by a vote of 84 to 15.

"The President announced the vote amid a solemnity that had something religious in it. Moved by the impulse of the moment, he asked a minister to invoke God's blessing on what had been done. The immense audience stood while he complied. Nor Cromwell's pikemen on the eve of battle felt their dependence on the will of Providence more than they. The prayer concluded, a dramatic incident came to relieve the tension. A gentleman entered the hall bearing a blue silk flag, in the center of which glittered a single white star. It had been made overnight by a Jackson lady, in anticipation of the action of the convention. He handed it to the President, who paused a moment and then waved it aloft with the exclamation that it was the first flag of the young republic. The audience broke into applause, rising to salute the emblem. Without were heard the salvos of artillery that greeted the new republic. The next night, it may be worth remarking, 'The Bonny Blue Flag' was sung in a local theater. It had been composed by Harry McCarthy, a comedian, immediately after witnessing the scene in the capitol.

"The convention knew its act meant war. Preparations were made for the conflict. Jefferson Davis was elected Major General of the State troops, and four Brigadier-Generals were chosen. Delegates to the Convention of the Southern States at Montgomery were also elected. The 'swelling prologue' to the theme of the Civil War was over as far as Mississippi was concerned.

The decision of the United Supreme Court in the Dred Scott case, fixing the status of the negro race, giving the owners of slaves the right to settle with them in the territories, was disregarded by abolition agitators. The substance of this decision was that the African slaves were not and could not be acknowledged as "part of the people," or citizens under the Constitution of the United States, and that Congress had no right to exclude citizens of the South from taking their negro servants as any other property into any part of the country.

Continued interference, the instigation of negro insurrection, the invasion of John Brown in Virginia to free the negroes, and the scattering of emissaries over sections of the South, coupled with past aggressions on Southern rights and efforts to deprive her of equality in the Union by discrimination in legislation, and denying them the right to settle with their slaves in the common territory in face of this decision of the highest tribunal of the land, created a deep feeling of insecurity and further inflamed the passions of the people. It was evident to the minds of Southern people that it was the policy of the abolitionists to irritate the South to the commission of an act to get an excuse to invade the country with the ultimate object of the abolition of slavery and the Africanization of the Southern States.

Pike County was not without its share of these sneaking abolition emissaries, going from plantation to plantation, secretly among the negroes, endeavoring to incite them to insurrection against their masters and families. This writer knows whereof he speaks on this matter in so far as Pike County was concerned. There was no more cruel and murderous intent perpretrated on a people than that attempted by Northern emissaries here in 1860; and it became necessary for the manhood of the South to be on the alert. On his father's estate on Topisaw the writer caught one of these scoundrels among the negroes trying to persuade them to rise and massacre his widowed mother and her children, which they refused to consider; and the same villian attempted the same thing on the plantations of Judge

James B. Quin, Hardy Thompson, Christian Hoover and others. This is localizing evidence and facts in a small radius. Put it thus over the entire South, where there were four millions of negro slaves, equal in number to the whites, what was there under these circumstances for the Southern people to expect? With twenty millions of white people in the Northern States, turned to be their enemies, sending their murderous emissaries among these four million slaves to incite them to massacre the four millions of whites in the South, thus placing the four million Southern whites at the mercy of the twenty million Northern whites and the four million negroes in their midst, what can be said against the South seceding and Southern manhood asserting itself for its own preservation? What constituted a greater incentive to manly and heroic effort to beat back the foe?

The Southern people were true Americans, and were not moulded from that class of the human race to stand idle and inactive while an insolent foe marched in among them to cut their throats or rob them of all the rights of freemen under a government which their fathers had given their best blood and brains to establish.

In 1859 H. E. Weathersby, the brilliant young lawyer previously mentioned, was elected to the State Legislature, and J. B. Crisman was elected to represent the counties of Pike and Laurence in the State Senate. They were gentlemen eminently qualified for these responsible positions. They were both men of ability and reflected honor upon the constituency they represented in these days of political commotion.

H. Eugene Weathersby was a young man born and raised in Amite County, and was educated at Centenary College in Louisiana. He was one of the class with Judge Thomas C. W. Ellis, of the Civil District Court of New Orleans, and a bosom friend. He was tall, handsome, talented, chivalrous and brave; and he had entered the practice of law in Holmesville at a period of life when noble aspirations fill the soul, and a laudable ambition urges one to seek the highest place among men; and it was at a time when trained and brilliant lawyers, in the floodtide of success, occupied the bar in South Mississippi, many of whose names have already been mentioned in these pages, and whose fame will go down to the ages. He became a partner with Hugh Murray Quin, a native of Pike County, and Thomas R. Stockdale, recently of the State of Pennsylvania, in the practice of law, and was the chosen orator of the day at the 4th of July celebration in 1860, the occasion of the presentation of the banner to the Quitman Guards. It was fitting that this should be the greatest celebration in Pike County, and it was fitting too that the gallant, the good, the chivalrous Weathersby should occupy such a conspicuous place in connection with the event, as it was the last for many years to come, and the young man who stood there the object of so much admiration, with his hands raised to high heaven, prophetically deploring the signs of the coming storm, became a sacrifice upon the altar of a principle he loved so well.

At the fall election in 1860 Robert Bacot was succeeded by the election of Louis C. Bickham as sheriff.

Louis Bickham was the son of Thomas Bickham, of Louisiana. His mother, Mrs. Elizabeth Bickham, becoming a widow by the death of her husband, became a resident of Holmesville and a conspicuous factor in its higher social life. She was a woman of queenly bearing, tender-hearted and kind, and delighted in the entertainment and happiness of young people. Her children, like herself, were all handsome and proud.

Louis C. Bickham married Margaret, one of the beautiful twin daughters of B. B. Lindsey, the noted millwright and mechanic. Her twin sister was named Jennie, whose first husband's name was McClendon. They were so nearly alike that even intimate friends were sometimes puzzled to tell which was Margaret or which was Jennie, when met separately. Louis Bickham's grandfather was Maj. Benjamin Bickham, who emigrated from South Carolina in 1811, in company with Benjamin Youngblood, the father of Joseph Youngblood, and John Brumfield, the father of Jesse and Isaac Brumfield, and settled in Washington Parish, Louisiana.

Louis Bickham was a man of delicate mould, handsome and friendly, but he was brave and fearless in the discharge of the duties of sheriff.

Among the original settlers of Summit and business men were William H. Garland, one of the original promoters of the building of the New Orleans, Jackson & Great Northern Railroad, as previously mentioned in the organization of that great enterprise.

Louis Alcus and Isaac Lichenstein became merchants there, also Hatch Hiller, James and Clint Atkinson, J. B. Wilson and John Cotton, J. D. Jacobowsky and Jake Hart, Sol. Hyman, Henry Lotterhos, John W. Huffman, dentist; Lemuel J. Quin, Ed. Mogan, I. Moiese, Henry Lotterhos, D. C. Packer, John D. Farnham, Algenon Sidney Mitchell, Isaac C. Dick, William McNulty, Sam Hyman, Louis and Isaac Scherck, Ben Hilburn, Rene H. Brunette, the Cunninghams, Boyds and Godbolts and James H. Wingfield.

Rene H. Brunette, previously mentioned as one of the original settlers of the town of Summit in 1856, was from the city of New Orleans, La. His wife was Susan Jane Thompson. They had four sons, Rene H., Jr., William M., Birkett Thompson and Frank.

At the commencement of the Civil War Rene, Jr., and William joined Charlie Drew's battalion of infantry, made up of some of the best young men of the city of New Orleans, which was immediately sent to Richmond, Va., with other forces to meet the invasion of the peninsula. They became engaged in a skirmish fight with the enemy near Newport News, July 5, 1861, at which time Charlie Drew was killed and it became a noted historical fact that he was the first field officer on the Confederate side to become a martyr to the cause of Southern independence.

In accordance with the terms of their enlistment the battalion was disbanded and the men given their discharge at Yorktown, in 1862, and Fenner's battery was formed from members of the battalion, and the two Brunette brothers from Summit became members of it when it was organized at Jackson, Miss., under orders, in May, 1862. William Brunette was killed at the battle of New Hope, Ga., May 24, 1864. Frank was too young to become an active soldier during the war. The family returned to New Orleans in 1866, where they engaged in merchandising. The elder son, Rene H., Jr., at this writing is over seventy years of age, in good health, active and strong and of superb memory connected with events of the Civil War. He married Miss Alice Shamwell, of New Orleans, and has one living son, Willam A. Brunette, of Gulfport.

The Reynolds family, also pioneer settlers of Summit, from New Orleans, returned to that city some years after the close of the war. One of the daughters of this family became the wife of Mr. Soule, of Soule's College.

Col. William H. Garland, one of the promoters of the New Orleans, Jackson & Great Northern Railroad, and founder of the town of Summit, was a widower from New Orleans with the following children: Lizzie, wife of Dr. James M. Ferguson, of Stockdale's Cavalry; David and William H., Jr., when he married the widow O'Callahan, with the following children: Baldwin (known as Bun), Harold and Mollie. Colonel Garland and his wife, Mrs. O'Callahan, were the parents of Sidney and Bettie Garland.

In 1859, while Robert Bacot was sheriff, Ralf Summers, a negro slave belonging to Jack Summers, the tanner, was killed by Green Wingo, a slave of Asa Wingo, for which the latter was hung after trial by jury in the circuit court. This killing occurred on the public road near the plantation of Andrew Kaigler, across the river from Holmesville.

Ralph Gibson, Capt. Westly Thomas and William Carr, who lived on Leatherwood, were members of Jefferson Davis' celebrated 1st Mississippi Regiment in the War with Mexico, noted for excellent services, crowning the American arms with success by the heroic efforts and gallantry of its illustrious colonel and his men.

William Sparkman, Joseph Page, Elijah Page, Felix Campbell, John and Josh Bishop and their father were the principal carpenters and builders in Holmesville.

William Sparkman was a fine violinist and furnished the music for the balls in Holmesville during his time when the California House was famous for these occasions.

Holmesville was the scene of many a happy gathering. An inland resort, the gay and the chivalrous came from near and far; distant States often lent their charmers, and there was no rural town or county that could boast of more attractive and lovable women.

One of the first fandangoes the writer visited while in his tender teens was at the residence of Joseph Luter, on the farm where he settled and lived on Varnal Creek. It was often the case that boys or young men from towns would attend these country dances, and they sometimes indulged in the habit of poking fun at the country lads and lasses. It was a fashion for them to wear fine red-top boots in attendance at these balls. The country girls were taught to dance all the fandango figures, "Virginia reels," "fisher's hornpipe," "heel and toe," "side shuffle," the "backstep" and "pigeon wing."

On this occasion, Flem Burkhalter, with his inimitable bow and fiddle and the magic pat of his foot, "filled the orchestra." The country boys fixed up a job—one of the relics of Pindar Ridge, in Washington Parish—on a youngster with red-top boots and a standing collar An old Virginia reel was arranged and partners chosen. One of the handsomest and best fandango dancing girls was robed in a homespun dress and kept in the background until the time came for the red-top boots to sidle out bantering for a vis-a-vee. Flem Burkhalter was "up to the game" and he laid his head down on his fiddle and went to work. A lithe, smiling figure tripped out in front of the red-top boots, her head leaning coquettishly to one side, a twinkle in her eyes, a happy smile upon her cheeks, with her homespun dress slightly tucked above the ankles. The knight of the red-top boots was amazed, he hesitated for a moment, but hands clapped, a shout went up. Flem Burkhalter came down vigorously with his bow, his foot went up and down, red-top boots took in the situation, and he proved to be a "clipper" in the art; but there was a match for him in the homespun dress. All the other dancers rested back on one foot in line, with their hands folded in front of them, eyes riveted on the performers. Flem Burkhalter sailed out from one tune to another for half an hour, and then plunged into Fisher's hornpipe. Red-top boots figured with the tune, and so did the figure in the homespun dress. The smile that lit her pretty cheeks was there yet, calm and beautiful, the head leaned from one side to the other, and there was not an error in the motion of the well-shaped, flexible limbs. She was one of "Flem Buck's" pupils; he knew the power of her endurance, and he fiddled to break down her opponent; but "red-top" was game; he was loath to yield to the pineywoods' smiling gazelle; great drops of fluid formed on his chivalric brow, his collar went limp, his linen was dripping. The nimble gazelle sidled him around; she wouldn't swing; it was a test of endurance, but red-top boots had to succumb, and he bent his obedience to his matchless conqueress in heroic fashion, and from that hour on, after she had donned her gayest attire, they were the charming leaders; took the first place at the magnificent supper prepared, wound up the fandango happy-hearted, and went their way rejoicing. The actress in this famous contest was Miss Louisa Burkhalter, an aunt of the wife of Irvin A. Quin.

The first man to receive a license to teach school in Pike County was W. D. Clarke, in the forties. One of his pupils, in the person of Hon. Henry S. Brumfield, still survives. In 1902, when these notes were compiled, Prof. Clarke was still living at the ripe old age of eighty-one, in the city of Springfield, Ill., and had recently written a beautiful letter to his pupil of the long ago.

The grading of the railroad was completed to Magnolia in 1856. The land upon which the town was built belonged to Ansel H. Prewett, and was laid off in town lots and sold to the settlers.

ANSEL H. PREWETT
The founder of Magnolia. Appointed Sheriff of Pike County by Governor Alcorn in 1870

Ansel H. Prewett was a son of Elisha Prewett and Ann Huckabee, pioneers from Georgia. His first wife was Julia Ann Raborn, and they were the parents of the following children: Sarah Ann, who first married Wesley Powell, and then Howell Dickey, second husband; Wm. Harrison Prewett, who married Polly Ann Vaughn; James Smiley Prewett, who married Elizabeth Vaughn: Martha Ann, who married Newton Nash; Elisha Taylor, who married Sally Harris,

Naomi Eviline, who married David Vaughn; Mary Ann, who married Cornelius T. Zachary.

His second wife was Miss Lucinda Barron, and they had an adopted daughter, Ann Elizabeth, who married Erasmus Nash.

Magnolia is ninety-eight miles from New Orleans, and is located on a gentle, undulating elevation sloping eastward with the little Tangipahoa flowing past its eastern border, and Ballards Creek, since called Minnehaha, marking its western boundary, emptying into the Little Tangipahoa below the town. The following are numbered as the original settlers of the town: Nick Sinnot, S. R. Jones, Capt. Robert L. Carter, W. H. Joiner, W. H. B. Croswell, Joseph Evans, Abraham Hiller, Bennett Carter, Evan McLennan, L. Gourny, Prof. Vincent, E. H. Pezant, Ira Cockerham, Dr. Hart, Dr. Snyder, Dr. T. J. Everett, Samuel Murray Sandell, John Carter, Henry Hall, Jasper Coney, Dr. J. H. Laney, Mr. Nurse, George Clarke, Mrs. Lagrue (Widow Marshall), Mrs. H. H. Hadden, Rev. W. H. Roane, Mrs. Emiline Coney, widow of Jackson Coney, and Eugene M. Bee, who was the first depot agent.

The Central House, erected by Dr. Clark and kept by Henry Gottig, was built in 1858.

Capt. Joseph H. Miller, the husband of Miss Rachel Coney, was a son of Ebenezer T. Miller and Miss Lucinda Davis, of Morgan County, Illinois. He came South in 1858 and located in New Orleans. At the breaking out of the war he joined the Washington Artillery and subsequently was stationed at Camp Moore as a drill master and assisted in organizing the 11th Louisiana, Colonel Marks, and went to the front as Captain of Company A. While in service he was wounded, and being thus disabled he was sent back to Mississippi as a recruiting officer, stationed at Holly Springs and Jackson, Miss. In the meantime he became acquainted with Miss Rachel E. Coney at Magnolia and married her in that town. At the close of the war he settled there and engaged in the mercantile business. He died February, 1874. He possessed a Washington Artillery pin with his name inscribed thereon, dated September 6, 1860, presented by S. H. to J. H. M., which is an heirloom of his family.

In order to ascertain what command Capt. J. H. Miller and Capt. A. LeBlanc belonged to during the Civil War, the writer addressed a letter to General John McGrath, of Baton Rouge, La., and received the following reply:

Mr. L. W. Conerly,   BATON ROUGE, LA., July 31, 1908.
   Griswold, Miss.
MY DEAR FRIEND:
   Yours of the 25th instant to hand, and in answer will say that I knew Capt. Miller and Lieut. Alex LeBlanc both. LeBlanc was second lieutenant of a company made up in Baton Rouge, but locally known as the Point Coupee Volunteers. The reason for the name was that the Pointe Coupee furnished the money to equip the company, which was officered as follows: Wiley Barrow, Captain; Thompson J. Bird, First Lieutenant; C. D. Favrot, Second Lieutenant;, and Alexander LeBlanc, Junior Second Lieutenant. The Eleventh Regiment was broken up in 1862, and the non-commissioned officers and men, after the formation of two companies of sharp shooters known as Austin's Battalion, were divided between the Thirteenth and Twentieth Regiments and the officers sent on provost and conscript duty. Under this arrangement, LeBlanc was sent to Magnolia, or that vicinity. I did not know much of Capt. Miller.
   There are no records of Confederates in Louisiana except a few old rolls in Memorial Hall.
   Regards to yourself and family.
                        Yours truly,
                               JOHN MCGRATH,
                                     Per M.

   NOTE.—Alex. LeBlanc, above mentioned, married Miss Jodie Coney, sister to Mrs. Joe Miller.

James Buchanan was President of the United States in 1860, and upon the assumption of her individual sovereignty, South Carolina demanded of the Federal Government a return to her the possession of Forts Moultrie and Sumpter, which were parts of her domain conditionally held by the United States Government, with a garrison in Fort Moultrie under Maj. Robert Anderson The secession of South Carolina and Mississippi was closely followed by Texas, Georgia, Alabama, Florida, North Carolina, Arkansas and Louisiana. A provisional government was formed and named the Confederate States of America. Virginia held back for some time in the interest of peace, and called a convention of States to meet in Washington for the purpose of trying to adjust the difficulties, but all her efforts were scorned by the Northern States, there being twenty represented.

Jefferson Davis, of Mississippi, who had served the United States conspicuously in the war with Mexico and as Secretary of War under President Franklin Pierce, and as United States Senator from Mississippi, a man of great ability and unblemished character, a gallant soldier and wise statesman, was chosen President of the Confederate States, with the provisional capital located at Montgomery, Ala., and Alexander H. Stephens, of Georgia, was chosen Vice-President.

The State of Maryland was handicapped and practically subjugated by an early invasion by Federal troops. The State had not seceded, but her people were in sympathy with her sister States of the South, and their enthusiasm, particularly in the city of Baltimore, was kindled to a high degree. The Secretary of War, by proclamation, had called on the States for their quota of troops to be used in the war about to be inaugurated for the coercion of the seceded States, and it was learned that troops from the West were to come through Maryland. On the 19th of April, 1861, a body of them landed at the depot in Baltimore and their further progress disputed. The soldiers were attacked with stones and many of them injured, when they fired on the citizens, killing a few and wounding others. This movement of the troops was in open violation of the United States Constitution; a provision incorporated in the States' Constitutions, to move troops through a State without the knowledge and consent of its Governor.

On the 11th of April, 1861, General Beauregard demanded of Major Anderson the surrender of Fort Sumpter, which he held, after secretly leaving Fort Moultrie, in violation of an agreement pending negotiations for a peaceful settlement, by order of his government, which he declined to do. In a second communication to General Beauregard, he offered to do so provided he should not receive before that time controlling instructions from his government or additional supplies. As it was known by General Beauregard that these controlling instructions had already been issued and the supplies expected every moment, and that the naval forces had already arrived off the harbor, and were prevented from coming in by a gale, there being no other recourse to prevent a conflict with the combined forces of the fleet and the guns of Fort Sumpter, General Beauregard notified Major Anderson, on the 12th of April, at 3:20-A. M., that he would open fire on his batteries in one hour from that time, which he proceeded to do. After a bombardment of over thirty hours the fort was partially destroyed and set on fire by shells and Major Anderson surrendered on the 13th.

The persistent and stereotyped rant of Northern demagogues and Southern haters about "firing on the flag" will not be considered by impartial students seeking the truth of history, as it is an undeniable fact of record that after Abraham Lincoln was inaugurated the most cunning treachery was practiced in the negotiations for the evacuation of these forts, and every principle of honor violated by government authorities, in communications with the commissioners representing South Carolina and the recently organized Confederate Government.

Horace Greeley, who was considered the best authority from a black Republican point of view, and who was considered fair and honorable, said: "Whether the bombardment and reduction of Fort Sumpter shall or shall not be justified by posterity, it is clear that the Confederacy had no alternative but its dissolution."

On the 5th of May following the scenes enacted in the city of Baltimore were followed up, and a body of United States troops were quartered at the relay House under General Butler, who subsequently took possession of Federal Hill and consummated the military possession of Baltimore, disarmed the people and placed that city under martial law. The police commissioners were arrested and the city marshal, George P. Kane, who had rendered effective service in preserving the peace, was sent to Fort McHenry by General Banks who succeeded Butler, and thus the State of Maryland was subjugated and wronged by the Federal Government at Washington in spite of the protests of her Governor and her people. A touching record of facts relating to the gross usurpations of Abraham Lincoln's government in direct violations of the oath of office he had taken may be properly inserted here from the pen of Jefferson Davis, in his "Rise and Fall of the Confederate Government:

"Henceforth the story of Maryland is sad to the last degree, only relieved by the gallant men who left their homes to fight the battles of State rights when Maryland no longer furnished them a field on which they could maintain the rights their fathers left them. This was a fate doubly sad to the sons of the heroic men who, under the designation of 'Maryland Line', did so much in our revolutionary struggle to secure the independence of the States; of men who, at a later day, fought the battle of North Point; of the people of a land which had furnished so many heroes and statesmen, and gave the great Chief Justice Taney to the Supreme Court of the United States."

During these eventful times Pike County had but one military organization, the Quitman Guards. The excitement produced by the aggressive acts of Abraham Lincoln after his inauguration on the 4th of March, 1861, was keenly felt and aroused the Southern people to a sense of the great danger threatening them. Lincoln could not be regarded by them as anything else but a revolutionist, heading the abolition party, by whom he was elected, and who had for long years been menacing the institutions of the South, not only in their incendiary efforts to raise insurrections among the negroes in the South against the whites, but the actual invasion of the State of Virginia by abolition filibusters, under the leadership of John Brown, who, after his capture and execution at Charlestown, was made a saint in the songs and prayers of his abolition followers and sympathizers throughout the North.

Many of the young men of Pike County immediately rseponded to the call of President Davis for troops to protect Pensacola; among them being James Bridges and Joe Quin, students at Holmesville, and Hugh Q. Bridges, Wm. J. Lamkin and Wm. Clint Barnes, and Alexander Mouton Bickham, students at Oxford, who joined the University Greys attached to the 11th Mississippi Regiment.

Upon polling the Quitman Guards it was found that a number of them, including Capt. Brent, could not immediately take the field if called upon, and it was determined to reorganize the company and

THE "BONNIE BLUE FLAG,"
Adopted by the Convention of Mississippi which passed th
Ordinance of Secession, January 9, 1861.

a call was made to make up the maximum of one hundred men allowed by the military regulations, and Captain Brent resigned, on account of his planting interests which he could not suddenly leave.

On the 15th of April, 1861, Abraham Lincoln issued his proclamation calling for seventy-five thousand men to suppress "combinations" opposed to laws "too powerful to be suppressed by the ordinary course of judicial proceedings or the powers invested in marshals by law," "the execution thereof obstructed, in the States of South Carolina, Georgia, Alabama, Florida, Mississippi, Louisiana, and Texas," "by virtue of the power in me vested by the constitution and laws," etc. It will be remembered here that in his correspondence with Alexander Stephens he said the South had nothing to fear from him.

The President of the United States had no such authority under the Constitution. This act of Abraham Lincoln was clearly an assumption of authority, a violation of the Constitution, which he had sworn to support, in the very beginning of his executive career; a preconceived revolutionary measure for the coercion of the Southern States and the abolition of negro slavery.

The Constitution of the United States clearly and emphatically says: "The Congress shall have power to provide for calling forth the militia to execute the laws of the Union suppress insurrection and repel invasions."

"Congress shall have power to declare war," says the United States Constitution, not the President, and when this man who had sworn to support the Constitution invaded Maryland and occupied her territory and shot down her people in the streets of Baltimore, and placed that city under martial law, arresting and imprisoning her civil officers, who had committed no unlawful act against the Government of the United States, it was a declaration of war upon a State of the Union which had not denied, nor attempted to deny, any lawful authority of the United States, nor attempted to obstruct the execution of its laws, certainly exceeded the bounds of his executive authority.

It was an act of revolution and invasion without a lawful excuse, and under the rant of firing on the flag at Fort Sumpter and the destruction of the Union, men flocked to his standard to defend *their* "liberties," "liberties" *assumed* to invade a peaceful State of the Union and to make war on and destroy others acting solely in self-defense. Seventy-five thousand men to suppress "unlawful combinations!" Sovereign States acting in the peaceful exercises of State rights. The earnest and impartial student of the political history of the United States cannot fail to be convinced that the Southern States were eminently correct in their attitude and acts in 1861. That Abraham Lincoln, who has been worshipped and lauded as a patriot and martyr to liberty, was a tool of abolition conspirators, a violator of the organic laws of the land, a revolutionist, a destroyer of the fundamental principles upon which the government was founded, acting in direct contravention to the action of the colonies in their exercise of the right to withdraw their allegiance to the British Government in 1776; the reverse of George Washington, with whom the feeble effort has been made to class him. In his own language I would say: "We cannot escape history."

These matters are here mentioned in order to prepare the mind of the reader for the future, and to show why the South was forced to resort to arms, and why Pike County, a mere speck on the map, became like other sections of the South, almost stripped of her gallant men and boys in the conflict which followed. The future pages contained in this work are embellished with their names—their deeds are recorded in story and song, in ably written histories of the land and in the published official reports of the armies.

When Virginia failed, through the convention of States called at Washington, to secure an amicable adjustment of pending difficulties, and seeing the hopelessness of her efforts and the determination manifested at Washington to invade and coerce the Southern States, she positively refused any aid for that purpose, but promptly withdrew from the Union and cast her destinies with the Confederate cause.

The secession of the Southern States was peacefully accomplished, and every effort consistent with honor was made by them to avoid war, but when they saw the treachery manifested over the Fort Sumpter affair and the determination of Lincoln to coerce them they determined to prepare for the issue as best they could.

SOME NOTES ON SECESSION.

It would seem proper just here to give some notes on secession, as the Southern States have had to bear the blame for the inculcation of the doctrine and for the "destruction of the Union," from a Northern point of view. We are at a period now when the Southern States are exercising the right of secession, not threatening to do so. Heretofore they had held fast to the Union, defended it and used every means in their power to sustain it in all its purity and in accordance with the rights declared by the Constitution.

As early as 1781 the New England States began the agitation of secession; only a few years after the Declaration of Independence, and from this time on down to 1845, a period of sixty years, prominent men supported and sustained by the people in New England advocated and agitated the question of secession and the formation of a Northern Confederacy.

Let us go back a little and see how history sustains this declaration:

Jefferson Davis has been scurrilously attacked by Northern writers and historians as the father of secession and the arch traitor of America, from the time imperial Abraham Lincoln displayed his infamous contempt for American institutions, founded on the independence achieved by the colonists in the revolution of 1776. If Jefferson Davis is the father of secession and the arch traitor who began the war between the North and South what name can be given to those who brought on the war against Great Britain? Who were the fathers of that great struggle? In other words, who were the grandfathers of the sin of secession? What Southern State ever made the threat of secession prior to 1860? Then what Northern State did? For the benefit of the reader it may be well even in this little history of Pike County to inform him on this subject. The historian says:

"While the thirteen States were living under the old Articles of Confederation, 1781-1788, threats of a new England confederation were loud and deep, and prominent men declared that if the Mississippi River were not closed up for twenty-five years the New England

States would secede from the perpetual 'Union' and establish a confederation for themselves," and this was because commerce of the country went out through that great highway instead of through the Eastern States. Mark the date, 1781–1788.

Lieutenant-Governor Wolcott, of Connecticut, made this declaration: "I sincerely declare that I wish the Northern States would separate from the Southern the moment that event (which was the election of Thomas Jefferson to the presidency) shall take place."

The election of Jefferson a cause of secession?

That was before Jefferson Davis was born. Some years later on, while negotiations were pending for the purchase of the Louisiana Territory from France, out of which five great States were carved, the Massachusetts Legislature passed the following resolution:

"*Resolved*, That the annexation of Louisiana to the union transcends the constitutional power of the government of the United States. It forms a new confederacy to which the States united, by the former compact, are not bound to adhere."

The North threatened to secede if the Embargo Act, which was passed to protect citizens of the United States on the high seas and the honor of the flag, were not repealed.

When Congress was considering the admission of Louisiana to the Union, in January, 1811, Massachusetts spoke out vigorously in the person of her representative, Hon. Josiah Quinsey, thusly:

"I am compelled to declare it as my deliberate opinion that if this bill passes the bonds of the Union are virtually dissolved, that it will free the States from their moral obligations; and, as it will be the right of all, so it will be the duty of some, to prepare for a separation." Another father of secession.

When was Jefferson Davis born? June 3, 1808, and he must have been learning his A, B, C's about this time at the point of a goosequill.

In the proceedings of the Hartford Convention, in 1814, the following has been preserved in history (some more Connecticut feeling):

"In cases of deliberate, dangerous and palpable infractions of the Constitution, affecting the sovereignty of the State, it is not only the right, it is the duty of such a State to interpose its authority for their protection in the manner best calculated to secure that end. States, which have no common umpire, must be their own judges and execute their own decision."

This was good secession doctrine for New England in 1814, but it was a crime in 1861 for the Southern States to act upon it!

When the Florida purchase was made by President Monroe in 1819, he was prevented from securing the Spanish claims west of the Mississippi River by "ominous threats of New England to secede."

We have not yet read of any Southern State doing this up to this time.

In 1845 Massachusetts again threatened to secede if Texas was admitted to the Union, when her Legislature passed the following resolution:

"The annexation of Texas will drive these States into a dissolution of the Union." What States? The Northern States. And down to 1845, including the threat to secede in case of war with England in 1812, the North made nine different threats to secede, and Jefferson Davis, though he had been admitted to a seat in Congress in 1845, had not been permitted the privilege of giving expression to his sentiments on secession, learned from the North, and we have not heard from South Carolina yet, except incidentally in asserting her sovereign rights.

New Hampshire spoke, through its Governor, in this wise in 1792: "All who are dissatisfied with the measures of government look to a separation of the States as a remedy for oppressive grievance."

"A war with Great Britain! We, at least in New England, will not enter into. Sooner would ninety-nine out of one hundred of our inhabitants separate from the Union than plunge themselves into this abyss of misery." Thus spoke Timothy Dwight, President of Yale College, in 1792.

Who fought the War of 1812–15 and beat back British invasion of our country? The South did.

Massachusetts presented a petition from citizens of that State in 1842, through John Quincy Adams in Congress, praying that Congress immediately adopt measures, peaceably, to dissolve the Union of these States; and one of the reasons given was that if the Union persisted in the present state of things it would overwhelm the whole nation in destruction.

The Southern States were not oppressing New England nor interfering with their affairs.

"Up to 1830 the right of secession was universally admitted," said Charles Francis Adams.

We have not heard from Jefferson Davis yet, though we have searched the records clear on down to Daniel Webster, in 1851. But Daniel Webster was of Massachusetts, and was regarded as a very wise man, a great statesman, and one whose opinion was considered correct. What does he say when the Dred Scott fugitive slave question was on? Here it is:

"I do not hesitate to say, and to repeat, that if the Northern States refuse wilfully and deliberately to carry into effect that part of the Constitution which respects the restoration of fugitive slaves, and Congress provides no remedy, the South would no longer be bound to observe the compact."

And the Northern States refused to obey the mandates of the Supreme Court, and according to Webster the South had a right to secede and set up a Southern Confederacy.

N. P. Banks, when Speaker of the House of Representatives in 1857, said:

"Under these circumstances I am willing to let the Union slide. If slavery is to continue the Union cannot and ought not to stand."

When one expedient failed to keep up the agitation the North adopted another, and the question of slavery was wrung in as an excuse for Northern secession and a free Northern confederacy.

"Let the wayward sisters depart in peace," said Gen. Winfield Scott, Commander of the United States Army, 1861.

Where was Jefferson Davis then? In the United States Senate pleading for peace, fair play, and for the security of the rights of the States composing the Union.

Col. Timothy Pickering said, as far back as 1804: "The principles of our revolution point to a remedy: A separation. A Northern confederacy would unite congenial characters and preserve fairer prospect of public happiness."

That is what the South thought in 1860–61, and acted upon it. Secession was good for the North when it suited the Northern case, but when it came to be necessary for the South to exercise the right peaceably to save herself, which she claimed, it then became an act of treason, and since we have arrived at that point let us hear something more.

William Lloyd Garrison, a representative of the North, and expressing Northern secession sentiment, spoke thus on the question:

"Justice and liberty, God and man, demand the dissolution of this slave-holding Union, and the formation of a Northern confederacy, in which slaveholders shall stand before the law as felons and be treated as pirates. No Union with slave-holders! Up with the flag of disunion, that we may have a free and glorious Union of our own. . . This Union is a lie; the American Constitution is a sham, an imposture, a covenant with death and an agreement with hell! Let the slave-holding Union go, and slavery will go with the Union down into the dust! If the Church is against disunion . . . then I pronounce it of the devil! I say let us cease striking hands with thieves and adulterers and give to the winds the rallying cry: 'No Union with slaveholders, socially or religiously, and up with the flag of disunion.'"

You may search the records in vain, you cannot find any such sentiments uttered by Jefferson Davis. Abraham Lincoln said:

"This country cannot remain half free and half slave."

He was nominated and elected by a party pledged to the abolition of slavery without compensation to the owners.

Charles Sumner said it was "a dog's job to obey it." Thaddeus Stephens said: "To hell with the Constitution," and Abraham Lincoln followed his advice from beginning to end.

William Lloyd Garrison failed to tell us who the slave pirates were. He passed over the fact that 360 Yankee vessels were at that very time engaged in the felonious act of kidnapping uncivilized negroes in Africa, bringing them over to the glorious, free, humane and religious North and criminally smuggling them into the Southern States, in violation of their established laws prohibiting the importation of African slaves from foreign ports. It was big money in the Yankees' pockets and a saintly avocation so long as it paid handsome profits; but slavery, which they established and kept up, like the Constitution which protected it, became "a covenant with death and an agreement with hell" as soon as the poor African was turned over to the Southern slaveholder and the Yankee pirate got the shining gold for him!

Who were the thieves, the adulterers, the pirates and felons that stimulated Mr. Garrison to raise the rallying cry of "No Union with slaveholders, socially, religiously, and up with the flag of disunion?" His own people of the New England States, and it is getting time for the people of the North to learn the truth, for in the language of their idol, "They cannot escape history."

In the face of these historical facts the South has been assailed by Northern writers, newspapers and historians as the hotbed of secession.

If the North was so anxious to secede and form a Northern confederacy which would give them security and peace, why did not they begin at the time they thought it essential to their interests to do so; and if the North desired a free confederacy God knows the South would have been glad of it, and what motive could they have to deny to the South that which they clamored so long for themselves, and what motive actuated them when the South felt aggrieved and formed a confederacy by peacefully withdrawing from the Union? Let history speak for itself.

The South tried to abolish foreign and ocean slave trade in a constitutional convention held in 1787, but the pious New England Puritans and African negro kidnappers defeated the effort; and while the abolition cohorts of the North and East were organizing their forces in 1859 and 1860, New York fitted out eighty-five ships, bringing over from Africa between thirty and sixty thousand negroes annually, to further stimulate the pious and moral fumigations of Abraham Lincoln and William Lloyd Garrison; and from the time of the constitutional limit against importation of slaves in 1808, up to 1860, it has been declared that 270,000 negroes were introduced into New England and smuggled into the Southern States by the pious abolition Yankees; and while they were doing this they were stealing from the Southern people the slaves they sold them, and they openly boasted of it, one Levi Coffin declaring that he alone had been the means of carrying away 2,500 slaves, valued at $2,500,000.

From 1770 Rhode Island maintained as many as 150 vessels, most of the time in the slave trade, to a few years before the outbreak of the Civil War. She probably quit the ocean business then to make other warlike preparations to help rob the Southern owners of all the others sold to them or to become saints when their kidnapping, smuggling and stealing back ceased to be profitable. And many of the palatial residences of the New England States stand as monuments to the slave trade which their owners followed.

As Massachusetts was the first to legalize slavery within her borders, it is nothing but justice to her to give her credit for it, by laws passed in 1641.

If the 2,500 slaves that Levi Coffin stole back from Southern purchasers were worth $2,500,000 it was a good business for the pious puritans, who have been classed by historians "Not mere slave-mongers. To themselves they appeared as the elect to whom God had given the heathen as an inheritance. In seizing and enslaving Indians, and trading for negroes, they were but entering in possession of the heritage of the saints."

Each cargo brought over by the eighty-five vessels fitted out in New York in 1859-60, ranging from 30,000 to 60,000 annually, represents so many millions of dollars, and if they were worth $1,000 each then the 4,000,000 slaves owned by the South in 1861 were worth four thousand millions of dollars taken from the Southern States, by force of arms, by the tender-hearted Abraham Lincoln who loved them so well.

Massachusetts was pious enough to pass a law abolishing the ocean slave trade about 1787, but Virginia preceded her by ten years. And Massachusetts kept up the institution until it ceased to be profitable, and sold them off to Southern people and got the money for them, and so did the other Northern slave States.

It is so hard to "escape history" that a few bits of advertising done later on in Boston and Philadelphia would be interesting. The *Boston Continental Journal* of 1799 advertised:

"FOR SALE.—A likely negro girl, sixteen years of age, for no fault but the want of employment."

"FOR SALE.—A likely negro wench, about nineteen years of age, with a child six months of age; to be sold together or apart."

The above matters are mentioned as a preface to what the New England States did in 1861–65 on the question of a "free Northern confederacy" versus a slave Southern confederacy.

It is intended that the reader should know that Massachusetts and the other New England States are responsible for the institution of slavery in this country, and that they plied the ocean trade in violation of the United States Constitution limitation of 1808 and in violation of the laws passed by Southern States prohibiting importation of negroes from Africa, and brought them into Northern and Eastern ports and sold them into Southern States.

As the secession of the Southern States began in December, 1860, the ocean slave trade of the New England States had to stop, and the millions of money flowing into their coffers from the South also.

Now let us see how many troops each of these self-constituted "elect to whom God had given the heathen as an inheritance," furnished for the next four years to abolish slavery in the South without compensation to their owners. We will try to be fair and give the statistics published as historical authority:

Massachusetts (army and navy)	159,165
Connecticut (army)	57,882
Maine (army)	70,107
New Hampshire (army)	32,750
Vermont (army)	36,755
Pennsylvania (army, exclusive of militia)	362,284
New York	448,850
Rhode Island	23,236
Total	1,191,029

And those pious, benevolent, kind, Christian kidnappers and abolition soldiers have had the gall to assert that the slaveholders got all they were entitled to out of the negroes and should ot be remunerated for them. This would be poor logic applied to themselves if they had thus been robbed. And the Northern States should be made to pay full value for every slave emancipated without compensation, and until they do it the crime of this stupendous robbery will hang over their heads and taunt them in the coming centuries. Physically the Union is restored; spiritually the Southern people cling to their ancient blood inheritance, and the crime of Southern invasion and coercion and their attendant disasters are unforgivable, and will haunt Yankee-doodle-dum until the crack of doom.

CHAPTER VI.

The exciting events leading to the secession of the Southern States, the formation of the Confederate government, President Davis' call for 1,500 troops to protect Pensacola, the fall of Fort Sumpter and Mr. Lincoln's call for 75,000 men to put down what he termed "combinations opposed to laws" "too powerful to be suppressed by the ordinary course of judicial proceedings," created a spirited military activity all over the south, and it was clearly seen that the cloud in the horizon "of the size of a man's hand" mentioned in Miss Rachel Coney's speech on the 4th of July, the year previous, was rapidly accumulating in volume. In response to the President's call there were immediately two companies, the Quitman Guards and the Summit Rifles, prepared for coming events. In April the Quitman Guards were reorganized with 107 members and the Summit Rifles with a lesser number.

CAPT. SAMUEL A. MATTHEWS
Quitman Guards

The following is the muster roll of the Quitman Guards mustered into the State service on the 21st of April, 1861:

1 Samuel A. Matthews, Captain
2 James M. Nelson, 1st Lieut.
3 Thomas R. Stockdale, 2nd Lieut.
4 S. McNeil Bain, 3rd Lieut.
5 Wm. M'Cusker, 1st Sergt.
6 R. J. R. Bee, 2nd Sergt.
7 Colden Wilson, 3rd Sergt.
8 Frank P. Johnson, 4th Sergt.
9 Luke W. Conerly, 5th Sergt.
10 Louis N. Coney, 1st Corp.
11 Dr. R. T. Hart, 2nd Corp.
12 Warren R. Ratliff, 3rd Corp.
13 Charles A. Ligon, 4th Corp.
14 E. G. Cropper, Ensign
15 Wm. Thad Tyler, Commissary

PRIVATES.

16 Andrew, E. C.
17 Ast, John
18 Ard, A. E.
19 Allen, George W.
20 Barksdale, John T.
21 Brent, J. A.
22 Brent, Geo. W.
23 Badon, H. B.
24 Burkhalter, John T.
25 Burkhalter, Charles
26 Breed, E.
27 Barr, Thomas M.

CAPT. JOHN HOLMES
Quitman Guards

28 Coney, William L.
29 Coney, John H.
30 Crawford, Jesse
31 Cook, Thomas D.
32 Conerly, Mark R.
33 Collins, Joseph W.
34 Carter, Harvey
35 Coney, Van C.
36 Fry, Charles H.
37 Friedrich, Phil. J.
38 Forest, Thomas Jeff.
39 Forest, Benjamin F.
40 Foil, J. D.
41 Finch, William
42 Finch, Milus
43 Garner, William
44 Gibson, Jesse F.
45 Guina, Asa H.
46 Gillespie, J. P.
47 Holmes, John
48 Holmes, Benjamin

49 Hamlin, O. C.
50 Harvey, W. Pearl
51 Hamilton, Thomas
52 Howe, Charles
53 Hewson, George
54 Irwin, James
55 Jelks, Eugene W.
56 Jewell, Collinwood
57 Jones, H. L.
58 Ligon, Lemuel T.
59 Lewis, Jesse W. B.
60 Lewis, Benjamin H.
61 Lewis, Martin L.
62 Laney, E. A.
63 Lamkin, Charles A.
64 Lamkin, Samuel R.
65 Leonard, David
66 Leonard, John
67 Lawrence, Irwin G.
68 Luter, William D.
69 McIntosh, D. M.
70 McGehee, William Frank
71 McGehee, Dr. J. G. L.
72 McGill, Henry
73 McCusker, John
74 McNabb, James
75 Mixon, Alex. R.
76 Matthews, George N.
77 Martin, William
78 May, William
79 May, Jared B.
80 Morgan, Green W.
81 Newman, Thomas H.
82 Neal, James N.
83 Netherland, Joseph N.
84 Pearson, Holden
85 Pendarvis, James
86 Page, James
87 Pearl, Seth W.
88 Root, George W.
89 Ratliff, Simeon
90 Regan, Thomas G.
91 Reeves, William R.
92 Rushing, Elisha T.
93 Stovall, Robert D.
94 Sutherland, Alex.
95 Simmons, George B.
96 Sandell, S. Murray
97 Sparkman, A. P.
98 Tarbutton, A. J.
99 Tarver, John E. J.
100 Travis, John Q.
101 Tisdale, Joseph M.
102 Walker, John A.
103 Walker, Anderson
104 Williams, W. L.
105 Winborne, Benjamin Frank
106 Wilson, R. D.
107 Yarborough, Wesley

Thus organized the Quitman Guards were mustered into the State service on the 21st of April, 1861, by Capt. Griffith, in front of the residence of John T. Lamkin, on the public square at Holmesville, in the presence of a large number of ladies; and on the 26th of May following the company embarked on the cars at Magnolia for Corinth, Miss., where they were ordered to rendezvous. On this occasion, Magnolia was the scene of a great gathering of the people from all parts of the county to witness the departure of the soldiers to the seat of war, as every precinct in the county was represented in the ranks of that company. Their names are all here, carefully preserved by this writer, ever since that eventful period.

Arriving at Corinth, the Quitman Guards were connected with the 16th Mississippi regiment, composed of nine other companies as follows, and designated Co. "E:"

Summit Rifles, Co. "A," Capt. Murphy, (succeeding Blincoe, resigned) of Pike County.

Westville Guards, Co. "B," Capt. Funches, Simpson County.

Chrystal Springs Southern Rights, "C," Capt. Davis, Copiah County.

Adams Light Guards, "D," Capt. Robert Clark, Natchez, Adams County.

Jasper Grays, "F," Capt. J. J. Shannon, Jasper County.

Fairview Rifles, "G," Capt. Moore, Claiborne County.

Smith Defenders, "H," Capt. W. H. Hardy, Smith County.

Adams Light Guards, "I," Capt. Walworth, Natchez, Adams County.

Wilkinson Rifles, "K," Capt. Carnot Posey, Wilkinson County.

Capt. Posey was elected Colonel, Capt. Robert Clark, of Co. D., Adams Light Guards, was elected Lieutenant Colonel and Lieut. Thomas R. Stockdale was elected Major. These troops all volunteered for one year, counting from the organization of the regiment at Corinth, May 27, 1861.

These troops were kept at Corinth in camp of instruction from this time until the 24th of July, after the news was received of the battle of Bull Run or First Manassas, July 18-21, 1861, when they were ordered to Virginia. Considerable sickness prevailed among them at Corinth, caused from the water they were compelled to use, being impregnated with lime, to which they were unaccustomed, and improperly cooked food. Provisions were given under the old army rules and really in greater quantities than necessary and a large number were stricken with diarrhea, and besides this the measles broke out among them, and the mortality was very great, and had a very discouraging influence in the ranks. The Quitman Guards were particularly unfortunate in this respect. The following members died at this place: Benjamin H. Lewis, F. P. Johnson, Pearl Harvey, Thomas Hamilton, Corporal Louis Coney, William D. Luter, and several were discharged from disability incurred.

On the 22nd of July, after the men had cooked and eaten their supper, the news came along the electric wires of the battle of Bull Run, and its results, which was received with vociferous shouts from the five thousand Mississippians stationed at Corinth, and on the 24th, Col. Posey received orders to repair with his regiment to Virginia.

DR. WM. J. LAMKIN
Gloster, Miss.
Quitman Guards, Co. E, 16th Miss. Regt.,
Harris' Brigade, Lee's Army

The following recruits were subsequently added to the Quitman Guards:

1 Andrews, Thomas J.
2 Boutwell, William
3 Bankston, Burton D.
4 Barnes, B. L.
5 Barnet, James A.
6 Conerly, Buxton R.
7 Coleston, John A.
8 Donahoe, John A.
9 Estess, William A.
10 Foxworth, George
11 Guy, Jesse W.
12 Guy, William Jefferson
13 Garner, Ransom
14 Holloway, T. P.
15 Holloway, Felix H.
16 Hartwell, Charles E.
17 Lamkin, William J., (transferred from 11th Mississippi).
18 Lamkin, Tilman S.
19 Lyles, John Y.
20 McGehee, Hans J.
21 Miller, George W.

22 Magee, William Levi
23 Newman, Joseph B.
24 Newman, John A.
25 Payne, William L.
26 Rushing, Warren T.
27 Rhodus, Reeves
28 Stanford, James D.
29 Sandifer, Hans D.
30 Sparkman, William L.

31 Scarborough, Henry
32 Simmons, Jeff. E.
33 Smith, C. C.
34 Smith, George
35 Smith, Dan J.
36 Welch, Samuel
37 Watts, Arthur T.
38 Wilson, Matthew

Thus it will be seen that the number of men belonging to this company was 145, but it was reduced by losses in transferred and discharged to the number of forty two.

The readers attention is called to the fact that some of the names of men who were discharged and transferred appear in the rolls of other companies from Pike County, subsequently formed. Some were transferred to other State regiments.

The following named persons ceased to be members of the Quitman Guards by being discharged on account of disability at the time of discharge or transferred:

1 Ast, John
2 Breed, E.
3 Barnes, J. A.
4 Barksdale, A. J.
5 Cropper, E. G. (over age).
6 Cook, Thomas D.
7 Coleston, John A.
8 Conerly, M. R.
9 Coney, William L. (under age).
10 Crawford, J. D.
11 Estess, W. A.
12 Forest, B. F.
13 Gibson, Jesse F.
14 Gillespie, J. P.
15 Hamlin, O. C.
16 Hewson, George (to Co. D, 16th).
17 Holloway, T. P. (over age).
18 Garner, Rans
19 Irwin, James
20 Laney, E. A. (to 15th Alabama).
21 Leonard, John
22 Lamkin, Charles A. (under age).
23 Ligon, Charles A.

24 Lawrence, Irvin J.
25 Lewis, Martin L.
26 May, William
27 Morgan, Green
28 McGehee, Dr. J. G. L.*
29 McCusker, John
30 McIntosh, D. M., (transferred to Co. C, 16th Mississippi).
31 Martin, William, (transferred to Washington Artillery).
32 Neal, James
33 Netherland, J. A.
34 Newman, J. B.
35 Pearl, Seth
36 Ratliff, Warren
37 Rushing, W. T.
38 Smith, C. C.
39 Sutherland, Alex.
40 Tisdale, J. M.
41 Welch, Samuel
42 Watts, A. T., (transferred to Summit Rifles).

The recapitulation of the Quitman Guards is as follows:

Enlisted 107	Died of disease 27
Recruited 38	Killed in battle 13
	Died of wounds 3
Total 145	Discharged and transferred 48
	Officers retired 4
	Men living and belonging to company May 1, 1865 50
	Total 145

QUITMAN GUARDS SURVIVORS KNOWN TO BE LIVING, APRIL 21, 1906.

1 Capt. John Holmes, Picayune, Miss., died 1907.
2 Lieut. John Q. Travis, Magnolia, Miss., died 1907.
3 Sergt. Elisha C. Andrews, Gloster, Miss.
4 Dr. Wm. J. Lamkin, Gloster, Miss.
5 Dr. A. P. Sparkman, Magnolia, Miss.
6 Simeon Ratliff, McComb, Miss.
7 Dr. R. T. Hart, McComb, Miss., died 1908.
8 Thomas Regan, Darbun, Miss.
9 Charles E. Hartwell, Wesson, Miss.
10 George W. Root, Linus, La.
11 Thomas M. Barr, Kansas City, Mo.
12 George Smith, Tylertown, Miss.
13 Warren Lafayette Payne, Tylertown, Miss.
14 John A. Walker, Magnolia, Miss.
15 Buxton R. Conerly, Marshall, Tex.
16 Luke W. Conerly, Gulfport, Miss.
17 Thomas Andrews, Monticello, Miss.
18 Hans J. Sandifer, McComb, Miss.
19 William Thad Tyler, Chattanooga, Tenn.
20 William L. Coney (later in Stockdale's Cavalry), Magnolia, Miss.
21 Chas. A. Lamkin (later in Holmesville Guards), Texas.
22 Irvin G. Lawrence, Pike Co., Miss.
23 Jared B. May, died 1907
24 Jefferson Guy, Texas.
25 Frank B. Forest, Texas.
26 B. F. Winborne, Columbia, Miss.
27 Eugene W. Jelks, Marion Co., Miss.

COLONEL SENECA M'NEIL BAIN.

Colonel Seneca McNeil Bain was a native of New York State. He married and emigrated to Mississippi in the early fifties with his wife and cousin, William J. Bain, and Miss Orrie Gillis. William J. Bain was a talented young lawyer and a popular man among the people, especially with the young men and young women at Holmesville. He died in Covington County while on one of his professional trips in 1860, during the heated season, deeply mourned by all his young friends.

Col. Bain engaged in school teaching with Miss Orrie Gillis at Holmesville, and was so engaged at the time of the breaking out of the Civil War. He and his wife had an only child, a little girl, that they named Dixie, and Dixie was a favorite song sung and played on their musical instruments by the family.

Col. Bain studied medicine and attended a course of lectures at the Medical Institute of Louisiana in New Orleans, during the term of 1860–1861, in company with Dr. A. P. Sparkman, Dr. C. P. Conerly and Dr. Joe Thornhill. He joined the Quitman Guards, was elected lieutenant and went out into the Confederate service with that company and fought through the war in Virginia. He was elected captain of the Quitman Guards in 1862 and rose to the rank of colonel of the regiment at the battle of "Bloody Angle," Spottsylvania Court House, May 12, 1864, and was the last colonel of the Sixteenth Mississippi Regiment. He was captured in the battle of Weldon Railroad, during the siege of Petersburg, August 21, 1864, and was held a prisoner until the close of the war, when he returned to his old home at Holmesville, where he remained until he finished his course in medicine. He subsequently removed to the State of Texas, where he remained until his death, about 1900. He was greatly loved by the members of the Quitman Guards and by the entire Sixteenth Mississippi Regiment. He was a quiet man, handsome, and genteel in his deportment, and as cool in battle while commanding his men as he ever was in the quiet control of his classes in the school room. His name will live in the history of the services of the Sixteenth Mississippi in the great conflicts in Virginia under Lee, along with Carnot Posey, Samuel E. Baker, A. M. Feltus and the intrepid Council, who lost their lives commanding that regiment in the sanguinary conflicts of Bristoe, Spottsylvania and Petersburg.

OFFICERS RETIRED APRIL 26, 1862.

1 S. A. Matthews, Captain.
2 James M. Nelson, 1st Lieut.
3 Thomas R. Stockdale, 2nd Lieut. and Major.
4 R. J. R. Bee, 3rd Lieut.

KILLED IN BATTLE.

1 Elisha T. Rushing, Bloody Angle, Spottsylvania C. H., Va., May 12, 1864.
2 Alex. R. Mixon, Brigade Ensign, Bloody Angle, Spottsylvania C. H., Va., May 12, 1864.
3 J. D. Standford, Turkey Ridge, Va., June 6, 1864.
4 Matthew Wilson, Sergt., Wilderness, Va., May 6, 1864.
5 A. E. Ard, Corp., Weldon Railroad, Va., August 21, 1864.
6 Tilman S. Lamkin, Weldon Railroad, Va., August 21, 1864.
7 William L. Sparkman, Petersburg, Va., April 2, 1865.
8 Robert D. Stovall, Sergt., Petersburg, Va., April 2, 1865.
9 James Page, in trenches, Petersburg, Va., October 9, 1864.
10 Asa H. Guina, Chancellorsville, Va., May 2, 1863.
11 John A. Newman, Chancellorsville, Va., May 2, 1863.
12 Westley Yarborough, mortally wounded, Cross Keys, Va., June 8, 1862.

KILLED IN BATTLE.

13 George W. Simmons, mortally wounded, Cold Harbor, Va., June 27, 1862.
14 Joseph W. Collins, Cold Harbor, June 27, 1862.
15 Lieut. Colden Wilson, mortally wounded, Sharpsburg, Md., September 17 1862.
16 Jesse W. Guy, Sharpsburg, Md., September 17, 1862.
17 Wm. R. Reeves, mortally wounded, Gettysburg, Pa., July 4, 1863.

WOUNDED IN BATTLE.

1 A. P. Sparkman, Cross Keys, Va., June 8, 1862.
2 Jared B. May, Cross Keys, Va., June 8, 1862.
3 Thos. Jeff Forest, Gettysburg, Pa., July 3, 1863, and in the trenches at Petersburg, July, 1864.
4 Samuel R. Lamkin, lost arm, August 21, 1864, Weldon Railroad.
5 J. Alex. Brent, Petersburg, Va., September, 1864.
6 Hans D. Sandefer, Bloody Angle, Spottsylvania, May 12, 1864.
7 L. W. Conerly, Bloody Angle, Spottsylvania, May 12, 1864, and at Sharpsburg, Md., September 17, 1862.
8 R. D. Stovall, Bloody Angle, May 12, 1864.
9 William J. Lamkin, Weldon Railroad, August 21, 1864; Second Manassas, August 30, 1862; also at Bull Run, July 21, 1861, while a member of 11th Miss.
10 Holden Pearson, Weldon Railroad, August 21, 1864.
11 John A. Donohoe, Petersburg, Va., July, 1864.
12 John A. Walker, Turkey Ridge, Va., June, 1864; Second Manassas, August 30, 1862.
13 Lemuel T. Ligon, Turkey Ridge, Va., June, 1864.
14 William Garner, permanently disabled, from which he subsequently died, Cross Keys, June 8, 1862.
15 George Root, Cold Harbor, June 27, 1862, both knees.
16 Lieut. John Holmes, Cold Harbor, June 27, 1862.
17 Wash L. Williams, arm off, Second Manassas, August 30, 1862.
18 Benjamin Holmes, Second Manassas, August 30, 1862.
19 Burton D. Bankston, Second Manassas, August 30, 1862.
20 Matthew Wilson, Second Manassas, August 30, 1862.
21 Lieut. Van C. Coney, Sharpsburg, September 17, 1862.
22 Reaves Rhodis, Sharpsburg, September 17, 1862.
23 David Leonard, Sharpsburg, September 17, 1862.
24 A. J. Tarbutton, Sharpsburg, September 17, 1862.
25 William McCusker, Sharpsburg, September 17, 1862.
26 A. E. Ard, Sharpsburg, September 17, 1862.
27 Thomas M. Barr, Sharpsburg, September 17, 1862.
28 Lieut. J. Q. Travis, Chancellorsville, May 2, 1863.
29 Simeon Ratliff, Chancellorsville, May 2, 1863.
30 W. L. Payne, Chancellorsville, May 2, 1863.
31 T. J. Forest, Chancellorsville, May 2, 1863.

HISTORY OF PIKE COUNTY, MISSISSIPPI 181

LIEUTENANT JOHN Q. TRAVIS
Second Lieutenant Quitman Guards, 16th Mississippi Regiment

JOHN QUINCY TRAVIS.

Lieut. John Quincy Travis was born in Amite County on the 30th day of December, 1832, near Travis Bridge, on the Amite River. His grandfather, John Travis, came to the territory of Mississippi in early 1800 from South Carolina, when his father, John Travis, was a small boy, and he came directly from the old pioneer stock of South Carolina, who plunged into the deep wilderness amid all its dangers and hardships to establish new homes as soon as Mississippi was constituted a territorial government. The name of Travis belongs to the history of the past, and is associated with all that excites the admiration for heroism and chivalry. It is stamped indelibly upon the recollection of the Texas revolution and the Alamo lives in history as a monument to its memory. John Travis, the grandfather of our subject, was a first cousin to the celebrated Travis of Alamo fame, who, while on his way to join the Texas patriots, stopped a few days in Amite County with him.

John Quincy Travis' mother was Polly Raiborn, daughter of Joseph Raiborn, who also came from South Carolina in the early 1800 and settled on Tangipahoa, about four miles from the town of Magnolia. In his boyhood Mr. Travis learned the carpenters' trade and in 1852, at the age of 20, he went to Holmesville and pursued his occupation there until 1855, when he went to Eastern Texas and lived until the breaking out of the war in 1861, then returned to Holmesville and joined the Quitman Guards as a private in the ranks, and went with the company to Virginia under Capt. Samuel A. Mathews. He was with the Sixteenth Mississippi Regiment in the celebrated Valley Campaign, as part of Ewell's command, who reinforced Stonewall Jackson and participated in the battle of Winchester on Sunday, May 25, 1862, which resulted in the defeat of N. P. Banks and his expulsion from Virginia. Previous to this battle, at a reorganization of the company, he was elected second sergeant. He participated in the battle of Cross Keys, when Fremont's forces were defeated, and then on through that wonderful movement of Jackson and Ewell to Richmond, when on the 26th of June, 1862, they struck McClellan's right, and, in the Seven Days' Battles, beat him back under cover of his gunboats. He was in the fight at Turkey Ridge and Cold Harbor. He participated in the battle of Second Manassas on the 30th of August, 1862, when the army of Northern Virginia, under Gen. Robert E. Lee, defeated the Federals under Pope and drove him back to Washington. It was at this battle that Sergeant Travis was recommended by Gen. Featherston for promotion for meritorious conduct on the field while the Sixteenth Mississippi was exposed to a deadly fire from the enemy's batteries. He was at the siege of Harpers Ferry, where Gen. Miles and his command of eleven thousand men were captured, and at Sharpsburg, Md., on the 17th of September following. He was at Hazle River with his command, in support of Gen. J. E. B. Stuart on the 10th of November, and at Fredericksburg on the 11th, 12th and 13th of December, 1862, where the Confederates under Lee so signally defeated Gen. Burnside.

At the battle of Chancellorsville, on the 2nd of May, 1863, he commanded the second platoon of the Quitman Guards on the picket line, when some hard fighting was done, Lieutenant Van C. Coney being in command of the company. They became exposed to a severe artillery fire of the enemy and it was here that Lieutenant Travis lost his right hand, thus commingling his blood on the same field made famous by the defeat, by Gen. Lee with 40,000 men of Gen. Joe Hooker with 110,000 men, and the loss by the Confederate army of the illustrious Stonewall Jackson. In this great battle, Lieutenant John Holmes acted major of the Sixteenth Mississippi Regiment. After returning home from the army Lieutenant Travis engaged in the occupation of farming. He married Sarah K. Coney, daughter of Jeremiah Coney and Emily Quin. In 1871 he was elected Sheriff of Pike County and served three terms, being elected by a good majority in the campaign of 1875. He was afterwards assistant postmaster at Magnolia for six years.

In the army he gave to the Confederacy, in behalf of his native State, all the spirit it was possible for him to give, sanctifying his devotion to duty with his blood upon the altar of its cause.

In his declining years he carried along with him the tender love of his surviving comrades and the esteem of his fellow citizens; and after an eventful life covering a period of seventy-six years, he passed from among them and was laid peacefully to rest in the cemetery at Magnolia.

SUMMIT RIFLES.

On the 20th of April, 1861, the Summit Rifles were organized and mustered into the State service by R. W. Bowen, in the town of Summit.

The following is the muster roll of that company as originally formed and afterwards recruited:

Capt. J. D. Blincoe resigned and did not enter service with company.
1 E. H. Murphy, 1st Lieut., promoted to Captain, died at Warrenton, Va.
2 L. R. Austin, 2nd Lieut., promoted to Captain, mortally wounded at Sharpsburg or Antietam, Md.
3 P. H. Thorpe, 3rd Lieut., transferred to Kentucky regiment.
4 C. H. Lyster, 1st Sergt.
5 D. B. Packer, 2nd Sergt.
6 George Ernst, 3rd Sergt.

7 4th Sergt., vacant.
7 T. J. Casey, 5th Sergt., killed at Weldon Railroad, Va.
8 H. Lotterhos, 1st Corp.
9 2nd Corp., vacant.
10 Thomas D. Day, 3rd Corp., wounded, lost leg.
11 Henry Bonner, 4th Corp.
12 Algenon S. Mitchell, Ensign, killed at Bulls Bluff, on James River, in fight three days after Lee's surrender.
13 B. T. Gatlin, C Guard.
14 S. D. Autie, C Guard.

PRIVATES.

15 Andrews, Robert
16 Adams, J. O.
17 Burk, M.
18 Byrd, James
19 Byrd, George W.
20 Black, Elisha, (killed.)
21 Brown, James, (promoted to Captain, killed at Malvern Hill, Va.).
22 Bales, Jesse

SUMMIT RIFLES—CONTINUED.

23 Boyd, James, (killed).
24 Clarke, A. S.
25 Conlon, T. M.
26 Connelly, P.
27 Collins, W. G., Captain, (resigned).
28 Carruth, John P.
29 Coon, W. C.
30 Coon, David
31 Coon, J. C.
32 Coon, Louis
33 Cole, Wash, (killed).
34 Collins, Calvin
35 Coffin, Sam T., (ex-Nicarauga soldier, under Walker).
36 Cook, C. P.
37 Carter, J. M.
38 Crocket, Joe, (killed).
39 Conden, Enos
40 Cummings, Charlie
41 Carter, Henry
42 Carter, Daniel
43 Dick, Isaac C., (severely wounded at Cold Harbor; subsequently transferred to the Washington Artillery, of New Orleans, La. At the battle of Cold Harbor he was color bearer of the Sixteenth Mississippi and was shot down in the charge made on the Pennsylvania Bucktails, who were routed and driven from the field.
44 Dunker, Henry
45 Dawling, W. M.
46 Dixon, James D.
47 Delaughter, Warren
48 Dick, Benj
49 Delaney, Ned, (killed).
50 Denman, W. C., (killed).
51 Davis, Charles
52 Ezell, Roulst
53 Farnham, John D.
54 Farrell, David
55 Folts, Henry
56 Felder, Hansford
57 Fronthall, Louis
58 Forester, C. H.
59 Fonden, Anderson
60 Ferguson, James M., (transferred. See Stockdale's Cavalry, Capt. Hoover).
61 Garner, Thos. A., (wounded; last captain of company).
62 Gunnels, N. R.
63 Gatlin, Thos. I., (died).
64 Gatlin, E. H., (mortally wounded; was captured at Bloody Angle, Spottsylvania C. H., Va., May 12, 1864).
65 Gerald, A. G., (killed).
66 Gibson, Ralph, (wounded; ex-veteran First Mississippi, under Jefferson Davis, in war with Mexico; severely wounded at Hazle River, Va.).
67 Huckaby, James, (died).
68 Hales, D. F., (killed).
69 Hoover, Christian, (wounded; see Stockdale's Cavalry—captain).
70 Hiller, Nathan
71 Hammond, W. C.
72 Harris, R. G.
73 Hooter, David
74 Hill, I. I.
75 Holloway, V. M., (killed).
76 Holmes, Crawford
77 Hart, Pincus
78 Hart, Morris
79 Hart, Nathan
80 Kruse, Charlie, (died).
81 Kennedy, T. E.
82 Louden, Andrew
83 Lenoir, John G., (killed).
84 Lanagan, Dan, (killed).
85 Lotterhos, Fred
86 Lewis, Martin, (from Quitman Guards).
87 Lenoir, D. C., (died).

SUMMIT RIFLES—CONTINUED.

88 Lea, Willie, (died).
89 Moise, I.
90 Mogan, Edward
91 McCloy, S. W.
92 Monaghan, James
93 Maples, John H.
94 Miller, Charles
95 McGowan, Pat C.
96 Maples, Erastus
97 Maxie, James L., (killed).
98 Montgomery, W. H.
99 Murphy, Pete, (killed).
100 McClosky, Dan
101 McColgin, M.
102 Miller, George, (killed).
103 McDavid, W. A.
104 Montgomery, William
105 Moak, A.
106 Newsom, James M., (died).
107 Newman, ——, from Chatawa.
108 Nall, Mike, (wounded).
109 Neeley, J. M., (killed).
110 O'Callahan, Baldwin (Bun).
111 Peterson, C. S.
112 Rodgers, C.
113 Rodgers, R. W.
114 Spicer, John Y.
115 Sipple, L.
116 Scherck, Louis
117 Shaw, G. M.
118 Standard, Geo. W., (wounded).
119 Turner, A. S., (wounded).
120 Tunison, Edward
121 Taylor, D. C.
122 Wadsworth, W. M., (killed).
123 Westrope, D. C.
124 Watts, Arthur T., (from Quitman Guards; lieutenant).
125 Wagoner, Louis, (originator of the word" bulldose," "bulldozer," "bulldoozer," as applied to that organization).
126 Westbrook, J. B.
127 Weil, Meyer
128 Wells, Columbus

The Summit Rifles was designated as Co. A, 16th Mississippi, and the Quitman Guards Co. E, of the 16th Mississippi Regiment.

Their first colonel was Carnot Posey, Captain of the Wilkinson Rifles, afterward Brigadier General of the 12th, 19th, 16th and 48th Regiments, mortally wounded at the battle of Bristoe Station, Virginia, October 14, 1863, General Posey commanded this brigade in the center of Lee's line against a brigade of United States regulars at the battle of Sharpsburg, (Antietam) Maryland, September 17, 1862. The brigade was then under Gen. W. S. Featherston, who had been wounded at Richmond.

The second colonel of the 16th Mississippi, was Samuel E. Baker, of the Adams Light Guards, from Natchez. He and Lieut. Col. A. M. Feltus, of the Wilkinson Rifles, were both killed in the fight at "Bloody Angle" or "Blood Bend" at Spottsylvania, C. H., Virginia, in retaking Lee's works captured by the enemy May 12, 1864.

The third colonel was Capt. Council of the Adams Light Guards, from Natchez.

The fourth and last colonel was Seneca McNeil Bain, of the Quitman Guards. Col. Bain survived the war, graduated in medicine and spent the remainder of his life as a practicing physician in Texas.

The Summit Rifles and Quitman Guards with their regiment, participated in the following campaigns and battles: Front Royal, Virginia, May 24th, and Winchester, Virginia, May 25th, 1862, under Ewell and Stonewall Jackson, against N. P. Banks, in the Shenandoah Valley; and Jackson's and Ewell's celebrated retreat from Harpers Ferry, after driving Bank's forces out of Virginia, eluding the junction of Fremont and Shields to intercept them at Strasburg.

Cross Key, Va., June 8, 1862.

Mechanicsville, Va., June 26, 1862.

Cold Harbor, Va., June 27, 1862.

Malvern Hill to the close of the seven days battles before Richmond against Gen. George B. McClellan.

The Maryland Campaign.

Second battle of Manassas, Aug. 30, 1862, against the Union forces commanded by Gen. Pope.

Siege of Harpers Ferry, Va., where the Union General Miles was forced to surrender with eleven thousand men.

Battle of Sharpsburg (Antietam), Maryland, against the army of Gen. George B. McClellan, Sept. 17, 1862.

Hazle River, with the 10th Alabama, in support of Gen. J. E. B. Stuart's cavalry, November 10, 1862.

Battle of Fredericksburg, Va., against the forces of Gen. Burnside. Featherston's brigade was stationed immediately in front of the town where the heaviest and most desperate assaults of the enemy were made by the "Red Shirt Zouaves," who were successfully beaten with great slaughter by the Mississippians. This battle began on the 11th and closed on the 14th of December, 1862. After this battle Col. Posey was promoted to Brigadier and put in command of the brigade, Gen. Featherston being sent to the department of Mississippi, Alabama and East Louisiana.

Battle of Chancellors, Va., May 1st, 2nd, and 3rd, against Gen. Joe Hooker, who succeeded Gen. Burnside, and whose army was completely routed.

The Pennsylvania Campaign, battle of Gettysburg, July 1st, 2nd and 3rd, 1863.

Battle of Bristoe Station, October 14, 1863, where Gen. Posey was mortally wounded.

Battle of Mine Run, Va., against Gen. Meade, November 30th and December 1st, 1863.

Campaign of 1864 and 1865. Battle of the Wilderness, May 5th and 6th, 1864, against the Union forces under Gen. Grant.

Shady Grove, May 8, 1864.

Spottsylvania Court House, Va., 9th, 10th, 11th and 12th of May, 1864. In this battle the brigade was commanded by Gen. Nathaniel H. Harris, colonel of the 19th Mississippi, who succeeded Gen. Posey, and was one of the brigades selected by General Lee to retake his lost works on the 12th of May, which had been captured by the enemy. Subsequently at Richmond, Va., Gen. R. S. Ewell wrote General Harris the following letter:

HEADQUARTERS DEPARTMENT OF RICHMOND, VA., Dec. 27, 1864.

Gen. N. H. Harris,
Commanding Brigade General.

I have omitted to acknowledge the valuable services rendered by your brigade on the 12th of May instant, at Spottsylvania, not from any want of appreciation, but because I want my thanks to rest upon the solid foundation of official reports. The manner in which your brigade charged over the hills to recapture our works was witnessed by me with intense admiration for men who could advance so calmly to what seemed and was almost certain death. I have never seen troops under a hotter fire than was endured on this day by your brigade and some others. Major General Edward Johnston, since his exchange, has assured me that the whole strength of the enemy's army was poured into the gap caused by the capture of his command. He estimates the force engaged at this place, on their side, at forty thousand, besides Birney's command of perfectly fresh troops. Prisoners from all of their corps were taken by us. Two divisions of my corps—your brigade and two others (one of which was scarcely engaged)—confronted successfully this immense host, and not only won from them nearly all the ground they had gained, but so shattered their army that they were unable again to make a serious attack until they received fresh troops. I have not forgotten the conduct of the Sixteenth Mississippi Regiment, while under my command, from Front Royal to Malvern Hill. I am glad to see, from a trial more severe than any experienced while in my division, that the regiment is in a brigade of which it may well be proud.

Very respectfully,

Your obedient servant,
(Signed) R. S. Ewell,
Lieutenant General.

In this battle the 16th Mississippi colors were perforated by over two hundred and fifty bullets. Alexander R. Mixon of the Quitman Guards, promoted to the rank of ensign, bearing the battle flag when they retook our works, waived it in the faces of the enemy and died on the breastworks an American soldier and a Mississippi hero. From this time to the investment of Richmond and Petersburg, and up to the surrender of General Lee at Appomattox Court House on the 9th of April, 1865, the army of Northern Virginia, under Lee, and the army of the Potomac, under Grant, confronted each other in line of battle. They fought at Hanover Junction on the 24th of May, 1864.

At Cold Harbor on the 3rd of June, 1864, the scene of the great battle in 1862.

They fought at Turkey Ridge, June 6th, 1864. On the 18th of June, 1864, they were put in the trenches at Petersburg.

In July they were taken out of the trenches, made a force march to Lee's right and whipped the enemy at the Davis House, near the Weldon Railroad, and then returned to the trenches.

On the 17th of August, they were again taken out of the trenches, went to Richmond and fought at New Market, on the 18th.

On the 19th returned to Petersburg, and on the 21st, engaged in a fight on the Weldon Railroad. In this fight the Quitman Guards lost two killed and fourteen captured. After the battle the brigade returned to the trenches and fought day and night until the 12th of November, 1864, when they were taken out and went into winter quarters, but were constantly on duty.

They fought at Hatcher's Run on the 5th and 6th of February, 1865, where they defeated an attempt to turn Lee's right.

On the 1st of March, they held the position vacated by Picket's Division between the Appomattox and the James Rivers.

When Sheridan began serious demonstrations on Richmond, they were sent to the aid of Stuart's and Causey's Virginia brigades and defeated his movements and then returned to their position between the Appomattox and the James, remaining there until the 2nd of April, when they were ordered to the right of Petersburg to reinforce troops who had lost their works and immediately went into action, but were compelled to retire before overwhelming numbers until the remnants of the 16th and 12th not killed, wounded or captured, took refuge in Fort Gregg, where they made a stand and fought with their usual desperate determination. A correspondent of the *London Fortnightly Review*, who was with Lee's army at the time, published the following article in reference to this struggle, putting the number of Mississippians in the fort at 250, while many of the survivors say there were not over 125, as the 19th and 48th regiments under General Harris made their escape, and the troops in Fort Gregg were of the 12th and 16th regiments with a few artillerists.

This correspondent says:

"The officer in command of Fort Alexander, which was fartherest away from the oncoming Federals, deemed it more important to save his guns than to try and help Fort Gregg. Receiving no assistance from its twin brother, Fort Gregg, manned by Harris' Mississippi brigade, numbering 250 undaunted men, breasted intrepidly the tide of its multitudinous assailants. Three times Gibbon's Corps surged up and around the works—three times, with dreadful carnage, they were driven back. I am told that it was subsequently admitted by General Gibbon, that in carrying Fort Gregg he lost five or six hundred men, or in other words, that each Mississippian inside the works struck down at least two assailants. When at last the works were carried, there remained out of its 250 defenders but thirty survivors. In those nine memorable days there was not an episode more glorious to the Confederate Army than the heroic self-immolation of the Mississippians in Fort Gregg, to gain time for their comrades."

In this episode Pike County's name became glorified in the names of Robert D. Stovall and Wm. L. Sparkman, of the Quitman Guards, who sealed their devotion with their lives in the last grand struggle that marked the closing end of the Confederacy. Col. Bain had been captured and Lieut. Col. Duncan, commanding the 16th, was severely wounded. Capt. Applewhite, of the 12th Mississippi, was next in command, and he and the following are present survivors: Buxton R. Conerly, Wm. F. Standifer, Bright Williams, Sam Howell, Joe Thompson.

CAPT. THOMAS J. CONNALLY
Bogue Chitto Guards

The Summit Rifles were especially unfortunate in the loss of officers. J. D. Blinco, who organized the company, resigned soon after. H. E. Murphy died at Warrington Springs, Va., in the winter of 1861-62, of consumption. James Brown, one of the most daring scouts in Lee's army, was killed at Malvern Hill (seven days battle before Richmond, 1862). It was ordered that the Summit Rifles, under his leadership, be mounted as scouts, but his death prevented it. Louis R. Austin, another gallant young officer, was mortally wounded in the battle of Sharpsburg, Md., September 17, 1862, in the desperate encounter of the Mississippians with a brigade of U. S. Regulars in the center. Lieut. E. H. Gatlin was mortally wounded at "Bloody Angle," Spotsylvania C. H., May 12, 1864. T. J. Casey, was killed at Weldon R. R. Thomas A. Garner, last captain, was shot through the cheeks and nose but lived many years after the war.

May 1, 1861, the Bogue Chitto Guards were organized and mustered in by Robert J. Bowen, with the following original officers and men:

1 R. S. Carter, Captain.
2 Thomas J. Connally, 1st Lieut.
3 Joseph Hart, 2nd Lieut.
4 G. A. Bilbo, 3rd Lieut.

PRIVATES.

5 Albrittan, R. R.
6 Albrittain, John M.
7 Brister, J. Milton
8 Bisbee, C. M.
9 Buett, Joseph
10 Buett, Thomas
11 Bount, A. A.
12 Brown, Robert M.
13 Brown, J. O.
14 Buster, John
15 Crosby, Thomas
16 Courtney, B. F.
17 Coon, Samuel
18 Gill, T. H.
19 Givin, W. J.
20 Gill, John J.
21 Gill, John A.
22 Hart, I. M.
23 Hart, John G.
24 Hart, H. L.
25 Hart, I. A.
26 Hart, Judge A.
27 Hart, James L.
28 Hampton, Jasper
29 Hodges, John C.
30 Hall, Thomas J.
31 Howell, James H.
32 Harrington, H. F. M.
33 Johnson, A. B.
34 Kinneally, Thomas
35 Kazza, James W.
36 Martin, James M.
37 Netherland, T. L.
38 Newman, Jasper
39 Price, Uriah
40 Prestridge, W. P.
41 Price, William
42 Prestridge, Zachariah
43 Price, H. H.
44 Richardson, Martin
45 Rawls, Jesse
46 Saper, Stephen
47 Sasser, Joseph
48 Terrell, Foster
49 Turner, Francis I.
50 Sasser, James S.
51 Price, T. M.

The above company was attached to the 7th Mississippi regiment, Gen. C. G. Dalhgreen.

THE DAHLGREEN RIFLES.

The Dahlgreen Rifles organized on Topisaw, by Capt. Parham B. Williams, and mustered in by him August 22, 1861, was also attached to the 7th regiment as Co. H, under Gen. Chalmers—Cheatham's division.

The following is the roll of the company:

1 Parham B. Williams, Captain, (killed in railroad collision at Ponchatoula, La.)
2 Joseph M. Thornhill, 1st Lieut., Asst. Surgeon.
3 Zebulon E. P. Williams, 2nd Lieut.
4 Jordan B. Williams, 3rd Lieut., (leg broken in collision at Ponchatoula, La.)
5 Elijah Cothern, Ensign.
6 Peter J. Felder, 1st Sergt., (killed in collision at Ponchatoula, La.)

THE DAHLGREEN RIFLES—CONTINUED.

7 John J. Sibley, 2nd Sergt., (discharged).
8 Wiott Thornhill, 3rd Sergt., (killed in collision at Ponchatoula, La.)
9 Isaiah Greer, 4th Sergt., (died).
10 William L. Walker, 5th Sergt., (appointed Lieutenant).
11 Harvey Boyd, 1st Corp., (substituted by Isaiah Boyd, wounded).
12 F. M. Coglin, 2nd Corp., (killed in collision at Ponchatoula, La.)
13 William Dunaway, 3rd Corp., (killed near Atlanta, Ga.)
14 William W. Gunnels, 4th Corp.

PRIVATES.

15 Adams, Joseph P., (killed in collision at Ponchatoula, La.)
16 Adams, John
17 Boyd, William, (killed in collision at Ponchatoula, La.)
18 Boyd, Jeremiah
19 Boyd, Thomas
20 Boyd, Jesse
21 Boyd, Thomas C.
22 Curtis, R., (killed at Murfreesboro, Tenn.)
23 Cothern, Joseph
24 Cothern, John
25 Coon, Craft
26 Coker, John W., (killed in collision at Ponchatoula, La.)
27 Coon, Louis
28 Coker, A. L.
29 Coglin, Thos. J., (killed in collision at Ponchatoula, La.)
30 Craft, Jackson
31 Coglin, Frank
32 Coglin, Jasper
33 Collins, Joe
34 Davis, Aaron
35 Davis, Arthur
36 Dunaway, Asa, (killed in battle at Harrisburg, Miss.)
37 Dunaway, Pearl, (killed in collision at Ponchatoula, La.)
38 Dunaway, Jesse F., (killed in battle at Atlanta, Ga.)
39 Dunaway, Stephen, (killed in battle).
40 Day, Pleasant
41 Davis, John
42 Dunaway, Osburn
43 Fortinberry, Jack, (transferred).
44 Felder, J. Smith, (wounded in collision at Ponchatoula, La.)
45 Gullage, G. C.
46 Greer, Newton
47 Greer, Francis
48 Hathorn, John, (transferred).
49 Hampton, Jasper
50 Hope, Cornelius, (wounded in collision at Ponchatoula, La.)
51 Jenkins, Jesse
52 Jenkins, Bill
53 Keen, Daniel
54 Keen, Charles, (killed in collision at Ponchatoula, La.)
55 Keen, Harvey
56 Kitt, Harrison
57 Morgan, J. H.
58 Morgan, William A.
59 McKinzie, A. N.
60 McClendon, Jack, (discharged).
61 Massey, Elisha, Jr.
62 McGallon, John J.
63 McGinty, Joseph
64 McDavid, William
65 McEwen, Silas
66 Leonard, Raford
67 Leonard, William
68 Leonard, Pleasant
69 Pollard, John R.
70 Pollard, Pleasant

HISTORY OF PIKE COUNTY, MISSISSIPPI

THE DAHLGREEN RIFLES—CONTINUED.

71 Pollard, Raford
72 Turpine, John
73 Thornhill, Wyatt
74 Thornhill, J. Martin
75 Thornhill, J. Newton
76 Thombs, George, (killed in collision at Ponchatoula, La.)
77 Wallace, J. B., (leg broken in collision at Ponchatoula, La.)
78 Wallace, E. H.
79 Saul, William J.
80 Slaven, John, (wounded in battle at Shiloh, Tenn.)
81 Reeves, Stephen, (killed in collision at Ponchatoula, La.)
82 Reddy, Mike, (killed at Harrisburg, Miss.)
83 Rutland, Cullen, (died at Corinth, Miss.)

This company met with a very serious accident during the war at Ponchatoula, La., by the collision of the train they were being transported on with another, which resulted in the death of Captain Williams and several of his men and wounding many others. It was charged that this was prearranged by persons controlling the trains for the purpose of killing the men, being northern men and in sympathy with the Union army. The engineer and others made their escape and kept out of the way until after the close of the war, else they might have paid the penalty of their crime.

In October, 1861, the McNair Rifles were organized with the following officers and men, attached to the 3rd battalion and 45th Mississippi, consolidated as Company E, Mark P. Lowry's brigade, Army of Tennessee.

McNAIR RIFLES.

1 Robert H. McNair, Captain, (promoted to Lieut.-Col.; killed at Shiloh).
2 William M. McNulty, 1st Lieut. and Captain.
3 James R. Wilson, 2nd Lieut., (resigned).
4 Isaac Scherck, 3rd Lieut.
5 Rialdo Downer, 1st Sergt., (mortally wounded at Shiloh, Tenn.)
6 James B. Martin, 2nd Sergt.
7 John H. Thompson, 3rd Sergt., (afterwards Captain; mortally wounded at Chickamauga.)
8 Robert Brown, 4th Sergt.
9 Dr. Busby, 1st Corp.
10 Clint J. Martin, 2nd Corp.
11 Alf A. Boyd, 4th Corp., (last Captain of company).
12 M. M. Murray, 1st Lieut., (close of war).
13 Samuel E. McNulty, 2nd Lieut., (close of war).
14 Dr. Boyer, Hospital Steward.
15 O. V. Shurtliff, Asst. Surgeon
16 Austin Hooker
17 Andrews, Robert
18 Byrd, Charlie, (died at Chicago, Ill., in prison).

MCNAIR RIFLES—CONTINUED.

CAPT. A. A. BOYD
McNair Rifles

19 Brown, Newton M., (killed at Chicamauga, Ga.)
20 Boyd, William
21 Borosky, Julius
22 Brown, Asa
23 Bigner, William
24 Bridges, C. B.
25 Causey, I. L., (died in prison at Camp Chase).
26 Carroll, James, (died at Triune, Tenn.)
27 Carruth, J. E., (prisoner at Camp Douglas).
28 Carruth, Robert M., (wounded at Lovejoy, Ga.)
29 Cutrer, Newt.
30 Carruth, James B., (killed at Shiloh).
31 Canter, W. D., (died at Shiloh).
32 Cornwall, F. M., (killed at Atlanta, Ga.)
33 Clark, Herbert
34 Chamberlin, Silas
35 Cosgrove, Thomas
36 Clarke, Thomas, (died at Bowling Green, Ky.)
37 Clark, Jessee
38 Dunica, Leon
39 Dunica, George
40 Daunis, A. J.
41 Dawson, D. A.
42 Day, Dave, (discharged).
43 Ezell, Tom
44 Flood, Martin, (prisoner at Camp Douglas).

MCNAIR RIFLES—CONTINUED.

45 Flowers, John H., (disch'd, over age)
46 Gardner, Seaborne
47 Gammon, Alex.
48 Gatlin, Elbert
49 Gatlin, Pinkney
50 Gotowsky, ———
51 Hyman, Sam
52 Hales, T. Benton
53 Hoover, Charles
54 Hodges, Sam J.
55 Hilborn, Benj.
56 Harvey, William, (wounded at Lovejoy, Ga.)
57 Hamil, Hugh J.
58 Johnston, William B.
59 Kinebrew, L. M.
60 Keen, John
61 Keen, F. M.
62 Keen, Cal L.
63 Keen, W. H., (killed at Franklin, Tenn.)
64 Latham, John P.
65 Latham, Nimrod
66 Martin, Frank M., (prisoner at Camp Douglas).
67 Martin, W. G., (died at Murfreesboro, Tenn.)
68 Miller, Poley
69 McGehee, Dunk, (mortally wounded at Shiloh).
70 Moak, Martin M.
71 McNulty, Hugh, (killed at Franklin, Tenn.)
72 McGehee, William
73 McKeating, William
74 Mason, M. M.
75 McComb, Ephraim
76 Ott, Frank M.
77 Pitman, Hardy
78 Powell, Abner D.
79 Powell, James (transferred).
80 Pitman, John
81 Roundtree, Starling (mortally wounded at Shiloh).
82 Reeves, Thomas (killed at Shiloh).
83 Richmond, A.
84 Richmond, ———
85 Simmons, Riddick
86 Steel, Jarvis (killed at Shiloh).
87 Smith, C. B., from Catahoula, La. (died at Shiloh).
88 Stevens, C. K.
89 Schreck, Louis.
90 Standard, Geo. (wounded).
91 Sharp, John
92 Sublett, T. J.
93 Turner, Wm. H.
94 Turner, Louis M. (killed at Jonesborough, Ga.)
95 Turner, Joseph, from Wilkinson Co., (killed at Franklin, Tenn).
96 Thompson, Silas (son of Hardy).
97 Thompson, Hugh (son of Hardy).
98 Terrell, Wm., (killed at Ringold Gap, Ga.)
99 Travis, W. J.
100 Terry, Benj.
101 Turner, Henry W.
102 Varnado, Felix
103 Varnado, Meredith
104 Wilson, Murdock
105 Wilkinson, R. B.
106 Wilkinson, S. C.
107 Williams, Jackson (son of Meyer Williams).
108 Williams, James (son of Meyer Williams).
109 Westrope, D. L. (mortally wounded at Perryville, Tenn.)
110 Williams, James (son of Sam, died in service).
111 Woodall, Hezekiah (killed at Shiloh).
112 White, Emmet A.
113 Woodall, Joe (died in service).
114 Wilson, Jasper
115 Quin, John H.

The author is indebted to Mr. Enoch Carruth, of Auburn, Lincoln County, for the entire memoranda of the above company given him from memory in 1902. It is not of record in the department of Archives and History, nor in the war department.

After the organization of the McNair Rifles, the people of Summit assembled at the Presbyterian Church, October 3rd, 1861, under the auspices of the Soldier's Friend Society, with Rev. Mrs. William Hoover, president, who was attended by the vice-presidents, Mrs. Phoebe Whitehead, Mrs. Dr. William Bacot, Mrs. Dr. John Huffman, Mrs. Helen Gracey and Miss Hattie Wicker, for the purpose of presenting a camp Bible to the company. Rev. D. W. Dillehay lead in prayer and Captain McNair introduced Rev. Mrs. Hoover, delegated by the society, to present the Bible, which she did, the Bible being received by William McNulty, subsequently captain, on the part of the company.

CAPT. MCNAIR
of McNair Rifles
Killed at Shiloh, Tennessee
Major of Regiment

CAPTAIN M'NAIR.

Capt. McNair was born in the city of New Orleans. He married Miss Columbia Sarah Sydnor, daughter of Col. Sydnor, a wealthy merchant of Galveston, Texas, who was regarded as one of the loveliest and most beautiful women that ever lived in Pike County.

Capt. McNair taught school in New Orleans, and was for a time Superintendent of Education in that city. He also taught in Amite City, and was induced by Col. Garland to settle in Summit. Here he erected a handsome college building east of the railroad, which was destroyed by fire and one of the students was lost in the conflagration. He rebuilt on a small scale, intending to erect a more handsome building than the first, but, the war coming on, he went into the army. He organized the company which bore his name, and on the 9th of November, 1861, left the town of Summit, via Natchez, for New Orleans, where they were mustered into the Confederate States' service and became attached to the Army of Tennessee, then under command of General Albert Sidney Johnston. He was promoted to Lieutenant-Colonel of the 45th Mississippi

Regiment, and was mortally wounded at the battle of Shiloh, at the same time his illustrious chief fell, crowned with the glorious victory over the superior forces of the enemy under Gen. U. S. Grant, the 6th of April, 1862. Col. McNair was a man of superior mold and his intellect was cultivated up to the highest standard, and his friends claimed that it was like an inspiration to be in his presence. He was cut down in life at a time when he had attained qualifications for the highest usefulness.

He died in the arms of Benjamin Hilburn, in the town of Corinth, where he was sent after he was wounded.

"Tell my wife that God will protect her," was a portion of his dying message.

COL. PRESTON BRENT
Brent Rifles,
Lt. Col. 38th Mississippi

BRENT RIFLES.

The Brent Rifles, 38th Mississippi Regiment, was organized on the 26th day of April, 1862, by Capt. Preston Brent, in the town of Holmesville, with the following officers and men:

1 Preston Brent, Captain (subsequently Lieutenant-Colonel).
2 Henry S. Brumfield, 1st Lieut.
3 David C. Walker, 2nd Lieut.
4 J. Cy Williams, 3rd Lieut.
5 Wm. E. Brent, 1st Sergt.
6 Jesse K. Brumfield, 2nd Sergt. (wounded).
7 W. H. H. Brumfield, 3rd Sergt. (wounded).

PRIVATES.

8 Andrews, Jack
9 Alexander, Henry
10 Alexander, Daniel (wounded).
11 Andrews, F. G.
12 Andrews, James.
13 Andrews, Mack

BRENT RIFLES—CONTINUED.

14 Allen, William
15 Brumfield, Elisha
16 Ball, Sampson E.
17 Bullock, Joel J.
18 Bickham, T. D.
19 Brumfield, W. N.
20 Blunt, S. S.
21 Burkhalter, J. Flem (wounded at Shiloh).
22 Brown, Wm.
23 Boyd, W. D.
24 Bacot, Levi.
25 Boyd, Benjamin
26 Boyd, Jefferson
27 Boyd, Jasper
28 Boyd, Newton
29 Beard, Thomas
30 Brumfield, Wm. Monroe
31 Brumfield, John
32 Blunt, James
33 Blunt, Balas
34 Brumfield, Jackson
35 Boyd, Andrew (killed April, 1862, at Shiloh).
36 Ball, John Ira
37 Ball, Jesse W., Captain (killed at Harrisburg, Miss.)
38 Brumfield, Geo. W.
39 Beard, C. D.
40 Breland, Elisha
41 Breland, Hillary
42 Coney, D. Aquila
43 Conerly, John M. (wounded).
44 Cavanaugh, J. N.
45 Clarke, John
46 Douglas, A. N.
47 Dillon, Clarke
48 Dillon, Willis R. (killed 1862 at Shiloh).
49 Dillon, W. R.
50 Dillon, Chauncey
51 Davis, Z. T.
52 Green, John
53 Ginn, Haverson

54 Hickman, Joshua
55 Holmes, Wm. Dort
56 Holmes, J. N. (wounded).
57 Holmes, Frank
58 Harvey, Henry
59 Holmes, Jackson
60 Hickman, Nitey
61 Irvin, Jack
62 Jones, Milton
63 Jones, W. T.
64 Lampton, Alexander Frank
65 Lampton, James (killed).
66 McEwin, Archie
67 McEwin, John
68 McCullough, Jasper
69 Magee, Irvin
70 Morris, Martin
71 Morris, Offie
72 McCalem, Simon
73 Magee, Fleet
74 Owens, W. R.
75 Parker, William (wounded).
76 Payne, Ed.
77 Payne, N. R.
78 Payne, Albert
79 Pigot, Wm.
80 Pigot, Ellis
81 Pigot, Charles
82 Pierce, Ed.
83 Page, Josiah W.
84 Pound, Daniel M.
85 Pinkerton, Sam
86 Quin, J. C.
87 Rollins, Chris.
88 Reeves, Joe
89 Smith, A. H. M.
90 Smith, Winston
91 Smith, Benton.
92 Smith, Jasper N.
93 Smith, J. R.
94 Smith, Ansel
95 Smith, G. W.
96 Sartin, Wesley
97 Sartin, Leander

BRENT RIFLES—CONTINUED.

98 Sartin, James
99 Sartin, Gus
100 Sartin, Robert
101 Sandifer, Wm. (wounded).
102 Sandifer, John
103 Sandifer, Peter
104 Sandifer, R. P.
105 Sandifer, Billie
106 Sandifer, Carroll
107 Stovall, Wm.
108 Stalling, John
109 Simmons, J. D.
110 Simmons, John
111 Simmons, B. F. (killed).
112 Simmons, J. M.
113 Smith, Ralph
114 Thornhill, H. C.
115 Thornhill, Isham
116 Thornhill, James
117 Walters, Newton
118 Walters, Pearl
119 Williams, Bose
120 Williams, Hamp
121 Williams, Ruben
122 Williams, S. C. (wounded at Shiloh).
123 Williams, Mac

In the siege of Vicksburg, Col. Preston Brent was severely wounded in the face.

Lieut. Jesse Ball and W. H. H. Brumfield were wounded and B. Frank Simmons killed.

At Harrisburg, Lieut. Jesse Ball and James Lampton were killed, and Capt. J. C. Williams, Sergt. J. K. Brumfield, Daniel Alexander, John M. Conerly, J. N. Holmes, J. F. Holmes, William Parker, Wm. Sandifer and one other——————were wounded.

Thirteen of this company went into the fight at Harrisburg and came out with two unhurt.

The same month and year, April, 1862, Nash's Company was organized in Magnolia. This company was commanded by William Monroe Quin, and was attached to Colonel Shelby's 39th Mississippi regiment of the Tennessee army. This is another one of Pike County companies that served in the Confederate army and did gallant service, which is not of record in the department of Archives and History.

The writer is indebted to the extraordinary memory of the Spinks Brothers, sons-in-law of Wm. Guy, for the entire list of names. Making it a special trip and a special business he stopped over night with them and thus procured them.

Nash's Company, 39th Mississippi, Tennessee Army, Colonel Shelby, Capt. Wm. Monroe Quin.

This company was organized in Magnolia, April, 1862, with the following officers and men:

NASH'S COMPANY.

1 Wm. Monroe Quin, Captain
2 J. A. Nash, 1st Lieut.
3 J. W. Sandell, 2nd Lieut.
4 Wm. D. Coney, 3rd Lieut.
5 Luke Magee, Orderly Sergt.
6 W. W. J. Magee, 2nd Sergt.
7 Wm. C. Vaught, 3rd Sergt.
8 Dickey, Howell, 4th Sergt
9 Alford, Raymond
10 Allen, Lafayette
11 Anders, Geo.
12 Buett, Emanuel
13 Barmister, Henry
14 Barnes, Webster
15 Brock, Alex.
16 Brock, William
17 Barksdale, Joe
18 Bankston, Ab.
19 Ballard, James
20 Ballard, Anthony
21 Carter, Henry Y.
22 Carter, Winston
23 Coney, Jasper, Lieut.
24 Cohn, The Shoemaker
25 Coney, Frank
26 Carter, Duncan
27 Carter, D. H.
28 Cliette, Harvey
29 Cook, Thomas
30 Cook, A. U.
31 Cook, F. A.
32 Dowling, James
33 Dickey, Wm.
34 Dickey, Seaborne
35 Dillon, the Fiddler
36 Estess, Thomas
37 Everette, T. J., Dr.
38 Ellzey, Benj. Frank
39 Ellzey, John
40 Ellzey, James
41 Foster, Joe
42 Feaney, ———
43 Guy, A. T.
44 Gibson, Cornelius C.
45 Harhill, Cliett
46 Hodges, M. G. L.
47 Haverland, Henry
48 Hamilton, Ardell
49 Johnson, Alex.
50 Jenning, B. B., Sr.
51 Lane, J. F.
52 Lea, J. F.
53 Lenoir, Josephus
54 Lenoir, Pink
55 McDaniel, Pink
56 McNeil, H. D.
57 Maples, Erastus
58 McCaffrey, James
59 McGehee, John
60 McGehee, Wm.
61 Magee, H. W.
62 Martin, J. S.
63 Martin, Jasper
64 McDaniel, George
65 Norman, Asa (killed at Corinth).
66 Nash, Erastus
67 Prewett, W. H.
68 Prewett, J. S.
69 Prescott, J. S.
70 Prescott, W. H.
71 Powell, J. O.
72 Phillips, Wm.
73 Pendarvis, Richard
74 Powell, John

NASH'S COMPANY—CONTINUED.

75 Phillips, John
76 Prescott, Frank
77 Quin, Frank M.
78 Quin, R. R.
79 Rayborn, James
80 Russell, Jessee
81 Roberts, Wm.
82 Schilling, Roderick
83 Stecky, I.
84 Stevenson, T. J.
85 Stevenson, W. M.
86 Simmons, Jackson
87 Simmons, Jack, Jr.
88 Simmons, Francis
89 Spinks, J. N.
90 Spinks, W. G.

91 Spinks, E. B.
92 Stuckey, Isaac
93 Smith, John
94 Smith, Wm.
95 Story, John
96 Tarver, Lum
97 Tuttle, B.
98 Tarver, Fred
99 Travis, Sim
100 Taylor, Marion
101 Varnado, S. H.
102 Varnado, Hardy
103 Varnado, Norval
104 Winborne, David
105 Williams, Harvey

CAPT. WILLIAM MONROE QUIN.

Capt. William Monroe Quin, who commanded this company, was a grandson of Peter Quin, Sr., who settled in Pike in 1812. His parentage has already been given. He married Miss ——— McKay, a daughter of Robert McKay and Eliza Harrell. Robert McKay came from Ireland and settled on Little Tonsopiho, but afterwards lived on Hurricane Creek, in the neighborhood of Muddy Springs.

Capt. Quin was the owner of a large cotton plantation and many slaves, located equidistant between the towns of Magnolia and Summit, at what was known as Quin Station after the railroad passed through the plantation, which is on Little Tonsopiho, between Fernwood and Whitestown. He and his wife had two daughters—Alice, who married Capt. Thomas A. Garner, and Nanny.

HOLMESVILLE GUARDS.

Holmesville Guards organized in Holmesville in April of 1862, by Capt. John T. Lamkin, attached to 33rd Mississippi Regiment (Co. E). Featherstones Brigade, Army Tennessee, commanded by Col. David W. Hurst.

1 John T. Lamkin, Captain
2 H. Eugene Weathersby, 1st Lieut.
  (killed at Franklin, Tenn., November 30, 1864)
3 John S. Lamkin, 2nd Lieut.
  (Captain close of war)
4 Robert H. Felder, 3rd Lieut.
5 Lenoir, George B.

HOLMESVILLE GUARDS—CONTINUED.

6 Miskell, Austin (killed at Peach Tree Creek, Ga.)
7 Quin, Lucius M. (arm disabled at Peach Tree Creek)
8 Richmond, Thomas Dilla (wounded at Peach Tree Creek)
9 Ratliff, Warren
10 Conerly, Wm. M.
11 Conerly, Dr. Chauncey Porter (hospital Steward and acting Assistant Surgeon 33rd Mississippi Regiment and Clerk of Chief Surgeon P. F. Whitehead, Loring's Division)

Hon. J. T. Lamkin

12 Lamkin, Wm. J. (son of Sampson Lamkin, killed in Georgia)
13 Abner Lamkin (son of Sampson Lamkin, killed in Georgia)
14 Briley, George (wounded at Peach Tree Creek)
15 Turnipseed, Clifton
16 Kavanaugh, Henry
17 Moore, George W.
18 Garner, David (killed)
19 Conerly, Owen L. (33rd Regiment Color Bearer, killed charging the enemy's works at Franklin, Tenn., November 30, 1864)
20 Conerly, Flem P. (wounded)
21 Conerly, James R.
22 Conerly, Mark R.
23 Price, Jasper A.
24 Harrington, James (killed)
25 Harrington, Wm. (killed)
26 King, Allen
27 Price, Wilson
28 Dunaway, Jesse

Dr. Chauncey P. Conerly
Holmesville Guards
Dr. Conerly was Acting Assistant Surgeon of the 33d Mississippi Regiment and Chief Clerk of Surgeon-General P. F. Whitehead of Loring's Division.

HOLMESVILLE GUARDS—CONTINUED.

29 May, Fred
30 Dunaway, Pink (killed at Franklin, Tenn., November 30, 1864)
31 May, John
32 May, Wm. (killed)
33 May, Richard H.
34 Lenoir, Joseph (died)
35 Magee, Wm.
36 Holmes, Wm.
37 Morgan, Green (killed at Peach Tree Creek)
38 Payne, Thomas (died)
39 Magaha, John (died)
40 Fisher, Christian
41 Bullock, Thomas (killed)
42 Bullock, Jeremiah (killed)
43 Rushing, Wiley
44 Rushing, Evan
45 Rushing, U. K.
46 Rushing, Matthew
47 Rushing, Novel
48 Carr, George
49 Dunaway, Dennis
50 Forest, Frank
51 Foil, Martin (died)
52 Lewis, Lemuel
53 Lewis, Samuel (died)
54 Holmes, David
55 Holmes, Raiford
56 Holmes, Jesse
57 Barnes, Pinkney L.
58 Felder, Rufus
59 Lee, Marion (wounded)
60 Ligon, Charles A.
61 Vanorten, John
62 Warner, John D.
63 McCormick, Ed.
64 Ware, Hiram (died)
65 Elliott, Dr. J. H.
66 Bacot, Adam,
67 Ginn, Newland (died at Grenada)
68 Lamkin, Charles A. (substitute)
69 Thompson, Hugh (died)
70 Hoover, Rev. Wm. (chaplain 33rd Mississippi Regiment)
71 Blackburn, Dr.
72 Hall, Thomas
73 Ratliff, Calvin
74 Ratliff, Green
75 Harvey, John (died)
76 Quin, Arthur
77 Ware, Frank
78 Bonney, Henry S.
79 Sandifer, Levi
80 Price, Alex (killed)
81 Booker, Wm.
82 Crosby, Thos (died)
83 Ball, Newton
84 Fritz, Chas. (died)
85 Hammond, Arrington
86 Rushing, Levi
87 Sandifer, Wallace (killed)
88 Sandifer, Joseph (killed)
89 Barr, Westley
90 Morgan, Frank
91 Dunaway, John (killed at Corinth)
92 Price, James

STOCKDALE'S CAVALRY.

Stockdale's Cavalry, Company I, 4th Mississippi Cavalry, organized at Holmesville, Miss., on the 1st of July, 1862, by Thomas R. Stockdale:

1 Christian, Hoover, Captain, Pike Co.
2 Dan Williams, 1st Lieut., Wilkinson Co.
3 Doug. Walker, 2d Lieut., Wilkinson Co.
4 Burrell C. Quin, 3d Lieut., Louisiana.

HISTORY OF PIKE COUNTY, MISSISSIPPI

STOCKDALE'S CAVALRY—CONTINUED.

5 H. N. Shaw, 1st Sergt. Amite Co.
6 Drew Godwin, 2nd Sergt., Amite Co.
7 W. M. Cain, 3d Sergt., Franklin Co.
8 F. Wall, 4th Sergt., Abbeville, La.

PRIVATES.

9 Anderson, B. F., Amite Co.
10 Anderson, Henry, Amite Co.
11 Andrews, Robert, Amite Co.
12 Andrews, Adam, Amite Co.
13 Bouie, Dan, Franklin Co.
14 Burrus, Enos, Franklin Co.
15 Briley, Benjamin F., Pike Co.
16 Barnes, W. Clinton, Pike Co.
17 Booker, Jim, Pike Co.
18 Bryant, Lewis, Wilkinson Co.
19 Berryhill, G. W., Amite Co.
20 Butler, Hugh, Amite Co.
21 Beam, Walter, Franklin Co.
22 Brown, George, Amite Co.
23 Bell, John, Amite Co.
24 Bell, A., Amite Co.
25 Criswell, M., Wilkinson Co.
26 Collier, Tobe, Wilkinson Co.
27 Cox, W. H., Amite Co.
28 Cain, Isaiah, Pike Co,
29 Cox, William, Amite Co.
30 Collins, Levy, Wilkinson Co.
31 Carey, Richard, Wilkinson Co.
32 Coon, Frank, Centerville.
33 Crozier, Robert, Wilkinson Co.
34 Cameron, ——, Centerville.
35 Causey, William, Amite Co.
36 Cassedy, Hiram, Franklin Co.
37 Crow, Thomas, Wilkinson Co.
38 Coney Wm. L. (Bose), Pike Co.
39 Crago, Doug., Wilkinson Co.
40 Caston, West, Amite Co.
41 Dies, Dave, Amite Co.
42 Davis, C. W., Wilkinson Co.
43 Dickerson, Jim, Pike Co.
44 Everett, W., Amite Co.
45 Everett, Alex., Amite Co.
46 Everett, J., Amite Co.
47 Everett, Chas., Amite Co.
48 Everett, Marshall, Amite Co. (killed at Harrisburg, Miss.)
49 Everett, James, Amite Co.
50 Flowers, E. W., Amite Co.
51 Ferguson, Jas. M. (Dr.), Pike Co.
52 Fenn, D. W., Amite Co.
53 Gatlin, W. M., Amite Co. (killed at Harrisburg, Miss.)
54 Garner, James, Amite Co.
55 Gildart, James, Wilkinson Co.
56 Garner, J, J., Amite Co.
57 Glass, J., Wilkinson Co.
58 Godwin, J., Amite Co.
59 Hurst, Wm., Amite Co.
60 Howell, Joe, Wilkinson Co.
61 Harkless, ——, Amite Co.
62 Howell, Henry, Amite Co.
63 Hart, Joe, Pike Co.
64 Huckleby, Dave, Pike Co.
65 Hamilton, Gus, Pike Co.
66 Huff, T. H., Amite Co.
67 Huff, Van, Amite Co.
68 Holland, Sam, Wilkinson Co.
69 Harris, Tom, Amite Co.
70 Harris, Enoch, Amite Co.
71 Jones, Pink, Franklin Co.
72 Jackson, Frank, Amite Co.
73 Johnson, Alex, Pike Co.
74 Jenkins, Wiley, Amite Co.
75 Kaigler, John, Pike Co.
76 Kaigler, Andrew, Pike Co.
77 Longmire, Wm., Amite Co.
78 Linton, Sam, Amite Co.
79 Lenoir, Walter, Pike Co.
80 Lusk, Joe, Amite Co.
81 Lusk, John, Amite Co.
82 Lewis, E. H., Wilkinson Co.

STOCKDALE'S CAVALRY—CONTINUED.

83 Ligon, Woodville, Miss.
84 Martin, Frank, Amite Co.
85 Martin, Wiley, Pike Co. (killed at Harrisburg, Miss.).
86 Martin, R. P.,
87 Morris, Monroe, Wilkinson Co.
88 McReady, Wilkinson Co.
89 McGehee, T. L., Amite Co.
90 McGehee, Lewis, Amite Co.
91 Moore, Bill, Amite Co.
92 Mays, Bill, Wilkinson Co.
93 McLain, E. B., Amite Co. (Gloster)
94 McLain, George, Amite Co.
95 Newsom, H. C., St. Helena Parish, La.
96 Nunery, Henry, Amite Co.
97 Netterville, Jesse, Wilkinson Co.
98 Noble, W. H., Wilkinson Co.
99 Posey, Jeff, Wilkinson Co.
100 Pascoe, W. H., Wilkinson Co.
101 Patterson, Wm., Wilkinson Co.
102 Prosser, Henry, Wilkinson Co.
103 Price, J. G., Pike Co.
104 Quin, Sherod R., Pike Co.
105 Rollins, Thad, Franklin Co.
106 Reeves, James, Amite Co.
107 Roberson, Thomas, Amite Co.
108 Roudolph, G., Amite Co. (South Carolina).
109 Rutland, Berry, Wilkinson Co.
110 Richardson, P. A., Wilkinson Co.
111 Riley, G. R., Wilkinson Co.
112 Rodgers, Robert, Wilkinson Co.
113 Roark, T. J., Wilkinson Co.
114 Simrall, Flem, Wilkinson Co.
115 Simrall, Scrap, Wilkinson Co.
116 Swearingen, Henry, Amite Co.
117 Smith, Wade, Amite Co.
118 Sample, William, Wilkinson Co.
119 Smith, R. K.
120 Stewart, Henry, Wilkinson Co.
121 Statham, Charles, Pike Co.
122 Sharpe, Ed., Amite Co.
123 Thornhill, J., Pike Co.
124 Tillery, D. W., Amite Co.
125 Thompson, Bell, Amite Co. (killed at Harrisburg).
126 Terrell, Griff, Amite Co.
127 Thompson, John, Amite Co.
128 Terrell, James, Amite Co.
129 Tolbert, Polk, Amite Co.
130 Vaught, W. W., Pike Co., Brigade Quartermaster.
131 Vaught, Wm. C., transferred from 39th Mississippi to 4th Mississippi Cavalry February, 1863, at Port Hudson.
132 Van, Norden, Pike Co.
133 Wright, Charles, Wilkinson Co.
134 Wright, E. A. Wilkinson Co.
135 Walker, Ed., Wilkinson Co.
136 Wroten, W. M., Pike Co.
137 Webb, P. C., Amite Co.
138 Weathersby, L. O., Amite Co.
139 Whittaker, James, Wilkinson Co.
140 Sleeper, Gardner, Amite Co.
141 Wilson, W. H., Amite Co.
142 Pandarvis, Dick, Pike Co. (killed at Harrisburg).

The above company was organized July 1, 1862, by Thomas R. Stockdale, who had served in Virginia one year as Major of the 16th Mississippi Regiment, then under Brigadier Isaac R. Trimble.

The company was first officered by Thomas R. Stockdale, Captain; Christian Hoover, 1st lieutenant; Dan Williams, 2nd lieutenant; W. W. Vaught, 3rd lieutenant.

It was formed into a battalion with W. Norman's company and

Thomas R. Stockdale was elected major, when it was known as "Stockdale's battalion" of Cavalry. This battalion was subsequently consolidated with Wilborne's batalion and formed into a regiment known as the 4th Mississippi Cavalry, with W. W. Wilborne, as colonel; Thomas R. Stockdale, lieutenant colonel and W. Norman, major.

W. W. Vaught was promoted to brigade quartermaster and B. C. Quin was elected 3rd lieutenant of the company. The company was first under Col. Frank Powers, as one of the companies of Stockdale's battalion, and afterwards in the spring of 1863 was consolidated with Colonel Wilborne's battalion and formed the 4th Mississippi Cavalry, and formed a part of Logan's cavalry brigade, which was composed of the 4th Mississippi, 14th Confederate, 11th and 17th Arkansas regiments, Roberts' Battery and Brown's Scouts.

Stockdale's cavalry company was in all the skirmishes in rear of Port Hudson; fought at Fayette against Elliot's marine brigade, fought Sherman from Vicksburg to Meridian and back. Skirmished with McPhearson's Corps from Big Black to Brownville and back. Fought around Oxford, was engaged in the battle of Harrisburg, Miss., having six men killed on the field and a number wounded, among them Lieut. Col. T. R. Stockdale, severely. Was in the celebrated raid with General Forest to Johnsonville, Tennessee, destroying over one million dollars of the enemy's property; captured and sunk three gunboats; was with Forest in the last campaign in Alabama, where Wilson made his celebrated raid destroying Selma, Ala., and Columbus, Ga., and finally surrendered at Gainesville, Ala., May 12, 1865.

The author is pleased to acknowledge his indebtedness to Hon. The. L. McGehee, for the muster roll of this company and valuable data and also to Dr. Wm. Monroe Wroten, and Wm. L. Coney for desirable information connected with its history, concerning which Dr. Wroten says in a note:

"I have carefully gone over the list and made all the corrections, assisted by W. L. Coney. I hope, by a little pains and patience on your part, you will be able to get things measurably correct. (Signed) W. M. WROTEN."

CAPT. KIT HOOVER.

Capt. Kit Hoover, who commanded Stockdale's cavalry company, was a son of Judge Christian Hoover, and his wife, Mary Newland Nails. At the beginning of the war he joined the Summit Rifles and served with that company in the army of Northern Virginia. Being severely wounded in one of his limbs, he returned home and joined Stockdale's Cavalry and became its captain. After the close of hostilities he graduated in medicine. He married Mary Virginia Barnes, daughter of Harris Barnes and his wife, Julia Lott, who resided at Columbia, in Marion County. Mary Virginia Barnes was a sister of Mrs. Emily Atkinson, of Summit. These young ladies were among the most accomplished in Marion County. They had two brothers, Allen and L. T. Barnes, and a sister, Mrs. David.

Capt. Hoover and his wife had two children, Harrie and Mamie.

CAPT. KIT HOOVER
Stockdale's Cavalry

DIXIE GUARDS COMPANY "H" THIRTY-NINTH MISSISSIPPI REGIMENT.

The Dixie Guards were organized and mustered into service May 5, 1862, with James R. Wilson, captain; Joseph B. Wilson, 1st lieutenant; Ned Bullock, 2nd lieutenant and Wm. Thompson, 3rd lieutenant. Lieutenant Bullock died and Lieutenant Thompson resigned.

The following is the roll of the company furnished the writer by Mr. John P. Carruth, of Auburn:

1 J. R. Wilson, Captain.
2 J. B. Wilson, Lieut.
3 J. B. Gatlin, Lieut.
4 J. J. White, Lieut.
5 J. P. Carruth, Sergt.
6 J. J. Sibley, Sergt.
7 Z. B. Gatlin, Sergt.
8 J. E. Denman, Sergt.
9 N. W. Gatlin, Sergt.
10 J. M. Jones, Corp.
11 W. T. Jones, Corp.
12 W. J. Wilson, Corp.
13 W. M. Small, Corp.
14 Adams, M. A.
15 Arnold, J. J.
16 Arnold, J. W.

DIXIE GUARDS—CONTINUED.

17 Alford, H.
18 Andrews, A.
19 Bowlin, W. L.
20 Bowlin, W. H.
21 Booth, R.
22 Barron, A. W.
23 Barron, R. B.
24 Bigner, G.
25 Bigner, W.
26 Edwards, J. E.
27 Edwards, D.
28 Freeman, I.
29 Gardner, S. R.
30 Hunt, F. J.
31 Huckaby, J.
32 Hancock, J. R.
33 Huffman, J. W.
34 Johnston, D. W.
35 King, W. A.
36 Lea, Z. Z.
37 Montgomery, W.
38 Montgomery, C.
39 Montgomery, J. A.
40 McManus, L. M.
41 McDonald, J.
42 Newsom, W. W.
43 Roundtree, E. R.
44 Rayborn, I. B.
45 Rayborn, J. J.
46 Sudduth, W. B.
47 Small, F. M.
48 Steel, A. P.
49 Turner, J. W.
50 Turner, F. E.
51 Terrell, J. N.
52 Terrell, J. A.
53 Travis, J. E.
54 Weathersby, L. L.
55 Wilson, J. D.
56 Wroten, E. W.
57 Wilkinson, T. W.
58 Westbrook, W. H.
59 Dr. Alex. Thompson, discharged.
60 Elisha Marsalis, died in service.
61 Newton Turner, died in service.
62 Walter Terry, killed in battle of Tallahatchie.

This company was engaged in the battles of Tallahatchie and Corinth, and was in the siege of Port Hudson. At the surrender of Port Hudson the officers of the company were retained in prison and the men were paroled and never reorganized as Company H. Some of them re-enlisted in other commands. One of the members, H. Alford, died during the siege of Port Hudson.

Dr. Wm. T. Coumbe was a member of Captain Nick's company (E), 22nd Mississippi regiment, from Amite County; also J. Dock Harrell, Nick Tate and Leander Varnado.

Capt. Josephus Quin, who married a Miss Murphy, of Kentucky, sister of Capt. Hatch Murphy, of the Summit Rifles, was killed at the battle of Harrisburg, Miss.

In 1862, N. G. Rhodes, from Baton Rouge, La., raised a company of cavalry at Osyka, known as Rhodes' Cavalry.

RHODES' CAVALRY.

1. N. G. Rhodes, Captain.
2. W. T. Wren, 1st Lieut.
3. R. B. Easley, 2nd Lieut.
4. W. B. Lenoir, 3rd Lieut.
5. W. H. Terrell, 1st Sergt.
6. H. Delemaer, 2nd Sergt.
7. R. A. Smith, 3rd Sergt (Pass Christian).
8. W. S. Gordan, 4th Sergt.
9. F. A. Way, 5th Sergt.
10. E. F. Loftin, 1st Corp.
11. D. M. Redmond, 2nd Corp.
12. D. W. Wall, 3d Corp.
13. J. D. McLain, 4th Corp.
14. Anderson, J. C.
15. Bridges, J. W.
16. Bastiern, C.
17. Bamler, James.
18. Briant, N. (Liberty)
19. Bradham, B.
20. Brown, A. M.
21. Covington, J. C.
22. Cutrer, E.
23. Cutrer, J. F.
24. Davis, J. B.
25. Duff, M.
26. Easley, E. W.
27. Easley, W. E.
28. Easley, N. Q.
29. Gordan, George (Raymond)
30. Honea, T. P.
31. Jones, D.
32. Kennedy, R.
33. Laird, L.
34. McDaniel, H.
35. McDaniel, J.
36. Miller, W.
37. Miller, B.
38. Morgan, S.
39. McCall, P. M. (Raymond)
40. Mulky, J. (Liberty)
41. Mixon, J.
42. Newman, G. P.
43. Owens, J. J.
44. Powell, H.
45. Rayborn, J. E.
46. Rayborn, A.
47. Stroud, P. S.
48. Smith, R.
49. Smith, Wm. (Liberty)
50. Stokes, G. W. (Clinton, La.)
51. Sleeper, G.
52. Sandifer, J. J.
53. Sandifer, J. W.
54. Sandifer, R. M.
55. Sandifer, W. E.
56. Spears, A.
57. Taylor, C. D.
58. Taylor, S.
59. Varnado, Lain.
60. Wall, L. C. (Gallatin)
61. Wright, E. A.
62. Wilson, S.
63. McLendon, M.

These men all enlisted at Osyka, except those marked in parenthesis. The above is a copy of the original muster roll on file in the Archives of History at Jackson, and the writer has been unable to get any other report of them.

Some time after the Holmesville Guards went out into the army, Capt. John T. Lamkin was elected to a seat in the Confederate Congress, sitting at Richmond, in which capacity he served until the close of the war.

John S. Lamkin then became commander of the company and served as such until the close of hostilities.

The following names have been preserved of men and boys belonging to the home militia stationed at Summit under Colonel Wingfield.

1. Andrew Kaigler, Captain.
2. Sampson Ball, Lieut.
3. Lamkin, James.
4. Payne, Lewis.
5. Applewhite, Alex.
6. Wroten, D. H.
7. Grabbs, Henry.
8. Guy, Luke.
9. Ellzey, Jack.
10. Turnage, R.
11. Bridges, Linus.
12. Vaughn, D. F.
13. Dail, John.
14. Martin, Will.
15. Curlett, George W.
16. Lamkin, Walter F.
17. McClendon, James.
18. Sandifer, James.
19. Brown, Abner.
20. Laney, Robert.
21. Lampton, Benj.
22. Andrews, Thompson.
23. Brent, John.
24. Bridges, R.

Robert S. Bridges belonged to Captain Bates' company of Col. Frank Powers' regiment.

Capt. Josephus R. Quin, who was killed at Harrisburg, was a citizen of Pike County.

Col. Oscar James Elizabeth Stewart, a lawyer, who lived many years at Holmesville, was stationed at Summit in charge of home military affairs. Colonel Stewart was ever zealous in the discharge of his duties as an officer of the Confederacy.

Capt. R. W. Duke, a saddler by trade, raised a company of boys under 16 years of age, whose main object was to preserve the status quo at home and protect their country from its assailants. They rendezvoused at Summit and went into camp and some of them were detailed on courier service for a few days. This new demand on the department commanders' commissirat caused him to make the threat that he would send them all to Virginia where some of them would get hurt. This caused a stampede from the headquarters at Summit and that place was thus deprived of the important services it might have had of Duke's command against the enemy.

CAPT. JAMES CONERLY'S COMPANY, MISSISSIPPI MILITIA.

1. James Conerly, Captain.
2. John B. Leggett, 1st Lieut.
3. E. Prescott, 2nd Lieut.
4. S. A. Blackwell, 3d Lieut.
5. D. H. Quin, 1st Sergt.
6. W. McDowell, 2nd Sergt.
7. John Magee, 3rd Sergt.
8. J. A. Crawford, 4th Sergt.
9. W. Rushing, 5th Sergt.
10. Stephen McLendon, 1st Corp.
11. Wm. Guy, 2nd Corp.
12. Wm. Boyd, 3rd Corp.
13. I. Smith, 4th Corp.

PRIVATES.

14. Aron, S.
15. Bond, J.
16. Brauss, R.
17. Bing, A.
18. Born, O.
19. Bickner, C.
20. Browning, W.
21. Clough, J.
22. Davis, C. P.
23. Felder, D. F.
24. Gardner, A. H.
25. Hall, H. R. M.
26. Hume, R.
27. Heirling, I.
28. Headen, H. H.
29. Harrison, W. H.
30. Huckabee, I.
31. Lenoir, J. H.
32. Lem, I.
33. McDaniel, H.
34. McElveen, M.
35. McElveen, S. D.
36. Miller, R. D.
37. Magee, S.
38. O'Quin, I.
39. Quin, Peter H.
40. Rushing, J. C.
41. Ryals, H.
42. Rehorst, J.
43. Rulphin, H.
44. Raburn, A.
45. Rushing, W. T.
46. Smith, G.
47. Stephenson, W.
48. Stephens, P.
49. Simmons, H.
50. Schnider, P.
51. Toby, W.
52. Varnado, I. E.
53. Wote, G.
54. Wroten, V. J., Dr.
55. Causey, I. B.
56. Fortenberry, B. T.
57. Hughs, W.
58. Sandifer, R. M.
59. Sandifer, W. E.
60. Sandifer, J. W.
61. Seal, E.
62. Sinott, N.
63. Waruke, I.
64. Calliard, I., substitute for A. H. Gardner.

The fall of Fort Sumpter and the surrender of Major Anderson soon transferred hostilities to Virginia and the seat of government was removed from Montgomery to Richmond. It was evident that Virginia would be the principal battle ground of the war. General Beauregard was stationed at Manassas Junction, on the Orange and Alexander Railroad, with a small force, and Joseph E. Johnston was sent to the Shenandoah Valley, which was threatened by a force under Patterson, and Manassas by a force under McDowell, who advanced and attacked Beauregard at Bull Run, on the 18th of July, and was defeated. McDowell, however, having a force double that of Beauregard, it was evident that he would renew the attack. Joseph E. Johnston was ordered by the President at Richmond to reinforce Beauregard at Manassas, which he proceeded to do, keeping his antagonist ignorant of his movement. McDowell attacked Beauregard again on the 21st of July, with 40,000 men, when a hard and bloody struggle ensued. Johnston's forces coming up in due time, however, McDowell's forces were put to flight and driven back across the Potomac at Washington. This was the great battle of 1861, which proved to the invaders that it was not as easy a job to capture Richmond before breakfast as they had claimed they would do, and no doubt believed they would do, as they brought along a good supply of ladies in carriages to participate in the great ball they were to have in Richmond, and some 20,000 handcuffs to put on the "Rebels" to be captured by them. After this battle the year 1861 was principally occupied by both parties in making preparations for the future with some minor demonstrations and engagements in different sections. The battle of Bull Run, or first Manassas, gave to the South a considerable quantity of small arms and some cannon which were very much needed. In view of the approaching magnitude of the conflict, the Congress of the Confederate States passed a conscription act approved February 17, 1862, requiring all male white persons of military age to become enrolled in the army. The men in the field at this time had volunteered for one year and in the face of a large invading force it was evident that it would be a calamity to the Southern States should these now trained volunteers return home at the expiration of their term of service. The conscription act was intended to meet this emergency as well as to bring a large force in the field to repel the enemy. The volunteers unhesitatingly volunteered again for the war, and were permitted at the expiration of their term of service to reorganize their companies and regiments.

The term of the 16th Mississippi regiment would expire May 27, 1862. They were in R. S. Ewell's division on their route to the Shenandoah Valley, to reinforce "Stonewall" Jackson for the purpose of expelling the Federal General, N. P. Banks, from Winchester, and were camped not far from the base of the Blue Ridge Mountain, on the route leading across Swift Run Gap. Here the reorganization took place which made the change in the official status of all the companies and of the regimental line.

As a matter of history with which Pike County is connected this circumstance is referred to. The election occurred on the 26th of April, the anniversary of its departure from Holmesville.

Colonel Posey was re-elected colonel; Capt. J. J. Shannon, of the Jasper Grays, lieutenant colonel; Samuel E. Baker, of the Adams Light Guards, major, thus retiring Lieut. Col. Robt. Clarke and Maj. T. R. Stockdale.

The Quitman Guards elected Lt. S. McNeil Bain, captain; Colden Wilson, 1st lieutenant; John Holmes, 2nd lieutenant; Van C. Coney, Jr., 2nd lieutenant, thus retiring Capt. S. A. Matthews, Lieut. J. M. Nelson and Lieut. R. J. R. Bee, who returned to their homes.

In the early part of 1862 events indicated that the Southern States were entering the boundaries of a tremendous struggle. Pike County was doing her duty. She had already sent out some of her boys with the University Grays attached to the 11th Mississippi regiment under Captain Lowry, who participated in the first battle of Manassas, and two companies of over 200 men to Virginia now engaged in active hostilities, and with the opening of the campaigns her other eight companies followed in rotation and were attached to the western or Tennessee army; over one thousand men out of a population of 11,135, including slaves. Patriots imbued with the common cause came out from every nook and corner of the county, from all classes of whites. They saw the giant with frowning brow looking on them and threatening them with destruction and they calmly and resolutely came and took their places in the ranks.

The formation of these companies well nigh stripped the county of its men, except those over military age and boys under the age, and among this class a large number were serving in the army.

There was one great problem to be solved and to be met by the people at home which fell upon the women and girls until the Confederate government could prepare for the necessity. The South had no manufactories and supplies of clothing must be had by the men in the army. They had no uniforms and they, of necessity, went out with such as would best suit the conditions. The task to supply these necessities naturally fell on the women and they took hold of the situation with a genius and a patriotic impulse which few, if any, women of any country or age has ever equaled.

The artisans who had come as pioneers from the older states in the beginning of the century had not come in vain. From John Barnes, the father of little Margaret, who floated down the Cumberland, Ohio and Mississippi rivers in a cypress canoe in 1798, William Ravencraft, who pulled his mill stones and turning lathes all the way from South Carolina to Magees Creek with cows, and from the Walker's and others down on the Bogue Chitto the lessons had been taught and handed down to the beginning of this conflict. The loom makers, slay makers, reel and spinning wheel makers were put to work to supply the needs and soon the hum of the wheel, the scratch of the cards, the flutter of the reel and the thump of the looms were heard in every household. The women and girls, and those who had slaves, the negro women and girls too, with creditable devotion, entered into the spirit of supplying the needs of the soldier as well as themselves.

From Indian Creek and the Darbun to Dillon town, from Hoover's to the Louisiana line; from Bogue Chitto to Osyka; from Clabber Creek to Bahala; from Topisaw and Leatherwood and Varnal; from Still Creek to the limits of the county on the western line, all through the hills and valleys of Pike County, amid the moaning of the pines, the thump of the loom and the buzz of the wheel was heard, chorused with the inspiring notes of the Bonnie Blue Flag, Dixie and the Homespun Dress.

The "Homespun Dress" was written by Lieutenant Harrington, an Alabamian, belonging to Morgan's cavalry command, who was killed in the battle of Perryville. It is said that the words were not printed during the war. However, it got rapid circulation and was generally memorized among the Confederate soldiers in the early part of the war, and was sung at home by the women and girls throughout the South to the tune of the Bonny Blue Flag. A writer in the Age-Herald of Birmingham says:

"While Morgan's army was in Lexington, Ky., the women of that city gave a ball one night in honor of Morgan's men. On this occasion it is said the women appeared in homespun dresses. Lieutenant Harrington, of Alabama, who was a member of Morgan's army and who attended the ball, was so deeply affected by the flower of Kentucky's young womanhood appearing at a ball gowned in homespun dresses that he wrote the words to the song: 'The Homespun Dress.'"

The following are the words:

> Oh, yes, I am a Southern girl,
>   And glory in the name;
> I boast of it with greater pride
>   Than glittering wealth and fame;
> I envy not the Northern girl
>   Her robes of beauty rare,
> Though diamonds deck her snowy neck
>   And pearls bestud her hair.
>
> CHORUS.
>
> Hurrah! Hurrah!
>   For the sunny South, so dear;
> Three cheers for the homespun dress
>   The Southern ladies wear!
>
> Now Northern goods are out of date,
>   And, since old Abe's blockade,
> We Southern girls can be content
>   With goods that's Southern made.
> We send our sweethearts to the war,
>   But, girls, ne'er you mind—
> Your soldier love will not forget
>   The girl he left behind.
>
> The Southern land's a glorious land,
>   And has a glorious cause;
> Then cheer, three cheers for Southern rights
>   And for the Southern boys!

> We scorn to wear a bit of silk,
>   A bit of Northern lace,
> But make our homespun dresses up,
>   And wear them with a grace.
>
> And now, young man, a word to you,
>   If you would win the fair,
> Go to the field where honor calls
>   And win your lady there;
> Remember that our brightest smiles
>   Are for the true and brave,
> And that our tears are all for those
>   Who fill the soldier's grave.

On the 25th of May, 1862, Stonewall Jackson and R. S. Ewell attacked the Union forces under General Banks at Winchester, and drove them pell'mell back across the Potomac. A large force under Gen. George B. McClellan, was threatening Richmond. At the battle of Winchester Jackson and Ewell's forces captured six hundred wagons with their horses and equipage, and a large quantity of small arms with some cannon and army supplies. In order to save all this valuable stuff and to elude the junction of Fremont and Shield at Strasburg, forty miles in his rear, Jackson made a rapid retreat back to Cross Keys and Port Republic and made a stand. Fremont and Shields came up and on the 8th and 9th of June, both of them were severely defeated and driven back down the valley, followed by a few squads of cavalry and daring scouts. In the battle of Cross Keys Jared B. May, William Garner and Dr. A. P. Sparkman were wounded and returned home, and Wesley Yarborough was mortally wounded and died. Immediately following Cross Keys, McClellan advanced on Richmond against the Confederate forces there under Gen. Joseph E. Johnston, Jackson and Ewell secretly, and by a most extraordinary rapid movement, put their commands in position in front of Richmond without the knowledge of Fremont and Shields in the valley, and the series of battles before Richmond lasting seven days, resulted in the latter part of June and early days of July.

At Cold Harbor, where Ewell's forces fought, Captain Brown, of the Summit Rifles, and Joseph W. Collins, of the Quitman Guards, were killed and George W. Simmons of the latter company mortally wounded. George W. Root and Lieut. John Holmes were wounded, and Ike Dick, of the Summit Rifles, badly wounded while bearing the colors of the 16th Mississippi in a desperate charge on the enemy's works. These series of battles resulted in the defeat of the enemy and forced them to abandon this line and fall back on Washington.

Gen. Joseph E. Johnston being wounded during this great conflict, Gen. Robert E. Lee was placed in command of the army in Virginia and then another series of battles ensued at Slaughter Mountain, Second Manassas, Harpers Ferry, Boonsboro, Md., Sharpsburg and Fredericksburg in this eventful year, and the roll of the killed and wounded and prisoners of Mississippians in Virginia was greatly enlarged. While all these stirring events were occurring in Virginia, Gen. Albert Sidney Johnston was organizing for the defense of the Southwestern department and the formation of the Army of Tennessee and the conflict was gathering with stupendous proportions.

The Bogue Chitto Guards under Captain Carter, were organized May 1, 1861. The Dahlgreen Rifles under Capt. Parham B. Williams, August, 22, 1861, and the McNair Rifles in October, 1861, and then followed the Brent Rifles on the 26th of April, 1862. Nash's company, Holmesville Guards, Dixie Guards, Stockdale's Cavalry and Rhodes' Cavalry following. Of these the McNair Rifles participated in the battle of Shiloh. General Johnston fought this battle with less than 40,000 men, while his antagonist is credited with over 49,000 men, reinforced by Buel with 21,579 men. The war had been carried into Missouri and elsewhere west of the Mississippi river and in Kentucky and Tennessee. Forts Henry and Donaldson on the Tennessee river, had fallen under combined land and naval forces of the enemy in February, 1862, by which the Confederacy lost some 15,000 men by surrender and in killed and wounded, and Gen. Albert Sidney Johnston concentrated all of his available forces near Corinth, with General Beauregard second in command. The success of the Union arms at Forts Henry and Donaldson caused President Lincoln to make U. S. Grant a major general in command of that department and the two armies came together at Shiloh

Church in Tennessee, on the 6th of April, when the great battle of that name was fought. The Union army under General Grant, was defeated and driven back under cover of his gunboats at Pittsburg Landing, Tennessee river, but in the hour of the triumph of his magnificent military genius the great Confederate general received a mortal wound and died on the field from loss of blood from a severed artery in his leg, which misfortune to the Confederate arms, occurring when it did, prevented the utter destruction or surrender of their enemies. The enemy claimed a victory at Pittsburg Landing, but the facts seem to indicate that their victory consisted in not being destroyed, which was prevented by the timely reinforcement of Buel with over 21,000 fresh troops. In the battle of Shiloh the Confederates lost 1,728 killed, 8,012 wounded and 959 missing or captured; total, 10,699.

The enemy lost 1,500 killed, 6,634 wounded and 3,086 missing or captured, total, 11,220.

The reader of these pages must not expect in them a history of the war or detailed account of battles. The events which have been mentioned are intended to call the attention of the uninformed more particularly to the character of the great war in the beginning of active hostilities at this period. The student must turn to works devoted to it in order to obtain correct information as to the causes and events following, and they can find no better works on the subject than Jefferson Davis' Rise and Fall of the Confederate Government and the Life of Albert Sidney Johnston, by his son, Wm. Preston Johnston. The year 1862 was frought with many hard fought battles, with a preponderance of numbers always in favor of the enemy, and the victory generally in favor of the Confederates. At the end of two years from the secession of the States, with all the blood and treasure which had been expended on both sides, the war appeared to have just begun. The South had garnered nearly, if not all, her resources in men and means to beat back her ruthless invaders. Her entire roll of men reached only 600,000 and from this enrollment was taken men for employment in every branch of the civil and military service outside of the field. Some Southern historians have claimed that the South had less than 400,000 actual and effective fighting men in the different fields of operation, while the enemy shows by published records of their own that they enlisted and put in the field 2,678,967 men, besides their militia and maritime forces against our people. These figures come from the Rebellion Records published by the government and are copied from Davis' Rise and Fall of the Confederate Government.

In Henry W. Rauff's Century Book of Facts, page 617, the reader will find the following figures:

Lincoln's Calls, 2,942,748.

Obtained, 2,690,401.

Number of men furnished by states in same table, 2,778,304.

These do not include the U. S. regular army and navy, nor several hundred thousand militia.

So persistent has some northern historians been in falsifying the true records that they cannot be relied upon. And this very same man Rauff in his Century Book of Facts is one of them, for he has stated that the North never had over 700,000 active men in the field at any one time. They have strained consciences and veracity to such a degree that they have tried to make it appear, and to falsely teach northern children, that the South outnumbered them in troops in the field, as shown by an essay written by a northern girl in which she stated that the Confederates numbered two-thirds of the Union soldiers, when the truth is they numbered about one-fifth.

What of this unequal contest? What age of the world has its like? Where is the argument or the record to justify the North's contemptuous boast of whipping the South? Four years for such a stupendous army and navy with unlimited means and armament, with the entire world to draw from, to overcome the South's 400,000 "ragged, barefooted, sickly, half-starved rebels," as they were sneeringly denominated in northern prisons to justify the inequality of prison deaths! History reveals the "Story of the Lost Cause." No people under the sun struggled under greater difficulties, or fought more desperately for the preservation of their rights and in defense of their homes and their beloved land, against such tremendous odds, cut off from the outside world, than those constituting the armies of the Confederate States.

When Thaddeus Stephens, the great abolition leader, gave the word to "beat the devil out of the South," it was the slogan for destruction; the obliteration of the South's manhood and womanhood; the piling up of hecatombs from her chivalric sons and daughters, and the fulfillment of a cruel conqueror's dream of an African domination constructed over the ruins of her temples and the embers of her Caucasian glory. "To hell with the constitution," which the South had revered, was the motto and the watchword in the coercion of the Southern States, with Abraham as their willing executive.

Mr. Lincoln stated in his first inaugural address that he had no constitutional right to interfere with the institution of slavery and that there was no purpose to do so; but there was just as much reason to believe this as there was to put confidence in anything which had transpired relating to the Fort Moultrie and Fort Sumpter affairs— a complete and cunning piece of official perfidy, from start to finish.

In his second inaugural address after he had issued his emancipation proclamation, he said: "All knew that this interest (slavery) was somehow the cause of the war," and he helped to make it so.

In 1833, at a meeting of the American Anti-Slavery Society, at Philadelphia, a declaration of sentiments was adopted as follows:

"We maintain that the slaves of the South ought to be instantly set free."

"We maintain that no compensation should be given to the planters emancipating their slaves."

When it is considered that this same year the British government had paid her planters the sum of one hundred ($100,000,000) millions of dollars for their slaves emancipated, and the South's slave property largely greater than this in value, the intelligent reader will admit that from a financial point of view alone, the South had a good cause for her fears and complaints. It was a consciousness of right that actuated them.

"I had rather be right than to be president," said an eminent Southern man.

"I may not be on the winning side, but I know I am on the right side," said a Southern Governor.

Vice-President Alexander H. Stevens, of the Confederate Government, a man acknowledged by all to be devoted to the Union and the Constitution at the period of the secession of Georgia, which he represented in the United States Senate, said:

"I am afraid of nothing on earth, or above the earth, or under the earth, except to do wrong."

"Duty is the sublimest word in the English language," said Gen. Robert E. Lee.

The declaration embodied in the resolutions of the American Anti-Slavery Society was an echo of the sentiment of England after it was found that there was no more kidnapping money to be made out of the Southern States, which had passed laws forbidding their nefarious crime. It was all right for the Eastern Yankee to steal Africans and sell them to the South, but it was wrong in their eyes for the South to be paid for them on emancipation.

A period frought with so many things to attract the attention of the historian cannot be given in a local record.

When all the men fit for military duty in Pike County were in the field, it must be plausible to the minds of the living, that the women had a struggle all to themselves that no man or woman of the present generation can comprehend. More than half of them had to depend on their own resources, for they were not slave owners. And with all their efforts for the maintenance of themselves and children came the reports, wafted by every breeze, of the great battles being fought, bringing tidings of loved ones killed or wounded. Distress and suffering broadened and deepened the chasm where sorrow found its habitation. Old men and women of pioneer fame who sprung from revolutionary sires, fell upon their knees in humble supplication to ward off the great affliction; but here in these pine hills, where joyous hopes had lived and brightened and beautified life, a deep wail went forth to gratify the ever insatiable maw of northern hatred and crime.

All the men in Pike County capable of bearing arms were in the field, as stated before, except a few men who were allowed under the conscription act of Congress to remain at home to manage negro labor in productions necessary for the support of the army. One-tenth of the home productions of all were exacted for this purpose, and those who had no slaves to help them on the farms were equally burdened with this tax, making it doubly severe on those unable to provide a sufficiency for themselves and helpless children. Some old men, subject only to militia duty as home guards, were detailed to look after those who were in dire distress and seek means for their relief. Human fortitude was taxed to the extreme point, but they never lost any of their chivalrous characteristics. Like their ancestors of the revolutionary period, they could and did often subsist on parched corn and roasted sweet potatoes.

In the year 1863, the Confederate Army may be said to have reached its full strength, about 600,000 men, while the enemy had called out nearly 3,000,000, and the prospect for peace was yet without hope. This preponderance of forces enabled the U. S. government to blockade all the Southern ports and in a manner cut them off from foreign communication, besides placing more than four times their strength against them in the field.

The enemy had captured New Orleans, thus cutting off the main depot of supplies for a large section of Louisiana and Mississippi. It was difficult to procure salt and the people had to dig up the dirt of their old smoke houses and boil it to extract the salt from it. At times it could be procured from the Avery Island, in Louisiana. Sugar was procured from Baton Rouge and other points by wagons and taken in exchange for cotton or other products. No means were at the command of the people at times, and it was a desperate condition which confronted them. Confederate money was greatly depreciated in value. Flour and coffee were out of the question with the masses far South, and even the wealthy could not procure them. Parched meal or corn and other things were used as substitutes for coffee. Sometimes the blockade, as it was termed, could be slipped through and coffee obtained from places within the enemy's lines. A woman with a house full of little children to support was at a great disadvantage in the struggle for existence.

The years of 1863 and 1864 were fruitful of desperate encounters. The enemy was straining every resource and power to accomplish the defeat of the Confederate armies. Thousand dollar bounties were given to enlist, and hundreds of thousands of foreigners from Europe flocked to their standard for the sake of the money to fight "mit the flag" and save the Union (?). After a most heroic defense, Vicksburg and Port Hudson were given up in 1863, and Lee, with his invincibles, penetrated into Pennsylvania and the swelling tide of the struggle seemed to be at its height; but there were no re-inforcements nor recruits to be had to replace the losses of the Confederates, while to destroy a thousand of the enemy might bring a hundred thousand more. Shut out from the whole world, with depleting ranks and scant rations, they fought on without a thought of defeat, and the whole land from the Potomac to the Rio Grande, and to the Gulf, was baptized in blood and marked with conflagrations and ruin.

A considerable force of the enemy's cavalry under Grierson, taking advantage of the absence of regular troops, marched diagonally across Mississippi through Meridian, tearing up the Vicksburg and Meridian and the Mobile and Ohio railroad tracks, destroying the town and committing other acts of vandalism, which was one of the peculiar characteristics of Yankee soldiers. They were notorious as robbers and thieves, when there were no forces in their way to oppose them, except a few squads of militia and women and children.

They passed through the town of Brookhaven, and of Summit, in Pike County, plundered the towns and destroyed all the business houses and some residences that belonged to men in the Confederate army, whose names are recorded in this book; men who were pursuing a civilized mode of warfare and not cowardly and disgraceful vandalism, perpetrated by these so-called United States patriots.

The small force of militia composed of men and boys exempt from the regular army stationed here under Colonel Wingfield did not feel it safe to risk a battle with the well equipped and trained troopers under Grierson, and they retreated across the Bogue Chitto at Hoover's bridge, while Grierson, after accomplishing his vandalism, proceeded on his route unmolested through the country to the Southwest.

Lieut. Sampson Ball, who had seen service in the regular army and had been discharged, made application for 100 boys belonging to the militia forces for the purpose of disputing the passage of the enemy across the Tangipahoa, but the application was refused.

Hoover Iron Bridge
Scene on the Bogue Chitto River

Lieutenant Ball related to the writer that he thought Grierson's forces had been greatly overestimated and with a bold attempt, coupled with a little strategy, he might have delayed and annoyed them sufficiently to have secured their surrender to other forces seeking to apprehend them on the line to Baton Rouge, but his application was refused.

The few conscripts stationed at Brookhaven, under Capt. S. A. Matthews and Lieut. A. M. Bickham, made a circuitous retrograde movement into the dismal regions of the Otopasas and thus eluded the Yankee cavalier, running rough shod over the unprotected women and children of Mississippi and Northeast Louisiana.

Grierson, like Sherman, in his celebrated, proudly heralded farce act through Georgia, against a similar foe, landed at Baton Rouge, covered all over with glory and wreaths of victory in the estimation of the Northern government.

When the civil war ended in 1865, the South was a land of desolation indeed, and those who survived its consequences were left without a ray of hope. All they had possessed was gone save the land they returned to, and that was offered by the Yankees to the negroes in sections of forty acres and a mule.

The great battles fought by the Army of Tennessee succeeding that of Shiloh, under the command of Gens. Leonidas Polk, Beauregard, J. E. Johnston, Bragg and Hood, on the fields of Marietta, Resaca, Peach Tree Creek, Mission Ridge, Chicamauga, Atlanta, Franklin and elsewhere, reduced their forces so much that when Lee surrendered, the others followed in quick succession.

During this war and previous to the general surrender, the Confederates captured Union prisoners to the number of 270,000 men; killed over 350,000 of them and caused over a million of them to be placed on the pension rolls from being disabled.

The Unionists captured 220,000 Confederates and according to a report made by Surgeon Gen. Barnes, of the 270,000 Union soldiers captured by the Confederates, 22,000 died in Southern prisons; and of the 220,000 Confederates captured by the Unionists, 28,000 died in Northern prisons.

Ever since the close of that war there has been a persistent attempt on the part of Northern writers to misrepresent the truths of history in order to cover up and hide the cruelties and inhumanity of united soldiers and its authorities from the knowledge of coming generations, but in the language of Abraham Lincoln, "we cannot escape history," they have charged that the Confederates were cruel and barbarous in their treatment to Union prisoners, and claimed that the rigors of the climate where Confederates were held was the cause of a larger proportion dying, though the South held over 50,000 more prisoners than they, when the North was possessed of everything and every means necessary to prevent the wholesale mortality which prevailed in their prison and the South did not.

The false assertions and arguments and mutilations of history, in the efforts to justify their ruthless invasion and coercion of the Southern States and to make Confederate authorities greater sinners than Northern authorities, has fallen stiffly to the ground, as dead and worthless literature, and repudiated by intelligent investigators in the face of official reports.

General Lee's army in Virginia was never beaten on a single battlefield, nor driven from one, from Bull Run, July 18 and 21, 1861, to the last days at Petersburg, and it never yielded to its foe until reduced by hard and constant fighting to a mere fragment as compared with its ever recruiting antagonist, surrounded by ten times its number. With the close of the career of this invincible body of men came the fall of the Southern Confederacy, as all the other armies agreed upon the terms arranged between General Grant and General Lee, approved by President Lincoln, who was shortly after assassinated by John Wilkes Booth, an actor, in Ford's Theater in Washington City.

President Jefferson Davis, of the Confederacy, was captured by a troop of Wilson's cavalry in Georgia and placed in irons and chained in Fortress Monroe, by General Miles, and tortured there for two years, with inhuman cruelty. He was subsequently released from custody under bond signed by Horace Greely and others, as the government of the United States was unable to make out a case against him. Many cruel things were done after the close of this war in a spirit of vindictiveness and many innocent men and women made to suffer death; among them Mrs. Surratt, of Maryland, an innocent and helpless woman, charged with complicity in the assassination of President Lincoln; and Captain Wirz, who was commander in charge of Union prisoners at Andersonville, Georgia. In the long years of hard fighting against great odds, the Southern armies, by the casualties of war, were reduced and overpowered. The Southern people had suffered much and might have quietly borne the disaster, but the end was not yet.

Capt. Henry A. Wirz, above mentioned, was a Switzer and was the commander of the Confederate prison at Andersonville, Ga. After the close of the war he was hanged at Washington, November 10, 1865, as the result of suborned testimony, or subordination of perjury, under pretense of conspiring to cause the death of Federal prisoners at Andersonville, but really for refusing to give evidence or perjure himself against Jefferson Davis. He was charged in conspiracy with Jefferson Davis, James A. Seddon, Howell Cobb, W. H. Winder and others to kill Union prisoners at Andersonville, in his keeping.

There was a conspiracy, known as the Conover conspiracy, gotten up in Washington City, to connect Jefferson Davis with the assassination of Abraham Lincoln, which failed; and the attempt to fix the other crime on him was made to secure his destruction; and Wirz was convicted on perjured testimony, and the effort was made to induce him to testify against Mr. Davis to save his own life, which he refused to do. His conviction was secured upon the perjured testimony of a Frenchman named Felix de la Baume, a grand nephew of Marquis Lafayette, who was given a position in the interior department as a reward for his perjury. He was shortly after recognized as a Saxon named Oeser, a deserter of a New York regiment, and was dismissed eleven days after the execution of the man whose life he had sworn away.

Sam Davis, of Tennessee, a young Confederate soldier caught within the Union lines, was executed under similar circumstances. He was a scout and penetrated the enemy's lines and was captured. Certain information found on his person, procured from a personal friend in the Union lines, caused him to be tried as a spy, though undisguised. His life was offered to be spared if he would turn traitor to his friends, which he refused to do, and he was hung in Tennessee.

The trial of Captain Wirz is of record and cannot be destroyed, neither can the records of the Secretary of war in reference to the test of the treatment and suffering of the prisoners of war North and

South, and will always be available to the historian; and any attempt to fix criminality on Southern leaders or men for cruel treatment to union soldiers will be met by these records. The writer of this book was for three months, while disabled for service in the field, detailed for service with an attending physician in the prisons at Danville, Va., and can testify from his own knowledge of kindness shown them by Confederate officers at that place in 1864. The necessities and conditions at the time compelled the crowding of them in smaller spaces than was conducive to their health, and the living was hard, but it was as good as that issued to Lee's veterans, confronting the powerful and preponderating forces under General Grant at Petersburg. The government at Washington had all the resources of the world at its command, which the Confederacy was cut off from, and the North claimed a more healthful climate, and yet, the deaths of Confederate soldiers in Northern prisons was 25 per cent. greater than that of Union prisoners in Southern prisons. It stands any ex-union soldier or Northern man in bad plight to attempt to fix such crimes upon Southern men and try to exonerate themselves from inhumanity and barbarity. This writer, a prisoner himself, knew of Southern soldiers at the old capitol building in Washington City, brutally murdered by the guards for thoughtlessly looking out the bars at the windows; and there was no necessity for starving them, as was done, and which every Confederate prisoner can testify to, while upon the other hand the South's resources were exhausted; but they gave their prisoners what their own soldiers had who were termed "poor, feeble, ragged rebels"—requiring nearly three millions of men with the resources of the world at their command four years to subdue. There is no question of doubt that the barbarity practiced on Confederates was vindictive and intentional in order to accomplish the attrition necessary to overcome them, as their immense armies could not subdue them on the field of battle, and the suffering and mortality of both Confederate and Union soldiers is due to the refusal of Northern authorities to exchange prisoners, which would have saved thousands of lives on both sides.

The fields of Virginia were spread with the dead and the line on the frontier, where the armies had so often clashed, was a mark of desolation. The hope of the country was centered on Lee and he knew the great responsibility. It was a heavy burden sustained as he was by his noble compatriots, but his master mind wavered not until the very climax of dissolution was forced upon him. When the opposing chief offered him the opportunity to surrender the little

GEN. NATHANIEL H. HARRIS

guard that was left him, he replied that the time had not yet come. His army had never been driven from a single battlefield, though always matched against superior numbers. The climax came when after eleven months incessant fighting his heroes had been taken from him by the force of overpowering numbers, and the last lingering hope died only, when in response to his order to "Hold the Fort at all hazards," it was entrusted to Harris' Mississippians, who went down at Fort Gregg.

BUXTON R. CONERLY

HOW FORT GREGG WAS DEFENDED APRIL 2, 1865.

BY BUXTON R. CONERLY,

One of its Survivors—Quitman Guards, Company E, Sixteenth
Mississippi Regiment, Harris' Brigade.

Fort Gregg was situated about two miles southwest of Petersburg, Va., and was one of the many earthworks or redouts that General Lee had constructed for artillery in the rear of his main line of defense covering the cities of Richmond and Petersburg.

Its form was semi-circular—a space was left open in the rear for the entrance of wagons and artillery. The earth was thrown up from the outside forming a ditch 12 or 14 feet wide and from 4 to 6 feet deep—the walls were from 6 to 8 feet wide at the top and the ground on the inside next to the wall was raised for the cannon and for men to stand on. A considerable amount of artillery ammunition was in the fort, consisting of grape, canister, bomb shells and solid shot, stacked in pyramid form.

The disaster on the right wing of General Lee's army at Five Forks, causing the loss of the South Side railroad, forced the evacuation of Petersburg and Richmond   The position at and near Fort Gregg evidently was and became of great importance at this time to that portion of our army in the trenches around Petersburg, as it covered the pontoon bridges that had been thrown across the Appomattox river, west of the town, over which the artillery wagon trains and troops were crossing in their retreat.

During the latter part of March, 1865, our brigade, composed of the 12th, 16th, 19th and 48th Mississippi regiments, commanded by Gen. N. H. Harris, occupied a position between the Appomattox and James rivers, watching and guarding the line from Dutch Gap on the James, southward in a deployed line.

About 2 o'clock on Sunday morning, the 2nd of April, 1865, we received orders to move, leaving about one-third of our men on the picket line in front of this position. We marched rapidly in the direction of Petersburg, following the Richmond and Petersburg Turnpike road until within about two miles of Petersburg we left the main road, turned to the right and crossed the Appomattox river on a pontoon bridge about two miles west of the town. We then crossed the South Side railroad and marched by the Forts Gregg and Alexander (or Whitworth, as it is called by some).

We moved to a position about four hundred yards in front of these Forts, and formed in line of battle with skirmishers well thrown out to the front. Every foot of ground was familiar to us, for here we had spent the greater part of the preceding winter and had guarded this part of our line for several months—our old uncovered winter quarters were just behind us. Long lines of Federal infantry were advancing on our front; batteries of artillery were coming into position, and as far as we could see to the right and left the enemy's guns and bayonets glistened in the rays of the morning sun now well up over the hills in the east. Our skirmishers soon became hotly engaged in our front, and the leaden hail was striking our ranks.

"Stand like iron, my brave boys,"

Said General Harris, as he walked along the line.

"Stand like iron."

Our skirmishers were soon driven in and our brigade opened fire on the advancing Federal line with deadly aim and effect. They gained the shelter of a sunken road about 150 yards in front of us. Continuous firing was kept up from this position for about one hour. On the right and left of this position the Federal troops continued to advance, threatening to enfilade us on both flanks. Quite a number of our men fell killed and wounded in this position. General Harris, seeing that our position was untenable, ordered us to fall back to the shelter of the Forts Gregg and Alexander. Leaving a skirmish line to hold the enemy in check, our brigade began the backward move in a storm of shot from the enemy's sheltered position in the sunken road and the crest of hills on the right and left flanks, behind which they were rapidly increasing in strength. General Harris led the greater part of the brigade into Fort Alexander and Lieut. Col. Duncan, of the 19th Mississippi regiment, led the remainder, about 250 men, principally from the 12th and 16th Mississippi regiments, into Fort Gregg. The enemy, discovering this movement, rushed forward with loud huzzas, and our skirmishers were pressed back over the open field by overwhelming numbers, but taking the advantage of every protection the ground afforded to rest a moment and load—they never failed to give them a parting salute as they retired from one position to another. During this time the men in the fort had gathered all the loose grass they could find scattered over the field around and near the fort. The Federal forces had advanced to this place early in the morning (before we arrived), but had been driven away by Gen. A. P. Hill, leaving quite a number of rifles scattered over the field. The men quickly gathered them together—not forgetting their experience in the "Bloody Angle" at

Spottsylvania, May 12, 1864, when they used the enemy's guns against them that they had captured, practically giving them the advantage of repeating rifles, as they had from two to four guns each, all loaded. In addition to the artillery ammunition in Fort Gregg, there were also several boxes of rifle ammunition, about 1,000 rounds to the box.

About the time that we were as well prepared as we could be under the circumstances, the enemy appeared in such overwhelming numbers that Colonel Duncan decided to evacuate the fort. We marched out of the fort to the rear about one hundred yards, where we met a carrier who handed Colonel Duncan a paper which he read aloud:

"Hold the fort at all hazards."

(Signed) R. E. LEE.

The men immediately returned to the fort, as no other order was necessary, and resumed their positions around the walls.

Our soldiers understood the conditions and every one knew that he must delay the advance of the enemy to gain time for his comrades. The Federal troops at this time had reached a point about 300 yards in front of Fort Gregg, and were moving on Fort Alexander at the same time behind or under cover of our old winter quarters, huts which had been set on fire, and the smoke obscured their movements. Fort Alexander (or Whitworth) was about 300 yards to the right of Fort Gregg, and was at this time under the command of General Harris. The fighting on other parts of the line to our right and left stops for a while as if the men were watching the results of the movements about Fort Gregg. Colonel Duncan watches the men and tells them not to fire until the word is given. With his sword flashing in the sunlight of that beautiful Sunday morning, he insists (with his appeals to the state pride of Mississippi) that we should obey his orders. All around the walls of Fort Gregg was the cry of the officers, "Keep down men, keep down,"—officers who had never quailed on any field from first Manassas to that hour—to name their record would be to write the history of the army of Northern Virginia soldiers that knew them, with their suspension drawn to a tension indescribable, yielded to the order, and waited with apparent patience until that magnificent line of Federal soldiers was within less than one hundred yards of us, and not the flash of a single rifle had yet defied them. The last order of our officers, "steady boys," was interrupted by the cracking of the rifles sending their death dealing missiles with telling effect. Gibbon's men fall fast and thick—his line staggers and finally breaks in confusion, seeking shelter behind the crest of a ridge. A great cheer went up from our lines on the right and left and our boys responded with their customary yell of triumph from Fort Gregg. Reinforcements were hurried forward by the enemy from their sheltered position behind the hill, and their second line came forward at a double quick, in broken and scattered ranks. We opened on them at a distance of three hundred yards, firing as fast as we could. They staggered up within one hundred yards of us, when the greater part of their line broke and ran back under cover. The balance, perhaps three or four hundred, reached the ditch in our front—they were not strong enough to take us and could not retreat without running the gauntlet of death. Before we could turn our attention to the enemy in the ditch, reinforcements were hurried to their assistance and a third line came rushing on us with loud huzzas, from their covered position behind the hill, but in broken and scattered ranks. The greater part of them succeeded in getting in the ditch and completely surrounding us. During this time the men in Fort Alexander assisted Fort Gregg to some extent with an enfilading fire from that fort. It seems that General Harris at this moment, seeing and believing that we were captured, evacuated Fort Alexander to save his men. Our men deployed so as to cover every part of the walls of the fort and detailed twenty-five men to hold the gate in the rear. Now the solid shot, cannon balls and bomb shells found in the fort came into use. Our men hurled them on the heads of the enemy in the ditch. The fuses of the bomb shells were fired and rolled on them. This work did not stop until all or nearly all of the solid cannon balls and shells were gone. Brick chimneys built to tents for artillery men were thrown down and the bricks thrown at the enemy. Numbers of efforts to scale the walls were made, but the Federal soldiers would not act together and consequently the most daring ones were shot down on the walls and fell on their comrades below. A color-bearer fell on the fort with his flag, falling over on our side. During all this time the men at the gate were engaged in a death struggle and the last one fell at his post. The Federal troops having no further resistance there began pouring in from the rear and firing as they came. So many of our men had now fallen that the resistance was weak all around, and the Federal troops began pouring over the walls where a hand to hand encounter ensued on the crest, and our brave men went down in death. Quiet soon followed and about thirty survivors were marched to the rear as prisoners of war and sent to Point Lookout prison.

General Harris evacuated Fort Alexander about the time we were surrounded and made his way to the balance of the army in the retreat to Appomattox C. H. The men of our brigade left on the lines between the Appomattox and the James also were in the retreat and the final surrender at Appomattox.

Our brave Lieut. Col. Duncan was left in Fort Gregg, wounded in the head in an unconscious condition, rolling in the blood of his fallen comrades, when we were marched out.

Our bullet-ridden flag that had been borne proudly on so many victorious fields had been planted upon its last rampart, waived its last defiance and gone down on the bodies and laved in the blood of its brave followers and defenders, who here made a chapter for the stories of the Army of Northern Virginia and left a gem for their mother State to place in the crown of her soldiers who had responded to her call to arms and faithfully performed their last duty.

HOW FORT GREGG WAS DEFENDED.

LIEUT.-COL. JAMES HENDERSON DUNCAN.

Lieut.-Col. James Henderson Duncan, who commanded at Fort Gregg in the last bloody struggle near Petersburg, was a son of Dr. Isaac A. and Isabella Lucinda Craig Duncan, and was born at Mount Pleasant, in Maury County, Tennessee, on the 15th of March, 1839, and was thirty-five years of age when

LIEUTENANT COLONEL JAMES HENDERSON DUNCAN
Who commanded the Mississippians at Fort Gregg

this battle was fought. In 1840 his father moved to Sarepta, Miss., in that portion of the State now Calhoun County. Col. Duncan was engaged in the mercantile business at Oxford when the war began, and at the first call of arms he enlisted as third lieutenant in Com3any A, Nineteenth Mississippi, under Capt. Dr. John Smith. Later he was promoted to captain and rose to lieutenant-colonel, by gradation. Dr. Isaac Alexander Duncan, Lieutenant-Colonel Duncan's father, was born in Smith County, Tennessee, in 1810, came to Mississippi in 1840, was member of convention in 1850, and served in the lower

House of the Mississippi Legislature from Calhoun County in 1858, 1859 and 1860. His father was from Maryland, and was a soldier of the revolution.

David Craig, the father of Colonel Duncan's mother, was born at Chapel Hill, N. C., and his father was a revolutionary soldier.

Colonel Duncan recovered from the wound received at Fort Gregg and returned, after the close of the war, to his home in Mississippi, where he died some ten or twelve years after the war.

The seeds of grief had been scattered all over the land and everywhere the mantle of sorrow was to be seen. Here where noble aspirations had been cultivated, where love lived, where beauty crowned the thresholds of the homes of Pike County, death had cast its sombre shadows. Men who had gone to the war flushed with majestic manhood, were shattered in health or driven to the ultimate fate which awaits those who offer themselves as a sacrifice upon their country's altar. Ages ago the heralds of destiny brought the messages that gave hope to a brave people, but here in the ruins which blackened the once beautiful South, a veil of gloom fell over the vision of those crushed by the hand of a powerful and unfeeling foe.

When the news came of Lee's surrender, mothers went down on their knees and prayed that their loved ones might be spared to crown their happiness in the years to come, but with many the Angel of Death had stalked and bowed them down in grief. Many waited and prayed in vain. The crucible of war had consumed the objects of their love and hopes. When the end came it was an end indeed.

The Southern cross that fluttered proudly and defiantly for four years, went down in a halo of imperishable glory; sanctified with the blood of the chivalrous and brave, and was furled forever at Appomattox April 9, 1865, and its tablet of memory, inscribed with the following lines written by the South's poet priest, Father Ryan.

THE CONQUERED BANNER.

Furl that banner, for 'tis weary;
Round its staff 'tis drooping dreary;
Furl it, fold it, it is best,
For there's not a man to wave it,
And there's not a sword to save it,
And there's not one left to lave it
In the blood which heroes gave it.
Furl it, hide it—let it rest.

Furl that banner! True, 'tis gory,
Yet 'tis wreathed around with glory
And 'twill live in song and story,
Though its folds are in the dust,
For its fame on brightest pages,
Penned by poets and by sages,
Shall go sounding down the ages—
  Furl its folds though now we must.

Furl that banner softly, slowly,
Treat it gently, it is holy,
  For it droops above the dead!
Touch it not, unfold it never,
Let it droop there furled forever,
  For its peoples' hopes are dead.

When the leaders of the Southern armies accepted the terms of surrender to the United States forces they bound their people to an observance of its authority and when the shattered remnants of those armies, yielding only to overpowering numbers, came back to their homes they meant to be true to the terms imposed upon them, but when the government itself disregarded the objects contemplated in the terms of surrender, the situation changed.

After the assassination of Abraham Lincoln, the Northern president, with which the South had nothing whatever to do, all the venom of a furious enemy was forced to the front to take revenge, the magnitude of which will scarcely be conceived by those living after the enactment of these horrible scenes. It was related to the writer by a gentleman who was closely connected with the Confederacy, and who was a prisoner at the time in Washington,(a bit of suppressed history) that at a meeting of nine Northern governors, headed by Governor Curtin of Pennsylvania, and members of the cabinet, that a resolution was passed to arrest and execute all Southern leaders from Jefferson Davis down. It was referred to General Grant, who refused to countenance it, but asserted he would use the entire army of the government to protect them and the men who had accepted his terms of surrender. R. S. McCollough, the renowned Confederate chemist, whose invented explosives sent so many Yankee vessels to the bottom, and who was one of the men included in the intended holocaust of vengeance, subsequently connected with the Louisiana State University, at Baton Rouge, in 1881, related this circumstance to the writer himself as a fact while a guest of his and his family in the suite of rooms occupied by them in the Jadot Hotel, in the city of Baton Rouge, and how his little daughter, Gracie, then only 9 years of age, went to see President Andrew Johnson, and, sitting upon his knees, begged that the life of her father be spared.

Colonel McCollough was captured at Richmond at the time of its evacuation by the Confederate forces and was conveyed to Washington in a closed carriage, confined there in prison and was informed of the conspiracy above alluded to. But when General Grant gave it the black eye—a crime so revolting and perfidious as to cast an eternal stigma on his own name and honor, the conspirators retired and suppressed a record of their meeting and resolutions. All Northern writers have carefully eluded any mention of it, if they knew of it. In later years some of them who have been disposed to be fair in speaking of President Davis' unjust imprisonment and treatment at Fortress Monroe, have hinted at it only, but in such terms as to indicate a knowledge of it.

CAPTURE OF DAVIS.

There were so many lies published in Northern papers immediately after the war and persistently continued and believed by a large class of Northern people about Mr. Davis being captured in the disguise of a woman's apparel, and pictures of the same scattered everywhere, and even pretended to be believed by some to this day, that it would be proper to insert the facts here.

He had fled from Richmond upon the evacuation of Petersburg by General Lee's army, with his guard, with the purpose of joining Kirby Smith or Magruder west of the Mississippi river, and was in camp near Irvinsville, Ga., where he had joined his family. On the rainy morning of May 18, 1865, the President's guard had surrendered and what followed is here reproduced from an article written by Mr. T. C. DeLeon, in New Orleans Picayune.

Through the dim pre-dawn a troop of Wilson's cavalry dashed into his camp by chance. His old instinct told him the truth and he whispered to his wife that they were regulars, and all was lost. Rapidly he told his plan, the troopers deployed and with leveled carbines. He would (with the old West Point trick) seize the foot of the nearest rider, hurl him from saddle and vault into it, flying for liberty or for quick death into the dense woods—thence, alone to the Mississippi. As he spoke, he grasped his pistol, creeping stealthily to the nearest horsemen's side. Already in the damp morning Mrs. Davis had thrown about his shoulders the light, sleeveless raglan from her own shoulders. While he spoke the last words, she threw about his neck the small, square shawl she wore.

But it was too late for the West Point trick, or for any escape, the destined object of attack wheeled his carbine and a dozen more centered on the one man, as locks clicked. With a scream, the wife threw herself between him and their muzzles, and the end had come.

But, in creeping up to the troopers in the dim light, the raglan and the shawl had both fallen from the husband's shoulders, yards away from the spot where he was seized.

As for the shawl, its "biography" is told by Mrs. Clem Clay Clopton, with all persiflage on dress subjects. In her book describing the trip of the prisoner to Fort Monroe, on the William P. Clyde, she tells that she and Mrs. Davis had two shawls so exactly alike that neither knew her own. One of these his wife had thrown about Mr. Davis' shoulders. She had picked it up when dropped unheeded by him. Both ladies had these shawls on the voyage to prison.

Mrs. Clay's diary was written while she was at sea, a guarded prisoner on a United States ship, and precluded from possibility of newspapers and the wild stories filling a superheated Northern press as to Mr. Davis' "disguise." She gives dates, facts and names. Her story has been in type for years. It is still uncontroverted.

When anchored off Fortress Monroe (the diary tells), two women were sent aboard the Clyde to search the persons of the female prisoners for treasonable papers. Then Lieutenant Hudson, of the guard, demanded of Mrs. Davis her shawl as proof against her husband.

She demurred; but, it being the only wrap she had, Mrs. Clay took her own duplicate shawl, folded it within Mrs. Davis' and gave them both to the officer. Later Mrs. Clay's shawl was returned, a maid of Mrs. Davis having identified hers, and that is the shawl formerly exhibited in Washington and recently "exhumed from a disused drawer in the War Department."

Few people noted its earlier exhibition along with the spurs, sleeveless raglan, etc. Nobody, North or South, cared a rush whether they had been refound or not. Time, the cure-all of ills, mental or moral, has passed the episode.

The war is ended. The union of states physically restored and the 14th and 15th amendments to the Constitution forced upon the South by Federal bayonets, through compulsion and fraud, stand as an insult and a curse to our people for which there will be no forgiveness until they are repealed.

CHAPTER VII.

The high price of cotton in 1865 and 1866 was a blessing to the people. Large quantities had been hidden away in nooks and corners where the Yankees could not find it, or failed to do so, by those who were exempt from military service, and in the fall after the surrender a small crop was gathered which brought the high price of fifty cents and over. This gave strength to the merchants who were thus enabled to help the farmers, struggling against the fretful conditions that prevailed. All the merchants in Summit, whose business houses had been swept away by the vandalism of Grierson's raiders, were rebuilding their stores, and those in Holmesville, Magnolia, Osyka and Tylertown endeavored to place themselves in condition to meet the necessities of their people. The demon of despotism was an ever haunting spector, and as time passed the evidences accumulated, showing the trend of the powers to subvert their cherished hopes. Every man who had been a soldier of the Confederacy was working to re-establish himself in the conditions had before the war, and all worked to rebuild their lost fortunes.

The evils which surrounded them at the beginning were measured by the power of endurance given them under the train of events which gave to their past a halo of glory. All the elements which went to form the nucleus of a powerful endeavor were centered in their great hearts. The wails of the widow and the suffering of her children were heard and given attention.

When freedom vanished with the fall of the stars and bars, the giant monster that had crushed them had no terrors for them save the dastard attempt to supplant them with the recently liberated negro slaves. They had been deprived of their arms, but a way was provided to place themselves in a position to meet the worst.

In his admirable book on the "Ills of the South" Rev. Charles H. Otkin, of Pike County, has given in his first chapter a description of conditions prevailing at this time, 1865, so truthfully and with language so appropriate that I am pleased to be permitted to copy from it as follows:

"CHAPTER I, PAGE I."

"THE CONDITION OF THE SOUTH IN 1865."

"Widespread desolation reigned in every portion of the South in 1865. The war of the States was ended. The South had staked all—lives and fortunes—upon a principle, and lost. The four years' struggle, with its hopes and its fears, was behind them; defeat, with all its vast significance, was before them. The Southern soldiers returned to their homes. It is not too much to say that a large majority of the soldiers of the Confederate armies had homes. But these homes of comfort and plenty in 1861 were not those to which they returned after the surrender. A great change had swept over them. Four years' ruthless war had left indelible marks. Time, with its ravages, the mismanagement of farms and plantations left largely in charge of the negroes, the vandalism of armies in the destruction of property, had made hideous alterations in the condition of the country. Dilapidated dwellings, fences out of repair and in many instances burned, sugar-houses and gin-houses damaged or in ruins, were seen everywhere. Farms once producing profitable crops were now grown up in broomsage. The chimneys of hundreds of comfortable dwellings furnished the only evidence that these places were once the abode of human habitation. Cattle and live stock of every description were largely diminished. Everywhere devastation met the eye.

"The Southern farmers commenced life anew under many and disheartening disadvantages. Not a few were well advanced in years, and had large families. There was mourning throughout the Southland. Many husbands, fathers, and sons slept on distant battlefields, never to return. Thousands of widows were left penniless. The gloom was appalling, and the people were poor. Those that had something left were ill-prepared to help their poorer neighbors. Hundreds returned maimed in body. There was nothing to relieve these scenes of ruin, save the brave, resolute determination to commence the hard struggle for existence."

The order of Thaddeus Stephens had been executed. The proclamation of Abraham Lincoln had been consummated at the cost of three billions of treasure to his government, a million of human lives of his own white race, and the widespread ruin of the fairest land on earth; the habitation of his countrymen, the descendants of those who had been the founders of the government he represented and devoted adherents to its principles. Four million negroes amancipated, valued at over two billion of dollars, without compensation to the owners, thus carrying out the resolution of the American Antislavery Society held at Philadelphia, all done under the cry of "save the Union."

Mr. Otken further says:

"Four million negroes were not only free, but were invested with civil rights. What a novel condition! What a tremendous experiment!"

At this stage a most novel condition was presented by the ex-negro slaves.

The sudden close of the war and the knowledge of emancipation struck the great mass of them with amazement. They were living with their families in comfortable homes, on the plantations of their masters, who had always provided for them. They had no knowledge of the responsibility which emancipation had cast upon their own shoulders. They had nothing on earth with which to begin life; not a mouthful of food, not a stitch of clothing, not a cent of money, not a shelter to protect them from the weather except that which came through the tender humanity of their former masters. The impulse was to leave their old homes and go somewhere else. Think of it! Four million ignorant slaves suddenly liberated and thus actuated and no provision made by the government to care for them. Were their old masters bound to do it? They were penniless, too. But the negro men by the thousands scattered hither and thither, leaving their wives and helpless children at the old plantation quarters to be taken care of by "de white folks." The majority of slave owners who could manage to provide for them tried to keep them at home to finish their crops with such wages as the conditions justified. Those who could not provide for them had to let them go, and they could not undertake to take care of the women and children when the men were gone and the bulk of the farm work left undone. They flocked to the military camps in great droves, men and women, with complaints of inhuman treatment and stories of barbarity, and the Yankee officer, who was bred and born and brought up to the period of donning the brass button in the belief that the negro was a peer of himself, believed these stories, and this resulted in squads of cavalry and infantry being sent over the country to investigate them, thus eternally harassing the white people and overturning their efforts to bring about a just equilibrium between themselves and these ex-slaves. Thus fell upon the authorities a new problem. They had just disbanded a couple of million of soldiers, but it was about to incur the greater responsibility of giving subsistence to four millions of ex-slaves who, if they ever had a thought of the necessity of labor for support, it was blotted out when freedom was announced to them by their old masters, and the "year of jubelo" had dawned, which condition was not mentioned in the emancipation programme. The military were driven to the necessity of organizing a written contract system in order to force the negroes to remain on the plantations and relieve themselves of the burden. This system, while it was the best that could be done at the time, was fruitful of great vexation and trouble. All infringements or violations of the contract must be referred to the military authorities.

The Southern white man and ex-Confederate soldier, in his management of the negro as a slave, was content only with obedience to his orders and instructions; but the negroes, having been received with the right hand of fellowship and brotherly love by the epauleted fraternity and his conceit galvanized, in the course of a very few weeks began to show his contempt for the "boss," and hence sprung an endless stir and flurry and military investigation of violated contracts. Under this system the negroes were required to procure passes from their employers when they wished to go away from the plantations. This was adopted to put a stop to their indiscriminate roaming and desertion of their own families and to give relief to the authorities. The pass system was productive of much good, but it was also productive of much evil.

At the close of the war the country was infested with many bad characters who had no regard for law and order, nor for the rehabilitation of the country. They were usually roaming characters, with no fixed abode, and whose means of support was a question to those who had borne the brunt of the struggle and had returned to their homes with their minds directed to the restoration of peaceful conditions and prosperity. The planters were not always strict about giving trusty negroes passes, and it occasionally happened when one should accidentally be met by the characters above alluded to it resulted in an inhuman flogging and sometimes a more severe punishment. Then the military were resorted to for redress, everybody in the region held accountable and the reins tightened on all. Social intercourse between the negroes and the Federal soldiers, without regard to color, became a fixed reality and their camps on Sundays and other times were scenes of social intercourse. Miscegination was openly inculcated and practiced, and the negroes were taught by the Yankee soldiers, in 1865 and 1866 what, in three hundred years, they had never learned from Southern white people. This may truthfully be said to be the beginning of race troubles after emancipation. The negro men seeing and having a knowledge of the intimate relations between white Federal soldiers and officers with negro women and openly taught equality, led them to desire an equal opportunity with white women, but there was a barrier that stood between them and the white women, and they knew it. It was a gun and a Southern white man behind it. There was no statutory law that could be brought into play to prohibit intermarriage, nothing except the inflexible principle and will of the Southron. But miscegination was conceived and born through the instrumentality of the Federal army stationed in the South—in Mississippi—in Pike County, and through an influx of Northern carpetbag negrophites who married negro women. There was one instance in Pike County where a white girl was persuaded to run away with a young negro man, which resulted in the parties being overtaken, the girl rescued and the negro escaped.

One can scarcely conceive how gradually, but how quickly, the situation dawned to excite the fears of the white people of the South in regard to dangers threatening their race. One who has lived through it and taken a part in the events and changes of the times can more fully, perhaps, appreciate the wide world calamity that stared them in the face then and which leads to a recital of circumstances following in these pages.

There was a chivalric principle implanted in the bosoms of those who had given their services in the cause which had succumbed to overpowering numbers, and the love they bore for their women who had passed through the crucible with them was such that nothing must come between them to contaminate their blood or mar their existing relations. The Confederate soldier, with trained eye and experience, saw with deep concern the danger which threatened and was increasing in the intimate relations and intercourse of Federal white soldiers and intermarriage of white men from the North with negro women and encouragement given to amalgamation of the races. The protection given the negroes, as they viewed it, by the soldiers, and the unmistakable partiality extended to them in all controversies between them and their late masters, made them insolant and created a spirit of defiance, encouraged by the Federal troops which was soon followed by insults and crimes. In the towns and cities Yankee white soldiers thought nothing of walking arm in arm with negro women, and negroes would shove white women off the banquettes. There was no redress to be had. Complaint to the military authorities was contemptuously ignored; protection was thrown around the culprit; insolence encouraged and white men and women turned aside in favor of the negroes. Amid these gathering disturbances the great Southern heart swelled with deep mortification and indignation and lifted itself above the ashes of desolation, and the impending degradation and ruin that seemed about to 'engulf their Caucasian civilization.

When the armies were disbanded and the Confederate soldiers who had survived returned to their homes, relying on the generosity of their former enemies, as manifested by General Grant at Appomattox, they believed that with the restoration of peace, and left untrammeled to the task of providing subsistence for their dependents and the rebuilding of their lost fortunes, the country would recover, in a measure, in a few years. But the vindictiveness of the Northern States was not yet abated, and the storm that arose over the unfortunate assassination of President Lincoln burst out with fury and revenge on the South as the conspirator and perpetrator of the crime. And hence United States soldiers were stationed everywhere in the South to overawe them and further crush their hopes. A company of negro troops were stationed at Holmesville, in Pike County. No white person was allowed to keep firearms of any description, and thus the people were forcibly reminded of the cold blooded answer of Abraham Lincoln when he was to issue his emancipation proclamation in 1863, and Mr. Wm. H. Seward, his Secretary, who had lived in the South, expressed his great fear of the horrors that would ensue by the insurrection of the negroes who might rise and butcher the wives and children of the Confederates behind their armies:

"It is time for us to know whether these people are for or against us."

Where should they turn for hope? What herald would bring them the tidings? Everything gone, disarmed, manacled, and the despot's heel stamping out the last glimmer of freedom! It was a solemn hour; their wives and sisters and mothers and daughters and widows and orphans of their dead comrades in the peril. Thousands wished themselves back in the fields where the conflict had raged in the past with chances of success.

"It is time for us to know whether these people are for or against us," echoed over the land. A cold blooded sentiment expressed by a man at the head of a government who looked Southward with the belief that four million negro slaves would rise up and with the maul and the axe and the dagger butcher four million helpless, defenseless white women and children of his own race, behind the Confederate armies, which would make his victory complete!

The answer was now given: "It is time for us to know, and we will see if these people are to rule over us and destroy our civilization."

A message came and gave to them a gleam of hope and with it came the mystic letters K. K. K.

It was an order of mysteries; one that carried determination and skillful planning by men who knew no fear in the face of despotic power. The issue was sprung. The fiat of self-preservation or death to the hilt or muzzle of the revolver. It was an order of masterful command, of obedience and discipline. It was the ego of duty.

It had for its object the salvation of the Caucasian race in the South, threatened with destruction, and the protection of its helpless women and children, the widows and orphans of Confederate soldiers.

Upon the threshold of a great calamity this organization arose, out of the bowels of the earth, as it were, and formed into a solid phalanx of oath-bound determined men.

Who were they? Whence came they? The shades of the dead who have passed the Styx of Dante's infernal regions, where they were sent for their inhuman crimes could not tell, nor the ghosts of the villains who wronged our helpless and defenseless women. It rose, it flourished, it performed its mission and disappeared as mysteriously as it came; this wonderful organization, The Ku Klux Klan.

The writer hopes that the readers of this volume will not consider him boastful nor egotistical when he tells them he was eminently familiar with the workings of the Ku Klux Klan. He does not have to draw on the imagination nor search the musty records of the past, nor cull from others what has been said of it. There lived a principle that swelled within the bosoms of every man who clung to and which was the motive power of this great order. It was the trying ordeals of the period which animated them to the verge of desperation. Around their homes and firesides there were those they loved, and the hand of barbarism, upheld by the conquering power of the United States Government, was raised to destroy the hopes of their country's future.

When the reader turns to the history of the South which glows with daring deeds, his soul will rise above the dastards who wrung freedom from its grasp. No people on earth who carry the principles of self-preservation within their bosoms will ever turn a deaf ear to a recital of the wrongs forced upon our beautiful South.

The organization of the Ku Klux Klan was so thoroughly systematized that all its movements were in harmony. Its secrets were so well guarded that its leaders and members were unknown outside of the organization. Its objects were summarized as follows:

"To the lovers of law and order, peace and justice, and to the shades of the venerated dead, Greeting:

"This is an Institution of Chivalry, Humanity, Mercy and Patriotism, embodying in its genius and principles all that is chivalric in conduct, noble in sentiment, generous in manhood, and patriotic in purpose; its peculiar object being, First, To protect the weak, the innocent, and the defenseless from the indignities, wrongs and outrages of the lawless, the violent, and the brutal; to relieve the injured and the oppressed; to succor the suffering and unfortunate, and especially the widows and orphans of Confederate soldiers.

"Second, To protect and defend the Constitution of the United States, and all the laws passed in conformity thereto, and to protect the States and the people thereof from all invasion from any source whatever.

"Third, To aid and assist in the execution of all constitutional laws of the land."

Their places of meeting were called "Dens of the Klan," and presided over by the Grand Cyclops, who was the presiding officer of the township or precinct.

The uniform or disguise for man and horse was made of a cheap domestic, weighing three or four pounds.

The white robes for the men were made in the form of long, loose gowns or ulsters, with capes, the skirts reaching to the ground and hanging below the stirrups when mounted. The men wore red belts which supported two revolvers. On each man's breast there was a scarlet circle within which was a white cross. The same appeared on the horse's breast and on his robe at the flanks, the mystic letters K. K. K.

Each man wore a white cap, from the edges of which floated a piece of cloth extending to the shoulders. Over the face was a white covering with eye holes and an opening for the mouth. On the front of the caps of the Hawks appeared the red wings of a hawk as an ensign of rank. From the top of each cap was a spire or spike 18 or 20 inches high, covered with the same white material and supported by wire. These uniforms were easily folded and concealed within a blanket and kept under the saddles without discovery. It was only a question of two or three minutes to dismount, unsaddle, doff the uniform and be on the move as if suddenly coming out of the bowels of the earth. The men were provided with various devices to create consternation among the superstitious. Their eyes looked like balls of fire at times, and sulphurous fumes emitted from their ranks. Several buckets of water was a commom draught for a man who suffered the intense thirst incident to the regions of heat below, where it was thought he made his abiding place. In companies of one and two hundred men, thus disguised at night, the spectacle was terrorizing, but the organization was composed of level headed men, trained Confederates who knew no fear.

The operations of the Ku Klux Klan were not confined to their own precincts altogether, as the United States soldiers were on the alert. They were ever watchful and any work to be done at home was often performed by those living many miles away, strangers to the community, who were notified by a relay system of couriers when messages could be sent long distances without any one being missed, except for a few hours, from the neighborhood. Louisianians worked in Mississippi, and *vice versa*, and so with counties and districts. If any serious work was to be performed it was sometimes prefaced by some public demonstration or amusement, when the home Klan had everything fixed, the criminal located and watched. The distant Klansmen appeared and mingled with the people, coming in from different quarters as others without a suspicion of their mission. Their mystic signs enabled them to recognize each other and to arrange the details of their operations. When night came they assembled in the vicinity and donned their disguises for themselves and horses, which were folded in their blankets, and a great apparition seemed to rise from the earth, and before the criminal suspected that danger lurked near him he was in their clutches. He was then taken to a place presided over by the Grand Cyclops, where witnesses were presented and a thorough investigation had. If adjudged guilty, when day dawned the culprit would be missing and sometimes found in his neighbor's yard, a dead proposition, or found dangling from the limb of a tree, and sometimes officials who were obnoxious and oppressive in their acts or exhibited a disposition to overawe the white people, were given the opportunity to breakfast on the carcasses of their unscrupulous henchmen and pets.

The thief and rapist, the murderer and the instigators of negro supremacy and self-importance had a poor show in the days of Ku Kluxism. Those who were under the ban of suspicion in minor cases were often warned by the mystic letters K. K. K. posted where they were sure to see them. They observed the laws which governed the different degrees of crime, but they executed those laws in their own way in proportion to the nature of the crime.

In May, 1865, Governor Charles Clarke called an extraordinary session of the Legislature to meet in Jackson, and the same month was arrested by General Osband, of the United States Army, and was sent to Fort Pulaski and there imprisoned, for the reason only that he had served the Confederacy and happened to be Governor at the close of the war of a State whose interests had been identified with that government. Judge Wharton, in describing his arrest, says:

"The old soldier, when informed of the purpose of the officer, straightened his mangled limbs as best he could and with great difficulty mounted his crutches, and with a look of defiance said: 'General

Osband, I denounce before high heaven and the civilized world this unparalleled act of tyranny and usurpation. I am the duly and constitutionally elected Governor of the State of Mississippi, and would resist, if in my power, to the last extremity the enforcement of your orders. I only yield obedience, as I have no power to resist.'"

A more glaring piece of tyranny and deviltry could not be thought of at this time than the infamous act of the officer who thus assailed a shattered veteran and legally elected Governor of a State, whose life was so nearly spent and whose beautiful character was conspicuous in the history of his country. A man worn with age and mangled beyond ability to walk without crutches, thus forced from his high position and carried under a military guard and imprisoned in a felon's cell at Fort Pulaski, beyond the borders of his own State. After the ejection of Governor Clarke the executive office was for the time being occupied by General Osterhaus.

Subsequent to the preformance of this disgraceful act the President of the Uuited States, Andrew Johnson, who had been inaugurated after the assassination of President Lincoln, appointed William L. Sharkey Provisional Governor. When he thus became the head of the executive department he called what has been termed "the Abortive Reconstruction Convention," August 14, 1865, which declared the ordinance of secession "null and void," and recognized the abolition of slavery in Mississippi. It also called a State election at which General Humphreys was chosen. But the military assumed the role of superior authority, and under it all persons were required to appear at the courthouse and record their oath of allegiance before they were allowed to pursue their regular avocations or transact any legal business. State sovereignty and individual liberty were wiped out. In Pike County Robert H. Felder had succeeded Louis C. Bickham as sheriff under Governor Clarke's administration. He held over until after the appointment of Governor Sharkey, when he was deposed by order of the military because he could not take the iron-clad oath. His brother, Levi D. Felder, was appointed and Robert filled out the term as his deputy.

Hon. Dunbar Rowland, in the Mississipi Official and Statistical Register of 1904, page 589, has the following to say of the Black and Tan convention in 1868, called during General Humphrey's administration in pursuance of the Congressional plan of reconstruction, which had been adopted when "General Ord, who had just completed revising the electorate of the State," called an election to determine whether there should be a Constitutional Convention. Of course the proposal was carried:

"Both the tragic and comic masks are needed to do justice to that notorious convention. It was a motley group, with a slender conservative membership, but composed chiefly of negroes and "carpet-baggers," both equally ripe for plunder. Ignorance and corruption combined, and there was such another revel as the "Broecken" could never match, This august body met in the Hall of Representatives on January 7, 1868. "Buzzard" Eggleston of Lowndes County, whose name bears witness to a certain unclean rapacity, was elected President. The compensation of members was the first question raised. A committee was appointed to report a schedule disposing of that important matter. Its report was most liberal in tone. Long and interesting were the debates, but it was finally decided that the president should receive $20 per diem and the members $10, exclusive of mileage. The official reporter and secretary were given $15 per day each, and a number of other superfluous officers were provided for at the rate of $10 per day. The hour had come and the harvest was ripe for the loyal Republican contingent. Protest against extravagance on the part of the few Democratic members was fruitless. One offered a resolution declaring the convention illegal, and the members not entitled to compensation. There was a long uproar and loud cries for his expulsion. Another suggested that after the expiration of twenty days each member should pay his own expenses. His language was denounced as "insulting" and he was requested to withdraw. A new spasm of indignation came when the superintendent of the city gas works sent the convention word that he would have to be paid in advance for all the gas used, as he doubted the solvency of the State and the convention. A resolution was passed declaring that no night sessions would be held. The convention triumphed only to be met by a new annoyance. It was observed that the newspaper reporters did not prefix "Mr." to the names of the negro delegates. The reporters were promptly excluded from the sessions after that."

"The important offices of the State were held by white Democrats. This called for reform. A resolution was offered appointing a committee of seven to memorialize Congress to declare all civil offices vacant and to vest the appointment in the convention, Heroic efforts were made to exploit the treasury under the guise of appropriations for the relief of indigent and suffering freedmen. The scheme failed because General Gillem, Military Commander, refused to sanction the appropriation."

"After a session of a month it occurred to several members that they were sitting for the purpose of framing a Constitution. They hastened to repair the oversight. A committee was appointed to prepare a draft and report in three days. Prompt at the time the report was made the franchise provisions, depriving a large section of the intelligence of the State of the right to vote, attracted main attention. They were debated long and bitterly, the few conservative members making a last vain stand. Fights were of frequent occurrence and feeling ran high. Finally the obnoxious provisions were adopted. The democratic members indignantly resigned and went home. Provisions were made for submitting the Constitution for ratification, and the convention adjourned on May 18th. It is a matter of history how it was rejected and adopted in 1869 without the franchise qualification. The convention had cost the impoverished State about a quarter of a million of dollars."

In June, 1868, General Adelbert Ames was appointed military Governor, who sent a body of soldiers under Colonel Biddle and ejected Governor Humphreys, taking military possession of the executive department himself, under instructions from General McDowell, military commander of the district.

The reader may be curious to know why this was done when the State had been moving along smoothly for some time under Governor Humphreys. The Constitution adopted by the Black and Tan convention was rejected in June following its adjournment. This was followed by the immediate appointment of a set of interlopers, more commonly known as "carpetbaggers," from Northern States, as officers to fatten on the spoils of war.

After Ames took forcible possession of the executive office he appointed Peres Bonney, an old citizen of Pike, Clerk of the Probate Court, ousting William M. Conerly, who had been legally elected. Bonney was a Republican and had been a member of the Black and Tan convention.

Levi D. Felder was ejected and superseded by the appointment of Charles B. Young as sheriff, a stranger to the people and an ex-Union officer, who, it was said, had commanded a negro regiment in the war against the South. Young was a Canadian Irishman, and was sent to Pike County by Ames to act as sheriff without bond.

His coming, under the circumstances, revived and stirred up the animosities of the people. His course in office, favoring negroes over whites and using them in the arrest of white people, intensified their animosity to a high degree. To be placed under the domination of negroes and held there by the powerful hand of the military was revolting, to say the least of it.

A man named Joseph W. Head, charged with the killing of Abraham Hiller, of Magnolia, was arrested by Young, assisted by negroes. Head was handcuffed by them and taken to prison. He had friends who sought revenge, as well as his release. After this Young mysteriously disappeared and was never seen nor heard of afterwards.

Various theories have been offered as to the manner of his taking off. The writer has traced all of them. The body of Charles B. Young never left Pike County. He was overhauled on the road leading from Holmesville to Magnolia and shot to death by men in sympathy with Head and with those he was sent to Pike County to oppress, and his body buried in a hole dug for that purpose in the southwest corner of Hardscrabble plantation, two miles south of Holmesville, and his grave can be located where mentioned.

It was discovered by the Board of Supervisors after Young's disappearance that he was defaulter in about twelve thousand dollars in warrants and money, about one thousand dollars in tax money. This was substantiated by inquiries being made by parties living in Canton, Miss., as to the value of these warrants on the market. Nothing was ever done toward their collection from the county, as the holders were advised that they had better not undertake it.

On one occasion, while making a speech, Governor Ames was asked by a man in the audience what about his sheriff Young in Pike County? His reply was: "I have information that the bones of Chas. B. Young are now bleaching in the Bogue Chitto Valley." The information obtained by the writer leads him to the conclusion that the usurping Governor was correct. It was a lesson to be duly heeded by him, as well as his successors. He saw the danger which threatened the commonwealth in his hands if he attempted to repeat the appointment of men not living in the county and not identified with its people, and it was a proof of the extremity to which men were driven to rid themselves of their oppressors and to counteract the desperate measures of the military authorities to overturn white supremacy and blot out Anglo-Saxon blood in the South.

James L. Alcorn being inaugurated Governor March 10, 1870, he reversed the policy of Ames. Governor Alcorn knew the temper of Mississippians, and his plan was to make appointments from the best who could meet the requirements under the Reconstruction Acts of Congress. He appointed Ansel H. Prewett, of Magnolia, as Young's successor, which gave general satisfaction.

This good man, while in the discharge of his official duties, conveying the prisoner Head to Vicksburg for safe keeping, until his trial could be had, was assassinated on the cars at Bogue Chitto Station, and his son, Elisha Prewett, and his deputy, W. L. Coney, wounded by Head's friends and rescuers, who held up the train for that purpose and all made their escape. It was said that they were formerly members of the noted Quantrell partisan rangers that operated in Missouri and the Trans-Mississippi.

At this critical period there was a man come to the front who exerted himself and wielded an influence to save Pike County from the scenes of blood that threatened it. Wherever Ames' policy was attempted to be carried out these chaotic conditions were multiplied. Negroes unaccustomed to being petted and given the hand of fellowship in equality with the white man, as they now were by the carpetbaggers and camp followers seeking their votes and their admiration, were growing insolent to those who had previously been their masters. This was a fatal step made by the powers at Washington. Had they left the negroes to be controlled by their late masters and gradually become acquainted with their new conditions the troubles would not have been so great. The efforts of their liberators to install them in the main offices of the government and to ecome the law making and law executing power was a thing too preposterous to be considered by the intelligence of the South. It was purely a fool's errand when the Government of the United States undertook such a task.

BENJAMIN LAMPTON
Of Tylertown
Appointed Sheriff of Pike County by Governor Alcorn
to succeed Ansel H. Prewett

W. H. Roane, a Presbyterian minister who resided in Magnolia, was elected to the Legislature in 1870, while Alcorn was Governor, and clung to the policy of Alcorn in appointing to office none but native or adopted white citizens whose interests were identified with the people.

With this policy carried out there would be less danger of a conflict between the races, which was daily threatening the entire commonwealth. Roane succeeded in having Benjamin Lampton appointed to succeed the lamented Prewett, and he appointed Peres Bonney Probate Clerk and Frederick W. Collins Circuit Clerk.

In 1871 an election was held. Wm. M. Conerly, Dem., was elected Probate Clerk and Fred. W. Collins, Rep., was elected Circuit Clerk, both serving until the fall election in 1875, when Conerly succeeded himself and Collins was succeeded by the election of Dr. A. P. Sparkman, who has held the office consecutively ever since.

Benjamin Lampton was succeeded in 1871 by the election of John Q. Travis, Rep., beating Robert H. Felder, Dem.

W. M. Conerly held the office of Probate Clerk until the fall election of 1879, when he was succeeded by the election of W. C. Vaught.

From the close of Ames' military administration, March, 1870, the expenditures of the State government were as follows:

In 1869, white rule...	$ 463,219 71
In 1870, negro rule...	1,061,249 90
In 1871, negro rule...	1,729,046 34
In 1872, negro rule...	1,596,828 64
In 1873, negro rule...	1,450,632 80
In 1874, negro rule...	1,319,281 60
In 1875, negro rule...	1,430,102 00
In 1876, white rule...	591,709 00

Here is a proof of the systematic robberies carried on by the powers of darkness and light mixed, and a proof of the utter incapacity of those forced upon the people to govern them, and the white people, not the negroes, had to meet these heavy expenditures.

The Reconstruction Act was a measure which disclosed all the venom that could be incorporated into a law, and with it came an army of adventurers in search of the spoils which they expected to obtain by the confiscation of property and by ingratiating themselves in the love and affections of the nation's wards. Adelbert Ames was the man to do their bidding, and when it became necessary to make appointments he favored those who were not of the manor born and gave to the newly enfranchised negro the same honors bestowed on the white carpetbaggers. Troops were quartered in different parts of the State to suit the necessities of the case upon the least complaint made by those in authority. A large body were kept at the State capital as a forcible reminder, and it was sometimes the case they were sent to places of public worship to overawe the people when ministers were dragged from the pulpit for declining to offer up prayers for the rulers and daring to protest against the wrongs perpetrated on the people.

As an illustration of the character of stories invented by the carpetbaggers to bring troops to places desired, the writer reproduces an article credited to the *Meridian Gazette*, printed in the *Magnolia Herald*:

"TERRIBLE VANDALISM IN JEFFERSON AND CLAIBORNE.

ALCORN UNIVERSITY DESTROYED—HORRIBLE DESTRUCTION OF HUMAN LIFE!"

"A body of White League Ku Klux from Louisiana, five hundred strong, well mounted and equipped with Winchester rifles and navy sixies, crossed the Mississippi River at Rodney, spreading terror and dismay to the peaceful inhabitants of that village. They moved upon Alcorn University, arriving there about daylight, where they are now bivouacked. Here have been enacted scenes at which humanity and civilization shudder.

"We are carried back to the days of cannibalism. This body of lawless invaders is under the command of Colonel Blood, a notorious desperado who has hitherto operated chiefly in Texas and Arkansas. As soon as they had tethered their horses and spread their tents in the beautiful groves of Oakvale, a detail of thirty men were sent into the chapel of the university, where all the pupils and professors were at prayers. Without a word they shot down the professors and pupils, and carried the little fat ones screaming to the camp. They alleged, amid coarse jokes and brutal laughter, that the old bucks were too tough for broiling purposes. They wanted tender steaks. When they reached the camp, these innocent youths were slaughtered and cut up into steaks and roasts, barbecued and eaten by the vandal host.

"Alas, that I should live to see a State in the American union relapse into cannibalism! I wish I had died before my eyes were blistered with such a sight, my ears pierced with such screams, my soul sickened with such horror! Alcorn University is no more! It has been eaten up by white cannibals.

"Not content with this terrible feast— this orgy of the demons—the same band are now scouring Jefferson and Claiborne Counties with blighting effect. All the tender little negro children are carried to the pot. They live only on human flesh and they are men of enormous appetites. An infant weighing twenty-five pounds will furnish food for one day for only four of these terrible gormandizers, and they all fastidiously refuse to eat tough meat. They shoot the men and drive the women in droves into the river, where, of course they are drowned. The colored population in this fertile but fated region has almost disappeared. This terrible band have killed six thousand men, drowned four thousand eight hundred and sixty women and eaten one thousand six hundred and seventy-five healthy children within the last five days.

"It is believed they have virtually cleaned out the illstarred Counties of Jefferson and Claiborne. Where they will now go, God only knows.

"It is believed in Jackson, in official circles, that the whole purpose of this Louisiana invasion was to intimidate the negro by a little so-called wholesome killing and eating and drowning, in order to enable the Democrats to carry the election. The facts have been presented to Governor Ames, and I understand the Governor will promptly despatch to the Attorney General of the United States and ask for troops. It is to be hoped he will succeed in getting the whole army of the United States in Mississippi, for all good citizens must deprecate such lawless and inhuman outrage as I have described.

"I send you this without signing my name, or indicating the place from which I write. Such is the reign of terror in this unfortunate section that my life would not be worth a button if it was known that I had given you these awful facts.

"P. S.—Since writing the above, I have visited the Southern portion of the State and find the same affairs existing there. In Wilkinson, Amite, Pike and Marion it seems as if the whole Ku Klux population of Northeast Louisiana, commonly known as the Florida parishes, had concentrated in these counties and are holding one grand barbecue of negroes. Such fearful and barbarous destruction of human life practiced there—it would seem past mortal description. At Rose Hill, in Amite County, they roasted seventy-five at one time and about two hundred of those Louisiana cannibals feasted on them; and out at a little place called Tylertown, in Pike County, where there are two water-mills, I am told they have been keeping about three hundred large sugar kettles stewing with negro hash, and then can scarcely supply the demand; and they tell me that the citizens in these localities have been thinking, for some time, of making application for troops. The fact is there is not a negro or white radical in this whole section of country that will dare to go to the polls unless the troops come, for Tylertown has always been noted for such remarkable events!"

The reader will understand that the above is a burlesque, but it is a fair sample of the reports circulated and presented to the authorities in order to induce the dispatch of troops to desirable points where there was any chance for the Democrats to carry the election, and there were thouasnds of people who actually believed the circumstances set forth in the above letter to be true, and it was a most excellent incentive to the military authorities to comply with the request. It may be safely said that truth is turned into burlesque by the ingenious framing of the *Gazette* article.

There was no fiction about the organization of the Ku Klux Klan, and the White League, nor in the determination of the white people of Mississippi and Louisiana to overthrow the regime of scandal that was besmirching the names of these great States. Side by side as sisters they had risen to a high fame and the destiny which awaited one must fall to the other. Their people were united by all the ties that could bind them to each other. It was a law of self-preservation that prompted them to act in harmony.

If the reader could see the inner chambers of the demon-like conclaves that secretly met in the night times everywhere when it was supposed all white people were asleep, they would be astounded. And with each of these secret negro carpetbag meetings held in some out of the way house, if you could look under you would see the figure of the Night Hawk of the Ku Klux Klan on duty, with his revolver in his hand, listening to the schemes concocted within. Nine out of ten of all the troubles that sprung up between the whites and the negroes were instigated at some of these secret meetings by the carpetbag politicians, inciting the negroes to acts that would bring trouble with the whites in order to have an excuse to apply for and bring troops into the county or precincts where elections were to be held.

The negroes were in a state of transition. When it was seen that they could be made to answer, as instruments to carry out the purposes of carpetbag freebooters, the plan was concocted and the negroes were made to bear the consequences to follow. The negroes were not to blame for these things, because they were led and controlled by white men who cared nothing for their welfare.

In Pike County the conditions were greatly ameliorated by the strong influence wielded over them by one man. Without this man there is no telling what may have been the fate of the negro in the county. His own people were as much concerned as the mass of citizens in the county in the careful control of the negro population under the new conditions. Many of his connections had been slave owners, and he belonged to a class of high respectability. He was too young to become a soldier in the war, but in his boyhood and young manhood he learned the lessons which should guide him for the right and he stood high in the estimation and friendship of Confederate soldiers who had safely passed through the war, as well as with all others who knew him.

On a little stream in the southeast portion of the county, where nature has given the sweetest hopes and the greatest joys to those who were ushered into life, a child was born whose ancestry was of a high class of Scotch people. In the morning of his life he imbibed from a Christian mother all the attributes of a pure and upright character. When the war closed he had not entered his majority, and when it became necessary to fit himself for higher duties he had to do so by his own exertions, as his father was unable to help him.

The name of Frederick W. Collins will go down to posterity as the one who saved his native county from the terrors of a race war. He had more influence over them than all the other Republicans in the county combined, and if he had not been firm with them and held them within his own grasp the doom of the negroes, wrought up by the influences of others, would have been sealed for the time in Pike County, and the day that W. H. Roane had him appointed Clerk of the Circuit Court, that day marked the salvation of the negroes in the county. If he had not thus been put forward it is likely no one else would have come to supply his place in the ranks of the Republican party, the bulk of which had no other influence over the negro than to incite him to wrong and to further their political schemes.

Fred Collins told them in their conventions that they knew not what they did, that they were "treading on coals of fire, which, if kindled to a blaze, would be the death knell of themselves and would sweep the negroes of Pike County from the face of the earth." He knew the temper of his Confederate soldier friends.

On one occasion when the feelings of the people were wrought up to an explosive point, one of the most dangerous and determined negroes was burning to begin a race war and was working his plans for that purpose, instigated by designing members of the radical party. Collins, being informed of it, immediately put a stop to it and informed his associates that such a thing should not be permitted to have encouragement. Another effort was made when the negroes attempted to dispossess the whites of their lands through the instrumentality of a set of scoundrels who came into the county under the pretense of locating the forty acres each of them was promised by the leaders of the Black and Tan government. This was an aggravating measure to stir up strife in order to compromise the white people and drive them to acts of desperation.

In this instance, as in others, the advice of Mr. Collins prevailed and trouble was happily averted.

Collins was a consistent conservative Republican, having at heart the best interests of the commonwealth, and as such he was in touch with the best people of the county; at the same time, by the force of his logic and influence, the negroes recognized him as their best friend and safest advisor, and he thus stood as a breakwater against race conflicts. The fact should also be recorded that no love existed between Fred Collins and the carpetbaggers.

FRED W. COLLINS.

Fred Collins was born on Magees Creek, or rather on Collins Creek, near its junction with the former stream in the southeastern portion of Pike County, on the 14th of September, 1846. His father was Chauncey Collins, of Scotch ancestry, a native of Salisbury, Connecticut, and came to Mississippi in 1842. His mother was Amelia Woodruff, who was a daughter of Elias Woodruff, a native of New Jersey, and Ailsey Collins, of Columbia, Marion County, Miss.

Fred W. Collins received his education in the common schools in the neighborhood of Tylertown. He grew up with the boys of his generation on Magees

Creek, a section of Pike County which has sent out into the world some brilliant self-made men. He was too young to enter into the Civil War.

At the age of twenty-three, on the 12th of January, 1870, he was married to Mary Elizabeth Smith, then eighteen years of age, a daughter of William Smith and Angeline Magee. William Smith was of German descent and a son

HON. FREDERICK W. COLLINS
Summit, Miss.
Collector of Port, Gulfport, Miss. From a late photograph.

of one of Pike County's original pioneers. Angeline Magee was a daughter of Sier Magee, who settled on Magees Creek, above the junction of Dry Creek with that stream, in 1811. It was from Sier and his brother Jeremiah that Magees Creek took its name. The Magees came from South Carolina; the Smiths came from Germany; the Collins and Woodruffs came from New England.

It was a very important epoch in the history of Pike County that brought Fred Collins to the front as a public man. It was the fiat of a necessity, and it was to save Pike County from carpetbagism. The Confederate soldiers were his warm personal friends. Governor Ames tried the experiment of appointing an alien Sheriff, who mysteriously disappeared. W. H. Roune, of Magnolia, member of the State Legislature, in support of Alcorn's policy of appointing native citizens (under the reconstruction acts) to office, had him appointed Circuit Clerk, to which position he was twice elected, while nearly all the other offices were filled by the election of Democrats. In 1870 he was elected Mayor of Magnolia and served as Deputy Sheriff under J. Q. Travis. He changed his residence to Summit and was elected by the Democrats of that town as its

VIEW ON F. W. COLLINS' FARM, LOOKING TOWARD THE JUDGE HOOVER PLACE, ON BOGUE CHITTO RIVER NEAR SUMMIT

Mayor. He held the office of postmaster of Summit for several years under appointment of President Hayes. In 1890 President Harrison appointed him United States Marshal for the Southern District. In 1892 he was a delegate to the Republican National Convention at Minneapolis, and a delegate at large to the St. Louis Convention. He was appointed Marshal by President McKinley in 1897. The Governor of Mississippi appointed him alternate commissioner to the World's Fair at Chicago.

Fred Collins was a Republican of wise and tactful conservatism, and an essential factor as such in Pike County, and occupies a conspicuous place in its history. There are few, if any, Republicans in the South who have been so warmly supported by Democrats and held office as long as he through their support. He knew how to be a Republican and at the same time merit the support of Democrats. Few men have such a record.

In June, 1900, he was sent as a delegate at large to the Republican National Convention at Philadelphia, that nominated McKinley and Roosevelt for President and Vice-President.

In 1904 he again served as a delegate from Mississippi at large in the Republican National Convention at Chicago, and supported Roosevelt and Fairbanks for President and Vice-President. He was also elected Chairman of the Republican State Committee, and assisted in managing the national campaign.

When Mr. Roosevelt succeeded to the presidency upon the death of President McKinley, he appointed Mr. Collins Register of the Land Office at Jackson, Miss. At the end of his four years' term, Mr. Roosevelt appointed him to the office of Collector of Customs for the District of Pearl River, in Mississippi, with headquarters at Gulfport.

Some of Mr. Collins' strongest political opponents have been his truest and sincerest personal friends. He has risen from circumstances in his career that called for peculiar merit and good ability.

The Clinton and Woodville riots, and the flame that burst out in Louisiana at Colfax, Coushatta, and other places leaped over the borders. The White League Ku Klux, as they were then termed, of Louisiana and Mississippi, were aglow with warmth and burning for action, and when it was seen that they would not submit to the efforts being made to Africanize their country, troops were stationed in every available locality to overawe them. In the county of Amite a deputy United States Revenue Collector had his headquarters and made it a special part of his duties to dodge about from place to place in order to create the impression that his life was in peril. He succeeded in having a detachment of cavalry sent to McComb City for the purpose of using them to intimidate the White Leaguers. These soldiers scoured the county for the purpose of arresting men who were under the ban of Ku Klux suspicion in forming associatoins to resist the government's policy.

A negro who had been a slave of the Sartin neighborhood, in the eastern portion of the county, assaulted his former master's young daughter while on her way to school and then cut her throat and left her for dead.

This brutal assault on an innocent and helpless child he had known from infancy, belonging to one of the first families of Pike County and descending from one of the first pioneers who came from the old historic State of Georgia and settled here, was an outrage which even to think of was revolting, much less the actual fact of the crime. In all the long years of slavery in Pike County no such a crime had been committed on a white girl by a negro, and when the news spread over the county among the people a body of determined men were ready to begin the work of extermination. It was a conclusion based upon this fact that led them to begin at once to rid themselves of a curse that was about to become their heritage. Knowing what would be the consequences to follow, the officers of the county promptly apprehended the negro and incarcerated him in a safe place until his trial could be had, which resulted in a verdict of assault and battery with intent to kill, and he was sentenced to the penitentiary for twenty years. The unfortunate girl recovered, but with the loss of speech for several years. From the very beginning of the outrages which cursed the South after the close of the Civil War, there was none perhaps which failed to meet its reward, but the public mind in Pike County has never been free from the stain it felt was left by not executing this negro at once.

Here the writer desires the indulgence of the reader for the purpose of referring to circumstances occurring in the sister State of Louisiana, which was felt by the people of Mississippi as concerning themselves.

A negro in Union Parish of that State was burned at the stake with the assistance of men of his own race, for a similar crime. He had been the outrager and murderer of a most estimable white lady and was caught, and after proof and confesson he was tied to a stake at the spot of his crime where his victim was found, and made to suffer death by cremation in the presence of over two hundred men. This lady, Mrs. Kidd, was the wife of one of the best young men in Union Parish and the mother of two beautiful children. Dragged from her horse while on the road to visit a sick neighbor in the afternoon, she was not seen again until found several days later chained to a tree, where she had been kept, and her brains knocked out.

There was another which occurred about the same time and which may be classed as the crowning of all outrages yet known in the annals of crime in this country.

In the Parish of Grant there lived a most estimable widow lady, Mrs. Lecour, who was the mother of a beautiful daughter seventeen years of age. They were relatives of one of the foremost families in the State of Louisiana and descendants of a high class of early Spanish and French settlers. Here in the midst of the presence of a body of United States troops under a Federal officer who bore the name of Colonel Decline, this young widow lady, with her daughter, were dragged from their home in the dead hour of night by nine desperate and brutal negroes and carried away into the adjacent swamp and there made to suffer the horrors of assault the whole night through, from which both died in a short while after being found by their friends.

When application was made to the officer in command of the troops at Colfax for assistance to arrest and punish the perpetrators of this revolting crime, he "declined," saying that he had come there for a "*higher* purpose." (?)

What action does the mind suggest to the reader when such outrages, so revolting in their nature, perpetrated in the very presence of United States troops, who were supposed to be there to protect the weak and defenseless and to keep the peace of the community?

When Colonel Decline, the commanding officer of these troops stationed at Colfax, refused the application for assistance to capture these criminals he was told that they would be caught and executed under his nose, if the State of Louisiana had to rise in solid mass and drive a devil like him from its borders to accomplish that end.

The news spread throughout the adjacent country with almost lightning rapidity. All through Rapids, Grant, Sabine and Natchitoches the news passed from house to house.

The organization that had been ushered into being and brought with it the flame that arose among the Scottish hills in the past came to the rescue to place the stamp of its order. Where was Decline's power then? Ask the little negro mulattoes rocked in the cradles of carpetbag concubinage in Grant Parish.

In the face of him and his troops and the "higher purpose" of his mission, these demons of his household were captured and made to suffer the penalty of their crime "under his nose."

And while these terrible crimes were being perpetrated on our white women by negroes upheld by Yankee troops, all the sympathy of Northern radical newspapers was given to the negro criminals and our white people assailed as barbarians for vindicating the wrongs, and the merciless power of the military invoked to punish them. Columbus Nash, the gallant young sheriff of Grant Parish, with his heroic posse cometatis of young men of Grant and Rapides, was hunted as an outlaw for trying to preserve order and protect the helpless.

When we go over the past and reflect we may wonder that there ever lived a people on earth who could be so controlled as not to rush into measures which might result into a sweeping destruction by again coming in conflict with the United States forces. This was one of the great characteristics of the Ku Klux Klan that stood forth to protect the weak and the helpless and to punish crime.

They were men who had been trained in war, recruited by youths of their own blood, and they were men who could control their own acts so as to avoid a conflict with the United States forces, yet they feared them not.

In all the cases where the negroes were concerned in these crimes they were or had been under the influence, openly and through secret channels, of carpetbaggers from the Northern States, who instilled in their minds that they were the special wards of the Government—the "children of Israel," led out of bondage by their Moses sent from God, cruelly assassinated in Washington, and by their Joshua who crushed the Philistines at Appomattox; that they were the masters now and could act with freedom as they regarded it.

The great riots of Grant Parish, where several hundred negroes were slain, and Coushatta, in Red River Parish, which resulted in the execution of the carpetbag leaders of that section, were the off-springs of Northern adventurers.

Referring back to the events connected with the negro government of Mississsippi the writer must be excused for indulging at length on these occurrences. They were the measures adopted by the carpetbaggers who came South to possess themselves of the wealth they thought existed among the white people, and they were men who believed the government would confiscate all the property of those engaged in the war on the Southern side and divide it out among those who had been instrumental in the overthrow of the Southern Confederacy; a concerted movement of rapine and plunder. This class of men put in their claims as deserving the rewards of the conqueror, and they were not scrupulous about how they obtained what they wanted. It mattered not to them if all the white people of the South were swept from the face of the earth, and they were men to do their dirty work through the ignorant negro.

The Southern armies had been overcome, and, returning to their homes, the Confederate soldiers cherished the hope of being able to retrieve their lost possessions, but within their hearts there was a spark of manhood left and it never became dimmed by anything that was offered by their enemies. The year following their capitulation was a time of deep distress among those dependent on them for the absolute necessities of life. They bore the indignities of the military rulers with a patience worthy of a race of freemen, but they never yielded a thought which they believed to be for their future welfare, and when the trying ordeal again came the reward of a faithful adherence to those principles which gave to them renewed hope and energy were realized.

A people that can be driven to the verge of desperation and then recover their lost liberties by the power of mind over matter are a people to stand the tests of any disaster. In the years that follow these events there will come to the surface conditions which will disclose all the virtues of a noble race. In the future there must rise a spirit which will animate them to the point of war or peace at all hazards, and in the conflict which shall be waged against the South's heroic warriors will come the requiem of a dead dynasty buried in its own polluted garments, which shall live in tradition and in history and story as the shame of the American Continent. For a more unholy piece of stupidity and oppression never cursed a people than the rule of the carpetbaggers and ignorant negroes, supported, defended and sustained by the military power of the Government of the United Northern States against the white people of Mississippi and Louisiana during this period.

It is well that the people of the South should persist in preserving the truths of history and keep before the civilized world the cruel enormities practiced upon them which their adversaries have endeavored to falsify and conceal from the rising generations, not only at the North, but in the South, and to force into the school books for the education of our children absolute falsehoods relating to events connected with the Civil War and the reconstruction era.

Under the fluttering folds of the vaunted star-spangled banner, held aloft as the emblem of freedom and hope and happiness for the oppressed of all nations, the very people whose genius made it famous, in what it represented, upholding it in times of peril, were made to suffer the most damnable coercion, subjugation and despotism, and to cover up their crimes against the South, blot out the records or mutilate history with glaring falsehood, while their poets feebly sing and their orators swell in recounting the "immortal deeds" of their invading armies whose vandalism was never equaled; fighting for FREEDOM, as the Hessians of England fought for it against us in the revolution of 1776, and in depopulating Nova Scotia of the unfortunate Acadians, scattering them along the bleak and wild gulf coast, as they fought for it in the subjugation of Ireland, and as the Spaniards fought for freedom in Cuba and elsewhere. Hundreds of books have been written and published by Northern men on events of the Civil War who have wilfully falsified the number of men enlisted and used in the subjugation of the South. The writer listened with amusement to an educated young man from the State of Michigan regaling a crowd of boarders on one occasion in the city of Wagoner, Indian Territory, on the history of the battle of Gettysburg, stating that there were forty thousand men killed on both sides in the battle, besides enumerating other wonderful things. Upon being asked where he learned that history he answered, "from an English Cyclopedia." His story was that Lee had 125,000 men engaged in the battle and Meade only 75,000, or thereabouts. He admitted he had never seen the "Rebellion Record," published by the Government. He asserted that the South had two million of men and the North had one million of men during the war. When I told him I happened to be present and "performed a part in that little skirmish" and corrected him with the official figures, more than he were struck with amazement. That if he would take off fifty thousand from Lee's forces and add them to Meade's he would come nearer to the truth of history; that the forty thousand included killed, wounded and prisoners captured on both sides.

It is well for the South to keep in mind the difference in the number of forces engaged, and for the benefit of those in whose hands this book may come in future years, I insert the following:

The South enlisted, all told, 600,000 men, which included those on post duty, hospital service and the men engaged in government service not actually on the field. From an article written by Gen. Stephen D Lee the following figures are gleaned:

"The North enlisted 2,864,272 men (not including three and six months' volunteers), giving them 2,264,272 men more than the South had altogether. To this must be added 600 vessels of war manned by 35,000 sailors used in the blockade of Southern ports, harbors and river warfare in support of their army. Against these marvelous odds the Southern armies fought for four years, successfully beating them back until by the casualties of war they were completely overpowered by the inexhaustible recruiting service of the Northern armies from Europe. There were only 100,000 effective Confederate fighting men for duty in the field when the war ended. The death roll of the Confederate armies numbered 325,000 men. They had contested every foot of ground against their enemies all over our beloved land on nearly two thousand battlefields.

"The death roll of the Yankee armies numbered 359,528 men, 275,000 of them buried beneath Southern soil.

"When the war closed the enemy had one million (1,000,000) men for duty in the field, or ten men to one Confederate, and a fabulous pension roll.

"The number of killed or mortally wounded of the Yankee Army in battle amounted to five per cent and the Confederates ten per cent of the numbers engaged, which is larger than any of the bloodiest wars of Europe, which has not been more than three per cent.

"In this great struggle the North owed its success to its continuous stream of recruits from Europe in quest of the $1,000 bounty and its ability to blockade our ports. If this contest had been narrowed down strictly to the two sections it is very questionable whether the South would ever been overcome; and it is left to the reader to judge if the Yankee armies have any room to boast of this prowess, or honors to claim in their invasion, and as to whether the judgment of the world is against them in favor of the South."

Bishop Charles B. Galloway, in speaking of this period some years later, said:

"The final test of Southern character was not displayed in laying the broad foundations of a new civilization; not in the solemn but tumultuous councils out of which was evolved our great system of government; not in the historic halls of State, where Titans struggled for mastery over national principles and policies; not in the splendid valor of her sons in the storm and red rain of terrific battle; not in the military genius of her peerless captains, pronounced by critics to be the greatest marshals of modern times; but in their serene fortitude and unyielding heroism and unconquerable spirit, after the storm of battle had ceased and they were left only 'the scarred and charred remains of fire and tempest.' Surpassing the splendor of their courage in battle was the grandeur of their fortitude in defeat. The sublime hour in the Southern soldier's life was the time of his pathetic home-coming. I have seen the painting representing the returned Confederate soldier, which, in my judgment, is not true to the facts of history. He stands, in tattered garments, amid the ruins of his home, the gate fallen from its hinges, weeds covering the doorsteps, leaning upon his old musket, with a downcast look and broken heart. As a matter of fact, he only waited long enough to greet the faithful wife whom he had not seen for four stormy years, and kiss the dear children who had grown out of his recognition, and then with grim determination put his hand to the stern task of reconstructing his once beautiful home, and rebuilding his shattered fortunes on other and broader foundations. Men of principle never falter, though they fail. They felt the bitterness of defeat, but not the horrors of despair. How those brave men, the sons of affluence, addressed themselves to the grinding conditions of sudden and humiliating poverty can never be described by mortal tongue or pen. And those pitiless years of reconstruction! Worse than the calamities of war were the 'desolating furies of peace.' No proud people ever suffered such indignities, or endured such humiliation and degradation. More heartless than the robber bands that infested Germany after the Thirty Years' War were the hords of plunderers and vultures who fed and fattened upon the disarmed and defenseless South. Their ferocious greed knew no satiety, and their shameless rapacity sought to strip us to the skin. As Judge Jere Black, with characteristic vividness and vigor, has said: 'Their felonious fingers were made long enough to reach into the pockets of posterity. They coined the industry of future generations into cash and snatched the inheritance from children whose fathers are unborn. A conflagration, sweeping over the State from one end to the other, would have been a visitation of mercy in comparison to the curse of such a government.'"

Such are the honors that go sounding down the ages the Yankee soldiers acquired in their so-called battle for liberty and the flag.

The Bishop further says:

"But no brave people ever endured oppression and poverty with such calm dignity and splendid self-restraint. And by dint of their own unconquerable spirit and tireless toil, they saw their beautiful land rise from the ashes into affluence. The South no longer 'speaks with pathos or sings miserere.' She has risen from poverty and smiles at defeat. Out of the fire and tempest and baptism of blood, our State has come, undaunted in spirit and unfaltering in the future. It is said that the green grass peacefully waving over the field of Waterloo the summer after the famous battle, suggested to Lord Byron, in his Child Harold, to exclaim:

" 'How this red rain has made the harvest grow!' So every battle plain that was once furrowed with shot and shell and wet with the blood of brothers, now waves with abundant harvest of a new and larger life. The refluent wave has set in. After a long and bitter night the morning dawns. 'It is daybreak everywhere'."

Following in the same line of thought Chief Justice Albert Hall Whitfield said:

"Cold in death our hearts must indeed be when they do not warm to our Tartan—the Confederate grey. What a civilization rushes upon our memory as we gaze upon you! We are with our ancestors of the sunny South of old! We see again that 'glorious loyalty to rank and sex,' that proud submission, that dignified obedience, that subordination of the heart, which kept alive, even in servitude itself, the spirit of exalted freedom. The unbought grace of life, the cheap defense of nations, the nurse of manly sentiment and heroic enterprise is there! And there, that sensibility of principle, that chastity of honor, which felt a stain like a wound, which inspired courage whilst it mitigated ferocity, which ennobled whatever it touched, and under which vice lost half its evil by losing all its grossness.

"It was a civilization which developed individualism; it magnified man, it enthroned woman. It imparted to the individual the sense of worth; the honor that preferred death to disgrace; fidelity to every trust; the sacred observance, as a matter of individual conscience, of every obligation, national, State and social, and it exacted of every official, from the highest to the lowest military and civil, that stainless standard of conduct, that lofty conception of public office as a public trust, which made every public servant tremble under the sense of responsibility, like the needle, into place. Cultivated, fired with the noblest patriotism, self-centered, used to power, the people of the South gave the United States, by this matchless statesmanship, a government strong in its justice at home, great in its dignity abroad, loved as the asylum of the oppressed of all lands, attracting at once the reverence and the affection of universal humanity. Such was the South in 1860. Illimitable wealth and boundless content were present everywhere. Her civilization was, in all that makes up the real blessings of civilization, the purest and loftiest time has ever yet known. Her people stood apart among the nations of the world. Their bosoms were the home of the most exalted honor. Whatever was mean, or low, or sordid, fled scorned from her borders. Majestic truth, imperial conscience, Olympian power, toned by the very courtesy of the gods, lifted its noble men and its glorious women far, far up, above the levels of all other civilizations. Content, happy, prosperous, moved always to splendid action by the highest ideal, if some god descending from superior worlds, in quest of the race most akin to his own, had swept with his vision the land of the South in 1860, he would have claimed us as his offspring, and here made his home. Soldiers of that elder and grander day, time and occasion do not permit reference to your achievements on the field of war. Rather let me hold in relief for the contemplation of your country a record nobler far than all the victories you have won.

"Other nations have greeted returning legions, victorious from the field, with triumphal arches, with marble monuments, with cheering thousands, with processions and bonfires; we, whose cause is said to have been lost, can bring alone the treasures of the heart.

"The Confederate soldier, when he left the final scene of surrender, passed before no reviewing stand, was greeted by the thunderous acclamation of no thousands and ten thousands of his fellow citizens, met no rejoicing multitudes on the way home, has since been sustained by no pension from the Federal treasury in his struggle with penury and want. I see the long, grey line melting back into private citizenship, when the sword of Lee was tendered.

" 'As some dark thunder cloud lowers upon the horizon, marshals its battalions and threatens all the landscape with ruin, yet is found, on the succeeding morning, in pearls of dew on flower and blade and grass, refreshing and beautifying God's earth,' so the Confederate soldier, after achieving immortal fame, and presenting the most matchless front that ever bore back invasion, became, when peace spread its banner o'er the land, the noblest, the safest, the surest citizenship that ever rescued civilization from night.

"Wearisome, I see him plod his way homeward. Finally, his eye rests upon the homestead, property all gone, in many instances blackened chimneys to testify how truly 'War is hell,' not a rose of the wilderness left on its stalk to tell where the garden had been. Does he murmur? Does he repine? Not so, my countrymen. He took up those burdens, he met those difficulties, the prospective statutes, the era of alien mastery and dominion. Repressing all tendency to lawlessness, restraining everything that passed the bounds of reason and prudence, curbing all passion in his onward march, he gradually but surely brought back, out of chaos, order

"From where Potomac's waters lave
  The tomb of Washington
To Rio Grande's distant wave,
  Beneath the setting sun,

the reign of beneficent laws.

"I know that McDonald led no grander charge at Wagram than did Pickett at Gettysburg; and I know that the bodies of dead Mississippians were found higher up that dread slope than those of any other State. I know that the awful shock at Chickamauga's field is not surpassed, if it is equaled, in the annals of tremendous and deathlike stubbornness of fighting. But, I tell you, my countrymen, that the grandest monument that the historian shall record, as rising in perpetuation of the name and fame of the Confederate soldier, is the record that he left through the days of reconstruction, the blessing which he gives us to-day of equal sisterhood in the union of States, with the privileges and laws and rights our fathers left us, intact and undiminished.

"But I want to ask, just here, the question: How far would the Confederate soldier have gotten in that magnificent effort if it had not been that he had beside him the inspiration of the Southern woman?

"Women of the South, you gave into his hands the banner of the free— you cheered and upheld him on 'the perilous edge of battle;' and when wounded or dying on the tented field, in the private home, in the hospital, you ministered to his wants, bound up his wounds, or closed the dying eyes, no more to see 'wife or friend or sacred home;' you were performing the very ministries of the angels themselves.

"It is a little thing to give a cup of water, but its draught of cool refreshment when drained by the fevered lips may give a shock of pleasure to the frame more exquisite than when nectarian juice renews the life of joy in happiest hours. It is a little thing to speak a word of common comfort, which, by daily use, has almost lost its sense, yet, on the ear of him who thought to die unmourned, 'twill fall like choicest music.

"There are those listening to me to-day who have ministered the comfort that should bring back to them the sweetest of memories. And when the war was over and the Confederate soldier returned, he was met not with reproaches, but with love, sustained by confidence, guided, upheld. God has so ordained that man may meet the brunt of some sudden storm, may live through and master some great crisis, but it is woman alone who can wear through the supreme crisis of individual or national life, by the endurance, the fortitude and the patience which she alone possesses.

"And so in the midst of the gloom, the women of the South rose resplendent to the occasion. She remembered that grief sanctified makes great. What, though she stood amid the wreck of desolated and dismantled homes, with the bright relics of princely fortunes strewn ruthlessly about her, the qualities of the eternal granite were integrated into her endurance. What, though her household Penates lay dashed to fragments on the hearthstone, her idols in the eternal silence, and the power of the despot attempted to bury in the grave of the slain the hopes of her country, set its seal upon the grave, rolled the rock upon the sepulchre and placed its watch. Her sublime faith has lived to see the resurrection angel of the South roll back the stone from the sepulchre, destroy the seal, break the fetters of political disability, shatter the bonds of industrial, agricultural and commercial subordination, and raise, radiant from the grave of the old, the figure of the new South, to stand in transfigured beauty, fronting the deepening glories of the Twentieth Century, 'like the winged god breathing from his flight.'

"She remembered that whatever was sublimest in the annals of Christianity looms o'er the ocean of time, like the Northern lights, more resplendent for the surrounding shadow of relentless persecution. She recalled that whatever is most glorious in the achievements of military heroes have been the triumphs of men who were cradled in storms and schooled by adversity. She remembered that whatever in literature is truly immortal, unvarying history proves the ripened products of intellects that have towered to the regions of perpetual sunlight, through atmospheres dark with clouds and tempests! And, remembering these things, she called her patience to her aid—she summoned her endurance to the tremendous task; she nerved the returning husband, father, or son, to the herculean task of the years that have just receded from us, and to-day, women of the South, if there be hope in this land it is due to your courage; if there be promise in the future it is the result of your faith; and if, my countrymen and countrywomen, if, I say, in the years that are to come, when we who stand under this evening sky shall sleep the dreamless slumber of the grave, when we shall no more be known amongst men, these Southern States shall fill with fifty millions of happy men and women—if the Isthmian Canal shall be gay with the merchantmen of every nation upon earth—if the Galveston of the future shall remember the Galveston of the tempest but as a nightmare dream; if New Orleans and Mobile and Savannah and Charleston and Wilmington and our own Gulfport and a hundred other marts shall become imperial 'cities, proud with spires and turrets crowned, in whose broad-armed ports shall ride rich navies laughing at the storm;' if, above all that, literature, and religion, and art, shall fill this land with temples and lyceums, and galleries glorious with immortal paintings and statuary, and with a knowledge universally diffused—if, I repeat, that glorious day shall come to this land we love, the land of the magnolia and the orange, the land of the mountain and the sea and of the tropic stars; the land of Lee and Jackson and of Davis; if the coming years shall bring these splendors to this clime, it will be due, women of the South, to the deathless fidelity with which you have held fast to the principles of justice and right and truth; immutable and eternal, because of the possession of which God has made the heart of woman, in every age, the last repository of the faith of every creed, and the patriotism of every land.

"Meet indeed it is, soldiers of the Confederacy, that your sons have determined to erect, in honor of the transcendent women of the South, whose inspiring patriotism made you in war the finest soldiery of time, whose love and sympathy and fortitude enabled you, through wreck and ruin, to preserve and perpetuate the liberties of your country, and who for forty years have annually covered the graves of your dead with flowers and tears of fadeless affection, a monument, the noblest in its proportions, the most exquisite in its carvings, the loftiest in its inscriptions, affection has ever reared to make virtue immortal! Let it rise in the purity of spotless white, against the dark background of our national sorrows, high up into the serene heavens! and through the ages to come, when garish day has gone, and with it the harsh clangor of commercialism, let the vast silence of the starry midnight steep it in holy, healing quiet!

"The Southland mourns her dead to-day
    And hangs a funeral pall
From Old Virginia's crimson plains
    To Pickens' gulf-girt wall.
Along her coasts, across her fields,
    And o'er her meadows fair,
She mourns to-day her chieftain dead,
    In earnest, sadd'ning prayer.
The humble and the low,
    The solemn sounds of heartfelt grief,
In fervent prayers now flow."

—*Emmet L. Ross.*

PEABODY PUBLIC SCHOOL, SUMMIT.

In 1868 one of the first public schools established in the State of Mississippi was located in the town of Summit. It was inaugurated under the provisions of the system devised in the will of the great educational philanthropist, George Peabody.

Rev. Barnas Sears, General Agent of the Peabody educational fund, visited Summit, and under an agreement for an equal amount of money to be raised by the people as an endowment for the support of an institute of learning, the Peabody School was established and its doors opened at the Episcopal rectory in November, 1868, which was leased for two years until a suitable building could be erected.

The Board of School Directors consisted of Wm. H. Garland, James B. Quin, James N. Atkinson, Thomas R. Stockdale and Chas. E. Teunison. Rev. Charles H. Otken, of Amite County, was chosen as Superintendent, with Mrs. Josephine Newton, Mrs. Mary B. Blincoe, Miss Emma Fourniquet and Miss Hattie Wicker, afterwards wife of Sheriff-Captain William McNulty, as teachers.

There were several causes that contributed to the difficulties in the beginning of this institution which were serious obstacles in the way of its Superintendent and teachers, as well as the authorities and citizen supporters of the town of Summit.

The country had been desolated by the war and there was a chaotic condition in the system of labor incident to the abolition of slavery. The farms had to be rehabilitated and agricultural industries made to prosper before other business or educational enterprises could succeed, except under the most trying circumstances. We were in the beginning of the ordeals of reconstruction. The Federal military were stationed in every county. Pike County had a negro military company stationed at its courthouse under an officer whose duties came under the plan of Thaddeus Stephens for the Africanization of the Southern States, which throttled the efforts of the people of Summit to establish the Peabody Public School in the beginning. But the men and women who were interesting themselves had passed through the crucible that tested their strength and their virtues, having lived through the flames of fire and the swelling streams of blood that characterized the Civil War.

After the first two sessions were over a handsome building, costing $5,000, was erected and the attendance rose from 142 in 1868 to 347 in 1871.

Among those already mentioned in connection with the institute will be found the names of C. L. Patton, Mrs. Annie Jackson, Miss A. T. Boyd, Miss Annie Flowers, Miss Octavia Johnson, Miss Annie Cunningham, Miss Ellen Hamerton, Miss J. B. Grant, Miss Caroline Augusta Lamkin, Miss G. Leonard, Rev. J. C. Graham, J. B. Winn, J. M. Sharpe.

Dr. Otken filled the place of Superintendent for nine years and successfully steered through the most difficult period of its existence. During the nine years of his services as principal the school directors were Wm. H. Garland, Thomas R. Stockdale, Jas. N. Atkinson, C. E. Tunison, J. L. B. Quin, I. Moise, W. A. Cotton, Wm. Cunningham, Dr. W. W. Moore, Gen. W. F. Cain, Chas. W. Bean, Ben. Hilborne, Rev. Wm. Hoover, Judge Hyram Cassidy, Sr., and after 1872 Col. Wm. Campbell and Mr. W. T. White served as members of the Board of Directors.

JUDGE HUGH MURRAY QUIN.

Judge Hugh Murray Quin was a son of Peter Quin, Jr., and Martha Catharine Moore. The Quins were from York District, South Carolina. Peter, Jr., married his wife in North Carolina. Her mother was a Miss Murray, whose brother was the author of Murray's Grammar.

They emigrated and settled in Holmesville in 1815, where Hugh Murray Quin was born on the 22nd of February, 1819, and where he grew up and was educated. In his young manhood he married Delilah Bearden. He settled on a farm purchased from Anthony Perryman, lying in the Bogue Chitto Valley, one mile and a half above Holmesville, where he lived, acquiring considerable property in land, slaves and stock. He was for many years clerk of the court at Holmesville and was admitted to the practice of law. During the Civil War he filled the position of Probate Judge, and after the close of the war, when county courts were established, he occupied the bench as Judge of that court, but was put out by order of the military and superseded by the appointment of Judge T. E. Tate. He afterwards, through the solicitation of the people, moved to the town of Summit, and was elected to the office of Mayor. At the expiration of his term he returned to his plantation near Holmesville, where he remained until his death in 1900.

With Delilah Bearden he raised the following children: Dr. Lucius M Quin, who married Courtney Magee; Wallace W. Quin, who married Neelie Williams; Emma Eoline, who married Luke W. Conerly; Lula, who married Charles H. Rowan; George, who married Alla Irvin.

Judge Quin was left a widower by the death of his wife in 1867, and subsequently married Nannie Sumrall, of Copiah County. With her he raised two children—Henry and Ina.

After returning to his plantation from Summit in the early seventies, he filled the position of justice of the peace for his district up to the time of his death, about twenty-seven years.

He was as well posted in the laws of Mississippi as any man who ever lived in Pike County. He was an excellent probate judge and practitioner in chancery. He was the soul of honor, broad minded, liberal to a fault, true in friendship, sympathetic, loving and kind, and his home was noted for being the place of unbounded hospitality, where the humblest wayfarer could always find a night's lodging and the hungry were never turned away from his gate unfed. He was a warm-hearted, devoted husband. He loved his own children tenderly and those who became members of his family by marriage. He was religious and a devoted member of the Methodist Church, and a Mason of high standing. He was sought far and near for advice, which was freely given, and few men have lived in Pike County whose death was more regretted and whose loss was more keenly felt. He died in the Christian faith, without a blemish upon his name or his character.

THE BURRIS MAGEE TRIAL.

One of the most noted criminal trials that occurred in Pike County after the close of the Civil War was that of J. Burris Magee, of Wilkinson County, charged with the killing of Connover in Summit. Magee had been a conscript officer in the service of the Confederate Government. A difficulty arose between the two men at the depot, Connover using violent language in the abuse of Magee. The latter withdrew from the depot, followed by Connover, who was armed with a heavy stick. Magee drew his revolver and leveled it at Connover, telling him to keep back, at the same time retreating across the street. As Connover advanced Magee fired one shot at his right arm with a view of stopping him, but he continued to advance with his uplifted club. Moving backward Magee stumbled in a ditch and fell, and as Connover with his stick raised over him, in his prostrate condition, Magee fired on him again, and killed him. The grand jury of Pike County indicted Magee for murder, though the preliminary examination disclosed the fact that it was not necessarily so, and he was given bail.

Magee secured the services of three of the most noted lawyers in South Mississippi, Judge Simrall of Wilkinson, Judge Hyram Cassidy of Franklin, and John T. Lamkin of Pike. It was as fine a legal team as could have been selected in the State.

At the trial the State was represented by H. F. Johnson, District Attorney, latterly President of the Whitworth College at Brookhaven, and Rev. W. H. Hartley, a Methodist minister, belonging to the Mississippi Conference, who felt it his duty and volunteered to assist in the prosecution of the case. The trial excited widespread interest. Judge Simrall's part of the programme was to dwell upon character, the reputation of the defendant and his people in the past. John T. Lamkin was to proceed on evidence and the testimony of witnesses in the case, and Hyram Cassidy was to close the defense with his inimical witticism, anecdotes and ridicule. The destruction of the court records by fire in Magnolia rendered it impossible to give the names of those concerned in the trial and the writer gives it entirely from memory, being present from first to last.

Judge Simrall's speech on character, in which he alluded to Judge Magee, the defendant's father, in Wilkinson County, a Christian gentleman and devoted adherent of the Methodist Church, whose house was always open for the hospitality of its ministers, was one of the finest ever delivered in the Pike courthouse. John T. Lamkin, in the magnitude of his superior genius on testimony and evidence, eloquence and moral influence, stood for three mortal hours before the jury in defense of a client who had acted solely in self-defense. Judge E. McNair was on the bench. A compact mass of humanity filled and surrounded the courthouse.

Judge Cassidy followed "Brother Hartley," as he spoke of him in the beginning of his address to the jury. All of his witticism, invective, anecdotes and ridicule, condensed and doubly distilled, as only Hyram Cassidy could do it, was hurled at "Brother" Hartley." He told the jury how the "Brother" had so often received the hospitality of Burris Magee's father, whose beautiful character Judge Simrall had portrayed, said grace at his table and eat the food his beloved and Christian mother had prepared for him, accepted his money and shared in the support he had given his church, and in the plentitude of his gratitude he had come here and volunteered his services in the prosecution of Judge Magee's son for doing only that which was the first law of nature, self-preservation.

Judge Cassidy stated, in closing his address, that out in Franklin County there was a certain cross roads where there was a whisky shop, a blacksmith shop and a race track, to say nothing of other matters that men indulged in where grand jurors were not generally allowed as guests or participants. About a mile west of this place was a farmer who had some noted breed of pigs, not long ushered into existence. About the same distance east of the cross roads was another farmer who wanted a pair of those pigs and had spoken for them. He owned an old negro named Ben. At the cross roads grocery the proprietor owned a gip that had recently presented the establishment with a hamper basket full of puppies. So neighbor Jones sent Ben over to neighbor Smith's with a basket to bring him the pair of pigs he had spoken for.

Ben stopped at the grocery, and in order to get a few dashes of "de side shuffle," and "de piggin whing," the boys gave Ben a good jigger of red eye, who, of course, was free to tell them what he was going over to Mr. Smith's for.

Ben went over and got a pair of the pigs from neighbor Smith, put them in his basket and tied a sack over them, but was inately persuaded to stop over at the cross roads for another drink, and while he was doing the dancing act to the old familiar tune of "Hogeye" the boys made the exchange and put a pair of puppies in Ben's basket in place of the pigs.

When Ben got home he was gladly welcomed by his good master Jones.

"Well, Ben, have you got my pigs?"

"Yasser, Master, and dey's fine pigs, too, dat dey is!"

Ben opened the basket.

"Why, Ben, these are puppies. I told you to bring me a pair of neighbor Smith's fine pigs."

Ben's eyes dilated. "Fore God, dey is puppies, fur a fac, but dey wus pigs when I put em in dar."

"Go back and tell Mr. Smith I want pigs, not puppies."

Ben shouldered the basket, but was again inclined to stop at the grocery.

"What's the matter, Ben?" asked the boys.

"Gwine back to Mr. Smith to git dem ar pigs Master sont me fur. When I got home wid em dey wus puppies."

The boys entertained Ben with another jigger and "old Jim Crow," while the puppies were exchanged for the pigs, the basket covered again and Ben sent on to farmer Smith.

"What's the matter, Ben, don't want the pigs?"

"Oh, yasser, Master says he wants de pigs, but dese is puppies."

"Take the cover off, Ben, and let me see," said Smith. "There, you dam fool nigger, don't you see they are pigs?"

Ben was astonished. "Fore God dey *is* pigs, but dey wus puppies when I got home wid em."

The same trick was repeated at the cross roads, and when Ben got home the second time and opened the basket there were the puppies. Farmer Jones got wrathy and told Ben to take them back. Ben was outwitted, but after a moment's philosophizing he raised himself up and said, "Master, fo God, if I wus you I wouldn't hab nutting to do wid dem tings. I fotch em here and deys puppies, I take em back and deys pigs; dey kin be eider pigs *or* puppies."

And, gentlemen of the jury, said Cassidy, this is the deplorable condition in which we find "Brother" Hartley. He can be either pig or puppy, and has acted both in connection with this trial. A minister of God's word, sharing the kindness and hospitality of this defendant's home, the tender ministrations of his devoted Christian mother, and then volunteers to prosecute her son and place the hangman's noose about his neck for doing that which he himself would have done under similar circumstances—to save his own life, take that of his antagonist, if he had a spark of manhood about him.

Magee was justly acquitted, but the previous record and notoriety of Pike County jurors in cases of the killing of a human being by another made it doubtful. There was a splendid animal standing near the public square waiting the verdict, which nothing in Pike County could overtake, in case its rider felt the necessity of fleeing from a cruel and unjust verdict.

David W. Hurst, who was a regular attendant of the Holmesville courts, was a citizen of Liberty, Amite County, in the zenith of his career as a lawyer. He was a man of great ability, and while a warm personal friend of John T. Lamkin he was usually his opponent in great contests before the courts in Holmesville, and more particu-. larly in cases against the New Orleans, Jackson & Great Northern Railroad Company. He was a persistent and stubborn fighter and full of sarcastic wit. He was a warm personal friend of Judge John E. McNair, but disliked one of the Chancellors (Berris), before whose court he had considerable practice. On one occasion they had a case up in which the rights of a girl minor were involved, and her advocate asked the Chancellor if she were entitled to a sewing machine. The Chancellor hesitated and stammered sew—sew—machine—machine—and asked one of the other lawyers if she did and he could tell. Hurst spoke up and said yes, of course she has, and then he casually remarked that the Chancellor was all right now, as he had something with peddles he could work with his feet, and didn't need any brains.

On one occasion he was examining a negro witness about a fight and asked what the man hit the other one with.

"With his fist," said the witness.

Then what did the man he hit with his fist do?

"Why, he retreated backward," was the answer.

Hurst, in commenting on the testimony of the witness, said he had often heard of retreats, but this was the first time he had ever heard of a retreat being made backwards.

After the close of the Civil War, Joe Tuff Martin engaged in the mercantile business in Magnolia in partnership with Capt. Jo. Miller.

Joe Tuff got into a scrap with Gen. William Cain. The General was too big a man for him and got him down and Joe fought and bit and scratched all he could and the best he knew how, until some of their friends pulled the big General off of little Joe Tuff. When Joe Tuff got up he said, "Well, by golly, I can say what no other man is able to say, and that is I am the only man who ever fought under General Cain, a distinction, by golly, that belongs only to Joe Tuff."

A negro named Martin Russell, who had served in the Yankee army, settled in Magnolia. He was a man of fairly good education and knew how to cultivate the friendship of the white people in order to further the interests of Martin Russell. He lived there during the exciting political campaign of 1876, and was used by the Democrats in the organization and leadership of negro Democratic clubs. Martin thought he could see that the future feathering of his nest depended largely on that of a brush pile, and to be set up in business, which he was after the campaign was over, but eventually failed and had to fall back on his book learning for a livelihood and engaged in school teaching for his race. His school grew so large that it became necessary for him to have an assistant. He was a good judge of human nature and was urged to go before the Board and plead his case for an assistant teacher, and he did so, making a forcible and polite address before that body, which it was decided by hearers would be effective and secure what he asked.

When he came out of the courthouse he was complimented on his sensible and forcible address by some of his white friends, who believed his speech was convincing and that he would get what he asked.

"I don't know, gentlemen," said he, "this Board aint got on any drawers," and he failed, as he expected.

Prior to 1861 Holmesville was a great place for horse racing. On one occasion a man came riding down Main Street from Louisiana leading a little long-haired, flop-eared Creole pony. The California House, which was then in its prime, had its complement of loafers and customers. Passing this place some one asked the stranger what he was going to do with that long-haired goat.

"Never mind about the goat, it can win all the money any of you may have to risk on a race."

The stranger put up his horses at Wm. Johnson's livery stable and stopped at his hotel, and then sauntered leisurely out on the streets and about the California House and got up some talk on horse racing. He boldly remarked, while in a drinking mood, that he would put up his "goat" pony against anything in the town on a quarter dash, wheel and go, without bridle or rider, and the boys took him up. Saturday was the day fixed for the race.

Eugene Weathersby had recently bought a large, long, active Tennessee horse from a drove, and the Holmesville sports decided to put this horse against the pony on the day of the race. The news got out in the country and the town was crowded. There was an old field below town and a level stretch from Owen Conerly's mill on the river below, and this was the place selected to make the run.

At the appointed hour Weathersby's horse was trotted out with one of the best jockey riders on his back. A little boy came afterwards leading the sleepy looking pony with a halter on and a red girth around its body.

Two to one on the horse, and bets went flying through the crowd that came in from the country. Hundreds of dollars were put up and the Louisiana stranger took every bet he could get offered against his pony.

After all the preliminaries were arranged the animals were taken down to the mill to make the start, the stranger leading his pony. They were placed in position with their heads in the opposite direction from which they were to run. At this moment the pony opened her eyes and cut them back in the opposite direction. Her master patted her on the neck and spoke a few words of kindness to her and she nerved herself for the contest. Weathersby's horse had won considerable money in other races and his backers felt sure of an easy victory. The owner of the pony unhooked the halter rein and at the word "Go" the pony reared and whirled on her hind feet and shot off like an arrow and was a hundred yards away before Weathersby's horse got fairly started, and as she ran out at the judges, stand, 300 feet in the lead, she kicked up her heels and, circling the grounds with wild prairie style, came trotting back to the stand.

CHAPTER VII.

NEWSPAPERS.

In 1840 Henry Smith Bonney first entered a newspaper establishment as apprentice in the office of A. W. Forsyth at Liberty, in Amite County. He was a son of Nancy Floyd and Perez Bonney, who were married at Soco, Maine, May 16, 1819, and immigrated to Holmesville in 1831.

Their children were William, Henry Smith, Samuel, Joel and Harriet, who married Major Gibson, and twin daughters, Mary Louise and Martha Elizabeth, dying young.

Perez Bonney was born in the Province of New Brunswick November 26, 1797.

Henry Smith Bonney married Miss Evelyn French Adonis, daughter of J. Q. Adonis and Pella Experience Davy, of Massachusetts. She was a sister of Lucy Whitmore Adonis, the wife of Curlette and then Henry Francis, the carriage maker at Holmesville, and subsequently the wife of Joseph Page.

NELSON P. BONNEY
Summit Sentinel

After serving his apprenticeship for two years at Liberty, Henry S. Bonney, in 1842, established a newspaper business for himself at Holmesville, calling it the *Holmesville Whig*, then the *Quarto Whig*, and later the *Planters' Free Press*. In 1847 he went to New Orleans and worked on the *New Orleans Bee* and the *Commercial Bulletin*.

In the meantime Barney Lewis and Robert Ligon established the *Southron* at Holmesville.

In 1851 Henry S. Bonney, after his marriage, returned to Holmesville and for the next two years was employed on the *Southron*, when he bought the material of the office and established the *Holmesville Independent*, which he continued up to 1862, when he joined the Holmesville Guards, organized by John T. Lamkin, who became Captain of the Company and was attached to the 33d Mississippi Regiment under Col. David W. Hurst, C. S. A. In 1869 he moved to Osyka and started the *Reporter*.

After the railroad entered the county and depots were located, John Waddill established the *Grand Trunk Magnolian* at Magnolia. This was succeeded by the establishment of the *Magnolia Gazette* by J. D. Burke.

After the close of the Civil War Fleet T. Cooper established the *Summit Times*, which subsequently fell into the hands of Capt. John A. Crooker and changed from a Democratic to a Republican paper. Crooker sold it to William H. Garland, Jr., who conducted it in the interest of the Republican party in 1875.

In 1870 Henry S. Bonney discontinued the *Osyka Reporter* and moved to Magnolia and began the publication of the *Eureka Centralian*. This enterprise, like its predecessor, was short lived and he moved everything to Summit, which was aiming to become the leading town in the county, and here he established the *Summit Sentinel*, which still lives as the grandchild in the fifth degree of the *Holmesville Whig*.

Henry S. Bonney was the pioneer editor and newspaper man of Pike County. He possessed persistent and staying qualities and was an acknowledged able and fluent writer, and down to the present time, for sixty-three years, his name and the influence of his papers, through his own long term of services, and that of his son, Nelson P. Bonney, has been associated with Pike County, the latter with the *Sentinel* for thirty-four years, but in fact with his father's business from childhood on the *Holmesville Independent*.

Henry Smith Bonney and Evellyn French Adonis were the parents of the following children: Nelson P. Bonney, editor *Summit Sentinel;* Mrs. E. E. Lavison, Washington, D. C.; Mrs. W. T. Head,

Terry, Miss.; Miss Flora A. Bonney, Summit; C. D. Bonney, New Orleans, La.; R. M. Bonney, Terry, Miss.

Nelson P. Bonney's wife, whom he married in 1881, was Miss Alexis A. Fournieque, of New Orleans, La.

In 1875 Luke W. Conerly, who was editing the *Amite County Democrat*, in Amite City, Tangipahoe Parish, La., was urged, by his old comrades and friends in Pike County, to establish a partisan campaign paper at Magnolia to aid in the defeat and overthrow of the Republican regime that had held sway since the close of the Civil War. He had for the previous eight years been connected with the stirring events of Louisiana in the struggle of her people during the reconstruction era and was at this time an adherent of the John McHenry State government, and was at the time commander of a company of young men at Amite City training for service in support of the White League. Louisiana was making the great struggle of her life and so was Mississippi to re-establish the supremacy of white rule now under the dominating power of Republican carpet-bag-negro rule, supported by the military of the United States Government over the Southern States.

Yielding to the solicitations of his friends, he bought an old extinct newspaper outfit at Ponchatoula, La., and shipped it to Magnolia. He was given a room in the store of Cornelius C. Gibson, and with the assistance of James Ballance, an experienced printer, on the 17th of September, 1875, he issued the first number of the *Magnolia Herald*, and continued as its proprietor and editor until 1878, when he sold it to Henry C. Capell and Charlie Lee. J. D. Burke afterwards got possession of the office material and revived the old *Gazette*.

In 1875 the *McComb City Intelligencer*, devoted to immigration and industrial pursuits, was established with W. H. Townsend as editor.

After the overthrow of the Republican regime in the county the *Summit Times* was consolidated with the *Sentinel* under the name *Times-Sentinel* and subsequently changed back to the *Summit Sentinel*.

Richard B. May, a little lad, picked up a card press in 1874 and procured some cards and paper and printer's ink, with a few words of encouragement from this writer, and began his newspaper career. He afterward drifted to New Orleans and learned book binding, and later on established the *McComb City Enterprise.*

After J. D. Burke's last venture with the *Magnolia Gazette* it was owned and edited by John S. Lamkin. It then became the property of D. M. Huff and from him it passed to H. H. Norwood.

CHAPTER VIII.

In Louisiana, a detachment of Federal soldiers, under one Colonel De Trobiand, marched into the legislative halls of that State, while in session, and forcibly ejected Louis A. Wiltz and Robert L. Luckett therefrom, at the point of the bayonet, without a substance of reason except that they were Democrats and dared to expose the infamy of those in control of the State government; and, in 1875, the further outrage of driving Governor John McEnery out of the executive office, to which he had been duly and legally elected by a majority of over 14,000 votes, and installing William Pitt Kellogg, an imported politician, were so criminal in their nature as to arouse the white people of Louisiana to a state of revolution. These circumstances, being a repetition of the scenes perpetrated in Mississippi, instigated by the most infamous designs on the liberties of the people, and the threatened destruction of their racial character, were the means of bringing to the front the perfect manhood and intellect of the two States.

Away from the scene of action one could not realize the efforts of those whose homes were involved and their masterful self-control. They had resisted every attempt to Africanize their States, and while doing so, carefully avoided coming again in conflict with United States troops, which was the only hope of the negro-carpetbag element. They could create a revolution in their own States and struggle on until the future should develop something to give relief. Nothing but the full power of the United States army among them could stay their determination to drive our their oppressors. Politically the negroes were a unit.

The White League and the Bulldoozer organizations were formed in both States, the latter being more on the order of the Ku Klux Klan. This organization had its origin in the early seventies, and was composed of the agricultural element of the country, whose property had been so repeatedly depredated on by thieves. They were unable to get redress through the courts in numerous instances, and, as a means of self-protection, they banded together and hunted down the criminals and punished them in their own way, which, in most cases, was done by a vigorous application of the bull whip; and "bull-whipped" got to be a common phrase and a common remedy to punish depredators on the live stock and fowls of the farmers.

In the roll of the Summit Rifles, recorded in this book, will be found the name of Louis Wagoner, who served through the war in Virginia as a Confederate soldier. He was a blacksmith and was living in the town of Clinton, in East Filiciana Parish, La., at the inception and beginning of the organization of Bull Whippers. Becoming irritated with some one on an occasion when he was in his liquor, he remarked: "Tam him, I'll bull dosch him." The word then grew to bulldose, then bulldoozer, and lastly bulldozer. This organization was a strong one and existed in the Florida Parishes of Louisiana and in the southern counties of Mississippi. It was made up principally of farmers, or those engaged in agricultural pursuits, and originated purely and simply for mutual self-protection of each other from the depredations of thieves and criminals. It has been wrongfully charged against the merchants of the Florida Parishes of Louisiana and of the Southern counties of Mississippi that they were responsible for this on account of their oppressions of the farmers and greed for gold, by driving them into such an organization. This proposition is simply one of theory set up by those who are practically unacquainted with the facts. It was natural for every merchant in Pike County and elsewhere to try to benefit his financial condition, and, being men of business experience, they knew their own welfare depended on the welfare of the intelligent farmers of the country. While there may have been a few cases of unjust and oppressive dealings which invited retaliation from the Bulldozer organization, or members of it, the fair minded, impartial reader will scarcely entertain the proposition that the merchants, on account of their worship of the god—gold, can be held responsible for this organization. In its very inception this writer became familiar with all the causes and fretful conditions which led to the necessity of a unity of action among neighborhoods to protect themselves from criminals. He got right in among these people at the time in East Filiciana, St. Helena, Tangipahoe and Washington Parishes and elsewhere, consulted with them and learned from their own lips the causes which made them feel the necessity of an organization which would give security to their property and their families. Arm chair philosophers, ministers of the gospel and newspaper theoretical writers, have been misled themselves and have indulged in false theories and given current circulation to false publications against the Bulldozer organization of South Mississippi and the Florida Parishes of Louisiana. A theory based on false premises is more sinful and has a more deplorable effect than the acts reputed to the Bulldozers. The writer is not summarizing on hearsay nor theory. There is a difference in obtaining facts by mixing with the operators, and basing conclusions upon reports received from afar off. In these days the country was flooded with criminals of all classes—whites as well as negroes. Horse-stealing, cattle and hog-stealing, and sheep-stealing pervaded the land

Negro camp meetings became a chronic disease; their zeal and enthusiasm in religion was encouraged by ministers of the gospel for their good. Their camp meetings extended through weeks at a time, becoming an unbearable nuisance, at which time the chickens, hogs and cattle of the white farmers who needed their labor were conspicuously thinned out. It was freedom, and these imitating worshippers assembling in large bodies for weeks at a time, must be fed, and they had little of their own to subsist upon; and while the mass of them were supposed to be conforming to the well-wishers of the various denominations, squads were scouring the surrounding country at night, doing the commissary act on chicken roosts and corn cribs, cattle herds, sheep ranches and pig sties. In one immense gulley in East Filiciana was found the heads of one hundred and fifty cattle, thrown in there by these negro camp meeting love feasters, stolen from the planters and farmers in the vicinity. The writer afterwards worked one of the leaders of this gamg on a sugar plantation in Louisiana.

The frequent mysterious disappearance of stock and products of the farm during these religious revelries made it necessary for the farmers to get together and make investigation and devise ways and means to check, if not entirely break up, these depredations. They were traced to the correct source and the farmers saw it was necessary to have some unity of action, and hence, formed into squads, and, as these criminals could not be reached with any certainty of punishment by the courts, they resorted to the whipping post, and to secure themselves against legal process for taking the law in their own hands, it became obligatory upon all the neighbors to become members of the law and order society. Hence the Bullwhippers—hence the Bulldozers. This organization continued to grow, but its inception and formation had no relation to the merchants at the time, nor to any political motive. It afterwards drifted in that direction and became identified with the White League. The White League organization was formed in every parish in Louisiana, its purpose being to overthrow the carpetbag and negro rule of the State.

In the State of Mississippi, in the fall of 1875, there was to be an election to fill the offices of State Treasurer, members of Congress, District Attorneys, State Senators, Representatives, Sheriffs, Chancery and Circuit Clerks, and on down, for all the county and precinct offices, and it was determined that no means should be spared to bring about a sweeping victory for the party supported by the native white people.

A long time had elapsed since the close of the Civil War and the carpetbag-negro government was held over them only by the power of military authority. At the close of the war they were powerless, but in the course of time, through agricultural means, they had become strong and self-reliant and were prepared to undertake a more radical course, and when the campaign of 1875 came on they were prepared to furnish proof of the power of intelligence over ignorance, vice and stupidity.

The removal of the court house from the town of Holmesville was a question which had agitated the entire population of Pike County, and one which created a strong enmity between two of the railroad towns. The main issue on this question was its central locality. The question was sprung as to the center of population, the railroad people holding that the western portion of the county, being more thickly populated, should have the court house, and the eastern people declaring that it should remain in its present geographical center, declared by law to be the permanent seat of justice.

Summit, which had acquired a larger population than any other town, was anxious to have the court house moved to that place. McComb was in its infancy, and, being made up largely of an immigrant population, was not in a position to make contention. Magnolia wanted it and Osyka, being in the extreme southern part of the county, favored Magnolia. The election decided in favor of Magnolia. The Board of Supervisors rented an old frame building in the lower part of town, near the railroad avenue, and had the records moved from the old clerk's office at Holmesville, and then the quarrel began over the insecurity of the records. The Board of Supervisors proceeded to advertise for the building of a new court house and for the issuance of bonds for the payment of the same. The town of Summit contended that the county was unable to build a new court house and an injunction suit was instituted, which was carried to the Supreme Court, but the removal of the court house and the proceedings of the Board of Supervisors were sustained. During this time the fever of animosity between the two towns had risen several degrees above the normal and the two were so stirred up as to make it absolutely unpleasant for a person living in one town to visit the other. The women even caught the infection and would toss their heads and shake their skirts in derision at each other, which was very hurtful to those of a tender and sympathetic nature. Society functions, in which our Southern women of aristocratic mould took delight, were greatly interfered with by this unhappy state of affairs, as a woman of one of the towns might refuse to take part or participate in, if a woman of the other had anything to do with it.

This was a local condition existing at the beginning of the campaign of 1875, and when the Executive Committee of the Democratic party began its preparations for the November election the county was in a turmoil over the court house question.

A recent edict of the Republican party indicated that a system of intimidation, as in the past, would be inaugurated, and then the Democrats, Bulldozers and White League determined to overthrow the negro-carpetbag government at all hazards, "peacefully if possible, forcibly if they must," and a regularly organized system of work was determined on.

One important thing was necessary to be done to insure success and to prevent the bloody scenes which were sure to follow, which was the immediate disbandment of Ames' negro militia, then under arms to intimidate them.

On the 13th day of October, 1875, in the town of Osyka, a meeting was held and addressed by David W. Hurst and Isaac Applewhite.

A set of resolutions were adopted and a club formed as an initial move to aid in the coming election. The club was composed of all the best men in the town and was the first to enter the campaign. Isaac W. Cutrer was elected its President and Joe Mallett its Secretary.

On this same day it so happened, by pre-arrangement, that a conference was held by a committee of citizens of different sections of the State, and Governor Ames, in the city of Jackson, when it was agreed that all the militia should be disbanded at once. This was a measure preconceived by the White League and which alone would prevent a bloody revolution throughout the entire commonwealth.

When the people of Pike County put out their ticket it was not certain how the election would terminate. It was so uncertain that a well organized party was necessary.

John S. Lamkin, who was Chairman of the County Executive Committee, issued a call for a meeting of the committee on the 15th of October, two days after the organization of the club at Osyka and the conference meeting at Jackson. The success of the party in Pike was so uncertain it was thought best to make an effort to employ or secure the services of a newspaper to be located at the seat of justice, if possible, to aid in the campaign.

In the town of Summit *The Sentinel*, edited and published by the able veteran pioneer newspaper man of Pike, stood alone. The Summit *Times*, established in 1866 by Fleet T. Cooper, had fallen into the hands of Capt. John A. Crooker, who converted it into a Republican paper. He sold it to William H. Garland, Jr. Garland had been associated with the Democratic party, but took up the *Times* in the interest of the Republican party and became a candidate for the State Senate. He was a son of William H. Garland, Sr., one of the original founders of the New Orleans, Jackson & Great Northern Railroad Company, now the Illinois Central Railroad Company, a leading man in this great enterprise and the first man to build a handsome residence in the town of Summit.

When young Garland began to make speeches and write strong editorials it was seen that something besides mere organization was necessary. John Quincy Travis was a candidate for Sheriff on the Republican ticket against R. H. Felder, Democrat; and Frederick W. Collins, Republican, was a candidate for re-election as Circuit Clerk against Dr. A. P. Sparkman, Democrat.

Dr. Achilles P. Sparkman
Quitman Guards
Wounded and disabled at the Battle of Cross Keys, Va., June 8th, 1862

Dr. Sparkman married Mary E. Vaught, daughter of Maj. W. W. Vaught, one of the charming girls who participated in the banner presentation in 1860. Dr. Sparkman was elected Circuit Court Clerk of Pike County in 1875, and has held that position consecutively since then, covering a period of thirty-four years.

Travis was an ex-Lieutenant of the Quitman Guards and had lost a hand at the battle of Chancellorsville, Va., May 2, 1863.

Sparkman had been a member of the same company and was dangerously wounded in the battle of Cross Keys in the Valley Campaign, under Ewell and Stonewall Jackson, in 1862. These facts were not lost sight of by the ex-Confederates of Pike County.

A delegation of citizens invited the writer, editor of the Amite City, (La.) *Democrat*, to Magnolia for a conference, the result of which was to establish a paper at once at Magnolia, which was done, and the *Herald* began on the 17th of September, 1875, with the writer proprietor and editor, and when the campaign was opened, its services were given to the candidates nominated by the Democracy.

Frederick W. Collins, the candidate on the Republican ticket, had been holding the office of Circuit Clerk since his appointment by Governor Alcorn and his election in 1873 and gave entire satisfaction to the people, and he was a hard candidate to beat. His magnetism and personal popularity was such that the party he belonged to even during this period of political animosity, was lost sight of by those with whom he had grown up, but in this election he was pitted against an ex-Confederate soldier—a member of the Quitman Guards—who had become disabled by a serious wound received in the battle of Cross Keys, Va.

R. H. Felder, the candidate for Sheriff on the Democratic ticket, had filled the office by election as the successor of Louis C. Bickham, had been put out by the military, had served as deputy for many years and was a popular man, but he was pitted against a handless veteran. Upon the above four men hinged the election in Pike County.

Upon general principles the issue was white supremacy

During this campaign, according to a correspondent of the New Orleans *Picayune*, the town of Columbus was fired in fourteen different places in one day by radical negroes. The fire was quickly extinguished and the citizens armed and placed the city under martial law. Four negroes were caught in the act of setting fire to the houses and they were immediately shot, and the New Orleans *Delta* stated that on the 4th of October a consignment of forty boxes of cartridges came in over the New Orleans and Mobile Railroad to William Pitt Kellogg, the usurper, of Louisiana.

These and other circumstances intensified the fever of excitement and a clash between the races was avoided only by the great self-control and counsel of the white leaders.

The campaign was short, but decisive, in its results for white supremacy. The Democratic party carried the State by forty thousand majority.

In Pike County the result was as follows:

State Senator—R. H. Thompson, Dem., over W. H. Garland, Jr., Rep.
Representative—James M. Causey, Dem., over C. W. Beam, Rep.
Sheriff—J. Q. Travis, Rep., over R. H. Felder, Dem.
Chancery Clerk—William M. Conerly, Dem., over Gideon Montford, Rep.
Circuit Clerk—A. P. Sparkman, Dem., over F. W. Collins, Rep.
Treasurer—Henry S. Brumfield, Dem., over C. S. Simmons, Rep.
Assessor—Samuel R. Lamkin, Dem., over P. F. Williams, Rep.
Surveyor—S. M. Simmons, Dem., over Peres Bonney, Rep.
Coroner and Ranger—E. P. Stratton, Ind., over H. S. Bonney, Dem. (complimentary vote).
Supervisors—First District, John G. Leggett, Dem.; Second District, Walter M. Lampton, Dem.; Third District, E. C. Andrews, Dem.; Fourth District, R. L. Lenoir, Dem.; Fifth District, William L. Coney, Rep.
Justices of the Peace—First District, J. M. Varnado, Dem., John A. Walker, Dem.; Second District, J. H. Crawford, Dem., A. F. Lampton, Dem.; Third District, E. L. Reeves, Dem., F. M. Walker, Dem.; Fourth District, S. A. Matthews, Dem., W. S. Mount, Dem.; Fifth District, W. C. Harrell, Dem., E. P. Stratton, Dem.
Constables—First District, L. T. Varnado, Dem., Andrew Jackson, Dem.; Second District, Harris Bullock, Dem., William Graves, Dem.; Third District, L. W. Sartin, Dem., Henry Jones, Dem.; Fourth District, H. H. Kuykendall, Dem., G. T. Smith, Dem.; Fifth District, Ed. Ricks, Joe Norris.

The Independent, a Republican paper published at Amite City by R. W. Reed, commenting on this election, said:

"*The Magnolia Herald* has had its effect. That town has gone Republican."

To which the *Herald* replied:

"Yes, '*The Herald* has had its effect.' Pike County has gone Democratic by 225 average majority, and the force of *The Herald* has been acknowledged. The town of Magnolia went Democratic. The Republican vote polled here did not live in Magnolia. Most of them were like the great mass of the Republican party: They were interlopers."

" 'Roll on, Thou Deep Blue Sea'!"

" 'As little as you may think of it,' says *The Magnolia Herald*, 'somebody is going to get beat next Tuesday.' And *The Herald* knows who it is just as well as it knows its own party."—*Amite* (La.) *Independent*.

Again:

"*The Magnolia Herald* and other Democratic organs of Mississippi think they have everything fixed to their own liking, and talk gushingly of the 'roll of the deep blue ocean.' The sea is too far distant to be of any service to drown the sorrow of their approaching defeat, but a mighty wave of another color will roll inward and produce some Democratic lashing and heaving that will put the salt water to shame."

To which the *Herald* replied:

"Your rotten radical concern has been shattered. The echoing thunders of a Democratic victory are heard all over the land and are caught up by the echoing voices of the deep! 'Roll on, thou deep blue ocean, roll!'"

And the white-capped waves rolled on.

FROM NEW ORLEANS.

Editor Magnolia Herald:

SIR: Yours of the 24th received. No "loud crowing cocks" in stock. The demand has exceeded the supply. Yours truly,

E. C. PALMER & Co.

"Mississippi is redeemed. Truth and honesty and intelligence have prevailed over falsehood, ignorance, fraud and oppression. The hand lifted to crush Mississippi has been paralyzed."

said the *Herald*.

"The immaculate Stephen A. Douglas, colored, who tried so hard to stick his finger in Pike County politics, did a little fingering over in Amite this time, and the last we heard of him, he was in Summit tracking it after Parker and his layout. He said he 'woods'd it' all the way from Liberty, and that if he dabbles in politics again he wants somebody to kill him. He had better go back to Massa Tom Green Davidson, of Louisiana,"

said the *Herald*.

The largest vote polled in Pike County was between James M. Causey, who received 1,414, against C. W. Beam, who received 1,188.

An important question to be considered by the farmers and planters of the county was a system of labor that could be relied upon, and a more perfect confidence among the negroes themselves in the duties to which their new conditions had brought them.

The last days of slavery were fraught with many troubles and the negroes were in a fearful condition of unrest, if such may be said, and when the events of the past were brought back to them, they again thought of the dangers of re-enslavement.

The carpetbagger was the barrier which prevented the prosperity that should follow the productions of the Southern States, under a peaceful management of the negro labor. His eternal intermeddling in the plans of the planters, by exciting them and diverting their minds, was an ever fruitful means of destroying the good that might have been done in the quiet control of the negroes under their former masters.

When the carpetbaggers were compelled to retire, the burden of responsibility to secure an equal protection to the negroes was given to the whites and they proved the certain fact that they were the better friends in all that pertained to their welfare.

In the year 1871, when the great school, which became a part of the State's charge, was put in a fair way to educate the children of the negroes, the voice of reason was heard and they began to see the light which previously had only shown to them in the temples of the strangers who had come to fatten on their ignorance.

Among all the great commonwealths of the South there are none which have given to the negroes a more liberal opportunity than the State of Mississippi.

In the fall of 1875, when the visions of departing freedom came to them, they trembled and felt the force of the white man's power, and when it was shown to them that their fears were groundless, a perfect confidence should thus have been a part of the outcome, but instead of this, it was broken into by the ever-prevailing incubus of political excitement. A better understanding had come to the surface and the negroes had understood, but not heeded. If such forces as those used in the past to convince were not necessary, it was considered to be so by the White League.

In a few months after the election, the executive committee gave notice that there would be a national election held in the coming fall and it was desired to keep up all organization and to arrange a plan to insure the success of the white man's party in the State. When we look back and see the condition of things, and see the success of the White League over the rule of carpetbaggers, held in power by the military, it shows the fallacy of not trying to make their past success a fixture; and when it is shown that the future welfare of both races must depend on the superior race now in power, it will be understood why the methods used were resorted to.

"Forget and forgive—this world would be lonely,
The garden a paradise left to deform,
If the flowers but remembered the chilling winds only
And the trees gave no verdure for fear of the storm."

Thus spake 1876 to 1875 as she assumed control over our ever changing destinies.

On the 10th day of January, 1876, the town of Magnolia, now the permanent seat of justice, held an election to fill the offices of mayor and councilmen.

At this election Frederick W. Collins, Republican, who had been defeated for the office of Circuit Clerk, was elected Mayor, and the following persons, all Democrats, were elected Councilmen: William M. Conerly, Cornelius C. Gibson, William M. Wroten, and Jonas Hiller; and Henry S. Copes, Secretary, Treasurer and Tax Collector.

Beginning with the new year, Hugh Q, Bridges' name was placed at the head of the *Summit Sentinel* as associate editor.

The new board of supervisors, composed of John G. Leggett, President; Walter M. Lampton, Elisha C. Andrews, Robert L. Lenoir, Wm. L. Coney, John Quincy Travis, Sheriff, and Willlam M. Conerly, Clerk, was organized on Monday, January 3, 1876.

Wm. Brown & Co.'s bond, contractors for the building of the new court house, was approved and filed.

Judge T. E. Tate, Republican, was confirmed as school superintendent by the State Senate.

Charles L. Patton became the owner of the *Summit Times* and the only newspaper ever published in Pike County in support of the Republican party, and negro government under military domination was expurgated, re-baptized in the folds of white supremacy.

Through the machinations of W. D. Redmond, Dr. Barrett, ex-Sheriff Parker, of Amite County, and a few of their sympathizers about Summit, a company of United States cavalry was stationed at McComb City, with orders, it was said, to protect Redmond and aid him in the discharge of his duties as United States Deputy Revenue Collector.

When the result of the election in Amite County was made known, Parker, Barrett and Redmond fled the county, under a pretended fear of assassination.

It was said that Parker and Barrett were particularly obnoxious to the people of Amite County, but it was denied that there was any animosity entertained toward Redmond, who was connected with a very prominent family of Amite by marriage.

After the election they had been dodging about between New Orleans and Jackson, under the pretense that their lives were in danger. Christmas week, a few planters went to Summit to sell their cotton and buy their supplies. They camped a mile or so from town and during the night were fired upon by a party of negroes and white men, and several of their number wounded. The following day a party of men from Amite County, hearing of the shooting of their friends, went to Summit to make an investigation of the affair and, if possible, learn who were the perpetrators of the deed. During the day more or less excitement prevailed. Some unguarded men became intoxicated and a small row occurred which was promptly quelled. After this another melee was raised at the market house, near the depot, which was quelled by General Cain, Chief of Police, and a few citizens. It was said that Redmond was present as a spectator and was not disturbed nor threatened. When the row ceased, the next day, Redmond stepped into the telegraph office and sent a message to Collector Shaunnessey, at Jackson, that he was being driven from county to county by an armed body of men, fifty or sixty in number, and that he could not perform the duties of his office without troops. Shaunnessey telegraphed to Washington, and upon his statement President Grant ordered the troops to be sent.

The citizens of Summit got up a statement of the facts in the case, signed by nearly all the white people of the town, including some leading Republicans, and corroborated by a certificate from Sheriff Travis and Chancery Clerk W. M. Conerly, falsifying Redmond's report of the necessity for troops, but this had no effect, and the troops were sent to McComb City and quartered there among its people.

A committee appointed by the State Legislature, composed of J. E. Leigh, Chairman E. A. Rowan, A. C. McNair and James W. Shattuck, reported that the only relieving excuse or feature provided to justify Redmond's charge that he was pursued from Amite County was that, in a drunken row at Summit, personal threats were made by one or more drunken men, who were not armed, against Redmond, which caused him to leave town, and that the charges alleged in his message to Shaunnessey were false and the demand for troops unwarranted by the facts.

This was regarded as the first step toward an effort in the future to reëstablish the carpetbag government in power. It was a repetition of what had been done in the past and the White League so regarded it, and a more perfect organization of the white people in Pike County was determined on.

In the month of February, 1876, T. W. Cordoza, the negro Superintendent of Education, was impeached and allowed to resign February 22.

In the month of March, A. K. Davis, the negro Lieutenant-Governor, was convicted of high crimes and misdemeanors and removed from office by the State Senate, sitting as a court of impeachment.

Charges for impeachment against Governor Ames were preferred and his trial begun. He was allowed to resign March 29th, 1876, and John M. Stone, President of the State Senate, became Governor.

On April 4th, 1876, Rev. William H. Roane died in the town of Magnolia. He was born November, 1826, near Huntsville, Ala.; was educated at Oglethorpe College, Georgia, and a member of the Presbyterian Church, North, and graduated in the Theological Seminary of South Carolina, preached the gospel upwards of twenty years and was a practitioner at the bar in Pike County. He was a member of the State Legislature and did all in his power for the well-being of the people. He was a classical scholar and a Mason, and deserves to be remembered as one who did much to ward off the perils of a race conflict and other bloody scenes threatened during the troublesome times previously mentioned.

After the impeachment of the negro Superintendent of Education, Cordoza, the negro Lieutenant-Governor, James K. Davis, the resignation of Governor Ames, and the instalment of a complete white man's government in Mississippi, the New Orleans, La., *Democrat*, edited by H. J. Hearsey, had this to say:

"Radicalism has literally gone to pieces in Mississippi. The Mississippians made a heroic fight and won their State. When their Legislature assembled and talked about impeachment, Morton endeavored to intimidate them by his threats, while fierce dispatches announcing that armies of troops were to be quartered in the State, were sent from Washington, in the New York *Herald*, and other journals of the same class, raised the stereotyped howl that the Southern whites were bent on revolution; that so soon as they got in power they began to make war, and other stuff. But the Mississippians didn't bully worth a cent. They told the New York *Herald* and the people of other States to attend to their own business, and, thinking it time enough to get scared when the troops came down on them with fixed bayonets, they went right ahead, drew up the charges against the rascals who had the State government, got full proof of them and impeached Davis and Ames. This did the business in Mississippi. So soon as it was evident that the Mississippians were in earnest and could only be prevented from doing their duty by being cleaned out *vi-et-armis*, the bullyism stopped, and radicalism went utterly to pieces. We wish Louisiana could charter the Mississippi Legislature for about a week or ten days."

On April 26th, 1876, the survivors of the Sixteenth Mississippi Regiment had a reunion at Summit. In view of that coming event, Capt. Thomas A. Garner, Capt. Alph A. Boyd, and Ed. H. Mogan, addressed a letter to Gen. W. S. Featherston, inviting him to come to Summit to deliver an address. The Sixteenth had been under General Featherston in Virginia prior to his transfer to the Army of Tennessee. It is considered proper to incorporate General Featherston's letter in this book, as the Summit Rifles and the Quitman Guards were members of this regiment and served under him while he commanded the brigade in Virginia, being succeeded by Gen. Carnot Posey:

JACKSON, MISS., April 7, 1876.

Messrs. T. A. Garner, E. H. Mogan, and A. A. Boyd.

GENTLEMEN: Your letter of April 4th, inviting me to address the survivors of the Sixteenth Regiment of Mississippi Volunteers at their reunion on the 26th day of this month, at Summit, has been received and duly considered.

Nothing would afford me more pleasure, gentlemen, than to be able to comply with your request. I should be proud to meet the survivors of that gallant and noble regiment of Confederate soldiers and shake them by the hand and talk with them about our common toils, sacrifices and sufferings in the past as well as of the virtues of our lamented comrades in arms, who fell on the field of battle. A better regiment I never saw under arms than the Sixteenth Mississippi. Patient under discipline, unfaltering in the discharge of duty, prompt in action and heroic and invincible in the face of the foe, it had no superior. But, gentlemen, I have been away from my family and private interests since September last, devoting my time entirely to public service.

When the Legislature shall adjourn, at the close of the next week, I shall be compelled to forego the pleasure of meeting you on the 26th at Summit, and return to my family and my home. Thanking you, gentlemen, sincerely, for the honor of this invitation, and wishing you and all the survivors of the Sixteenth Regiment prolonged lives of happiness and usefulness, I am very truly, your friend and obedient servant,

W. S. FEATHERSTON.

General Featherston, a representative from Marshall County, had been conspicuous in the Legislature in offering a resolution for a committee to be appointed to inquire into the official conduct of Adelbert Ames, acting Governor of the State of Mississippi, which was adopted and he was appointed on that committee, which resulted in the impeachment, trial of and resignation of Ames and the reinstalment of white supremacy.

May 9, 1876, a meeting was held at the court house for the purpose of fixing on some plan of demonstration to be given upon the day of laying the corner-stone of the new court house, which was fixed for Saturday, May 27th following, and Dr. George Nicholson, Deputy Grand Master of the Seventh District of Mississippi, was invited to conduct the ceremonies according to the usages of the Masonic order. John S. Lamkin, Samuel E. Packwood, Thomas R. Stockdale, and Isaac Applewhite were selected orators of the day. C. C. Gibson, Henry Gottig, W. W. Vaught, A. LeBlanc, and Frederic W. Collins were appointed a Committee of Arrangements.

It was thought that this occasion would be an opportune time to heal the differences existing between the towns of Summit and Magnolia over the court house question, and Thomas A. Garner, Mayor of Summit, was directed by its citizens to convey to the people of Magnolia, through Hon. Fred W. Collins, Mayor of that town, their sentiments of friendly regards on the occasion of laying the cornerstone, the centennial year of American independence. Following is the account given by the Magnolia *Herald* of June 2, 1876:

LAYING THE CORNER-STONE.

On Saturday last, May 27th, 1876, as previously advertised in the papers, the people of Pike County assembled at Magnolia to participate in the ceremonies of laying the corner-stone of their new court house, now in process of erection. At an early hour in the morning, though the weather threatened to be unfavorable, the people came pouring in, in squads, from all points of the compass, thus indicating that there would be a large gathering.

At about half-past nine o'clock, Capt. Travis' excursion train from Brookhaven, conveying a large number of citizens from that town, Bogue Chitto, Johnstons Station, Summit, McComb City and Quin Station, arrived, and were received by the anxious crowd assembled at the depot, amid enlivening strains of music from the Jolly Brothers' cornet band, of Summit, engaged for the occasion.

At about eleven o'clock, the excursion train from Osyka, heavily freighted with the beauty and chivalry of that lovely town, moved up, while hundreds of handkerchiefs waved on high and sweet music swelled the breeze and bade them welcome.

By this time the town was crowded with people from all parts of the county, as well as a few from Lincoln and Amite Counties, and Tangipahoa Parish, La.

The doors of the Central House and private residences were thrown open for the reception, convenience and comfort of guests and friends, and the entire place was alive with masses moving to and fro, inspecting the town and the preparations which had been made on the picnic grounds and elsewhere to add to the beauty of the surroundings and to the comfort and pleasure of the people.

At about half-past eleven o'clock, Sincerity Lodge No. 214, F. & A. M., and Tangipahoa Lodge I. O. O. F., of Magnolia, emerged from their places of meeting and formed in procession in the following order:

S. A. Matthews, Grand Marshal, aided by Jonas Hiller and C. C. Gibson.

Henry Swan, Tyler of Sincerity Lodge No. 214, F. & A. M., of Magnolia, accompanied by Tylers of other lodges.

Stewards, with rods.

Master masons.

F. Prescott and M. Day, Deacons, with rods.

A. L. Lazar, Secretary, and E. T. Prewett, Treasurer *pro tem*.

R. H. Dickey, Senior Warden *pro tem*.

Mark Master Royal Arch Masons.

Royal and Select Masters.

Knights Templar, as escort to Grand Lodge.

Jolly Brothers' cornet band.

C. H. Lyster, Grand Tyler.

John Holmes and J. H. Monfourt, Grand Stewards, with white rods.

H. Q. Bridges, Grand Secretary, and N. Greener, Grand Treasurer.

Walter Cowart, Grand Pursuivant.

Bible, square and compass, carried by Joseph Mixon, supported by stewards.

J. W. Sandell, Grand Chaplain, and E. P. Stratton, Grand Lecturer.

W. Fleet Simmons, with five orders of architecture.*

Representatives of the press.

W. M. Conerly, Junior Warden, with silver vessel of oil.

H. M. Quin, Senior Grand Warden, with silver vessel of wine.

A. A. Boyd, Deputy Grand Master, carrying golden vessel with corn.

J. S. Lamkin, Master of oldest lodge, carrying book of the constitution.

George Nicholson, Grand Master, supported by J. M. Thornhill and P. C. Kennedy, Deacons, with rods.

C. A. Zackary, Grand Sword Bearer.

---

*These five orders of architecture were drawn in spatter work by the accomplished and talented Miss H. May Lamkin, daughter of John S. Lamkin, Esq., of Magnolia, and were presented to Sincerity Lodge No. 214. They were tastefully and beautifully executed, evidencing superior artistic skill, and are highly appreciated by the members of the lodge.

Thus arranged they moved to the front of the sheriff's office, on the corner of Railroad Avenue and Myrtle Street, where the order of Odd Fellows filed in at the rear, the procession moving up Myrtle Street to Clarks Avenue, down Clarks Avenue to Bay Street and down Bay Street to the court house square, filing in beneath the triumphal arch prepared at the entrance of the square. Upon arriving on the square, the Masonic procession opened to the right and left, uncovering the grand master and his officers, who repaired to a temporary platform ercted upon the foundation of the court house (in front of which was constructed a beautiful evergreen arch bearing the inscription, "Centennial"), where they were surrounded by the rest of the brethren. Dr. George Nicholson then read a letter from the Grand Master of the State, authorizing him to perform the ceremonies of laying the corner-stone, which stated that Sincerity Lodge No. 214 had the matter in charge. He then delivered the proclamation as laid down in the Masonic ritual. Then followed a lesson from the Scriptures, and prayer by the Grand Chaplain, after which, accompanied by a splendid organ, the choir rose and sang in sweet harmony, to the tune of "Arlington :"

> When Solomon, with wondrous skill,
>   A temple did prepare,
> Israel with zeal his courts did fill,
>   And God was honored there.
>
> Celestial rays of glorious light,
>   The sacred walls contained;
> The pure refulgence day and night
>   With awful force remained.
>
> O may Thy presence, gracious Lord,
>   In our assembly be;
> Enlighten us to know Thy word,
>   That we may honor Thee.
>
> And when the final trump shall sound,
>   To judge the world of sin,
> Within Thy courts may we be found,
>   Eternally til'd in.

A tin casket had been prepared, in which was deposited the following articles:

Three copies *Magnolia Herald*.
One copy *Summit Sentinel*.
One copy *Summit Times*.
One copy *Easy Chair*, published at Summit.
One copy *Young America*, published at Summit.

A list of officers and roll of members of Sincerity Lodge No. 214, F. & A. M., and the constitution and by-laws of the order.

One nickel coin U. S. currency, valued at five cents.

One Prussian silver coin, valued at twenty cents.

One five-dollar note, Mississippi cotton money.

One ten-dollar note, Confederate money.

One silver coin U. S. currency, valued at five cents.

A list of officers and roll of members of Company F, Third Regiment U. S. Infantry.

A list of county officers of Pike County.

Copy of programme of the day's exercises.

The box was then deposited in a vault prepared for it, and the corner-stone was lowered and laid in accordance with the usage and solemnity of the Masonic order, covering the box containing the above mentioned articles, which was cemented in its vault, and concealing them from the sight of man for ages, perhaps, to come ere they shall be admitted to the light of day.

Inscription on the stone:

>North side—LAID MAY 27, 1876.
>CENTENNIAL YEAR.

>East side— C. C. GIBSON,
>ARCHITECT & BUILDER.

The choir then sang to the tune of Old Hundred, the following stanzas:

>Master Supreme! to Thee this day,
>Our corner-stone with praise we lay;
>And resting on Thy word fulfilled,
>To Thee, O Lord! our house we build.

>Nor build we here with strength alone
>Of carven wood or sculptured stone;
>But squarely hewed, and broadly plann'd,
>Our lines we raise, like ashlars grand.

>By Thee, O Lord! our work design'd,
>The widow's son his help shall find;
>And we shall frame, for trembling youth,
>The winding stairs that lead to Truth.

>In Faith we toil—in Hope we climb
>To Charity—our Arch sublime;
>And evermore the Keystone see,
>O Master! Lord! in Thee—in Thee!

The benediction pronounced, Hon. T. A. Garner, mayor of Summit, was introduced, who read a letter (previously prepared for the occasion), to Hon. F. W. Collins, mayor of Magnolia, presenting him (on the part of the good people of Summit) with a bronzed hatchet, to be buried in token of a cessation of sectional animosity hitherto existing and brought about by the removal of the court house from Holmesville to Magnolia, and as an evidence of a restoration of harmonious feelings and unity of purpose.

The following is Mayor Garner's letter:

SUMMIT, May 27th, 1876.

To Hon. F. W. Collins,
Mayor of Magnolia, Mississippi.

SIR:

I am directed by the people of Summit to convey, through you, to the people of Magnolia, their sentiments of friendly regard on the occasion of laying the corner-stone of the new court house.

The question of "removal or no removal," which once so seriously agitated the public mind, and which unfortunately created sectional jealousies, not unmixed with sectional animosities, has been happily set at rest, and the people of Summit, in token of their magnanimity, desire to manifest their entire acquiescence in the logic of events, as well as their complete reconciliation over the late "bone of contention." With this view they have delegated me in their behalf to unite with you in conducting the present public demonstration, and to deposit in the cavity of the stone some suitable token of their harmonious feelings. To give expression of their wishes, I have selected the accompanying implement, which, in the earlier history of our common country, was not unfrequently used as a symbol of *buried* animosity, and which besides has been made historic by the father of our country.

It is fitting that in the centennial year of our existence as a republic the burying of the hatchet, which has more than once performed the conspicuous office of securing profound and permanent peace for the nation, should now serve to allay sectional feeling, and mark the era of perfect peace and complete reconciliation in our county affairs.

In humble imitation of this rude custom of our forefathers, I have the honor to place at your disposal this bronzed implement, to be used, if you please, in the manner, and for the purpose above indicated, with the additional assurance that it is our common desire that the people of this county shall henceforth, like brethren, dwell together in unity. I have the honor to be

Very truly,

T. A. GARNER,
Mayor of Summit.

Mr. Collins, on the part of the citizens of Magnolia, accepted the hatchet from Mr. Garner, with the following well timed impromptu reemarks:

Ladies and Gentlemen: The document just read, by Hon. T. A. Garner, Mayor of Summit, fully explains itself. For and in behalf of the people of Summit, he presents to me, as the representative of the people of Magnolia, this ancient symbol, this hatchet, desiring that we bury with it, after the ancient custom, all the jealousies and animosities generated by the vexed court house question. I am not prepared to make any extended remarks upon this important occasion, but suffice it to say that I, on the part of the people of Magnolia, accept it in good faith—I accept it in the spirit in which it is presented.

We will now deposit it in the cavity of the corner-stone of the court house, where we hope, and have every reason to believe, it will ever rest undisturbed.

Capt. John S. Lamkin, Hon. S. E. Packwood and Hon. I. Applewhite were each respectively introduced and delivered addresses appropriate to the occasion.

It was announced that dinner would be served on the island picnic grounds. The procession of Masons and Odd Fellows returned to their respective lodges, disbanded, and at two o'clock, as stated in the programme, the people repaired for refreshments.

At the foot of Magnolia Street, over the west end of the bridge leading to the island, inscribed on an evergreen arch were observed the following words:

"As citizens of Pike County, we give you a kindly greeting."

Near the end of the bridge leading from the island to the Central House, was another, containing the inscription:

"Our wish is that together we may work for the good of our county."

The people had contributed generously, and seven long tables were laden with provisions prepared principally by the hands of the fair ones, sufficient for at least two thousand people. A large quantity of fresh meat—beef, mutton, kid and pork—was barbecued, supervised by our esteemed fellow citizen, William Stevenson, assisted by his son.

We heard it frequently remarked by old "barbecued meat eaters" that this was the best they ever saw or tasted. Everthing was arranged systematically—the ladies being invited to the table first and the men afterward. It was calculated that, allowing two feet for each person, these seven tables would accommodate more than six hundred persons.

The carving table, supervised by W. G. Tyler, John F. Lieb, B. F. Winborn, Mr. Lloyd, a worthy guest from New Orleans, J. H. Stevens, and others, was elegantly managed.

Among the many large baskets noticeable, was one sent by Mr. George Folsom, which came as neat being a cart-load of good things as any we ever saw.

W. W. Vaught, table manager, A. LeBlanc and H. Gottig were particularly active in their respective duties; while many others are equally deserving of mention, but not having been furnished with their names, we can not give them from memory.

Mrs. Roane, and the ladies who assisted her in the decorations, deserve especial mention for the part they performed; and to the ladies generally, who so generously contributed in labor and provisions to the occasion, the thanks of the people are due.

Particular mention is also due the ladies' table committee for the part they performed in so tastefully arranging the tables.

According to the published schedule, Capt. J. Q. Travis returned to their homes the good citizens of Osyka, Carters Hill, Chatawa, and those living at the various stations between Magnolia and Brookhaven, by his excursion train.

At seven o'clock the doors of the Central House hall were opened for the ball, and when the twilight shades had passed away, the brilliant chandeliers spread their light over the most magnificent array of beauty and chivalry, attired in gorgeous suits, upon which our eyes ever feasted, and amid dulcet strains of music from that splendid "Jolly Brothers' Cornet Band," terpischorean lovers, with joyous hearts, "whiled the happy hours away." The ball was arranged and conducted under the auspices of W. M. Conerly, and was managed with judgment, skill and perfect order.

At midnight the ball ceased, and our friends from McComb City, Quins Station and Summit were conveyed home by special train.

The press, on this occasion, was represented by the handsome, good-natured and talented editor of the Brookhaven *Ledger*, Mr. R. H. Henry; Capt. J. D. Burke, formerly of the Brookhaven *Citizen*; Hon. H. Q. Bridges, H. S. Bonney, and N. P. Bonney, of the Summit *Sentinel*; Col. W. Lee Patton, and his corps, of the Summit *Times*; and the members of *The Herald* office.

We were pleased to observe present Sam Henderson, Esq., of New Orleans, and several friends from Tangipahoa Parish, La.; Hon. J. B. Deason, from Brookhaven; and several handsome and accomplished young ladies from Amite County, among them Misses Safford, and Miss Raiford, daughter of our old friend, William Raiford, of Liberty.

We were also proud to see so many of the good people of McComb City present. The ties of friendship between them and the citizens of Magnolia are growing stronger and stronger as time and again they are thrown together in social gatherings.

To the people of Osyka, Johnstons Station, Summit and all intermediate stations, Holmesville and throughout the entire county, the compliments and hearty good wishes of Magnolia are extended. May they in the future be bound together in stronger ties of friendship, and work with more united hearts for the good of the county and for the elevation and prosperity of the people.

For order, harmony of action, good feeling, plenty to eat and general satisfaction among the people, the occasion of the 27th of May, 1876, can safely be said to have had no equal since *ante bellum* days, and it is a forcible evidence of what can be accomplished and the satisfaction that can be enjoyed when there is a common object in view and a common purpose among the people. May they ever work together.

At a meeting of the committee of general arrangements, held in this town on Wednesday, 31st ult., concerning the proceedings had on the 27th ult., the following resolution was adopted:

Resolved, That the undersigned committee of general arrangements for the picnic and barbecue given in this place on the 27th ult., tender sincere thanks to the various auxiliary committees for their kindly and prompt assistance in carrying out the various details of the day's programme. We especially return thanks to the venerable William Stevenson, and to his son Thomas, for their vigilant and untiring services and complete success in barbecuing the meats, and to the ladies who so kindly and beautifully decorated the grounds. We know no words commensurate with our appreciation of their noble services.

                C. C. GIBSON,
                H. GOTTIG,
                F. W. COLLINS, Committee.
                A. LeBLANC,
                W. W. VAUGHT,

The occasion thus described in the foregoing article of the *Herald* was a great love feast in which the bitterness engendered over the court house question was softened and sweetened by forgetfulness of the past. Mayor Garner and Mayor Collins shook hands over the "blood chasm" and cemented the bonds of friendship by the burial of a genuine hatchet, deposited in the vault of the corner-stone of the new court house. A good old time lady of direct pioneer descent, wearing an ancient pair of spectacles, held on by a cord around her head, remarked to the writer:

"I am so glad the people of Magnoly and Summit is made up. I do hate these bickerins. I always heard it said that a man's love, and a woman's, too, for all-er that, was down his throat, and now I knows it. I bleve this dinner has had a powerful influence in settling the fuss."

In the early days of reconstruction the negroes were in a transitory condition, so to speak, and wholly unfit to perform any of the functions of government.

A more stupid effort to force them to the equality of the white man was never made by any civilized or enlightened government on earth. It would be bad enough now, with all the care and all the advantages of enlightened Christian education, to put them in possession of government with white people. To do so at the end of the Civil War, just liberated from slavery, was a crime of so great proportions as to stamp it the STUPIDITY of the Nineteenth Century.

The negro was a child of the jungles in his native land, far below the Indian in America, and never knew the value of anything. His ancestry for thousands of years was no wiser than those brought to Jamestown on a Dutch vessel in 1620 and sold into slavery for the ponderous sum of 150 pounds of leaf tobacco.

A race so deficient in intellect as the native African in the jungles where life exists only as that of the wild beasts, that have not advanced higher in thousands of years, are not expected, by people acquainted with negro characteristics, to become fit for rulers in a few centuries, even with the advantages of educational training under the higher civilizing influences and care of the Caucasian. In the nature of the creature there is no redeeming quality to fit him for self-government or the position of ruler over the white race. He is a child of the hour and concerned only about his stomach and comfort. His progress, little as it is, in the United States, has been forced upon him by the white man. His civilization here is due entirely to the discipline and training, for three hundred years, to the institution of slavery improving him gradually each generation in the manner the superior intellect has evolved the intelligence of animals of the brute creation. He cares no more for the general welfare nor the upbuilding of a community now than he did thousands of years ago in his native jungles. As a race he cares nothing for law and order nor the attainment of the higher attributes of civilized man. A creature of the hour and present surroundings.

The very idea of a people like those of the Northern States, with their claims of superior education and general attainments, marshaling an immense army, spending billions of treasury and sacrificing hundreds of thousands of lives, murdering women and children of their own race, devastating a vast territory occupied by enlightened citizens, to put a race of savages over their white brothers and drive them to destruction, is a crime so vast and so unforgiving that it must be classed as the demon age of American history.

In the past as well as the present the negro as a race has shown only the characteristics of the creature that sleeps with utter unconcern in the jungles where the God of Nature planted him.

If the reader of this book will do as this writer has done in order to fit himself for a proper conception and truthful exposition of negro character, he will easily understand. No one possessed with an impartial desire for truth can go into the negro quarters of large cities or small towns and investigate their condition, habits and characteristics without a feeling of disappointment and disgust after forty years of freedom and special care given them under the efforts of Northern missionaries and under the educational advantages forced upon them by the white people of the South. And this is the creature, who, without having had these special intellectual advantages thrust upon them, just emerged from slavery, that the power of the military under Northern domination, holding the reins of government of the United States, put over our people to crush them and destroy their racial character, supervised by a horde of Northern adventurers, worshiping at the shrine of negro superstition, ignorance and idolatry. As a slave the negro could be controlled for good purposes; as a ruler he was the curse of the hour. In this the negro was not so much the criminal. It was his foster white brother, the Northern carpetbagger, political adventurer, so-called philanthropist, and fortune seekers. These observations and those in a previous chapter are given to show to the reader why the white people of the South took the steps they did to re-establish their supremacy and hold it at all hazards.

The Southern people are persistently charged, by a certain class of Northern writers and historians, as being responsible for, and the founders of, the institution of slavery in the United States; when it is a fact beyond contradiction that one of the very first acts of the founder of the first colony in Georgia was to prohibit the introduction of slavery; and later on the question began to look so serious that South Carolina and other States had to pass stringent laws to prohibit further importation of slaves. The very first act creating the territorial government of Mississippi prohibited the importation of slaves from any foreign port, and as late as the secession of Alabama that State made the initiatory move for the abolition of slavery, which was referred to the Confederate government, but, the war coming on, it was not considered practicable to do so, as organized labor and their services were needed in the production of crops to sustain the armies;

and, besides, the Southern people held to the belief of gradual emancipation in twenty years, and compensation to their owners, while Northern abolitionists held to immediate manumission without compensation.

CHAPTER IX.

Ex-Governor Adelbert Ames, before the Congressional Committee of investigation on Mississippi affairs, testified to a general system of intimidation, frauds and violence on the part of the white people, by which voters in Republican counties were prevented from voting. He found it impossible, without a bloody collision between the masses (he should have said between the races), as he was not supported by the troops, to secure the negroes in their rights in the recent election. He testified that there were riots, shootings and threats, and that the pretext set up by the white citizens of Mississippi of robbing the State by excessive taxation was wholly ungrounded—that taxation in Mississippi was only seventy cents per head, against sixteen dollars in New York. He failed to draw the comparison between the people of New York, possessed of billions of wealth, and those of Mississippi, whose fortunes had been swept away by the conflagrations and vandalism of an invading army in which he aided, succeeded in its system of plunder by the military government set over them of which he assumed executive authority. In order to contradict the testimony of Governor Ames, given after he had been deposed, a few statistics will be valuable for the enlightenment of those in search of truth.

The constitution of Mississippi did not authorize the executive to involve the State in debt, but at the expiration of his authority the debt of Mississippi is shown to be $2,631,804.24.

Land assessed to owners..$83,774,279
Land held for taxes.. 12,099,218
Assessed valuation of personal property........................ 35,639,555

    Grand total...$131,513,052

THE RATE OF TAXATION,

In 1865	$ 1.00 on	$1,000—white rule
In 1866	1.00 on	1,000—white rule
In 1867	1.00 on	1,000—white rule
In 1868	1.00 on	1,000—white rule
In 1869	1.00 on	1,000—white rule
In 1870	5.00 on	1,000—negro rule
In 1871	4.00 on	1,000—negro rule
In 1872	8.50 on	1,000—negro rule
In 1873	12.50 on	1,000—negro rule
In 1874	14.00 on	1,000—negro rule
In 1875	9.25 on	1,000—negro rule

In the foregoing it will be seen that the rate of taxation under the government of Ames, in 1874, was fourteen times greater than under white rule, and under military domination, the five years previous to negro rule supported by the military, and in 1875, the last year of his term, it was nine and one-fourth times greater; and in the face of these figures he goes before a Congressional committee and testifies that the charge made by the only taxpayers (the white citizens) of Mississippi, of robbing the State by excessive taxation, was wholly ungrounded.

It was a source of pleasure to the white people of Mississippi, after so many years of excitement and peril, to have at the head of the executive department such a man as John M. Stone. Governor Stone was born in Tennessee and entered the Confederate service as Captain of the Iuka Guards. He distinguished himself by his gallantry at the first battle of Manassas, in July, 1861, and became commander of the Second Mississippi Regiment. His career as a Confederate soldier and his personal courage was such that with him as Governor, and freed from Federal interference, the people of Mississippi felt confidence in maintaining white supremacy; but there must be no relaxation of vigilance and organization, not only to make secure the possession of the State government, but to work for the success of the national Democratic ticket in the coming fall of 1876.

On May 5th, John S. Lamkin, Chairman of the Democratic Executive Committee of Pike County, issued a call to the Democrats of the county to meet in general convention on the 3rd of June to take into consideration matters recommended by the State Executive Committee.

At this convention the executive committee was reorganized by the election of W. F. Simmons, F. M. Lea, E. C. Andrews, A. A. Boyd, Ephraim Prescott, and Capt. John S. Lamkin, again chosen as President, and Hugh Q. Bridges, Secretary.

The following delegates were chosen to the State convention to assemble in Jackson on the 14th of June: Dr. George Nicholson, W. Fleet Simmons, Benjamin Lampton, Ralph Regan, W. C. Barnes, R. H. Felder, W. Lee Patton, James Greener, W. W. Vaught, and Joe Mixon.

To Congressional convention: Dr. George Nicholson, W. Fleet Simmons, J. H. Crawford, Thomas J. Hall, R. J. Boone, Parham Thompson, D. W. Hurst, H. Q. Bridges, S. E. Packwood, and W. D. Davidson.

A resolution was passed urging the various political clubs to keep up a thorough organization.

The club at Osyka was organized with Joseph Mixon as President and Joe Mallett Secretary.

The club at Tyletown was organized with Benjamin Lampton, President; Jesse K. Brumfield, First Vice-President; George Smith, Second Vice-President; F. M. Lea, Treasurer, and J. H. Crawford, Secretary.

The club at Magnolia was organized with Gen. E. McNair, President, and William C. Vaught, Secretary.

On June 4th, 1876, the Hancock Democratic Club of Osyka was organized, with W. D. Davidson, President, and Meyer Wolf, Secretary, and a membership of sixty-seven, with ten negro members, being the first negroes to join a Democratic club in Pike County. The following are their names: Rev. William Greenfield, Rev. G. Robertson, Henry Woods, Henry Roberts, T. B. Commons, Jacob Halfin, Henry Tate, Robert Brumfield, William Brumfield, Bird Braxton.

Two large clubs were formed in the Silver Creek district, whose patriotic citizens were ever in the line of duty. The Tilden Democratic Club was formed with the election of C. W. Simmons, President; S. M. Simmons, Vice-President; and R. L. Simmons, Secretary. Two negroes, Scott Barnes and Thomas Robertson, joined the club. H. W. Sandifer was elected Corresponding Secretary.

The Tilden, Hendricks and Hooker Club was organized at Carters Creek on the 25th of July, 1876, with Joel J. Bullock, President, and John May, Secretary.

The Tilden Colored Democratic Club was organized in Magnolia August 1, 1876, with Samuel Madden, President; Thomas Jefferson, Vice-President; James Scott, Treasurer; Martin Russell, Secretary; and Joe Singletary, Captain of the Club, and twenty-seven colored members. The men composing this club were the most influential of their race in the precinct, and went to work to organize this club of their own accord and without any influence used on them by the white people. They had lived ten years under the rule of the military and carpetbagism, which created only a feeling of unrest and a clashing of interests with the white people, and they were willing to make the change in harmony with those upon whom they must depend for peace and protection to themselves and their families. The Freedmans Savings Bank, the offspring of the system of carpetbag robbery of the negro race in the South, and the total failure of a delivery of the gift of forty acres and a mule, had impressed themselves on their minds and caused an awakening which placed them in line with their old masters to free the State from misrule.

Simmons Precinct Democratic Club was organized July 29, 1876, with the election of Benjamin Franklin Ellzey as President, and A. S. Smith, Secretary. Resolution inviting colored members adopted.

On the 12th of August, the Holmesville Democratic Club was organized at Holmesville, with John G. Leggett, President, and Hugh Murray Quin, Secretary. A resolution inviting colored members was adopted. David C. Walker, Robert S. Bridges and H. M. Quin were elected delegates to the Central Club organization in Magnolia, third Monday in August.

At the National Democratic Convention held in St. Louis, Mo., on the 27th of June, 1876, Samuel J. Tilden, of New York, was nominated for President and Thomas A. Hendricks for Vice-President of the United States.

Rutherford B. Hayes, of Ohio, was nominated for President and William A. Wheeler for Vice-President by the Republican Convention.

In the organization of the Democratic party of Mississippi in 1876, for the final overthrow of carpetbagism and military interference in State affairs, the people had much to convince them that their late defeated opponents were using every effort possible ro reëstablish themselves and negro rule in power. John R. Lynch, negro, in the national House of Representatives, from Mississippi, said:

"I desire to make what may be a final appeal. I use the word 'final' because, as little as you may think of it, the condition of the colored people of the South to-day, if not of the whole country, is a seriously critical one. We are standing, as it were, upon the brink of our political and, I may add, personal destruction. When we look to the right we find the angry billows of an enraged democracy seeking to overwhelm us. When we look to the left, we find that we are crushed to the earth, as it were, with an unjust and an un-Christian prejudice. When we turn to the rear, we find the assassin in certain portions of the country ready to plunge the dagger into our hearts for a public expression of our honest conviction. We turn our faces to you as our friends, our advocates, our defenders and our protectors.

"The Democratic party has an armed military organization in several of the Southern States called the White League. This organization has been brought into existence for the sole and exclusive purpose of accomplishing with the bullet that which can not be accomplished with the ballot; for controlling public opinion and carrying popular elections by violence and force of arms; for the purpose of destroying the freedom of speech, the freedom of opinion, the freedom of the press and the protection of the ballot. Its mission is to accomplish practically within the union that which could not be accomplished through the madness of secession."

This sable representative in the United States Congress, sent there by his carpetbag and negro supporters of Mississippi, forgot to say that the white people of the State had been for ten years held under the yoke of a military despotism, and made to pay all the taxes, and assume the burden of debts thrust upon them without their consent. This speech was simply one of the old appeals for United States troops.

The Deputy United States Revenue Collector, D. M. Redmond, had succeeded in getting a troop of cavalry stationed at McComb City, and to put a finishing touch to the speech of John R. Lynch, a white preacher of the gospel who had made his home in McComb City, and shared the kindness and hospitality of its people, Rev. H. M. Church, presiding elder of the African Episcopal Church, came out in a slanderous letter published in the New York *Witness*, on the election of 1875, against the white people of Amite and Pike Counties, so full of vehement slander and falsehood as to excite the contempt of all Northern people who had settled in McComb, and who, from a sense of justice to themselves and those with whom they had cast their destinies, felt compelled to publish a statement contradicting this intermeddlers' statements.

The Magnolia *Herald* copied Church's letter at the time and characterized him as a man of mischief, sleeping and eating with negroes, and inciting them against the white people

Bishop Haven, of the Northern Methodist Church, published a letter in which he stated that at a conference of the A. M. E. Church, he was told how a certain Louisiana representative was brutally murdered by the white people. The representative referred to was John Gair, a notorious thief and murderer, who caused the poisoning of Dr. Sanders of Clinton, La., and H. M. Church was Bishop Haven's informer.

The McComb City *Intelligencer*, published by a Northern gentleman,* commenting on the scathing editorial of the Magnolia *Herald* on Church's slanderous letter and that of Bishop Haven, said:

"This is true. Our community here is composed of Northern men and Southern men and people of both political parties and the various Protestant and Catholic denominations, and we believe the feeling is universal that Church, when he resided with us, was a strife-making nuisance. His letter to the New York *Witness*, defaming the very people who, in another portion of it, he admits have treated him with hospitality and kindness, is characteristic of the man."

Fred Barrett, who had figured in Amite County, sent out the following in an open letter in the *Southern Republican*, published by him at Jackson:

---

*W. H. Townsend.

"By becoming fiends infuriate, devils incarnate, as our enemies did last year, we could spread consternation and dismay, ruin and death, in our course; we could soon teach the enemy the full force of his favorite resort, VIOLENCE."

GRANT MUST CALL OFF HIS DOGS.

The New York *Herald*, in the following language, insisted that President Grant must be made to "take his heavy hand off the South."

"In this canvass one demand should be made by all who love their country, irrespective of party sentiment—let Grant take his heavy hand off the South. Of our soldiers we may say to him, as Richard III. said to Stanley, 'What do they in the South when they should serve their country in the West?' Why should Mississippi be strongly garrisoned while troops are wanted to fight Sitting Bull in Dakota and all that region which is now threatened with a cruel and possibly disastrous war? Senator Bayard, in a recent debate, showed how Mississippi has suffered under one of the worst governments ever known, and how much moderation and wisdom are wanted to enforce the much needed reforms. The views of Mr. Bayard are not extreme in this case. Mississippi and the whole South, indeed, are orderly enough, and a presidential campaign is not the time when large bodies of troops should be stationed in any State, when they are needed to fight the common enemy. There is a dividing line between caution and rashness, and we hope the administration may find it."

Rainey, the negro member of Congress from South Carolina, said if they failed to get troops in the South to control the election, he would advise his people to arm themselves and to sell their lives as dearly as possible. "Then," he added with a snap of his jaws, "if we are not strong enough to fight that way, by the living God, we will bring the torch into combat, and burn out all who seek our destruction."

Gen. Phil A. Sheridan, the "Rough Rider" of the Shenandoah Valley, in Virginia, who, with five thousand troops, passed up that section and desolated it, at a time when there were none to defend it, making war on its unarmed and helpless inhabitants, it was announced by telegram had been appointed military commander of the States of Mississippi, Arkansas, Louisiana and Alabama.

The apprehension of the people in consequence of this appointment could not be appreciated. It was evident to them that President Grant and the radical party intended again to place the Southern States under military rule in order to control the coming fall election.

Sheridan's connection with the Louisiana troubles and his denunciation of our people as banditti, and having advocated that they be tried as such and shot, gave room for the most serious consequences. Another military despotism, presided over by a man whom they regarded as destitute of civilized sensibilities, a brute in character as a commander, the slaughterer of a camp of sick Indians, was considered to be willing to perpetrate any outrage that might be desired of him by his master against the white people of these States in order to reëstablish negro supremacy.

Just at this time a great fever of excitement was raised by the news from Wilkinson County and West Feliciana Parish, La.

One Weber, a member of the Louisiana Legislature, instructed the negroes that the only hope for the success of the radical party in that State, was to prevent the Democrats from organizing and break up their club meetings by armed force. Learning a club was to be organized at Dr. Perkins' place, seven miles south of Woodville, at the State line; about forty armed negroes went there to break it up. Finding no club and no one else to kill they murdered Max Aronson, a Jew storekeeper, and wounded his colored clerk.

Gains, the negro leader, seconded by Swazey and Ben King, two other negro leaders, proclaimed war and began to increase his force.

In the meantime Col. Mose Jackson raised a small body of men and on Sunday engaged in a lively skirmish with the negroes, about six hundred strong. On Monday it was ascertained that the negroes had concentrated a force of about eight hundred men at Fort Adams. Col. Jackson was heavily reinforced, and was joined by two large companies of cavalry, under Col. Powers. The negroes were attacked and routed with severe loss. Gains, the leader, was captured and hung.

All these circumstances, with some little local disturbances caused by negroes insulting white ladies, created intense anxiety among the people of Pike County and convinced them that the time had not yet come when they should cease to be on the alert or relax their energies in the coming political contest.

If the reader will bear with the writer in this recital it will be shown that all the means that could be brought to bear in Pike County would not prevent an utter destruction of the negro race at this moment if the same circumstances surrounding other communities had been forced upon the white people here. It has already been said that a great influence was wielded by one man in Pike County, which few people appreciated at the time. The very first outbreak on the part of the negroes would have been the death knell of the race in Pike County. At Tylertown a negro named Dick Tyler, who has been mentioned in a former chapter as an obedient and trustworthy slave, insulted some white ladies in that community. It was a wise precaution taken by twenty men of his own color to provide themselves with the necessary outfit for his punishment, which resulted in his leaving the country.

The Democratic Club at Tylertown was presided over by Benjamin Lampton, a man well beloved by all people, and it was composed of members that would not permit an insult to a white lady by negroes. They had invited the negro men of the community to join them and aid in the effort to restore amicable political relations with them. The negroes were dependent for homes, for labor to earn their support, for the food they ate, for the clothes they wore, for medicines and medical attention, for the education of their children, wholly upon the white people, and it was time for them to cease obstructing the avenues which led to peace and happiness and prosperity. When these things could be impressed upon their minds, it was then and then only that a future security for them could be assured. On one occasion, the most important perhaps that ever occurred in that little village, a voice was heard that awakened an interest in the future course of the negroes at Tylertown. When the Democratic Club told them that their rights were not in danger and that they should be made secure in all that pertained to good citizenship, the voice of reason should have come to them for once. They had never attended a Democratic political speaking. It had been the policy of their leaders to hold up to their view the ever frightful and cadaverous skeleton constructed from the corpse of slavery.

In the next few weeks succeeding the one mentioned here a case occurred in the adjoining county of Lawrence which gave a backset to the efforts made to smooth over racial conditions. A negro committed an assault upon a white lady, but was promptly hung for the crime.

The radical papers all over the South began the publication of the most extreme and incendiary editorials, advising the negroes to acts of desperation, calculated to incense the Democratic press and cause them to retort in an equally threatening and vindictive spirit.

These were some of the conditions presented at the opening of the campaign of 1876, and they were conditions to be met with a firm resolve.

When the white people saw the character of the forces arrayed against them it was determined to be fully prepared and conduct a campaign under the most aggressive conditions. The executive committee arranged a plan of campaign and all the clubs in the county held weekly meetings. Hon. Samuel E. Packwood, Hugh Q. Bridges and the editor of the Magnolia *Herald* were appointed speakers to visit the clubs and address the people on public occasions. Thomas R. Stockdale, Samuel A. Matthews, David W. Hurst, Isaac Applewhite, Harry Applewhite, John S. Lamkin, James C. Lamkin, all able speakers, entered in the work to secure the success of the party.

An effort was made to break up the negro Democratic Club at Magnolia by putting the negro women forward to abuse its members, and threats were made by the "inconvincible" negroes, as they were termed, but the Democratic whites gave them protection and put a stop to it at once. Pike County had its share of irreconcilable and obstreperous negroes who needed something more than gentle persuasion and argument, and, while the white clubs in all the election precincts were offering inducements to them to come with them, it was determined never again to be placed under negro domination. The carpetbagger and negro had been on top for some years and held the guns while the white people had to pay the bills and feed them. The whites were on top now and held the guns and they were going to continue to hold them at all hazards. Argument and reason had failed to convince them in the past. It was time for a practical illustration of Caucasian manhood and tutelage by object lessons.

The negro club at Magnolia worked so earnestly and faithfully against the threats and intimidations offered them by men and women of their own color that they were honored by the white people of Magnolia with a public banner presentation. The banner was received on the part of the club by Martin Russell, the Secretary. Russell was an ex-Union soldier, an educated man and a good judge of human nature.

It was a curious fact that all, or nearly all the great newspapers at the North were wholly in sympathy with the carpetbaggers and negroes against the white people of their own race and blood. All of the so-called savage barbarity, outrages and crimes claimed to have been perpetrated in the Southern States, were laid at the door of the white people. The negro was the innocent lamb led to the slaughter pen, and the carpetbaggers were the persecuted missionaries and Christian martyrs to the cause of humanity, and it gave unction to their benighted souls when the military interceded to oppress the Southern whites.

In every single instance within the knowledge and experience of this writer, where there was a clash between the negroes and whites, the negroes were the beginners and aggressors. It is so to-day.

During this political campaign, in 1876, there is only one instance to be recorded where Democratic speakers succeeded in drawing the attention of a negro audience at a public meeting in Pike County. The club at Tylertown extended a special invitation to S. E. Packwood, Hugh Q. Bridges and the writer to deliver addresses at that place. Packwood was well known as a forceful speaker; he had lived among them for twenty-five years. Hugh Bridges was a captivating orator and the editor of the *Herald* was born and raised among them. A large number were present.

At the beginning of the speaking they stood afar off, but were gradually coaxed up around the stand during the closing address, when they received enlightenment on the forty acres and a mule and the Freedmans Bank swindles, with an illustration of how they obtained their pork and beans at the hands of Benjamin Lampton, the President of the Tylertown Club, whose interests they had been casting their votes to cripple; and if the members of this club who they had voted against in the past were to cut off their supplies, they, with their wives and children would starve to death in ten days, unless they went to stealing, which would result in every one of them being hung.

This was an opportune occasion and the first and only one when a Democrat got a shot at them from his mouthpiece, and they were admonished that the time had come when there must be a change in their attitude toward those who gave them houses to live in and furnished them the necessities of life; and there was going to be a change if every negro had to be swept from the face of the earth; and before the dawn of the day of the November election they would hear it thunder as it had never thundered before in Pike County.

The writer does not say it boastfully, but he was almost constantly in the saddle or on other conveyance visiting clubs and arranging details to make sure of the result on the day of the election. A large amount of powder was obtained for different neighborhoods and election precincts to be used the night before the election. A torch light horseback procession was arranged to make a circuit from Holmesville around by China Grove to Tylertown and return. This procession was headed by Jesse K. Brumfield and the editor of the Magnolia *Herald*, who rode side by side the entire circuit of over thirty miles. The pine tree cannonading began about ten o'clock and continued through the night. The torch light procession proceeded by China Grove and stopped for a few minutes at the residence of Hon. A. S. Bishop, where there was an exchange of courtesies in which Mrs. Bishop and some other ladies participated with most gracious hospitality and kindness. From here it proceeded to Tylertown, recrossing Magees Creek and passing by the old Smith place and the old home of Sampson L. Lamkin. During this time the horse of Jesse Brumfield took fright and lunged against the horse of the writer, causing a severe and painful sprain of his left knee. Some little excitement was produced in the ranks by the report that a body of negroes were in ambush, but nothing checked the procession. Rans Lewis, the only negro in Pike County who had never voted the Republican ticket, but always voted the Democratic ticket, was with this procession from start to finish.

The procession arrived at Tylertown about twelve o'clock, where a large crowd of people, containing some negroes, awaited it. Mrs. Benjamin Lampton had prepared supper for a few. After partaking of this last supper with a much beloved aunt, the writer was forced to respond to repeated calls.

During the year and through the campaign of 1876 the White League and the Bulldoozer organizations were kept up in Louisiana and in Mississippi. The most persistent and bitter opponents and denouncers of these organizations were the carpetbaggers—political adventurers, seekers after the flesh-pots, and ambitious negro politicians. The United States military and government authorities were not on friendly terms with them either. It was a bold peasantry indeed that would arm themselves and assert their inherent rights against such tremendous odds. Mississippi had complied with the terms of the reconstruction laws. It was self-government they claimed and the overthrow of a system which was bankrupting the taxpayers, who were the white, bona fide citizens of the State.

The State of Louisiana had been trampled under foot and the right of self-government completely overthrown by an insolent soldiery and it was deliberately approved by nearly a unanimous vote of the Republican majority in the United States Senate.

In his message to Congress in February, President Grant proposed the invasion of Arkansas and the overthrow of the government of that State, then in the hands of the men he had already recognized. What then could be expected for Mississippi, even after she had deposed the military and impeached the usurping Governor Ames?

An incident occurred in the town of Magnolia during this time to indicate the cool determination of the White League and Bulldoozer organizations. One of their number had been arrested and confined in the county jail at Magnolia. John Q. Travis was Sheriff, F. W. Collins, First Deputy, and Dave Walker, Under Deputy. A band of about seventy-five White Leaguers, said to be from Louisiana, unexpectedly appeared just on the outskirts of the western part of town and went into camp on the Minnehaha Creek, in old time cavalry fashion, late in the afternoon. The Sheriff and his deputies were unable to cope with such a body of men so unexpectedly appearing at the county seat, even if they had attempted or committed an overt act. They simply went into camp and proceeded to broil their meat and cook their hoecakes and procure feed for their horses, "very deliberately." After dark the Sheriff sent his Deputy, Dave Walker, and one or two other persons out to spy and scout around to ascertain their objects. Walker was captured and held a prisoner all night. Scouting parties of this command were sent all over Magnolia making inquiries for the Sheriff, after night set in. It was a bright moonshine night. The Sheriff took refuge in the residence of Rev. Farris, a Baptist minister, and went to bed. Deputy Sheriff Collins became the guest of the editor of the Magnolia *Herald*, who had the reputation of being the Bulldoozer mouthpiece. The whole town of Magnolia soon got into a fever of excitement over the invasion of the Louisiana Bulldoozers and their determined effort to capture the Sheriff of Pike County and his deputies. After assuring Mr. Collins of perfect security and protection at his home, the editor of the *Herald* walked out on the streets and encountered several squads and conversed with them. They said they wanted to find the Sheriff to get the jail key to get their friend out of jail and they intended to have him or tear the jail open, if they could not get the key. The editor suggested to them that they all retire to camp and wait till after breakfast time in the morning; that they could not find the officers even by searching every house in town, perhaps; to go back to camp and tell their commander to wait till morning and ride in to the court house square; that the Chancery Clerk was authorized under the law to fix the amount of the bond and they could get their comrade out of jail without violence and that there were some people in the community who would be pleased at their success in order that they themselves might escape apparent danger. The suggestion was adopted and the following day the bond was fixed and the prisoner released, when the troop disappeared as mysteriously as it came.

It is estimated that over forty thousand negroes were enrolled in the Democratic ranks and voted the Democratic ticket in the fall election of 1876. A tremendous majority was given in the State for Samuel J. Tilden for President.

In Pike County there was a clear gain of six hundred votes for the Democratic ticket over the returns of the election of 1875.

From the very first pioneer who settled in Pike County territory, in 1799, there had not been any census of the county taken or reported until 1820, when the population was shown to be 4,438, five years after the county was formed. In 1860, it was shown to be 11,-135; in 1870, 11,303; in 1880, 16,688; in 1890, 21,203; and in 1900, 27,545.

In consequence of the ravages of war and the revolutionary conditions prevailing the next five years after its close, the increase of the population of the county from 1860 to 1870 was only 168, while the next ten years showed an increase of 5,365.

After the re-establishment of authority and government by the white people and the restoration of peace and confidence, the gain was commensurate therewith, and the growth in population, prosperity, wealth and happiness that followed, the fulfillment of the aims of the leaders and the rank and file of the White League.

Tilden and Hendricks were elected President and Vice-President at this election by a large popular vote and by a majority of the electoral college, but so determined were those of the Republican party in control of the executive and legislative branches of the United States government to keep the Democratic candidates out that a measure was passed by the Congress to render the decision of the election in a manner contrary to the provisions of the Constitution, and so stultifying in its character as to stamp the Republican candidate who was declared elected by this fraudulent act, as "His Fraudulency R. B. Hayes," thus adding another chapter of scandal to the name of the United States government, in its shameful record throughout the war against the Southern States and the reconstruction era.

Infamous as the crime was in making R. B. Hayes President, it will always be remembered of him that he exerted himself in a laudable way to harmonize the bitter feeling of the Southern people engendered during Grant's administration, by removing the United States troops and stopping their interference in State affairs; and from his administration dates the beginning of the rehabiliment of Mississippi.

Let the recollections of the past be a lesson for those who come in the future to teach them to love their country and adhere to the fundamental principles upon which the government and their liberties were founded though the heavens fall.

> "Ill fares the land to hastening ills a prey,
> Where wealth accumulates and men decay;
> Princes and lords may flourish or may fade,
> A breath can make them as a breath is made.
>
> But a bold peasantry, their country's pride,
> When once destroyed can never be supplied;
> 'Tis yours to judge how wide the limits stand
> Between a splendid and a happy land."

WILD JIM BARNES.

In its early history there existed in the State of Mississippi a band of outlaws, and many were the scenes enacted that gave rise to exaggerated sensational reports of lawlessness which frustrated the authorities as to the methods best to be adopted to defeat the schemes concocted by them to further their aims in depredating on the live stock and other movable property of farmers and others that the organization operated on.

There was an organization known as Copeland's Clan. This clan had a line of operation from Alabama, through Mississippi, Louisiana, Arkansas and Texas, and along this line there lived a class of farmers who were in league with the clan, aiding and abetting their work and harboring the active operators. A system of relays was established so that a horse could be stolen from a community and, during the night, hurried off twenty miles to the next man and the actual thief back at the place of theft without being missed from the neighborhood and the horse hurried on to the next relay and so on until he was entirely out of reach, without the owner being able to get trace of him, and thus back and forth through a wide area the work went on for many years, until finally it was broken up by the Governor of Mississippi, who put a detective at work among them. They were sometimes called "Border Beagles" and a book was published bearing that title, giving a history of their operations. But there was what we may call a tail end to this clan which revived some years after the main head had been chopped off, that operated in scattered sections, almost every county in the State being more or less troubled at times with its work. This is reverted to in order to reach the subject of this article, who, many thought, back in the fifties, belonged to an organized clan during that time.

Wild Jim Barnes was a native of Marion County and in his early training was given advantage of a good education. He sprang from one of the best pioneer families of that county and was considered to be a young man of model characteristics up to a certain period of his life, when he was set adrift in pursuit of a livelihood by his own exertions. In connection with his excellent education he possessed a most remarkable memory, and was considered a prodigy in this particular gift. Everything he heard was indelibly stereotyped on his brain, and, like the graphophone, had only to be wound up for the occasion to reproduce whatever he wished, and with this remarkable talent he was possessed of the gift of oratory, witticism and sarcasm to a wonderful degree. Whenever the occasion presented itself he could and would reproduce any speech or sermon he ever heard and even in his early manhood he got to be a regular encyclopedia of sermons, speeches and prayers. He figured in Pike County to some extent and gave to the writer, in his boyhood, a lesson he never forgot. He was a prisoner in 1858, in the town of Holmesville, and was kept under guard until a trial could be had on the charges preferred against him, as the county jail had been destroyed by fire when the only prisoner in it at the time was cremated in the building. The writer was one of the guards appointed by the Sheriff to watch at night, and this fact gave rise to the information which this article contains.

He was arrested at the instance of Robert Ligon, a justice of the peace, in the town of Summit, charged with grand larceny. His witticism was pointed and side-splitting at times. He was a great talker and always commanded an attentive audience. He ridiculed the officer who had him arrested on such a charge and characterized his court as a nonentity. A famous expression fell from his lips in which he stated that "a bright idea has as much room for navigation in that officer's brain as a frog has in Lake Erie."

On one occasion he was taken to jail and delivered an interesting sermon to a large crowd, on cucumberology, taking "the cool cucumber" as his text, and declared, with vehement emphasis, eloquence and convincing argument that the cucumber was as apt to be saved as some of the gourd-headed upstarts who had filed affidavit against him on charges they could not prove, based upon the best of their knowledge and belief, which was merely a freak of their imagination.

Wild Jim Barnes traveled from Alabama to Texas, and back and forth, which gave rise to the supposition that he was following an unlawful avocation and belonged to one of the numerous gangs of horse and negro thieves that infested the South in those days, and it took considerable means to pay expenses. Horseback was the principal mode of traveling, on account of the character of the roads, trails and by-paths that had to be followed to reach given points in sparsely settled sections. There were no railroads nor telegraph lines, and the facilities for the transmission of news was through the slow process of the mails carried on horseback or by stage, and the outlaw or the one engaged in a questionable avocation could out travel these and be far away before the news would reach a point desired. Jim often got hard pressed for money to meet his demands, but he was resourceful, and when he got into a good neighborhood it was said he would hold divine services, either Baptist or Methodist, as occasion fitted, prayer meeting, protracted meetings and Sunday sermons, for the betterment of the community and particularly for the betterment of his empty pocketbook, and he always left full handed. Whether Wild Jim Barnes was the originator of this style of raising funds for the depleted finances of the ministry in South Mississippi and elsewhere, there is no positive proof, but it was practicable and Jim may have been the originator of it for aught we know. It is said at times, when he wanted to "raise a flush," he would sell his horse and then hold a big meeting, make a poor mouth to the brethren about having lost his horse, being on his way to fill a mission or attend a special call at a great distance. He proved his mission by his ability to preach and would hold meetings and give them some of his fine sermons, and his gift of oratory and entertainment never failed him. He would stir up their religious feelings and sympathy and always got a new horse, and then when he reached a suitable village or town he was ready for a game of poker, or a horse race.

One of his impressive sermons, for the "hat act," was on the subject of homes, the text being taken from the 5th chapter and 9th verse "of the gospel of our Lord, by Isaiah."

"In mine ears said the Lord of hosts, of a truth many houses shall be desolate, even great and fair, without inhabitant." Care was taken to impress upon his hearers that a homeless man was a sad subject to contemplate and how wholly dependent the servant of the Lord was on the brethren of the church for sustenance and support to enable him to satisfactorily discharge his duties to his flock. God had given to us all the privilege to locate a home and build a house and be the possessor of all that we need; but when we thought we had reached the height of our desires for comfort and happiness, a wave of illness would spread over the land and the angel of death appear, and behold the house made desolate. It is the house well provided and administered that gives the happiness He intended we should enjoy on this earth, and when we believe in Him and do His will, we will be rewarded abundantly, as was the case with Job, until he fell into the meshes of the devil. When we lay aside the will of the Lord that moment the devil reaches out and takes us by the hand and leads us astray from the paths of righteousness and we become sorely afflicted. Job was always patient, so say the Scriptures, and he believed it was for his own good that affliction was put upon him, and it was well that he believed this that he might bear his affliction with more patience. But I am not exactly prepared to say that I would feel as Job did.

"Of a truth many houses shall be desolate, even great and fair, without inhabitant," says the text, and in the palace as well as in the hovel there shall be desolation.

"And the mean man shall be brought down, and the mighty man shall be humbled, and the eyes of the lofty shall be humbled," says the prophet, Isaiah, and we see it all through our lives.

No man or woman should fail to perform the duties devolved upon them in responding to the calls made upon them by one of the Maker's servants who has laid aside all he possessed to administer to the spiritual needs of His children. Christ has said: "Sell all thou hast and follow me," and now there is an opportunity presented for those whose alms should be freely given, if they would escape affliction and torment, and desire to obtain everlasting life, lest the house become desolate. Let your light SHINE so that it will be acceptable to the Lord, that you may feel the consolation that you have given freely of your great abundance to advance His Divine Will." And then Brother Barnes would submit his distressed condition to the congregation through one of the deacons whom he had previously coached to make the call for help. Success always crowned his efforts.

When the Civil War broke out Wild Jim Barnes joined a compnay that became a part of the Thirty-third Mississippi Regiment, commanded by Col. David W. Hurst, Featherston's Brigade, Loring's Division, of the Army of Tennessee, C. S. A., and performed the duties of a faithful soldier. But he kept up his old practice of preaching for profit in the army, taking up collections to buy blankets for the boys, and gambling. Whenever a chance offered, when near a large town, he would have it announced that Brother Barnes of the 33rd Mississippi would hold divine services in one of the churches and he would preach one of his most stirring sermons, and always made a good hit and a good haul, in Confederate money, which he divided generously with the members of his company, and when monotonous camp life was on and the boys wanted something refreshing, they would call on him to hold a meeting. He always responded as sincerely and earnestly as if he had been a regularly ordained minister.

A man who could thus command the wages of a minister of the gospel and be a mischievous runabout and sportsman was an enigma to all who knew Wild Jim Barnes. He may have lived in its atmosphere as happily as any person performing the regularly ordained and acknowledged functions of the Church, and perhaps more so. We have no evidence that he ever gave a thought to anything of greater value to himself or to the world. While he was a genius and a man qualified to stand aloof from such conduct as that attributed to him, he never gave to mankind any evidence of heroic self-abnegation that belongs to those whose lives are free from stain. If he possessed talents to advance a great cause it would seem reasonable that there is something in the personal influence of a Creator on man for special purposes.

Here we have a man with power of thought, of language, eloquence and witticism and great memory traveling over the country as itinerant minister at times and at others filling the roll of a gambler, or of a vagabond from established moral society. He performed the farce act for the ministerial department of churches on his own hook at a time when ignorance and superstition predominated a large class of the people in sections where he operated, a representation of hypocrisy, of a class who believe *they only* were the elect and saints on earth and who abused the power entrusted to them by humbugging the people, as illustrated by Wild Jim Barnes, who gave to the world the picture of saintly ministry for personal profit as proof of a plan which has dominated the ministerial forces of the Christian churches, as evidenced in later history, and which with thinking men has damaged the cause of Christianity; and religion has been prostituted in the glow and glitter of costly edifices and paraphernalia for the edification of the rich and haughty, while the poor and meek and the lowly are driven to the hovels, beshamed and denied association with those they can not reach in personal adornment. The religion of the holy Jesus who was born in a manger and whose teachings and examples were of the purest simplicity and suited to all mankind has been superseded by the glamor of costly temples, where wealth revels and where souls that are earnest and sincere are denied entrance without pay; and to raise means to sustain these establishments and their belongings, great advertisements and bill posters are sent abroad announcing protracted revival meetings which are turned into collection bureaux, while millions are starving on account of the taxation. In the widespread competition for supremacy every Christian Church is struggling to outclass its rival in gorgeous temples of worship.

Beneath the starry dome of heaven, the blue canopy above us, nor in the woodland groves where nature spreads out in wholesome glory, are not good enough places to commune with God. We live in an age when wealth stands as the personification of all that is great and good, and the mean man who has a rented pew set aside for his own exclusive occupancy is not disposed to worship and commune alongside of his neighbor whose bank account is inferior to his own.

And this reminds us of a story told on Bob Ingersoll. While a country lawyer in Illinois, he visited a large city, and, as was his custom, he attended church to get new material for his lectures and seated himself in the first convenient pew. Soon afterward the renter of the pew walked in, faultlessly dressed, and seeing his pew occupied by a stranger, drew a card from his pocket and wrote upon it the following: "You are occupying my pew; I pay $500 a year for that pew." This he handed to the old pagan through the usher. Ingersoll reversed the card and wrote the following: "You pay too damned much," which he handed to the five hundred dollar pew man and walked out.

Wild Jim Barnes gave to the world all that was necessary to illustrate what has been written, and he made a point which cannot be refuted, and in doing this, he may have performed the work assigned to him by his Creator.

The great war lifted a veil from the eyes of the world. The combatting forces have passed into the annals of fame and the sterling worth of those who have been spared through eventful scenes is yet a synonym of glory. In the line that fame has rewarded there are a few who are the survivors of its immortal heritage. We who look back to the desolation wrought and the blazing glory which enshrines the epoch in which they acted, can scarcely conceive the wonderful advancement that has crowned our Southland from the Potomac to the Rio Grande. They mastered themselves and sustained the principles they struggled to maintain and they have achieved a still greater glory in establishing a firm moral character on their descendants. It is seen in all the avenues of trade and the productive achievements of the country and the strength of the government under which they live. They are its support in conflict or in peace, and they live to adorn the present with their examples.

LITTLE JOE LEWIS' FAREWELL SERMON.

Little Joe Lewis was the son of Joseph Lewis, one of the pioneers who settled on the west side of Magees Creek, some miles below and south of the present site of Tylertown, on the plantation still known as the Joe Lewis place, where Little Joe, as he was familiarly called by his friends and neighbors, was born, and who had acquired distinction as a local Baptist preacher, officiating at the old New Zion Church, in the southeastern corner of Pike County, located on or near the Pushepatapa Creek. This meeting house was one of the first erected in that section of the county by the early settlers of the Baptist persuasion, and was constructed, like all other early meeting houses, of small logs for the main body and subsequently enlarged by the addition of wide sheds around it, so as to give accommodation to the increasing population of whites and negro slaves adhering to the Baptist faith and living in the neighborhood. Little Joe's father had officiated here in the early settlement of the community, and, in connection with the Rev. Willis J. Fortinberry, had organized and built up a Christian fellowship that has lived and flourished ever since. The war had come on in the sixties and was progressing with all its incident suffering and horrors. Nearly all the men of military age had gone to the scenes of the conflict, leaving the very old men and boys and the women and children to struggle along as best they could, and very many of these were in great distress for reasons growing out of the war.

In his childhood and boyhood Little Joe had to work hard on the farm, shell corn and go to mill at Tyler's or Conerly's, on Dry Creek, to have it ground into meal and hominy, and sometimes to the tannery of Chauncey Collins, over on Collins Creek, to carry hides in payment of shoes for the family. He was a sturdy, good boy of practical common sense and grew up so under pious surroundings. In his young manhood he became strongly impressed in religious duties, and though acquiring a limited education, such only as could be acquired in the country pay schools at that time, felt that it was his duty to enter the ministry and preach the gospel, and in a measure fill the mission inaugurated by his distinguished father, and hence officiated at New Zion during the Civil War. He announced at one of his well attended meetings that on a certain Sabbath in the future he would deliver his farewell sermon at his home church at New Zion. When the time came it was a cold, bleak, drizzly day and the shivering winds were howling around the houses and moaning through the pines and were too much for those whose apparel was worn and thin from the absence of means in these awful war times to supply something better. Confederate money was at par—that is, it was worth dollar for dollar of the same sort of currency and scarce in this neighborhood, too, and greenbacks had not circulated to any extent. Hence a small congregation appeared to listen to Little Joe's farewell sermon. He was greatly disappointed at the small gathering as manifested in his remarks and as depicted on his countenance when he arose and spoke as follows:

"MY DEAR FRIENDS: When I last had the pleasure of appearing before a congregation in this house, I announced that on this day I would be here to preach my farewell sermon before taking my departure to the State of Texas, here I expect to reside in the future.

"Under all the circumstances I had hoped and expected to be greeted by a large congregation, but, behold, the seats are empty!

"Now, my dear friends, if I had announced that on this day I would be here for the purpose of distributing ten thousand dollars, what scrouging! What scrouging!! What scrouging!!!

"I had intended to give a discourse on a certain passage of Paul's Epistles to the Corinthians, but under the circumstances I shall content myself with a few general remarks.

"In the first place, my dear, dying congregation, I desire to warn you that the salvation of your precious souls is of greater value and of greater concern to you than the acquirement of a few paltry dollars; for what doth it profit a man to gain the whole world and lose his own soul?

"I feel sure that if this idea had been properly impressed on the minds of my people I would to-day stand in the presence of the largest congregation ever assembled on these grounds.

My friends, I am a plain spoken man, and when I give an illustration I want it to illustrate.

"Church people are not always what they ought to be and sometimes some of them are not what they appear to be. They sometimes remind me of the great and grand forests. We go out and into them and view and admire the beautiful foliage, the symmetrical poplars and stately oaks. They all appear to be sound, but lo, when the axman comes to cut into them he finds many of them doty and filled with worms, and some of them hollow at the butt.

"I shall not expect you to be in a very pious mood on this day, as the shivering winds are rumbling about us and bringing the cold damp of death from the mountains in the far off North where our soldiers are standing guard in defense of our country.

"I wish I could see the effect of a spiritual uprising, so that we could feel the flow of God's love and mercy in our hearts. I always felt that God was a merciful and loving God, and that he would one day lift our benighted souls into a realization of His desires, but it seems to me now that He has forgotten or withdrawn the care He has previously bestowed upon us, as I see so few here to-day who seem concerned about which way the contest ends.

"I am a lover of the country which gave me birth and the privilege of worshiping the Lord according to my idea of it, and I desire to impress upon you the full import of the duties you should perform. I am at a loss to understand why I should thus become the innocent victim of the devil's schemes to rob a people of its inheritance.

"We are at a stage of life when all the virtue that is in us should be manifested in the true Christian spirit. It is so important to us that all of us should join in the refreshing services of a day when our souls can be free to exert themselves. I always love to meet my people on the Sabbath when the cares of the workshop, the store and the farm can be laid aside and we can come together and fulfill the mission of our lives in the blessings of the gospel of Jesus Christ. I shall live to remember the saddest day of my life when it became necessary for me to depart from them. Oh, my people, where are the loved ones gone now? What sacrifices you are called upon to make, and yet deny yourselves the blessings of the Maker!

"If God has given the people a chance to become the children of righteousness and they prefer the ways of the devil instead, it is all right with me and I will depart in peace.

"If Paul, when he spoke to the Romans, had flickered in the least the devil would have given him due compensation; but Paul was a man of power and great thought, who could give the devil his dues and at the same time give the Lord His dues; but here, in my home church, where I have labored long and listened to the wails of suffering and sorrow and the sacrifices of the women of our land in the trying ordeals which beset our country, I am confronted with the person of the DEVIL, who has been promulgating his desires in the midst of my people! I at least desired a full congregation so that a voice from heaven might hover over them upon my departure and give them a special blessing, but lo, the seats are empty where once the fond father and the pious mothers, brothers and sisters sang the songs of the blessed Redeemer. If it is the will of Him who sent me to preach to them, to go to a distant land and there unfurl His banner, I shall not tarry here with those who have thus forgotten me and disobeyed His will. Away over yonder in the sunlight of His glory I shall be found in that day when the angels call us hence.

"This occasion, my dear, dying congregation, reminds me of a song which was always a harvest of joy and so refreshing that I am constrained to call it up now:

> Jesus, lover of my soul,
> Let me to thy bosom fly;
> While the nearer waters roll,
> While the tempest still is high.

"My dear, dying congregation, I had almost said my dead congregation!

"In the morning of the resurrection I shall be glad to greet my people if they can come to the throne of grace and get forgiveness for the shortcomings of this occasion, but if they do not, there will be wailing! There will be wailing! There will be wailing and wailing!

"I admonish you to-day that in the quiet hours of the night you repair to your secret closets and there ask God to give you love and happiness and salvation. It will stay the torrent of human disasters and torment that afflict the wicked. The evils which beset us is the stumbling block on the road to the heavenly mansion, and it is this which must be removed if you ever expect to get to the land of everlasting life, hope and happiness, and if you don't do it there will be stumbling and falling, falling and falling!

"Oh, foolish Galatians, who hath bewitched you that ye should not obey the truth, before whose eyes Jesus Christ hath been evidently set forth, crucified among you?

"Oh, New Zions, 'Are ye so foolish?'

"Who hath warned you to flee from the wrath to come?

" 'Have ye suffered so many things in vain?'

"'And let us not be weary in well doing,' saith Paul to the Galatians, written from Rome.

"'For behold the day cometh that shall burn as an oven; and all the proud, yea, and all that do wickedly, shall be stubble, and the day that cometh shall burn them up,' saith Malachi.

"My dear, dying congregation, I shall not detain you any longer than it is necessary to illustrate by illustrating that the sinner who dies in his or her sins will be damned. He or she is destined to be plucked out from the elect and plunged down into the depths of hell, lapped in the lambent flames of an eternal damnation, in company with the devil and his angels, forever and forever, and forever and ever!

"My dear, dying congregation, let the blood of the Lamb be the guiding star of your lives and when I have departed it will give you comfort and joy.

"I am in the condition of the wolf in the fold. It is said that once a wolf got in among the sheep and the sheep put up a job on him. He became enamored of a beautiful fat lamb and lay down by its side and became very affectionate toward it, but in the course of time the lamb began to smell something unusual and to feel that it was in the wrong place. It didn't like the smell of the wolf and got up and started away. When the wolf discovered this he made a nab at the lamb and tried to catch it by the tail, but all the other sheep scrouged in on the wolf and scrouged him to death, and this is about the fix I am in to-day. It was a loving beginning, but turned out to be a bad job in the end. They seem to have smelt a wolf, and I feel that I am scrouged to death.

"I shall give you another illustration, so that you may forsake your sins and come to the throne of grace. It is too much for a man to be betrayed into the fold where such treatment follows, and I shall illustrate it further by saying that all who shall hereafter seek the Lamb of God that taketh away the sin of the world had better be pure in heart, wash off the scent of the wolf and be ready to receive the blessings of the fold instead of being scrouged to death before departing to the other place of residence in the eternal hereafter.

"I hope these few remarks will live in the memory of my few hearers on this day and that a day will come when they shall fill their place in the history of this church and this congregation.

"I am not inclined to be in a timid mood any longer. I am at a stage to speak out and act as my mind tells me, and I am going to depart from this neighborhood with the free will and consent of the people as manifested on this occasion. I expect some of them will feel hurt when I say to you that it is a sin and a shame for me to be denied their presence on this the last day of my stay among them. I desire to be emphatic. The Sabbath is the holy day of the Lord, and in the light of the great rivers of blood which are now flooding our land from the Potomac to the RioGrande, blighting homes, breaking hearts, bringing death and desolation, making thousands of widows and orphans, creating starvation, sorrow and distress everywhere, it is as little they could do to come out and let the Lord see who they are. I know He will remember them in the day of judgment, as I expect to do.

"I sincerely hope to meet you all in the land of the redeemed. God is the giver of all good and the devil is the giver of all the evils and sorrows that afflict humanity.

"A sinner is a sinner, and he or she is a sinner every time he or she fails to perform the duties of life as set forth in Paul's Epistles to the Corinthians and to the Galatians. I shall not detain you any longer. It is the will of God that a day is to be given to his services and it is due to Him to perform its functions in the manner set forth in the Scriptures.

"I want it understood that what I have said is intended in the warmest friendship and true Christian spirit and for the sake of your never-dying souls.

"In the morning of the resurrection I shall come to the throne of God and there I shall lay my case before the Messenger who was sent to us to fulfill His mission here. I am now at a loss to know just how I shall be fitted for the place He has prepared for me, but I am going to try to do my duty as I think it should be done.

"If any of this congregation feel that a wolf is in the fold I should like for them to intimate it by doing as the lamb did when it smelt the wolf, and I shall then understand that my presence is not wanted any longer. I shall feel as though I had been in the same fix as the wolf unless I am admonished otherwise. I am not disposed to let the opportunity pass, however, to prove my fidelity and tender feelings for those whom I have served so long and for whom I have prayed so much.

"Brethren, sing the Doxology.

> Praise God from whom all blessings flow,
> Praise Him all Creatures here below;
> Praise Him above, ye heavenly host,
> Praise Father, Son and Holy Ghost.

"And may the blessings of God rest and abide with you all forever. Amen."

And Little Joe, big-hearted Little Joe Lewis, took up his hat and saddlebags and bid his few hearers farewell forever on this earth, leaving this in their memory as a fulfillment of his wish and prayer that it would become a part of the history of that congregation.

This sermon made such an impression upon the few who were present as to cause it to be considered one of the most celebrated ever delivered in that community. It was so forceful and earnest in its delivery that most of the survivors who heard it remember its context to this day, and this fact has enabled the writer to reproduce it and incorporate it in these reminiscences of Pike County.

MRS. MARTHA L. J. HOOVER.

Mrs. Martha L. J. Hoover, wife of the late Rev. William Hoover, was a daughter of Alexander Thompson 3d and Dorothy Pryor Womack, and was born in Amite County November 20, 1834. The Thompson ancestors were from Scotland. Some of them settled in New York, North Carolina and Georgia. Alexander Thompson, Sr., and son James, fought in the battle of King's Mountain. He was wounded in the head. A man named Griffith was shot and he stooped to raise him up when a ball struck him in the forehead, passed over his head under the scalp and came out at the back of the neck, which prevented the hair from growing where the scar was left. Alexander Thompson 2d came to Amite County in 1818 with the Epps, Powells and Wells. They organized the Pisgah Presbyterian Church with Rev. Robt. Smiley pastor. This church is now in Summit with all its records.

Alexander Thompson 3d, father of Mrs. Hoover, who married Dorothy Pryor Womack, of St. Helena Parish, La., removed from Amite County and settled on the Tickfaw River, where he raised his family and four of his sons participated in the battle of Shiloh. D. W. Thompson, his eldest son, at the age of 15 was in the war with Mexico and fifteen years later raised a company for the Confederacy, and one of his brothers, 15 years of age, was a member of it.

MRS. MARTHA L. J. HOOVER

Dorothy Pryor Womack, the mother of Mrs. Hoover, was the mother of five sons: Diotician, Robert, Jefferson, William and J. P. Street Thompson, and three daughters: Martha, Virginia and Amelia. Virginia married John J. Wheat and is the mother of Judge Wheat, of Beaumont, Texas. The other daughter died in the Sacred Heart Convent, St. James Parish, La.

The Womacks were from Georgia. Abraham and his brother Jacob Womack, relatives of Mrs. Hoover, on the mother's side, belonged to the Louisiana militia in the War of 1812-15, and were present at the battle of New Orleans. Jacob was in the battle and claimed to be the man who shot General Packingham from behind a bale of cotton.

Mrs. Hoover was a highly intellectual woman, devoted Christian and religious worker and was a great aid to her husband in his ministerial work.

MASONRY. A MYSTERIOUS FIND—A MASONIC EMBLEM FOUND IN AN INDIAN MOUND IN PIKE COUNTY.

The Masonic historian has found many evidences of the existence of Masonry without, however, finding sufficient data to establish a clear and continuous record from the time Masons first arrived at the places where such evidences are found.

Much rise is therefore given to speculation and the mind of man creates fantasies which frequently are accepted by those who do not give careful study to the subject as facts.

When Masons first trod the soil of our State and that of our sister Mississippi may never become known. From time to time there are found relics which establish clearly that some of the Craftsmen penetrated deep into the wilds of the unexplored domain—perhaps lived in peace and amity with the Indians, possibly infusing into some of these sons of the wilderness the principles and teachimgs of Masonry.

We take pleasure in placing before our readers an evidence of that kind. The stone in question is in possession of Brother Brittain B. Purser, of Osyka, Miss., to whom we are indebted for the following lines descriptive thereof:

BROTHER BRITTAIN'S LETTER.

Among the many Masonic curios which show the antiquity, and as well the universality of Freemasonry is the carved stone represented herein. This piece of shale or soft stone was found in its present condition, carving and delineations, in a plowed up Indian mound some twenty miles east of Osyka, Pike County, Miss. It was picked up by Alex. Hughes, who at the time of finding was about nine years old, and it has been in his keeping since, until a few months ago when he gave it to the writer. Mr. Hughes is now a grown, settled man, with a son as old as he was when the stone was found.

A description calling attention to the various delineations will show the correctness of the knowledge of the maker, and prove beyond the shadow of a doubt that he was not only a fellow-craftsman, but was in possession of the exact knowledge of all three degrees.

On the obverse side of the stone are delineated two oblongs, the one smaller and within the other, the sides of the two being parallel and the angles are indicated each by an arc of ninety degrees. Thus in this we have the form of the Lodge, horizontals, perpendiculars and right angles. Within the two oblongs, and nearer one end, is delineated a small part of the Masonic pavement. Nearer the other end, and within the oblongs, are delineated a square and compass, so arranged that one point of the compasses is elevated above the square, the other being concealed beneath. One leg of the square is longer than the other, indicating the carpenter's rather than the stonemason's square.

On the reverse side are delineated the two oblongs, the angles of ninety degrees, but in the inner oblong we now see a symbol beyond the two on the obverse side, for there is delineated a human heart pierced by an arrow.

The stone itself is carved to represent a closed book, and while there are no letters or characters to indicate the fact, one's first thought on seeing the shape is of "The Book of the Law."

The clear indications of a knowledge of all three degrees would bring the making of this curio to within something less than 175 years; the square being that of the carpenter rather than the stonemason, would indicate French origin, while the arrow in place of the sword on the reverse side, and as well the finding in an Indian mound, and with no other evidences of civilization, would indicate an Indian origin. We would therefore suppose that this stone was carved by some old French brother and from him came into possession of the Indians, and was placed in the mound as a talisman. Or, possession may have passed to the Indian because of ties of blood, for in the earlier days of this section of country matrimonial as well as fraternal and commercial treaties were made between the French and Indians. Of this, however, we are certain, deep down in the heart of some resident or visitor to this district, in the earlier days when the undying principles of the ——————— and in his handiwork we see the signs of his advancement from darkness unto light, and though his heart may now be stilled by the touch of man's last and best friend, Death, yet across the gulf, adown the years comes a message from him to us, for in the imperishable stone he has given us the signs of his deliverance from the bondage of darkness, and we may well believe that with all the brethren who have gone before this way he is now resting from his labors in the celestial Lodge above, where the G. A. O. T. U. presides.

BRITTAIN B. PURSER.

Osyka, Miss., September 8, 1902.

Brother Purser is a young, highly intelligent and progressive Mason, a scion of noble ancestry. He is a son of the lamented Rev. D. I. Purser, who sacrificed his life in the discharge of his sacred calling during the epidemic which visited our city in the autumn of 1897.

When and how this stone came into an Indian mound, among arrows and other evidences of Indian origin, may never be explained. We place this fragment of historical evidence on record for the benefit of future explorers.—*Square and Compass.*

It was the good fortune of the editor of the *Enterprise* to see this curiosity and decipher its well illustrated emblems. The cuts given in this article are about one-half the size of the original stone.

MRS. L. W. CONERLY, *nee* IDA M. FARMER.

Mrs. Conerly is a daughter of Zachary T. Farmer and Mary J. Byars, of Sharon, Madison County, Miss., and was married on the 4th of May, 1909. Her father was a member of the Second Missouri Light Artillery, King's Battalion, Armstrong's Brigade of Cavalry, Jackson's Division, and surrendered with Forrest at Gainesville, Ala., 1865. She had two uncles, Henry Clay and Franklin Pierce Farmer, in the Confederate army, both killed during the Civil War. Her grandfather Farmer was a Confederate soldier also. Her grandfather, Philip Byars, was a member of Company H, Ninth Mississippi Volunteers, and was killed at the battle of Franklin, Tenn., November 30, 1864, and was buried on the battlefield.

Mrs. Conerly was born January 3, 1870, at Sharon.

Mrs. Eloise Chisholm
Holding Quitman Guards' Banner

SEQUEL TO THE QUITMAN GUARDS BANNER.

At a reunion of the Sixteenth Mississippi Regiment in Summit, in 1876, William Frank McGehee was appointed custodian by members of the Quitman Guards, and kept it in his possession for twenty years. Having removed to Texas, he returned the flag to Capt. S. A. Matthews, the first captain of the company, who led it to Virginia, in 1861, and after his death his widow kept it in her possession until April

W. Frank McGehee
Quitman Guards

21, 1906, when it was returned to the survivors of the Quitman Guards by the granddaughter of Captain Matthews, Miss Norma Dunn, the fourteen-year-old daughter of Hollis G. Dunn and his wife, Mamie Matthews, of Summit, at a reunion in the town of Holmesville,

Lieut. Van C. Coney
of the Quitman Guards
Served with distinction through the Civil War
He was severely wounded in the Battle of
Sharpsburg, Md., Sept. 17th, 1862

and was received by Capt. John Holmes, the last and surviving captain of the company, the writer acting as spokesman for Captain Holmes. It was decided to have this banner framed between two large glasses and a record of it and of the company written, to be attached to it and to be placed in the Hall of Fame at Jackson, and the writer was appointed its last custodian and historian to do this work, and to convey the banner to Jackson and deposit the same with the Director of Archives and History. After preliminary addresses delivered by Capt. S. C. Walker, of the Brent Rifles, and the writer, Rev. I. H. Anding was called on and spoke as follows:

THOMAS M. BARR
In original uniform of Quitman Guards, 1861.

Mr. Barr is a son of Joseph Barr, and was born on Magee's Creek, near China Grove. He was wounded in the battle of Sharpsburg, Md., Sept. 17th, 1862, and was detailed and appointed Postoffice Inspector for the Confederacy, which position he filled during the remainder of the war. He is now a citizen of Kansas City, Mo.

Survivors of the Quitman Guards, Ladies and Gentlemen: The eloquent addresses to which we have just listened, followed by the strains of music to the air, "Home, Sweet Home," rendered so beautifully by the band, stirs my soul. Were I a poet I should feel constrained to compose a lyric inspired by the scenes which surround us and the occasion which calls us together. Memories of the past come trooping before our mental vision. Well do I recall, though younger in years than you veterans, an April day, forty-five years ago, next Saturday, when a dear brother, strong and intellectual, gentle and brave, embraced our mother and kissed us all good-bye and went away in response to his country's call to the Virginia fields, where on the 21st of August, 1864, he fell in the bloody fight at Weldon Junction. Some of your comrades fell in that fierce conflict. We leave a tribute of praise to their valor.

To-day our surroundings are inviting; nature smiles propitiously upon us, the skies bend lovingly over us. On this April morning the breezes gently fan our brows, the leaves of these grand old oaks dance and rustle to the breeze; the grass gives us a carpet of velvet green; the flowers charm us with fragrance and loveliness; the birds carol their praises to their Maker; the waters of our valleys go murmuring and sparkling to the sea. This is a beautiful world in which we live. Were it given to me to choose an orb for a permanent abode, I think it would be this earth arrayed in its sinless beauty, with the friends and companions I have known in other days and those I now know, to walk by my side. "Sentiment," you say; yes, there is beauty, too, in sentiment, that kind of sentiment which denotes fixed opinions nurtured by feelings that are pure, strong, noble and good. The occasion of this hour is full of that sort of sentiment, and to me it is beautiful. We have after nearly a half century, the opportunity of looking upon a relic that recalls the long ago—a relic which tells us in silent speech of the loving hands and hearts that gave it, as a memento of their patriotic fervor and constant devotion to their country's cause and to the boys who were to wear the gray.

It is my delightful privilege to introduce one who will recommit this sacred relic to the survivors of as gallant a company of Southern braves as ever raised the battle cry or marched to death or victory—the gallant Quitman Guards. The one who is to present this flag to you today is fittingly selected, since she is the granddaughter of your first captain, who led you forth in answer to country's call—Samuel A. Matthews—who, a few years ago, at his home in Summit, Miss., surrounded by loved ones and friends, fell into the dreamless sleep. She is also the granddaughter of Mathew A. Dunn, one of the bravest of the brave, who fell on Franklin's bloody field.

GEORGE W. ROOT
Quitman Guards, (E), 16th Mississippi
One of the gallant young men from the State of Connecticut
Wounded through both knees in the seven days battles before Richmond, Va., and disabled
Now a resident of St. Helena Parish, La.

Survivors of the Quitman Guards, Ladies and Gentlemen:

Allow me to present one who is a special favorite of mine, and I know she must be to you and to all who know her, the daughter of our most excellent citizen of Summit, Mr. and Mrs. Hollis G. Dunn.

I present with pleasure Miss Norma Dunn:

Miss Norma Dunn

SPEECH OF MISS NORMA DUNN RETURNING BANNER TO QUITMAN GUARDS:

The occasion we celebrate today is in honor of the Holmesville Quitman Guards, a few survivors of whom are present today to do honor to the memory of the 107 who left for the field of carnage forty-five years ago.

In 1859 the Quitman Guards were organized as a home military company, by Capt. Preston Brent, with Chauncey P. Conerly, Samuel A. Matthews, Wm. J. Lamkin, John Holmes, Luke W. Conerly, H. Eugene Weathersby, Henry S. Bonney, William Garner, A. P. Sparkman, Senaca McNeil Bain and others as menbers at that time.

In 1860, the Ladies of Holmesville, and surrounding country, some of whom I can mention:

Madams J. T. Lamkin, S. A. Matthews, Dr. Jesse Wallace, H. S. Bonney J. C. Williams, H. M. Quin, Dr. D. H. Quin; H. F. Bridges, Dr. George Nicholson

Owen Conerly, Preston Brent, Wm. Ellzéy and Jackson Coney, made up by subscription $250, and purchased a silk banner, and appointed Rachel E. Coney, who named Emma Ellzey and Fanny Wicker as maids of honor to make the presentation. The three named Thomas R. Stockdale as their escort, and on this very spot, where we stand today, Rachel E. Coney presented the banner and it was received on the part of the Quitman Guards by the Hon. H. Eugene Weathersby, who was an honored member. Of those who were

CHARLES E. HARTWELL
Quitman Guards, Co. E, 16th Mississippi
One of the young boys who joined as a recruit,
serving in the sanguinary conflicts in Virginia
from the Wilderness May 6th, 1864,
until the fall of Petersburg and
Richmond in 1865

members at that time and present at the presentation of the banner, we can only recall the names of Capt. John Holmes, Luke W. Conerly, Dr. A. P. Sparkman, Dr. W. J. Lamkin and Wm. E. Brent, who are living today. So much for 1859 and 1860.

In 1861, forty-five years ago today, after a call of President Davis for troops, the Quitman Guards were reorganized with 107 members and elected S. A. Matthews, Captain; James M. Nelson, 1st Lieutenant; Thomas R. Stockdale, 2d Lieutenant, and Senaca McNeil Bain, 3d Lieutenant.

DR. R. T. HART
Quitman Guards
Wounded in Virginia
Subsequently appointed Assistant Surgeon in
the Western or Tennessee Army

Thus formed, they left Magnolia on the 26th day of April, and were mustered into service on the 27th day of May, 1861, at Corinth, Miss., as Company

E, 16th Mississippi Regiment. This company was sent to Virginia and formed a part of the Army of Northern Virginia, remaining with Lee's army from 1861 to 1865, and participated in the battles of Manassas, Petersburg, Gettysburg, Spottsylvania, Sharpsburg, Weldon Railroad and all of the great battles of that country.

This scene to you, noble survivors of that heroic band, must recall the halcyon days of the long ago, when on this village green your steps were blithe, your hearts were glad, and your eyes spoke love to eyes of those who call you brave and true, and to whom you tenderly referred as your "sweethearts pretty girls." Now five and forty years ago, a voice from the past tells of the brave heroic deeds of those who fell upon the firing line, and of those who, after the storm of strife had passed, returned to the ordinary pursuits of life to fulfill their mission and then go over to meet their brothers on fame's eternal camping ground. Let us here place the chaplet of praise to the memory of every one of them, and permit me to make personal reference to one whose memory you sacredly cherish, and whose name you will pronounce with a thrill of pride to your posterity, the truest type of Southern blood, and the very impersonation of dauntless courage. I refer to the gentle, the generous, the tried and true, the gallant, the intrepid Frank McGehee. Should a monument ever be erected on this spot to the memory of the gallant braves of the Quitman Guards, let the name of "Shanks," as he was lovingly called by his comrades, stand out in bold relief, the synomyn of Southern manhood, and the highest type of the Confederate soldier; this single reference is made, not to detract from others just as noble and brave, but to do honor to one who for twenty years was the custodian of this flag and who represented the chivalric spirit of the Quitman Guards. And now as a direct descendant of him who led you as your first captain under the bugle call to arms in the great civil strife—Capt. S. A. Matthews—it is my happy privilege through the esteemed honor, you, the survivors of the Quitman Guards have conferred on me, to recommit this banner to your sacred care and keeping. It tells its own story. Time, with its corroding touch, has dimmed its material luster, but not its inherent glory. It speaks emblematically today of Southern chivalry as crystalized in the hearts of the many fair young daughters of our noble old county of Pike. In its fold, as in your hearts, are enshrined the memories of mothers, sisters, sweethearts, whose faith in your gallantry has been your inspiration on many a hard fought field. Pathetically, though triumphantly, it tells of those ever living principles for which our dear Southland poured out its most precious blood. Though our flag went down in defeat these principles can never die. Silently this flag symbolizes them today, as when our fathers donned the gray.

To you, Capt. John Holmes, the worthy survivor of the comrades who honored you as their leader and followed at your command into the thickest of the fight, I commit this sacred relic, the grandest and most characteristic symbol of that liberty for which our fathers and your brothers gave their lives; keep it, and guard it for the sake of those who first gave it to you. Care for it for the sake of those who followed its bearer, preserve it for the sake of those principles it silently, but emphatically, represents. In the words of another

> "Lift up your boy on your shoulder high,
> And show him the faded shred,
> Those bars would be red as the sunset sky
> If death could have dyed them red."
> Off with your hats as the flag goes by,
> Uncover the youngest head,
> Teach him to hold it holy and high
> For the sake of the sacred dead."

And now, may you honored sir—and few but faithful who survive with you and share these reminiscences of a deathless past, together with all of us who love our new South, our country and its flags, may it not be ours to hear again the beat of drum which calls to mortal combat, or feel the chilling shadow of the storm cloud of war, but when at last we strike our tents from the old camp ground of this life, may we go over as loyal soldiers to the great Captain of our salvation, to drink from the springs of everlasting peace and to hear from His sacred lips the glad "Well done!"

Miss Dunn was replied to by the writer in a short appropriate address in behalf of Captain Holmes, to whom the banner was returned, during which a crown of flowers was placed on her head by Miss Fredirica Bongard, and she was adopted as the daughter of the survivors of the Quitman Guards, and, in the language of the Magnolia *News*, "Thus bringing to a sublime ending in a most befitting way one of the most noted historical events of Pike County."

The good man into whose hands this relic was again placed has since passed and gone where the echoes of war shall not be heard and now sleeps the dreamless sleep in the cemetery at Magnolia beside his own beloved Alvira, who in the very midst of the storm of the great conflict gave her heart and hand to him; and Lieutenant John Q. Travis, too, the handless veteran, who stood by his side, succeeded to the command of the last remnant of the old guards, only to cross over the river in a few weeks after.

MISCELLANEOUS LEGAL AND FAMILY RECORDS PERTAINING

TO THE AREAS OF PIKE AND WALTHALL COUNTIES,

MISSISSIPPI

13TH REGIMENT (NIXON'S) OF MISSISSIPPI MILITIA

Captain John Bond's Company
Lieutenant William Bond's Company
Captain David Cleveland's Company
Captain Moses Collins's Company
Captain Francis B. Lenoir's Company
Captain James McGowen's Company

Captain James Phillip's Company
Captain Henry Quin's Company
Captain Harmon M. Runnel's Company
Captain William Smith's Company
Captain William Spencer's Company

Adison, Hiram, private
Akin, John, ensign
Alexander, Isaac, private
Allen, Barnabas, sergeant
Allen, Garret, private
Allgood, Wiet, private
Andrews, James, private
Andrews, William, private
Applewhite, Stephen, private
Ard, Thomas, private
Armstrong, Abner, private
Armstrong, Jesse, private
Armstrong, Jonathan, private
Ashton, Henry, private
Askue, Henry, private
Bagley, William, sergeant
Bailey, James, private
Bailey, Thomas, private
Ball, Sampson E., private
Ballard, Lewis, private
Ballard, Nathan, private
Ballard, Reuben, private
Banks, Levi, private
Barksdale, Collier, private
Barrett, George, private
Batson, James, private
Batson, Peter, private
Batson, Seth, private
Batson, Thomas, private
Beard, William, private
Beasley, William, private
Becot, Labon, serg.
Bell, Thomas, private
Berry, James, private
Blue, Angus, serg.
Blue, Daniel, private
Bond, Gedion, corp.
Bond, Henry, private
Bond, James, private
Bond, John, captain
Bond, Robert, private
Bond, William, lieut.
Bohannon, Wily, private
Braddy, William, private
Breland, Hillery, serg.
Brent, Charnel, private
Brent, John, private
Brent, Merideth, ensign
Brent, Thomas, private
Bridges, Sampson, private
Brister, John, private
Brown, Daniel, private
Brown, John, private
Brown, Moses, sergeant
Brown, Robert, private
Buckaloo, John, private
Buckaloo, Richard, private

Buckley, James, private
Bullin, William, private
Bullock, David, private
Bullock, James, private
Bullock, Silas, private
Burge, Nathaniel, private
Burge, Washington, private
Burns, Reason, serg.
Butler, Luke, private
Cagle, John, private
Calbert, Richmond, private
Canady, Nathen, private
Carpenter, John, private
Carpenter, Wm. private
Carson, John, Jr., private
Carson, John, Sr., private
Carter, Allen, private
Carter, Burrel, serg.
Carter, George, private
Carter, Hardy, private
Carter, Marcus E., private
Carter, Michael, private
Carter, Wm. lieut.
Catching, Jonathan, private
Catching, Joseph, corp.
Catching, Philip, private
Chesnut, David, private
Cleveland, David, captain
Clower, Daniel, private
Clower, John, private
Coats, Pollard H., private
Collins, Joshua, private
Collins, Moses, captain
Collins, Seaborn, private
Cook, Green, private
Cook, Green B., private
Cook, Matthew, private
Cooper, Hambleton, private
Cooper, John, private
Cooper, John, private
Cooper, Joseph, private
Cooper, William, private
Cooper, William, private
Coore, John, corporal
Cossey, Solomon, private
Cothin, Asea, private
Crawford, William, serg.
Croft, Jesse, private
Cutrer, John, private
Danaway, Joseph, private
Davis, I. W., serg. major
Davis, John, private
Davis, Samuel, corp.
Davis, Zacheus, corp.
Day, James, private
Deer, John, private
Denman, Joel, private

Denman, Thomas, private
Dickerson, Caleb, private
Dickerson, John, private
Dickerson, Thomas, private
Dickson, David, Jr., surgeon
Dillon, Clarkson, private
Dillon, Theophilus, private
Dillon, Willis, trumpeter
Doddle, James, private
Drake, Britain, private
Dukes, Jeptha, private
Dunahoo, Daniel, private
Dunahoo, John, serg.
Dunahoo, Wm., private
Dunkley, Richard, private
Dunn, John, private
Edmondson, Amos, private
Elliot, Wm., private
Elliott, Samuel, private
Ellis, George, private
Ellis, Owen, corp.
Ellis, Stephen, private
Ellis, William, private
Fairchilds, John, private
Fatheree, Readen, private
Fatheree, Hilliard, corp.
Fatheree, Levi, ensign
Felder, John, private
Fergerson, Aaron, private
Fergerson, Eli, private
Fergerson, Moses, private
Fielder, Wm., private
Flippin, Merrit, private
Ford, David, private
Ford, Preserved, private
Foxworth, Stephen, private
Garrel, Horatio, private
Gates, Joshua, private
Ginn, Jeptha, private
Gipson, James, private
Gipson, Wm., private
Goff, Nathaniel, private
Golman, Bedey, private
Golman, William, corp.
Golman, Young, private
Graham, William, private
Grantham, Daniel, private
Grantham, Matthew, private
Graves, Isaac, private
Graves, James, private
Graves, John, ensign
Green, John, private
Green, John, private
Green, Leonard, private
Hains, Noble W., private
Hall, Wyatt, private
Hambleton, Thomas, sergeant

Herrington, Thomas, private
Harvey, John, Jr., private
Harvey, John W., Serg.
Harvey, Nehemiah, 2nd lieut.
Harvey, Thomas, private
Harvey, Thomas, Sr., private
Harville, Edward, private
Harvy, Thomas P., private
Heard, Thomas, serg.
Helton, John, private
Herrington, Hardy, private
Hill, Harty, private
Hollingsworth, Isaac, corp.
Holmes, Liberty, private
Honea, Wilks, private
Hoover, Christian, private
Hoover, John, private
Howell, Henry, private
Howell, Samuel, private
Hubert, David, private
Hufman, Daniel, private
Hunly, John, private
Isaacks, Elijah, private
Isaacks, Samuel, private
Isle, William, corp.
Isles, Demsy, private
Jackson, Andrew, private
Jacobs, Walter, private
Jenkins, Allen, private
Jenkins, Davis B., private
John, ---, private waiter
Johns, John, private
Johnson, George, serg.
Johnson, John, private
Jones, Britain, private
Jones, Lewis, private
Jones, Samuel W., private
Jones, Thomas, private
Jones, William C., private
Kinchin, Henry, private
King, David, private
King, James, private
King, Jessee, private
King, John, private
King, John F., private
King, William, private
Kinchen, John, private
Kinschen, Mathew, private
Kirkland, Obediah, ensign
Lea, Alexander, private
Lee, James, corp.
Lee, Major, private
Lemmons, James, private
Lenoit, Francis B., Capt.
Lewis, Arthur, private
Lewis, Britton, private
Lewis, William, private
Lewis, William, private
Loftin, Ezekiel, private
Lott, Abraham, private
Lott, Arthur, Jr., private
Lott, Arthur, Sr., private
Lott, John, Jr., private
Lott, John, Sr., private
Lott, Luke, private
Lott, Nathan, private
Lott, Simon, serg.
Lott, Solomon, private
Lott, William, Jr., lieut.

Lott, William, Sr., private
Love, Robert, serg.
Lovin, Bailey, private
Low, John, private
Lowe, Lunchford, corp.
Lumkins, Hendrick, private
Magee, Daniel, private
Magee, Elisha, private
Magee, Fleet, private
Magee, George, private
Magee, Henry, private
Magee, Jacob, private
Magee, John, private
Magee, John, private
Magee, Nehemiah, private
Magee, Robert, private
Magee, Sire, private
Magee, Solomon, private
Magee, Willis, private
Marshall, Matthew, private
Martin, Aaron, private
Martin, Cornelius, private
Martin, Derrell, private
Martin, William, private
Massey, Benjamin, private
Mathewes, John, private
Mathewis, Shadrach, private
Mathews, Silas, private
May, Benjamin, private
May, Berry, ensign
May, Etheldredge, private
May, Green, private
May, John, private
May, Joseph, private
McAnulty, James, private
McAnulty, Robert, private
McAnulty, William, corp.
McComb, William M., private
McCrary, Matthew, private
McCullie, Benjamin, private
McCullie, James, private
McCullie, Mathew, private
McDaniel, John, private
McElvin, Moses, private
McElvinn, John, private
McGowen, Hugh, private
McGowen, James, captain
McGowen, William, private
McGraw, James, private
McGrew, Alexander, private
McGuffee, Alfred, private
McGuffee, John, major
McKinsey, private
McNeal, Hector, private
Merrel, Edmund, private
Merret, Joel, corp.
Mikell, James, private
Mikell, John I., corp.
Miller, Jacob, private
Minor, John, private
Mitchell, Wright, private
Mixon, Cornelius, corp.
Mixon, John, private
Mixon, William, private
Moke, Andrew, private
More, William, private
Morgan, Davis, private
Morris, Selathiel, private
Moses, ---, private waiter

Myers, Isaac, private
Netherlin, Levi, private
Netherlin, William, private
Nichols, David, private
Nichols, Noah, private
Nixon, Geo. Henry, lieut-
   col.
Noble, Levi, lieut.
Noble, Mark, private
Norman, Hiram, private
Norman, James, private
Norris, Acquilla, private
Oats, John H., private
Odam, William, private
Odum, Richard, private
Oneal, Ransom, private
Peak, Stephen, adjutant
Pelatta, Francis, private
Perkins, Samuel, private
Petty, Presley, private
Phillips, Elias, private
Phillips, James, captain
Phillips, Thompson, private
Pleasant, Washington, corp.
Pope, Benjamin, private
Pope, James, private
Prescott, Michael, private
Prescott, Nathan, private
Prescott, Willis, private
Prestredge, Howel, lieut.
Prestridge, John, private
Prestridge, Robert, private
Prestridge, Samuel, private
Price, Stephen, private
Prichard, Wm., 1st lieut.
Pullin, John, private
Quin, Daniel, lieut.
Quin, Henry, captain
Ragland, Henry, private
Raiborn, James, private
Ralls, Harris, private
Ratliff, James, private
Rawls, Briant, private
Rawls, Charles, private
Rawls, Jabez, ensign
Rawls, James, serg.
Read, James, corp.
Redman, Jesse, private
Redmon, Wilson, private
Reives, Alfred, private
Reives, John, private
Reives, Thomas, serg.
Richmon, Andrew, private
Rizer, Adam, private
Roberts, James, private
Roberts, Thomas, private
Robertson, Nathan, private
Robertson, Reason, private
Ross, John, private
Ross, Richard, private
Rowel, Lewis, private
Rule, Thomas, corp.
Runnels, Harmon M., capt.
Runnels, Hiram G., serg.
Saville, Aaron, private
Seale, Daniel, serg.
Seale, Eli, fifer
Seale, Lewis, private
Seale, William, private

Shaves, John, private
Silmon, Elias, private
Simmons, John, private
Simmons, Josphus, private
Simmons, Ralph, private
Simmons, William, private
Simmons, Willis, private
Simpson, Samuel, private
Sims, Robert, private
Slaughter, David, private
Slaughter, John, private
Slaughter, George, private
Slaughter, Richard, private
Slaughter, Robert, private
Slaughter, William, corp.
Smith, Alexander, private
Smith, Eli, private
Smith, Ezekiel, private
Smith, Henry, major
Smith, Hugh, private
Smith, Isham, lieut.
Smith, James, private
Smith, J. Carter, private
Smith, Jeremiah, private
Smith, John, private
Smith, John, private
Smith, Levi, private
Smith, Thomas, private
Smith, William, captain
Smith, William serg.
Smith, William, private
Somner, Owen, sergeant
Sones, Henry, private
Sorrel, Washington, serg.
Sparks, Richard, ensign
Spencer, William, captain

Steen, James, private
Steen, Nathaniel, serg.
Steen, Robert, ensign
Steen, William, corp.
Sterling, Allen, serg.
Sterling, John, Jr., private
Sterling, John, Sr., private
Stigler, Benjamin, serg.
Stigler, George, private
Stone, Marvel, private
Stovall, Charles, quartermaster serg.
Stovall, Gilbert, private
Stovall, John, corp.
Stovall, Lewis, private
Strickland, Robert, private
Strong, John, private
Strong, Thomas, private
Summerall, Jesse, corporal
Tarver, James, private
Taylor, Daniel, private
Taylor, John, private
Tellis, John, private
Tellis, Silas, private
Terrill, Philomon, private
Thomas, Charles, private
Thomas, Daniel, serg.
Thomas, James, private
Thompkins, Thomas, private
Thompson, Archibald, private
Thompson, Jesse, 1st serg.
Thompson, Siemon, private
Thornhill, William, private
Tilley, Drury, private
Tolar, Henry, private
Tomlinson, Jacob, lieut.
Tompkins, John B., private

Toney, James, private
Trailor, Matthew, private
Trailor, William, private
Tynes, Fleming, private
Tynes, Minor, private
Vardaman, Jeremiah, private
Varnado, Leonard, private
Varnado, Moses, private
Walker, Charles, private
Wallace, Oliver, private
Wallis, Thompson, private
Warren, Daniel R., lieut.
Warren, John, private
Warren, John, Jr., private
Warren, Joseph, private
Warren, Joseph, private
Warren, Solomon, private
Waterhouse, John I., private
Watson, Harrison, private
Weatherby, George W., serg.
Weathersby, Isham, private
Welcher, Duke W., private
Wells, John, private
Wells, Nathaniel, Major
Westfall, Samuel, private
Williams, John, private
Williams, Reuben, private
Williams, Samuel, private
Williford, John, private
Woldredge, William, private
Woodall, William, private
Woods, John, private
Wright, Reuben, corp.
Young, Green, private
Youngblood, Benjamin, priv.
Youngblood, Henry, private

The above data was taken from the PUBLICATIONS OF THE MISSISSIPPI HISTORICAL SOCIETY, VOLUME IV, edited by Dunbar Rowland, LL.D., 1921, chapter entitled "Rolls of Mississippi Commands in the War of 1812," pages 200-205. The rolls printed above covered all of Marion and Pike Counties.

NAMES INADVERTENTLY OMITTED FROM LIST:

Runnels, Howell W., quartermaster
Rutland, Asa, private
Sadler, Isaac, private
Sandal, Daniel, private
Sanders, Travis, private

ABSTRACTS OF PENSION RECORDS FOR VETERANS

OF THE WAR OF 1812

Complete files for men listed in this brief presentation may be secured from the National Archives, Washington, D.C. When ordering, cite the BLWT or Pension number given directly behind the veteran's name. Not all men listed hereafter served in the unit which went from the Pike County area to the famed Battle of New Orleans, 1814-1815, but in some way each person listed was connected with the area under consideration.

ADAMS, John BLST 34460-80-50
    Served as Pvt. in Capt. Thomas Bickham's Co., La. Mil. Enl. 1/1815, discharged 3/1815. On 6/5/1851 he apprd. before Barney Lewis, J.P., of Pike Co., and stated that he was 74 yrs. old; served under Watson in Col. Abram Womack's command; that he was "pressed" into service when a res. of St. Tammany Par., La. (then Washington), and was dischgd. at the Navy Yard in Madisonville, La., in or abt. the middle of Mar., 1815. Paper wit. by John S. Lamkin. He pet. for bounty land. Application attested by H. Murray Quin, Cl. of the Probate Ct., Pike Co.

ALFORD, Edwin BLWT 27,446
    Served as Pvt. in 12/13th Consolidated La. Inf. On paper dated 4/12/1855 addressed from Washington Par., La., he stated that he was 64 and living at that time in Osyka, Pike Co., Miss. In 1874 he certified that he md. Martha Smith on 12/20/1818 in Pike Co.

ALLBRITTON, Richard S.O. 4,856 S.C. 9,674
    Served as Pvt. in W. Watson's Co., La. Mil. Enl. 12/28/1814, discharged 3/10/1815. In 1850 a resident of Pike Co. where he d. 8/13/1876. Wife Nancy Richardson whom he md. in Bullock Co., Ga. 12/14/1809.

ANDREWS, Micajah (widow Sarah) W.O. 42,993 W.C. 34,523
    Served as Pvt. in Capt. Wm. Kincaid's S.C. Mil., enl. 10/21/1814, dischgd. 3/6/1815. Vet. lived in Amite Co., Miss., 1852-1856. In 1883/1886 widow lived at Summit in Pike Co. Andrews md. 1) Margaret Delaney; 2) 10/5/1854 in Franklin Co., Miss., to Sarah Nettles, the widow Smith. Andrews d. in Summit on 11/12/1865.

APPLEWHITE, Seth (or Stephen?) S.O. 30, 014
    Served as Pvt. in Wm. Spencer's Co., Miss. Mil. (No data in file)

BAGLEY, William (widow Mary) W.O. 44,707 W.C. 35,027
    Served as Pvt. in Capt. Brandon's Co., Miss. Mil.; enl. 9/21/1812, dischg. 3/21/1813. In 1851 and 1855 vet. lived in Covington, St. Tammany Parish, La.; in 1888 in Pensacola, Fla. Vet. md. 1) Elizabeth Goygle (?); 2) 1/27/1825 in New Orleans, La., to Mary Merritt. Soldier d. 11/3/1871 in Pensacola. Widow d. ca. 1891.

BARNETT, Mark S.O. 29,452 S.C. 21,298
    Served in Capt. Zachariah Lee's Co., Miss. Mil.; enl. 9/19/1812, dischgd. 3/21/1813. Resided in Pike Co. in 1851; Lawrence Co, 1855 to 1873. He was unmarried.

BRELAND, John R. (widow Mary) S.O. 27,965 S.C. 19,710
                                W.O. 32,195 W.C. 24,660
    Served in Capt. John Goff's La. Mil.; enl. 9/30/1814, dischgd. 3/31/1815. In 1851 resided in Pike Co.; in 1857 in St. Tammany Par., La. In 1878 widow had an Osyka, Miss., mailing address but lived in Tangipahoa Par., La. Wife's maiden name was Mary Lewis whom he md. 1/13/1839 in Pike Co., Miss. Vet. b. in S.C. and md. 1) Luranna Rogges (or Rogers) who d. ca. 1838. He md. 2) Mary Lewis in ceremony performed by Re. Wm. Fortenberry. Vet. test. on 11/3/1851 before Sampson L. Lamkin that he was 58 yrs. old. He d. 5/14/1875 in St. Tammany Par., La.

BRUMFIELD, Davis (widow Cynthia) W.O. 20,259 W.C. 11,307
    Served as Pvt. in Capt. Wm. Bickham's Co., La. Mil.; enl. 12/23/1814, dischgd. 3/10/1815; resided in Pike Co., Miss., in 1851. Widow had Conerly P. O. in Pike Co. in 1878. Vet. md. 11/23/1823, in Pike Co., to Cynthia Holmes—md. by Thomas

Pleasants, J.P. Vet. d. 4/23/1863 in Pike Co. Vet had been 6' tall, had black hair, and blue eyes. Jesse Day of La. (Wash. Par.) cert. that he was in the unit with Brumfield.

COLLINS, John (widow Mary A.)   S.O. 7,753   S.C. 5,026
                                W.O. 30,320 W.C. (rejected)
        Served as Pvt. Capt. Samuel Leaven's Co., La. Mil.; enl. 12/24/1814; discharged 3/31/1815; resided in Washington Par., La., in 1856; by 1871 a resident of Lawrence Co., Miss.; md. 10/14/1837 in Pike Co. to Mary A. Stringfield. Soldier d. 2/5/1873 in Lawrence Co., Miss.

CUNNINGHAM, Elijah   S.O. 21,478   S.C. 15,307
        Served as Pvt. Capt. John Porter's Tenn. Mil.; md. 5/30/1827 in Pike Co., Miss., to Mariah M. Burton. 1851-1871 lived in Copiah Co., Miss.

DAY, Jesse (widow Dicy)   W.O. 1,240   W.C. 726
        Served as Pvt. in Capt. Wm. Bickham's Co., La. Mil. In 1850's lived in Washington Par., La.; md. 11/11/1808, Wells Cr., Franklin Co., Miss., by Mr. Black to Dicy Estes (Estess). Vet. d. 11/11/1857 (or 58) in Pike Co. On 6/19/1855 in Washington Par., La., vet. certified age as 69 yrs. old. His widow on her application papers claimed to be 80 yrs. old in 1871. Hezekiah Magee and James Graham of Pike Co. certified to her papers. David M. Day, son of the vet., gave statement and said that he was b. in Aug., 1815.

DILLON, Theophilus (widow Lucy)   S.O. 29,373   S.C. 21,362
        Served as pvt. in Capt. John Bond's Miss. Mil.; enl. 1/3/1815, dischgd. 4/2/1815. Lived in Pike Co. 1850 and 1860; 1874 resided in Franklinton, Washington Par., La.; md. 2) 11/6/1866 in Washington Par., La., to Lucy King.

EAGER, Robert (widow Hannah)   W.O. 29,683   W.C. 25,294
        Served as Pvt. in Capt. T. C. Moreland's Co., S.C. Mil. Resided in Pike Co. in 1857; d. 6/29/____ at Cherry Springs, Tenn. Wife's name: Hannah A. Prince who d. in Summit on 6/10/1880.

EDWARDS, Joseph   S.O. 8,780   S.C. 13,604
        Served as Pvt. in Capt. P. Barnett's Co., Miss. Mil.; enl. 9/25/1814, discharged 3/23/1815; lived in Amite Co., Miss., 1852 and 1859; lived in Pike Co. in 1871; md. 3/1821 at Johnson's Station to Margaret Johnson.

FELDER, David (widow Jane)   W.O. 31,816   W.C. 15,928
        Served as Ensign in Capt. Barnett's Miss. Mil, enl. 9/25/1814; discharged 3/22/1815; md. 6/17/1819 in Amite Co. to Jane McMorris; vet. d. 10/1/1842 in Livingston Par., La. Widow d. ca. 10/1/1882.

FELDER, John (widow Martha)   W.O. 28,906   W.C. 17,896
        Served as Pvt. in Capt. H. Quin's Co., Miss. Mil., enl. 1/6/1815, discharged 2/5/1815. In 1856 lived in Pike Co.; in 1878 widow lived in Lawrence Co. Vet. d. 12/20/1876. He md. 1) Patience Allen; 2)____ Stanfield; 3) 7/19/1855 in Copiah Co., Miss., to Martha Douglas.

GIRTMAN, Bartholomew (widow Elender)   W.O. 80,632   W.C. 4,585
        Served as Pvt. in Capt. Barnett's Miss. Mil., enl. 9/25/1814, discharged 12/31/1814; md. 3/11/1811 in Barnwell Dist., S.C., to Elender O'Quin. Vet. d. in Pike Co., 3/31/1834; widow d. 5/31/1875.

JONES, John   S.O. 32,588   S.C. 23,129
        Served as Pvt. in Capt. Robert Spencer's Miss. Mil.

MAPLES, John A. P.
        Served as Pvt. in Capt. Wm. Bickham's Co., La. Mil.; discharged at Naval Yard at Madisonville, La. Served on W. bank of Miss. R. under Gen. David B. Morgan. In 1871 vet. lived at Summit; drew pension from U.S. and the state of La. Original application in archives, St. Tammany Parish Courthouse, Covington, La.

MAYFIELD, Edmond (or John)   BLWT 71,870
        Served as Pvt. in 12th/13th Consolidated La. Inf. On 5/28/1852, aged 57, was in Pike Co., Miss. In 1860 lived in Hinds Co. On 2/6/1887 one N. Shirley of Bogue Chitto wrote Pension Bureau (Washington, D.C.) that John Mayfield d. at his home and left a Bounty Land Warrant among his effects. In 1852 John Adams certified

that he served in the unit with Mayfield and that he (Adams) received bounty land.

MIKELL, John J. (widow Mary) W.O. 5,930
    Served as a corporal in Capt. Wm. Spencer's Miss. Mil.

RAWLS, Jabez (widow Kesiah) W.O. 28,373 W.C. 34,384
    Served as Ensign in Capt. Wm. Spencer's Co., Miss. Mil. On 5/28/1878 when widow filed a claim for pension as a resident of Marion Co., when she was 83 yrs. old, she stated vet. enlisted for the war in 1813, discharged in 1815; at the time of enlistment vet was 21 yrs. old, a farmer, native of N.C., of medium height, light hair, blue eyed, light complexion (ended statement with when they md.--so age probably fit marriage and not enlistment date). Her maiden name was Maria Felder and she md. 5/4/1819 by Thomas Nixon M.G. Vet. d. 7/22/1834. From time of discharge until 1828 lived in Marion Co.; then moved to Hinds Co. where he remained 5 yrs; then back to Marion Co. William E. Rawls aged 56 and Allen B. F. Rawls aged 58 (in 1878) were supporting witnesses for Maria. (Certified copy of marriage in papers--from Pike Co.) Widow d. 9/29/1886.

REDMOND, Jesse (widow Elizabeth) S.C. 23,931 W.O. 13,097 S.C. 15,656 W.C. 7,503
    Served in Capt. Wm. Spencer's Co., Miss. Mil.

REEVES, John (widow Martha) W.O. 28,456 W.C. 23,314
    Served as pvt. in Capt. Spencer's Co., Miss. Mil.

REID, James (widow Mary) W.O. 27,939 W.C. 14,982
    Served as Pvt. in Capt. John Bond's Co., Miss. Vols. Vet. md. in Marion Co., Miss., 11/27/1816 to Mary or Polly Newsom. Widow d. near Monticello, Lawrence Co., Miss., 3/4/1884. She applied for a pension on 6/3/1878. Ezekiel Reid, aged 70 in 1878, and L. A. Pevy aged 66 certified her application as being long personal acquaintances and near neighbors. Conflict arose over her last pension check. One witness to the voucher was Zebulon Pendleton Jones, aged 40 yrs., on paper dated 3/22/1887, sd. he served thinking the money was to be given to Miss Page, a granddaughter of the deceased. A similar statement signed by Pleasant Zebulon Jones, 16 yrs old in 1886, who said that he thought money was to have gone to Miss L. A. Page, granddaughter of the deceased pensioner. Numerous papers over the voucher with several merchants called into question over the false payment.

TATE, Harvey BLWT 18,527
    Served as Pvt. in 12th/13th Consolidated La. Inf. In 5/20/1871 vet. was 85 years old and a resident of Osyka, Pike Co., Miss.; he md. Elizabeth Bruce in St. Helena Par., La., in Jan. 1824.

TATE, John (widow Martha) BLWT 95,051
    Served as Pvt. 12th/13th Consolidated La. Inf., Pike Co., Miss.; 9/23/1859, John G. Tate aged 29 certified that soldier d. in St. Helena Par., La., 4/21/1850; his widow Martha d. 12/27/1852. Their children (according to the file) were: Harvey b. 6/15/1816; Obidiah b. 8/27/1818; Mosella b. 2/15/1833; and Elizabeth b. 9/27/1835. On Nov. 12, 1862, Harvey Tate, aged 62, and Mary Newman, aged 62 (twins) stated that they were a brother and a sister to John and certified to his service.

TAYLOR, David BLWT 77,650
    Served as Pvt. in 12th/13th Consolidated La. Inf. Vet. d. in St. Helena 5/20/1853; vet. md. in Pike Co., Miss., 3/1/1843 to Elizabeth Westmoreland. On 8/7/1855 widow, then a resident of St. Helena, stated she was 46 yrs. old. Papers certified by Abner Womack in Pike Co., Miss., 9/29/1857; and Jacob Womack, William and Elizabeth McElvin, John Bankston (aged 63) and John G. Gates aged 29, presented papers of verification.

TONEY, Drury (widow Elizabeth) S.O. 21,092 S.C. 17,780
                       W.O. 37,740 W.C. 28,213
    Served as Pvt. in Capt. John Goff's Co., La. Mil.; enl. at Englishtown (English Turn), La. (below N.O.) in 9/1814; discharged at Jackson Square in N.O. 3/10/1815. In 1871 lived at Bogue Faliah, La.; md. 10/9/1827 in Pike Co., to Elisa Boutewell. Vet. d. 1/8/1872. Vet. was 5' 10" tall, had dark complexion, black hair, gray eyes--but lost eyesight in old age. Clerk of Pike Co. made statement that record of this marriage was not found as many records were lost during the Civil War when records were transferred from Holmesville to Brookhaven, Miss.

THORNHILL, William (widow Mary) W.O. 27,978   S.C. 18,551
        Served as Pvt. Capt. Moses Collins Co., Miss. Mil.

VARNADO, Leonard   BLWT 62,300-160-55
        Served as Pvt. in Capt. Quin's Co., Miss. Mil. (overall command of Col. Geo. M. Nixon), pressed into service in Pike Co. on the 15th or 20th (Dec?) 1814, stationed at Fordsville for war. Discharged 3/15/1815. No other data.

VARNADO, Samuel (widow Kesiah)   S.O. 27,781   W.C. 28,016
                                 W.P. 29,251
        Served as Pvt. in Capt. James Harris's Co., Commanded by Abner Womack, 12th/13th Consolidated La. Inf. Regt. Drafted 12/1814, discharged at Madisonville, La., 3/1815. Vet. md. 3/2/1813 in Marion Co., Miss., by Labon Bacot, J.P., to Kesiah Newsom. Vet. d. 9/20 (or 26), 1874. Widow was 86 yrs. old on 2/14/1871 when she applied for pension on strength of husband's service. Vet. had been 5' 10" tall, had fair complexion, black hair and black eyes.

WALLACE, Thompson (widow Elizabeth)   W.O. 38,925   W.C. 29,299
        Served as lieut. in Capt. Wm. Bond's Co., Miss. Mil.

WARREN, John (widow Angeline) W.O. 40,457
        Served as Pvt. in Capt. John Bond's Co., Miss. Mil.

1816 CENSUS OF PIKE COUNTY, MISSISSIPPI

Key: White Males Over Twenty One Years Old.
White Males Under Twenty One Years Old.
White Females Over Twenty One Years Old.
White Females Under Twenty One Years Old.
Total of White Inhabitants.
Total of Free People of Color.
Total of Slaves.
Total of Inhabitants.

Lazarus Reeves	1210 4 00 4
Allen King	1310 5 03 8
Robert Sims	1315 10 01 11
James Anders	2100 3 07 10
Elias Silmon	1010 2 00 2
Isaah Hamilton	1713 12 05 17
Abraham Bryley	1213 7 04 11
Jeremiah Smith	1415 11 01 12
John Strawther	1314 9 04 13
Isaac Sadler	2212 7 01 8
Lewellin Leggit	1413 9 00 9
Moses Collins	1521 9 06 15
Samuel Williams	1311 6 01 7
John Newman	1411 7 00 7
Barnabas Allen	1010 2 02 4
Benjamin Youngblood	1425 12 07 19
Edward Gatland	2324 11 0 15 26
John Williams	1112 5 00 5
John Warren	1116 9 01 10
Jonathan Carter	1222 7 00 7
George Ellis	1312 7 00 7
Vincent Gannir	2312 8 06 14
Nathaniel Wells	1413 9 08 17
Henry Quinn	2202 6 08 14
Gabriel Allen	1112 5 06 11
Jesse King	1312 7 01 8
John Bond	1010 2 00 2
John Bond Junr.	2212 7 00 7
Philip Catching	1313 8 0 11 19
Joseph Catching	1411 7 0 10 17
James Roberds	1112 5 00 5
James Hope	1214 8 00 8
John Smith	1313 8 03 11
Thomas Heard	1101 3 00 3
William Love	2211 6 04 10
Robert Bond	1101 3 00 3
William Beard	1312 8 00 8
Thomas Arthur	2412 9 00 9
Francis Ross	1313 8 01 9
Joshua Stockstill	2315 11 00 11
John Atkins	1111 4 00 4
Robert Fairchilds	1514 11 00 11
Walter Jacob	1113 6 00 6
Brice Miller	1811 11 00 11
John Stallians	1211 5 00 5
David Morgan	1412 8 08 16
Willis Simmonds	1412 8 00 8
Thompson Wallis	1114 7 00 7
Gideon Bond	3117 12 00 12
Nathaniel Goff	2111 5 00 5
Robert Smith	1212 6 00 6
David Bullock	2102 5 00 5
Silas Bullock	1111 4 00 4
Frederick Craft	1123 7 00 7
James Craft	0101 2 01 3
Joseph Lane	1001 2 00 2
Peter Batson	1111 4 00 4
William Isles	1111 4 00 4
Archibald Thompson	2010 3 00 3
Brandford Kemp	1414 10 00 10
Thomas Batson	1315 10 00 10
Robert Strickland	1612 10 00 10
Keen Milton	0201 3 00 3
Eli Batson	0101 2 00 2
Isaac Milton	1011 3 00 3
Polly Riley	0310 4 00 4
John Hinson	1211 5 00 5
Seth Batson	1111 4 00 4
James Batson	1112 5 00 5
Henry Bond	2403 9 00 9
John Thompson	1024 7 03 10
Daniel Houghman	1311 6 00 6
Thomas Bell	1212 6 01 7
William Bond	1412 8 00 8
Nancy Mullins	0311 5 00 5
David Hines	1412 8 00 8
John McDaniel	1110 3 00 3
Moses McCelvin	1101 3 00 3
John Davis	1010 2 00 2
John Hinson	1312 7 00 7
Benjamin Zachery	1214 8 00 8
William Faris	0102 3 00 3
James Daugherity	1212 6 00 6
Asa Rutland	1011 3 00 3
Ann Simmonds	1515 12 07 19
Daniel McDaniel	1411 7 00 7
Zachariah Redmon	1010 2 00 2
Thomas Batson	1010 2 00 2
Peter Felder	1222 7 0 16 23
Peter Felder, Jr.	1110 3 02 5
Mark Cole	1212 6 00 6
Jacob Summers	1312 7 00 7
Michael Prescot	1001 2 00 2
William Sellers	3011 5 00 5
Laban Bacot	1105 7 00 7
Ephraim Prescot	1021 4 07 11
Nancy Roberson	0014 5 00 5
Nathan Prescot	1111 4 00 4
Henry Pigot	1114 7 00 7
Isaac Carter	1412 8 017 25
Sarah Pendarvas	0110 2 00 2
Leonard Varnado	1410 6 00 6
Moses Varnado	1313 8 00 8
Samuel Varnado	1215 9 02 11
Samuel Carter	1513 10 00 10
Hardy Carter	1001 2 00 2
William Carter	1111 4 02 6
John Cutrair	1012 4 00 4
Daniel Dunnahoo	1211 5 00 5

John Dunnahoo	0210 3 00 3
Samuel Isaacs	1010 2 00 2
William Jenkins	1514 11 00 11
Samuel Barbar	1112 5 00 5
John Sherrin	1111 4 00 4
Catherine Addison	0132 6 01 7
Elijah Isaac	1315 10 00 10
Abner Barksdale	1222 7 09 16
William F. Barksdale	1111 4 00 4
William Cooper	2113 7 00 7
William Dunnahoo	1110 3 02 5
Richardson Bowman	1011 3 01 4
John Low	2002 4 012 16
James Y. McNabb	3322 10 00 10
Cornelius Martin	1310 5 00 5
Clark Hall	1110 3 00 3
Jeremiah Cawley	2213 8 00 8
Daniel Sandal	1001 2 00 2
Nicholas Yawn	1112 5 00 5
James Ballard	1510 7 00 7
John Ballard	2242 10 00 10
Henry Dickerson	1213 7 04 11
James Gordan	1211 5 00 5
William Green	1210 4 00 4
George Hartsuck	1611 9 011 20
Henry Sandal	1311 6 00 6
John Dickerson	2422 10 00 10
Daniel Sandal	1312 7 00 7
Lunsford Law	2112 6 02 8
Frederick Law	1110 3 03 6
John Smith	0101 2 00 2
Thomas Cook	1311 6 05 11
Jeremiah Thomas	1711 10 00 10
Green Cook	1214 8 01 9
Peter Quinn, Sr.	1010 2 06 8
Joel Denman	1110 3 05 8
Obed Kirkland	2313 9 01 10
Swan Thompson	3114 9 03 12
Thomas Thompkins	2011 4 00 4
Peter Quinn, Jr.	1212 6 05 11
David McGraw, Jr.	2512 10 011 21
Benjamin Bagley	2313 9 03 12
William Bullock	1512 9 04 13
John H. Marsh	2101 4 00 4
Robert Love	1014 6 02 8
Loften Fairchilds	1012 4 03 7
Isaac Foster	1414 10 00 10
Thomas Roberts	1115 8 00 8
Enous Daughtery	1103 5 00 5
Elizabeth Hoover	1412 8 06 14
Joseph Brown	2216 11 00 11
John Brown	1310 5 00 5
Daniel Quinn	1511 8 04 12
Bartholemew James	1110 3 01 4
Joseph Strong	1614 12 00 12
Robert Gray	1010 2 00 2
Thomas Rule	1212 6 00 6
Richard Smith	1312 7 00 7
Paul Toosing	2010 3 03 6
Polydore Coats	1001 2 00 2
Gideon Smith	1120 4 07 11
Richard Parker	1113 6 00 6
Jesse Bell	4020 6 06 12
Dred May	3112 7 00 7
Eleazer Bell	2211 6 09 15
John Oquinn	2211 6 00 6
John May	1214 8 00 8
Bartholomew Girtman	1112 5 00 5
Jacob Cawley	1012 4 00 4
Solomon Causey	2512 10 00 10
Richard Stone	1011 3 00 3
Joseph Thornhill	1513 10 00 10
Jeptha Ginn	1328 14 00 14
Jacob Magee	1612 10 06 16
Henry Magee	1211 5 00 5
James Dawdle	1213 7 00 7
Lemuel King	1315 10 00 10
Lawrence Dillen	1113 6 00 6
John Hilton	1312 7 02 9
Mary Smith	0140 5 01 6
Clarkson Dillen	1412 8 00 8
Richard Dillen	2012 5 011 16
Samuel W. Jones	1122 6 00 6
John Stallians	1110 3 00 3
Nathan Morris	1213 7 01 8
George Magee	1012 4 01 5
Abraham Breedeland	1210 4 00 4
Willis Magee	1312 7 01 8
Lewis Rowel	1001 2 00 2
Daniel Makenzie	1213 7 00 7
David Makenzie	1014 6 00 6
Joseph Lewis	2613 12 00 12
John Magee	4214 11 010 21
Solomon Magee	1010 2 04 6
David Murr	1312 7 00 7
John Carr	2121 6 08 14
Seth Cawley	0101 2 02 4
John Night	1423 10 01 11
Owen Ellis	2412 9 00 9
Duke W. Wilcher	2211 6 00 6
John Ship	1011 3 00 3
Mathew Cook	2212 7 00 7
Benjamin Toney	1512 9 00 9
Richard Odum	1000 1 00 1
William Thornkill	1221 6 00 6
William Odum	1011 3 00 3
William Eliott	1112 5 00 5
Thomas Jones	1012 4 00 4
Robert Thornhill	1010 2 00 2
William Prichard	1211 5 00 5
Hannah Collis	1220 5 09 14
John Sartin	1210 4 00 4
Joseph May	1111 4 010 14
William Barnes	2513 11 00 11
James May	1211 5 00 5
Evin Harvey	1011 3 03 6
Michael Harvey	1712 11 00 11
Daniel Clower	1001 2 00 2
Reuben Ponder	1111 4 00 4
Ralph Stovall	2325 11 07 18
Frederick Newsom	1214 8 00 8
Marble Stone	1012 4 00 4
William Ellis	2112 6 00 6
Hans Hamilton	1311 6 00 6
John Tullis	1211 5 00 5
Briton Drake	1211 5 00 5
Temple Tullis, Jr.	1212 6 00 6
Wiloby Tullis	1111 4 06 10
Temple Tullis	3422 11 00 11
William Smith	0201 3 02 5
Temple Tullis	3422 11 00 11
William Smith	0210 3 02 5
James Anders, Jr.	1210 4 02 6
John Brent, Sr.	3111 6 01 7
William Tait	1301 5 00 5
John Brent	2113 7 00 7
James Day	1012 4 00 4
Abel Simpson	1111 4 00 4

Daniel Davis	1312	7	01	8	Charles Rials	1211	5	02	7
Hiram Normon	1010	2	00	2	Andrew Moke	1312	7	00	7
James Normon	1010	2	00	2	Joel Merrill	1012	4	00	4
Abraham Trewit	1113	6	00	6	Jacob Coon	1211	5	00	5
James McCillie	1211	5	00	5	William Forgey	1214	8	00	8
Presley Normon	1312	7	00	7	William Morrow	1110	3	00	3
William Williams	1023	6	00	6	John Wells	1312	7	00	7
Zachariah Williams	1112	5	00	5	George Johnson	1213	7	00	7
Isaac Alexander	1011	3	03	6	Nathaniel Johnson	1613	11	00	11
Robert Middleton	1013	5	00	5	Andrew Richmond	1411	7	00	7
William Rolan	1311	6	00	6	George Whaley	1002	3	00	3
Caleb Bright	1312	7	00	7	Thomas Richmond	0101	2	00	2
Peter Glover	1013	5	07	12	Samuel Boyd	1511	8	00	8
John Hickman	1212	6	00	6	Joseph Turner	1414	10	02	12
Amiziah Vardeman	1010	2	00	2	Mathew Turner	1010	2	00	2
Jeremiah Vardeman	1012	4	01	5	Bedy Goldman	1113	6	00	6
Mathew McElvin	1110	3	00	3	Josiah Martin	1411	7	016	23
Jacob Miller	1012	4	00	4	Hendrick Vaughn	1011	3	00	3
Andrew Boyd	1510	7	00	7	Elijah Martin	1214	8	00	8
Joseph Dunnaway	1211	5	00	5	Moses Miller	0101	2	00	2
William McCullie	2312	8	00	8	William Woodale	1212	6	00	6
John Wood	1210	4	00	4	John Gordon	1510	7	00	7
William Gates	1314	9	01	10	Richard Conn	1323	9	010	19
John Walker	1311	6	00	6	Joseph C. Smith	1112	5	00	5
Jacob Keen	1001	2	00	2	David Smith	1212	6	00	6
Howel Prestidge	1211	5	00	5	William Garner	1012	4	00	4
Nehemiah Williams	1010	2	03	5	William Martin	1001	2	01	3
Alexander Harper	1422	9	06	15	James Roberson	1413	9	08	17
Absolom Harper	1410	6	01	7	William Dunnahoo	1111	4	00	4
Jesse Harper	1210	4	01	5	William Barbar	1311	6	00	6
John Mathews	1513	10	00	10	William Goldman	1001	2	00	2
John Hog	1313	8	00	8	Young Goldman	1001	2	00	2
Nathan Sims	1311	6	03	9	John Felder	1111	4	01	5
William McAnulty	1001	2	00	2	Elizabeth Findley	0213	6	00	6
Britton Jons	1310	5	00	5	David Chesnut	1001	2	00	2
James Leggett	1110	3	00	3	Lewis Howel	2412	9	00	9
Thomas Gatland	1011	3	00	3	Hendrick Lumpkins	1112	5	00	5
James McAnulty	2211	6	01	7	Salathiel Morris	1011	3	00	3
Spellsby Trebbles	1114	7	03	10	Henry Hale	1411	7	00	7
Jonathan Catching	1112	5	04	9	William Vincent	1012	4	00	4
Charles King	1111	4	08	12	Isham Alldridge	1422	9	00	9
Allen Carter	1123	7	02	9	Charles White	1413	9	00	9
Reuben Williams	1101	3	00	3	Mary Trentham	0211	4	00	4
Thomas Warren	1312	7	00	7	David Bruland	1010	2	00	2
Caleb Wordley	1511	8	00	8	Daniel Thomas	1000	1	00	1
Isaac Tabor	1112	5	00	5	Berry May	1112	5	00	5
Ephraim Esthers	1110	3	00	3	William Newsom	1312	7	012	19
John Johnson	1001	2	00	2	Isaac Newsom	1212	6	06	12
Thomas Reives	1010	2	00	2					

Note: The names in this list were printed in the MISSISSIPPI OFFICIAL AND STATISTICAL REGISTER, CENTENARY VOLUME, 1917, by Dunbar Rowland, LL.D., on pages 134-138. The following names were found to be omitted when the original census was checked. The original is in the Dept. of Archives and History, Jackson, Mississippi.

Henry Ragland	2113	7	010	17	David McGraw Senr.	1311	6	016	22
James Gibson	1112	5	01	6	Wyley Rolon	1211	5	00	5
Hans Hamilton	1412	8	15	14	Henry Goldmon	1413	9	01	10
Thomas Hamilton	2214	9	02	11	William Miller	1417	13	00	13
Crenshaw Parkman	1414	10	01	11					

I do hereby certify the pages 1, 2, 3, 4, 5, 6, 7, 8, 9, 10 to contain the true enumeration of the census of Pike County, taken by me as assessor of taxes for said county for the year 1816, agreeable to an act in that case made and provided.

David Cleveland

1820 CENSUS OF PIKE COUNTY, MISSISSIPPI

Key: First six figures represent Free White Males, aged 0-10; 10-16; 16-18; 16-26; 26-45; 45 and upwards.
Second five figures represent Free White Females, aged 0-10; 10-16; 16-26; 26-45; 45 and upwards.
First figure after dash represents those engaged in agriculture, unless followed by a "C" and those are in commerce. The last figure is the total number of slaves.

Name	Figures	Name	Figures
Young Goldman	100100 00100-1-0	Tho. Norman	30000 21010-2-0
Joel Denman	200020 00200-2-1	Jno. Wilson	101101 01000-7-7
Robert Sims	021110 40010-4-1	Danl. Sistrunk	110010 10010-1-0
Wm. Green	000101 00001-3-0	Wm. Chandler	220101 21110-5-0
Margaret Penn	110100 01301-5-3	Wm. Hodges	100010 20100-0-0
Allen King	200010 11010-2-4	Ephr. Bridges	300100 10200-1-0
Alexr. Harper	110101 01001-4-4	Moses Bridges	121301 30001-6-2
Jno. Cater	000100 10100-2-1	David Burford	200200 00200-2-0
Spilesbee Tribble	001101 32010-2-4	Leml. T. B. Hall	001201 10100-3-0
Jefse Harper	300010 10010-2-1	Frances Petelfiles	200000 10010-0-0
Jas. Andrews Junr.	300010 00010-3-7	Ezek. Norris	200010 20010-1-0
Rachl. Hamilton	010100 00001-3-2	Danl. Taylor	000010 30100-2-1
Hance Hamilton	210411 21010-6-5	Tho. Warren	130010 30010-4-0
Judith Hamilton	411300 01110-6-7	Jas. Norman	200110 00100-2-0
Abr. Briley	101101 02110-8-9	Wm. Wroten	011101 20001-2-0
Barnab Allen	100010 10010-3-4	Wiley Wroten	300010 20010-1-0
Tho. Gullidge	020101 50110-3-0	Jefse Grier	100010 30010-1-0
Eliz. Hamilton	110000 32010-0-1	Amos Grier	202301 00110-6-0
Jas. Ellis	000100 00100-0-0	Thompson Brister	000001 21201-1-0
Geo. Ellis	120001 20101-4-0	Wm. McDavid	000100 00100-1-0
Thos. Crews	000101 01100-4-6	Edmond Hodges	100010 10010-1-0
Jno. Brent Senr.	000201 10001-4-3	Drure Hodges	000001 00001-0-1
David G. M.Graw	200101 00100-2-0	Henry Davis	000100 10100-1-0
Jno. Ammons	110201 01201-4-0	Jno. Hickman	110001 11010-2-0
Meredith Brent	200110 10100-1-0	Danl. Davis	120001 01100-4-2
Jno. Crews	100010 00100-1-0	Jno. White	000100 00100-0-0
Jno. Brent Junr.	300010 31010-2-1	Wm. Bullock	020201 10101-6-8
Wm. Carter	000010 00001-1-0	Wm. Bowman	100001 01101-1-0
Aaron Beard	100100 10100-1-0	Martin Holland	000010
Wm. Cothen	410010 11010-3-0	Arch. Stinson	000010
Wm. Gates Junr.	420010 11010-6-3	Jno. McCafety	000010
Jno. Strother	200001 12101-2-3	Leroy Bowman	100100 20010-1-0
Wm. Gates Senr.	200101 12010-5-2	Abi Trewit	010001 11010-2-0
Mary Newman	220000 00101-5-2	Andrew Boyd	410001 00010-0-0
Jno. Craft	021201 30001-9-5	Jas. McCullough	400110 01010-3-0
Jonath. Carter	001101 21010-3-1	Sally Norman	211100 21101-2-0
Wm. McCullough Senr.	111101 11101-2-1	Jno. Warren	400110 42110-6-4
Wm. McCullough Junr.	000100 01000-1-0	Jno. Taylor	300010 10100-3-2
Jno. Woods	110010 20010-3-0	Jno. Walker	210110 21010-3-0
Geo. Dunaway	100001 31010-1-0	Danl. Taylor Senr.	010111 00001-3-4
Jas. King	111110 22110-4-0	Swan Thompson	000301 02101-5-6
Jos. (?) Dunaway	210020 20011-2-0	Parris Thompson	000301 12210-3-0
Wm. Howard	100010 20010-1-0	Mat. McEwen	100021 20010-2-0
Abner Silman	200010 21010-2-0	Archd. McEwen	100010 00100-1-0
Jonath. Dunaway	110011 31010-2-0	David Montgomery	000001 -1
Tho. Silman	400010 10010-2-0	Crensh Parkman	211201 21210-5-4
Benj. Thomas Senr.	011201 00002-3-1	Steph. Tatum	100110 12020-3-2
Jefse Thomas	200100 10010-1-0	Sidney Hodges	210000 11010-2-0
Malachi Thomas	100100 00100-1-0	Tho. Wroten	100100 00100-1-0
Jas. Thomas	100010 30100-1-0	Elisha Tyler	100010 10100-1-0
Benj. Thomas Junr.	000100 00100-1-0	Jos. Sanderfer	100100 10100-1-0
Elias Silman	000010 00100-1-0	Jane Bright	310000 01001-0-0
Benj. McCullough	000100 10100-1-0	Peter J. Glover	000101 01201-4-9
Simeon Thompson	000100 10100-1-0	Nichl. Vaughn	200010 11010-1-0

Name	Col1	Col2
Am. Vardeman	000110	10010-2-0
David Ott	200010	11010-1-0
Aaron Spell	100010	00100-1-0
Jerem. Vardeman	000110	40010-2-1
Abs. Harper	310010	10000-1-0
James Howell	310010	10210-0-0
Jefse Hodges	000100	10100-0-0
Jas. May	200010	20010-1-0
Jno. Merchant	200201	01301-3-1
Richard Odom	000100	00010-1-0
Archd. Tullos	100100	00100-1-0
Benj. Rasberry	000100	10100-1-0
Wm. Rasberry	100010	20100-2-1
Wm. Tullos	000010	10100-2-1
Wm. Boon	220010	11010-3-0
Sarah Boon		00401-0-0
James Tullos	300010	10010-1-0
Thos. Harvy	200010	10010-1-1
Steph. Tullos	001100	00100-1-0
Danl. Sullivan	020101	20301-4-0
Jno. Sistrunk	001200	00101-1-0
Willibe Tullos	000001	00001-3-9
Temple Tullos Junr.	310010	11010-4-0
Tho. Fletcher	420001	10010-3-0
Jno. Tullos	200010	20010-1-0
Tho. Tullos	000010	00100-1-0
Temple Tullos Senr.	011211	00211-5-0
Reuben Ponder	300310	10010-3-0
Richd. Ratliff	310010	21010-10-12
Leroy Tatum	000100	21010-1-1
Tho. Ponder	100010	11010-1-0
Lewis Stovall	100100	10200-1-0
Wm. Ellis	010010	40010-2-0
James Gordon	121301	31010-5-0
Francis Pelotte	100010	00010-1-0
Jas. Walling	000010	10100-1-0
Geo. C. Hamlet	200000	20010-1-0
David Breland	000110	10100-1-0
Jas. M. Breland	100010	10200-1-0
Aquilla Donaho	210010	30010-2-0
Tho. Harvy	100110	11000-1-1
Tho. Jones	100100	10100-1-1
Jos. Newsom	010010	21101-2-0
Jas. Reed	100100	10010-2-0
Ralph Stovall	200020	12110-5-8
Eliz. Doughty	000000	00101-0-2
Jno. May	210010	30010-1-0
Evan Whitington	010010	02010-4-6
Richard Richardson	100110	21010-3-6
Jno. T. Spencer	000100	10100-1-0
Michl. Harvy	321401	11010-5-1
Benj. Jones	010101	21111-3-5
Wm. Pleasant	000001	00001-3-6
Saml. Williams	310010	10110-4-7
Richdson. Bowman	100010	20010-2-4
Richd. Davidson	110010	11010-0-1
Jno. Sertin (?)	400010	11100-1-0
Owen Ellis	420010	00010-4-1
Danl. Thomas	100010	00100-1-0
Green B. May	000100	01000-1-0
Moses Collins	321110	10011-5-10
Duke W. Welcher	210010	20010-2-0
Peter Sanderfer	210201	00210-3-0
Seaborn Collins	200100	00100-2-4
Richd. Carr	000100	
Tho. Boutwell	210001	21010-3-0
Jos. May Senr.	000121	00001-8-13
Robt. Williams	300010	20010-2-1
Jas. Chamberlain	000010	11010-3-0
Jas. Day	220001	11010-3-0
Jonath Kent	410210	00210-4-0
Wm. Odom	100010	20100-1-0
Laban Kent	320010	11010-3-1
Wm. Legget	020011	00001-2-0
Claiborne Rushin	000100	00200-1-0
Wm. Elliotte	200010	20100-1-1
Matth Cook	110110	11001-2-0
Willis Brumfield	000010	10100-1-0
Wm. Thornhill	000100	20100-1-0
Wm. Cook	200010	20010-1-0
Jos. Thornhill	221101	11010-4-0
Sier Magee	000010	00100-1-0
Richd. Stone	000001	20010-1-0
Danl. Thomas	100200	00100-2-2
Jas. Toney	200100	00010-1-0
Sarah Elliotte	000000	00001-0-0
J. Abr. Breland	100001	10101-1-0
Robert Elliotte	300010	20011-4-3
David McKinza	200010	40010-1-0
Wm. Lewis	100010	00100-1-0
Jos. Lewis	111301	12101-5-0
Willis Magee	320010	20010-5-2
Henry Magee	200010	10010-2-3
Wm. Fortenberry	220001	00011-3-0
John Jones	501201	21110-2-1
Lobn. Magee	000001	00001-2-6
Danl. Clower	000100	20100-1-0
Thompson Miller	100010	00100-1-0
Elisha Holmes	320301	03010-5-1
Stephn. T. Dallis	000010	00010-0-1
David Myers	301101	11010-2-0
Jas. Holmes	000100	10100-1-0
Philip Sherby	100001	11000-0-0
Eliz. Ginn	210000	01010-0-0
Jno. Magee	001221	01101-8-0
Penelope Ginn	210000	32010-1-1
Richd. Graves	200001	20100-7-7
Tho. Rule	000010	31010-3-1
Isaac Roberts	411110	20010-4-4
Saml. Davis	000021	10101-5-8
Jonas Cawsey	000010	20010-?-1
Little B. May	200010	20200-1-0
Peter James	210011	00101-?-0
Eleazer Bell	111102	10011-2-12
Jas. Cawsey	000100	01000-1-1
Lobn (?) Cawsey	121101	20110-3-2
Hardy Sanderfer	311301	02101-3-4
Armsted Hall	210010	21110-4-0
Jno. Oquin	100111	00001-3-3
Jehu Oquin	200010	00100-2-1
Jacob Owens	000010	41010-2-0
Benj. Kenady	140001	30010-3-0
Jas. Carr	100030	20100-2-0
Hilry Breland	000100	00200-1-0
Wm. Thornhill	000201	01102-3-0
Robert Thornhill	100010	10020-2-1
Wm. Prichard	110020	10110-4-1
Jacob Williams	000001	30010-1-0
Wm. Smith (Gideonite)	200200	00010-2-1
Peggy Hale	000000	10010-0-0
Pollard H. Coats	200100	00100-1-1
Major Craft	000100	10100-1-0
Jerem Bearden	300010	10100-1-0
Isaac M. Graw	000100	00100-1-0
Uriah M. Graw	300010	10010-5-5
Jonath. Smith	000010	10010-1-0
Wiley P. Harris	000100	01001-3-4
Wm. Barnes	300001	11001-2-9

Name	Col1	Col2
David M. Graw (Taf)	121111	10101-8-1
Jas. Gibson	200020	11010-1-0
Robert Love	000010	31100-4-7
Saml. Barker	000100	00100-1-0
Robert Rose	000010	
Isham Akin	000120	00010-0-1
Jno. Williams	010010	30010-1-1
Saml. Higginbothan	000101	00100-0-1
Nath. M. Graw	000001	00010-0-0
Wm. Wilson	100010	20010-1C-0
Aley Savage	010010	00100-0-2
Maj. Lea	101210	00100-0-1
Wm. Orr	000010	
Saml. C. Barlow	000100	
Jno. Matthews	310101	01100-3-0
Wm. Martin	000100	00000-3A-1C-5
Buckner Harris	000100	
Jno. C. Weeks	000100	10100-1-1
Isaac Saddler	011111	01110-5-4
Peter Quin Junr.	311230	20010-5-10
Jas. C. Dickson	100200	00100-2A-2C-4
Wm. Rymes	110101	42010-3-0
David Cleveland	010110	00011-14-14
Antho. M. Perriman	000100	00000-1C-0
David M. Graw Senr.	000001	00001-7-16
Derrel Martin	000012	00000-6-9
Vincent Garner	120001	30010-4-6
David Dickson	301200	20100-3-6
Jas. Andrews Senr.	000001	00000-2-3
Jno. Akin	300110	10100-0-1
Laban Bacot	000110	02300-1-0
Laz. Reeves	000201	30011-3-0
Jno. Reeves	000010	00100-1-0
Jas. Legget	300100	10100-1-0
Jno. Dickenson	200100	00100-2-0
Mary Win	000200	01001-1-0
Wm. Danning	210010	21010-2-0
Jno. Arlidge (?)	000100	
Saml. Wilson	230001	10001-4-0
Isaac Simmons	100010	30100-1-0
Jno. Simmons	200010	40010-1-0
Chas. Walker	100010	22210-1-0
Jno. Laurence	420010	21010-3-1
Jas. McAnuilty	110010	21010-2-2
Nathan Sims	120010	30010-4-5
Lewallen Leggett	101301	11101-4-0
Edward Gatlin	210201	02011-11-21
Edward Bullock	000100	00100-1-0
Howell Prestige	200010	30010-2-0
Wm. McAnulty	100010	10100-1-1
Abr. Atwood	000100	01000-1-0
Rolly Little	200100	00100-1-0
Meshack Matthews	000110	00100-2-1
Shadrack Matthews	100100	10100-1-0
Michl. Ammons	500110	10100-4-0
Hudson Howell	200010	10010-2-0
Saml. Cupsted	000010	00100-1-0
Jno. Dismukes	200010	10100-1-0
Jno. Chapman	000010	00100-1-0
Jacob Coon	400010	01010-1-0
Joel Merril	000010	20010-1-0
Andrew Moake	220010	11110-4-0
Jno. Johnston	100010	10100-1-0
Eliz. Ryals	020000	30010-2-0
Jas. Rollins	310010	01010-4-1
Reubin Williams	200010	10100-1-2
Ezra Estes	100100	10100-1-0
Wm. Little	000201	00111-5-6

Name	Col1	Col2
Allbritton Jones (Sones?)	210020	20011-3-2
Floyd Williams	400010	11010-1-1
Nathl. Wells	330010	12010-10-16
Tho. Gatlin	100010	20200-1-0
Tho. Richmond	200100	10100-1-0
Geo. Johnston	100101	11101-2-0
Nathl. Johnston	411101	20110-3-0
Nathl. Johnston	000100	00100-1-0
Jno. Wells	130010	20110-4-0
Jefse Edwards	100110	00100-2-0
Caleb Burton	200110	02200-8-14
Jas. Boyd	000100	10100-1-0
Tho. Bradshaw	211201	11001-2-2
Silas Hollis	000010	00100-1-1
Wm. Morrow	000001	00001-1-9(?)
Wm. McComb	100100	00100-1-0
Robert Wilson	100100	00100-1-0
Sarah Montgomery	010000	01001-1-0
Wm. Forgy (?)	010001	10101-2-0
Tho. Reaves	100010	20010-1-0
Jno. Queen	100010	30110-1-0
Nicho. Clarke	200100	10100-1-0
Mary Clarke		00201
Jane Luthrell	110100	02010-1-0
Andrew Richmond	320011	10001-4-0
Math Turner	000011	01001-1-0
Jos. Turner	210011	12101-5-2
Bede Goldman	300101	01300-4-0
Moses Clarke	311201	12010-4-0
Wm. Hampton	100110	40100-4-5
Jas. Cammel	000001	
Wm. Clarke Senr.	001301	11101-3-0
Jno. Clarke	100010	10100-1-0
Wilson Clarke	000010	01000-1-0
Benj. Ezel	100010	10100-1-0
Josiah Powel	301110	22110-4-8
Jno. Martin	200201	01101-2-1
Josiah Martin	130011	10010-1-19
Wm. H. Laurence	100100	00100-0-0
Benj. Bagley	011101	02000-4-3
Peter Quin Senr.	000001	00001-4-8
Henry Goldman	310101	10110-4-1
Steph. Huff	000001	00101-5-5
Henry Quin	200010	30100-7-13
Elizabeth Glafs	100000	44010-1-0
Jas. Y. McNabb	410010	11010-2-1
Elijah Martin	300011	01201-3-0
Wm. Martin	200120	00100-5-2
Wm. G. Cooper	410020	20010-2-1
Wm. Clarke Junr.	400010	10100-1-0
Abner Barksdale	100211	02011-7-9
Wm. F. Barksdale	200010	20010-1-0
Martin Crowe	400010	20010-3-0
Jas. Gordan	100010	30100-2-2
Lewis Battard	000010	10100-1-0
Elij. Isaaks	101201	32010-3-0
Lucy Donaho	100100	20010-3-2
Wm. Earle	300001	00200-1-0
Derrel Young	000010	00100-2-0
Jno. Sharon	000001	00001-1-0
Willis Prescot	000010	10100-2-1
Allen Carter	110010	30010-4-2
Henry Clarke	410010	00010-2-0
Wm. Jenkins	210001	21100-2-0
Danl. Jenkins	000100	00100-1-0
Jas. Neale	000100	10100-1-0
Wm. Donaho	000001	00000-1-1
Daniel McKinza	310010	21010-2-0

Nehemiah Newman	130110 10010-1-0
Jno. Cutrer	200100 30010-2-1
Jefse Webb	200010 30010-2-0
Jos. Rodrigarz	000010
Tho. Neale	221101 00010
Mark Cole	110001 01101-3-0
Nathl. Prescot	200010 30010-2-1
Elij. Roberts	100010 00001-1-1
Chas. Tate	000010 00100-1-0
Saml. Varnado	200010 20100-1-0
Abel Dyches	120101 00101-3-0
Patrick Young	000100 10101-3-2
Jno. Stevenson	200010 21010-3-0
Saml. Varnado Senr	100101 22101-5-4
Saml. Carter	101201 02110-4-0
Hardy Carter	100010 20100-3-3
Jacob Summers	220101 11001-3-0
Danl. McDaniel	021101 00001-3-0
Benj. Zachery	010101 11101-3-0
Robt. Griffin	000100
Zach. Redmon	000101 00002-2-0
Thompson Wallis	300010 41010-1-0
J. Elbert Hinds	100110 10100-1-0
Wm. Carter	100010 20100-3-2
Barnot Drees	000010 00000-0-1
Geo. Carter	100010 10100-1-0
Jno. Zachery	110201 03050-5-0
Isaac Melton	000101 00101-2-0
David Hinds	100201 10013-2-0
Wm. Pendarvis	400110 20010-4-2
Henry Bond	110201 01110-3-0
Jno. Huckebe	100010 00100-1-0
Jefse McClendon	220010 11010-4-5
Jerem. Huckebe	000010 10010-1-0
Fred. White	100100 10100-1-0
Nelson Higginbothan	310010 32010-3-0
Gideon Bond	010001 42010-2-0
Geo. M. Trotter	000010
Jane Huffman	120000 00010
Wm. Andrews	100100 10000-3-2
Early Harris	500010 00010-8-14
Edwd. White	310020 20010-3-1
Elbert Burton	000010 10100-1-2
Sandra Burton	100010 00111-4-6
Tho. Tomkins	200010 01010-1-2
Robt. Higginbotham	101201 33010-7-5
Zadock Turner	100010 10100-1-0
Barnes C. Arthur	000010 10100-1-0
Walten Jacob	200110 31010-2-0
Jno. Bond	000001 00001-1-0
Tho. Arthur	220101 11001-4-0
Jos. Hughes	101300 30111-3-0
Tho. Seale	210201 00001-3?-5
Benj. Morgan	000010 00100-1C-1
Lewis Elza	010101 01001-8-8
Abr. Hughes	100010 30010-1C-0
Hene Lumpkin	000011 21010-0-0
Jas. Roberts	100010 21010-2-0
Jno. Weeks	200010 10100-1-0
Wiley Weeks	200100 10100-1-0
Reuben Vaughan	000100 10100-1-0
Nathl. Goff	210010 01010-4-2
Jas. Batson	000100 00000-1-0
Jas. Craft	200100 21100-2-1
Jas. Weeks	020001 00001-1-0
Moor Kenady	000010 00000-0-1
Simeon Morris	100100 10010-1-0
Benj. Morris	221201 02201-4-0
Nath. Morris	110010 12010-3-0
Jerem. Smith	121101 51110-7-4
Wm. Weeks	100100 00100-1-0
Jas. Weeks	000010 10100-1-0
Leml. Bullock	000100 20100-1-0
Edwin Alford	100010 00100-1-0
Benj. Kent	200100 00100-1-0
Saml. Howel	100010 00100-1-0
Edward Abby	110001 10301-2-0
Jos. Knight	000010 00000-1-0
Tarner (?) Lewis	221101 01010-3-0
Susan Whorton	320000 21201-5-3
Jno. Crow	100010 10100-1-0
Danl. Allday	000010 01010-1-0
Richd. Findley	200010 10100-4-3
Nancy Mullens	020100 20010-3-0
Peter Batson	200010 10010-1-0
Tho. Batson	000001 00001-0-1
Jas. Beasley	320101 11011-7-4
Jno. Beasley	000100 20100-1-0
Jno. Miller	100100 10100-1-3
Wm. McMorris	100010 10100-2-0
Aquilla Coney	211110 31010-9-7
Betsey Batson	120100 21110-2-0
Allen Strickland	000010
Polly Riley	210010 00010
Robert Strickland	120201 10101-5-0
Brice Miller	311310 01010-6-0
Jas. Rymes	100100 20100-1-0
Wm. Beard	120001 21010-2-0
Jno. Hinson	300001 30010-3-0
Saml. Ferguson	221110 31011-5-0
Tho. Bell	110020 20010-3-4
Daves Barron	000200 00100-1-1
Jane M. Kisick	000200 00001-2-0
Mos McElveen	200010 20100-0-0
Jno. McDaniel	200100 00010-1-0
Wm. Sanderfer	000010 00100-1-0
Jno. Sanderfer	110010 21010-6-8
Ann Simmons	031200 21110-8-10
Jas. Daugharty	120011 40010-2-0
Saml. Holman	000100 10010-1-0
Simon Osteen	121101 40020-3-0
Leond. Varnado	311220 00020-3-1
Burrel Carter	200100 10100-2-1
Derrel Carter	100100 00010-2-1
Isaac Carter	020001 01001-5-14
Abden (Alden?) Tyler	100010 20100-1-0
Sarah Pendarvis	000100 00000-1-0
Ephr. Prescot	100010 02113-4-4
Michl. Prescot	000010 10100-1-1
Harwood Jones	010101 -6-8
Jacob Lockhart	000100 30010-1-0
Henry Sandel	010101 -3-0
Danl. Felder	000010 10100-1-0
Peter Felder Junr.	200010 10100-3-4
Peter Felder Senr.	000101 10201-8-17
Jno. Kelly	000001
Henry Dickerson	110001 21010-3-5
Jno. Ballard	000201 00231-1-0
Jas. Ballard	410010 10010-3-0
Jno. Felder	200010 20101-3-0
Jno. Dickerson Senr.	000301 00310-4-0
Tho. Dickerson	000010 10100-1-0
Michl. Morris	000001 00001-3-5
Lunsford Lowe	010110 11010-4-6
Jno. Crum	000101 01211-2-0
Jerom Corley	201101 21010-3-0
Jacob Corley	000010
Danl. Sandel	100010 00100-1-0

Name	Code	Name	Code
Sarah Bankston	010100 00210-2-0	David Strong	100010 11010-1-0
Jno. Neighbors	000001	Wm. Sibley	100010 20010-2-0
Jno. Lowe Senr.	200101 00100-17-22	Saml. Roberts	100110 21010-2-0
Jas. Robinson	110101 31010-12-16	Laurance Dillon	100010 31010-2-1
Tho. Cook	410010 10010-11-14	Saml. Jones	000100
Richd. Quin	400010 10010-9-9	Eml. King	320001 12110-2-0
Polly H. Lenior	400010 22010-6-10	Jno. Stallings	100010 10010-1-2
Saml. Barron	100001 32010-0-1	Danl. Graves	000100 00100-0-1
Wm. Woodall	120110 21010-4-0	Jane Helton	220000 30010-2-0
Jno. Richmond	000001 00001-1-0	Baily Smith	100010 20100-1-1
Sherod Gray	100110 10100-2-0	Geo. Smith	200010 11101-2-1
Jonath. Catching	010010 11010-6-8	Clarkson Dillon	211110 21010-4-13
Jno. Woods	000010	Richd. Dillon	000001 10011-6-0
Goodman Trawick	020010 00001-3-0	Willis Dillon	200010 10010-1-0
Jas. Bridges	110010 01010-4-6	Susanna Jones	300000 11011-0-0
Wm. Faust	310001 31000-3-0	Britton Lewis	000100
Danl. Smith	110010 20200-2-0	Ann Jackson	000000 00111-0-0
Isaac Foster	201201 13010-3-2	Jno. Fowler	000010 -0-1
Isaac Milsaps	000100 10100-2-1	Wm. Smith	100200 10100-0-1
Tho. Roberts	210010 41110-2-0	Henry Hale	410111 00100-5-0
Enos Daughtery	010001 00200-1-0	Little Jno. Rymes	200010 00100-1-1
Jas. Waddle	100121 00100-3-1	Willis Simmons	221100 20010-4-1
Britton Smith	310200 21010-7-7	David Morgan	111110 32011-5-10
Jno. Brown	300010 20010-2-0	Loften Fairchild	400010 11010-3-5
Martha Stanfield	200000 01010-0-0	Wm. Love	011102 00201-9-6
Benj. Kenady	000100	Robt. Bend	100010 20100-1-0
Tho. Denmon	200200 00100-2-6	Tho. Heard	100010 20100-1-3
Chas. King	000101 01000-4-4	Jno. Smith	210010 22010-5-6
Jas. McMullen	000010 10100-1-0	Jas. Hope	111110 32010-4-1
Jefse King	310010 11000-3-1	Jos. Catching	221110 00010-7-13
Zach. Davis	100010 00100-1-0	Philip Catching	300110 12010-6-12
Robert Fairchild	310201 10301-4-0	Esther Ragland	100010 02010-5-11
Richd. Smith	010201 01101-5-1	Anne Allen	100010 01101-4-10
Wm. Elza	000110 20100-2-1	Garrel M. Allen	000100 00100-1-3
Jos. Strong	511301 12010-5-1	Wm. Dickson	100010 10100-5-8

Laban Bacot, assistant to the Marshall of Mississippi, certifies to the correctness of this report on June 15th, 1820. There were 4438 inhabitants in the county at that time.

Mr. Bacot in his transcribing the names on this census omitted the small "c" in all names beginning with "Mc." The "c" was so affixed to the following letter that it appeared non-existant. In copying this enumeration I omitted the "c" in all of the McGraw names. ERW

EARLY LISTS OF MEMBERS OF THE BOGUE CHITTO OR CRAIN'S CREEK

BAPTIST CHURCH, PIKE COUNTY, MISSISSIPPI, 1824-27 & 1834

The lists below were copied from the original minutes of the church now on file in the Library, Mississippi College, Clinton, Mississippi.

NAMES OF BRETHREN IN FELLOWSHIP UP TO AUGUST 1st, 1834:

1. Thomas Gulledge
2. Nathan McGraw
3. Green Rasberry
4. Wm. Gulledge
5. Thomas Grant
6. Henry Simmons
7. Dempsey McGraw

NAMES OF THE MALE MEMBERS BELONGING TO THE CHURCH 8th DAY OF JUNE, 1827

1. John Warren, Deacon
2. Thomas Gulledge, Deacon
3. William Carter
4. David Cleveland
5. Hanse Hamilton
6. Nathan McGraw
7. Wm. W. Sheppard
8. John K. Marsh

NAMES OF FEMALE MEMBERS BELONGING TO THE CHURCH THE 8th DAY OF JUNE, 1828

1. Priscilla Warren
2. Sarah Walker
3. Grace Cleveland
4. Jane Gulledge
5. Judah Hamilton
6. Lucy King
7. Mary Catchings
8. Mary Magdalen
9. Sarah Thompson
10. Jelowen Perryman
11. Betsey Carter
12. Mary Carter
13. Thezia Beard (Kesia Beard)
14. Hannah Strother
15. Elizabeth Gates
16. Nancy Barkerly (?)
17. Susannah Brown

NAMES OF FEMALE MEMBERS BELONGING TO THE CHURCH SEPTEMBER 5th, 1828

1. Priscilla Warren
2. Sarrah Walker
3. Gracey Cleveland
4. Jane Guilledge
5. Judith Hambleton
6. Mary Magdalen
7. Sarrah Thompson
8. Flower Perryman dec.
9. Elizabeth Carter
10. Polly Carter
11. Kezia Beard
12. Hannah Strother
13. Elisabeth Gates dec.
14. Nancy Barker
15. Mary Norman Exp.
16. Martha Gulledge Exp.
17. Frances Hale

THE 1834 LISTING OF FEMALES IN THE CHURCH WAS THE SAME AS THE ABOVE.

- - - - - - - -

SOME EARLY MEMBERS OF NEW ZION BAPTIST CHURCH IN PIKE COUNTY,

NOW WALTHAL COUNTY, MISSISSIPPI, 1823-1830

1. John Bennit
2. Elizabeth Breland
3. Francis Breland
4. James Breland
5. Chrisiana R. Fortenberry
6. Hannah Fortenberry
7. Violette Kennington Fortenberry
8. William Fortenberry
9. William Fortenberry
10. John Jones
11. Mariann Jones
12. Joseph Lewis Senior
13. Joseph Lewis Junior
14. William Lewis
15. Willis Magee
16. Daniel McKinzy
17. Nathan Morris
18. Abigail Pierce
19. John Pierce
20. Reuben Pierce
21. Elizabeth Powell
22. Starlin Powell
23. Absolem Roberts
24. Martha Roberts
25. Bilbra Ryall
26. Hardy Ryall
27. James Thigpen
28. Joel Bullock

SOME EARLY MEMBERS OF NEW ZION BAPTIST CHURCH ON A LIST

PRIOR TO THE NOVEMBER MEETING IN 1866

The names above were extracted from the original minutes of the church which are now in the Library at Mississippi College, Clinton, Mississippi. The members listed above were <u>not</u> the only members of the church during this time. The following list seems to be a <u>complete</u> list for the period prior to 1866

1. Joseph Lewis, dec.
2. Calvin K. Fortenberry, dec.
3. Daniel Smith
4. Hugh Bullock
5. Sire Magee died 1867
6. Leonard Magee
7. Alfred Morris
8. Ivin M. Fortenberry
9. Everit Pittman
10. Willis Fortenberry
11. Thomas Pigott Jr.
12. Samuel Blackwell
13. John R. Breland
14. Louiza Magee
15. Rebecca Magee
16. Anna Magee
17. Lucy Faulk
18. Caroline Fortenberry
19. Sarah Ann Morris
20. Nancy Pigott
21. Vina Blackwell
22. Louisa Fortenberry
23. Saml. Lewis
24. Vilotte Fortenberry d. 1858
25. Elizabeth Breland
26. Mary Ann Jones
27. Mary Ryall
28. Mary Dillon
29. Susanna Green
30. Clarissa Smith
31. Nancy McKenzie
32. Luerisisa Smith
33. Tabitha Smith, dec.
34. Elizabeth Carson
35. Sarah Rowell
36. Abashaba Rowell
37. Mary Breland
38. Elizabeth Jones
39. Siller Jones
40. Emily Jones d. 12/1861
41. Cathern Smith
42. Caroline Bullock
43. Norcecy Fortenberry
44. Isebella Fortenberry
45. Olevia Fortenberry
46. Mary Carter
47. Cordelia Crain
48. Nancy Holmes
49. Molsey Pittman
50. Nancy Ruching
51. Gatsey Magee
52. Sarah Webb
53. Nancy De Laughter
54. Adarren Fortenberry Davis
55. Mary Fortenberry
56. Jane Blackwell
57. Martha McQueen
58. Mary Smith
59. Susan Rowell
60. Rutha Passman
61. Jacob, colored man
62. George, colored man
63. Rose, colored woman
64. Samuel, colored man
65. Delila, colored woman
66. William Rowell
67. Robbert, colored man
68. Virgil, colored man
69. Eliza, colored woman
70. Charlotte, colored woman
71. Isreal McKenzy
72. Jules McKensey
73. Samuel McQueen
74. Ephraim Rushing
75. Thomas Pigott Senior
76. Rebecca Pigott
77. Polly Futch
78. Alfred Fortenberry
79. Mary Ann Passman
80. Abraham Breland
81. Frances Rowell
82. York, colored man
83. April, colored
84. Lucinda L. Rodgers
85. Sidney Platt
86. Margaret Carson
87. Mary Rodgers
88. Emily Rodgers
89. Nancy Willis Broomfield
90. Adaline Jones
91. Emmah, colored woman
92. Leonard Taylor
93. Warren Mitchell
94. Nancy Taylor
95. Pamelia Rowell
96. Mary Magee
97. Rebecca, colored woman
98. Nowel E. Rushing
99. Julia E. Rushing
100. Selean (?) Carter
101. Chalop, colored man
102. Jonus L. Causey
103. Seretta Causey
104. Gemimi Hambleton
105. Sarah Blackwell
106. George W. Fortenberry
107. Harriot Dillon
108. Nancy Rushing
109. Tyre J. Magee
110. Emily Fortenberry
111. Charles B. Davis
112. Emily S. Davis
113. Martha Hughes
114. Nancy Smith
115. Nancy Webb
116. Granberry Blunt

117. Mary Blunt
118. Warren, colored man
119. Rebecca Pope
120. Gracy Hobgood
121. Nathaniel Graves
122. Benjamin Dunkin
123. Mary Thomas
124. Granberry Blunt
125. Mary Jane Blunt
126. Jane Davis
127. John Smith
128. E. W. Pigott
129. Elizabeth Fortenberry
130. William Robbins
131. Jane K. Robbins
132. Levie Rushing
133. Nancy A. E. Rushing
134. Calvin Smith
135. Sarah Smith
136. Margret Smith
137. Emily M. Smith
138. Nancy Pigott Morris Ball
139. Cyntha Pigott Warner
140. Ann Mitchell
141. J. W. Smith
142. Anizi Mitchell
143. Warren Mitchell
144. Leonard Taylor
145. Elizabeth, colored woman
146. Pernecia Bullock
147. Martha Ann Magee Branch
148. Sileta E. Davis Smith
149. Sarah M. Holmes Dunkin
150. Lucrecia A. Breland Passman
151. B. F. Branch
152. Adeline Jones
153. Adarine Magee, colored
154. Elvy Magee, colored
155. Mary Erwin
156. I. J. Jones
157. Lucy Jones

158. Lucy Jones Holmes
159. Edward Pierce
160. Elisabeth Pierce
161. Samantha McAlister Dillon
162. Mary Magee, colored
163. Dafney Holmes, colored
164. Louisa Bernard
165. Ellen Beard
166. Wm. L. Davis
167. Narcissa A. Davis
168. John M. McAffrey
169. Sarah A. J. Smith
170. George Smith
171. Brandon Ryall
172. Martha R. Ryall
173. William Smith
174. Martin P. Duncan
175. Benjamin Duncan
176. Richard O. Cowart
177. Willis N. Brumfield
178. Nancy Brumfield
179. Eliza Bullock Tyner
180. Elizabeth Green
181. Agga Bullock, colored
182. Martin Mitchell
183. Joseph Ginn, colored
184. Dafney Holmes, colored
185. Eliza Jones
186. Vilet Holmes, colored
187. Cloah Guy, colored
188. Everet Pittman
189. Jerden Gay
190. Charlotte Broomfield, colored
191. Levinia Rushing
192. John C. Rushing
193. William A. Rushing
194. Anna Rushing
195. April Broomfield, colored
196. Malinda Pigott
197. Mary Green

1825 TAX LIST FOR PIKE COUNTY, MISSISSIPPI

Key
name
acres of owned property
location (waterway)
white taxables
slaves
total tax paid

Abbreviations
Baily Chitto--Bai. Ch. Leatherwood--Lthd.
Bogue Chitto--Bo. Ch.
Tangipahoa River (spelled Taunchepaho
  on original)--Tnch.
Little Tangipahoa--L. Tnch.
Topesaw--Top.
Magee's Creek--Mag. Cr.
Terry's Creek--Tr. Cr.
Silver Creek--Sil. Cr.
Glovers Creek--Gl. Cr.

Page 1

Name	Acres/Location	W	S	Tax
Barna C. Arthur	240 Bai. Ch.	1	0	1.03
Jno. Akin	160 Bo. Ch.	1	0	3.95
Wm. Andrews	240 Bo. Ch. & L. Tnch.	1 5		5.70
Frank Ammond		1	0	.75
Ashley Arnold		1	0	.75
Jas. Arnold		1	0	.75
Wm. Arnold	160 Bo. Ch.			.33
Michl. Ammond				
Jas. Andrews	160 Bo. Ch.	1	6	6.53
Isham Akin	160 L. Tnch.	1	1	1.66
Micaj. Andrews	80 Tnch.	1	0	.95
Lanty Armstrong		1	0	.75
Hyram Addison	160 Tnch.	1	2	2.65
Hudson Andrews		1	0	.75
Daniel Allday		1	0	.75
Edwin Alford	160 Bo. Ch.	1	0	1.55
Jno. Ammons	80 Top.			.16
Michl. Ammons Jr.		1	0	.75
Felix Allen	240 Bo. Ch.	1	6	7.
Lanson Boutwell	80 Mag. Cr.	1	0	.83
Laban Bacot	320 Bo. Ch.	1	6	7.35
2 lots in Holmesville				2.50
Saml. Bacot	234 Bo. Ch.	1	0	1.60
Dav. Bullock		1	2	2.25
Tho. Burton		1	0	.75
Jas Boid		1	0	.75
Saml. Burron (Burros?)		1	1	1.50
Robert Brown	160 Bo. Ch.	1	1	1.56
Hugh Brown		1	0	.75
John Brown		1	0	.75
				$57.15

Page 2

Name	Acres/Location	W	S	Tax
Bartlet Bird		1	0	.75
Thomp. Brister		1	0	.75
Hocketta Brister	160 Top.	0	2	1.90
John Bigner		1	0	.75
Shadr. Boit		1	0	.75
Edwd. Bullock	160 Bo. Ch.	1	2	2.40
Wm. Bullock	860 Bo. Ch.	0	8	10.16
Jno. Bullock		1	0	.75
Abr. Briley		1	0	.75
Rob. Bond	160 Bo. Ch.	1	1	2.46
Jno. Black	160 Bo. Ch.	1	3	6.40
4 lots in Holmesville				16.00
Same for Sar. Barton		0	3	2.25
Robt. Barton 1 lot in Holmesvl.				1.75
Same for Est. C. Barton	260 Bo. Ch.	0 19		15.70
Berry R. Bridges		1	0	.75
Reub. Ballard	80 L.Tnch	1	0	1.06
Jas. Ballard	160 L. Tnch	0	0	.64
Lewis Ballard	80 Tnch.	0	0	1.00
Benj. Bagley	240 Tnch.	0	6	5.70
Same for Est. of H. Vaughan (?)	160 Tnch.	0	0	.80
Uriah Beeson		1	0	.75
Abner Barksdale	160 Bo. Ch.	0	8	6.20
Wm. F. Barksdale	320 Bo. Ch. & Tnch.	1	0	1.10
Wm. Braddy		1	0	.75
Jno. Bankston		1	0	.75
Henry Bond	240 Bai. Ch.	1	0	2.20
Preston Bond	160 Bai. Ch.	1		.96
Tho. Bell	160 Bai. Ch.	0	6	6.05
Edwd. Barron		1	3	3.00
Agese lous Barron	160 Bai. Ch.	1	0	9.50
				$91.46

Page 3

Name	Acres/Location	W	S	Tax
Davis Barron	160 Bai. Ch.	1	1	1.70
Jno. Beesley	80 Sil. Cr.	1	1	1.90
Peter Batson		1		.75
Jno. Bennet		1		.75
Robert Berryhill		1	0	.75
Archd. Brown		1	0	.75
Jno. B. Barker	320 Top.	1	2	3.25
Mered. (?) Brent	160 Top.	1	2	2.45
Jno. Brent	160 Top.	1	3	3.80
Tho. Brent	160 Top.	1	1	2.30
Preston Brent	160 Top.	1	1	2.30
Aaron Beard	30 Top.	1	0	.88
Jno. Boid		1	0	.75
Isaac Boid		1	0	.75
Mos. Bridges	480 Gl. Cr.	0	5	4.95
Same for Vinzant	160 Gl. Cr.			.80
Wm. Bridges		1	0	.75
Ephr. Bridges	80 Gl. Cr.	1	0	1.05
Jno. Bridges		1	0	.75
Peter Q. Bridge		1	0	.75
Byrd Buford	240 Gl. Cr.	0	0	.80
Param Buford		1	12	9.75
David Burford	160 Gl. Cr.	1	1	1.66
Fredr. Brese (?)		1	1	.75
Saml. Barker	160 Lthd	1	1	1.70
Wm. Bearden		1	0	.75
Jerem. Bearden	160 Lethd	1	1	1.74
Tho. Barnes		1	0	.75
Danl. Buckhalter		1	3	3.00
Richdson Bowman	240 Mag. Cr.	1 11		22.45
Richd. R. Bridges		1	0	.75
				$76.98

Page 4

Name	Acres	Location			Value
Jas. J. Bridges	160	Bo. Ch.	1	7	6.16
Tho. Burnes			1	0	.75
Jesse Blackbourn	240	Bo. Ch.	1	4	4.10
Jno. Breland			1	0	.75
Jas. M. Breland			1	0	.75
Hillary Breland			1	0	.75
Ann Cathe Bell			0	7	5.25
Nath. Ballard			1	0	.75
Tho. Cook	480	L. Tnch.	1	27	23.40
Abr. J. Currell			1	0	.75
Eza. Cates			0	1	.75
Mos. Clark	160	Tnch.			9.60
Willis Clark			1	0	.75
Benj. Clark			1	0	.75
Wilson Clark	320	L. Tnch.	1	1	2.00
Saml. Colston			1	0	.75
Jacob Corley	160	Bo. Ch.	1	0	1.03
Jno. Cleveland			1	0	.75
Wm. Crouswell	160	Bo. Ch.	1	2	2.40
Caleb Coker	160	Bo. Ch.	1	0	.90
Saml. Cubsted (?)	80	Bo. Ch.	1	0	1.23
Jacob Coon	155	Bo. Ch.	1	0	1.63
Same for Est. Ryals	160	Bo. Ch.	0	0	1.28
David Cleveland	800	Bo. Ch.	1	26	23.94
Same for Jas. Gray	1 lot in Holmesville				1.00
Jerom Corley	160	L. Tnch.			.20
Godfrey Clement	80	Tnch.	1	0	1.00
Mary Carrel				1	.75
Henry Clark	80	Ter.Cr.	1	0	.94
Mark Cole					.48
Saml. Carter	160	Tnch.			.62
Wm. Carter	160	Tnch.	1	3	3.96
					91.48

Page 5

Name	Acres	Location			Value
Allen Carter	400	Tnch.	1	4	5.83
Richd. Carter	160	Tnch.	1	0	1.55
Hardy Carter	160	Tnch.	1	4	4.70
Derrel Carter	160	Tnch.	1	4	4.54
Nancy Carter			0	6	4.50
Israel Carter	240	Tnch.	0	5	5.20
Harvel Carter	160	Tnch.	0	3	3.04
Burrel Carter	160	Tnch.	1	3	3.80
Jno. Collins			1	0	.75
Benj. Catching	160	Bai. Cr.	0	1	1.70
James Craft	160	Sil. Cr.	1	1	2.46
Rachel Coney	160	Sil. Cr.	0	6	5.46
Wm. Coney	160	Sil. Cr.	0	0	.20
Jos. Catching	320	Bo. Ch.	1	15	13.60
Philip Catching	480	Bo. Ch.	1	15	16.80
Jesse Craft	160	Top.	1	2	2.48
Same for Thos. Creed (?)	400	Top.	0	0	.50
Wm. Cothern	160	Top.	1	0	.95
Jonath. Carter	292	Top.	1	3	4.45
Saml. Craft	80	Carter's Creek	1	0	.95
Jno. Craft	160	Carter's Creek	0	4	3.20
Jno. Chandler			1	0	.75
Wm. Chandler	320	Gl. Cr.	1	0	.75
Eli Coker			1	0	1.82
Wm. Carter (Topesaw)			1	0	.75
Johnston Carnes			1	0	.75
Major Craft			1	0	.75
Jno. Craft Junr.			1	0	.75
Pollard H. Coats	160	Lthd.	1	3	3.40

Page 6

Name	Acres	Location			Value
Jas. Car			1	0	.75
Philip Cawsey			1	1	1.50
Same for 1824			0	1	.75
					100.13
Jonath. Catching	160	Bo. Ch.	1	12	10.70
Wm. Catching	240	Bo. Ch.	1	5	4.98
Wm. Caster, Dillon's Settlement			1	0	.75
Matth. Cook	160	Mag. Cr.			.20
Same for 1824	160	Mag. Cr.			.20
Jonas Cawsey			1	2	2.25
Mos. Collins	160	Mag. Cr.	1	13	11.30
Burton Collins			1	0	.75
Seab. Collins	160	Mag. Cr.	1	5	5.45
Wm. Car			1	0	.75
Jas. Cawsey			0	4	3.75
Solm. Cawsey	240	Mag. Cr.	0	5	4.94
Jno. Dismukes	80	Bo. Ch.	1	0	1.06
Henry Davis			1	0	.75
Daniel Davis	160	Top.	0	2	1.66
Steph. T. Davis			1	0	.75
Jeto (?) Dickerson	160	L. Tnch.	0	0	.64
Jas. Dickerson			1	0	.75
Martin Dickerson			1	0	.75
Owen Dickerson			1	0	.75
Tho. Dickerson			1	0	.75
Henry Dickerson	160	L. Tnch.	0	6	5.45
Jas. Delany			1	0	.75
Wm. Dykes			1	3	3.00
Wm. Dickson	160	Bo. Ch.	1	9	8.78
Same for J. Dickson 3 lots Holmesville	80	Bo. Ch.	0	6	8.98

Page 7

Name	Acres	Location			Value
Jos. Dunaway			1	0	.75
Seab. J. Durham	80	Mag. Cr.	1	2	2.65
Wm. Donaho			1	0	.75
Aquila Donaho	160	Mag. Cr.	1	0	.90
Thos. Denham	95	Bo. Ch.	1	2	2.46
Zacheus Davis	160	Bo. Ch.	1	2	3.05
					91.42
Laur. Dillon	160	Mag. Cr.	1	11	9.48
Willis Dillon	160	Bo. Ch.	1	1	2.30
Richd. Dillon	160	Bo. Ch.	0	5	4.47
Clarkson Dillon	320	Bo. Ch.	1	4	4.50
Theo. Dillon	320	Bo. Ch.	1	3	3.85
Richd. Dillon	320	Mag. Cr.	1	14	11.60
Saml. Davis	160	Mag. Cr.	1	1	2.30
Jno. Davis			1	1	1.50
Ballard Eppes	160	Tnch.	1	3	3.48
Benj. Ezel	160	L. Tnch.	1	0	.95
Wm. Ellza			1	0	.75
Jesse Edwards	160	Bo. Ch.	1	0	1.38
Eza Estes	80	Bo. Ch.	1	0	1.21
Lewis Ellza	320	Bo. Ch.	0	8	7.91
Benj. Eddens	3 lots Holmesville		1	0	2.35
Lewis Ezell			1	0	.75
Owen Ellis	320	Mag. Cr.	1	2	2.70
Lowry Ellis			1	0	.75
Steph Ellis	80	Mag. Cr.	1	0	1.00
Michl. Elliott	160	Mag. Cr.	1	0	.90
Wm. Estes			1	1	1.50
Tho. Ellza			1	0	.75

Name	Acres	Type			Value	Name	Acres	Type			Value
Wm. Ellza	160	Bo. Ch.	1	1	2.46	Mary Hart			0	2	1.50
Jno. Ellza			1	0	.75	Jno. Hart	236	Bo. Ch.	1	4	5.43
Jno. Everet			1	0	.75	Jas. Hart	80	Bo. Ch.	1	2	2.65
Wm. Elliott	160	Mag. Cr.	1	5	4.70	Josiah Hart			1	1	1.50
Jos. Forgy			1	0	.75	Wm. Herrington			1	0	.75
Wm. Forgy	160	Bo. Ch.	0	0	.96	Wm. Hall			1	0	.75
Jno. Felder	160	L. Tnch.	1	4	3.95	Edmond Hodges			1	0	.75
Isaac Felder	160	L. Tnch.	1	3	3.95	Jno. Hoppman			1	0	.75
Elizabeth Felder	160	L. Tnch.	0	2	2.46	Christian Hoover	320	Bo. Ch.	1	7	7.60
Jane Felder			0	2	1.50	Lewis Harper			1	5	4.50
					88.71	Jesse Harper	160	Bo. Ch.	1	4	5.03
						Seab. Harper	240	Bo. Ch.	1	2	3.25
Page 8						Alexr. Harper			0	2	1.50
Tho. Gullege	240	Top.	0	0	.36						86.15
Maria Felder			0	1	.75						
Peter Felder	480	Tnch.	1	9	9.74	Page 10					
Adrian Frick	160	Tnch.	1	4	4.00	Jno. Hamilton	160	Bo. Ch.	1	3	3.96
Richd Forrest	320	Sil. Cr.	0	8	7.00	Hance Hamilton	400	Bo. Ch.	0	4	4.40
Richd Findley	160	Sil. Cr.	1	5	5.14	Same for Elizabeth					
Loften Fairchild	160	Bo. Ch.	1	7	7.28	Hamilton	240	Top.	0	1	1.95
Jas. Fletcher	160	Bo. Ch.	1	5	4.66	Tho. Hamilton	160	Top.	1	0	1.70
Danl. Farie (Faris)			1	0	.75	Judith Hamilton	320	Bo. Ch.	0	10	9.25
Green Fan	160	Gl. Cr.	1	0	.90	2 town lots in Holmesville					.75
Tho. Francis			1	0	.75	Tho. Hamilton			1	0	.75
Jno. Fisher			1	0	.75	Tho. Heard	320	Bo. Ch.	1	3	4.92
Edwd. Gatlin	400	Bo. Ch.	0	24	19.80	Jos. Hughes			1	0	.75
Henry W. Gober			1	0	.75	Jefferson Hughes			1	0	.75
Majr. Gatlin			1	0	.75	James Hughes			1	0	.75
Jno. Gatlin	320	Bo. Ch.	1	3	4.60	Chas. Harris	160	Bo. Ch.	1	1	1.66
Wm. Gordon			1	2	2.25	Wiley P. Harris	2 town lots				
Tho. Gordon	160	Bo. Ch.	0	6	4.60	in Holmesville			1	2	3.45
same for J. J. Denmon											6.00
	160	Bo. Ch.			.80	Jas. Houston	80	Tnch.	1	4	6.63
Tho. Gatlin	160	Bo. Ch.	1	0	.90	Jno. Huckaby	160	Bai.Ch.	1	0	1.40
Golifer			1	0	.75	Jas. Hope	160	Bai. Ch.	1	0	.95
Vincent Garber	240	Bo. Ch.	0	8	7.68	Henry Howel			1	1	1.50
Amos Greer	160	Bo. Ch.	1	0	1.40	Lewis Howel Junr.	80	Sil.Cr.	1	0	.85
Mos. Greer			1	0	.75	Jno. Henson Senr.	80	Sil.Cr.	0	0	.48
Jacob Gibson			1	1	1.50	Abr. Hughs			1	0	.75
Jos. Gibson			1	0	.75	Robt. Higgenbothom	160	Bo.Ch.	1	4	4.55
Jas. Gibson			1	0	.75	Sol. Higgenbothom			1	0	.75
David Gordon			1	0	.75	Henry Higgenbothom			1	0	.75
Jos. Garret			1	0	.75	Jas. Howell			1	0	.75
Wm. Gullege	80	Top.	1	0	1.15	Aaron Hickman			1	0	.75
Jos. Gates			1	0	.75	Jesse Hodges			1	0	.75
Eliz. Gates	113	Top.	0	2	2.61	Drury Hodges	80	Gl. Cr.	0	2	1.83
Jno. Greer	80	Top.	0	0	.83	Wm. Hodges			1	0	.75
					96.95	Hyram Hughes			1	0	.75
						David Hughes			1	0	.75
Page 9						Michl. Harvy	160	Mag. Cr.	0	1	1.15
Peter J. Glover	240	Gl. Cr.	0	8	6.24	Thos. C. Harvy	160	Mag. Cr.	1	1	1.66
Jesse Greer	80	Top.	1	0	.83						62.04
Jas. Gordon	240	Top.	1	4	4.15						
David Glass			1	0	.75	Page 11					
Jas. Gordon	480	Mag. Cr.	0	0	2.40	Elisha Holmes			0	4	3.00
Rob. Gordon			1	0	.75	Benj. Holmes	80	Mag. Cr.	1	0	1.22
Jno. Gordon			1	0	.75	Elisha Holmes Junr			1	0	.75
Danl. Graves	160	Bo. Ch.	1	3	3.40	Jno. C. Holmes	80	Mag. Cr.	1	0	.86
Josiah Gale	320	Mag. Cr.	1	14	11.56	Benj. Hazewood					
Penelope Gin	80	Mag. Cr.	0	3	2.45	Hagewood ?			1	0	.75
Mary Grubs			0	3	2.25	Armsted Hall			1	4	3.75
Henry House			1	2	2.25	Tho. Johnston			1	0	.75
Wm. Hampton	160	Tnch.	0	0	.96	Geo. Johnston	160	Bo. Ch.	0	0	.96
Jerem. Hucksby			1	0	.75	Robt. Johnston			1	0	.75
Benj. Herring	80	Bo. Ch.	1	2	2.65	Nath B. Johnston			1	0	.75
Chas. Hoover	470	Bo. Ch.	1	0	3.62	Jno. Johnston	160	Bo. Ch.	1	0	.90
Jas. Herrington	160	Bo. Ch.	1	1	1.70	Same for Jos. Ryals					
Reason Hood			1	0	.75		160	Bo. Ch.	1	0	.80
Jos. Hart	80	Bo. Ch.	1	1	1.98	Renny Julian			1	0	.75

Name	Description				Name	Description			
Wm. Jones		1 0	.75		Same for W. Gordon	160 Tnch			.96
Wm. Jenkins	160 Ter. Cr.	0 0	.80		Same for R. McCoy	240 Tnch			1.28
Harwood Jones	160 Tnch.	0 3	3.20		Same for Est. of R. Williams				
Marsten G. Jones		1 0	.75			320 Bo. Ch.			1.20
Walter Jacob	240 Bo. Ch.	1 0	1.75		Same for Jas. Y. McNabb				
David Jourdon		1 0	.75			320 Tnch.			.72
Oliver R. Ingram		1 0	.75		Berry May	160 Mag. Cr.	1 1	2.30	
Benj. Jones	480 Mag. Cr.	0 7	6.30		Josiah Martin Junr.		1 0	.75	
Tho. Jones	160 Mag. Cr.	1 1	1.66		Saml. Melton	2 lots Holmesville			
James Jones		1 0	.75			(sold 10,000 in mdse)			
Jas. Kelly	160 Bo. Ch.	1 0	1.			@3.75	1 1	22.25	
Allen King	480 Bo. Ch.	1 1	2.94		Andrew Moke	240 Bo. Ch.	1 0	1.95	
Tho. King	80 Bo. Ch.	1 1	1.65		Shadr. Matthews	160 Bo. Ch.	1 0	.90	
1 town lot Holmesville			.25		Jas. Matthews		1 0	.75	
Gilbert Keen		1 0	.75		Sarah Monk	160 Bo. Ch.	0 1	.90	
Josiah Keen		1 0	.75		Philip Martin	80 Bo. Ch.	1 2	2.65	
Jas. Kilborn		1 0	.75		Derrel Martin	160 Bo. Ch.	1 9	9.70	
Jas. King	240 Top.	1 0	1.94		Isaac Morgan		1 0	.75	
Danl. King	160 Top.	1 0	1.70		Jas. Mastin		1 0	.75	
Uriah Kent		1 0	.75		Phebe McGraw	2 town lots Holmes-			
			45.73			ville @4.00	0 1	1.54	
					Wm. McGuppee		1 0	1.75	
Page 12					Michl. Morris	160 L. Tnch.	0 4	3.80	
Jesse King	320 Bo. Ch.	1 1	3.42		Elij. Martin	160 Tnch.	0 0	.20	
Laban Kent	480 Mag. Cr.	1 2	2.73		Wm. Martin	320 Tnch.	1 1	1.90	
Elias D. Kent	160 Mag. Cr.		.16		Wm. G. Martin	160 Tnch.	0 1	1.54	
Jon. Kent	240 Mag. Cr.	1 0	1.83		Josiah Martin	640 Tnch.	1 20	18.95	
Jas. Legget	160 Bo. Ch.	1 0	1.40		Hyrom Miller		1 0	.75	
Reub. Lea		1 5	4.50		Alexr. Miller		1 0	.75	
Jno. Lowe Junr	160 L. Tnch.	1 22	18.20					97.71	
Same for Est. of L. Lowe									
	100 L. Tnch.		.40		Page 14				
Polly H. Lenoir	480 L. Tnch.	0 10	9.30		Calvin McDaniel	160 Tnch.	1 0	1.15	
Major Lea		1 1	1.50		Middleton McDaniel		1 1	1.50	
Barton Lea		1 0	.75		Danl. McDaniel	80 Tnch.	0 0	.48	
Clenth. Legget	160 Bo. Ch.	1 0	.95		Wm. Miller		1 0	.75	
Wm. Little	160 Bo. Ch.	0 2	2.46		Jesse McClendon	160 Tnch.	1 5	4.70	
Saml. Little		1 0	.75		Willis Mullin		1 0	.75	
Jno. Laurance	160 Bo. Ch.	1 0	.90		Lawrance Mullen	160 Tnch.	0 0	.24	
Wm. Love	480 Bo. Ch.	0 7	7.33		Moses McElveen	160 Tnch.	1 0	.95	
Wm. Lundy	200 Bo. Ch.	1 5	5.70		Asa Miller		1 0	.75	
Jane Lowe	60 L. Tnch.	0 19	15.53		Brice Miller	160 Sil. Cr.	1 0	1.55	
Franklin Love		1 0	.75		Benj. Morris		1 0	.75	
Henry Long	320 Bo. Ch.	1 3	4.60		Simeon Morris		1 0	.75	
Jno. Lowe	320 L. Tnch.	0 19	9.86		Nathan Morris	160 Bo. Ch.	1 0	1.71	
Wm. Legget		0 2	1.50		David Morgan	240 Bo. Ch.	1 12	11.20	
Abram Lundy	400 Bo. Ch.	1 2	3.93		Benj. Morgan	800 Bo. Ch.	1 9	13.05	
Robt. Love	400 Bo. Ch.	1 9	9.86		(sold 1190 merchandise)				
Posey Legan	160 Top.	1 0	.90		Jos. P. Morgan		1 0	.75	
Jos. Lewis	80 Mag. Cr.	1 0	.90		Benj. McCollough		1 0	.75	
Wm. Lewis		1 0	.75		Wm. McCollough	240 Top.	1 0	1.75	
Henry Lewis		1 0	.75		Jos. McCollough		1 0	.75	
Wm. McMorris	160 Bo. Ch.	1 5	4.66		Elisha Masse		1 0	.75	
Jno. Martin Junr.		1 0	.75		Pool Masse		1 0	.75	
Jas. P. McAnulty	160 Bo. Ch.	1 6	5.04		Calvin Masse		1 0	.75	
Wm. M. McComb	160 Bo. Ch.	1 0	1.55		Jas. McCollough	160 Top.	1 0	.88	
			115.11		Archd. McEwen	160 Top.	1 1	2.46	
					Matth. McEwen	160 Top.	1 1	2.46	
Page 13					David McGraw		0 3	2.25	
Ralph Mason		1 0	.75		Zach. McGraw		1 1	1.50	
Joel Merret	310 (?)				David G. McGraw	80 Bo. Ch.	1 0	.95	
	Bo. Ch.	1 0	2.66		Tho. McGaller		1 0	.75	
Benj. Masse	160 Bo. Ch.	1 0	1.70		Jno. May		0 1	.75	
Jas. Martin		1 0	.75		Jas. May		1 0	.75	
Nehamiah Magee	160 Mag. Cr.	1 0	1.71		Jos. May Junr.	160 Mag. Cr.	1 4	4.23	
Sier Magee	240 Mag. Cr.	1 1	2.54					63.51	
Same for Est. of									
E. Magee	160 Mag. Cr.	1 0	1.71		Page 15				
Jas. Y. McNabb	240 Tnch. & Bo. Ch.				Jas. Merchant		1 0	.75	
		1 9	7.90						

Name	Acreage/Description			Amount
Jno. Merchant	80 Mag. Cr.	0	6	4.74
Ethd. May	160 Mag. Cr.	1	3	3.20
Norman McLeod		1	0	.75
Ruphus Massee	1 lot in Holmesville	1	0	.95
Jos. May	320 Mag. Cr.	0	13	11.34
Isaac Millsaps		1	1	1.50
Michl. McCafry		1	0	.75
Henry MaGee	180 Mag. Cr.	1	5	4.70
David McKinza		1	0	.75
Willis MaGee	400 Pushpetappaw	1	6	6.20
Solm. MaGee	160 Mag. Cr.	0	1	1.07
Thomp. Miller		1	0	.75
Richd. Magee	320 Mag. Cr.	0	1	2.10
Same for Est. Jno. Magee	160 Mag. Cr.	0	10	8.23
Betheny MaGee		0	3	2.25
Solm. Newman		1	0	.75
Cary Napp		1	0	.75
Jas. Norman	160 Top.	1	4	4.54
Nehem. Newman		1	0	.75
Mary Newman	160 Top.	0	2	2.34
	1 town lot			
Furny Norman		1	0	.75
Tho. Norman	160 Top.	1	5	4.70
Sarah Norman	160 Top.	0	0	.80
Jno. Norman		1	0	.75
Jos. Newsom	160 Mag. Cr.	1	0	.95
Dawson Obanyon	160 Bo. Ch.	1	0	1.71
David Ott		1	0	.75
Dnl. Osten		1	0	.75
Jacob Owens	80 Mag. Cr.	1	1	1.66
Jno. Oquin	160 Mag. Cr.	0	0	.64
				73.28

Page 16

Name	Acreage/Description			Amount
Dnl. Oquin		1	0	.75
Shadr. Odom	160 Mag. Cr.	1	0	.90
Richd. Odom		1	0	.75
Elisha Prewit		1	0	.75
Jno. Parker	320 Bo. Ch.	1	0	1.22
Saml. Prestige	240 Bo. Ch.	1	1	3.10
Robert Price	155 Bo. Ch.	1	0	1.70
Jos. Price	240 Bo. Ch.	1	0	1.95
Wm. Price	240 Bo. Ch.	1	0	1.83
Howel Prestige	320 Bo. Ch.	1	0	1.15
Wm. W. Pearson	80 Tnch.	1	2	2.52
Josiah Powel	640 Tnch.	1	9	10.38
Nathn. Prescot	160 Ter. Cr.	1	3	3.80
Michl. Prescot	160 Tnch.	1	1	2.30
Ephr. Prescot		0	1	.75
Penelope Prescot		0	2	1.50
Even Pendarvis		1	0	.75
Francis Parsons	280 Bo. Ch.	1	2	3.20
Wm. Pendarvis	160 Bo. Ch.	1	2	2.45
Tho. Pleasant	480 Mag. Cr.	1	4	4.38
Francis Pelotte	160 Mag. Cr.	1	0	.90
Tho. Pain		1	0	.75
Wm. Pritchard	100 Mag. Cr.	1	10	9.21
Nelson Pain		1	0	.75
Stephn. Peak's Admrs.	160 Mag. Cr.	0	9	6.90
Saml. G. Pool		1	0	.75
A. M. Perryman	2 town lots Holmesville (sold 15000 merchandise)	1	12	44.84
				110.23

Page 17

Name	Acreage/Description			Amount
Jno. Queen		1	0	.75
Peter Quin	380 Bog. Ch.	1	20	26.14
	6 lots in Holmesville @20.55			
Same for Est. Peter Quin	774 Tnch.	0	3	6.08
	2 lots in Holmesville @.50			
Judith Quin	80 Bo.Ch.	0	3	8.18
	6 lots in Holmesville @28.00			
Richd. Quin	720 L. Tnch.	1	11	13.31
Henry Quin	320 Tnch.	1	21	18.10
Danl. Quin	545 Bo. Ch.	1	7	8.42
Tho. Queen		1	0	.75
Jno. Reeves	160 Bo. Ch.	1	0	1.55
Zach. Reeves	160 Bo. Ch.	1	1	2.30
Alfred Reeves		1	0	.75
Wm. Rodus	160 Bo. Ch.	1	0	.95
Tho. Richmond		1	0	.75
Andr. Richmond	320 Bo. Ch.	1	0	1.86
Tho. Reeves	160 Bo. Ch.	1	0	2.02
Harris Rolls	160 Bo. Ch.	1	1	2.46
Chas. Ryals	160 Bo. Ch.	0	0	.86
Jas. Rollins	80 Bo. Ch.	1	1	1.84
Jas. Robinson	560 L. Tnch.	0	14	11.20
Wm. Richmond		1	0	.75
Henry Richardson	160 Tnch.	1	4	4.55
Henry Richardson & Co. (1740 merchandise sold)				3.50
Jno. Reppe		1	1	1.50
Elij. Roberts	320 Ter. Cr.	1	0	2.34
Mary Robinson		0	1	.75
Eliz. Robinson		0	1	.75
Asa Rutland		1	0	.75
Zach. Redmon	160 Tnch.	0	0	.20
Jesse Redmon		1	0	.75
Jas. Rymes	160 Tnch.	1	1	1.70
Jas. Roberts	160 Bo. Ch.	1	2	2.40
Jas. L. Reed	160 Top.	1	0	.90
				129.03

Page 18

Name	Acreage/Description			Amount
Jas. Reed	160 Mag. Cr.	1	0	.95
Nathn. Rule	160 Bo. Ch.	1	0	.90
Richd. Ratliff	160 Mag. Cr.	1	17	14.14
Wm. Rasberry		1	1	1.50
David Roberts	160 Mag. Cr.	1	0	.90
Tho. Roberts		1	0	.75
Christopher Riabon?		1	0	.75
Isaac Roberts	160 Mag. Cr.	1	6	6.21
Same for E. Roberts	320 Bo. Ch.	0	0	1.60
Tho. Rule	80 Mag. Cr.	1	4	4.40
Jno. Riggins		1	0	.75
Claib Rushin		1	0	.75
Ephr. Rushin		1	0	.75
Jno. G. Roset		1	0	.75
Jno. Ready		1	0	.75
Nathan Sims	240 Bo. Ch.	1	7	7.20
Jesse Suddeth		1	0	.75
Jno. Simmons		1	0	.75
Littleton Seal	160 Bo. Ch.	1	1	2.30
Wm. Sibley	160 Bo. Ch.	1	0	1.70
Henry E. Symons		1	0	.75
Reddeck Sparkman	160 Bo. Ch.	1	2	3.20
Danl. Sandel	160 L.Tnch.	1	0	.95
Wm. Spenks		1	1	1.50
Wm. Strickland		1	0	.75
Jno. Stephenson	160 Tnch.	1	0	.95
Jno. Sommers		1	0	.75

Name	Land			Amount
Wm. Sanderfer	160 Tnch.	1	1	1.66
Wm. Simmons	160 Tnch.	1	0	.90
Ann Simmons	8 Tnch.	0	10	7.74
Jno. Simmons		1	0	.75
Henry Stogner		1	0	.75
Robert Strickland	160 Tnch.	1	0	1.55
				70.55

Page 19

Name	Land			Amount
Jno. Strickland		1	0	.75
Henry Strickland		1	0	.75
Jas. Strong		1	0	.75
Willis Simmons	240 Bo. Ch. & Sil. Cr.	1	2	2.54
Same for C. Doolin	80 Sil. Cr.	0	0	.20
Jerem. Smith	720 Bo. Ch.	0	6	9.98
(2 wheeled vehicles)				
Jno. Smith	320 Bo. Ch.	1	10	10.16
Jno. Strother	267 Top.	0	5	5.20
Jemmerson Strother		1	0	.75
Abner Sitmon	80 Top.	1	0	.84
Aaron Spell		1	0	.75
Jno. Sistrunk		1	0	.75
Jacob Sistrunk		1	0	.75
Noah Strickland		1	0	.75
Danl. Sistrunk	80 Gl. Cr.	1	1	1.66
Wm. W. Shepherd		1	0	.75
Wm. Smith		1	5	4.50
Jno. Sartin		1	0	.75
Patrick Sulivan		1	0	.75
Danl. Sulivan	80 Mag. Cr.	0	0	.16
Lewis Stovall	160 Mag. Cr.	1	3	3.20
Ralph Stovall	720 Mag. Cr.	1	26	21.75
Britton Smith	240 Bo. Ch.	1	10	9.45
Richd. Smith Jr.		1	0	.75
Richd. Smith Senr.	80 Bo. Ch.	0	1	.83
Pleas. Smith		1	0	.75
Jno. Stallings	160 Bo. Ch.	1	2	3.20
Same for Est. of E. Stallings		0	1	.75
Geo. Smith	320 Bo. Ch.	1	4	5.35
Jno. Stallings Junr		0	4	3.
Danl. Smith	80 Mag. Cr.	1	1	1.66
Peter Sandeford	160 Mag. Cr.	0	3	3.05
				97.21

Page 20

Name	Land			Amount
Amos Sandeford		1	0	.75
Rob. Sandeford		1	0	.75
Jas. Sandeford		1	0	.75
Burw. Scott	400 Mag. Cr.	1	8	8.60
Matth. Turner	160 Tnch.	0	0	.80
Jos. Turner	160 Tnch.	1	3	3.20
Balis Turner		1	0	.75
Alexr. Thompson	80 (?)	1	2	2.37
Jas. Thompson		1	0	.75
Jesse Terver		1	0	.75
Steph. Thompson	160 Bo. Ch.	1	0	.95
Danl. Taylor Junr	640 Top and Bo. Ch.	1	3	4.12
Benj. Thomas		0	1	.75
Jesse Thomas	2 lots in Holmes @5.00	1	0	1.75
Isaac Taber		1	0	.75
Chas. Tate		1	0	.75
Abden Tyler		1	1	.75
Geo. M. Troller	240 Tnch.	1	0	2.30
Paris Thompson		1	0	.75
Param Thompson		1	0	.75
Hugh Thompson		1	0	.75
Simeon Thompson	160 Top.	1	2	2.45
Steph. Tatum	160 Top.	1	4	3.95
Abr. Trewit	80 Top.	0	0	.40
Swan Thompson	320 Top.	0	7	6.84
Wm. Thompson		1	1	1.50
Jno. Taylor	80 Top.	1	4	4.15
Danl. Taylor Senr.	80 Top.	0	4	3.48
Jos. Taylor		1	0	.75
Nath. Thomas		1	0	.75
Marg. Tullos	160 Mag. Cr.	0	0	.64
Steph. Tullos	160 Mag. Cr.	1	0	.95
Tho. Tullos	80 Mag. Cr.	1	0	.83
				62.03

Page 21

Name	Land			Amount
Temple Tullos	80 Mag. Cr.	0	0	.32
Leroy Tatum	80 Mag. Cr.	1	6	4.74
Abr. Tullos		1	0	.75
Rolin Tullos		1	0	.75
Elisha Thornhill	80 Mag. Cr.	1	0	1.
Goodman Trawick	80 Bo. Ch.	1	0	1.06
Danl. R. Thomas		1	0	.75
Wm. Thornhill Senr		0	1	.75
Wm. Thornhill Junr.		1	0	.75
Jos. Thornhill	160 Mag. Cr.	0	0	.80
Brian Thornhill	80 Mag. Cr.	1	0	1.15
Spillsbe Tribble	160 Bo. Ch.	0	4	3.16
Henry Varnado		1	0	.75
Saml. Varnado	160 Tnch.	0	5	4.70
Leond. Varnado	240 Tnch.	1	0	1.47
Saml. Varnado Junr	80 Tnch.	1	0	1.
Jas. D. Williams	160 Top.	1	0	1.
Tho. Wroten		1	0	.75
Arick Wilson		1	0	.75
Jos. Wigley (Wigby?)		1	0	.75
Wm. Woodall		1	0	.75
Susa Williams (?)	240 Bo. Ch.	0	0	.86
Jno. Wells	160 Bo. Ch.	1	0	1.55
Robt. Wilson		1	0	.75
Nathl. Wells	400 Bo. Ch.	1	16	15.15
Jno. Wainwright	80 Bo. Ch.	1	0	.95
Saml. Wilson		1	0	.75
Tho. Whitaker		1	0	.75
Andr. Wicker	320 Tnch.	1	8	8.33
Adam Wicker	160 Tnch.	1	1	2.30
				64.31

Page 22

Name	Land			Amount
Fredr. White		1	0	.75
Thompson Wallace	160 Tnch.	1	0	.95
Jno. C. Weeks		1	0	.75
Wm. Weeks		1	0	.75
Benj. Wills		1	0	.75
Jno. Woods	80 Top.	1	0	1.15
Rolin Williams	80 Top.	1	0	.95
Jno. Wilson	80 Top	0	8	6.20
Wm. Wilson		1	2	2.25
Joshua Wooly		1	0	.75
Tho. Warren	80 Top.	1	0	.95
David Windborne		1	0	.75
Tho. Willingham	160 Top.	1	0	.95
Jno. Warren	240 Top.	1	4	4.87
Jno. Walker	160 Top.	1	0	1.54
Evan Whittington	160 Mag. Cr.	1	8	7.
Deek (Duk?) W. Wiltshire	160 Mag. Cr.	1	2	2.48
Chas. Wiltshire		1	1	1.50
Jas. Waddle		1	0	.75
Saml. Williams	160 Mag. Cr.	1	8	6.90

```
Elias Woodruff                    1  1  1.50
Robt. Williams     80 Mag. Cr.    1  0   .95
Wiley Zachery                     1  0   .75
David Zeagler      80 Tnch.       1  0   .95
Nichs. Yaugh (Yaugn)80 Top.       1  0   .83
                                        48.68
```

Signed by Laban Bacot Assessor and Collector

1835 TAX LIST, PIKE COUNTY, MISSISSIPPI

(Selected Columns Only)

Name	Abbreviations	
Acres	Baily Chitto--Bai. Ch.	Terry's Creek--Tr. Cr.
Value	Bogue Chitto--Bo. Ch.	Silver Creek--Sil. Cr.
Situation	Tangipahoa River--spelled Tanchapaho--	
White Polls	Tnch.	Glover's Creek--Gl. Cr.
Slave Polls	Topesaw--Top.	Leatherwood--Lthd.
	Magee's Creek--Mag. Cr.	Dry Branch--D.B.
	Pushapatapp--Push.	Carter's Creek--Car. Cr.

```
James W. Aills                        1        Simeon Boyd         80 $160 Top.      1  0
Thompson Andrews                      1        Peris Bonney                          1  0
David Alexander                       1        John Brent Sent    480 $720 Top.      0 10
James Andrews                         1 10     Gideon Bond         80 $ 80 Bai.Ch.   0  2
Hanceford Addison                     1        Payton Bond                           1  1
John Akin          160 $240 D.B.      1  4     Daniel Burkhalte                      0  5
Micajah Andrews                       1        Cornelius Beasley                     1  0
Richard Allbritton                    1        Jesse Brumfield     80 $ 80 Mag. Cr.  1  4
Seabourn Alfred     70 $105 Bai.Ch.   1        Henry Baddan        80 $160 Mag.Cr.   1  2
William Andrews    160 $240 Tnch.     1  8     Robert M. Brown     80 $160 Bog.Ch.   1  3
Canty Armstrong                       1        William Brown       80 $ 80 Bo. Ch.   0  0
Edwin Alfred       160 $240 Bo.Ch.    1  4     Abner Barksdale     80 $160 Tnch.     0  7
William Alfred     160 $240 Bo.Ch.    1  1     Wm. F. Barksdale                      1  0
Hiram Addison Est                     0  1     Thomas Bond                           1  0
Rebecca Addison                       0  1     Lewis Ballard       81 $160 Tnch.     1  0
Felix Addison                         0  1     Isaac Brumfield                       1  6
Uriah Bowman                          1  1     Preston Bond       160 $320 Bai.Ch.   1  0
Henry Bond         240 $480 Bai.Ch.   0  0     James Brock                           1  0
Jeremiah Bearden    80 $160 Lthd.     1  6     Eli P. Brock                          1  0
Holloway Bishop                       1  2     Quinny (?) Bullock 160 $240 Sil.Cr.   1  0
Robert Bond        160 $320 Bo.Ch.    0  0     William Biles                         1  0
Isaac Boyd                            1  0     John Bankston                         1  0
Edward Bullock      80 $ 80 Bo.Ch.    1  7     William Bates    2 town lots          0  0
George Byerly                         1  0     James J. Bridges    4 $  4 1 town lot
Zechariah Bullock                     1  0                          Holmesville     1  1
John P. Branan (?)                    1  0     Henry T. Burkhalter                   1  0
Henry Barran                          1  0     Davis Brumfield     80 $160 Mag.Cr.   1  2
Aaron Beard         30 $ 30 Car.Cr.   1  0     Hugh Brown         160 $240 Bo.Ch.    1  0
Nathan Ballard     240 $480 Tnch.     1  0
William Boyd                          1  0     Page 3
John Brent Jr.                        1  0     Shadrack (?) Boyet 160 $160 Top.      1  0
Wm. Bullock Est    290 $580 Bo.Ch.    0  6     Thompson Brister    80 $160 Top.      0  0
                                               Uriah Botton (?)                      1  0
Page 2                                         Andrew Boyd         80 $ 80 (not given
Leroy Bowman                          1                                              0  0
David Bullock      255 $765 Bo.Ch.    1  6     Mark Burney        160 $160 Top.      1  0
William Barnes                        1  0     James Brumfield     80 $160 Mag.Cr.   0  4
James Boyd                            1  0     Jackson Booker                        1  0
Thomas Brent       160 $320 Top.      1  4     James A. Boutwell                     1  0
Laban Bacot        160 $240 Bo.Ch.    0  7     Frederic Boon                         1  2
Samuel Bacot       240 $480 Bo.Ch.    1  0     Richardson Bowman  248 $480 Mag.Cr.   0  0
Hillory Breland                       1  0     Jesse Ball          80 $160 Mag.Cr.   1  1
William Brisler     80 $160 Top.      1  0     James Breland       80 $ 80 Push.     1  0
```

N. W. Bosworth		0	2
Joel J. Coney		1	0
Joseph Catching	800 $1200 Bo.Ch.1	1	15
Jonathan Catching	180 $270 Bo.Ch.	0	0
S. M. Catching		1	5
S. M. Catching & Co.	7500 Mdse	0	0
Drury Cook Snr		1	3
Jeremiah Coney	160 $321 Bai.Ch.1	1	4
William Coney	160 $240 Bo.Ch.	1	5
James Craft		1	1
A. P. Cunningham	332 $664 Bo.Ch.	1	18(?)
Michael Cook	160 $320 Bai.Ch.1	1	7
Russel Craft		1	1
James E. Cunningham	320 $440 Bo.Ch.	1	12
Drury Cook Snr.	160 $320 Tnch.	1	0
Elizabeth Corley	80 $ 80 Tnch.	0	0
Hardy Carter	400 $800 Tnch.	1	11
Isaac Carter Snr.	80 $160 Tnch.	0	0
Johnson Carnes	80 $160 Car.Cr.1	1	0
Elbert Cook	320 $640 Tnch.	1	7
John Carroll		1	4
Richard Curtis	160 $240 Tnch.	1	2

Page 4
Matthew Cook		1	0
Willis Clark		1	0
Thomas Coon		1	0
Moses Carter		1	0
Elijah Cothern		0	0
Margaret Conn	160 $160 Bo.Ch.	0	39
David Cleveland	800 $1100 Bo.Ch.	1	0
Henry Clark		1	0
Austin Corby		0	0
Moses Clark Snr	240 $360 Tnch.	1	0
Bennet Carter		1	0
Charles Carter		1	0
John Carrouth		1	0
Moses Clark Junr		1	0
Aran Clark		0	1
Catherine Cutrer (?)		1	5
Israel Carter	220 $440 Tnch.	1	4
Allen Carter	320 $960 Tnch.	1	2
Isaac Carter Jnr.	160 $320 Tnch.	0	7
Nancy Carter		1	0
Henry Carter	160 $160 Tnch.	1	0
Joseph Cutrrar		1	0
John Carter		0	0
Godfry Clement	80 $160 Tnch.	1	7
Burrel Carter	160 $160 Tnch.	1	5
Derrel Carter		1	1
Michael Clowers		0	0
Cornelius Carr	80 $ 80	0	30
Thomas Cooks Est	900 $1350		
1 town lot Holmesville		1	4
Harvil Carter	80 $160	0	1
Jackson Goflin		1	0
James Coon	80 $160 Bo.Ch.	1	0
Samuel Cubstead	80 $121 Bo.Ch.	1	0
Jacob Coon	155 $310 Bo.Ch.	1	0
Jacob Curtis		1	0

Page 5
Ulysses Clark		1	0
Moses Clark		1	0
Susanna Clark	80 $160 Top.	0	1
Jonas Causey	320 $560 Mag.Cr.0	0	4
William Cooper		1	0
Owen Connerly	160 $320 Mag.Cr.0	0	8
Charles Cooper		1	0
(Next three names marked out)			

David Girtman		1	0
A. R. Green		1	0
Henry Goldman's Est.160 $240 Tnch.		0	0
Gatkin S___ (Marked out)			
George W. Dickey		1	1
Clarkson Dillon	320 $320 Bo.Ch.	0	6
Fielding Dunaway		1	0
Laurence Dillon	400 $600 Mag.Cr.	0	9
Pearl Dunaway	80 $160 Car.Cr.	1	0
Richmond Dunaway		1	0
George Dunaway		1	0
Martin Dickinson Junr		1	0
Allen J. Davis		1	0
James Dickerson		1	0
Owen Dickerson	180 $160 Tnch.	1	0
Martin Dickerson Snr.		1	0
Richard Daniels		1	0
Paul Davis		1	0
Enos Daughtery		1	2
Rebecca Davis	160 $320 Mag.Cr.	0	2
John Davis		0	2
Benj. Delaughter		1	0
Everett Dillon		1	0
Willis Dillon	160 $320 Mag.Cr.	1	3
Ann Dillon Est		0	1
Theophilus Dillon	640 $960 Mag.Cr.	1	2

Page 6
John Ellsey		1	2
Jesse Edwards	160 $160 Bo.Ch.	1	2
William Ellsey	160 #240 Louis Cr.		
		1	10
Thomas Ellsey	80 $160 Lthd.	1	12
B. F. Epps	160 $240 Tnch.	1	7
Ezra Estess	160 $320 Mathises Cr.		
		1	0
Benj. Ezell Est.	80 $120 Tnch.	0	0
Matthew Edwards	80 $160 Tnch.	1	0
John D. Estess		1	0
William Estess	80 $160 Bo.Ch.	1	0
William Elliott		1	0
Michael Elliott		1	0
Richard Forrest	160 $240 Sil.Cr.	0	7
Peter Felder	505 $875 Tnch.	1	21
Adrian Frick	240 $480 Tnch.	0	3
Isaac Felder	320 $640 Tnch.	1	6
Jacob Faust		1	0
G. C. Fortenberry	160 $320 Sil.Cr.	1	1
Richard Finley	160 $160 Sil.Cr.	0	0
William Fortenberry		0	1
John Felder	80 $ 80 Bai.Ch.	1	4
Calvin Fortenberry		1	0
David Girtman		1	0
A. R. Green		1	0
Henry Goldman Est. 160 $240 Tnch.		0	0
Gatlin Sparkman & Co.			
(4600 merchandise sold)		0	0
Thomas Guinea 2 lots Holmesville			
4000 merchandise sold		1	0
James Gatlin	160 $320 Bo.Ch.	1	5
W. H. Gibson		1	0
Shered Gray	320 $480	1	13
John Garner		1	3
Daniel Graves		1	4
Ephraim Greer		1	0
Jesse Greer Junr		1	1

Page 7
Jesse Ginn		1	1

Name	Acres	Value	Location			Name	Acres	Value	Location		
Nancy Gordon	480	$720	Mag.Cr.	0	0	D. L. Harvey				1	0
Jacob Gibson				1	1	Harris Harvey				1	0
Smith Greer				1	0	Wm. M. Hall				1	0
William Gulledge	80	$ 80	Bo.Ch.	1	0	Christian Hoover	400	$600	Bo.Ch.	1	13
Elizabeth Garner	400	$800	Bo.Ch.	0	8	James R. Hamilton	240	$480	Bo.Ch.	1	0
Jesse Gates				1	0	Judith Hamilton	320	$640	Bo.Ch.	0	8
Thomas Gulledge	185	$185	Bo.Ch.	0	0	V. F. Hamilton				1	5
John Gatlin	320	$480	Bo.Ch.	1	6	John Huffman				1	0
Edward Gatlin's Est.	800	$1600									
3 lots in Holmesville				0	25	**Page 9**					
William Gordon	560	$850	Bo.Ch.	1	4	James Hart	80	$ 80	Bo.Ch.	1	4
Reubin Gill				1	0	John B. Hart				1	0
John Gwin	400	$800	Bo.Ch.	1	0	Wesly Hampton	80	$ 80	Top.	1	0
Henry Goldman	80	$ 80	Bo.Ch.	1	0	Drury Hodges	75	$ 75	Top.	0	3
John Greer	160	$220	Vapasan (?)			Aaron Hickman	80	$160	Top.	1	1
				0	1	James Howell				1	0
Wm. K. Godwin				1	0	Benj. Holmes	160	$160	Mag.Cr.	1	1
Alexander Glann (Glover?)				1	0	William Holmes				1	0
Jesse Greer Senr				1	1	James Jones				1	0
Peter J. Glover's Est.	160	$320	Vapasan			Michael Jones	260	$520	Mag.Cr.	0	7
			(Vapasaw?)	1	10	Benj. Jones	240	$240	Mag. Cr.	0	7
Joseph Gates	190	$285	Vapasaw (?)			Wiley Jones				1	0
				1	1	David Jordan	80	$ 80	Top.	0	0
Gilbert Grubs				1	0	Reni Sulivan				1	0
Meredith Grubs	65	$ 65	Mag.Cr.	1	0	George Johnson	240	$360	Bo.Ch.	0	0
Sebastian Ginn				1	0	James Johnson				1	0
Penelope Ginn	80	$160	Mag.Cr.	0	4	William Jenkins	160	$320	Ter.Cr.	0	0
William Green				1	0	Elijah Jenkins				1	0
John Hamilton			Bo.Ch.	1	2	William Jenkins Jnr.				1	0
Jemima Hamilton				0	0	Milton Jones				1	0
Jesse Harper	160	$320	Bo.Ch.	1	9	Thomas Jones				1	7
Thomas Howell				1	0	Hutson Jones				1	0
H. S. Hope				1	0	Michael Jones				1	1
Elmore Harper				1	0	Jesse King	320	$640	Bo.Ch.	0	0
John Hampton				1	0	David King				1	0
John Huckaby	240	$240	Bai.Ch.	0	0	Jeremiah King	85	$170	Top.	1	1
David Huffman				1	0	John C. King				1	0
Alexander Hamilton				1	0	James Kent				1	2
Mary Hamilton				0	1	Cairy Knapp				1	0
			(marked out)			John Kaigler	560	$1120	Bo.Ch.	1	10
						Joseph A. Kirkland				1	8
Page 8						Allen King Est.	311	$311	Bo.Ch.	0	0
William Hall	80	$ 80	Top.	1	2	William Keath				1	0
Armstead Hall	320	$640	Bo.Ch.	0	6	James Kelly				1	0
Henry Hickman				1	0						
Elisha Holmes				1	0	**Page 10**					
Edmond Hodges				1	0	Robert Love	787	$1180	Bo.Ch.	0	12
William Hodges				1	0	Amasa Lish				1	0
Isaiah Hart				1	1	William Leonard				1	0
Joseph Hart	160	$160	Bo.Ch.	1	3	Noble Lea				1	0
Joseph J. Hart	80	$160	Bo.Ch.	0	0	Barton Lea	81	$162	Tnch.	1	0
Charles Hoover	315	$630	Bo.Ch.	1	0	H. B. Lawrence				1	0
Susanna Herring	80	$160	Bo.Ch.	0	1	Jefferson Love				1	6
Wm. Hampton	160	$160	Tnch.			William Love	321	$640	Bo.Ch.	0	4
John Huffman				1	0	Benj. W. Leggett	400	$600	Bo.Ch.	1	5
D. C. Henderson	80	$160	Tnch.	1	0	Luke Lea-				1	0
Thomas Hallman	160	$240	Tnch.	1	0	W. P. Leggett	160	$160	Bo.Ch.	1	5
H. P. Howard				1	0	James Leggett	320	$320	Bo.Ch.	1	2
Hunt	160	$320	Sil.Cr.	0	0	Franklin Love	4 lots Holmesville				
William Hinson				1	0					1	1
Nancy Hinson	80	$ 80	Sil.Cr.	0	0	L. C. Leland				1	0
J. B. Hinson				1	0	Major Lea	120	$360	Tnch.	1	2
James Houston	400	$800	Tnch.	1	11	Polly A. Lenoir	390	$585	Tnch.	0	7
Teletha Harless				0	3	William Lenoir				1	1
Abner Hope	6	$ 12	Bo.Ch.	1	0	John Lain	160	$240	Tnch.	0	4
Hugh Hall				1	0	Middleton Lain				1	0
A. Hope & Co.				0	0	John M. Lain				1	0
Michael Harvey	240	$240	Mag.Cr.	0	3	Reubin Lea	80	$120	Tnch.	1	4
Daniel Harvey				1	0					(or 6)	

Name	Acres	Value	Location			Name	Acres	Value	Location		
Wm. Lea				1	0	John McGowers				1	2
W. B. Legon	80	$160	Mag.Cr.	1	1	Andrew Moke	400	$400	Bo.Ch.	1	0
(7448 mdse. sold)						Joel Merrit	310	$120	Bo.Ch.	0	0
Jacob Lute (Luter)				1	0	Henry Moke				1	0
John Laurence	240	$360	Bo.Ch.	1	0	Archibald McEwen	160	$320	Top.	1	1
Joseph Luter				1	0	Matthew McEwen	160	$320	Top.	1	0
Wm. Lewis	160	$160	Kirkland Cr.			Elisha Massey				1	0
				1	1	Uney Massey	80	$160	Top.	0	1
Joseph Lewis	160	$240	Mag.Cr.	1	3	Benson McClendon				1	0
Geo. G. McNabb				1	0	Sier Magee	440	$660	Mag.Cr.	1	8
James Y. McNabb	480	$960	Bo.Ch.	0	7	Hiram May				1	3
	2 lots Holmesville					Berry May				1	0
Robert McKay	240	$360	Tnch.	0	0	John May				0	1
Michael McAnulty	160	$320	Bo.Ch.	1	2	Zachariah McGraw				1	0
John W. Moore				1	0	Joseph May	160	$240	Mag.Cr.	0	12
Zachariah Martin	160	$160	Tnch.	1	3	Etheldred May				0	12
						Polley May				0	2
Page 11						Calvin Magee				1	4
Wm. G. Martin	160	$320	Tnch.	1	5	Richard Magee	240	$360	Mag.Cr.	1	4
Charles McDermott				1	0	Nehemiah Magee	160	$320	Mag.Cr.	1	5
Calvin McDaniel				1	0	Willis Magee	260	$260	Mag.Cr.	1	6
Uriah McGraw				1	0	Sier (Seir) Magee Sr.				1	0
David McGraw				0	2	Henry Magee	720	$1440		1	19
Dempsey McGraw				1	0	Chapman Magee				1	1
Henry Meng				1	0	Haverson Magee				1	0
Gabriel Mullens	80	$160	Bai.Ch.	1	0	John C. Martin				1	0
Benj. F. Morgan	160	$240	Bo.Ch.	0	0						
Lawrence Mullens				1	0	**Page 13**					
Willis Mullins				1	0	William Newman	80	$160	Ter.Cr.	1	0
Henry McDaniel				1	0	Elizabeth Newsom				0	2
David Morgan	240	$420	Bo.Ch.	0	13	William Newsom				1	0
Josiah T. Martin	140	$320	Tnch.	1	5	Benj. F. Neyland				1	0
Sarah Monk				0	1	M. H. Newman	160	$320	Top.	1	3
Martin McCullough				1	0	Thomas Newman				1	1
Jesse McClendon				0	3	Joseph Newsom	80	$160	Tnch.	1	0
James R. Martin	160	$160	Top.	0	0	Nehemiah Newman	80	$160	Tnch.	0	0
Wm. Miller				1	0	J. L. Neyland				1	0
Joseph P. Morgan				1	0	James Neale				1	0
Peter McDonald				1	0	John Neace				1	0
Joseph McClendon				1	0	Mary Norman	400	$600	Top.	0	4
Elbert Matthews				1	0	Josiah Neale	72	$144	Top.	1	0
Middleton Moke				1	0	Samuel Neale	160	$160	Top.	1	0
Wm. Montgomery				1	0	Joshua Neyland	80	$80	Mag.Cr.	0	0
Wm. M. McComb	158	$158	Bo.Ch.	0	0	Richard Odom				1	0
James McAnulty	160	$320	Bo.Ch.	0	7	Jacob Owens	80	$80	Bo.Ch.	0	0
Josiah Martin				1	0	Dawson Obannion	160	$320	Mag.Cr.	0	0
James B. Martin	320	$320	Tnch.	1	5	Daniel Oquin	80	$160	Mag.Cr.	1	2
James Martin				1	0	David Ott				1	0
John McDaniel				1	1	Margaret Ann Odom				0	0
Middleton McDaniel				1	2	Ancel Prewit				1	0
Daniel McDaniel				1	0	Josiah Powell	960	$1440	Tnch.	0	16
Micajah McDaniel				1	0	William Powell				1	0
Isaac McCullough	80	$80	Oushneyroot Cr.	1	0	Wm. W. Pearson	80	$160	Tnch.	0	6
						Malachi Pearson				1	0
						Wm. E. Pearson				1	0
Page 12						Thomas Powell	80	$160	Tnch.	1	1
Jacob Moke				1	0	Nelson Payne				1	2
John Morgan				1	0	Elisha Prewet	160	$320	Tnch.	1	2
Simeon Morris	80	$180	Bo.Ch.	1	0	Alexander Price				1	0
Benj. Morris	160	$240	Bo.Ch.	1	2	Elijah Prestridge				1	0
Thompson Miller				1	1	Samuel Prestridge	320	$640	Bo.Ch.	1	110
Ubane (?) McClendon				1	1	Ellsey Prestridge				1	0
Alexr. Miller				1	0	James Pittman				1	0
Moses McElvin				1	0						
Zacha. McDonald	80	$160	Bai.Ch.	1	0	**Page 14**					
Nathan McGraw	2 lots in Holmesville			0	1	Francis Passans (?)	480	$720	Bo.Ch.	0	0
						Jesse J. Prescott				1	3
William Mellon's Est.	1 lot in Holmesville			0	0	Willis Prescott				1	1
						William Pearce	80	$160	Mag.Cr.	1	1

Name	Value1	Col1	Col2	Name	Value2	Col1	Col2
A. M. Perryman's Est.1408 $2112				Littleton Seale		0	2
8 lots in Holmesville		68		Willis Simmons Jr.		1	0
Pike Co.		s1		William S. Strother		1	1
Wm. A. Price		1	0	Wm. Strickland	240 $720 Tnch.	1	0
Allen Price		1	0	**Page 16**			
Robert Price	149 $159 Bo.Ch.	0	0	Darius Sandel		1	0
William Price	160 $240 Bo.Ch.	0	1	Daniel Sandel	80 $ 80 Tnch.	1	2
Joseph Price	320 $480 Bo.Ch.	0	2	Peter Sandel		1	0
John B. Parks		1	0	John E. Sibley	120 $240 Lthd.	1	3
Gatney (?) Pollard		1	0	Wm. Smith		1	0
Wm. Pendarvis		0	1	John Summers	91 $182 Bo.Ch.	1	4
Etheldred Peters	400 $800 Mag.Cr.	1	0	Henry Sandel		1	1
Joseph Parker		1	0	John J. Sandifer		1	0
R. Quin & Sons 9257 merchandise sold		0	23	Stewart & Hargroves	240 $240 Top.	0	0
James B. Quin 2 lots in Holmesville		1	1	Willis Simmons Sr.		0	8
Peter A. Quin		1	0	Jilson Y. Seale		1	0
Elizabeth Quin	485 $727 Tnch.	0	21	William Spinks		1	0
William Quin	40 $ 80 Lthd.	1	3	John Sertain		1	4
Arthur G. Quin		1	3	John Simmons		1	0
Daniel Quin	560 $720 Bo.Ch.	0	9	Wm. Suttons Est	400 $800 Bo.Ch.	0	0
Richard Quin	1040 $1560 Tnch.	0	26	Jesse Sudduth		1	0
4 (?) lots Holmesville				Lewis Sudduth		1	0
Peter Quin	660 $990 Bo.Ch.	1	22	John Stephenson	80 $120 Tnch.	0	0
11 lots Holmesville				Simeon Stephenson		1	0
Judith Quin	80 $ 80 Bo.Ch.	0	3	Wm. Stephenson		1	0
6 lots in Holmesville				John Smith Est.	480 $720 Bo.Ch.	0	17
Sarah Richardson	115 $233 Tnch.	0	0	Richard Story		1	0
John Richmond		1	0	Wm. Simmons		1	1
William Rodus		1	0	Henry Simmons		1	0
Jesse D. Rimes		1	0	Joseph Smith		1	0
Lightel Roberts		1	0	Wm. Self	160 $160 Bo.Ch.	0	4
Henry Rollines		1	1	Barney Seale		1	2
John Reaves	160 $240 Clear Cr.	1	0	Eli Smith	160 $160 Bo.Ch.	1	1
				Wyatt Smith		1	0
Green Rhasberry	320 $640 Top.	1	1	Jeremiah Smith	880 $1760 Bo.Ch.	0	8
				William Snell		1	0
Page 15				Mayson Simmons	160 $240 Sil.Cr.	1	0
Lewis Rowell		1	0	John Simmons	160 $240 Bai.Ch.	1	0
Moses Roberts		1	0	George Simmons		1	2
David Roberts		0	1	Thomas Simmons		1	2
Martin P. Roberts		1	0	Calvin Smith		1	0
Ephraim Rushing		1	1				
James Richmond		1	0	**Page 17**			
Andrew Richmond	240 $480 Bo.Ch.	0	1	Wm. Y. Sandifer		1	2
Harris Rawls	310 $465 Bo.Ch.	0	1	Wm. N. Sandifer		1	1
Jasper S. Rawls		1	0	Nancy Simmons		0	2
Thomas Reams	160 $320 Bo.Ch.	1	0	Wm. Simmons		1	2
Alfred Reams		1	2	Robert Strickland Sr.		1	0
Zachariah Reams	160 $240 Bo.Ch.	1	3	Henry Strickland		1	0
Jesse Redman		1	0	Meredith Strickland	80 $120 Bai.Ch.	1	0
Elijah Roberts	400 $600 Ter.Cr.	1	0	Jeremiah Strickland		1	0
Jeptha Roberts	80 $120 Ter.Cr.	1	0	Robert Strickland	160 $240 Bai.Ch.	0	0
John Rippy	80 $160 Ter.Cr.	1	0	Peter Sandifer Jr.		1	0
James Riley		1	0	Peter Sandifer Sr	160 $320 Mag.Cr.	0	6
Joseph Rice		1	0	Henry Soan		1	10
Joseph Raybourn	240 $480 Tnch.	0	33	Brittan Smith	240 $240 Bo.Ch.	0	0
Washington Raybourn	80 $160 Tnch.	0	0	Hugh Smith	320 $640 Bo.Ch.	0	0
Richard Ratliff	160 $160 Mag.Cr.	0	13	John Sistruck		1	0
Claborn Rushing		1	0	Thomas Smith	80 $160 Bo.Ch.	1	2
Tery Rembert		1	0	Wm. Sibley	320 $480 Bo.Ch.	1	4
James Rollins	240 $480 Bo.Ch.	0	4	James Stallings	160 $320 Bo.Ch.	0	0
John Reddy		1	0	John Stallings	80 $160 Mag.Cr.	0	4
William Reed	160 $320 Mag.Cr.	0	3	Daniel Smith Sr.	80 $ 80 Mag.Cr.	0	0
Willaby Ryals		1	0	Robert Sandifer	80 $160 Mag.Cr.	1	1
William Rogers	80 $160 Mag.Cr.	1	0	John Smith	160 $320 Mag.Cr.	0	7
N. R. Sparkman		1	1	Hannah Strother	280 $420 Top.	0	6
L. H. Strother		1	0	Major Sertain		1	0
R. T. Sparkman	398 $796 Bo.Ch.	1	8	Jacob Smith		1	2
John Strickland	80 $200 Bai.Ch.	1	0	Mary Smith Est	80 $160 Mag.Cr.	0	3

Name	Value1	Value2	Type	C1	C2
John H. Sandifer				1	0
William Sandifer				1	0
Daniel Smith Jr.	160	$160	Mag.Cr.	1	3
Clary Smith	320	$320	Bo.Ch.	0	6
Soloman Thornhall	160	$320	Mag.Cr.	1	0
Cornelius Trawisk				1	0
Grant R. Taylor				1	3
Wesley Thomas				1	0

Page 18

Name	Value1	Value2	Type	C1	C2
Elisha Tedder				1	0
Alexander Thompson	120	$240	Tnch.	1	9
James Thompson Est.	200	$400	Tnch.	0	5
Jesse Thomas				1	0
Harris Turnipseed				1	0
Elisha Thornhill				1	0
Abraham Tullos				1	0
Evan Thornhill				1	0
Joseph Thornhill Jr.				1	0
Hiram Terrell	80	$160	Tnch.	1	7
Nancy Terrell				0	4
Joseph Turner	160	$320	Tnch.	0	5
Joseph W. Turner				1	0
Balis Turner				1	1
Matthew Turner	160	$240	Tnch.	0	1
Charles Tate	160	$160	Ter.Cr.	1	2
David Taylor	160	$160	Ter.Cr.	1	5
Trask & Fetters (?)	1 lot in Holmesville			0	0
Joseph Thornhill Sr.	160	$320	Mag.Cr.	0	0
Swain Thompson	560	$840	Top.	0	10
Eustatia Travis				0	1
Wm. Thornhill				0	0
Temple Tullos				1	0
Margaret Tullos	160	$160	Mag.Cr.	0	0
Thomas Tullos				1	0
Patric Thornhill				1	0
Hugh Thompson	160	$320	Mag.Cr.	1	4
Mitchell Varnado				1	0
Wm. Varnado				1	0
Emmanuel Varnado				1	1
Samuel Varnado				1	0
Leonard Varnado	80	$160	Tnch.	0	1
Lewis Varnado				1	0

Page 19

Name	Value1	Value2	Type	C1	C2
Samuel Williams Jr.	160	$240	Bo.Ch.	1	2
Hezekiah Williams				1	0
Wm. Walker				1	0
Jeremiah Walker	190	$435	Car.Cr.	1	1
John Walker	240	$480	Top.	1	1
Sam. Williams Sr.	80	$160	Mag.Cr.	0	11
Enoch G. Wicker				1	0
Andrew Wicker Est.	320	$320	Tnch.	0	3
Henry Williams				1	1
Thompson Wallis	80	$120	Sil.Cr.	1	0
Moreton Wigley				1	0
John Williams	430	$860	Top.	0	7
David Winbourn	160	$240	Top.	0	0
W. M. Williams	80	$160	Top.	0	1
George Wells					
Patric Wallace					
Dickson Wainwright					
John Wells	160	$160	Bo.Ch.	0	0
Nathaniel Wells	400	$800	Bo.Ch.	0	15
Susanna Williams	160	$240	Bo.Ch.	0	4
Thomas Wroten				1	0
Adam Wicker	160	$160	Tnch.	1	3
Joseph Winningham				1	0
James Woodward				1	3
John Wallis				1	0
Moses C. Williams				1	1
H. L. Williams				1	0
Reuben Warren				1	0
Thos. C. Warren (?)				1	0
Sanders Walker				1	0
John Williams	160	$160	Bo.Ch.	1	0
Robert Williams				1	0
William Walker				1	0
Elias Woodrough				1	2

Page 20

Name	Value1	Value2	Type	C1	C2
Henry Youngblood	320	$320	Mag.Cr.	1	3
Franklin Young	160	$240	Bo.Ch.	1	2
Cullin Yawn				1	0
Nicholas Yawn				1	0
Berry Zachery				1	0
David Yeagher (?)				1	1

1843 TAX LIST FOR PIKE COUNTY

Taken by David Winborne

From this list which enumerated items such as money loaned with interest, watches owned, carriages, bowie knives, etc., only the columns with the white taxables and the slaves have been copied.

Andrews, Burrell	1	0	Beard, John	1		Carter, Allen	0	7
Alford, Seborn	1	0	Boney, Peris	1	0	Cutrur & Allman		
Anderson, Arthur	1	0	Bishop, Holoway	1	1	Caruth, John	1	2
Adams, Anderson	1	6	Bearden, A. J.	1	0	Crawford, Thomas	1	0
Alexander, Robert G.	1	0	Bowman, Jesse	1	0	Carter, Harvel	1	14
Andrews, John	1	0	Bowman, Leroy	1	0	Coglin, Jackson	1	1
Alford, Edwin	0	8	Burns, John	1	0	Corley, Wyitt (Wyett)	1	0
Adams, C. W.	1	0	Brown, Hugh	1	1	Coon, John	1	0
Allbritton, James	1	0	Brown, T. T.	1	0	Coney, Eliza	0	6
Allbritton, Richard	0	0	Bigner, John M.	1	0	Coney, Jeremiah	1	8
Adams, William	1	0	Bigner, John	1	0	Catching, S. M.	1	21
Adams, Bedy	0	0	Brown, E. G.	1	0	Catching, Joseph	0	23
Allen, Felix	0	18	Beard, Aaron	1	0	Cook, Thomas	1	5
Andrews, Williamson	1	0	Brent, Jesse	1	0	Cook, Elbert	1	4
Adams, Anna	0	2	Brent, John	0	14	Care of T. Brumfield		
Anderson, Thomson	1	4	Brent, William	1	0	sherif		7
Aford [sic], Warren	1	0	Bond, Preston	1	1	Crawford, Jesse	1	4
Alford, Ira	1	0	Bond, Hugh Cenr (?)	0	1	Carter, William	1	0
Adison, Hirums Est.	0	2	Bond, John	1	2	Cawsey, Mary	0	4
Allen, Chestain	1	0	Bond, Henry, Jr.	1	0	Collins, Chancy	1	1
Alford, Wm. C.	1		Ballard, Rubin	1	0	Carson, John W.	1	2
Alford, Wm.	0	0	Barron, John	1	0	Carson, Samuel	1	0
Busby, Ezekiel	1	0	Brown, Jane	0	0	Conerly, John R.	1	3
Boyet, Anderson	1	0	Brumfield, John G.	1	0	Conerly, Owen Jr.	1	2
Boyd, William	1	0	Booty, C. B.	1	0	Carney, Elijah	1	1
Boyd, Henry	1	0	Bond, Peter	1	0	Certain, Joseph	1	2
Boyd, Jackson	1	0	Bankston, J. J.	1	0	Certain, Alfred	1	0
Boyd, Semeon	1	0	Buckhalter, Henry	1	6	Certain, William	1	0
Burch, Edward	1	0	Breland, James	0	1	Craft, James	1	5
Bullock, Edward	1	15	Brown, John P.	0	0	Cutrer, Clifton	1	0
Bullock, Zaceriah	1	2	Breland, Thomas	1		Carter, Torrent (?)	1	0
Bullock, J. L. W.	1	0	Breland, John R.	1	0	Carter, Derrel	1	0
Bacott, Laban	0	15	Badon, Henry	1	2	Carter, Henry	1	0
Bingham, Hugh	1	0	Ball, Daniel	1	3	Carter, Minton M.	1	4
Bridges, A. F.	0	12	Boon, Skinner	1	2	Caruth, Samuel	1	0
Brister, William	1	0	Boutwell, James A.	1		Carrol, John	1	5
Butler, John D.	1	0	Bales, Noel	1	9	Cutrere, Catherine	0	1
Bullock, Luiza	0	14	Barksdale, Wm. F.	0	1	Carter, William A.	1	3
Brent, John A.	1	9	Bradham, Zaceriah	1	1	Carter, John	1	0
Brumfield, Jesse	1	11	Carter, Bennet (?)	1	1	Cutrere, Joseph	1	0
Booker, H. J.	1	0	Coon, Luis	1	0	Courtney, Robert	1	0
Bank, Commercial			Clark, Moses	1	0	Dickson, C. T.	1	0
Brent, Thomas	0	0	Coon, Samuel	1	0	Davis, Jesse E.	1	0
Bonney, William	0	4	Certain, John	0	7	Dunaway, Pearl	1	0
Bonney, Henry	1	0	Cuningham, A. P. gard			Davis, Benjamin	1	0
Bridges, L. H.	1	0	(guardian?)	1	4	Dunaway, George	1	0
Brumfield, Davis	1	4	Coon, Thomas	1	0	Dunaway, Richmond	1	0
Buckhalter, W. J.	1	0	Cook, Michael	1	7	Dunaway, Fielding	1	0
Bays, G. W.	1	0	Clark, Willis	1	0	Davis, Samuel	0	1
Brumfield, Isaac	1	10	Cook, Taylor	1	4	Dickey, Georg W.	1	6
Brumfield, James	1	5	Coker, James	1	0	Dickerson, Owen	1	0
Barksdale, Fleury S.	1		Clark, Joseph	1	0	Dillin, Clarkston	0	10
Berry, Seborn	1		Curtis, Jacob	1	5	Dillin, Evret	1	3
Brent, Michael	1	1	Coney, J. J.	1	9	Dickerson, Martin Senr.		
Burnet, Harison	1	0	Conerly, Cullin	1	4		1	0
Ball, Liberty B.	1	1	Carter, Burrel	1	16	Davis, D. B.	1	0
Brock, James	0	2	Caruth, Robert A. (?)	1	2	Davis, William A.	1	0

Dickerson, William	1	1	Greer, Jesse Jr.	1	0	Johnson, Kinza	1	0
Dickerson, Martin Junr.	1	0	Girtman, George D.	1	0	King, Jeremiah	1	0
Day, David	1	0	Gipson, Wm. E.	1	1	King, Charles	1	0
Dillin, James T.	1	0	Gilchrist, David	1	0	Kaigler, Wm. W.	1	2
Dillin, Ransom	1	0	Gray, Sherard	0	19	King, F. M.	1	0
Daniels, Richard T.	1	0	Girtman, David	1	0	Koil, John	1	0
Dillin, John T.	1	5	Goldman, Henry	1	0	Kent, James W.	1	2
Dillin, Theophilous	1	3	Green, John	0	0	Lamkin, John T.	1	8
Dillin, Leroy	1	0	Garner, Elizabeth	0	2	Lea, David	1	0
Dillin, Willis	0	3	Guenea (?), Thomas	1	1	Lea, Barton	1	0
Dillin, Willis, as guardian for the estate of Sarah Graves		3	Goolin (Gosin?), Martha	0	5	Love, Franklin	1	3
						Lundy, William	0	1
			Ginn, Jesse	0	0	free person of color		
Davis, John	0	2	Green, William	1	0	Lane, Midleton	1	4
Deer, Joseph	1	0	Gatlin, Katherine	0	15	Luis, William	0	2
Dougless, Edward	1	0	Gill, Ruben	1	0	Legett, B.W.	1	5
Davison, Samuel	1	0	Girtman, John	1	0	Literal (?), John	1	0
Deer, John	1	0	Gray, Mejamin (Mesamin?)	1	0	Luis, Joseph	1	3
Deer, Ann	0	5				Leget, William P.	1	6
Delaughter, Benjamin	1	0	Graves, Daniel	1		Lea, Rubin	1	2
Delaughter, James	0	1	Gin, Sebastian	1	2	Lenear, Robert	1	5
Dunahoe, Hiram	1	0	Gin, Seleman	1	3	Lenear, Wm. H.	1	2
Estes, William	1	0	Grubs, Gilbert	1	0	Legget, John	1	0
Estes, Elisha	1	0	Garber, Ledford	1	18	Luiza, Hamilton	0	1
Elsey, John H.	1	2	Hodges, Edmond	0	1	Legan, J. J.	1	0
Elzey, William	0	17	Hodges, John C.	1	0	Lane, John	0	8
Elsey, James	1	1	Hampton, John	0	0	Legget, Josiah	1	0
Estes, Ezra	1	0	Harper, Edwin	1	0	Luis, John	1	0
Elsey, Thomas	1	10	Hall, William	0	3	Lundy, Alfred	1	
Elsey, John	1	2	Hickman, Aaron	1	0	free person of color		
Eliot, Robert	0	6	Hales, Joel	1	0	Lundy, Robert	1	
Eliot, Barnet	1	2	Hervey, Harris	1	1	free person of color		
Earle, John	1	0	Hodges, James W.	1	0	Lazarre, Abraham	1	0
Estes, John D.	1	0	Hall, John J.	1	0	Luis, Joseph B.	1	0
Edwards, Matthew A.	1	0	Houston, James	0	29	Legan, Robert B.	1	2
Felder, Wiat	1	0	Hoover, Joseph S.	1	0	Legan (no other entries)		
Felder, Gabriel	1	0	Hampton, Wesley	1	0	Luter, Joseph	1	0
Felder, John	1	3	Holms, John C.	1	3	Luter, Jacob	1	0
Farris, Elbert	1		Harper, Alexander	1	0	McCombs, Joseph	1	0
Fenn, Gabriel H.	1		Hall (Hobbs?), James	1	0	McCombs, William	1	0
Felder, David	1	6	Heart, James M.	1	0	Megee, Obed	1	2
Felder, J. J.	1	9	Heart, James Senr	0	5	McCollough, William	1	0
Foil, William	1	0	Heart, Joseph	0	2	Miskel, R. H.	1	0
Frick, Adrian	0	5	Hart, Daniel	1	1	MCollough, Isaac	1	0
Felder, Isaac	1	15	Huffman, John	1	1	McEwen, Matthew	0	0
Faust, N.	1	0	Hather, Isaac A.	0	0	McEwen, Thomas	1	0
Faust, John	1	0	Huckeby, John	0	0	Martin, Josiah	1	9
Faust, William	1	0	Harper, Jesse	0	13	More, John W.	1	2
Fortenberry, G. C.	1	1	Hinson, Isham B.	1	0	Massey, Uny	0	2
Felder, Peter	0	19	Hayworth, J. H.	1	0	Megee, Nehemiah Junr	1	0
Fortenberry, Calvin	1	1	Hall, Armstead Senr.	0	9	Mekinza, Wm.	1	0
Fortenberry, William	1	3	Hall, Ezekiel B.	1	0	Megee, Chapman	1	2
Fortenberry, Burrel	1	0	Hughs, James	1	2	McEwen, James W.-	1	5
Farmer, William	1	0	Hervey, Michael J.	1	0	Montgomery, W.	1	0
Fletcher, James	1	0	Hall, Hugh	1	0	Morgan, William	1	2
Flowers, Henry	1	1	Holms, Benjamin	1	2	Megee, Haverson	1	3
Flowers, John H.	1		Holms, Elisha	1	0	Merret, Joel	0	1
Greer, Jesse Senr	0	2	Herreld, Benjamin	1	0	McDaniel, Daniel	1	0
Goodwin, Benjamin	1	0	Hoover, Christian	1	33	Megrew, Zaceriah	1	2
Green, Equilla	1	0	Isrel, Greenberry	1	0	Meclendon, Benson	1	1
Guledge, Thomas	1	0	Jones, Wiley	1	0	Meclendon, Stephen	1	1
Giledge, Willins	1	0	Jones, Michael	1	1	Moke, Andrew	0	1
Green, Beams (?)	1	0	Johnson, James	1	0	Maning, Melia (?)	1	1
Gipson, Gilbert	1	0	Johnson, George W.	1	0	McEwen, Archibald	0	3
Gatlin, James	1	11	Jones, Wyley Junr.	1	0	Mcanulty, Michael	1	19
Gatlin, Alfred	0	3	Jones, James	1	0	Mathews, William	1	0
Gatlin, William R.	1	0	Jones, Isham	1	0	McDaniel, Calvin	1	0
Garner, John	1	5	Jones, Benjamin	0	4	Ming, Henry	1	1
Gallond (?), A.	1	0	Jones, Milton	1	1	Moke, Henry	1	0

Michel, Alexander	1	0	Parker, Joseph (Josept)			Rushing, Claiborne	1	0
Moke, Middleton	1	0		1	0	Rowel, Luis	0	0
Montgomery, Neill	1	0	Price, N. E.	1	0	Rials, Wiloby	0	0
Matthews, John	1	0	Parnet (Parnel?), Daniel			Raiford, N. B.	1	10
McNabb, John G.	1	6		1	0	Ratliff, Richard	0	30
Mullens, Laurence	1	0	Price, Joseph Senr.	0	5	Reed, Ezekiel	1	0
Miller, William	1	2	Price, Joseph Junr.	1	0	Reed, Joseph	1	0
Martin, John C.	1	0	Price, Uriah	1	0	Revencraft, Joseph	1	0
Megee, Pope	0	1	Price, Uriah	1	0	Rippy, John	1	0
Morris, Simeon	1	0	Price, Robert	0	0	Roberts, Barzilla	1	0
Morris, William B.	1	0	Prestredge, Samuel		19	Roberts, Elijah	1	0
Morris, James	1	0	Prestridge, Simeon	1	0	Roberts, Jepthah	1	0
Morris, Benjamin	1	5	Prestridge, Elijah	1	1	Smith, Calvin	1	3
Miller, Thomson	0	4	Prestridge, Elsey	1	0	Stricklin, William	1	0
Miller, Thoms J or T	1	0	Price, Alexander	1	0	Sims, Julia	1	0
Meclendon, Urbin	1	1	Powel, Joseph	1	1	Sims, Nathan	0	11
Mullens, Gabriel	1	0	Prescot, Gusiar			Seals, Elie	1	0
Martin, Sarah	0	5	(Susiar--Susan?)	0	1	Statum (?), R. Y.	1	0
Martin, Mary	0	3	Prescot, Ephraim	1	0	Sandel, Henry	1	1
Megrew, Phebe	0	2	Pounds, Julia	0	2	Simmons, Willis	0	14
Megrew, Wiley	1	0	Pearsons, Reding	1	0	Simmons, William J.	1	3
Megee, Henry	0	10	Purvis, Clemens	1	0	Stricklin, Henry	1	1
Miller, Fleet M.	1	0	Pearce, Humphrey	1	1	Summers, John	1	9
Megee, Syre	0	9	Quin, James B.	1	13	Stricklin, Jeremiah	1	0
Megee, John	1	1	Quin, Urvin	0	12	Smith, Thomas	1	3
Megee, Nehemiah	1	8	Quin, Patsey	0	21	Summers, Henry	1	1
Megee, Syre Junr	1	2	Quin, A. G.	1	0	Sandel, Daniel	0	7
Megee, Calvin	1	6	Quin, Peter A.	1	9	Sandel, Gabriel	1	0
Megee, Willis	1	4	Quin, William	1	4	Sandifer, John J.	1	3
Mekenza, A.	1	0	Quin, Daniel	0	5	Sandifer, Hardy	1	0
Megraw, Dency	1	0	Quin, L. J.	1	0	Sasser, James G. H.	1	4
May, Etheldred	0	20	Quin, H. M.	1	8	Sparkman, R. T.	0	0
May, Joseph	0	26	Quin, Peter G.	1	7	Stanley, Charles T.	1	0
May, Joda	1	0	Quin, Elizabeth	0	14	Sutton, Allen	1	2
Mekinza, James	1	0	Quin, Monrow	1	0	Suduth, Charles A.	1	3
May, Green	1	0	Quin, Richards Est.	0	21	Suduth, Luis	1	1
May, Rebecca	0	3	Raby, Gayoso	1	0	Smith, John	1	0
McCoy, Robert	1	0	Rollins, James Junr	1	0	Sasser, Luis	1	0
Miller, John	1	0	Raibourn, Luis	1	1	Smith, Joseph	1	0
McDaniel, Micejah	1	0	Roberts, Martin	1	1	Stricklin, Sophronia	0	1
Mixon, Obed	1	0	Roberts, Jackson	1	0	Sandel, Peter	1	2
Newsom, Joseph	1	1	Rollins, Jesse	1	0	Statume, John B.	1	0
Nicholson, George	1	4	Raibourn, John	1	0	Stephens, Elisha	1	0
Nicholson, Robert	1	0	Richmond, John	1	13	Stallings, John	0	4
Neal, Daniel	1	0	Richmond, James	1	0	Sartwell, B. F.	1	0
Newman, Smylie	1	0	Richmond, Andrew	0	1	Smith, Jeremiah	1	0
Newman, Carrol	1	1	Rawls, Jasper S.	1	5	Smith, Wiat	1	1
Nease, John	1	0	Rushing, John C.	1	0	Simmons, G. W.	1	0
Newsom, Elizabeth	0	3	Roberts, David	0	2	Simmons, Mason	1	3
Newsom, William	1	0	Reaves, Thomas	0	2	Simmons, John R.	1	2
Neal, William P.	1	2	Reaves, John Junr.	1	0	Snell, William	0	2
Newman, Samuel	1	0	Reaves, John Senr. (over			Seals, Jilson	1	2
Newman, Thomas	1	1	age and no taxable			Simmons, William	1	4
Ott, Jepthah	1	0	property)			Sandifer, William Y.	0	5
Ott, John A.	1	0	Reaves, Alfred	1	3	Sandifer, William E.	1	0
Ott, A. D.	1	0	Ripple, Henry J.	1	0	Self, William	0	7
Oquin, Jehue	0	1	Roberts, William	1	0	Self, Elijah	1	2
Owens, Jacob	0	0	Riley, James	1	0	Sandifer, Benjamin	1	1
Oquin, Daniel	1	0	Rodus, William	0	0	Simmons, George	1	1
Paddeford & Catchings			Reaves, William	1	0	Simmons, John	1	0
Paddleford, T. D. or Q.	1	0	Reaves, Zacheriah	1	5	Sandifer, Wm. N. Est.	0	0
Pearson, Malikia O.	1	2	Rimes, Jesse D.	1	0	Stricklin, John	1	0
Pruet, Elisha	0	0	Rice, Joseph	1	0	Sandifer, Martha	0	1
Pruet, John	1	0	Raibourn, Joseph Junr.			Shoupe, J. T.	1	2
Powell, Howell	1	0		0	4	Sandel, Darious	1	0
Pruet, A. H.	1	4	Raibourn, Joseph Senr.			Stallings, James	1	1
Powel, Thomas	1	3		0	18	Smith, Wm. D.	1	0
Prier, James	1	0	Raibourn, Quincy	1	4	Smith, Jeret	1	0
Price, James	1	0	Rogers, William	1	0	Smith, Newel S. (?)	1	0

Smith, Cleary (?)	0	9	Terrel, J. L.	1	0	Warren, Thomas	1	0
Smith, Daniel	1	5	Thomson, Parham	1	0	Williams, Nehemiah	1	1
Smith, John Junr.	0	9	Thomas, Jesse	0	3	Walker, John	0	3
Smith, William	1	2	Thomson, Hardy	1	14	White, John	1	0
Sibley, John	1	4	Thomson, Sarah	0	1	Waters, Urven	1	0
Statham, Sherwood	1	0	Tyler, William G.	1	2	Williams, Samuel	1	5
Sandifer, Peter Senr.	0	9	Thornhill, Elisha	1	0	Wallis, Patrick	1	0
Sandifer, Robert	1	2	Thomson, Hugh	1	11	Wooward, James H.	1	4
Sandifer, John	1	0	Thornhill, Even	1	0	Wroten, Lever	1	3
Smith, William	1	0	Thornhill, Joseph	1	0	Williams, Elisha	1	0
Stovall, Thomas P.	1	2	Thornhill, Henry H.	1	0	Wilborne, Ebert	1	0
Smith, Susanna	0	9	Taylor, David	0	7	Williams, James	1	2
Sibley, William	0	6	Vawes (Vower?), Josiah			Whaley, George	0	3
Sterling, Samuel C.	1	0		1	6	Wells, Nathaniel	0	16
Spinks, William	1	0	Varnado, Imanuel	1	6	Williams, John	0	11
Stephenson, William	1	0	Varnado, Michel	1	0	Wroton, Thomas	1	2
Tate, Charles	1	3	Varnado, Isham	1	0	Walker, Jeremiah	1	1
Taylor, Jourden W.	1	0	Varnado, Samuel	0	5	Walker, Elijah	1	1
Taver (Tarver?), Elijah	1	4	Varnado, Leonard	0	7	Young, Franklin	1	6
Terrel, Hirum	0	11	Varnado, Luis H.	1	0	Williams, Hezekiah	1	0
Terrel, William	1	2	Wallis, John C.	1	0	Yeager, David	1	5
Terrel, Bird	1	0	Winborn, H. (?)	1	0	Zacherry, John	1	0
Terrel, John G.	1	1	Walker, John E.	1	0	Zacherry, G. B.	1	0
Terrel, Josiah	1	0	Winborne, Jepthah	1	0	Whitington, Moses	1	0
Thomas, Wesley H.	1	0	White, H. S.	1	0	Whitington, Charles	0	0
Turnipseed, Harris	1	6	White, Henry H.	1		Wainwright, Sebern	1	1
Turner, Jackson	1	1	Wallis, Wm. H.	1		Williams, Parham	1	1
Taylor, Edward	1	9	Wells, George	1	3	Woodreff, Ailsey	0	4
Turner, Balis	1	3	Wilson, Bruse M.	1	2	Winborne, Jesse F.	1	0
			Wicker, Adam	1	10			

*NOTE: Throughout this list the title <u>Senior</u> following a name was consistently spelled <u>Cenr</u>.

MARRIAGE AND DEATH NOTICES FROM THE MAGNOLIA GAZETTE

published at Magnolia, Mississippi

12/14/1872 Gibson, Mrs. Nancy, d. in Magnolia 11/19/1782 of pulmonary consumption, ill 6 mos.; nee Nancy Raiborn. Writer of obit. first met her in Jackson, La., when she was a student of his at age 12 (1849). She md. 1) Dr. William N. Sandell with whom she lived 7 yrs and who d. in 1859. James Sandell of Magnolia was a son by that marriage. She md. 2) C. C. Gibson of Magnolia in 1860 by whom she had 2 daus. and 1 son. She united with church in 1857; buried at 3 P.M. on 11/21/1872 about ½ mi. W. of Magnolia. (Written by her pastor)

1/4/1873 Lumkin/Hurst, md. at res. of bride's father on Thurs., 1/2/1873, by Rev. Wm. Hoover, James C. Lumkin of Holmesville and Kaloolah Hurst of Summit.

Marshall, Col. L. L., d. in Magnolia on Tues., 12/31/1872 at 1 o'clock A.M.

McCurker, William, d. in Holmesville, Wed., 1/1/1873 at 6 A.M.

2/7/1873 Quin/Williams, md. in Summit on Wed. 2/5/1873 at res. of bride's mother by Rev. M. Otkin, Wallace W. Quin of Holmesville to Cordelia M. Williams of Summit.

2/14/1873 Lavisson/Orr, md. at Oskya Thurs., 2/6/1873 by Rev. Father Schuttelhofer, Rector of St. James, Jules Lavisson and Mrs. E. E. Orr of Magnolia.

Mikey, Mrs. Elizabeth J., aged 35 yrs., d. in Magnolia at 5:15 A.M. 2/11/1873.

Packwood, Mrs. Catherine S., d. at res. of her son J. H. Packwood at China Grove on Mon., 2/3/1873, aged 70 yrs.

3/7/1873 Notice that James Dent, who killed Daniel Wailes at Osyka last yr., had been arrested and sent to Holmesville for trial.

4/11/1873 Clark/Gennison, md. by W. C. Harrell, J.P., at Osyka, at his res., Sun. the 6th Inst., P. C. Clark to Miss C. A. Gennison, both of New Orleans, La.

4/25/1873 Smith/Rushing, md. at Conerlys, Pike Co., 4/17/1873, Charles Smith to Laura Rushing.

5/2/1873 McGehee, Dr. W. C., a citizen of Osyka for several yrs., d. suddenly Sat. night; had been on the road during the day, returned to Osyka by train, and d. that night--former res. of Amite Co.

5/9/1873 Philippe, Alfred, a Frenchman, committed suicide by taking arsenic 7 P.M. last Wed.; lived in Magnolia 2 or 3 yrs. at Central House; a barner by profession; served with gallantry in the Confederate Army.

5/16/1873 Altercation at Carter's Hill Mon. afternoon between Charles Hannan and James Dent--the latter shot in abdomen and d. last Tues. at 1:15 P.M. After being wounded Dent got on the train and went to Osyka where he died. Hannen voluntarily surrendered to the law.

5/23/1873 Hannen's trial procedure published.

5/30/1873 Hill, Mrs. A. S. of McComb City shot by Frank Moran last Sunday evening.

6/6/1873 Hill, Mrs. A. S. of McComb not long since shot, d. Fri. morning.

6/20/1873 Moran, Frank B., charged with murder of Mrs. Hill at McComb City, d. in Vicksburg jail a few days ago--refused to eat so supposedly d. of starvation. (False report--his trial soon followed for the above mentioned murder. ERW)

6/26/1873 Lindermann, Henry, late proprietor of the Lindermann House at Osyka, d. at this place (Magnolia) the 23rd Inst., after a long painful illness.

10/17/1873 Owen/McKinney, md. at res. of bride's father on Wed., 10/15/1873, by
Rev. O. L. Johnson, Benjamin F. Owen and Fannie M. McKinney, both of Pike Co.

10/31/1873 Kuykendall/Addison, md. at res. of Dr. Wm. Jones, at Osyka, Sun., 10/26/1873, by Rev. W. E. Tynes, Morgan T. Kuykendall of Summit and Sarah M. Addison of Osyka.

11/7/1873 Roark, Joseph, d. at Osyka Mon., 11/4/1873, aged 50 yrs., 17 days.

11/14/1873 Magee/Hall, md. by Rev. H. P. Lewis on 11/6/1873, Nelson Magee to Useba Jane Hall, both of Pike Co.

O'Quin/Hall md. by Rev. H. P. Lewis on 11/5/1873, William J. O'Quin to Mary E. Hall.

Barr/Allen, md. by Rev. H. P. Lewis 10/30/1873, R. Wesley Barr to Catherine O. Allen.

Curleit/Murray, md. at Magnolia Bapt. Ch., Thurs., 11/6/1873 at $7\frac{1}{2}$ P.M. by Rev. W. E. Tynes, George W. Curleit and Mattie C. Murray of Magnolia.

Lazar/Quin, md. Thur., 11/16/1873 at res. of bride's father by Rev. W. H. Roane, Andrew J. Lazar to Virginia T. Quin of Pike Co.

Gatlin, Mrs. Amanda Adelaide, nee Spenser, aged 24 yrs., wife of Capt. E. A. Gatlin, d. 10/26/1873, at Osyka.

11/28/1873 Hord/Joyner, md. at Bapt. Ch. by Rev. W. E. Tynes on 11/20/1873, John T. Hord and Mrs. M. A. Joyner, both of Magnolia.

12/19/1879 (new series of the Magnolia Gazette)
Sandell, Daniel, oldest citizen of Pike Co., d. at Magnolia 12/13/1879, aged 87 yrs., 9 mos., 21 days; lived at his old homeplace for 60 yrs.

Williams/Whittington, J.P. Williams and Miss M. A. Whittington md. at Summit a few days ago.

Runnels, Picket, d. at Summit on 13th Inst. (from Summit Sentinel)

Quin, Mrs. L. M., d. at res. of Dr. W. M. Wroten at this place (Magnolia) Thurs., 12/11/1879.

2/6/1880 Varnado/Sipple, md. at Epis. Ch. in Osyka Thurs., noon, 1/22/1880; by L. D. Brainerd, Rector; H. H. Varnado and Barbara Sipple, both of Osyka.

The oldest record on file in the Chancery Clerk's Office for Pike Co. in 1880 was dated June 5, 1816--a document filed when the area was still a territory.

4/9/1880 Andrews, Miss Maggie, d. at McComb City last Tues., remains carried to Magnolia for interrment; funeral by Rev. J. C. Graham last Wed.

5/21/1880 Draughon/Wilson md. at res. of bride's father 5/11/1880 by Elder J. R. Farish, W. W. Draughon and Amanda Wilson, both of Tangipahoa, La.

Ferguson, Mrs. Pinkey, late consort of William Ferguson, d. near Summit 10 A.M., Mon. 5/17/1880.

6/4/1880 Fredericks, Mrs. Victoria, wife of C. S. Fredericks of McComb City, d. the 28th Inst.; funeral conducted by Rev. J. R. Farish of Magnolia, 10 A.M. Sat.

7/2/1880 Fitzpatrick, young Mr., of McComb City committed suicide last Mon. by taking strychnine.

Stratton, Dr. E. P., d. Sat. 26th Inst., at 9 A.M.; b. in Va.; came to state 45 yrs. ago; strict member of the Presbyterian Ch. and an Odd Fellow for 40 yrs. Upon invitation of the IOOF Lodge of Tangipahoa, lodges from Magnolia, McComb, and Summit participated in funeral. Rev. J. C. Graham, assisted by Rev. Mr. Wykoff of New Orleans, conducted the service.

7/30/1880 Lenoir, Alice Betha, dau. of Robert L., and Sarah Ann Lenoir, d. near McComb on Thur., 7/27/1880.

Pitts, Col. T. T., who once published the Magnolian at this place, d. in Little Rock, Ark., a few days ago.

9/10/1880 Mr. Quinea Lewis, who lives near Homesville [sic], a pensioner of the War of 1812, was in town last Sat. He is 87 yrs. old and was 19 when he entered the army.

Marsh/Fisher, md. in McComb City 9/1/1880, at res. of Mrs. E. E. Lee by Eld. J. R. First, James D. Marsh and Miss Lon Fisher.

9/17/1880 Poindexter, Josie Caruthers, 12 yrs. old, d. at Magnolia 3½ A.M., Sun. 9/12/1880, dau. of Margaret E. and Herbert E. Poindexter.

11/5/1880 Memorial to J. C. Cary, late of McComb City, signed by Luther Manship, chairman of committee, W. H. Tegadden, O. S. Parker, and O. B. Quin.

11/26/1880 Easterling, Andrew, drowned trying to ford Strong R. at Albritton's Ford, 2 mi. S. of Magnolia on Sat. morning.

Frost, Dr. Ebenezer, d. in Perry Co., Miss., 11/1/1880 in his 60th yr., b. in Wayne Co., Miss.; grad. from Medical College in old U. of La. in N.O.; moved to Ark., but lived in Magnolia for several yrs.

12/10/1880 Varnado/Brooks, md. in Osyka a few days ago, W. L. Varnado of Osyka to Emily Brooks of New Orleans.

Dicks, Mr. and Mrs. Dicks of Summit lost 2 children within the span of a few days.

12/31/1880 J. B. Simmons brutally murdered near Raymond a few days ago by a "colored man" named Granville Harrell.

1/21/1881 Sandell/Lenoir, md. at res. of bride's mother near Magnolia, Tues. 1/18/1881 by Rev. J. W. Sandell, James M. Sandell and Nannie F. Lenoir.

1/28/1881 Manship/Phelps md. Wed. 5 P.M., 1/26/1881 in Magnolia, at res. of bride's father by Rev. Dr. Douglass, Luther Manship of McComb and Miss Belmont Phelps of Magnolia.

Walker, Jeremiah, an old citizen who lived near Topisaw in the Carter's Cr. Ch. neighborhood, d. Sun. night the 23rd Inst.; he was nearly 70 yrs old, father of our postmaster W. L. Walker. Mr. Quinea Lewis, an aged man, preceded him only a few days before.

2/4/1881--brief obit. for Quinea Lewis submitted by H. P. Lewis (see more details in the obits. from the N. O. C. A.)

County Clerk issued 176 marriage licenses in 1880; but Dr. Sparkman, the clerk, said 1880 was not a good year for marrying.

2/11/1881 Varnado/Gibson, md. Wed. 2/8/1880 [sic] at res. of bride's father Mr. William Gibson of McComb City, Hezekiah Varnado and Ellen Gibson.

3/4/1881 Albro/McNiff, md. in the Cath. Ch. in Magnolia, Mon. 2/28/1881 at 8:30 P.M. by Rev. F. Kennedy of Amite City, La., assisted by Rev. Father McDonald, Samuel Albro of McComb City and Mary McNiff of Magnolia; Josie McGrath of Brookhaven and Jonathan Iles (Gile or Niles?) of McComb were attendants.

Wamble/Quin, md. in McComb City Wed. 2/16/1881, Frank Wamble and Lizzie Quin.

Persell/Cotten md. in Summit Wed. 2/24/1881 by Rev. Charles H. Otkin, S. H. Persell and Emma C. Cotton of Summit.

Richardson/Sippel md. in the Epis. Ch. of Osyka, Tues. evening 2/22/1881, by Rev. W. K. Douglass of Dry Grove, F. S. Richardson of Selma, Ala., and Louise Sippel of Osyka.

Sibley, Miss Lizzie, d. in Magnolia Tues morning, 1/1/1881.

Gardner, Sylvester, d. 2 mi. N. of Magnolia, Sun. night at 8, 2/27/1881.

Gibson, Della Estella, d. in McComb City, 2/11/1881, dau. of W. H. and M. A. Gibson, aged 2 yrs., 1 mo., 11 days.

3/25/1881 Hiller/Levy, md. in Magnolia at Jonas Hiller's res., Sun. 3/20/1881, by Rev. J. L. Lencht of N.O., Daniel Hiller of Canton, Miss., and Julia Levy of Bastrop, La.

Smith, Nellie E., d. Osyka on Tues., 3/15/1881, aged 19 yrs.

4/8/1881 H. Y. Newsom, who killed Anthony Melville in McComb last week, has been admitted to bail.

4/22/1881 Sibley, Miss Lizzie, d. 3/1/1881 in her 34th yr. at res. of her brother-in-law C. C. Gibson in Magnolia; suffered much of her life; lived with sister Nanie Gibson and took care of the latter's house after her death. She joined Methodist Ch. in 1874. (Obit. by J. W. Sandell)

5/6/1881 Tynes, Mrs. T. E., d. near Osyka at res. of Judge T. E. Tate on Mon. 5/2/1881. She was dau. of Judge Tate; funeral preached from his res. last Tues. by Rev. J. R. Farish.

5/13/1881 Packwood, S. E., son of J. H. Packwood of China Grove, d. at Oxford Un. on Thur., 5th Inst; remains arrived Sat. and taken to China Grove for burial.

5/20/1881 Gillaspy/Lieb, md. on Thurs. 3/12/1881 at 3 P.M. at the res. of bride's father in Magnolia by Rev. Mr. Monroe of Crystal Springs, J. R. Gillaspy of Crystal Springs and Tillie Lieb of Magnolia.

Battles, H. A., d. Colorado Springs, Colorado, on the 9th Inst., of mountain fever; went there few yrs. back to seek his fortune. Family and mother-in-law Mrs. Mary R. Lee left to join him last Oct.

Packwood, Samuel Franklin b. 7/31/1863 and named for uncle S. E. Packwood, believed then to have been killed at Gettysburg; d. at Oxford 5/5/1881 from effects of measles; buried at China Grove.

5/27/1881 Gibson, Dr. P. L., d. in an accident between 11 & 12 P.M. last Mon. night. He was a dentist. He decided to go to McComb after making arrangements to stay at the Magnolia Hotel, even if he had to walk up the RR track; he either laid down or fell down on the rails and was run over by the 11:15 train.

6/17/1881 Weirauch/Frith, md. in Magnolia, 3 P.M. Wed., 6/15/1881 at T. H. McGowin's res. by Rev. J. R. Farish, E. P. Weirauch & Sallie Frith of Summit.

6/24/1881 Deaton/Watts md. at res. of W. R. Harvey of McComb, 6/14/1881 by Eld. J. R. Farish, George Deaton of Hazlehurst and Fannie Watts of McComb.

8/5/1881 Grunewall, Renzo, d. at Chatawa Fri., 7/19/1881 at 5 P.M. of "Pyemia (?)" after a long illness; native of Bavaria, aged 52 yrs.

In memory of Dena Sprich, b. 2/7/1871, d. 7/20/1881, b. in Liberty, Amite Co., moved to Pike Co., only short time before death. Family data not given.

8/19/1881 Jones, J. J., d. in N. O., Sun. 8/7/1881; native of Galway Co., Ireland; lived in N. O. for 30 yrs.; res. of Magnolia for the past 6 yrs., aged at death, 54 yrs.

9/9/1881 Lenoir, Albert d. at Central House in Magnolia 3 P. M., Sun. 9/4/1881.

Copes, Mrs. Eveline Rebecca, widow of late Henry S. Copes, d. Wed. 9/7/1881 at 5 P.M. at res. of bro.-in-law in Brookhaven, Mr. E. M. Bee, who accompanied body to Magnolia for interment next to her "young devoted" husband who d. 2 yrs. ago.

9/18/1881 Walter B. Lampton of Tylertown lost his wife Sat. 9/10/1881. His mother-in-law arrived from Kentucky about the same time and discovered her dau.'s death.

9/23/1881 Stewart, Samuel d. on Magee's Cr. with typhoid at age 29; buried at China Grove with Masonic Honors (letter from J. A. Quin dated 9/14/1881 from China Grove).

Brent, Joe Lee, d. at res. of Preston and Fannie Brent, his parents, 10 mi. E. of Summit 9/10/1881 of congestion of the brain, aged 10 yrs., 2 mos., 5 days.

Womble, B. F., d. at Warm Springs, N.C., the 12th Inst., 35 yrs. old; memorial from the McComb Dramatic Club.

10/7/1881 Bickham, James A., d. at Marianne, Ark., 9/30/1881, aged 26 yrs., 8 mos., son of Lewis C. and Maggie A. Bickham, formerly of Summit. James was killed in a shooting affair between himself and J. D. Rogers.

11/25/1881 Webb/Lezar, md. at res. of bride's mother in Magnolia 11/24/1881 by Rev. B. F. Flowers, Dr. J. W. F. Webb of Liberty and Victoria V. Lezar of Magnolia.

Atkinson/Kearns md. in New Orleans, Wed. 11/23/1881, by Father Nethart, Jesse W. Atkinson of Summit and Ella C. Kearns of New Orleans.

12/2/1881 Powell/McMillian, md. at res. of Mrs. Dr. Gullet, Amite City, La., 11/17/1881, J. M. Powell and Laura McMillian.

Ford/Walshe, md. at res. of Mrs. P. McGehee of Osyka 11/22/1881, Dr. J. D. Ford and Mrs. Josephine Walshe, by Rev. J. R. Farish.

Bacot, Jesse, son of Dr. William Bacot and Myra C. Atkinson, d. Fri., 11/25/1881, aged 24 mos.

12/13/1881 Varnado/Martin, md. Wed., 12/22/1881, at res. of bride's father J. T. Martin, by Rev. J. R. Farish, Eugene Varnado and Florence Martin, all of Pike.

Guy/Prewitt, md. Wed., 12/22/1881, at res. of bride's grandmother Mrs. Vaughan, by Rev. J. W. Sandell, Monroe Guy and Julia Prewett of Pike Co.

2/3/1882 Williams/Simmons, md. Thurs., 1/26/1882 at res. of bride's mother on Silver Cr., by Rev. M. S. Shirk, J. R. Williams, of Amite Co., and Ida I. Simmons of Pike Co.

Davis/Wroten, md. Wed., 1/25/1882 at res. of bride's father Dr. V. J. Wroten, by Rev. J. W. Sandell, Charles Davis and Katie Wroten.

6/29/1882 McCloskey/Henderson, md. Wed., 6/14/1882 at St. Alphonsus Ch., N.O., George McCluskey to Kate E., only dau. of John Henderson, Jr.

Pike County Courthouse burned Sat. morning 7/1/1882--all records lost.

7/14/1882 (in Tylertown items) McElveen, Mrs. Mary, wife of J. R. McElveen d. at 6 A.M. on the 12th Inst.

7/21/1882 Marshall, Mrs. Mary Clay, d. Wed. at 6 P.M. 7/12/1882. She was a Martin from Edgefield Dist., S.C., a dau. of the Revolution, being in her 96th yr. She left 5 sons and 3 daus. Her father and eldest brother fought for Independence. (D. in Magnolia?)

9/22/1882 Reed, William G., aged 41 yrs. native of Louisville, Ky., d. Fri. 9/15/1882. He was deaf and dumb and had only one arm, in Magnolia for a very short time; left a wife and 3 destitute children.

10/27/1882 Adams, Col. R. L., native of Va.; many yrs. in Miss., d. at Summit 5 A.M. 10/18/1882 after long illness in his 76th yr. He was one time editor of Yazoo Banner, sheriff several times of Yazoo City, served two terms in Miss. Legis. as Rep. from Yazoo Co; md. 2 times, 1) dau. of Gabriel Swayze of Yazoo Co.; 2) Miss Bridgeport, also of Yazoo.

11/2/1882 Kramer, Mrs. Eugenia Esker, wife of John B. Kramer, d. in Magnolia 10/28/1882, aged 32 yrs, 4 mos., native of Mason (?), Dept. of Ettlingen, Badem,

Germany; left husband and 3 children.

11/23/1882 Prewett, Joe, d. last Tues., 21-yr.-old son of Smiley Prewett, d. from hemorrhage of the lungs while out squirrel hunting.

12/21/1882 O'Quin/Brownlee, md. in Magnolia, Wed. 12/20/1882 by Rev. J. R. Farish, J. M. O'Quin of Pike Co., and Belle A. Brownlee of New Orleans.

Vaught/Bacot, md. Wed., 12/20/1882 at res. of bride's father Dr. William Bacot near Summit, by Rev. J. T. Nicholson, W. O. Vaught and Anna M. Bacot, both of Pike Co.

2/1/1883 Gibson/Matthews, md. in Hazlehurst 1/29/1883 at home of bride's father J. R. Matthews, C. C. Gibson of Magnolia and Laura Matthews of Hazlehurst.

Lenoir, Bessie, dau. of V. T. and Nannie Lenoir, aged 2 yrs., 3 mos., 8 days, d. 1/29/1883.

2/22/1883 Rice/Hoke, md. in Magnolia Thurs., 2/15/1883 at res. of bride's father F. M. Hoke, by Rev. L. Scofield, Robert J. Rice of Amite Co., and Lizzie J. Hoke of Magnolia.

3/1/1883 Ellzey, Oscar J., d. Thurs., 2/22/1883 at res. on Silver Cr., bro. of W. F. Ellzey, bookkeeper for Smith and Simmons of Magnolia.

3/15/1883 Ellzey/Gatlin, md. in Magnolia 3/8/1883 at res. of bride's father John B. Gatlin by J. T. Nicholson, W. F. Ellzey and Mollie Gatlin both of Magnolia.

Anderson/Barrett, md. in Summit 3/13/1883 at res. of Mrs. Reynolds by Rev. Upton B. Bowden, W. C. Anderson of Summit Times and Intelligencer and Claude F. Barrett. (?)

4/12/1883 Causey, Hon. J. M., d. near McComb, Sun., 4/8/1883; native of Amite Co.; moved to Pike Co. 12-15 yrs. ago; elected to Leg. is 1875 and re-elected in 1877, representing Pike Co. for 2 terms; he was also a trustee of the Agricultural and Mech. College of Miss., a director of the Miss. Valley Co., and a member of the Grange.

4/26/1883 The old Courthouse at Holmesville built over a half century ago burned Fri. 4/20/1883. Used at the time by A. W. Crawford (as a store?) who housed a "stock of goods" therein.

Vaught, Harrison Hobart, d. in Magnolia on Mon. 4/28/1883 at 11:30 P.M. aged 3 yrs. and 24 days; son of W. C. and Charlotte D. Vaught.

7/12/1883 Nicholson, Dr. George, of Holmesville, old and respected citizen, d. last Sat., aged 74 yrs., buried with Masonic Honors.

8/30/1883 Evans, J. P., age 50 d. at Summit Tues. night 8/22/1883

9/20/1883 Lenoir, William H., 70 yrs. old, d. at Magnolia Thurs., 9/13/1883.

Davidson, W. D., d. at McComb on Sun., 9/15/1883.

Rehorst, Miss Josephine, d. at Osyka 9/11/1883, aged 20 yrs.

11/8/1883 Jones/Slade, md. 11/1/1883 at res. of bride's father near Magnolia by Rev. J. T. Nicholson, J. E. Jones and Ida G. Slade.

Yopp-Loch, md. at the Cath. Parsonage 10/16/1883 (in Magnolia?), Nicholas Yopp and Maggie Loch of Magnolia, George Yopp and Mary Budde, Attendants.

3/13/1884 Curtis/Safford, md. at res. of Mr. and Mrs. Lloyd Clarke at Mt. Pleasant, N.J., 3/11/1884, Thomas C. Curtis and Hettie Blanche Safford, dau. of Judge E. Safford of Magnolia, Miss.

4/17/1884 Coney, Mrs. Bessie, wife of Van Coney, d. last Sun. morning, the 13th Inst. She was dau. of Mr. D. C. Walker.

5/23/1884 Coney, Mrs. Emeline, d. at Magnolia at 6:40 A.M., Sat., 5/17/1884, aged 64 yrs.; a native of Pike Co.; member of the Bapt. Ch.; wife of Jackson Coney, who d. several yrs. ago; buried in family burial ground 5 mi. E. of town. Funeral by Rev. C. H. Otken.

6/5/1884 Sandifer/Brown, md. near Holmesville at res. of bride's father 5/28/1884 by Eld. R. J. Boone, J. T. Sandifer and Angie Brown.

Steppe, Jessie Lot, d. at Anding, Miss., 5/16/1884, 6 mos. old, infant of J. P. and M. E. Steppe.

6/19/1884 McClutchie/Travis, md. at Natchez 6/12/1884, Will McClutchie of Natchez and Mamie W. Travis, formerly of Magnolia.

7/10/1884 Hoke/Moffat, md. in New Orleans 7/5/1884, Andrew J. Hoke of Magnolia and Henrietta Moffat of N.O.

7/31/1884 Brumfield, _____, an old landmark of Amite Co., d. Fri., father of Pike Co. treasurer, Henry S. Brumfield.

8/28/1884 Kaigler, William W., killed in an accident last Thurs. evening when run over by wagon loaded with 1650 pounds of goods near Vaughan's Mill. He was 64 yrs. old. Remains carried from home of Dr. Sparkman to China Grove for burial last Mon. morning.

OBITUARIES FROM THE

BOGUE CHITTO BAPTIST ASSOCIATION

OF MISSISSIPPI

1872 - 1910

MINUTES OF THE THIRD ANNIVERSARY OF THE BOGUE CHITTO BAPTIST ASSOCIATION, October 26, 1872.

Morgan J. Coney . . . born in Pike Co., Miss., 1828, united with the Baptist Church, Salem, in 1858; dismissed by letter and joined to the Boguechitto Church, Oct. 5, 1861; elected Clerk March 5, 1864. For five years or more he faithfully served his church. He died Oct. 10, 1872, at his residence, of congestion, aged 41 years, 11 months and 10 days. MT. ZION

MINUTES OF THE FOURTH ANNIVERSARY OF THE BOGUE CHITTO BAPTIST ASSOCIATION, October 25, 26, 27, 1873. Printed by the Summit "Times" Print.

No obituaries reported.

MINUTES OF THE FIFTH ANNIVERSARY OF THE BOGUE CHITTO BAPTIST ASSOCIATION, October 3, 1874. Printed by the Southern Baptist Publication Society.

William Lewis . . . was born in Georgia, July 11, 1791, where he was raised, and removed from thence in 1811 to Miss., where he like many others, engaged in redeeming the State from Indian rule and enabled it to assume its place among its band of civilized sisters. He was baptized into the fellowship of New Zion Church in 1824 and from that time to the day of this death remained a consistent Christian. He was ordained a deacon in New Zion Church and remained such through his career. He died Sept. 28, 1874, being 83 years, 2 months, and 17 days old. NEW ZION

MINUTES OF THE SIXTH ANNUAL MEETING OF THE BOGUE CHITTO BAPTIST ASSOCIATION, October 2, 1875. Printed by the Southern Baptist Publication Society Print.

No obituaries reported.

MINUTES OF THE SEVENTH ANNUAL MEETING OF THE BOGUE CHITTO BAPTIST ASSOCIATION, October 2, 1876. Printed by the Southern Baptist Publication Society Print.

No obituaries reported.

MINUTES OF THE EIGHTH ANNUAL MEETING OF THE BOGUE CHITTO BAPTIST ASSOCIATION, October 8, 1877. Printed by the Southern Baptist Publication Society.

William Marselas . . . was born in 1806; emigrated to Miss. in 1810 from Ga.; married Lucy Drimmen in 1829; united with Mar's Hill Church in June, 1835; in 1841 he moved his membership to Mt. Pleasant and then back again to Mar's Hill, in 1847 where he remained a member till his death Oct. 2, 1876. He served for many years as Deacon. He leaves a second wife and one daughter of the second marriage. MAR'S HILL

Jacob Curtis . . . was born in this State in Feb., 1813, and for the past 35 years was a citizen of Pike Co. He first embraced religion at a revival meeting held in a school house four miles east of Summit, in 1850. A quorum of the Mt. Pleasant Conference being present at the time, he was made a member of that church, and in 1851 he moved his membership to Bogue Chitto Church. After serving 6 years as Clerk of Friendship, he became a member of Bogue Chitto, the second time, 1875, where he remained until his death May 10, 1877. BOGUE CHITTO

Alfred Reeves . . . born in Barnwell District, S.C., June 12, 1796; moved to Miss. in 1811; was married to Sarah Thompson June 8, 1821; professed conversion and was united to the Friendship Church, 1833; moved his membership to Bogue Chitto Church in June, 1840, where he remained until his death Jan. 31, 1877. McCOMB CITY

William S. Holmes . . . was born in Ga., Nov. 12, 1806, and died on Dec. 30, 1876, aged 70 years, 1 month, 18 days. He was the husband of Jane P. Holmes, deceased. He leaves 10 children, 49 grandchildren, and 1 great-grandchild. He left the state of Ga. at the age of 6 years and emigrated to Pike Co., Miss., where he spent his life remaining there. He joined the Union Baptist Church on Aug. 2, 1851. UNION

MINUTES OF THE NINTH ANNUAL MEETING OF THE BOGUE CHITTO BAPTIST ASSOCIATION, October 5, 1878. Printed by the Times Power Press Print.

E. P. Williams . . . was born in Lawrence Co. in 1841, where he remained until the commencement of the late war. He was married to Miss Rozilla Felder, Dec. 14, 1864. He united with the Shady Grove Baptist Church in 1871 and became a member of this Association and remained until he died Sept., 1878. SHADY GROVE

MINUTES OF THE TENTH ANNUAL SESSION OF THE BOGUE CHITTO BAPTIST ASSOCIATION, November 1, 1879. Printed by the Martin & Winkley Book and Job Print.

No obituaries reported.

MINUTES OF THE ELEVENTH ANNUAL SESSION OF THE BOGUE CHITTO BAPTIST ASSOCIATION, October 2, 1880. Printed by the "Conservative Times" Print.

William Gulledge . . . was born Nov. 3, 1799. He died at his home in Pike Co., Miss., Sept. 20, 1879. He united by experience with Bogue Chitto Church (Miss.) July 6, 1833. He served his church for a number of years, referred to as a model of Christianity. BOGUE CHITTO

John W. Bishop . . . was born Oct. 18, 1855. He united with the Church at Smyrna, July 15, 1876. He died Aug. 5, 1880. He leaves a wife and child. SMYRNA

MINUTES OF THE TWELFTH ANNUAL SESSION OF THE BOGUE CHITTO BAPTIST ASSOCIATION, October 1, 1881. Printed by the Charles Winkley, Steam Book & Job Print.

Jeremiah Walker . . . was born in Hickman Co., Tenn., Sept. 11, 1808. His father moved to Pike Co., Miss., June, 1814. When he was 27, he married Louisiana Williams, with whom he lived the remainder of his life. He died Jan. 23, 1881, aged 72 years, 4 months and 12 days. He leaves her and 7 children. In 1837 he joined the Bogue Chitto Church, and in July he was ordained Deacon of the church, an office he used well upwards of 32 years. BOGUE CHITTO

John Simmons . . . was born in Barnwell Dist., S.C., Sept., 1803; moved to Pike Co., Miss., with his parents when quite young. He united with the Silver Creek Baptist Church in 1835, withdrew to go into the constitution of the Mt. Zion Church, in July, 1838, and was elected Clerk. He served many years as Clerk and resigned on account of being hard of hearing. Several years after, he removed his membership back to Silver Creek Church and shortly after was elected Deacon. Then he withdrew his letter to help constitute the Balochitto Church, Oct. 12, 1873, and was elected Deacon. He died June 27, 1881. He leaves a widow and several children. BALACHITTO

S. O. Magee . . . was born in Pike Co., Miss., in Nov., 1816. In June, 1839, he united with Silver Creek Baptist Church. At the August meeting, 1842, he was elected Deacon and ordained Mar., 1843 and served the church until he drew out his letter to go into the constitution of the Balochitto Church on Oct. 12, 1873; he was elected Deacon at the same time. He died Apr. 27, 1881, at the age of 65 years. He was twice married. He leaves a widow and 2 children by his first marriage. SILVER CREEK

MINUTES OF THE THIRTEENTH ANNUAL SESSION OF THE BOGUE CHITTO BAPTIST ASSOCIATION, September 30, 1862. Printed by the Baptist Record, Book and Job Print.

John E. Sibley . . . joined Sept. 1, 1861, by letter, died Jan. 27, 1879.

Nancy Boyd . . . joined July, 1841, died 1879.

Mary Gulledge . . . joined Sept. 9, 1859, died Oct., 1879.

Permelia Dunaway . . . joined July 9, 1856, died Jan. 29, 1880.

Mary Turnipseed . . . joined Aug., 1852, died Mar. 16, 1880.

Bethany Alexander . . . joined Sept. 7, 1873, died May 3, 1880.

Elizabeth Thompson . . . joined July 8, 1856, died Sept. 7, 1880.

Barbara Turnage . . . joined July 7, 1873, died April 1, 1881.

Samantha Raiborn . . . joined July 5, 1876, died 1880.

Susan Sibley . . . joined April 3, 1837, died Mar. 20, 1882.

Eliza Boyd . . . joined July, 1844, died Mar. 24, 1882.

R. B. Morris . . . joined by letter, Mar. 2, 1873, died April 10, 1882.

Minda Cothern . . . joined July 10, 1856, died May 31, 1882.

THE ABOVE JOINED THE BOGUE CHITTO CHURCH

Rosa E. Fortinberry . . . was a daughter of Bro. Jackson Brumfield, born Mar. 2, 1856, near Franklinton, Washington Parish, La. She was married Dec. 5, 1878, to Bro. Benjamin C. Fortinberry, after which she moved to Pike Co., Miss., where she lived until her death July 26, 1882. She united with Mt. Hermon Church Oct., 1879, received and baptised by Eld. W. J. Fortinberry. Funeral sermon was preached by Bro. Willis J. Fortinberry. She leaves a husband and 2 children, a father, mother, 3 brothers, and 5 sisters. MT. HERMON

Jacob M. Ott . . . was born Aug. 28, 1821, near where Amite City, La., now is; lived there with his parents till he was eleven years old, after which they moved to Silver Creek where he remained until his death. At the Union Schoolhouse he was received and baptised in the year 1857. He then united with Mt. Zion Church, Pike Co., Miss., on a certificate of baptism from Bro. Jesse Crawford, where he remained till the constitution of Mt. Hermon Church in 1863 of which he died an honored member. He was married to Miss Nancy C. Simmons, Nov. 30, 1854. He died July 20, 1881. He leaves a wife, daughter, and son. His funeral sermon was preached by Eld. C. Felder Crawford. MT. HERMON

MINUTES OF THE FOURTEENTH ANNUAL SESSION OF THE BOGUE CHITTO BAPTIST ASSOCIATION, September 15, 1883. Printed by the Baptist Record Publishing House.

Emanuel D. Varnado . . . was born in Barnwell Dist., S.C., Jan. 16, 1807; moved to the Mississippi Territory in 1811. In 1828 he was married to Miss Sarah Simmons. Joined Beulah Baptist Church, Washington Parish, La., in 1837. In 1838 he went into the constitution of the Mt. Zion Church where he remained a member. He died Oct. 20, 1882, aged 75 years, 9 months and 4 days. MT. ZION

T. A. Moak . . . was born in Pike Co., Miss., Dec. 9, 1839. He was married to Miss Julia Sasser Oct. 3, 1866. He united with Mt. Pleasant Church Sept. 23, 1871, and was elected Clerk. He died Dec. 18, 1882; he leaves a wife and 6 children. MT. PLEASANT

Eliza Schilling . . . was born in the State of Ga., Aug. 5, 1809; moved to Livingston Parish, La., when small and thence to Washington Parish. She was married to Michael Schilling in the fall of 1825, was baptised into the fellowship of Mt. Hermon church by Eld. W. J. Fortenberry, Nov. 12, 1864. She died Aug. 23, 1883, aged 74 years, 18 days. She leaves 3 sons and 3 daughters, besides grandchildren and great-grandchildren. MT. HERMON

Sallie Fortenberry . . . was born Feb. 5, 1810, in Ga. She married G. C. Fortenberry Oct. 11, 1833, and then moved with her husband to Silver Creek, Pike Co., where she remained. She united with the church in 1850 and was baptised by Eld. Jessee Crawford. She went into the constitution of Mt. Hermon Church Dec. 12, 1863. Two daughters and one son preceded her to the spirit world, while 5 daughters and 1 son survive her. She died July 19, 1883, aged 73 years, 5 months and 14 days. MT. HERMON

Oscar J. L. Ellzey . . . born Jan. 31, 1854. Joined the church at Mt. Hermon, Oct., 1874. He died Feb. 22, 1883, aged 29 years, 22 days. He leaves a wife and 3 children. His funeral services were conducted by Rev. W. J. Fortinberry. MT. HERMON

MINUTES OF THE FIFTEENTH ANNUAL SESSION OF THE BOGUE CHITTO BAPTIST ASSOCIATION, September 20, 1884. Printed by the Baptist Record Publishing House.

Richard Story . . . age 86. MAGNOLIA

Emiline Coney . . . age 65. MAGNOLIA

M. R. Lea . . . age 65. MAGNOLIA

V. W. Champlin . . . age 38. MAGNOLIA

Nannie Martin . . . age 19. TANGIPAHOA

Thomas Whittenton . . . age 28. TANGIPAHOA

Brother Delaughter . . . age 84. MT. PLEASANT

Elijah Prestidge . . . age 74. MT. PLEASANT

Rebecca Sandifer . . . died Dec. 2, 1883, age 84 years, 6 months, and 7 days. She was born in Barnwell Dist., S.C., May 26, 1799, moved to the Mississippi Territory in 1812; was married to Hiram Addison in 1821. He died 13 years afterward. She joined Silver Creek Church, Aug., 1837, withdrew in 1838 to go into the constitution of Mt. Zion Church; was married a second time to Benjamin Sandifer in 1838 and again left a widow in 1850. MT. ZION

G. C. Fortenberry . . . was born in South Carolina, July 16, 1805; died at his home in Pike Co., Miss., June 21, 1884; joined the Baptist Church at Silver Creek and was baptised by Eld. Jesse Crawford August, 1837. He moved his membership to the constitution of Mt. Hermon Church in 1864 where he remained. He leaves one son and five daughters, besides two brothers and one sister. His funeral services were conducted by Eld. W. J. Fortenberry and E. M. Schilling. MT. HERMON

Maria Fortenberry . . . was born in the city of New Orleans, Feb. 22, 1846; died at her home in Washington Parish, La., Feb. 4, 1884. She joined the Baptist church at Silver Creek, Pike Co., Miss., Aug., 1862, and was baptised by Eld. Ben A. Crawford. She lost her father when they moved from New Orleans to Miss. Her mother moved from Pass Christian, Miss., and from thence to Pike Co. She married Brother W. Frank Fortenberry, Apr. 24, 1867. She moved her membership from Silver Creek to Mt. Hermon church in 1867 and became a deaconess. She leaves a mother, husband, and seven little children. Her funeral services were conducted by Eld. E. M. Schilling. MT. HERMON

MINUTES OF THE SIXTEENTH ANNUAL SESSION OF BOGUE CHITTO BAPTIST ASSOCIATION, September 19, 1885. Printed by the Baptist Record Book Print.

L. D. Cook . . . was born in Amite Co., Miss., Mar. 8, 1844; moved from there to Pike Co. in 1859 or '60, where she resided. She married P. A. Cook on Feb. 22, 1864. In Sept., 1879, she was baptised by Eld. R. N. Crawford. She died May 14, 1885; she leaves a husband, 7 children and an aged mother. TANGIPAHOA

H. Eugene Varnado . . . died Oct. 29, 1885. He was born in Pike Co., Sept. 26, 1856. He united with Mt. Zion Church in Aug., 1880, and was married to Miss Florence Martin Dec. 21, 1881. He leaves a wife, 1 child, mother and father, brother and sisters. MT. ZION

Sarah Varnado . . . died June 23, 1885. She was born in Pike Co., Miss., Jan. 4, 1814. She was married to Emanuel D. Varnado, Jan. 10, 1828. She withdrew in 1838 and went into the constitution of Mt. Zion church in the same year. She was a loving companion and mother. MT. ZION

L. W. Ott . . . died May 6, 1885. He was a devoted husband and father. He was born May 3, 1831. He lived and died on Silver Creek, Washington Parish, La. Joined the Baptist church at Mt. Zion and was baptised June 1, 1862, by Rev. C. R. Crawford. He afterwards moved to Mt. Hermon. His funeral was preached by Rev. E. M. Schilling. MT. HERMON

Naomi Ott . . . died Mar. 17, 1885. She was born Oct. 9, 1805, in Orangeburg Dist., S.C. She migrated with her parents to La. in 1818. She joined the Baptist church at Silver Creek, Pike Co., Miss., in Aug., 1837, but was baptised into the fellowship of Beulah church by Eld. Jesse Crawford. She moved her membership to Mt. Hermon church May 13, 1865, where she remained. Her funeral services were conducted by Rev. W. F. Eady. MT. HERMON

S. E. Parker . . . died May 29, 1885. She was born Jan. 9, 1842. Joined Mt. Hermon church May 13, 1865, where she remained until her death. She leaves a husband and several children. MT. HERMON

MINUTES OF THE SEVENTEENTH ANNUAL SESSION OF THE BOGUE CHITTO BAPTIST ASSOCIATION, September 18, 1886. Printed by the Baptist Record Book & Job Print.

J. E. Simmons . . . died Tuesday, Aug. 3, 1886. Julia Elizabeth Pound, eldest daughter of Daniel M. and Jane Pound, was born Oct. 31, 1856. She united with the Silver Creek Baptist Church when she was 16; removed her membership and joined in the organization of Balachitto Church; was married to D. Monroe Simmons, Jan., 1876, after which she removed her membership to Mt. Zion Church. She leaves a kind husband, three little children . . . MT. ZION

Jeremiah Strickland . . . died Feb. 5, 1886. He was born in Ga., Feb. 12, 1812. He married Matilda Varnado, Dec. 11, 1834. He united with this church and was baptised Nov. 15, 1841. He has left a wife and two orphan grandchildren. MT. ZION

Bettie Small . . . died Mar. 1, 1886. She was baptised Aug., 1884. She was born in Amite Co., Aug. 5, 1860. She leaves a mother to mourn her loss.

David Edwards . . . was born in Amite Co., July 20, 1838; was married Dec. 22, 1859. He united with Tangipahoa church on Saturday before the 2nd Lord's day in Sept., 1871, and received baptism by Eld. B. A. Crawford. He died June 7, 1886. He leaves a wife and 5 children. TANGIPAHOA

Rebecca Fitzgerald . . . united with Magnolia church, June, 1879, and died Sept. 11, 1885, age 55 years and 25 days. MAGNOLIA

Mary Prewett . . . died Nov. 5, 1885. She was born May, 1848, and joined the church in 1864. She was a loving mother, a devoted wife and an untiring worker in the church. MAGNOLIA

MINUTES OF THE EIGHTEENTH ANNUAL SESSION OF THE BOGUE CHITTO BAPTIST ASSOCIATION, September 17, 18, and 19, 1887. Printed by the Weekly Gazette Book and Job Print.

Jesse F. Dunaway . . . united with the Providence Church, Lawrence Co., Aug. 20, 1871, and afterward united with Bogue Chitto Church, Pike Co. He withdrew from Bogue Chitto Church and went into the organization of Enon Church, Sept. 14, 1884. He was born in the State of Miss. He leaves a wife and 6 children. ENON

Annis J. Dunaway . . . was born July 31, 1817. She united with Bogue Chitto Church in July, 1844, drew a letter and joined in the organization of Enon Church. She leaves a husband (Fielding Dunaway), 8 children. ENON

Pearley Cothern . . . united with Enon Church, Aug., 1885, and received baptism at the hands of Eld. J. L. Chandler. He died Aug. 9, 1887, age 27 years. ENON

Margaret Ann Ott . . . daughter of Thomas Tate, born at Clarksburg, Va., Mar. 20, 1813, moved to Washington Parish, La., when quite young where she lived until her death June 7, 1887. She united with the Baptist church in 1835 and was a devoted Christian. At the age of 13 she married Charles Ott. She leaves 6 sons and 5 daughters. The funeral services were conducted by Rev. J. F. Hailey of Tenn. BAPTIST

MINUTES OF THE NINETEENTH ANNUAL SESSION OF THE BOGUE CHITTO BAPTIST ASSOCIATION, September 15, 16, 17, 1888. Printed by the Weekly Gazette Book and Job Print.

Celia Magee . . . Celia Roberts was born in Washington Parish, La., Mar. 9, 1833, and died Sept. 22, 1887. She joined the Baptist church at Mt. Zion, Pike Co., Miss., in Oct., 1860, and moved her membership to Mt. Hermon, Washington Parish, La., in 1866, where she remained a member until her death. She was married to Nehemiah Magee in 1849 and remained his loving wife until his death Feb. 3, 1868. She leaves 4 sons and 2 daughters. MT. HERMON

Saline Wilson . . . was born Aug. 5, 1818, died Nov. 23, 1887. She was received into the Tangipahoa Church by letter on the 4th Lord's Day in Aug., 1886. TANGIPAHOA

Dan Cook . . . united with Tangipahoa Church in Aug., 1886. Departed this life the 6th day of June, 1888, at the age of 29 years, 10 months and 17 days. TANGIPAHOA

Amon A. Kennedy . . . was shot by an assassin or assassins on the night of May 10, 1888, and died on the night of May 14, 1888. He was born in Washington Parish, La., Oct. 25, 1856. United with the Bala Chitto Baptist Church in Aug., 1879. He married Miss Virginia A. Pound Dec. 22, 1880. He left a wife, 3 small children, mother, brothers, sisters. BALA CHITTO

Isabella Mullins . . . died Mar. 24, 1888. Her maiden name was Hinson. She married Brother L. Mullins Dec. 8, 1853. She united with the Silver Creek Church Aug., 1872; withdrew from said church to go into the constitution of Bala Chitto Church. She was born Mar. 31, 1820, in Pike Co., Miss. She has 2 children with her aged husband still living. BALA CHITTO

Lizzie R. Mullins . . . daughter of L. Mullins and Isabella Mullins, died Mar. 11, 1888. She was born June 20, 1860, in Pike Co., Miss. She joined the Bala Chitto Baptist Church in 1879 where she lived a faithful member until her death. BALA CHITTO

Elijah Cothern . . . died Jan. 23, 1888. He united with the Bogue Chitto Baptist Church many years ago. He afterward withdrew from Bogue Chitto Church and went into the organization of Enon church where he remained. ENON

Martha C. Boyd . . . united with Bogue Chitto Church in July, 1868; withdrew her letter and joined the organization of Enon Church. She leaves a husband (Lewis B. Boyd), and 7 children. ENON

James Williams . . . was born in Miss., Pike Co., Dec. 29, 1813; and was married to Judith Shateric, Nov. 24, 1836. He united with the Friendship Church Aug., 1856, under the administration of Eld. W. Clark and elected deacon of that church in April, 1862. Ordained April, 1866, and lived an earnest worker for the Lord until he and his wife drew letters and joined the Moak's Creek Church July 25, 1876. He died Feb. 2, 1888. He leaves a wife and friends. MOAK'S CREEK

Nancy Simmons . . . died July 17, 1888. Was born near the French Broad River in E. Tenn., Oct. 2, 1807. She married William Simmons in Oct., 1824. She joined the Baptist church at Beulah in 1835; withdrew and went into the constitution of Mt. Zion Church in 1838 and was elected deaconess. The funeral ceremonies were conducted by the Rev. I. Allmand and Rev. E. M. Schilling. MT. ZION

MINUTES OF THE TWENTIETH ANNUAL SESSION OF THE BOGUE CHITTO BAPTIST ASSOCIATION, September 14, 15, and 16, 1889. Printed by The Weekly Gazette Book and Job Print.

Clarenda Cothern . . . joined the Baptist Church at Providence, Lawrence Co., Miss., after which she removed her membership to Bogue Chitto Baptist Church and after the organization of Enon she removed her membership there where she remained a member. She married Bro. John Cothern in 1883 and was the mother of 4 children. ENON

Eliza Cook . . . was received into the church by baptism during our annual meeting in Aug., 1887. She died on June 6, 1889, leaving a husband and little babe. TANGIPAHOA

Janie Jones . . . united with us by letter in Nov., 1884, and met her death in Apr., 1889. She leaves 3 children and a husband. TANGIPAHOA

Narsisa Thompson . . . was born in 1844. She united with the Bethel Baptist Church in 1872 where her membership remained until 1885. She removed from there to Topisaw Church where she remained until her death. She died Apr. 11, 1889, leaving a husband, 10 children. TOPISAW

William Thompson Busby . . . was born Dec. 8, 1835, in Washington Parish, La. He was the son of Ezekiel and Sarah Wallace Busby. He united with Shady Grove Baptist Church, then drew his letter and united with Pleasant Hill church, Lawrence Co., in 1882 he went into the constitution of Topisaw Church. He was married to Emily Jones Dec. 17, 1860. He died Apr. 16, 1889. He leaves a wife and 9 children. TOPISAW

Hugh M. Norman . . . was the youngest son of Hiram and Isabel Norman. He was born in Pike Co., Miss., May 29, 1858, and on Dec. 11, 1879, he married Miss Martha A. Curtis. He joined the Moak's Creek Baptist Church in Aug., 1882. He died July 14, 1889. He leaves parents, wife, and 4 children. MOAK'S CREEK

Mary J. Price . . . daughter of A. B. Hammons and wife of S. E. Price, was born Nov. 1, 1848, and united with Moak's Creek Church, Aug. 2, 1871. She was married to S. E. Price Jan. 3, 1872. She died Nov. 7, 1888. She leaves a husband, 4 sons, and 2 daughters. MOAK'S CREEK

Rosaline Martin . . . died Feb. 28, 1889. She was born near Magnolia, Pike Co., Miss., Jan. 10, 1839. She was a daughter of William Coney; was married to Clinton Martin Dec. 26, 1855. She united with the Baptist Church at Tangipahoa, Amite Co., in 1872, in which she lived a true and worthy member until she was granted a letter in 1886 and united with Moak's Creek Baptist Church Aug. 29, 1887. She leaves a husband and several children. MOAK'S CREEK

Mary Ann Simmons . . . died July 20, 1889. She was born near Savannah, Ga., Mar. 24, 1809; was married to George Simmons Jan. 18, 1830. She joined Beulah Church and was baptised about 1837 and joined Mt. Zion Church by letter Jan. 11, 1840. MT. ZION

MINUTES OF THE TWENTY-FIRST ANNUAL SESSION OF THE BOGUE CHITTO BAPTIST ASSOCIATION, October 25, 26, 27, 1890.

Catharine Reeves . . . wife of Zachariah Reeves, died at Pike Co., Miss., May 13, 1890, aged 68 years and 10 months. She leaves a husband, 7 children. She lived and died a Christian. She united with the Baptist Church in 1856. She was taken sick Sept. 26, 1889, and suffered until death relieved her. MOAK'S CREEK

Lucinda Hall . . . was born in Coweta Co., Ga., Nov. 25, 1857; moved to this state with her widowed mother Mrs. Robertson in 1859; was married to Mr. Wiley W. Hall Nov. 18, 1874. She joined Pleasant Hill Church Aug. 13, 1876, and afterwards joined Moak's Creek Church by letter Sept. 25, 1885. She leaves a husband and 4 children. MOAK'S CREEK

Eugenia C. Martin . . . daughter of Labon and Elizabeth Moak and wife of Thomas J. Martin, died Sept. 7, 1890. She was born June 11, 1860; joined Moak's Creek Baptist Church Aug. 10, 1874. She leaves a husband and 5 little children. MOAK'S CREEK

Clara Thomas . . . died Sept. 21, 1890. She was the daughter of Fritz and Lena Lottery and wife of George W. Thomas. She was born in New Orleans Apr. 3, 1856; joined Moak's Creek Church Sept. 14, 1889. She leaves a husband and little babe. MOAK'S CREEK

Isabel Simmons Varnado . . . was born in Pike Co., Miss., Dec. 13, 1831, and died Oct. 3, 1889. She joined the Baptist Church at Mt. Zion Nov. 4, 1857. She was married to Newton B. Varnado Jan. 8, 1852. She leaves 5 sons and 5 daughters. MT. ZION

Sarah Jane Strickland . . . daughter of W. N. and Caroline Varnado, was born Nov. 19, 1851, and was married to R. C. Strickland Apr. 2, 1869. She united with Mt. Zion church and was baptised in Sept., 1872. She died Sept. 30, 1889. She leaves parents, a husband, and 8 children. MT. ZION

Jane Whaly . . . daughter of Andrew Richmond, was born in S.C., Jan. 26, 1797; moved to Miss. with her father in early life and married Mr. George Whaly. She united with the Baptist Church and remained a member until her death May 17, 1890, age 95 years. FRIENDSHIP

Victoria Barron . . . wife of Bro. Wm. Barron, was born in Amite Co., Miss., on May 20, 1838, and united with Zion Hill Baptist Church where she remained a member for 17 years, moving from that community. She united with the Tangipahoa Church by letter July 1, 1882, and died Sept. 23, 1889. She leaves a husband and others. TANGIPAHOA

Martha Everett . . . was born in Amite Co., Miss., Oct. 17, 1837; united with Mt. Zion Baptist Church, Franklin Co., Jan. 25, and received baptism by Eld. Z. Reeves. She withdrew from thence and went into the organization of the Baptist church at Tangipahoa in April, 1868, and died Feb. 17, 1890, leaving an aged mother, brothers and sisters. TANGIPAHA

Lea Wilson . . . was born near Savannah, Ga., Feb. 1, 1808, and united with Mar's Hill Baptist Church and was baptised by Eld. James Newman in July, 1882, and remained a member there until July 1, 1883. He withdrew his letter and united with the Tangipahoa Baptist Church. He died June 30, 1890. Funeral services were conducted by Eld. E. P. Douglass. He leaves an aged wife and relatives. TANGIPAHOA

James Edwards . . . was born in Amite Co., Miss., Sept. 28, 1830, and united with Tangipahoa Baptist Church in 1870; was baptised by Eld. B. A. Crawford and died Sept. 5, 1890. Funeral services were conducted by Eld. E. P. Douglass. He leaves a wife and relatives. TANGIPAHOA

Richmond Dunaway . . . died July 22, 1890, aged 82 years, 4 months, and 15 days. He was born in Augusta, Ga. After moving with his father from Ga. to Miss. in 1815, he settled in Pike Co., Miss., where he remained until his death. In 1830 he married Miss Jane Beard with whom he lived happily 59 years. God gave them 16 children. In Aug., 1843, he joined the Baptist Church at Bogue Chitto, Pike Co., Miss. BOGUE CHITTO

Patsy Gulledge . . . was born in Franklin Co., Ga., Mar. 21, 1809. Died Sept. 4, 1890, aged 87 years, 5 months and 13 days. She had 6 sons and 5 daughters, of whom 5 survive her. She united with Bogue Chitto Baptist Church in Oct., 1833. BOGUE CHITTO

B. S. Turnipseed . . . was born in Pike Co., Miss., July 6, 1846; was baptised and became a member of the Bogue Chitto Baptist Church Sept. 2, 1867. He was elected clerk of the church in Nov., 1870, and of the Bogue Chitto Association in 1874, and was ordained as deacon in Jan., 1871. He died Apr. 25, 1890. He leaves a wife and relatives. BOGUE CHITTO

Betsy Dunaway . . . died Aug. 4, 1890, was the daughter of Richmond and Jane Dunaway, and was born in Pike Co., Miss., Mar. 17, 1832. She united with the Bogue Chitto Baptist Church July 7, 1872. BOGUE CHITTO

MINUTES OF THE TWENTY-SECOND ANNUAL SESSION OF THE BOGUE CHITTO BAPTIST ASSOCIATION, September 19, 20, 21, 1891. Printed by the Weekly Gazette Book and Job Print.

Robert Harkness . . . age 68 years. He joined Zion Hill Baptist Church; then moved his membership to Mar's Hill, Amite Co., and there lived a faithful member until he joined us Aug. 4, 1888. It seems the dear old brother was destined to be alone in the world. He moved to Texas and there buried his wife and 8 children; they died of measles. He returned broken-hearted. A few years ago he married Mrs. Amanda Shadrach. She lived only a few years and he was again left with no one. MOAK'S CREEK

Elizabeth Clark . . . daughter of Thomas and Sophia Walker, and wife of Willis Clark, was born in Ga., May 13, 1809, and moved to Mississippi with her father while a child. She married Willis when she was 19. She united with Friendship Baptist Church in 1856 and lived a devoted member until her death Dec. 5, 1890, aged 82. FRIENDSHIP

Asa Boyd . . . was born Jan. 25, 1854, died Jan. 14, 1891. He joined the Baptist Church at Magee's Creek, Sept., 1871, after which he joined Salem by letter Sept. 22, 1883. He leaves a wife and 7 children. SALEM

Matilda L. Traylor . . . was born in Holmes Co., Miss., June 10, 1842; joined the church in Clinton, Miss., while at school in her 18th year. She was baptised by Eld. J. B. Hamberlam; married to Brother J. J. Traylor Dec. 9, 1863; moving to Pike Co. in 1858 and united with Holmesville Baptist Church Feb. 10, 1889. She died Jan. 14, 1891. She leaves a husband, 5 daughters and 3 sons. HOLMESVILLE

Annie Everett . . . was born near Barnwell, S.C., in 1808. She was married to Thomas Everett July 30, 1828; united with the Baptist Church at East Fork, Amite Co., Dec., 1838. She died Mar. 12, 1891. She leaves 100 children, grandchildren and great-grandchildren. TANGIPAHOA

Elizabeth Causey . . . united with the Baptist Church at Tangipahoa, Amite Co., Miss., Aug., 1878, and was baptised by Eld. T. J. Everett. She moved to Louisiana afterwards. She married Mr. Sam Galoway Jan. 7, 1882, and died Jan. 10, 1891. She leaves a husband and 5 children and a father, sisters and brothers. TANGIPAHOA

Catherine Whittington . . . wife of Bro. N. Whittington, was born in Edgefield Dist., S.C., Mar. 12, 1815. She moved to Miss. when young, united with the Baptist Church at Mar's Hill, Amite Co., Miss., Aug., 1858. She was baptised by Eld. Z. Reeves. She moved her membership to Tangipahoa Baptist Church in 1878. She died Jan. 31, 1891. She leaves a husband and relatives. TANGIPAHOA

Matilda Varnado Strickland . . . was born Dec. 17, 1814, and died Jan. 14, 1891. She was married to Jeremiah Strickland in 1834, united with Mt. Zion Church and was baptised in Mar., 1840. She left 3 sons and 2 daughters. Two sons and 3 daughters and her husband have passed away before her. MT. ZION

Nancy Jane Rhodus . . . died at her home near Osyka, Miss., Aug. 13, 1891. She was born July 11, 1859; joined Mt. Zion Church and was baptised Sept. 10, 1875. She was married to Wm. L. Rhodus Dec. 12, 1877. She leaves a husband and 3 children, a mother, brothers and sisters. MT. ZION

Margaret Hope Varnado . . . died at her home in Osyka, Miss., Sept. 1, 1891. She was born Aug. 4, 1815; was married to Isham E. Varnado, Feb. 28, 1834; was baptised into the membership of Mt. Zion Church Nov. 12, 1850. She leaves 5 sons and 3 daughters behind, 4 sons and 1 daughter having gone before her. MT. ZION

Jane Albritton . . . died Nov. 19, 1890; was born in Washington Parish, La., June 27, 1821; united with Mt. Pleasant Church Nov., 1857, and was a member until her death. She leaves one brother and one sister and relatives. MT. PLEASANT

Matilda A. Moak . . . wife of Zachariah Moak, died at her home in Lincoln Co., Miss., Jan. 30, 1891, age 34 years. She leaves a husband and six children and relatives. MT. PLEASANT

J. R. Roberts . . . was born in Pike Co., Miss., in 1850; united with Mt. Pleasant Baptist Church in Aug., 1868; was married to Frances Albritton in Dec., 1873, and died at his home in Lincoln Co., in sight of where he was born and raised on June 14, 1891. He leaves a wife and three children. Funeral services were conducted by Elder B. A. Crawford. MT. PLEASANT

H. A. Wallace . . . was born in Pike Co., Miss., Aug. 13, 1855; united with Mt. Pleasant Church July 18, 1873, and was baptised by Elder B. A. Crawford; married Adaline Maples in 1874 and died May 18, 1891. He leaves a wife and 6 children. MT. PLEASANT

Lucinthia Rushing . . . was born in Scott Co., Miss., in 1813. Her maiden name was Price. She moved to Lawrence Co. where she married Jacob Rushing. She united with Union Hall Baptist Church in 1841, where she lived a Christian until Aug., 1883. She moved her membership to Mt. Pleasant. She died in Vicksburg, Miss., Jan. 23, 1891, aged 78 years. She leaves 12 children and 176 grandchildren and great-grandchildren. MT. PLEASANT

MINUTES OF THE TWENTY-THIRD ANNUAL SESSION OF THE BOGUE CHITTO BAPTIST ASSOCIATION, September 17, 18, 19, 1892. Printed by the Weekly Gazette Book and Job Print.

C. B. Freeman . . . was born in Macon, Noxubee Co., Miss., Aug. 17, 1849. He united with the Methodist Church in June, 1865. In Nov., 1869, he began a course of study for the ministry at Summerville, Ala. In 1870 he was baptised by Rev. H. S. Valandingham into the fellowship of Macon Baptist Church and was licensed to the ministry in Aug. of the same year. He graduated from Mississippi College in 1875 and in Aug. of the same year was ordained to the full work of the ministry by Elder J. T. Freeman and Eld. Moore. On the following Nov. 17 he married Miss Katie Miller of Hazlehurst. His first pastorate was at Bastrop, La., but he accepted a position as principal of Concord Institute at Shiloh, La., in 1877. At the request of the Board of the La. State Convention, he resigned and in 1882 entered on the work of Home Missionary in the region of Alexandria. After 18 months he located at Steen's Creek as principal of a high school and as pastor of the church after which he became principal of Kavanaugh College. At our Aug. meeting he with his wife and eldest daughter united with the Holmesville Baptist Church. His last sickness dates from Feb. 10, 1892, from which he died June 11, 1892, and was buried at Hazlehurst. He leaves to survive him a wife and children besides four sisters and three brothers. METHODIST

Noah Whittington . . . was born in Amite Co., Miss., May 17, 1811, and died Oct. 13, 1891. He was received into the Tangipahoa Church by baptism in Aug., 1873. TANGIPAHOA

W. A. Rawles . . . leaves a mother, two brothers and one sister, a wife and 7 children. He was born Aug. 24, 1850, joined Shady Grove Baptist Church Sept., 1867; was married to Elizabeth Roberts Nov. 15, 1870, and moved his membership to Moak's Creek April 11, 1874. He died Mar. 8, 1892. MOAK'S CREEK

C. A. Cast . . . another of our beloved sisters. C. A. Norman was born Sept., 1852, and was married to Thomas Cast in 1869. She joined Wesson Baptist Church in 1876; joined Moak's Creek by letter July 15, 1889, where she lived until Mar. 20, 1892, when the summons came for her. She leaves a husband, children and a host of friends. MOAK'S CREEK

Mrs. Elizabeth Woolley, dau. of Daniel and Sarah McKenzie, united with Zion Hill Church in 1838, and was baptised by William Fortenberry. She was born Jan. 19, 1824, married James Wooley Jan. 18, 1840, and died Sept. 3, 1892. ZION

Charlotte Brown . . . died Dec. 16, 1891. She was born in Pike Co., Miss., Feb. 6, 1840. Her maiden name was Charlotte Felder. She first united in marriage to H. E. Thornhill on July 11, 1858. After his death she was married to Brother Thomas Rollin of Lincoln Co. in 1864. After his death she again married to Brother William Brown Dec. 31, 1878. She first united with the church at Shady Grove in Sept., 1866, after which she moved her membership to Moak's Creek Church Aug. 25, 1872. She leaves 5 children, a husband, and many relatives and friends. MOAK'S CREEK

Mary A. Andrews . . . daughter of Willis and Elizabeth Clark and wife of August Andrews, was born Jan. 22, 1835, and was raised in Pike Co., Miss. She was united with the Friendship Baptist Church Aug., 1877, and lived in honor of her profession. She died Dec. 6, 1891, 56 years of age. She leaves a husband and children. FRIENDSHIP

J. E. J. Hart . . . was born Jan. 29, 1818, in S.C. He moved to Miss. while young; married Mary Guin in 1835; and united with Mt. Pleasant Church in 1859. Soon after that time he was chosen deacon. He died May 29, 1892, at the old age of 74 years and 4 months. MT. PLEASANT

Mary Johnston . . . was born in this county Mar. 13, 1855; married Mr. R. Albritton Dec. 18, 1870, who preceded her to the grave several years. She united with Mt. Pleasant Church July, 1873, and married Bro. W. H. Johnston about 1879. She leaves a husband and 6 children to mourn her loss. She died Apr. 20, 1892. MT. PLEASANT

Martha Clark . . . was born in Amite Co., Miss., Mar. 9, 1820. Her first marriage was to Hugh Montgomery in 1838. She united with Mar's Hill Church May 6, 1843; dismissed from said church Apr., 1844; united with Mt. Pleasant Church in June, 1844. She married Wm. Clark about 1849 and died June 2, 1892, aged 71 years and 3 months. MT. PLEASANT

MINUTES OF THE TWENTY-FOURTH ANNUAL SESSION OF THE BOGUE CHITTO BAPTIST ASSOCIATION, September 16, 17, 18, 1893. Printed by The Weekly Gazette Book and Job Print.

Jesse Maxwell Price . . . son of Emanuel and Amanda Price, was born July 25, 1852; united with Moak's Creek Baptist Church in 1871; married Miss Julia Elizabeth Rollins on Dec. 14, 1871. He died July 29, 1893. He leaves a wife and 8 children and many relatives and friends. MOAK'S CREEK

Elizabeth Bowman . . . was born May 2, 1816, and died Aug. 13, 1893. She united with the Mt. Pleasant Baptist Church in July, 1841, and was baptised by Elder Zachariah Reeves. She was connected with Shady Grove, Pleasant Hill and Moak's Creek Churches by letter, the latter of which she was a member at the time of her death. She leaves a husband and son. MOAK'S CREEK

Nancy Reeves . . . was born Aug. 21, 1816, in Pike Co., Miss., and was married to Jacob Moak about 1836. He lived but a few years afterwards. She married second Wm. Reeves in 1844. She united with Mt. Pleasant Church in July, 1843, and died July 21, 1893, at the age of 77 years. She leaves 4 daughters and 2 sons. MT. PLEASANT

Zillia Ann Mullins Addison . . . was born in Pike Co., Miss., June 2, 1828; was married to Richard H. Addison Feb. 1, 1844, and soon after moved to Washington, now Tangipahoa, Parish, La. Her son's name was Bro. Richard M. Addison. She was blind for several years before her death Dec. 2, 1892, at the age of 64 years and 6 months. She leaves 5 children and a large number of grandchildren and great-grandchildren.

Mary Forrest . . . died Jan. 18, 1893. She was born in Carroll Co., Tenn., about 67 years ago. Her maiden name was Edwards. She married Bishop M. Forrest. She united with Mt. Zion Church and was baptised July 12, 1852, by Elder Jesse Crawford. MT. ZION

Lula Schilling Fortinberry . . . was born Apr. 14, 1871; baptised by her father Rev. E. M. Schilling into the fellowship of Silver Springs Church Oct. 4, 1884; married James Felder Fortinberry Mar. 24, 1888, and died Aug. 30, 1893. She leaves father, mother, sisters, husband and 3 little children. Her funeral services were conducted by Rev. J. N. Fortinberry. SILVER SPRINGS

P. C. McDaniel . . . was born in Pike Co., Miss., in 1832; married Miss Sarah Jane Schilling in 1859 and was baptized into Silver Creek Church by Rev. B. A. Crawford Aug. 26, 1860. He died July 30, 1893, leaving a wife and 7 children. SILVER SPRINGS

Angeline M. Gatlin . . . was born in Copiah Co., Miss., July 11, 1817. Her maiden name was Allen. She married W. R. Gatlin in 1834 and died July 23, 1893, at the age of 76 years and 11 days. She united with the Friendship Baptist Church Aug., 1876. The funeral was conducted by Eld. B. A. Crawford, who baptised her. She leaves 8 children, 6 sons and 2 daughters, and a number of grandchildren. FRIENDSHIP

Joseph Roberts . . . died near Johnson's Station, Miss., Apr. 21, 1892, aged 39 years, 1 month and 2 days. He was born in Pike Co., Miss., on Mar. 19, 1853. He united with Mt. Pleasant Baptist Church in July, 1873. On Aug. 5, 1877, he married Miss Julia Albritton. He leaves a wife, 5 children, a father, 2 brothers and 2 sisters. MT. PLEASANT

Aaron Banister . . . died June 30, 1893. He was born Jan. 25, 1824, and was married to Miss Elizabeth Statham, Jan. 25, 1853. He united with the Baptist Church at Mt. Hermon in Oct., 1866. He leaves a wife and 6 children. MT. HERMON

MINUTES OF THE TWENTY-FIFTH ANNUAL SESSION OF THE BOGUE CHITTO BAPTIST ASSOCIATION, September 22, 23, 24, 1894. Printed by The Semi-Weekly Gazette Book and Job Print.

James Herrington . . . was born December 15, 1829, on Myres Creek near Bogue Chitto Station, Lincoln Co., and died Oct. 1, 1893. He was married to Elizabeth Hodges Sept. 17, 1854. She died and he married Sarah M. Yarbrough Dec. 6, 1860. In 1877 she died, and he married again on Jan. 1, 1891, to Martha Rowlins. He united with the Shady Grove Baptist Church in 1850, after which he went into the constitution of the Pleasant Hill church where he remained until 1870. He went back to Shady Grove by letter and in 1873 went by letter into the Mt. Pleasant Church. He leaves a wife, 6 children and a host of friends. MT. PLEASANT

Willis Bowman . . . was born in Pike Co., Miss., Oct. 30, 1822. He died Dec. 22, 1893, aged 71 years, 1 month and 33 days. He was married to Elizabeth Price Dec. 6, 1848. He united himself with the Pleasant Hill Baptist Church Aug. 2, 1870, and was baptised by Rev. W. H. Bailey. He moved his membership to Shady Grove Church and then to Moak's Creek. He was totally blind before his death. MOAK'S CREEK

Elizabeth Hughes Rhodus . . . was born Jan. 13, 1839; married Thomas Rhodus Jan. 27, 1876, and moved from Pike Co., Miss., to Tangipahoa Parish, La. She united with Mt. Zion Church and was baptised by Eld. E. M. Schilling Aug. 7, 1890. She died July 11, 1894. She leaves 2 children, 1 grandchild, 5 brothers and 2 sisters. MT. ZION

J. Marshal Varnado . . . son of Bro. Emanuel and Sister Sarah Varnado, died Aug. 12, 1894. He was born in this county Feb. 9, 1837. He united with Mt. Zion Church and was baptised Nov. 4, 1857. He married Miss Jane V. McDaniel Jan. 12, 1860. He leaves a large family of children, brothers and sisters. MT. ZION

Thedras Scarbrough . . . was born Sept. 19, 1841. She united with Rameh Church after which she came to our church with letter in 1887. She leaves a husband and 6 children to mourn her loss. MT. PLEASANT

Mary Elizabeth Price . . . daughter of Jesse and Elizabeth Price, was born Aug. 20, 1876. She joined the Shady Grove Church Aug., 1891, and united with Moak's Creek by letter in 1892. She died Oct. 1, 1893, leaving a mother, 4 sisters, and 3 brothers to mourn her loss. MOAK'S CREEK

William Stephenson . . . died Apr. 28, 1894, in Pike Co., Miss. On May 19, 1837, he married Elizabeth Strickling. Both were baptised into the Salem, now Magnolia Baptist Church. After she died, he married Elizabeth Ballard. After she died, he married Mary E. Reagan. He leaves a widow and 17 children. When he died he was 82 years of age. Funeral services were conducted by Rev. W. P. Price. MAGNOLIA

Adline Wallace . . . was born June 17, 1855, in Amite Co., Miss. She united with Mt. Pleasant Church July 3, 1874, and was baptised by Bro. B. A. Crawford. She married H. A. Wallace in Nov., 1875. She died in Feb., 1894, leaving 6 children. MT. PLEASANT

Judith Williams . . . daughter of Richard Shateric and wife, was born Dec. 27, 1813. She married James Williams Nov. 24, 1836, and died July 16, 1894. She and her husband drew their letters from Friendship Church and united with Moak's Creek July 25, 1876. Her husband died Feb. 2, 1888. MOAK'S CREEK

Zachariah Moak . . . died Mar. 2, 1894, son of Andrew and Susan Moak. He was born Sept. 18, 1830, in Pike Co., Miss., and married Sept. 12, 1859, to Serena Brown, who with 10 children survived him. He joined Moak's Creek Baptist Church by letter Oct. 2, 1870. MOAK'S CREEK

J. D. Johnston . . . son of William and Emiline Johnston, was born in Lincoln Co., Miss., Oct. 3, 1869. He married Thedius Moak, dau. of M. M. and Frances Moak, Nov. 12, 1887. He united with the Mt. Pleasant Baptist Church July, 1886. He died Oct. 13, 1893, leaving a wife and children. MT. PLEASANT

Matilda King . . . was born in Pike Co., Miss., July 9, 1830; was married to F. M. Price Jan., 1851. She united with Mt. Pleasant Church Oct. 26, 1860, and was baptised by Eld. S. W. Bullock. She married J. F. King in 1865. She died July 18, 1894, leaving 2 sons and 1 daughter. MT. PLEASANT

MINUTES OF THE TWENTY-SIXTH ANNUAL SESSION OF THE BOGUE CHITTO BAPTIST ASSOCIATION, September 20-23, 1895. Printed by the Clarion-Ledger Printing Establishment

Lula Price . . . daughter of J. A. and Eliza Thomas, and wife of S. E. Price, died May 1, 1895, age 26 years. She married Dec. 3, 1890, and joined Moak's Creek Church Aug. 26, 1886. MOAK'S CREEK

Nancy Moak . . . was born Aug. 15, 1821; married John Moak in 1845. She joined Moak's Creek Church July 31, 1871. She died May 19, 1895, leaving 1 brother, 1 sister and a large family of children and grandchildren. MOAK'S CREEK

Ella Barron . . . dau. of Napoleon and Malissa Wilson, was born in Amite Co., Miss., Nov. 20, 1864. She joined the Tangipahoa Baptist Church in Aug., 1881; was baptised by Eld. I. Aldmand; married Bro. W. W. Barron Nov. 4, 1884; died Sept. 18, 1894. Her funeral services were conducted by Eld. J. H. Lane. She leaves a husband and 4 little children, 7 brothers, 3 sisters, and an aged mother. TANGIPAHOA

Virginia L. Causey . . . died June 15, 1895. She was born May 5, 1830, and joined the church at the age of 20. MOAK'S CREEK

Louisa Johnston . . . wife of Benton Johnston, died July, 1895. She joined Moak's Creek Church Feb. 27, 1875. She leaves a husband, 1 sister and friends to mourn her. MOAK'S CREEK

Sarah E. Traylor . . . died in Pike Co., Miss., Aug. 6, 1835. She was the dau. of Bro. J. J. and Sister Matilda Traylor. She was born in Jasper Co., Miss., Mar. 12, 1873. She came to Pike Co., Miss., in Nov., 1888, and united with Holmesville Baptist Church in Aug., 1891, baptised by Elder M. S. Shirk. She leaves her father, 3 brothers and 4 sisters. HOLMESVILLE

Bernettie Harrell . . . wife of Bro. W. J. Harrell. She was born Aug. 23, 1866; joined Mt. Sinai Baptist Church, Sept., 1888; was married to W. J. Harrell Dec. 11, 1884; united with Friendship Church by letter in May, 1894. She died Apr. 17, 1895, age 28 years, 7 months, and 26 days. She leaves a husband and 6 small children to mourn her loss. The funeral services were conducted by Rev. J. R. G. Reeves. FRIENDSHIP

Clara Jane Coney . . . died Dec. 12, 1894; was the wife of Bro. M. W. Coney, clerk of Holmesville Baptist Church. She was the dau. of Henderson and Francis Alford, born Mar. 1, 1856. She united with the Bogue Chitto Baptist Church in Aug., 1893 and was baptised by Rev. B. A. Crawford. She married Marshall W. Coney Dec. 25, 1876, and soon after united with Smyrna Church. Her funeral was conducted by Rev. A. F. Davis. She leaves a husband, 4 daughters, 1 son, mother, step-father, 7 brothers and 5 sisters. SYMRNA

Fannie J. Brown . . . died Jan. 30, 1893. She was the dau. of Huldy Brown, born in Neshoba Co., Miss., on Apr. 8, 1876. When she died, she was 17 years, 9 months, and 22 days old. She united with Vernon Church Sept., 1892, and was baptised by Eld. J. M. Hutson. She leaves a mother, 2 brothers, and 2 sisters. VERNON

Zachie Wooley . . . son of Joseph W. and Martha Wooley; was born in Lincoln Co., Miss., May 7, 1874; died Mar. 18, 1895. He united with Topisaw Church Aug. 26, and was baptised by Eld. J. H. Gambrell Aug. 10, 1890. He was 20 years, 10 months, and 11 days old when he died. He leaves a father, 1 brother and sister. TOPISAW

Eliza R. Bulloch . . . was born Oct. 5, 1829, and died Oct. 2, 1894, age 65 years. Her maiden name was Bickham. She was twice married, first to Wm. Bixler Jan. 8, 1853; then to Joseph J. Bullock Jan. 25, 1869. She joined the Methodist Church in early life and then united with the Bogue Chitto Baptist Church of La., July, 1874, from which she drew her letter and united with Topisaw Baptist Church. TOPISAW

John Kenzie Reeves . . . died Apr. 11, 1895, at the age of 36 years, 3 months, and 17 days. He was born in Pike Co., Miss., Dec. 24, 1858; moved to Lincoln Co., 1875, and was baptised into the fellowship of Moak's Creek Church by Eld. B. A. Crawford in 1878. He was married to Miss Keziah Beard Dec. 22, 1880, and moved his membership to Pleasant Hill Church in 1881; drew his letter from there and went into the constitution of Topisaw Church Nov. 13, 1882. He leaves father, mother, 5 brothers, 3 sisters, a wife and 3 children. TOPISAW

D. W. Reeves . . . was born Mar. 3, 1874, and united with Topisaw Baptist Church Aug. 31, 1890. He died Mar. 14, 1895, at the age of 21 years and 11 days. He was married to Miss Jennie Belle Wadley Dec. 23, 1894. He leaves a wife and relatives to mourn his loss. TOPISAW

Minerva Roberts . . . dau. of Wilson and Lucy Bradham, was born in Amite Co., Miss., Feb. 18, 1851; united with Terry's Creek Church; removed her membership to Mt. Pleasant Church in 1892; married James Roberts Mar., 1882. She died Sept. 10, 1895. The funeral services were conducted by Eld. B. A. Crawford. MT. PLEASANT

M. M. Moak . . . was born in Pike Co., Miss., on May 10, 1847; married Francis Sasser Jan. 2, 1865; united with Mt. Vernon Church in 1883; remained there until he moved his membership to Mt. Pleasant. He died Apr. 5, 1895. He leaves a wife and children. MT. PLEASANT

Quincy C. Shilling . . . son of E. M. and E. E. Shilling, was born June 1, 1877; died Feb. 17, 1895; was baptized into the fellowship of Silver Springs Baptist Church July, 1891. Services were conducted by Bro. J. N. Fortenberry. He leaves a father and mother, 6 brothers and 3 sisters. SILVER SPRINGS

J. D. May . . . was born Feb. 2, 1852; joined the church at Bogue Chitto, Pike Co., Miss., on July 8, 1872. Moved from there to Moak's Creek Church. He died on Apr. 14, 1894. He leaves a wife and 7 children. MOAK'S CREEK

Fielding Dunaway . . . was born May 2, 1811, joined the Bogue Chitto Baptist Church July, 1844. In 1884 he drew out and went into the organization of Enon Baptist Church. He died July 5, 1895. ENON

MINUTES OF THE TWENTY-SEVENTH ANNUAL SESSION OF THE BOGUE CHITTO BAPTIST ASSOCIATION, September 25, 26, 27, 28, 1896. Printed by the Semi-Weekly Gazette

Frank McElrath . . . was born Apr. 20, 1864; united with the McComb City Baptist Church in May, 1887; obtained a letter from said church and united with the Tangipahoa Baptist Church in Feb., 1895. He married Miss Annie Holmes July 7, 1887. He died Mar. 10, 1896. He leaves a mother, sister, wife and little son. TANGIPAHOA

Dr. Hatten Isomweathersby . . . was born in Amite Co., Miss., July 4, 1837, and died July 9, 1896. He joined Mt. Zion Baptist Church, Franklin Co., Miss., in 1866. He moved into the neighborhood of Tangipahoa Church Dec., 1895, and he and 5 children joined said church by letter Jan., 1896. He leaves 9 children. TANGIPAHOA

Hettie F. Ellzey . . . dau. of B. F. Ellzey, wife of James Felder Fortinberry; was born Apr. 4, 1872; united with Silver Springs Church May, 1896; baptized by Rev. E. M. Schilling. She died Dec. 22, 1896, age 23 years, 8 months, and 18 days. Her funeral services were conducted by Rev. E. M. Schilling. SILVER SPRINGS

William Brock, Sr. . . . was born Apr., 1840; married to Miss Clara H. Smith, Dec. 15, 1858; united with Silver Springs Church and was baptized by Rev. E. M. Schilling, Oct., 1884; died Jan. 14, 1895. He leaves a wife, children, relatives and friends. SILVER SPRINGS

Rachel Schilling . . . was born Dec. 23, 1840; joined Silver Creek Church, Aug. 24, 1858; married to ----- Smith, son of Wyatt Smith, Oct. 12, 1859. After he died in service, she married Mr. B. P. Schilling Jan. 25, 1865; died Jan. 12, 1896. She leaves husband and 7 children and 13 grandchildren to mourn her loss. Her funeral service was conducted by Rev. E. M. Schilling. SILVER SPRINGS

Cullen C. Wilson . . . son of R. S. Wilson, was born Aug. 11, 1881; united with Silver Springs Church July 3, 1895; was baptized by Rev. E. M. Schilling; died Dec. 30, 1895. He leaves his parents, brothers, sisters, relatives and friends. His funeral service was conducted by Rev. E. M. Schilling. SILVER SPRINGS

Telitha I. Sandifer . . . was born May 23, 1854, and died Sept. 1, 1896, age 42 years, 3 months and 8 days. She joined Bala Chitto Baptist Church Aug. 16, 1878; drew her letter from that church Oct., 1895, and went into the organization of Bluff Springs Church Oct. 27, 1895. She leaves an aged father and mother, 3 brothers, a sister and many relatives and friends to mourn her loss. BLUFF SPRINGS

Zillia A. Kennedy . . . wife of Bro. Robert Kennedy, was born Mar. 5, 1837; died May 7, 1896, age 59 years, 2 months and 2 days. She united with the Bala Chitto Church Oct., 1837. She leaves a husband, 7 sons, 4 daughters. BALA CHITTO

Lucie Simmons . . . dau. of Cyrus S. and Rosa Tate Simmons, was born Sept. 23, 1873. She joined Mt. Zion Church and was baptized Aug. 7, 1885. She leaves her family and relatives. BALA CHITTO

George Cater . . . died Apr. 6, 1896; was born Dec. 7, 1820; married Miss Caroline Allen in 1856. He joined the church and was baptized in Aug., 1870. He was ordained deacon which office he filled for several years. He joined Bala Chitto Church by letter in June, 1895. BALA CHITTO

Victory Kendrick . . . united with Union Church and was baptized by Eld. E. M. Schilling. She died Mar. 28, 1896. She leaves a husband and 6 children, relatives and friends. UNION

Mary Turnipseed . . . was born Mar. 26, 1843; was married to B. S. Turnipseed Dec. 20, 1864. She died Feb. 19, 1896. She joined the Bogue Chitto Baptist Church of Pike Co. in 1867 or '68 and moved her membership to Friendship Baptist Church in Mar., 1893. FRIENDSHIP

Julia Ann Wallace . . . was born Nov. 8, 1849, in Pike Co., Miss.; married Wm. Wallace Jan. 17, 1867. She was baptized by Eld. J. B. Lewis into the fellowship of Mt. Pleasant Church July, 1868. She died Sept. 22, 1885, age 45 years, 10 months, and 14 days. She leaves a husband and 9 children to mourn for her. The funeral service was conducted by Eld. Zach Loftin. MT. PLEASANT

Mrs. T. C. Welch . . . died June 8, 1896. She was born Dec. 2, 1873, and united with Mt. Pleasant Baptist Church in July, 1893. She was the dau. of Mr. G. W. and Levenia Hart. She married Mr. J. P. Welch Jan. 18, 1894. She leaves a husband, 1 child, 6 brothers, 5 sisters and relatives. MT. PLEASANT

James Jackson Sandifer . . . was born May 3, 1825; married Jane A. Rhodus Feb. 3, 1848. After she died, he married Delia E. Sandifer May 3, 1884. He died July 15, 1896. He joined Mt. Zion church and was baptized by Elder Jesse Crawford Nov. 8, 1854. He leaves a wife, 2 brothers, 1 sister. MT. ZION

MINUTES OF THE TWENTY-EIGHTH ANNUAL SESSION OF THE BOGUE CHITTO BAPTIST ASSOCIATION, September 25-27, 1897. Printed by the Semi-Weekly Gazette

Ellie Cothern . . . was born Mar. 8, 18--; united with the Enon church in 1894. She leaves a husband and 2 children, many relatives and friends to mourn her loss. ENON

Marguerite Jones Greer . . . died May 10, 1897. She was born Feb. 2, 1832, and united with Shady Grove Baptist Church, Lincoln Co. in 1866; was married to John A. Greer Feb. 8, 1849. She leaves 6 children, 40 grandchildren and 3 great-grandchildren. ENON

Lula May . . . died Aug. 21, 1897; was born Oct. 3, 1872. She was baptized into the fellowship with Bala Chitto Church by Eld. E. M. Schilling. She was married to Mr. Dan May, Mar. 18, 1888. She leaves a husband, 4 children, 1 brother, 2 sisters, relatives and friends. UNION

Telitha A. Felder . . . wife of C. C. Felder, died Apr. 24, 1897. She was one of a family of 13 children, the dau. of Isham E. and Margaret Varnado. She was born on Oct. 3, 1840 and married Columbus Felder in 1860. She leaves a husband and 6 children. She united with Mt. Zion Church and was baptized by Rev. C. F. Crawford Sept. 4, 1867. Funeral services were conducted by Rev. M. S. Shirk. UNION

Mary Williams Finch . . . died Feb. 8, 1897; was born Sept. 8, 1845; joined the Shady Grove Baptist Church, Lincoln Co., Miss., July, 1867. She was married to Bro. Joel Finch Oct. 29, 1867. She leaves a husband, 1 daughter, 3 sisters, 3 brothers. UNION

Dora Emmics . . . died June 4, 1897. She joined Tangipahoa Church in June, 1887. She leaves a husband and one child to mourn her loss. TANGIPAHOA

Mary Woodall . . . born Sept. 2, 1823, married John Reeves and then married Isichiah Woodall in Jan., 1853. She united with Mt. Pleasant Church Oct., 1834, and was baptized by Eld. L. A. Wroten. She died May 20, 1897. She leaves 8 children to mourn her. MT. PLEASANT

F. B. Erwin . . . was born in Washington Parish, La., Nov. 19, 1828; married Mary Clark in 1850. She died in 1870 leaving him with 13 children and him a cripple for life having lost a leg in the War of the States. He united with Mt. Pleasant Church in Sept., 1871; married Sarah Albritton Nov. 21, 1871. He died Dec. 18, 1896. The funeral was conducted by Eld. B. A. Crawford. He leaves a wife and 13 children to mourn for him. MT. PLEASANT

Margaret Bigner . . . was born in South Carolina Jan. 16, 1827; moved to Pike Co., Miss., in 1830; married William Bigner in 1850. She united with Mt. Pleasant Baptist Church in Aug., 1879. She died Jan. 16, 1897. She leaves 3 sons and 3 daughters to mourn for her. MT. PLEASANT

Oveta Dykes . . . dau. of Lemuel Dykes, was born July 20, 1871; joined Mt. Zion Church and was baptized by Bro. E. M. Schilling Aug. 7, 1886; married Jackson Sanders Dec. 24, 1895. She died Nov. 21, 1896. She leaves father, mother, sister, husband. MT. PLEASANT

Rev. B. W. Bullock . . . died at Summit, Miss., Nov. 27, 1896. He was born Dec. 11, 1825, in Edgefield Dist., S.C., and when about 2 years old moved to Monroe Co., Ga. In 1844 he united with Macon Baptist Church. In 1848 he moved with his parents to St. Helena Parish, La., and in 1850 to Rankin Co., Miss., where he united with Mill Creek Church by letter and was licensed to preach. He married about 1864 to Martha Huckabee and in 1867 moved his membership to Mt. Pleasant Church where he remained a member until death. He leaves a wife, four daughters and several grandchildren. MT. PLEASANT

MINUTES OF THE TWENTY-NINTH ANNUAL SESSION OF THE BOGUE CHITTO BAPTIST ASSOCIATION, September 24-26, 1898. Printed by the Semi-Weekly Gazette

Carrie Pound . . . daughter of Daniel M. and Jane Leggett Pound, died July 4, 1898, age 24 years, 5 months and 9 days. She united with Bala Chitto church and was baptized in Aug., 1889, where she remained a member until her death. She leaves her parents, brother and sisters. BALA CHITTO

Nancy Moore . . . was born Mar. 3, 1827, and died Feb. 17, 1898. She joined Friendship Church July, 1897, and leaves a host of relatives and friends. FRIENDSHIP

Adonia Ellzey . . . died Dec. 18, 1897. She was born in Hinds Co., Oct. 21, 1849, and joined the Baptist church in early life. She leaves her husband and friends to mourn for her. The funeral was conducted by Rev. E. M. Schilling. SILVER CREEK

Ben McCullough . . . died on May 10, 1898. He was born Aug. 24, 1824; was married to Sister Savilla Gunnell in 1846; joined the Bogue Chitto Baptist Church in 1849 and was baptized by Brother Zachariah Reeves; drew out of the Bogue Chitto Church and was in the organization of Shady Grove Church in 1852. He was married twice. After the death of his first wife, he married Sister A. A. Boyd, Dec., 1867. He leaves a widow and several children, grandchildren, relatives. His funeral was preached by Rev. Allmand. SHADY GROVE

Ezekiel Busby . . . was born Apr. 16, 1839, in the State of Louisiana. His parents moved to Pike Co., Miss. He joined the Shady Grove Baptist Church, Sept., 1859, and was baptized by Bro. Samuel Bullock. He was married to Sister Clarenda Hodges, Nov. 15, 1860. He died Mar. 24, 1898. He leaves a wife and 3 sons and 3 daughters. The funeral was preached by Brother B. A. Crawford. SHADY GROVE

Lizzie Johnston . . . died Apr. 10, 1898. She was the dau. of B. F. and Virginia Clark and was born Mar. 22, 1873. She married W. C. Johnston Oct. 22, 1889. She united with Mt. Pleasant Church July, 1889. She leaves her family, husband and children. The funeral service was conducted by Eld. J. L. Price. MT. PLEASANT

Caroline Thornhill . . . was born Oct. 23, 1882. She united with Enon Church in 1895; married J. P. Thornhill Feb. 14, 1897, and died Sept. 12, 1898. She leaves a husband and one child. ENON

MINUTES OF THE THIRTIETH ANNUAL SESSION OF THE BOGUE CHITTO BAPTIST ASSOCIATION, September 23, 24, 25, 1899. Printed by the Semi-Weekly Gazette

Jordan Dykes . . . died Feb. 23, 1899; was born in Tangipahoa Parish, La., Mar. 4, 1821; married Angeline Smith Hope Jan. 6, 1849. He united with Mt. Zion Church and was baptized July 14, 1852. He leaves a wife, children, relatives and friends. MT. ZION

Emma Dickey Sandifer . . . was born May 19, 1869; joined Mt. Zion Church and was baptized Aug. 7, 1885; married Dr. H. W. Sandifer Dec. 23, 1885; died at her home in Pike Co., Miss., Mar. 25, 1899. She leaves a husband, brothers, relatives and friends to mourn for her. MT. ZION

N. B. Varnado . . . died April 15, 1899. He was born June 26, 1827, in Pike Co., Miss.; married Miss Isabel Simmons Jan. 8, 1852, and was the father of 12 children. He was baptized into the fellowship of Mt. Zion Church Oct. 11, 1860. He leaves a brother, sister, children and grandchildren. MT. ZION

Zachariah Reeves . . . was born Jan. 3, 1829; married Catharine Moak Dec. 10, 1846. He united with Friendship Church and was baptized by Elder Wilson Clark in Aug., 1855. He dismissed from Friendship and united with Mt. Pleasant in Feb., 1856; was ordained deacon July, 1857; dismissed from Mt. Pleasant and returned to Friendship in Apr., 1859; dismissed from Friendship and united with Moak's Creek in Mar., 1882; and in 1892 withdrew from Moak's Creek and again united with Mt. Pleasant. He died July 15, 1899, at the age of 70 years, 6 months and 12 days. After the death of his wife, he married Amanda Alexander, Dec. 9, 1890. His funeral was conducted by Eld. J. L. Price. MT. PLEASANT

Sarah Prestridge . . . died Dec. 17, 1899. She was born Nov. 1, 1814; united with Fair River Church; moved her membership to Mt. Pleasant in Jan., 1858. She married Elijah Prestridge Sept. 23, 1832. The funeral was conducted by Elder B. A. Crawford. MT. PLEASANT

Ideller Brown . . . dau. of Matthew and Mary Albritton, who was born July 31, 1874. She united with Mt. Pleasant Church July, 1890, and was baptized by Elder Zachariah Lofton. She married Franklin Brown Apr. 29, 1897, and died Sept. 8, 1898. She leaves a husband, 1 sister and a host of relatives and friends. MT. PLEASANT

David Coon . . . was born Nov. 20, 1841; was married to Sophronia Reeves Jan. 16, 1868; united with the Mt. Pleasant Church July, 1886. He died Nov. 14, 1898. He leaves a wife and 9 children. The funeral service was conducted by Elder B. A. Crawford. MT. PLEASANT

Eliza Jane Fortinberry . . . dau. of John and Elizabeth Ellzey, was born in Pike Co., Miss., Sept. 5, 1830; married to Burl T. Fortinberry, Aug. 15, 1850; united with Silver Creek Church Aug. 26, 1858; died April 3, 1899. Her funeral service was conducted by Rev. Willis J. Fortinberry. She leaves her sons, brothers, sisters, and friends to mourn for her. SILVER SPRINGS

Mary A. May . . . was born in Simpson Co., Miss., in 1856; joined the Baptist Church at Bogue Chitto, La., and was baptized by Rev. E. M. Schilling in 1873; married to P. W. Pierce Nov. 2, 1876. Her husband P. W. Pierce died in 1887. She married again to Brother A. G. May, Nov. 14, 1889. She died Oct. 14, 1898, leaving a husband, 3 children, and relatives. SILVER SPRINGS

Mary Alice Walker . . . daughter of Bro. W. R. and Sallie Walker, was born Oct. 28, 1871, and died Dec. 8, 1898. She united with Bala Chitto Baptist Church in Aug., 1887, and was baptized by Eld. T. C. Schilling. She leaves parents, brothers, sister and friends. BALA CHITTO

Hampton E. Walker . . . was born July 20, 1873, and died June 13, 1899. He leaves a wife and one child and many relatives. He united with Bala Chitto Baptist Church in Aug., 1893, and was baptized by Bro. T. C. Schilling. The funeral was conducted by Bro. W. K. Red. BALA CHITTO

Francis Simmons . . . was born Aug. 1, 1824, in Lowndes Co., Ala. She married Reuben Simmons in 1844. She joined the Methodist order at the age of 18 but connected herself with the Baptist Church at Line Creek, Amite Co., Miss., and finally moved her membership to Union Church, Pike Co., Miss. She died Oct. 18, 1898. Funeral services were conducted by Eld. J. M. Hutson. She leaves an aged and afflicted husband, 4 sons and 2 daughters. UNION

I. M. Phelps . . . died Feb. 24, 1899. He was born in Alabama, Jan., 1821; moved to Mississippi and married Miss Caroline Parker. After she died, he married Mrs. Annie Land in Feb., 1865. He was baptized in fellowship with Bala Chitto church by Eld. E. M. Schilling, 1873. In 1892 he drew a letter and organized with Union church. He leaves an aged and broken hearted companion and 7 children. UNION

Mamie Stella Curtis . . . died July 25, 1899, age 22 years, 5 months, and 19 days. She was born in Pike Co., Miss., and joined the Friendship Baptist Church in July,

1892. The funeral was conducted by her paster, Bro. S. W. Sibley. She leaves her parents. FRIENDSHIP

Margaret F. Reeves . . . dau. of Elijah J. Reeves, was born Dec., 1860, in Pike Co., Miss., and married Thomas G. Warner Jan. 4, 1877. She died Sept. 4, 1899, the mother of 7 children. She united with the Baptist church at Friendship, Pike Co., Miss., Aug., 1879. She leaves a husband and children. FRIENDSHIP

Sarah Elizabeth Jones . . . wife of Bro. J. M. Jones and dau. of Rev. John Wroten and Mrs. Judy Pate, was born in Mississippi in 1842. She married Mr. Joseph Whittington in 1858. After he died, she married J. M. Jones. She died Oct. 25, 1898. She joined the church at Friendship, Pike Co., Miss., in 1887, and was baptized by Rev. Isaiah Allmand. She leaves a husband and 10 children. FRIENDSHIP

Margaret Causey . . . dau. of Willis and Elizabeth Clark, was born Oct. 12, 1848; married to W. S. Causey some 24 years ago. She was baptized into the fellowship of the Summit Baptist Church Nov. 21, 1863. In 1881 she united by letter with Friendship Baptist Church. She died Aug. 21, 1898. FRIENDSHIP

W. J. Price . . . was born Mar. 13, 1833; married M. J. Hart, Dec. 25, 1856. He joined the church at Mt. Moriah July, 1858; from thence he moved to Pleasant Hill and from there to Moak's Creek in the organization of that church where he lived a member and deacon until his death Apr. 7, 1899. He leaves a wife and 7 children. MOAK'S CREEK

Delitha Laurence . . . was born Sept., 1866. She united with Enon church in 1891. She died in 1899. ENON

Fannie Rayborn . . . was born Mar. 29, 1878. She united with Enon church in 1893 and remained there until her death. She leaves a husband and one child. ENON

Webster McKenzie . . . died Mar. 9, 1899. He was the son of Bro. John T. and Sister Jane McKenzie. He was born Mar. 2, 1874, and joined Salem Baptist Church July 23, 1894, and was baptized by Rev. C. P. Shepard. The funeral service was conducted by Rev. A. F. Davis. SALEM

George B. Marshall . . . was born on St. Helena Island May 28, 1824. He was married to Mary A. Edwards Jan. 24, 1867, and united with the Tangipahoa Baptist Church, Dec., 1885, and was baptized by A. G. Felder. TANGIPAHOA

D. B. Brewer . . . died Sept. 1, 1899. He was born June 17, 1861, in Washington Parish, La., and moved with his parents to Pike Co., Miss. He joined the Society Hill Baptist Church in Aug., 1879; moved his membership to Silver Springs Church in Nov., 1891, and again in July, 1897, moved his membership to Bluff Springs Church. He married Olivia J. Webb, Oct. 18, 1888. He leaves a wife, 5 children. BLUFF SPRINGS

MINUTES OF THE THIRTY-FIRST ANNUAL SESSION OF THE BOGUE CHITTO BAPTIST ASSOCIATION, September 22, 23, 24, 1900. Printed by the Enterprise Steam Print

B. A. Crawford . . . was 72 years of age and had spent the greater part of his life in the Gospel ministry, having united with the Baptist Church in early life. MONTGOMERY

Sarah Branch . . . wife of Bro. H. M. Branch, died at Vossburg Springs, June 24, 1900. She was about 30 years of age, the mother of 8 children, 2 of whom preceded her and one who died since her death. She leaves her husband and 5 children. She was born in Amite Co., Miss., about 1870, and joined Mars Hill church in early life. In Aug., 1899, she joined Friendship Baptist Church by letter and remained a member until her death. FRIENDSHIP

Olive Reeves . . . dau. of Wm. and Sarah McCullouge, was born near Felders Campground, Pike Co., Miss., June 15, 1829. She was one of a family of 21 children, some 17 of whom preceded her to yonder's World. She married Jesse J. Reeves, Dec. 28, 1848, and had 12 children. She died Jan. 13, 1900. The funeral was conducted by Rev. S. W. Sibley, her pastor. FRIENDSHIP

Katie Brown . . . was the dau. of Washington and Lavenia Hart, born Nov. 16, 1886; united with Mt. Pleasant Baptist Church Mar. 23, 1890; died Apr. 1, 1900. She leaves a husband and 8 children, 6 brothers and 4 sisters to mourn for her. MT. PLEASANT

Cintha Brown . . . married J. I. Brown, Dec. 5, 1850. She was born Jan. 28, 1830, and died Nov. 6, 1899. She united with the Mt. Pleasant Church Sept. 22, 1860, and was baptized by S. W. Bullock. In 1894 she drew her letter and joined the Montgomery Church where she remained until her death. She leaves a husband, 2 brothers, 11 children, 51 grandchildren, and 2 great-grandchildren, and 3 sisters. MT. PLEASANT

Janie Hart . . . was born Feb. 12, 1870, in Lincoln Co., Miss.; married J. L. Hart, Dec. 15, 1888. She united with Mt. Pleasant Church, July 17, 1887, and was baptized by Eld. Zack Lofton. She died Jan. 18, 1900. She leaves a husband and children. MT. PLEASANT

Mattie Stoks Eaton . . . died May 8, 1900; was born Oct. 30, 1860. She married Rube Eaton, Jan. 1, 1880; joined the Baptist church at Mt. Moriah, Lincoln Co., July, 1880. Afterwards she placed her membership in Shady Grove Baptist Church. Her funeral was conducted by Rev. I. B. Anding. She leaves a husband and 4 children. SHADY GROVE

Emily Coney . . . Grandma Coney as she was called was born Sept. 1, 1816, and died Nov. 30, 1899, age 83 years, 2 months and 29 days. She joined Rocky Creek Baptist Church, Nov., 1852. She leaves 3 sons and 5 daughters. BALA CHITTO

Adam Bacot . . . was born Jan. 14, 1834. He married Miss Jane Sibley and united with Enon Church and was baptized July 4, 1896. He died Jan. 4, 1900, leaving a large family and a host of friends. ENON

MINUTES OF THE THIRTY-SECOND ANNUAL SESSION OF THE BOGUE CHITTO BAPTIST ASSOCIATION, September 21, 22, 23, 1901

Van Crawford Coney . . . died June 26, 1901, age 60 years, 7 months, and 16 days. He joined Salem Church and was baptized Aug. 24, 1860. He went into the organization of Bala Chitto Church, Oct. 12, 1873. He married Miss P. A. Dickey, Mar. 21, 1867. He leaves a wife to mourn his loss. BALA CHITTO

Maggie Pound Holmes . . . Maggie E., youngest dau. of Daniel M. and Jane Pound, was born July 31, 1876, and died May 3, 1901. She joined Bala Chitto Church and was baptized by Rev. T. C. Schilling in Aug., 1891. She married Mr. B. Oscar Holmes, Jan. 7, 1895. She leaves 2 daughters, a husband, father and mother, one brother and 3 sisters to mourn for her. BALA CHITTO

Hinton Cade Weathersby . . . was born on June 4, 1879. In Aug., 1897, he united with the Tangipahoa Baptist Church where he remained until his death, Feb. 13, 1901. He leaves his orphan brothers and sisters to mourn for him. TANGIPAHOA

Ester Magee . . . died April 20, 1901. She was born May 31, 1829, in Marion Co., Miss., and joined the Baptist church in early life where she remained until her death. She married Willis Magee Dec. 6, 1849. At the time of her death, she was a member of Smyrna Church. She leaves 3 sons and 2 daughters, 2 step-sons and 1 step-daughter. SMYRNA

Sarah Lang . . . whose maiden name was Phelps, was born in Newton Co., Miss., Nov. 30, 1853, and died July 30, 1901. She married W. P. Lang Sept. 20, 1868. She united with Bala Chitto Church in 1872, was baptized by Rev. E. M. Schilling, drew a letter from Bala Chitto and came in the constitution of Union Church. She leaves a husband and 6 children and 3 sisters. UNION

Theodocia McDaniel . . . died Apr. 12, 1901. She was born in Amite Co., Miss., Nov. 8, 1830, and was married to Winston McDaniel, Dec. 12, 1849. She united with old Salem Church, was baptized by Rev. Calvin Magee Apr., 1851, and was received into the Mt. Zion church by letter May 1, 1858. She leaves 10 children, grandchildren, and relatives. MT. ZION

Susan R. Schilling . . . died Dec. 1, 1900. She was born Jan. 18, 1837; married to John B. Schilling Dec. 10, 1854. Nine children were born to them, seven of whom are living and are members of our church. She was baptized by Rev. Willis Fortenberry and went into the constitution of the Mt. Hermon church Dec. 12, 1863; was dismissed from that church by letter July 12, 1890, and was received into the Mt. Zion Church

Aug. 2, 1890. She leaves her children, grandchildren, and relatives to mourn for her. MT. ZION

Lona Sandifer . . . was born Jan. 9, 1868, joined Mt. Zion Church Aug. 8, 1885; married to J. H. Sandifer Dec. 22, 1886; moved her membership to Bluff Springs, Nov. 24, 1895; died Oct. 24, 1900. She leaves a husband and two children. The funeral service was conducted by Rev. E. M. Schilling. BLUFF SPRINGS

D. E. Sandifer . . . was born July 24, 1861; joined Union Church Sept. 7, 1880; married J. J. Sandifer, May 3, 1884; moved her membership to Mt. Zion Nov. 1, 1884, and thence to Bluff Springs Sept. 6, 1896. She married B. F. Simmons and died Feb. 28, 1901. She leaves a husband and two children. BLUFF SPRINGS

MINUTES OF THE THIRTY-THIRD ANNUAL SESSION OF THE BOGUE CHITTO BAPTIST ASSOCIATION, September 26, 27, 28, 29, 1902.

Alice Jackson, Tangipahoa
Cordelia Wood, Mt. Zion
Emanuel Price, Celistine Price, and Frank Brown, Moak's Creek
Martha Jane Gulledge, Rebecca Beard and Courtney Boyd, Bogue Chitto
Matilda Templeton, Mt. Pleasant
W. D. Cony, May Simmons, and Caroline Kavanaugh, Bala Chitto
Mary Starkey, Bro. M. A. Reeves, Topisaw
Brother James M. Jones, Friendship
Bro. Louis Fortenberry, Sisters Ophelia Walls, and Milly Morris, Silver Springs
Bro. Jesse L. Yawn, Holmesville
Sister Susan West, Union
Sisters Margret Ellzey, Emily Bearden, Smyrna
Sister Louminda Sandifer, Bluff Springs
Sister Julia Bell Reeves and Bro. Emanuel Moak, Montgomery
Mrs. J. I. Cain, Mrs. Hailey, Mrs. S. Akers, McComb
Sisters Fannie Stockdale, Sophronia Andrews, Summit
Sister Sarah E. Heley, East McComb

MINUTES OF THE THIRTY-FOURTH ANNUAL SESSION OF THE BOGUE CHITTO BAPTIST ASSOCIATION, September 26-28, 1903. Printed by the Enterprise Steam Print

Deaths reported:

William Brown and Elizabeth Montgomery, Moak's Creek
Mary Clark, Sarah Greer and Virgil Conn, Shady Grove
Elizabeth Crittenden, Whitestown
Reuben Simmons and S. E. Pittman, Union
Ella L. Allen, Bluff Springs
Miss Mattie Cook, South McComb
Mary Yawn and Willie Walker, Holmesville
Josephine Walters, Courtney Alexander, Louisa Beard and Permelia M'Manus, Bogue Chitto
Ida Gill Price and Mrs. T. E. Gill, Magnolia
John D. Simmons, Silver Creek
Sister Able, J. A. Beard and Mrs. C. S. Sternbuger, McComb City
Mary Pate, Sophronia Andrews, Dr. R. E. Gatlin, Dr. W. H. Reuben, Summit
Joel Moak, Friendship

MINUTES OF THE THIRTY-FIFTH ANNUAL SESSION OF THE BOGUE CHITTO BAPTIST ASSOCIATION, September 22, 23, 24, 1904. Printed by the Enterprise Steam Print

Sister A. S. Brent, Jesse Greer, I. R. Hodges, Shady Grove
Sophronia Simmons, Angeline Dykes, Eugene Wall, Mt. Zion
Abraham Roberts, Wade Roberts, Sarah Coon, Rosa May, and Angeline Thomas, Moak's
    Creek
John W. May and Elizabeth May, Bogue Chitto
Mrs. E. M. Baugh, Mrs. Mahala Pendarvis, Mrs. Jane R. Cutrer, Mrs. N. E. Walker, and
    John A. Walker, Magnolia
J. M. Sutton, James A. Moak, Cleveland Wallace, Sophrona Coon, and Moses Rushing,
    Mt. Pleasant
John Cothern, Enon

Robert Kennedy, Bala Chitto
Mr. J. E. Booty and Liddia Simmons, Silver Springs
Della Traylor Comfort and D. C. Walker, Holmesville
Oscar Quin, Elizabeth Breland, and Myrtis Rushing, Salem
Annie A. Philips and Annie May, Union
L. T. Bullock, James Bearden, and Lula Bearden, Smyrna
Clara Miller, Feliciana Webb, Bluff Springs
Emma A. Porter, Johnson
Miss Roberta Givens, East McComb
W. W. Williams, James McDaniel, and Mrs. A. Frith, South McComb

MINUTES OF THE THIRTY-SIXTH ANNUAL SESSION OF THE BOGUE CHITTO BAPTIST ASSOCIATION, October 19, 20, 21, 1905. Printed by the Enterprise Print

Leona Barron, D. H. Jackson, Tangipahoa
J. F. Burkhalter, Emmett F. Simmons, and Sister Arkansas Brumfield, Silver Creek
Sister Mary Williams, Moak's Creek
Sister Rhoda McKelvin Hagg, Bogue Chitto
Henry Roberts, Magnolia
W. N. Varnado, S. S. McElveen, and Sister Katie McElveen, Mt. Zion
D. M. Pound, D. Write Pound, and Sister Lula Reagan, Balachitto
Willie Boyd, Elisha Thornhill, Sister Elevia Talbot and Sister Lura Alexander, Enon
J. J. Reeves and John Pierce, Friendship
B. F. Ellzey, Sisters Sarintha Ellzey, Clarenda Brock and Lois Brumfield, Silver Springs
Bledso Addison, T. W. Lea, Chas. Penny, J. B. Gill, J. D. Cutrer and Sisters Julia Addison, Mattie Ott, and Sarah Cutrer, Osyka
Joseph Bearden, Smyrna
Fleet Fortenberry, Sister Christina Breland, Bluff Springs
Sisters E. D. Solomon and Mary A. Bolling, McComb
Sister E. A. Porter, Johnston
Dewitt Smith, South McComb

MINUTES OF THE THIRTY-SEVENTH ANNUAL SESSION OF THE BOGUE CHITTO BAPTIST ASSOCIATION, October 26, 27, 28, 1906. Printed by the Enterprise Print

Sarah A. Moak, Tangipahoa
A. J. Coghlin and Miss Carrie Eaton, Shady Grove
Jane Brock Simmons, Silver Creek
P. X. Simmons, L. W. Simmons, Isaac Rhodus, Mt. Zion
Emily Walker, Bogue Chitto
Mary V. Blount and Francis E. Garner, Magnolia
A. C. Wooley, Mt. Pleasant
D. M. Walker, Malissa Allmand, Balachitto
James Reid, Lottie Cothern, Susie Tolbert, Enon
Esther Gunnels, Friendship
Cathern Bearden, Smyrna
Mrs. T. J. Zealy, Mrs. Vernon Robbins, Mrs. J. B. Alford, Rosa Robinson, McComb 1st.
Mrs. V. P. Mercier, Johnston
Victoria McKennon, East McComb
James R. Davis, Bell Pope, Minerva Crawford, Marshal Booty, Tylertown

MINUTES OF THE THIRTY-EIGHTH ANNUAL SESSION OF THE BOGUE CHITTO BAPTIST ASSOCIATION, October 23, 24, 25, 1907. Printed by the Enterprise Print

John G. Leggett Sr., Oscar Alford, Silver Creek
Elisha Beard, Bogue Chitto
Louise C. Simmons, Union
Nora Johnson, Salem
Sophia Reeves, Frank Boggs, John Boggs, Friendship
Emily Richmond, Viola Dunaway, Smyrna
W. H. Ellzey, Nancy Lyles, East McComb
Lula McGehee, Mt. Zion
J. W. Thornhill, Tylertown
Sister M. J. Kennedy, Bluff Springs
Seth J. Coney, Martha Tull, Hiram G. Lambert, Magnolia

Emily Ellzey, Lizzie Schilling, Josephine Fortinberry, Mary Ellzey, Emma A. Schilling,
   Silver Springs
D. M. Redmond, Jennie Cutrer, Susie Carsey, Osyka
Hattie McNulty, Summit
Webster Albritton, Ophelia Albritton, Annie Wooley, Hester Alfred, Mt. Pleasant
Wm. L. Dickey, Clementine Magee, Monroe Johnson, Bala Chitto
Robert Andrews, Sister Rebecca Harrison, W. D. Robbins, McComb 1st
Sister S. M. Wilson, South McComb

John G. Leggett, Sr., . . . was born in Pike Co., Miss., Sept. 25, 1831, and died
Aug. 13, 1907. He spent his life in his native county except the time he was in the
Civil War. He united with Silver Creek Church Aug., 1851, where his membership
remained until his death. He was in the organization of the Bogue Chitto Assoc.,
Oct. 22, 1870, and was the first clerk. He served as county supervisor, as a member
of the school board, and in the state legislature. On May 26, 1857, he married Miss
Mary Simmons, who died some years ago. To their union were born ten children, five
of whom survive their parents. SILVER CREEK

MINUTES OF THE THIRTY-NINTH ANNUAL SESSION OF THE BOGUE CHITTO BAPTIST ASSOCIATION,
October 22, 23, 1908. Printed by the Enterprise Print

J. W. Bales, R. L. Smith and R. D. Weathersby, Tangipahoa
Ester Price, Lonore McCullough, Lourend Busby and Fred Greer, Shady Grove
Judson McDaniel, Mettie McKenney, Silver Creek
S. O. Simmons, J. M. Forrest, Rachael Simmons, L. Ann Rhodus and S. Jane Varnado,
   Mt. Zion
Martha Coon, Moak's Creek
S. C. Boyd and Lucy Norman, Bogue Chitto
Lorinda Martin, Nelson Webb, Martha Walker, Magnolia
O. S. Dunaway, Enon
Mollie Sanders, Silver Springs
Mary Shirk, Osyka
W. E. Sandifer, N. E. Kennedy, Bluff Springs
T. J. Clark, Mrs. W. A. Knight, Mrs. A. J. Hackett, Z. T. Terrell, Ben F. Alvarez
   and R. B. May, McComb 1st
Horace N. Porter, Johnston
Martha Bales, South McComb
Macy Dunaway, Navilla
Lottie Conerly, Tylertown
Fanny Dickerson, Emma Clark and Trusie Hart, Mt. Pleasant

MINUTES OF THE FORTIETH ANNUAL SESSION OF THE BOGUE CHITTO BAPTIST ASSOCIATION,
October 21, 22, 23, 1909

Mrs. S. E. Dickey, E. T. Wall, Tate Lea, Osyka
Yancy White, Susan Finch, East McComb
W. G. Melton, Bluff Springs
W. L. Coney, Bennie F. Holmes, Johnston Station
C. R. Cook, Mrs. Elizabeth Cartalan, South McComb
Susan Rayborn, Elizabeth Gulledge, Bogue Chitto
Jas. Costley, Jno. H. Marsh, Mrs. S. H. McDonald, Summit
Samantha E. Simmons, Mt. Zion
Deacon Chas. Galvant, Mrs. Ida G. Jones, Magnolia
Dorothy Strickland, Ollie W. Alford, Bala Chitto
Courtney Ann Boyd, Enon
Viola Moak, Tangipahoa
Wallace Greer, Shady Grove
William Reeves, Moak's Creek
Hester Boyd, Tylertown
Mrs. N. R. Hemphill, Mrs. M. H. Richardson, Mrs. C. R. Hodges, Ruby Brewer,
   Dr. J. H. Plunkett, McComb City
Needham Holmes, Holmesville

MINUTES OF THE FORTY-FIRST ANNUAL SESSION OF THE BOGUE CHITTO BAPTIST ASSOCIATION, October 20, 21, 22, 1910. Printed by the Enterprise Print

Sisters Arminda M. McCullough, Inez Greer, Shady Grove
Sisters Mary Ann Rhodus, Delia White, Bro. M. M. Simmons, Mt. Zion
W. A. Moak, Moak's Creek
A. S. Walker, Rachel A. Brewer, Bogue Chitto
Mrs. Martha Hodges, Miss Florence M. Daniel, Magnolia
Sister Ann Brown, Bros. Esaac May and Wiley Brown, Mt. Pleasant
H. D. Strickland, Telitha Slaven, Belle Allen, Balachitto
Louranie Thornhill, Enon
Annie Curtis, Friendship
Dr. L. M. Quin, Holmesville
Mrs. O. S. Magee, Edgar Spears, Osyka
Alice Bullock, Victoria Thornhill, Smyrna
Bro. C. L. Simmons, Sisters Josephine Rayborn, Mary Williams, Bluff Springs
R. H. Hays, F. M. Lee, Sister May Sutphen, Dr. J. W. Naul, McComb, First Church
Dr. B. F. Holmes, Johnston
Bro. J. W. Cotton, Sister Golda Haley, East McComb
T. U. Gill, Cain Smith, South McComb
Nettie Erwin, Navilla
Mrs. Lizzie Dykes, East Fork
Oscar Rime, Norris Davis, Tylertown
J. C. Lang, Mary Lang, Union
Brothers F. Marion Boyd, J. W. Brumfield, Silver Creek
Brothers W. W. Boyd, J. M. Boyd, Salem

Rev. Theodore C. Schilling . . . died Mar. 3, 1910. He was born in Washington Parish, La., Jan. 23, 1853; joined Mt. Herman Baptist Church in 1870; was licensed in 1873 and ordained in 1876. On Feb. 3, 1876, he was married to Angie D. James, who with five sons and three daughters survive him. Bro. Schilling was elected vice-president of the Mississippi Baptist Convention in 1895 and was a member of the State Mission Board for some time. MT. HERMON

MARRIAGES AND DEATHS (OBITUARIES) ABSTRACTED FROM THE
NEW ORLEANS CHRISTIAN ADVOCATE,
(the official organ for the Methodist Church)
For Pike County, Mississippi, 1853 to 1910

1853 Germany/Gatlin: Rev. B. B. Whittington md. 5/10/1853, Rev. Willis H. Germany
      to Miss Martha E. Gatlin of Pike Co., Miss.

1855 Ellzey/Barr: Rev. John A. B. Jones md. 3/1/1855 at Holmesville, Miss., Mr.
      DeWitt Ellzey to Amanda Sophia Palatiah Pulmoglover Barr of Pike Co., Miss.

1856 Rask/Elliott: Rev. Calvin McGee md. 4/15/1856, R. S. Rask M.D. of Lunenburg
      Co., Va., to Miss Elizabeth Elliott of Pike Co., Miss.

1859 Leney/Ellezy: Rev. A. B. Nicholson md. the 7th Inst (Aug?) 1859, Rev. James
      H. Leney of the Miss. Conf. to Miss Caroline A. Ellezy of Pike Co., Miss.

1859 Connerly, Rev. Luke, d. of consumption of La., Sabine Parish, at his res.
      9/8/1859, aged 66 years. He was beloved by his friends. He was willing to
      die. He said to his wife, not long before he died, he would soon be where he
      would have the best of society, while she would be so lonely; but not to grieve,
      for they would soon meet again. He was sick about five weeks. He left a wife
      and a large number of friends to mourn.

2/15/1860 Farmer/Lee: the 25th Inst. at the res. of Noble Lee, William M. Farmer
           of Copiah Co., md. Miss Sophronia Lee of Pike Co., Miss.

2/15/1860 Foxworth, Nancy, wife of Samuel G. d. 2/10/1860, b. Jan. 22, 1810. She
           left 9 sons, son died 5 days later on 2/16/1860 (name not given).

1860 Ligon, Angeline E., wife of R. B. Ligon Esqr., d. at Summit, Miss., 3/14/1860.
      B. in Pike Co., 3/12/1820, dau. of Jermiah Bearden. She md. Ligon on 2/11/1841
      and joined Meth. Ch. in 1846. (Nashville papers were requested to copy)

1860 Wilson/Thompson: Tues. the 3rd Inst. (April?), at res. of bride's father
      Hardy Thompson, Esqr., by Rev. H. J. Harris, Mr. Joseph B. Wilson to Miss
      Malissa J. Thompson, all of Pike Co.

1860 Conerly, Owen d. in Pike Co. 6/2/1860, aged 42 years.

1860 Alford, Sophia Elizabeth dau. of Seaborn and Mary Alford b. 4/20/1842, md.
      J. Williams on 12/14/1858, d. 4/12/1860, in Pike Co.

1/19/67 Thompson, Hardy: d. at his Pike Co. res. on 11/26/1866, b. Georgia 2/5/
         1802, moved to Miss. in 1818 with his parents; md. Nancy McMorris in Amite
         Co., and removed to Pike.

1868 Downer, Mrs. C. M.: d. Oct. 10, 1868, at her res. at Forest Home, Pike Co.,
      Miss., aged 66 years. Note about her death in a subsequent issue (10/11/1868)
      written by her son Rev. Robert B. Downer. She d. 10 min. past 3 p.m.

1869 Sibley, Mrs. Mary: mother of 10 chld. (7 sons, 3 daus) all of whom survive
      except oldest and youngest sons; d. 12/3/1868. Signed by R. A. Sibley.

1870 Finch, Bro. Sidney: d. at Holmesville 2/11/1870, aged 21 yrs. 10 mos., 16 days.
      Converted last summer by Rev. R. B. Downer.

8/10/1871 May, John: d. Fri. 6/30/1871, in Summit, 59 yrs. old, native of Germany
           b. in Great Hoosen on 5/1/1813; came to U.S. when 26 and converted to Methodism
           in New Orleans. Left wife and child.

9/28/1871 King, Mrs. Ann: dau. of Aaron and Jemima Spell of Pike Co., Miss.,
           b. 8/24/1822, md. William L. King of Holmes Co., 5/25/1838, mvd. to Yazoo Co.
           in 1845 where she d. 10/19/1871.

10/19/1871 Neusome, Sister (name not given), of Summit, d. 8/7/1871; b. Amite Co., Miss., 8/4/1808.

11/30/1871 Haynes, Mrs. Delia, d. at Summit 10/19/1871, dau. of Robert & Eliza McCoy, b. in New Orleans 5/19/1822, mvd. to Pike Co. where she md. Bythell Haynes on 10/21/1847, of Clinton, La. Subsequent obit. stated that she left one dau., Eliza wife of H. Q. Bridges.

1871 Guy/Martin: At res. of bride's father in Pike Co. on 11/23/1871, Louis Guy of Amite Co., to Sarah Martin.

1871 Richmond/Dickey: At res. of bride's father 11/13/1871, A. R. Richmond to Miss A. E. Dickey, all of Pike Co.

2/22/1872 Murray: d. near Magnolia 1/6/1872, son of Rev. Wesley and the late Mrs. Louisa Sandell Murray, aged 14 yrs--ran over by a team-driven vehicle.

2/22/1872 Gray/Barr: Md. 2/8/1872 at res. of W. B. Ligon in E. Baton Rouge Parish, La., by Rev. William H. Leith, Ruffin A. Gray and Mollie W. Barr.

4/11/1872 Lowery, Mary Angeline, d. in Claiborne Parish, La., 1/25/1872, aged 41 years, dau. of William O. & Sarah Bullock, b. in Pike Co., Miss.; moved to Claiborne Parish when young; md. George W. Lowery in 1850.

11/28/1872 Barr, Sister Mart A., wife of R. W. Barr of Pike Co., dau. of J. B. & Mahala Lewis, b. 2/11/1837, d. 9/25/1872; md. 1/20/1857; joined Meth. Ch. in 1859. D. at 15 till 3 A.M. (H. P. Lewis)

2/13/1872 Brown, Mrs. Margaret E., wife of Wiley, dau. of Jesse & Mary E. Edwards, b. Pike Co., 8/16/1831, d. of pneumonia 1/21/1873; md. 10/24/1854; jnd. ch. in fall of 57; conv. in 1863; left 4 children. (By N. B. Brown of E. Baton Rouge Parish, La.)

1873 Yarborough, Rebecca Clark, b. in S.C. 12/30/1797; mvd. to Ga.; md. Wm. Yarborough in 1812; mvd. to Marion Co., Miss., in 1818; jnd. Meth. Ch. in 1826; d. in St. Helena Parish, La., 1/28/1873 at the home of her sons John & Elijah.

8/7/1873 Sims, Mrs. Olivia J., widow of the late Louis A., dau. of Rev. Stephen Ellis, d. at home near Franklinton, La., 6/30/1873, aged 41 years.

8/28/1873 Bullock, Jerry J., d. of consumption in Pike Co. 8/1/1873, aged about 53 years; left wife and 2 children.

11/16/1873 Lewis, Hugh, b. Marion Dist., S.C., May 22, 1800; in 1812 he and parents mvd. to Marion Co., Miss.; md. at age to Miss Elizabeth Ball; mvd. to Copiah Co. In 1840 mvd. to Madison Co.; wife d. soon after; md. 2) Mrs. C. E. Magruder who survived him and by whom he had 3 children. Of his children, 4 of the 1st set and 2 of the last survived; joined church in 1823.

11/13/1873 Marsalis, Mrs. Letitia, consort of Ephraim, d. at Johnston's Station on 9/13/1873, age 52 yrs. Born and reared in Amite Co.

Barr/Allen md. by Rev. H. P. Lewis on 10/30/1873, R. W. Barr to Catherine O. Allen, all of Pike Co.

Magee/Hall md. by H. P. Lewis on 11/5/1873, Nelson Magee to Useba J. Hall, all of Pike Co.

OQuin/Hall md. 11/5/1873, William J. OQuin to Mary E. Hall, all of Pike Co.

Hathorn/Stateham md. on 11/20/1873, N. L. Hathorn to Miss N. E. Stateham, all of Pike Co.

Curtis/Norman: 12/4/1873, at 1 o'clock P.M. at the res. of the bride's father H. M. Norman, Esrq., by Rev. Benjamin Crawford, Mr. T. M. Curtis and Miss Mattie D. of Pike Co.

4/2/1874 Jenkins, Mr. L., d. at res. of Mr. J. W. Kinabrew of Johnston's Station, 112 miles from New Orleans on the New Orleans Great Northern Line, a gentleman and stranger here from Kentucky. He had a badly affected left side and used crutches.

Gray/Ligon: Md. at res. of Rudolph Ligon, E. Baton Rouge Par., La., 2/25/1874, by Rev. Robert B. Downer, Joseph E. Gray to Mary Louise Ligon.

4/16/1874 Ligon, Robert B., b. in Miss. in 1848; d. at his res. near Baton Rouge, La., wife, child, brothers & sisters survive.

4/30/1874 Martin, Loyd, b. Anne Arunda Co., Md. 1/15/1816, d. in Summit, Miss., 12/17/1873, son of Wm. and Harriet Martin. Lloyd taught school 11 yrs. then journeyed west and then south. Taught school in Jefferson Co., Miss., and moved to Summit in 1872.

5/18/1874 Godbolt, Gabriel Pickren, d. Apr. 24, 1874, near Summit after several weeks suffering and paralysis. He left large family of Methodist friends.

5/25/1875 Regan, Elizabeth, b. Roberson [Robeson] Co., N.C., 3/22/1802, md. Stephen A. 1/8/1818; jnd. Meth. Ch. shortly afterwards, d. _____. Though Sister Regan was old and infirm, she never ceased to work for the Glory of God.

7/2/1874 Conerly, Harriet Elizabeth, dau. of Culen F. and Mary J. Conerly of Vernon Par., La., d. 4/23/1874, aged 3 yrs. 4 mos., 3 days.

10/15/1874 Crawford, Sarah M., wife of James C., d. of heart disease 8/28/1874 at Johnston's Station in her 60th year. B. in Rutherford Co., Tenn., dau. of Elizabeth & John Hall. Her father d. when she was a year old; 2 yrs. later her mother moved to Pike Co., Miss. (1818); 5 years later moved to Copiah Co. In 1829 Sarah md. J. C. Crawford by whom she had 10 children, 4 of whom were left to mourn her loss. She jnd. Methodist Ch. in 1835.

Quin/Kaigler, md. on 9/31/1874 by Rev. H. P. Lewis, at res. of bride's mother, Charles W. O'Quin to Miss Jane V. Kaigler.

1/22/1875 Prewett, Polly Ann, d. near Magnolia, Miss., wife of Harrison Prewett, dau. of A. J. Vaughn in the 28th year of her age; jnd. Meth. Ch. when 15; md. in 1868 to Mr. Prewett and had 6 children, of whom 4 survive. Polly Ann was a twin.

Powell/Martin, on 12/10/1874, at res. of bride's father F. A. Martin, near Magnolia, by Rev. J. W. Sandell, Mr. Joseph W. Powell & Miss Eliza R. Martin.

Lenoir/Cook, on 1/26/1875 at res. of bride's mother near Magnolia by Rev. J. W. Sandell, Pinckney Lenoir & Miss Rosalie Juliette Cook.

3/18/1875 Lewis, Mrs. Martha, dau. of the late Philip Spear, b. Robertson [Robeson] Co., N.C., on 10/10/1801, md. Quinea Lewis 9/22/1816 (?); jnd. Meth. Ch. at Union Academy on Pearl River in 6/1820 under Rev. Thos. Griffin. She was her husband's sweet counselor & his inseparable companion for 57 years. She raised 10 children to be grown, 6 of whom survive--2 sons in Meth. ministry. She leaves about 100 children, grandchildren. She d. 1/31/1875 at her home near Holmesville. She was called Aunt Pattie.

4/8/1875 Lewis, Bro. Barney, eldest son of Quinea & Martha Lewis, b. in Robertson [Robeson] Co., N.C., 9/28/1818, emigrated with his parents to Pearl River in Marion Co., Miss., in 1820. Md. Kezia Lamkin, eldest dau. of S. L. Lamkin on 1/15/1846; mvd. to Scott Co. 12/1856 and to Brookhaven in 1868 and to Crystal Springs in 1871 where he d. of chronic diarrhea 1/30/1874; jnd. Meth. Ch. under Rev. George C. Light in 9/1857; thereafter served as classroom leader for 10 to 12 years. Obit. written by Barney's younger brother H. P. Lewis.

Lewis, Henry Tilman, son of Barney & Kezia Lewis, b. 2/3/1867, d. 1/10/1875.

4/22/1875 Johnson, Jordan Denson, b. 4/22/1821, md. Miss E. M. Roberts, dau. of Rev. James Roberts, 12/22/1842, d. 4/7/1845; md. 2) Miss E. J. Pounds on 10/28/1845; d. 7/17/1866; md. 3) Miss Julia Stanley 9/4/1866. He was licensed

to preach at Darlinton, St. Helena Par., La., 9/1857; ordained by Bishop
Paine 11/25/1864 at Crystal Springs; ordained Elder by Bishop Kavanaugh at
Hazlehurst 1/9/1869. Paralyzed in 1/1875; d. 3/11/1875. (Obit. by Thomas
Simmons)

5/6/1875 A second obit. for Mrs. Martha Spears, wife of Quinea Lewis.

6/24/1875 Harrell, James P., eldest son of Kearny & Maria B., b. Madison Co., Ala.,
10/31/1844, d. Osyka, Miss., Pike Co., 2/9/1875, 30 years, 3 mos., 9 days.
Soldier of the Confederacy and later worked on the Jackson RR.

7/8/1875 Ligon, Mrs. Mary Louisa, dau. of Dr. Wm. G., and Martha E. Austin, b.
Woodville, Miss., 7/23/1846, d. at res. of parents in New Orleans 6/8/1875;
md. George V. Ligon 12/1867; husband and son survive.

8/19/1875 Lampkin, William Griffin, b. 9/30/1819, md. Susan Stevenson 1/23/1845;
a Meth. for 30 yrs.; d. 6/25/1875, buried by the Masonic Fraternity in the
Odd Fellows Cem., Starkville, Miss.

10/28/1875 Gatlin, Charlie, at father's res. at Magnolia, 15 yrs., 2 mos., 6 days
old, son of John B. His mother d. when he was a child with a sister younger
than he; father md. 2nd time. (J. W. Sandell)

11/11/1875 Germany, Ella Ethel, dau. of Dr. W. H. & M. E. Germany, b. 9/17/1872,
d. 9/13/1875.

1/13/1876 Winborne, little Hubart Ottaman, son of B. F. & Louise Winborne, b.
6/1874, d. 9/13/1875.

Abney, R. R., d. at res. of son in Marion Co., Miss., 10/25/1875, from infirmity
of age, 65 yrs., 28 days; b. Maury Co., Tenn., 8/28/1810, moved with father
to Warren Co., Miss., in 7/1830; md. Mary Ann Roberts in 1836; moved to Jasper
Co. where he remained until a few mos. before death.

1/13/1876 Felder/Byrd, on 12/27/1875 at res. of Bro. Felder on Topisaw, Pike Co.,
Miss., by Rev. E. R. Strickland, Wm. I. Felder & Isabella M. Byrd.

1/27/1876 Howard/Regan, 1/5/1876 by Rev. H. P. Lewis, Rev. P. Howard of the Miss.
Conf. md. Mrs. M. E. Regan of Pike Co., Miss.

Vaughan/Prewett, 1/12/1876 by Rev. H. P. Lewis, D. F. Vaughan md. Eva Prewett
of Pike Co., Miss.

2/10/1876 Felder, John, d. 12/20/1875, in Pike Co., Miss. Converted at a camp
meeting where Magnolia now stands in 1811 when 18 years old (on 5/7th.) In
1830 he moved to the Topisaw. (This data combined with a second obit. which
appeared in the issue of 3/23/1876.) He md. 3 times: 1) Elizabeth, by whom
he had 7 children; 2) Mrs. Simmons by whom he had 1 child; 3) Mrs. Stanfill
still living (in 1876). Among his survivors (sons and nephews) were six
preachers in the Meth. Church in La., Miss., Texas, and other states. John
was the son of Peter Felder, who migrated to Miss. in 1810 from S.C. landing
his boat at Natchez. John and the other sons came through the Indian Nations
with horses to the Tangipahoa [River] about 1½ miles from Magnolia. John then
went on to Natchez to meet his parents who in turn were a week late in arriving.
John was then 17 years old. (J. W. Sandell)

2/24/1876 Douglas, Lee H. D., on the Topisaw in Pike Co., son of Newton & Mary Ann
Douglas, b. 4/27/1866 (?), d. 12/20/1875.

Douglas, Robertson B., son of Newton & Mary Ann, b. 10/6/1875, d. 11/20/1875.

5/11/1876 Holmes, little Ransom Chalman, grandson of John & Sarah E. Yarborough,
son of J. T. L. & Sarah E. Holmes, b. Pike Co. 7/5/1872, d. 3/14/1876, 3 years,
__ mos., 9 days.

10/12/1876 Applewhite, Mrs. Mary Ann, d. in Carroll Co. 7/17/1876, at the home of
her son Dr. J. A. Applewhite, widow of Rev. James Applewhite, pioneer Meth.
preacher. She was b. in Roberson [Robeson] Co., N.C., 11/10/1797, moved with
father Rev. John Regan & settled in Marion Co., Miss., in 1811; joined Meth.

Ch. while young; she md. on 4/17/1817. (W. H. Holmes)

Crawford, Francis William, son of H. H. & H. A. Crawford b. 7/30/1869, d. of congestion at Johnston's Station, 10 A.M. Sunday 9/10/1876. He was called Willie.

11/2/1876 Carruth, John, d. 8/22/1876, at Johnston's Station, aged 27 yrs. Md. by the writer to Miss Almeda L. Seal of Rankin Co., Miss. He was reared as a Presbyterian but joined the Meth. faith at Summit. (J. E. Jagers)

12/21/1876 Smith, Sister Angeline, d. 8/10/1876 near Tylertown, wife of William (?) dau. of Sara (?), and Jno. ___, aged 50 years.

3/1/1876 Toney/McGowan, at res. of bride's mother, Mrs. Lucy Lampton, on 1/3/1877, by Rev. P. Howard, Thomas Toney md. Mrs. Elizabeth McGowen, all of Pike Co.

Sumner/Lewis, at res. of bride's father J. W. Lewis, 2/8/1876, by Rev. P. Howard, George C. Sumner of Smith Co., Miss., md. Miss Alice Lewis of Pike Co.

Smith, Lemuel Osman, son of B. B. & Margaret Smith, b. 8/28/1873, d. 1/15/1877, after a 43-day illness at China Grove. (P. Howard)

3/22/1877 Ott/Magee, at the home of Mrs. Celia Magee on 2/14/1877, by Rev. Ruffin T. Davis, Walter T. Ott md. Leah D. Magee of Washington Par., La.

4/5/1877 Regan, Elizabeth Span, d. at res. of her son Joseph Bryan in Bienville Par., La., 2/15/1877, dau. of Joseph & Dorethy Regan of Lumbertown, Robeson Co., N.C., b. 10/20/1798; md. 1) Joseph Regan (confused and perhaps incorrect facts) 11/11/1818; moved to Gregg Co. [sic], Ga., where she was widowed with 2 sons; md. 2) 9/19/1825 to Redric Bryan also with 2 sons in Houston Co., Ga.; moved to Claiborne Par., La.

5/10/1877 Lewis, Pamela Ann, consort of Lemuel Lewis, d. in Brookhaven, Miss., 6 A.M. 2/7/1877.

Crawford, James C., d. 3/11/1877 at Johnston's Station, Summit Circuit. Resolution to his memory signed by W. H. Germany.

8/16/1877 Felder, Bro. W. W., b. in Pike Co., 5/16/1815, md. Cynthia Isabel Hope in 1835 by whom he had 4 daus. & 2 sons. She d. 2/17/1848. He md. 2) in 11/1848 to Mrs. Sarah Curtis Felder by whom he had 3 sons & 2 daus. He d. 6/21/1877 at Myrtle Place, Miss.

9/20/1877 Wallace, James, d. 6/25/1877, only child of G. W. and Lucy Norman, aged 1 yr., 3 mos., 13 days.

10/18/1877 Felder, Zebulon Pipkin, d. at res. on Topisaw Creek, Lincoln Co., 8/23/1877, after 29-day illness, aged 27 yrs, 8 mos, 12 days. Joined church in 1865. Left wife and 2 daus.

11/29/1877 Felder, Amanda Jane, dau. of Levi & Martha; b. Pike Co., 10/3/1853, md. Wm. Matthew Tyler in 12/1871, d. 9/22/1877.

1/3/1878 Wordsworth, Rev. Wm. d. on Christmas Eve, 1877, member of the Miss. Conf., transferred to the Scotland Conf. a few weeks before.

Thomas/Regan, 1/1/1878, by Rev. P. Howard, Jesse G. Thomas md. Miss Sallie M. Regan, all of Pike Co.

1/17/1878 Williams/Lampton, near China Grove, 12/27/1877, by Rev. P. Howard, Henry P. Williams md. Miss Lucy Lampton.

1/24/1878 Wordsworth, Rev. Wm., b. near Jackson, Hinds Co., Miss., in 1830. In 1836 moved to La., converted in 1847. (Long obit.)

7/18/1878 Prewett, Elizabeth, wife of Smiley, d. near Magnolia 5/13/1878, in the 32nd year of her age. She was the dau. of Mrs. A. J. Vaughan. Sister Betty was a twin to sister Polly, who d. nearly 4 yrs. before. She was brought up by her poor mother. Converted at the age of 15.

7/25/1878 Henington/Martin, on 7/16/1878, at res. of bride's father at West Station, Holmes Co., by Rev. George W. Brown, L. F. Henington of McComb City to Miss Mollie E. Martin.

8/29/1878 Martin, Mrs. Medora A. (nee Huffman), b. Pike Co., 10/3/1859, d. Bogue Chitto in Lincoln Co., 8/6/1878 after a painful 3-day illness. She md. on 12/28/1876 to John O. Martin. Called Dora, she joined the Baptist Ch. at age 11. She became the mother of a son on 8/4 and named him John for his father. Died from effects of birth.

9/5/1878 Warren, Jesse M., b. Baldwin Co., Ga., 4/27/1811, d. at res. in Coffee Co., Ala., 6/10/1878. Conv. at Flat Woods camp meeting in Green Co., Ga., & joined Meth. Ch. in 1837.

Connerly, Sister Margaret O., wife of W. W. Conerly & dau. of Price & Mary Connerly, d. of paralysis at her home in Tylertown, Pike Co., 6/5/ buried 6/6/1878 in the 67th yr. of her age. Member of the Methodist Ch. for nearly 50 yrs.

(No papers found for 1879)

3/11/1880 Crofford/Brent md. at res. of Col. Brent 12/24/1879, by Rev. H. P. Lewis, Dook (Dock?) Crofford & Mollie Brent, all of Pike Co.

Conerly/Simmons md. at res. of bride's mother, 2/12/1880, by Rev. H. P. Lewis, C. W. Conerly & Miss Dixie Simmons, all of Pike Co.

Kenny/Germany, md. at res. of bride's father at Johnston's Station, 2/20 (or 26?), 1880, by Rev. H. P. Lewis, John M. Kenny & Julia Germany, all of Pike Co.

Conerly, Wm., b. Duplin Co., N.C., 8/11/1810, emigrated with parents Owen & Mary Conerly in 1822 to the Pushapatappa in Marion Co., Miss.; joined church at Waterhold about 1826 and conv. at camp meeting 6 mi. north of Holmesville, Miss., at Gatlin's camp meeting. Md. Caroline Stares in 1833 & lived at China Grove until 1847. Moved to Sabine Par., La., where he lost his 1st wife in 1851; moved back to Miss. in 1853. Md. 2) Miss Margaret O. Connally with whom he lived happily till 6/5/1878 when she d. He d. at his res. 11/19/1879.

3/11/1880 Sandell, Daniel, b. Orangeburg Dst., S.C., 2/22/1792, d. Magnolia 12/13/1879 in his 88th year. Son of Henry Sandell & Catherine Nobles, who moved from S.C. to near Magnolia in 1812 and were parents of 7 children, viz: John, Daniel, Henry, Darius, Elizabeth and Louisa. Daniel survived all the family; md. Elenor Corley, dau. of Jeremiah, who migrated to Miss. from Barnwell Dist., S.C., on 9/17/1815, before formation of Pike Co. In 1816 he settled place where he spent the remainder of his life. Fathered 5 sons: Gabriel, Nelson, Wesley, Monroe, and Murray; and 2 daus: Mary and Martha. He outlived all his children except John Wesley Sandell of the Miss. Methodist Conf. and Mary Terrell of DeSoto Par., La. Daniel Sandell was first a farmer; his first son a mechanic; the second a physician, the 3rd a farmer, and the 2nd md. Jepthia Winborne, a preacher. Daniel Sandell joined the Methodist Ch. in S.C. in 1812. In Miss. he belonged to Felder's Ch. 1 ½ mi. south of Magnolia for 65 years. In 1837 his 1st wife died leaving him with 7 children. He md. 2) in 1845 to Mrs. Sarah Martin, widow with 6 children. She survived him.

4/8/1880 Alford, John Wesley, son of Seaborn J. & Mary C. Alford, b. in Pike Co., 6/25/1836, d. of pneumonia 11/27/1879 at his home in Denton, Texas.

6/10/1880 Huffman, Sister L. O., b. 2/1/1844, d. 1/4/1880, joined Methodist Ch. in 1878, md. P. M. Huffman in 1866. (No locations given; obit. by M. D. Mills.)

8/26/1880 Simmons, Rev. Thomas, b. in S.C., 7/11/1806; moved with father's family Pike Co., Miss., in 1812; joined Methodist Ch. in 1826; md. Barcana Hope 9/10/1824; licensed to preach in 1831 (?) and ordained deacon by Bishop Waugh in New Orleans in 11/1841; moved to Copiah Co. in 1842; ordained Elder in 12/1847 by Bishop Paine at Canton, Miss.; joined Methodist Protestant Ch. in 1879. Died 8/9/1880 aged 74 years, buried at the Providence Com. One son mentioned in obit, Rev. W. W. Simmons of the Miss. Conf. (By A. M. Widney)

9/30/1880 Gates, Sister Louisa, b. Pike Co., 5/24/1824; joined Methodist Ch. at Grove Creek, now Port Vincent, La., in 1856; maiden name Felder, dau. of David Felder & Jane McMorris, who came from S. C. in 1830; settled in Livingston Par., La., near Amite River; joined church under Rev. Beverly Tabor; md. Wm. Jefferson Gates on 2/11/1851. He d. in 1855, leaving 2 children.

1/6/1881 Ferguson/Gibson md. on 12/23/1880, by Rev. H. P. Lewis, Wm. B. Ferguson and Mrs. M. E. Gibson, all of Pike Co.

2/3/1881 Lewis, Quinea, b. Lenoir Co., N.C., 5/28/1794; d. Holmesville, Pike Co., 1/13/1881, in his 87th year; md. Martha Spears 9/22/1816; came to Miss. and settled on Pearl R. in Marion Co. In 1843 he settled on Magee's Cr. in Pike Co. In the winter of 1856/57 he came to Holmesville where he and his wife died. Called "Uncle Quinea" by all classes in the community. His last illness was short. He was a soldier for a short time in the War of 1812 and a pensioner at the time of death. He was brought up by a Baptist mother, but he became a Methodist at Union Academy, Marion Co., Miss., under influence of Revs. Thomas Griffing and Miles Harper on 6/15/1822. He had 10 children; two sons, H. P. and W. B., are ministers of the Gospel in the Methodist Church. (By J. W. Sandell)

3/3/1881 Sibley, Miss Lizzie, d. 3/1/1881 in her 34th year, at res. of her brother-in-law C. C. Gibson in Magnolia. She joined Methodist Church in Magnolia in 8/1874. Lived in Texas for a period where she had gone because of poor health.

Carr, Mrs. Maranda A., b. Sumpter Dist., S.C., in 1816; d. 2/4/1881 of consumption; maiden name Rhrodus. Reared as an orphan by the Baxter family; moved to Lowndes Co., Ala.; md. there to John Peter Carr 9/9/1840 and mothered a child.

4/7/1881 Baker/Purdy md. at res. of bride's father in McComb City on 3/22/1881, by Rev. W. W. Hopper, F. W. Baker & Miss M. A. Purdy of McComb.

5/5/1881 King, Kittwood, b. Pike Co., Miss., Oct. 4, 1814; md. John Ballard 3/4/1836, d. 12/3/1880, dau. of Rev. Jesse King and niece of Rev. Peter James of sacred memory. She md. Ballard in Amite City, La.; moved to Livingston Par. and settled near Springfield where she died. Left a son and six daus.

5/19/1881 Gatlin, Mrs. Rosalba, b. Pike Co., 1 mi. from Johnston's Station on a spot a little distance from the old residence which stands in front of Judge Magee's place; reared in the same old dwelling where she married. She was b. 6/10/1814; md. James S. Gatlin 10/6/1831. After marriage they lived on Bogue Chitto River 6 mi. above Holmesville. In winter of 1856 moved to Amite Co.; in Jan., 1872, moved to Johnston's Station. Reared by pious Presbyterian parents; joined Methodist in 1848. She was stricken with paralysis in 2/1879, d. 1/3/1881. She knew much suffering. Her 3rd son was wounded at Richmond, Va. 5/12/1864, d. in Franklin Co., 6/25/1864. Her 4th son d. at Bienville Hospital in Richmond 11/26/1861. Her 6th son killed at Battle of Harrisburg 6/14/1864. Her husband Col. Gatlin was away at the time of her death. (By W. W. Hopper, Pastor)

5/20/1881 Broderick/Tegarden, md. at Episcopal Church in Summit by Rev. W. W. Hopper, M. H. Broderick and Miss M. Key Tegarden.

6/23/1881 Packwood, Samuel Franklin, b. Pike Co., son of J. E. (or J. B.) and Mary Packwood, b. 7/3/1863, d. from effects of measles while at school at Oxford, Miss., 5/1/1881.

7/21/1881 Conerly, Miss Virginia, d. at res. of writer in Vernon Par., La., wife of J. W. Conerly, dau. of Thomas B. and Mary Connerly, b. in Ala., Oct., 1853 (or 63?); moved to La. while young; became Methodist under Rev. James M. Franklin in 1868. (By John Franklin)

9/29/1881 Williams, Mrs. Courtney, dau. of Wyatt Felder and Cynthia Hope; b. 6/6/1842, d. 8/9/1881; md. Jackson Williams in Pike Co. 12/13/1866; joined Baptist Church after marriage; member of Moak's Creek Church at death. (M. L. J. Hoover.)

11/17/1881 Smith, Wyatt, son of Brittain and Elizabeth Smith, b. Pike Co., Miss., 7/1/1820; moved to Holmes Co. with parents when 7; md. 1) Mary C. Robbs in

1845 who d. in 1847; md. 2) Hester Ann Waters in 1848, who d. in 1857 leaving 4 children; md. 3) Sue D. Waters in 1858 (who survived) leaving 4 children.

11/24/1881 Martin, Wayne S., d. 8/17/1881, in McComb City, eldest son of Lloyd Martin and L. J. McNeill. He was b. 12/7/1862 in Wilkinson Co., d. aged 18 yrs, 8 mos.

1/15/1882 Hart/Moak, md. on 12/8/1881 near Holmesville, Thomas A. Hart and Miss M. S. J. Moak.

Brown/Williams, md. 12/13/1881, at Summit, W. M. Brown and Miss E. L. Williams.

Gerald/Hayman, md. 12/15/1881, at Summit, E. W. Gerald and Miss R. J. Hayman.

Mara/Regan, md. 12/22/1881 at China Grove, C. R. O. Mara and Miss L. J. Regan.

Coney, Mrs. Nancy U. E., wife of John E. Coney, dau. of Rev. James R. and Mary C. Langston, b. Drew Co., Ark., 11/21/1819, d. Webster Par., La., 11/21/1881. Leaves husband and 5 children.

2/16/1882 Whitaker, Mrs. E. Carolina (nee Saunders) b. 7/8/1824, d. Dec., 1881, in Wilkinson Co., Miss., md. in early life to John Whitaker.

2/16/1882 Parrsons/Nix, md. 1/24/1882, at the res. of Seaborn Covington near Summit, F. C. Parrsons and Miss Della Nix, all of Pike Co.

3/2/1882 Brown/Nesom, 2/7/1882, at the res. of the bride's mother, by Rev. I. W. Cooper, Mr. J. L. Brown of Pike Co., Miss., to Miss L. J. Nesom.

3/30/1882 Lewis, Miss K. A., b. 8/27/1861; d. 12/31/1881; joined church at Crystal Springs in 1875; converted by sermon of writer at old China Grove 9/20/1881; buried on 1/2/1882. (W. W. Hopper)

4/6/1882 Downing, Mrs. Alice Maria, d. at Raymond, Miss., 3/5/1882, 2nd child of James L. and Philonia Tynes, now of Hinds Co.; b. in Pike Co., Miss., 3/8/1850; joined church at age 10; md. 2/9/1876 to William W. Downing of Raymond. (D. P. Drake)

4/20/1882 Vaughn, Mrs. Aby Jane, b. 1/26/1819, in Pike Co., d. near place of birth 4/4/1882; md. 4 times; 5 children--4 daus. and 1 son, of whom 2 daus are dead, each leaving a family.

5/18/1882 Magee, David, b. Washington Par., La., 11/25/1825, md. Elizabeth Peak; d. of consumption 12/19/1881; left 4 children.

7/27/1882 Catchings, Mrs. Emma A. (nee Smith), b. Pike Co., 12/17/1833; d. 5/30/1882; md. J. Noel on 12/17/1883.

8/30/1883 Parnell, George Washington, b. 4/15/1815, in Robinson [sic] Co., N.C.; when 18 moved to Ga. where he remained until 1846; in 1844 md. in Columbus to Emma Curtis (who survived him); in 1846 moved to Ala. where he remained until 1870; thereafter moved to Summit, Pike Co., Miss., where he d. of cancer on 8/2/1883. Joined Meth. Ch. in 1857.

10/18/1883 Terrell, Josiah Martin, b. Amite Co., Miss., on 2/14/1818; when 10 moved with parents to Pike Co.; md. in fall of 1844 to Ann Morgan; in 1849 moved to DeSoto Par., La.; wife d. in 1857 leaving him with 5 small children. In 1858 joined Methodist Ch. under Rev. S. B. Surratt; moved to Ark. in 1861 and back to DeSoto Par. in 1862; joined Confederate Army; d. 9/19/1883.

10/5/1882 Pittman, Willie Henry, son of W. W. & Martha, b. 1/5/1881; d. 8/21/1882 aged 1 yr., 7 mos., 6 days. (By R. A. Sibley)

11/23/1882 Toomer, David R., son of Wiley & S. A., b. Magnolia 11/9/1861; d. at res. of father at Pearlington, Miss., 10/20/1882; md. 11/6/1881 to Mrs. Virginia Leonard by whom he leaves an infant dau. (By J. W. Sandell)

12/7/1882 Stevens, John C., son of A. C. & Mary, b. Pike Co., 7/9/1858, d. Jackson Co., Miss., 9/11/1882, aged 24 yrs. 3 mos. 19 days. Conv. at Salem Camp, 1879.

1/23/1883 Felder, Mrs. Jane; maiden name McMorris; d. at res. of her son R. K. Felder near Port Vincent, La., 11/9/1882, aged 87 yrs., 2 mos., 5 days. Born S. C.; moved with parents to Miss. in 1812; md. David Felder 1819; moved to La. in 1830; lost husband in 1841. Left a large family.

2/22/1883 Lea/McGehee, md. at Methodist Ch. in Summit, 1/2/1883, Alfred Lea and Tenia McGehee, all of Pike Co.

3/8/1883 Youngblood, Adelia Virginia, dau. of Joseph and Mary E. O'Mara and wife of Henry Youngblood, b. 5/16/1856; joined Methodist Ch. at Sartins in 1874 under Rev. H. P. Lewis; md. Oct., 1880; d. at China Grove 10/1882; left mother, father, brothers and sisters, husband and a motherless child.

5/24/1883 Sandell, Mrs. Sarah, d. at res. of her son Clinton Martin, near Johnston's Station, 3/13/1883. Born S.C. 10/10/1805; md. William Martin in 1823 and 2) Daniel Sandell in 1845 (of whom is Rev. J. W. Sandell of the Miss. Conf.) who d. at Magnolia 12/13/1879. She joined Methodist at Terrals near McComb City in 1840. (By W. G. Backus)

6/7/1883 Middleton/Reynolds, md. at Summit (Methodist Ch.) by Rev. William B. Hines, 5/16/1883, Charles Middleton and Annie Reynolds.

6/23/1883 Youngblood, George Henry, son of Rev. W. T. and Nancy J. Youngblood, b. near Homewood in Scott Co., Miss., d. China Grove 3/22/1883, aged 30 yrs., 11 mos., 16 days; moved to Pike Co. in 1878; md. in 1881 to Miss Adelia V. O'Mara, who d. 10/1882, leaving a daughter.

9/20/1883 Russ, Mrs. Effie, wife of J. L. Russ, b. Rankin Co., Miss., 12/8/1858; d. at Osyka, Pike Co., 8/8/1883; dau. of Dugald Leach and wife Fannie W. Shaw, who came to Miss. from the Carolinas. Parents d. of yellow fever in 1878. She was baptized at Canton by Rev. W. E. Tynes. She md. Bro. J. L. Russ 10/14/1879. She visited her brothers and sisters at Canton, came home ill on July 31, and died Aug. 8. (By B. Jones)

9/27/1883 McLean, Eliza Jane (nee Wildblood), b. 10/20/1846, in Washington Par., La., d. Jackson, E. Feliciana Par., 7/9/1883; md. John W. McLean of E. Feliciana.

10/4/1883 Felder, Sarah Curtis, b. near Liberty, Miss., 8/23/1816, md. 1) Ira Felder. In 1848 she md. Wyatt W. Felder and d. in Pike Co. 7/31/1883. She was reared Baptist but became Methodist in 1847. She left 5 children. (By M. L. J. Hoover)

11/1/1883 O'Mara, J. Laney, son of Joseph and Mary E. O'Mara, b. Pike Co. 4/28/1863, d. of typhoid 9/20/1883; joined Methodist Ch. in 1873 under min. of Rev. H. P. Lewis; converted at Topisaw Camp Meeting in 1882. (By W. W. Simmons)

11/29/1883 Russ, Jasper L., b. near Covington, La. 6/24/1845, d. Osyka 10/10/1883, son of S. P. and Mary Russ of New Orleans. He attended Centenary College; joined Confederate Army when 17, in N.O. when it fell to Federals. He escaped and joined army of Trans-Mississippi Dept. of Confederate Army. He was converted in 1873 at Seaborn Camp Mtg; md. 1) Mary E. Armstead of Pearlington, Miss., who d. Feb., 1878, leaving 2 sons (one since deceased); moved to Osyka for mercantile trade; md. 2) 10/1879 to Miss Effie Leitch of Canton, who d. 8/8/1883 only 2 mos., 2 days before his death.

Felder, Dora Mabel, dau. of Byrd Felder and Jane Greer, b. 7/15/1881, d. 7/31/1883.

Felder, Clifton Lee, son of Byrd and Jane Greer Felder b. 10/10/___, d. 10/5/1883. (By L. S. Hoover)

2/14/1884 Buckley, Capt. James, b. Lawrence Co., Miss., 11/10/1830, (d. date not given); md. on 4/1/1856 in Pike Co., Miss., to Bethany Craft with whom he lived till death. Studied law with Judge Vanesson; in 1862 elected Chancery clerk of Lawrence Co., served until 1869; moved to Brookhaven; elected Chancery Clerk in 1872, served until 1879; moved to Jackson when apptd. deputy auditor for State of Miss. Left children.

3/13/1884 Felder, Emma, dau. of Rufus K. and Sarah, b. 5/25/1868, d. with meningitis near Port Vincent, La., 1/26/1884.

4/10/1884 Howell, Mrs. Mary, d. 1/14/1884, at res. of son-in-law N. G. Irby in Jackson Par., La., aged 69 yrs.; maiden name May, b. either in Yazoo or Pike Co., Miss., on 10/29/1815; md. Mr. Howell at age 19 yrs. He d. in 1847.

4/24/1884 Catching, Dr. Joseph B., b. Pike Co. 5/13/1822, md. Martha Bridges, dau. of H. F. and Margaret, near Georgetown (Miss.?), 12/9/1847; joined Methodist Ch. in 1849; d. 12/21/1883. (Resolutions adopted by the Providence Circuit)

6/12/1884 Lee, Bro. John P., d. at Jefferson Co., Miss., 2/18/1884, aged 55; b. Pike Co., Miss., joined Methodist Ch. at Nebo in 1859 under Rev. Wm. B. Johnson. Left wife and 7 children.

6/12/1884 Alford, Seaborn J., d. of typhoid pneumonia on 2/7/1884, b. near Osyka on 10/11/1807. His father was Jacob Alford who came to La. shortly after he and his twin brother were born. Their father soon died leaving their mother and little sons when they were quite young. He stayed to help his mother until he was about 24 years old. After then he md. Mary C. Felder by whom he had "several interesting children." He md. 2) on 12/8/1864 Mrs. Mary S. Wadsworth, widow of the lamented Daniel M. Wadsworth, with whom he lived until death.

6/26/1884 McClutchie/Travis, md. at Wesley Chapel, Natchitoches, La., 6/13/1884, William G. McClutchie, formerly of Jefferson Co., Miss., and Mary Travis, formerly of Pike Co., Miss.

7/10/1884 2nd Obit. for Seaborn J. Alford, written by H. Walter Featherstun. The obit. stated that Alford was buried at Old Topisaw Graveyard. He md. Mary C. Felder on 12/29/1831; md. 2) Mrs. M. S. Wadsworth on 12/8/1864; d. 2/7/1884. He was converted to Methodism at the old Warner Camp Ground near present-day Warnerton in Washington Par., La., by old ministers Pipkin, Clinton, and John G. Jones. He was licensed to preach in 1866 & served at Topisaw, Johnston's Station, Bethany, and Brisler Churches. He taught his children to love the same religion.

7/17/1884 Regan, Rebecca Jane, widow of Joseph Regan, eldest dau. of Samuel and Mary Ann McRee, d. at the home of her brother J. J. McRee, Marion, Union Par., La. She was b. in Copiah Co., Miss., in 1833, d. age 51 yrs.

7/31/1884 Barnes, Mrs. Mary A., b. Marion Co., Miss., 2/15/1815; d. 1/21/1884, at son-in-law's C. C. Hartzog's res. in Texas.

9/25/1884 Barnes, Harris, son of William Barnes and Mary Spears, b. Robinson [sic] Co., N.C., 10/30/1813, moved with parents to Marion Co., Miss. He remained with his widowed mother and seven children. Md. 4/17/1839 to Julia A. Scott by whom he had 8 children, of whom 3 survived (in 1884). The wife d. 5/14/1858. His 1st son James Allen Barnes aged 20 yrs. d. 8/14/1868--a CSA veteran who suffered 2 wounds. Barnes Sr. md. 2) 3/25/1861 at res. of late Judge C. Hoover in Pike Co. to Annette Equen of New Orleans--she was a twin to the Rev. Mrs. Downer, by whom he had seven children, the eldest barely of age in 1884. (By M. L. J. Hoover)

10/30/1884 Harper, Sister Winafred, b. Pike Co. 8/12/1827, md. Laban B. Harper, 10/1/1884; d. at 9 a.m. on 9/20/1884, aged 57 yrs., 1 mo., 8 days. Survived by husband, 2 sons, and 1 dau.

11/27/1884 Holloway, Mrs. Caroline Frances (nee Ford) b. Marion Co., Miss., 12/24/1829, md. William B. Holloway 12/4/1848; joined Methodist Ch. in 1861, d. Silver Cr., Lawrence Co., Miss., 7/18/1884; left husband, 3 daus., & grandchild.

12/4/1884 May, Willie W., son of John D. & Julia C. May, b. 2/10/1868 in Pike Co., Miss., d. 10/3/1884, aged 16 yrs., 7 mos., 23 days.

Mullin, George W., b. Samson (Sampson?) Co., N.C., 10/27/1821, md. Mary L. Majors 12/18/1843, d. Marion Co., Miss., 2/9/1884.

1/29/1885 Colquhone, Sister Mary Ann, wife of John Colquhone, dau. of Cullen and Lavinnia Conerly, b. Marion Co., Miss., 10/15/1835, d. Simpson Co., Miss., 12/11/1884; md. in Amite Co., Miss., 12/5/1855. Had 12 children--7 sons, 5 daus.--all of whom survive.

2/12/1885 Godbold/Felder, md. at res. of Gabriel Felder in Pike Co., 1/22/1885, by Rev. Wm. B. Hines, Gabriel Godbold and Ella Felder.

3/5/1885 Conerly/Stringer, at res. of Nash Stringer near China Grove 1/15/1885, by Rev. W. W. Simmons, Eugene Conerly and Flora Stringer.

Martin/Johnson, md. at res of Mr. Falls, China Grove, by W. W. Simmons, J. W. Martin and Julia Johnson (no date).

Magee, Minnie Ella (nee Berry), b. Osyka 12/15/1860, d. near McComb City 12/13/1884; funeral preached on her 24th birthdate from home of mother at Johnston's Station. On 5/16/1883 she md. J. A. Q. Magee; joined church in 1875.

3/19/1885 Seymour, Sarah A., wife of William, dau. of David Talley and Mary, his wife; d. 2/1/1885; b. on W. Pearly R. on 11/15/1862; md. Wm. Seymour by Rev. N. B. Young 11/15/1883.

5/21/1885 Fant, Annis (Annie?), consort of S. A. Fant of Pike Co., b. 10/31/1859, d. of congestion of stomach 3/18/1885 in her 25th yr. Dau. of Judge Ransom Magee (decd.); md. 5/27/1880 to Samuel A. Fant whom she left with two sweet little boys. Conv. by Rev. C. F. Thompson in 1876; member of church at Johnston's Station.

7/23/1885 Godbold, John F., b. Franklin Co., Miss., in 1860, d. 6/29/1885, md. Jessie Ligon in Summit in 10/1882.

9/3/1885 Ellis, George, b. in La. 10/7/1807, d. Utica, Miss., 3/9/1885; parents moved to Miss. when he was a child; md. Elizabeth Wade in 1843 and moved to Hinds Co. next year. Joined Methodist Ch. 7/27/1853. (Obit. mentioned son Dr. G. H. Ellis.)

11/5/1885 Fant/Gatlin, md. at res. of bride's father by Rev. J. A. B. Jones, Samuel A. Fant and Miss Lula Gatlin, all of Johnston's Station.

Brumfield, Andrew Jackson, b. Pike Co., 12/25/1830; moved with grandparents to Marion Co., Miss., where he remained until he d. 10/5/1805; md. 9/11/1851 to Martha Lewis, who with 3 children survive. Joined Methodist Ch. in 1853 under Rev. James Shelton.

11/4/1886 Barnes, Mrs. M. E. (nee Ford), b. Hinds Co., 3/21/1837, md. Richard Flowers Barnes 1/25/1855, d. McComb 8/29/1886.

12/9/1886 Rollins, Jeremiah, b. Pike Co. 7/15/1825, md. Martha A. Alford by Rev. P. E. Green, at res. of her father Rev. Seaborn Alford 9/1/1853; joined ch. at Topisaw Camp Mtg. 8/28/1881. Died at home in Lincoln Co., Miss., 9/5/1886, buried at Topisaw.

12/30/1886 Hoover, Dr. C. B., Pike Co., 1/19/1840, served in CSA, Capt. in Cavalry, graduated in medicine in N.O. in 1866. Md. Miss Mary V. Barnes of Columbia on Apr. 16, 1867; joined Methodist in 1875; d. at McComb 8/28/1886.

Lewis, Sampson Henry, infant son of Q. M. and N. A. Lewis, b. near Johnston's Station on 2/25/1885, d. 8/4/1886.

2/3/1887 Rawls, Mrs. Kesiah (nee Felder), b. S.C. in 1795, md. Jabez Rawls of Pike Co., Miss., on 5/20/1818, d. near Hattiesburg, Miss., 9/29/1886.

2/10/1887 Germany, Dr. William H., M.D., d. at his home at Johnston's Station 1/21/1887. (Resolution passed by the Summit Quarterly Conf.)

Wallace, Courtney Marcella, youngest dau. of Peter and Martha Quin, b. Holmesville 8/19/1833; md. Dr. Jesse Wallace on 3/14/1850; joined Methodist Ch.; shortly after marriage moved to McComb. D. at dau.'s home, Mrs. Julia Castello (nee Wallace) on 7/21/1886. (By J. T. Nicholson)

3/10/1887 Taylor, Eva B., dau. of Thomas S. and L. Taylor b. in Pike Co., 10/3/1868, d. Freestone Co., Texas, 2/21/1887; joined Methodist Ch. a few mos. before death.

5/26/1887 2nd Obit. for Rev. Willis H. Germany, M.D., who d. of pneumonia 1/21/1887 near Johnston's Station; licensed to preach when 18 yrs. old and travelled 8 yrs. as an itinerate minister. Wife has since died.

5/2/1887 Germany, Mrs. Martha, b. Pike Co., 3/3/1836, dau. of Col. James Gatlin and wife, who in early life md. Dr. Willis H. Germany. No death date given. Buried at Johnston's Station.

8/11/1887 Regan, Ralph, b. Marion Co., 3/11/1819, d. near China Grove 6/11/1887, son of Stephen Regan, a local preacher. His mother was a devoted Christian. Ralph md. 1) Tabitha Warner, who d. after 1st year; md. 2) Abigail Lewis, dau. of Quinea & Martha Lewis & sister to Rev. H. P. Lewis and W. B. Lewis of Miss. Conf. She had 12 children. One son was a preacher; a dau. Mrs. P. Howard of Centerville also dedicated life to Christian work.

8/18/1887 Ott, Mrs. Margaret Ann Tate, widow of Charles Ott, dau. of Thomas and Ingaba Tate b. 7/20/1813 in Clarksburg, Va., d. 6/7/1887 in Washington Par., La.

9/1/1887 Lewis, Lemuel, b. Lenoir Co., N.C., 9/8/1804, d. near China Grove 7/16/1887; parents moved to Robertson [Robeson] Co., N.C., when he was an infant. At age 16 he moved to Miss. with 3 older brothers: Martin, Quinea, and James. While there the father died, so Lemuel returned home to care for the mother. At her death he md. Polly Williams in 1826 and in 1831 moved back to Miss.; the next yr. he became a Methodist. (By R. S. Gale)

9/22/1887 Simmons/Vaught, md. at Magnolia 9/13/1887, by Rev. J. W. McLaurin, T. C. Simmons and Mary H. Vaught.

Magee, Rosa Jane, d. Aug. 23, 1887, in Washington Par., La., dau. of Mrs. Celia Magee, aged 25 yrs., 5 mos., 20 days.

10/20/1887 Sartin/Willoughby, md. at res. of bride's father Bro. Wm. Willoughby at China Grove on 9/25/1887, by Rev. R. S. Gale, Alonzo Sartin to Emily F. P. Willoughby.

12/8/1887 Tarver, William Allen, son of Rev. Elijah Tarver, b. Pike Co., 3/16/1838, "born again" when 15 at camp meeting near Liberty, Miss., md. 12/17/1867 to Julia A. Muse, dau. of Rev. and Hon. James H. Muse of La.; fathered a number of sons and daus--4 died earlier, 6 with wife survive. Died in Amite Co. on Sunday morning 10/30/1887.

Jones, John Walton, son of Jesse T. and Nannie Jones d. at Summit, aged 1 yr., 10 mos., 19 days.

12/15/1887 Barnes/Lewis, md. at China Grove, 11/24/1887, by Rev. R. S. Gale, C. C. Barnes and Beulah B. Lewis.

12/29/1887 Conerly, Bro. Cullen F. b. in Marion Co., Miss., 12/27/1842, d. in Vernon Par., La., 11/13/1887, son of John R. and Elizabeth Conerly, old pioneer Methodists. Volunteered in the late war where he became the victim of lung disease which proved fatal. Md. in 1870 to Mary Koonce; in 1877 served on the police jury and in 1879 elected sheriff of Vernon Parish.

1/5/1888 Alford, Mrs. Mary S., b. in Tenn., 1/29/1836, d. 9/1/1887, at home near Johnston Station, Pike Co., Miss. Her maiden name was Kirk. In 1860 she md. Rev. Daniel M. Wadsworth of the Miss. Conf., who died shortly after their marriage. In 1864 she md. Seaborn J. Alford, who died 3 years ago. She left orphans.

1/19/1888 Carruth/Nix, md. 1/5/1888, Samuel E. Carruth of Lincoln Co., to Miss Z. L. Nix of Pike Co.

1/26/1888 Wadsworth, Judge John, d. Franklinton, La., on 1/2/1888, aged 65 yrs., 4 mos., 22 days. Judge of the Parish, 1872-1874.

2/23/1888 Magee, Mrs. Celia, widow of Nehemiah Magee, d. 9/22/1887. Left 4 sons, 2 daus., 2 sisters, and 2 brothers. She was 54 yrs. old. Funeral by Rev. Eady.

5/3/1888 Holmes, Nancy Elizabeth, b. 12/28/1854, in Marion Co., oldest dau. of John M. & Lucinda Conerly; md. Wesley Holmes 2/1880, d. 3/27/1888. Became Methodist at China Grove 7/1874 under influence of Bro. H. P. Lewis.

Conerly, Col. James B., Marion Co., Miss., 2/7/1831, d. 12/25/1887 at Tyler Town; born of Methodist parents; md. 10/20/1853 to Mary Lamkins with whom he lived 35 yrs and fathered 6 children, all of whom lived to maturity except 1. He and wife joined Methodist Ch. at China Grove in 1855/1856; Mason in Tyler Town Lodge; buried with Masonic Honors 12/26/1887.

7/5/1888 Raiford, Wm. B., d. at Gloster, Amite Co., Miss., 5/24/1888, on his 59th yr.; b. Goldsboro, Wayne Co., N.C.; moved to Pike Co., Miss., in 1850; md. Jane Tarver, dau. of Elijah Tarver of Amite Co., on 12/27/1853; became merchant in Amite Co. (Long article about his career)

3/7/1889 Simmons, Mrs. Harriet Cecelia (nee Warner), d. at Tangipahoa, La., 11/23/1888, aged 54 yrs.; md. Joseph M. Simmons in Pike Co., 1/29/1852; converted during the Civil War and first joined Baptist ch.

3/14/1889 Felder, Katie (Miss), d. 2/15/1889, b. 2/3/1869 near Topisaw Camp Ground.

7/4/1889 Godbold, Rowan P., d. at Summit June 7, 1889, aged 30 yrs., 8 mos., 9 days; joined Methodist Ch. in 1880 under inf. of Rev. W. W. Hopper; left wife, aged mother, 2 bros., and 2 sisters.

12/5/1889 Lewis, Mrs. Susan, dau. of Joseph and Hannah Warren, b. Marion Co., Miss., in 1832; md. 1853 to Iddo Lewis; d. of hematuria 10/22/1889, 30 yrs. a Methodist. Left a husband and 4 children.

Sistrunk, George W., b. Pike Co., 3/22/1827, d. Crystal Springs 6/7/1889; left wife.

12/19/1889 Felder, Eula, youngest dau. of George and Iowa Felder, d. Port Vincent, La., 9/6/1889, aged 1 yr., 1 mo., 6 days.

7/3/1890 Tynes, T. F., b. Marion Co., 5/10/1822, d. 2/1/1890 of dropsy.

9/18/1890 Smith/McNulty, md. at Summit, Prof. Maxy Smith and Sady McNulty (no date).

11/13/1890 Dear, Hardy, b. Columbia, Marion Co., Miss., d. Poplarville, Miss., 9/20/1890, aged 69 yrs.

1/22/1891 Nelson/Strickland, md. at res. of Rev. E. R. Strickland in Pike Co., 1/8/1891, by Rev. J. W. Ellison, Fred Nelson and Ella F. Strickland.

2/12/1891 Lewis, W. Ben, d. at China Grove 6:45 P.M., 1/15/1891, aged 46 yrs., 2 mos., 8 days, d. within a mile of his birthplace; b. 11/7/1847. A Methodist and a Confederate Soldier; joined China Grove 20 yrs. ago; left wife and 7 children, 4 of whom were members of China Grove.

3/12/1891 Bridges, Hugh Franklin, b. 11/25/1805; md. Margaret Smith; lived last yrs. with dau. Mrs. Martha Catchings near Georgetown, Miss.; d. 11/4/1890.

Franklin, Rev. Thos., d. Vernon Par. on Anacoco, 2/3/1891; b. 1/8/1826; md. Martha Ann Davis 12/15/1853; licensed to exhort 1854 and to preach 1855.

4/9/1891 Felder, Lula S., dau. of Mr. and Mrs. R. H. Felder of Topisaw, b. 9/12/1867, d. 12/16/1890, converted at Topisaw Camp Meeting in 1881.

4/23/1891 Lenoir, Walter A., b. Marion Co., Miss., 8/31/1821, d. same county 1/24/1891; md. Harriet Foxworth 8/3/1847; had 12 children, 7 surviving at his death. Joined church at Topisaw Camp Meeting.

6/18/1891 Jennings/Combs, md. at Holmesville 7/1/1891, A. W. Jennings and Miss. A. A. Combs.

Wright, Sister M. J., wife of Capt. D. C. Wright, d. Apr. 28, 1891. She and sister converted at old Carrollton Camp Ground; md. in 1850; left a dau.

7/9/1891 Havers/Sharp, md. at Summit, E. P. Havers and Effie A. Sharp (no date).

10/29/1891 Selman, W. R., d. 7/9/1891, b. on 1/22/1824 in Pike Co.; md. Kate Baker 9/25/1851. She was from Franklin Co., Ala. In 1868 settled in Lawrence Co.

and raised a large family.

12/3/1891 Gatlin, Willie, son of Z. B. Gatlin and Martha Hoover Gatlin, b. 3/20/1867, baptized by Rev. E. A. Flowers in 1889; d. in Pike Co. 10/15/ ?, 1891.

1/21/1892 Magee/Warren, md. at res. of bride's father in Summit 12/22/1891, Lem. L. Magee and Addie E. Warren.

Elliott, S. T., b. Pike Co., 1/6/1866, d. 1/5/1892 at home of brother-in-law Capt. S. B. Williams.

3/31/1892 Rice/Prewett, md. at Magnolia, T. J. Rice to Maybell Prewett of Pike Co.

5/12/1892 Calhoun, Lucious, d. in Holmesville at home of parents 4/7/1892, aged 14 yrs., 8 mos., 7 days.

Tynes, James L., b. Marion Co., 1/3/1820, d. at home of son-in-law T. C. Harvey in Terry, Hinds Co., 3/14/1890; md. 11/10/1849, to Miss P. G. Collins; joined Methodist Ch. in 1856.

5/26/1892 Lewis/Alford, md. on 5/1/1892, Q. C. Lewis of Placquemine, La., and Emma B. Alford of Pike Co., Miss.

6/16/1892 Gibson/Foot, md. at res. of bride's father C. C. Foot, McComb City, on 5/31/1892, by Rev. L. Burton, Rev. C. C. Gibson and Miss Minnie E. Foot.

7/14/1892 Gorman, Mrs. E. A. (nee More), d. near Osyka 4/4/1892, leaves husband M. D. K. Gorman of Crowley, La.; joined Methodist E. Ch. at Pipkin's Chapel in St. Helena Par., La.

Hunt, Nancy Anne, b. 2/3/1850, in Miss.; md. W. H. Hunt 5/13/1875, d. in Vernon Par., 5/14/1892; left husband and 6 children.

7/21/1892 Magee/Alford, md. at Magnolia, W. C. Magee of Franklinton, La., to Lena Alford of Pike Co.

7/28/1892 Strickland, Rev. Erastus Root, of Miss. Conf., d. at Summit 2/25/1892; b. Delaware Co., N.Y., 4/6/1807; converted at Maple Ridge, Orleans Co., N.Y., at age 22; came to Miss. Conf. in 1838.

8/11/1892 Anders, Michael b. Gloster, Miss., 1/18/1813, d. 6/16/1892; md. Susan E. Roberts 4/6/1841; had 11 children, 6 of whom were dead by 1892. Converted at old Vernon in 1880. (By W. W. Simmons)

8/18/1892 Stafford, Joshua, b. Clarke Co., Miss., 11/6/1852, d. near Magnolia 6/14/1892; joined church when young. Funeral preached by Revs. V. V. Boone and W. F. Harden.

5/15/1892 Regan, Alif Farrar, b. Franklinton, La., 10/20/1827; md. J. A. Regan 1/5/1843; had 5 daus., 2 sons; d. Natchez 7/22/1892; left husband, 1 son, 2 daus., 6 grandchildren and 1 great-grandchild.

10/3/1892 Smiley/ Copes, md. at home of bride's mother on 9/28/1892, by Rev. V. V. Boone, Edward Smiley of Ramsey, La., to Mary Copes of Magnolia.

11/3/1892 Wroten, Dr. Vincent J., d. at home near Magnolia 10/7/1892 in his 75th yr.; b. in Pike Co. 5/1818; graduated in medicine in 1841; md. Miss Elizabeth Quin in 1845; converted in 1847; joined Methodist Ch. in same year. Survived by 2 sons and 2 daus. (By J. W. Sandell)

11/10/1892 Brown, Mrs. Charlotte, dau. of late Wyatt and Cynthia Hope Felder, b. Pike Co., 2/6/1840; md. 1) H. E. Thornhill 7/11/1858 by whom she had 2 children who died young. Thornhill d. 6/26/1862. She md. 2) Thomas Rollins d. 1877 by whom she had 3 daus. Md. 3) 1/31/1878 to Wm. Brown. She d. 10/16/1892 in Lincoln Co.

11/24/1892 Conerly, Little Davie Edna, dau. of Dr. T. S. and Courtney Conerly b. 11/25/1891, d. 10/24/1892 at China Grove.

Applewhite, Little Marvin, son of Dr. E. L. and Lou Applewhite, d. at China Grove (no dates given).

2/16/1893 Simmons, sister Mollie H., Memorial from Ladies Aid Society of the Methodist Ch. of Magnolia signed by Mrs. A. Gatlin for committee.

3/2/1893 Simmons, Mrs. M. H., eldest dau. of W. C. and C. D. Vaught, b. 12/31/1864, d. at home in Magnolia after lingering suffering 12/23/1892; md. T. C. Simmons 9/13/1887; left 3 children--Clara, Oliver, and Clinton.

3/9/1893 Smith/Jourdan, md. at res. of Mrs. Gottig in Magnolia on 2/22/1893, Rev. C. F. Smith of the E. Texas Conf., to Miss L. D. Jourdan of Magnolia.

4/13/1893 Jenkins/Impson, md. in McComb on 4/2/1893, John L. Jenkins of Summit to Mrs. Martha J. Impson.

McLean/Britt, md. in McComb on 3/3/1893, Charles Earl McLean (McLeon?) to Sarah McLaurin Britt, all of McComb.

Weidmer/Bronson, md. at res. of bride's father R. C. Bronson of McComb, Frank Weidmer to Roche Irene Bronson of McComb.

Holmes/Godbold, md. at McComb on 2/28/1893, J. F. Holmes to Mrs. Jessie I. Godbold of Summit.

4/27/1893 Bennette, Elisha Coleman, b. 3/12/1861, d. 11/20/1892, md. Mattie D. Holmes on 12/1/1880. (By E. H. Rook)

8/24/1893 Hudson, Brother (first name probably not given), b. Lumbardy Grove, Va., 12/19/1841, d. Summit, Miss., 5/9/1893; moved to Ala. in 1845 and to Monticello, N.C., in 1856; joined Methodist Ch. at Greensboro when 16; served in the Southern Army under Capt. Daniels, Co. G 44th Regt; surrendered with Lee at Appomattox; went back to N.C.; in 1870 to Mattie Young; in 1876 md. 2) Mrs. Ann J. Moore and moved to Durant, Miss., in 1887 and to Summit in 1888.

9/7/1893 Gatlin, Zebulon Butler, son of James Gatlin and Rosalvia Wells Gatlin, b. Pike Co., 8/20/1832; md. Martha Hoover, dau. of late Judge C. Hoover and Mrs. Mary Neyland Nailer, by Rev. Peter Green, 9/16/1852; d. Pike Co. 6/16/1893; a Confederate Soldier and a Christian, converted by Rev. Ephraim Flowers.

10/12/1893 Godbold, Bro. P. B., b. Franklin Co., Miss., 4/4/1829, d. at Summit 8/14/1893; joined church at Ebenezer, Franklin Co., md. Mary Ann Cloy on 5/24/1848 by whom he had 7 children, 3 of whom preceded him to Glory Land.

Germany, Willie Laura, b. 1/31/1891, d. 8/21/1893; and Germany, Zebbie Lee, b. 7/20/1889 (?), d. 8/25/1893, child of Bro. and Sis. Wm. Germany of Johnston's Station, Miss.

1/11/1894 McDaniel/Dillon, md. at Franklinton, La., Methodist Parsonage on 12/21/1893, Wiley McDaniel and Jane Dillon, both of Pike Co., Miss.

1/18/1894 Lewis, Quinea Monroe, son of Barney and Kesiah Lewis, b. at Holmesville, d. at Norfield, Lincoln Co., Miss., 9/16/1893, aged 44 yrs., 5 mos., 29 days. (By Rev. H. P. Lewis)

2/1/1894 Butler/Stewart, md. at res. of bride's father George Stewart of Summit, 12/19/1893, D. P. Butler to Miss Willena Stewart.

2/8/1894 Tyler, Wm. Glanville, b. Cops Hill, City of Boston, 5/18/1804, d. in Tylertown, Pike Co., 11/23/1893. When he was 3 his parents moved to Landover where he grew up. In 1833 he came south and lived in New Orleans and Covington, La., then moved to Columbia in Marion Co. and on to an area of Tylertown in 1836. Md. 1) Mary L. Connally in 1837 by whom he had 5 children; md. 2) Mrs. Nancy Sandifer who lived only 2 years afterwards. Tyler spent his last years with his children and the last 2 with his son-in-law Bro. D. N. Ball. (By M. J. Miller)

2/15/1894 Sandell, Permelia L., b. in Magnolia 4/3/1836, d. Magnolia 12/12/1893, dau. of Thomas and Almira Powell; md. 1) W. J. Martin who d. in the late war;

md. 2) Rev. J. W. Sandell of the Miss. Conf. on 9/9/1865.

Warren, G. W., b. 11/19/1852, d. 8/26/1893, left wife and 6 children. (No location of residence given.)

6/7/1894 Barnes, W. W., b. in Robinson [Robeson] Co., N.C., 10/22/1814, d. in Miss. 3/2/1894; moved to Miss. in 1831; joined church in 1834 at a camp meeting at Crystal Springs; md. in 1838 to Eliza M. Risher.

6/28/1894 Jones, William Hugh, son of Wm. D. and Emma Adelaide Bertis Jones, b. 11/17/1883, d. 6/7/1894 in McComb.

7/26/1894 Sartin, Alfred, b. Pike Co. 2/6/1818, d. 2/21/1894, md. in 1837 to Miss T. Powers; md. 2) Mrs. Frances Newton.

Sartin, Louisa A., dau. of Dr. E. and Mrs. P. J. Cowart, d. in McComb City, 5/29/1894; she was b. in Lincoln Co. 9/17/1863; md. Selph Sartin 9/17/1880.

8/30/1894 Ramsey, Thomas Y., infant son of Josiah B. and Sallie Carey Ramsey, b. in McComb City 2/14/1894, d. 7/6/1894, aged 4 mos., 22 days.

11/1/1894 Felder, Rufus K., b. Pike Co., Miss., 4/26/1820, d. 7/30/1894; md. Sarah Singletary 12/8/1855; joined Methodist-Epis. Ch. in 1845.

12/20/1894 Armstrong, Mattie Regina, dau. of John O. and Kate C. Armstrong, b. 12/3/1876, d. in McComb City 11/22/1894; joined Baptist Ch. 10/1892.

3/28/1895 Rankin, George W., b. Marion Co., Miss., 3/31/1830; md. Ann E. Flynn 10/4/1855; joined church summer of 1863 while a soldier in Tenn.; d. 6 mi. south of Columbia, 1/31/1895.

4/4/1895 Hayman, Wm. M., b. 3/16/1867 near Summit, d. at the old home 12/12/1894; leaves mother, 5 brothers, 2 sisters, wife and 3 small children.

5/9/1895 Bethea, Mrs. Mary Eliza (nee LeGette), b. Marion Dist., S.C. in 3/1832, d. at Summit, Miss., 2/19/1895; md. Rev. R. C. Bethea M.D. in 1852 by whom she had 4 sons, 2 daus.; joined Methodist Ch. at old Centenary Camp Ground, Marion Dist., S.C.

10/24/1895 Yarborough, T., b. Marion Co., Miss., 3/4/1852, d. Liverpool, La., 1/8/1895, leaving wife, 5 children, aged parents, 3 bros., and 1 sister.

1/30/1896 Lewis, Mrs. Kesiah, eldest dau. of S. L. and Narcissa Lamkin [sic], b. Ala. 8/21/1831, came as child with parents to Magee's Cr. near Tylertown; father d. at Holmesville in 1875. She md. 2/23/1846 to Barney Lewis, eldest son of Quinea and Martha Lewis. Barney published the paper at Holmesville called "The True Southern." In 12/1855 moved to Leake Co.; then to Brookhaven; from there to Crystal Springs where husband d. in 12/1874. She moved to Dayton, then Rosetta, Miss., where she d. 11/23/1895. H. P. Lewis, author of the obit., stated that he had also written her husband's obit. and officiated at her mother's funeral "in August last." Lewis also conducted Kesiah's funeral.

2/27/1896 Magee, Andrew G., b. Washington Par., La., 1/7/1850, d. 11/16/1895.

Warner, Mrs. Laura D. (nee Holmes) b. 2/9/1842, d. 3/11/1895, md. Daniel C. Warner 9/26/1864 and became a Methodist soon after.

4/2/1896 Whittington, Mrs. Addie R. (nee Bazzoon), b. St. Helena Par., La., 1/2/1866; joined Methodist-Epis. Ch. in 1891; md. B. F. Whittington on 5/7/1893; d. in McComb City 2/12/1896. The writer, Rev. J. T. Abney buried her child on 9/15/1895.

5/28/1895 Beeson, Mrs. Evaline Lenora (nee Collins), b. Washington Par., La., 5/25/1826, d. 4/16/1895; md. on 3/25/1847 to Rev. B. A. Beeson who survives her. She mothered 17 children, of whom 13 survived her; joined church at Topisaw Camp Ground. (By B. W. Lewis)

May, Mrs. Rachel Ann (nee Collins), b. Pike Co. 5/21/1839, d. 4/6/1896, md. Enos D. May on 1/16/1860. Survived by her husand and 5 children.

7/2/1896 Fountain, J. B., of Columbia, Miss., b. 2/2/1821, d. 6/7/1896; member of Baptist Ch. for 45 years. Survived by wife, 2 sons and 2 md. daus.

7/16/1896 Gibson, Hattie E., b. Pike Co. 8/18/1859, d. at Summit 3/12/1896, aged 36 yrs., 8 mos., and 28 days, dau. of Major and Harriet Gibson. Her father d. in 1883; survived by mother, 1 brother and several sisters.

10/22/1896 Powell, Mrs. Eliza (nee Marton) b. 10/8/1856, near Magnolia, md. J. W. Powell 12/10/1874, joined Methodist Ch. 9/5/1874, d. 7/3/(?), 1896.

Martin, Eugene F., b. 1/5/1859, in W. Feliciana Par., La., moved to Pike Co., joined Methodist Ch. at Muddy Springs 9/17/1879; d. 7/6/1896. (By J. T. Abney)

10/29/1896 Stafford, Joshua Joseph, b. 1/20/1890, d. at mother's home 9/30/1896. No location given.

12/5/1896 Turnipseed, Mary Huffman, dau. of late John Huffman and Mrs. Mary Glass Huffman, b. Pike Co., 3/26/1843, md. Berkly S. Turnipseed 12/20/1864. He d. 4/25/1890. She d. 2/19/1896. Obit. mentioned her sister-in-law Mrs. Brylie.

11/26/1896 Pound, Mrs. Edna, dau. of W. F. and S. P. Sparks, b. 12/8/1870, d. at Nettleton, Lee Co., 9/7/1896; md. R. L. Pound 6/17/1890.

4/29/1897 Gatlin, Col. James S., b. in Ala. 4/20/1811, d. at Johnston's Station, Miss., 2/21/1897. When 4, his parents moved to Miss. where he grew up and md. His wife d. in 1881, by whom had a large family. Two sons survived in 1897--N. W. Gatlin (with whom he lived in last yrs.) and John Gatlin of Magnolia.

9/9/1897 Felder, Virginia Harrison, dau. of George M. Kirk and Mrs. Nancy Sessums Kirk, b. Hardeman Co., Tenn., on 5/28/1840. As a child, she and parents moved to Ark. and to Biloxi, Miss., where she was reared and educated. During war refugeed in Amite Co., Miss.; md. Ira Felder of Pike Co. in 1/1870, mothered 8 children--2 sons died in infancy, 5 sons and 1 dau. survived her. She d. Sun., 5/9/1897 in Pike Co. (By Mrs. M. L. J. Hoover)

12/16/1897 Godbold, Irvin, d. at 3 yrs., 2 mos., on 10/19/1897. Obit. by "Aunt Belle."

1/6/1898 Ball, D. N., of Pike Co. [Tylertown], b. 2/24/1833, d. 12/20/1897, converted in early manhood; md. 8/30/1855 to Miss M. E. Tyler by whom he had 15 children; 9 with his wife survive him. One son was sheriff of the county; 1 son, a physician in Alexandria, La.; 2 daus. md. Methodist preachers--Rev. W. M. Stevens of the Miss. Conf. and Rev. L. E. Alford of the La. Conf. (By F. G. Hocutt)

2/3/1898 Terrall, James Landrum, b. Amite Co., Miss., 2/10/1821, son of Hiram Terrall and Isabell Glass, one of 9 sons and 3 daus. raised to maturity. In his childhood parents moved to Pike Co. Md. on 12/22/1842 to Mary M. Sandell. She and 3 daus survive him. In 1847 moved to La. and settled near Mansfield. He served in Confederate Army and came home in bad health. Was farmer by profession. (By his daughter)

5/12/1898 Ford, Mrs. Mattie, dau. of the late Mr. and Mrs. Wm. Ligon, b. Pike Co., near China Grove, 5/13/1849; joined Baptist Ch. when 13 yrs. old. Md. on 1/25/187_ to D. C. Ford, then became Methodist; d. at Summit 3/24/1898. One dau. died in 1894; survived by 6 sons, 2 daus. and her husband. (By H. P. Lewis)

7/28/1898 Moore, Thomas G., b. Greensborough, Ga., 8/3/1832, d. at Magnolia 5/3/1898, parents moved to Miss. near Houston, where he was converted. On 5/20/1861 he married Mary E. Garner near Summit. She, 1 dau. and 2 grandsons survive him.

8/11/1898 Powell/Bales, md. at res. of bride's parents, J. A. and Janette Bales of McComb City on 7/20/1898, by Rev. R. B. Bales, W. L. Powell and Nellie Bales.

10/27/1898 Brown, Rosie, dau. of James L. and Lon J. Brown, b. Holmesville 9/23/1883, d. near Pine Grove Methdoist Ch., St. Helena Par., La., 2/7/1897; survived by parents, twin sister Lillie, 3 older sisters, 3 bros., and an aged grandmother.

12/8/1898 Applewhite, Mrs. Prudence, b. 6/16/1816, md. Thomas Applewhite 1/19/1836, d. 10/19/1798. (By Vashti Hodges of Cotton Valley, La.)

Huffman, Mrs. Abi Elizabeth, dau. of Levi and Martha Felder of Pike Co., b. 5/31/1849, d. at her home 7 mi. from Summit 8/17/1898; md. George W. Huffman 1/10/1867 by whom she had 6 children, one of whom died in infancy. Last illness was severe. (By V. V. Boone)

12/15/1898 Barnes, Willis, b. Robeson Co., N.C., 6/8/1816, d. Crystal Springs 11/2/1898; moved to Miss. in 1834, to Crystal Springs in 1871; converted at age 10 by Rev. Hardy Mullins. At age 21 md. Mary M. Hennington who d. 15 yrs. ago. In 1887 he md. Mrs. Kate Long, who survived him.

12/22/1898 Roberts, Abraham Jasper b. Amite Co., Miss., 6/1/1830, d. near Bewelcome (?) 11/11/1898; md. on 1/7/1851 to Catherine Anders by whom he had 8 children, 6 sons and 2 daus. Wife and 4 children survived him.

Barnes, Mrs. Missie King, b. 11/14/1870, md. J. A. Barnes of Benton, Miss., 11/3/1897, d. 11/9/1898.

7/27/1899 Fant, Elmise, infant dau. of Bro. and Sis. F. A. Fant of Johnston's Station, b. 7/19/1898, d. 5/3/1899. (By J. A. More)

8/3/1899 Pool, Mrs. Malinda C., b. Pike Co., 4/6/1825, removed to Copiah Co. when young; converted at early age; twice md. 1) A. Y. Lord in 1849; 2) A. D. Miller.

Dear, Virginia Coffman, dau. of Dr. C. R. and Mrs. V. E. Rencher, b. Enterprise, Miss., 2/3/1871, baptized by Bishop Paine 6/4/1871; professed religion at age 12; d. 6/13/1899; md. H. M. Dear of Enterprise 12/16/1898.

8/17/1899 King, James H., b. Pike Co., Miss., 4/26/1819; moved to Tangipahoa Par., La., near Amite City in 1836; md. Evilene Dean in 1839; had 8 children, 2 of whom died in infancy. In 1854 moved to Pine Grove, La.; 1st wife d. 9/1868; md. 2) 10/12/1877 to Mary A. Tabor who gave him a son. Joined Methodist Ch. at age 10. (By F. N. Sweeny)

9/21/1899 Franklin, Sister Martha A., (nee Davis), d. Vernon Par., La. 8/3/1899, b. 4/26/1834; md. Thomas Franklin on 12/15/1853; her husband Rev. Thomas Franklin was a local deacon in Methodist Ch. for many yrs. Her husband died some yrs. ago. She left children.

Carruth, Mrs. Emma, b. 3/18/1876, d. 7/23/1899, dau. of Mr. C. W. Beam, a preacher for many years on the Adams circuit; baptized in infancy by grandfather, Dr. John Sample. Joined Methodist Ch. at Ebenezer at age 12; md. on 9/1/1898 to J. A. Carruth and had twin sons who were only 2-3 weeks old at mother's death. Left husband, father, 2 bros., 5 sisters, and infant sons. (By B. H. Rawls, Tylertown)

9/28/1899 Causey, Mrs. _____ Lucy, dau. of Bro. J. R. & Sister M. E. Conerly, b. Tylertown on 9/19/1879; moved to Gloster. At age 7 converted at China Grove Camp Meeting; held membership of church in Tylertown until she moved to Gloster; d. _____; left a baby only 2 weeks old and 4 step-children. (By M. M. Black) [Obit. unclear on film.]

10/5/1899 Boston, Mrs. Mattie Warren (nee Dunman), b. near McComb City on 9/30/1874; d. Franklin, Ky., 8/15/1899; when 13 converted at Houston, Texas, under ministry of Rev. J. L. Hendry, now a missionary to Cains (?); lated joined Baptist Ch. On 5/26/1892, md. in Meridian, Miss., to John Boston of Bowling Green Ky.; spent 4 yrs. of marriage in McComb; ill last two years of life. (M. M. Black, Gloster, Miss.)

11/2/1899 Marshall, Mrs. Amanda, dau. of Wm. and Eliza Black, b. near Gallman, Miss., 8/24/1847, d. at home near Fernwood, Miss., 10/10/1899; md. in 1869 to Dr. C. C. Marshall, who d. in 1883. She was a good Methodist; buried by husband at Hazlehurst, Miss.

11/9/1899 Fant, Little Joe Van, son of S. A. and Lula G. Fant, b. 6/26/1888, d. of typhoid at Johnston's Station 8/16/1899. (By J. A. Moore)

12/28/1899 Beam, Mrs. Mollie, b. 10/9/1844, dau. of Alexander and Lucretia Carruth; had 6 bros. and 2 sisters, all yet living except 1 brother; all were Methodist. She was converted 10/28/1864; joined Presbyterian Ch. at Summit; md. 12/13/1883 to C. W. Beam, a widower with several children, some of whom were small; had children of her own. D. at home in Summit after a week's illness on 8/28/1899. (By B. H. Rawls, Tylertown)

2/8/1900 Boone, Mrs. Dela, b. 12/8/1842 near Carthage, Leake Co., Miss., dau. of Taylor Williams; md. J. F. Boone in 1867; she d. at Magnolia 12/16/1899. She had 4 children, 3 sons and a dau. who d. at 5 mos. The sons, Rev. V. V. Boone of Miss. Conf., Emmett of Texas; and Daniel "of this place" still living. Miss Florence Grogan, a niece, was taken into the family at age 10 and took the place of the dau. Family moved to Magnolia in 1894. (By J. W. Sandell)

2/22/1900 Hubbard/LeNoir, md. at res. of Bro. Brown, McComb, on 2/14/1900, by Rev. Isaac L. Peebles, George Hubbard to Mary LeNoir of Magnolia.

3/22/1900 Quin, Judge H. Murray, d. early morning, Thursday, 3/1/1900; b. in Holmesville where he lived for almost half a century (54 yrs.); md. 1) Miss Bearden; md. 2) Nannie Sumrall by whom he had 2 children. Survived by children, grandchildren, and great-grandchildren. He was in public office almost all his life--began as Clerk of Court in Pike Co., then was a lawyer, probate judge (turned out of office by the "carpet-bag" governor Adelbert Ames), mayor of Summit, last part of life a Justice of the Peace for area around Holmesville. (Long feature article)

3/29/1900 Scarborough, Sister Sarah Elizabeth, dau. of Bro. and Sister Power b. near Pearl R. in Washington Par., on 10/15/1867; md. Charles Scarborough on 2/10/1887; joined Methodist Ch. Aug., 1895. (By Robert Randle P. C., Franklinton, La.)

3/19/1900 Ramsey/Rhymes, md. at Methodist Parsonage in McComb, 3/25/1900 by Rev. Isaac L. Peebles, W. M. Ramsey and Miss T. E. Rhymes of McComb.

4/12/1900 Alford, Mrs. Anne or "Aunt Anne," d. 1/30/1900 at home of her son Rev. N. E. Alford near Magnolia; devoted member of Methodist Ch.; mother of 11 children, most of whom went on before her. (By Mollie Carter, her granddaughter, Lumberton, Miss.)

4/26/1900 Ford, Mrs. Olive H., wife of W. F. Ford, dau. of J. M. and Frances L. Foxworth, b. at Hopewell, Columbia Circuit, Marion Co., on 10/24/1871, d. 3/14/1900, at Balltown, La., md. M. F. Ford 10/16/1895. (By W. M. Williams)

5/3/1900 Alford, Mrs. Celia A. (nee Lewis), b. 11/6/1822, d. 1/13/1900, dau. of Quinea and Martha Lewis; md. in 1840 to Warren Jackson Alford who preceded her to the grave by 2 mos., 19 days; she had 11 children, all living except a son and a dau. Joined Methodist Ch. when about 18. She had 2 brothers in Miss. Conf.--W. B. and H. P. Lewis. Her son Rev. N. E. Alford is a local Methodist preacher. (B. H. Rawls, Tylertown)

Thompson, Jesse, Sr., b. near Columbia, Miss., 7/1/1812, d. near Spencer in Copiah Co., 2/20/1900; md. 5/10/1835 to Nancy Rembert; md. 46 years. Mrs. Thompson d. 9/17/1881. He md. 2) on 7/21/1882 to Mrs. Eliza Jones, who survived him.

5/10/1900 Barr, Sister Sarah H., dau. of Judge Christian Hoover and Mary N. Nailer; b. Pike Co., 3/30/1838; md. T. C. S. Barr on 6/10/1856; d. at 1:30 P.M. 3/31/1900, 62 yrs. and 1 day old. Mother of 3 children; 1 son died in infancy and another son Thomas C. Barr and his sister Mrs. Mollie Johnson administered unto her until the end. (D. P. Drake, Summit)

6/7/1900 Yarborough, Mrs. Susan, b. in Marion Co., 4/5/1837, dau. of Judge Lemuel and Polly Lewis; joined Methodist Ch. when 20; converted when 18, in 1854 md. Jabez Yarborough by whom she had 4 sons and 1 dau. She spent her last years in home of son-in-law B. A. Bummer [sic--Summer?], d. in Buford, Marion Co., Miss., and buried at China Grove. (B. F. Rawls P.C., Tylertown)

6/21/1900 Elzey, Lizzie Lamkin, b. Columbus, Ga., 2/13/1835; dau. of Sampson L. and Narcissa Lamkins who moved to Holmesville, Miss.; united with Methodist Ch. when young; went to Cokesburg College for ed.; taught for 20 years; md. Rev. E. L. Tarver in 4/1883 with whom she lived 7 years, being widowed on 5/12/1890. On 6/18/1891 she md. R. A. Elzey of McComb who survived her. Buried in family cemetery near Adams Church, Lincoln Co., Miss.

7/5/1900 Hines, Mrs. Jane Fletcher, b. in N. C., 11/3/1822; d. at Summit, Thursday, 4/19/1900; dau. of Charles Caster Coppedge and Azzle Kendall whose fathers were from Va. and settled in N.C. Dr. Coppedge (her father) was ed. to be a doctor, but ill health forced him from the profession; he became sheriff of his home city. Both parents were Methodist. After Dr. Coppedge's death, the widow moved to Miss. to be with relatives near Grenada. Jane md. W. B. Hines, a young medical student, who 5 years later answered the call to preach and joined the Miss. Conf. After 59 years as a wife and 54 years as a preacher's wife, she was a widow. She had 10 children of whom 6 preceded her to the home above. Several died young, but the son Edward was taken in the flush of youth; Dr. John H., the skillful physician, in the maturity of strength and usefulness. She spent last yrs. with dau. Mrs. Millie Reed. (By Clara B. Drake)

6/16/1900 Brown, Elbert, b. 12/27/1822, united with Methodist Ch. at Pine Grove, Pike Co., 9/1855; moved to Pine Grove, St. Helena Par., La., in 1860; lived there 40 yrs.; d. 4/1/1900; left wife and relatives.

7/26/1900 Raiford, Mrs. E. J., b. Pike Co., 4/4/1833, d. Gloster on 7/1/1900; wife of Hon. Wm. B. Raiford, who preceded her to the "beautiful beyond." Left children and grandchildren.

8/9/1900 Webb, Sampson C., Jr., son of Dr. S. C. and Margaret A. Webb. b. at Liberty 5/8/1876; md. Bertha Barnes of Pike Co. 10/21/1896; d. Gloster 5/2/1900.

8/23/1900 Brumfield, Wm. son of Thomas and Sister Brumfield; b. Washington Par., La., 2 md. NE of Franklinton 3/30/1859; joined Methodist in 8/1890; d. 5/27/1900.

9/6/1900 Felder, Bro. Levy, b. 9/28/1822, md. 12/16/1847; joined Methodist 10/1848; d/ 4/24/1900; wife Mary and 4 children and grandchildren survive him. Funeral preached by Rev. J. J. Golden of Topisaw Ch. He was a founder of the Topisaw Camp Meeting, one of the oldest campgrounds in Miss. (H. P. Lewis)

11/1/1900 Huffman, Joseph L., b. 8/31/1878, d. 8/15/1900; joined Methodist when 9 at Topisaw under influence of Rev. R. S. Gale; 4th Sun. in Oct., 1899, md. Belle Coney; leaves wife, father, 3 sisters, 1 brother.

11/5/1900 Geiger, Lewis, d. at Silver Cr. 5/2/1900, age 75; b. Jessup, Wayne Co., Ga., 3/1/1826; moved to Miss. when 15 yrs. old; md. 1849 (ca.) to Elizabeth Bush of Simpson Co. (who d. in 1860), leaving 8 children--5 still living; joined Methodist Ch. in 1880. (By J. Early Gray, Silver Creek)

12/6/1900 Akin, Rev. John, b. Pike Co., Miss., 12/2/1815; d. at home of son Wm. in Union Par., La., 9/16/1900; joined Methodist in 1825; md. Susan Garlington 10/25/1836; licensed to preach by Elder R. R. Alexander in 1855 in what is now the Salem and Summerfield charges.

2/21/1901 Felder, Mrs. Clara (nee Williams), b. 7/29/1875, d. 12/5/1900; joined Church in 18__; 2/3/1896 md. John Henry Felder and same summer united with the Methodist Ch. at Topisaw. Left husband and 2 sweet little daus. (By J. J. Golden)

3/7/1901 Bridges, Mrs. Elize, wife of E. V. Bridges, and dau. of John and Janie Sistruck; d. at Beach Grove in Copiah Co., Miss.; moved with parents to Copiah Co. when 4 yrs. old; md. 12/28/1869; left husband and 3 sons with their wives and families.

4/4/1901 Beam, Charles Walton, b. 8/12/1836; d. at Summit 12/17/1900; md. 6/30/1867 to Fannie Sample; had 9 children; wife and mother passed to reward on 8/29/1882; on 12/13/1883 he md. 2) Mollie Carruth by whom he had one child. (By M. L. Burton)

4/11/1901 Muggah, Katella Edith, dau. of Capt. Thomas R. and Addie Fash Muggah; b. Summit 6/23/1864; d. Patterson, La., 3/4/1901 after a 3-day illness; joined Methodist at the Felicity St. Ch. in N.O.

5/30/1901 Hayman, John T., b. Pike Co., 4/1/1847; d. 1/8/1901; left wife and children. (By R. L. Webb)

6/6/1901 Williams, James H., b. Covington Co., Miss., 1/31/1848; d. Silver Springs, Miss., 2/11/1901; joined Methodist-Epis. Ch. at Mt. Zion; 10/28/1869 md. Thirzah Ann Dale by whom he had 6 children.

7/11/1901 Creel, Robert, b. Scott Co., Miss., d. at McComb City 3/8/1901, 57 yrs. old. (R. L. Webb)

7/18/1901 Bowman, Claiborne, in his 82nd yr., d. at res. of son in Yazoo Co., Miss., b. in Pike Co., son of Judge Richardson Bowman, who with wife and 2 daus. settled land in Yazoo Co. in 1828--land still in family in 1901. In 1835-37 Claiborne was employed on land plat called Manchester; father d. in 1834; mother, in 1840, thus making him the head of the family. He md. in 1853 to Mrs. Elizabeth Hays, widow of W. C. Hayes, dau. of Robert Stephens, by whom he had dau. named Rebekah, who md. Dr. Henry Yandell. Wife d. 3/15/1853 (dates conflict) leaving Rebecca and infant son named Richie. On 3/21/1871 Claiborne md. 2) Susan S. McCann, a Presbyterian of S.C., who d. in 1898. The Yandell family moved to Washington State in 1889. Thereafter Claiborne lived with son. He was ill the last yr. and cared for by Dr. Yandell Swayze (his nephew) and Dr. J. W. C. Smith, C. C. Evans and J. D. Burks. Survived by son and dau., a sister Mrs. Mary Jenkins of Holmes Co., and 2 bros., Judge Robert Bowman of this place and another not named in article. (By XX of Yazoo City)

8/15/1901 Mixon, Mrs. Milberry R., wife of Miliard F. Mixon, b. Pike Co., 12/17/1855, d. 7/13/1901; joined Methodist Ch. when 30 yrs. old; left husband, 2 sons, and a dau. (By J. W. Sandell)

9/12/1901 Newman, Mrs. Mary Magdeline (nee Mixon), d. 30 yrs., 7 mos., 3 days, 6/18/1901 (?); converted 9/1882 by Rev. J. T. Nicholson. (No locations given; by R. L. Webb)

10/17/1901 Howard, Mrs. Alice (nee Regan), b. near China Grove 3/29/1869, md. Robert Howard on 8/30/1888, d. at Holmesville 9/22/1901, joined church at old China Grove while young. Converted by W. W. Simmons.

2/20/1902 Kellam, Myra (nee Powell), b. 8/29/1875, d. 10/12/1901, at home of father J. S. Powell of Pike Co. (R. L. Webb)

2/27/1902 Cook, Drury, b. Pike Co., Miss., 10/3/1860, d. Magnolia 9/15/1901

4/17/1902 Brown, A. N., b. at China Grove, 3/6/1859; d. Lake Arthur, Texas, 7/10/1901; joined Methodist Ch. at age 12; moved to St. Helena Par., La., with parents; md. Filona Branch 1/1/1879, who d. 1882 leaving 1 dau., Mrs. George Mack of St. Helena Par.; md. 2) in 1887 Birthnella Mack, who d. 1898, by whom he had 4 chld.

5/22/1902 Lewis, Lemuel, b. Marion Co., Miss., 9/23/1827, d. in New Orleans 4/26/1902, 2nd son and 4th child of Quinea and Martha Lewis; served CSA in Co. A, 33rd Miss. Regt; reared large family; oldest son was Stephen A. Lewis, conductor on the Southern Div. of the ICRR. Lemuel was older brother of H. P. and W. B. Lewis of the Miss. Conf. Buried at Brookhaven on Sunday 4/22/1902.

8/14/1902 Sandell, J. Darius, d. in Sabine Par., La., 5/2/1902; b. 2/23/1855; cared for widowed mother with the 5 children; father d. when he was young; md. 3/2/1882 to Anna Davis, who gave him 5 children.

Powell, Otis Argyle, d. near Magnolia 11/19/1901, son of J. W. and Eliza Powell; ill for 4 years; member of Muddy Springs Methodist Ch.

9/8/1902 Lewis, Mrs. Beulah Ball, dau. of B. B. Lewis, b. in Marion Co., Miss., 11/15/1869; converted at China Grove in 1879; joined church at Waterhole Cr. She and husband moved membership to Columbia, Miss.; md. Charlie C. Barnes 10/1887; d. at home of parents in Columbia 8/19/1902 of Bright's Disease. Left 2 sons, 2 daus., parents, 3 bros., 1 sister.

10/30/1902 Alford, Mrs. May L., b. Lauderdale Co., Miss., 9/17/1850; d. Magnolia 7/9/1902, dau. of Abram and Frances Stafford; md. Rev. N. E. Alford 1/7/1869 and became mother of 12 children, 10 of whom survived. Two sons are members of the La. Conf., and the 3rd preparing for ministry. When 12, parents moved to Lauderdale Co. from Washington Par., La.; joined church when 17 at Bethel Ch. under influence of Rev. Hyde.

11/27/1902 Dillon, Mrs. Annie Elizabeth, wife of John Dillon, dau. of Elisha R. & Sarah Margaret Clark, b. 4/7/1876, d. 10/12/1902 at Mt. Herman, La.; joined Methodist Ch. summer of 1892 under W. M. Sullivan; md. 11/16/1899 and left son.

[No papers found for 1903]

1904 Terrell, Mrs. Mary, b. Pike Co., Miss., 11/14/1822, d. at Mansfield, La., 12/8/1902, dau. of Daniel and Charity Eleanor Sandell, who reared 5 sons and 2 daus., the writer being the only survivor. The death of their mother left the subject to care for the family. She md. James L. Terrell 12/22/1842; converted at age 14. She left a brother, 3 daus., and many grandchildren. (By J. W. Sandell)

1904 Simmons, Bro. Dave W., b. Pike Co., Miss., 10/26/1838, son of Rev. Thomas Simmons and bro. of Rev. W. W. Simmons of Miss. Conf. CSA, Co. G, 6th Miss. Regt; wounded at Port Gibson 5/1/1863; md. in 1874 to Fannie Bonie (?); d. 1/27/1904 of pneumonia.

1904 Felder, Martha Matilda (nee Williams) of Pike Co., b. in Lawrence Co., Miss. 1/18/1831; joined Methodist Ch. in 1847 at Old Smyrna, Pike Co., md. Levi D. Felder 12/16/1847; left 7 children, 3 sons and 4 daus.; all lived to be grown except 1; d. 2/3/1904 at 9:45 P.M. while sitting in her rocker leaning her head on her pastor's hands. (By her pastor P. H. Howse)

1904 Henderson, Martha (nee Ford) b. at Old Ford Home on Pearl R. 12/21/1821, dau. of Rev. John Ford Jr., d. 4/21/1904 in Keithville. Funeral conducted by J. M. Alford; survived by 1 dau. and 2 sons. One son, W. F., is head of the Miss. Conf.

1904 Franklin, T. J., b. 11/16/1847 (?), d. Sabine Par., La., 3/6/1904; md. 1870 to Caroline Ryans; 7 children, 5 surviving; buried with Masonic Honors.

1904 Franklin, Elizabeth b. _____ 1818, d. Vernon Par., La., 2/20/1904, aged 85 yrs., 8 mos., 4 days; survived by 150 grand and great-grandchildren; joined church in 1850; 2 sons are preachers--J. M. Franklin of Bienville, La., and John of Range, La. Funeral conducted by Rev. C. B. Carter of Leesville.

1905 Tait, Mrs. Eliza C., b. Miss. 8/20/1822, twin to Judge R. J. Bowman of Alexandria, La., with whom she spent her 83rd birthday; moved to Alexandria in 1869. No death date given.

1905 Simmons, Mrs. Eliza A. (nee Webb), b. Ga. 6/2/1831, d. Pike Co., at res. of son W. J. Terrell 8/6/1905; md. 1) John Holiday in 1847, who d. 3 yrs. later. In 1859 she moved to Amite Co. In 1860 she md. 2) M.W. Terrell, who d. in 1864 leaving a son; md. 3) May 14, 1869, to Wm. Simmons, whom she lived with until 4/6/1892 when he died. Left a son J. W. Simmons. (By N. E. Alford)

1906 Gibson, Mrs. Harriet Newel (nee Bonney), d. at Summit 3/15/1906, aged 83 yrs., 9 mos., 15 days; only dau. of Peres and Nancy Bonney, late of Holmesville; b. in Portland, Maine; when 6 she came to Holmesville; 60 yrs. ago md. Major Gibson who d. yrs. ago. Survived by 7 children, 2 dead. (H. P. Lewis of Vicksburg)

8/23/1906 McEwen, M. R., b. Pike Co., 8/12/1845, md. Minerva Felder in 1870; d. at Topisaw 7/23/1906; left wife, 5 children; joined church at Topisaw in 1873. (By R. Bradley)

9/13/1906 Brumfield, Mrs. Martha, b. Robeson Co., N.C., 11/18/1830; moved with parents Lemuel and Polly Lewis to McComb, Miss.; md. Andrew Jackson Brumfield 9/11/1851, who d. 20 yrs. ago; she d. 7/8/1906; buried by grandson Orison F. Robins, infant son of Dr. E. D. and Martha Robins. Member of Waterhole Ch.

1906 Summer, Bro. Buford A., b. 6/14/1850; d. 7/23/1906, originally a
Lutheran; joined church when 11; in early life was a photographer; in 1876 moved
to China Grove to farm; md. 2/6/1878 to Celia Yarborough; moved to Marion Co.;
later built Summer's Chapel at his expense; buried at China Grove.

9/20/1906 Lewis, G. W., son of Lemuel and Polly Lewis, reared in Marion Co., 10 mi.
W. of Pearl R., where Waterhole Ch. stands; father was city judge in Marion
Co. for 30 yrs; b. 1/14/1833; joined church in 1843; md. Rebecca Yarborough
[sic] 4/1855 with whom he lived 50 yrs. They had 10 children, 4 sons and 6
daus.; 8 with mother survived at Bogue Chitto. (H. P. Lewis Sr.) [No death
date given]

11/29/1906 Connerly, Mrs. Maggie (nee Ratliff), b. 5/8/1875, near China Grove Camp
Ground; joined China Grove when 12; md. Baxter Connerly 9/22/1898, d. 10/29/1906,
leaving husband and 3 small children.

3/7/1906 Franklin, Rev. J. M., of Alberta, La., d. 2/3/1907, b. 9/14/1836 in the
Anacoca settlement in Natchitoches Par., La., now Vernon Par.; md. in 1856
to Malissa Conerly by whom he had 1 son; in 1860 licensed to preach; in 1862
joined CSA; in 1866 joined itineracy; in 1868 1st wife died; in 1860 ordained
deacon; md. Mrs. Martha Talley and had 7 more children; late in life moved to
Fort Jessup. [Long obit.]

3/14/1907 2nd obit. for Rev. J. M. Franklin.

5/2/1907 Wroten, Mrs. Elizabeth Hugh, b. Pike Co., 10/7/1826; md. Dr. V. J. Wroten
12/5/1844, d. 4/4/1907; dau. of Henry and Elizabeth Quin, who were among
the 1st settlers of Pike Co., settled about 5 mi. W. of Magnolia; reared 4
sons and 3 daus: Peter, Arthur, Henry, Minerva, Amanda, Mary and Elizabeth.
The subject of this sketch, Elizabeth, reared 5 children, 2 sons and 3 daus.:
Wm. Monroe, DeWitt, Maggie, Kate, and Eloise; all survived except DeWitt.
All the former generation are gone. Joined church at Muddy Springs where she
was a member of 60 years; moved membership to Magnolia when church founded there.

5/16/1907 Coney, Mrs. Elizabeth Salena, b. near Huffman near Summit, 9/25/1838; md.
Wm. J. Coney 12/4/1860, d. at Columbia 4/8/1907; husband joined CSA in 1862
and d. soon after far from home leaving her with 1 child, a dau. wife of J. J.
Magee of Columbia; she was a Methodist for over 50 years. She had taken care
of her parents in her old age. (Could she have been a Huffman instead of
being born at or near Huffman?) (H. W. Featherstun)

10/10/1907 Connerly, Bro. M. H., b. 11/3/1874, near China Grove Ch., md. 12/25/1900
to Aletha Owen, d. 1/7/1907, leaving a wife and 3 children.

1/2/1908 McEwen, Mrs. Mary P. (nee Lenoir) b. in McComb 1/8/1850, joined Muddy
Springs Ch. under pastorage of Rev. Andrew Day; md. 12/18/1871, to G. M.
McOwen; d. 9/21/1907. Had 9 children, 2 of whom died young. Writer was her
son-in-law for 8 years. (By J. T. Abney)

1/30/1908 Thompson, John Harvey and wife Ann Watson, b. Marion Co., Miss., born
the 1st in 1818 and the 2nd in 1821; moved to Copiah Co. in 1842. After Civil
War moved to Beauregard. He d. several yrs. back; she, in 1908. Survived
by 3 children: Mrs. Julia T. Christmas of Houston, Tex.; Hon. R. H. Thompson
of Jackson; and Mrs. Margarett Butker, a prominent lawyer, of Brookhaven.

5/20/1908 Ferguson, Wallace B., d. of measles at father's home near Holmesville,
3/18/1908, aged 25 yrs., 18 days.

1/14/1909 Godbold, Mrs. Sarah J. (nee Rawls), b. 8/12/1829, md. 11/19/1846 to
Levi R. Godbold, d. 12/13/1908; md. at age 17; left children, 4 sons and 4
daus.

12/6/1909 Boyd, Mrs. C. A., d. 5/18/1909, aged 59 yrs.; former principal of Summit
High School, dau. of Judge John Lamkin; b. Holmesville; moved to Summit and
md. Capt. A. A. Boyd and left 3 brothers, 3 step-children.

12/23/1909 Brown, Thomas Jefferson, b. 10/28/1833, at Holmesville, d. Mt. Peller,
La., 6/18/1909; md. Marian Grubbs in 1855, who died leaving him 5 children;
md. in 1870 to Mrs. Pernus Bullock by whom he had 2 sons.

3/24/1910 McLean, Mrs. Clarissa Mary (nee Wildblood), b. Washington Par., La., 8/16/1844; md. on 3/1/1864, to W. A. Skinner; md. after his death to J. W. McLean 4/16/1884, d. 12/4/1909. No children of her own.

2/26/1910 Badon, Mrs. Madeline M. (nee May), d. at 8 A.M. Sat. 3/5/1910, in Oackvale, Miss., b. at Darbun, Pike Co., Miss., 4/30/1834; md. 11/11/1852 to Wm. G. Ellzey, widowed after 5 yrs and left with 3 children; md. 2) 12/6/1863 to Henry B. Badon and left with 4 children by him. (By Hilary Westbook)

6/16/1910 Roberts, George W., d. at Muddy Springs Ch., on Sun. 4/3/1910; b. Magnolia, Miss., 11/15/1842; served in CSA; after war at age 28 md. Janie Guy on 4/1/1870, who died years ago. Left children.

11/10/1910 Kellner, Carl William, son of Wm. and Emma Kellner, b. at Fernwood, Miss., 4/7/1910, d. 9/25/1910

12/29/1910 Ford, W. A., b. in Marion Co., Miss., 11/26/1839, d. at Balltown, La., 10/20/1910; md. 1) Martha H. Warren; md. 2) Martha A. Ball; md. 3) Martha Ford; left last wife and 10 children.

5/11/1911 Felder, Lewis Raynor, son of W. H. and Laura Felder, b. 7/26/1893, d. at Topisaw on 1/7/1911.

ALBRITTON

The Albrittons of Pike County, Mississippi, (and the neighboring parishes of Louisiana) descend from a Richard Albritton, who died in St. Helena Parish in 1816/17. This Richard was the father of the Richard Albritton, veteran of the War of 1812, who married Nancy Richardson in Bullock County, Georgia, in 1808, and died in Pike County on 8/13/1876.

The Albritton family originated (seemingly) in York County, Virginia. One Francis Albrighton appeared in that area ca. 1650. He left a will dated 4/9/1667 under the name of Francis Albrighton but actually signed it Albritton. His descendants thereafter signed as Albritton.

Francis Albrighton, or Albritton, named seven children in his will in 1667 (York Co., Bk. 4, p. 132 (156) as follows: Richard, Francis, Elizabeth, George, John, Anne, and Margaret. Of these, George was born ca. 1630, supposedly fathered a son named Ralph b. ca. 1655/56. [Ralph's age was proved in January, 1689, when he gave a deposition before the York County Court in which he said he was 33 years old. See York County, Book 8, p. 385 (406)]

Ralph was later a parishioner in the Charles Parish Church in York County. Having married ca. 1680 to Mary _____, he and his wife had a son named Thomas baptized in the church in 1682. He had been born 8/1/1682. In addition, others baptized at that church were:
    2) Edward Albritton b. 12/17/1686
    3) John Albritton b. 9/2/1688
    4) William Albritton b. 7/7/1691
    5) Ralph Albritton b. 7/10/1696
    6) Richard Albritton b. 4/19/1698
    7) Benjamin Albritton b. 7/22/1700
[See Landon C. Bell, Charles Parish, York County, Virginia, History and Registers--Births 1648-1789; Deaths 1665-1787 (Richmond, Va., 1932), p. 42-43.]

The Charles Parish Church Register denotes that several Albrittons died in the 1680's and 1690's. Since ages were not given, it can be confusing. Perhaps the death records applied to Ralph Albritton's children--or perhaps to adults in his family--such as Ralph Albritton d. 1/21/1701. Was this the father or the son?

The deaths were as follows:
    Benjamin Albritton d. 8/29/1702
    Charles Albritton d. 1/18/1692
    Edward Albritton buried 9/6/1688
    John Albritton d. 8/25/1689
    William Albritton d. 12/6/1692
If this list applied to the children of Ralph Albritton's children, only the son Thomas survived--and that was possibly so.

Thomas Albritton md. ca. 1704 to Agnes _____ and had issue (baptized at Charles Parish):
    1) James Albritton b. 9/17/1705
    2) Agnes Albritton b. 3/13/1707
With no other entries recorded for Thomas Albritton after 1707, it is apparent that he left Charles Parish. It is possible that he is the identical Thomas Albritton who left a will in Princess Anne County, Virginia, in 1730.

The James Albritton b. in 1705 was possibly the one and same James Albritton who appeared in Pitt County, North Carolina, about the time of that county's creation. He, as did most of his sons, followed the profession of saddler (or Saddle maker). With a wife possibly named Ami or Amy, he was alive in 1769 but dead by 1774. He sired at least the following sons (as proved by the Pitt County Deeds).
    1) Thomas Albritton, saddler (F-75)
    2) James Albritton, saddler (F-75)
    3) Peter Albritton (F-75)
    4) Matthew Albritton, inholder, of Onslow County (F-75)
    5) George Albritton who md. Lydia ___

6) Henry Albritton (H-140)
7) Richard Albritton (I-253)
8) John Albritton

Of these Albrittons, George, Thomas, and Richard were of age by the 1770's as their names appear on varied militia lists (especially July 1775----Richard had been in the militia as early as 1771). See N.C. State Records, X, pgs. 62, 63, 38, and 221. In the period just prior to the American Revolution, Thomas and Peter served on the Committee of Safety. There was a Matthew Albritton who served as a private in Evans' 10th Regt. N.C. Mil, dischg. 4/20/1783 after a service of 18 months. (N.C. State Records XVI, p. 1008)

The third son Peter, named above, was dead by 1799 in Pitt County at which time his property was divided among his heirs. He was father of:
  a) James Albritton, decd. by 1799 (O-335)
  b) Elizabeth (Betsy) wife of Gardner Mayo
  c) Mary or Polly, wife of Matthew James
  d) Adam Albritton
  e) Jonathan Albritton
  f) Luke Albritton
  g) Joel Albritton
  h) Peter Albritton Jr. (O-17)
  i) William Albritton (possibly)

Sons 7 and 8 of James Albritton of Pitt supposedly migrated to the area of Effingham County, Georgia, shortly after the American Revolution. Richard Albritton b. ca. 1750 (if 21 years old when he served in the militia in 1771) got grants in Effingham in 1784 and 1793. He lived in Bullock County by 1797 when he obtained a fourth grant. (Actually he never moved; Bullock was just carved off of Effingham.)

It is asserted that Richard Albritton, b. ca. 1750 in North Carolina, died in St. Helena Parish in the summer of 1817; md. 1) in 1776 to Mary Lanier b. 12/25/1759, d. in Bullock Co., Ga., after 1800, to dau. of Benjamin Lanier, granddaughter of Byrd Thomas Lanier.

This Richard was quite active in Screven County as early as 1794 when he recorded his mark and (1795) was a Justice of the Peace in that county. After his residency in Bullock County, numerous deed records exist for Richard--but they are too numerous to review.

Richard Albritton and Mary Lanier had a large family as follows:
    a) Lanier Albritton b. ca. 1777 (Richard's will did not name a son Lanier. Perhaps he was paid off before Richard left Georgia. This Lanier served in the 2nd Battn, 2nd Regt. Ga. Mil. in 1794--and was later a justice in Burke Co. Too, Lanier could have died without heirs before his father made his will.)

    b) Nancy Albritton md. John Richardson (came to Louisiana, but finally migrated into Mississippi and then to Texas.)

    c) Mary Albritton md. Reddick Sibley b. ca. 1775, d. in 1851 at Toro in Sabine Parish, La., and had issue:
        1) Richard Sibley d. before his father.
        2) Robert F. Sibley (called Junior--named for his uncle)
        3) John I. Sibley
        4) Sarah or Sally Sibley md. Henry Stagner
        5) Mary Ann Sibley b. 3/24/1809 in Ga., d. in Pike Co., Miss., 7/20/1889 md. George Simmons b. 1808, d. CSA 4/1862, and had issue:
            a) Jefferson E. Simmons b. 11/12/1830, d. 6/17/1919, md. 1) 3/25/1867 to Epsa Ann Corley d. 3/25/1867; 2) in 1871 to Elizabeth Stoker, widow of John Coleman Sibley.
            b) Mary Elizabeth Simmons b. 3/9/1832, d. 3/22/1895, md. 5/26/1857 to John Goff Leggett.
            c) Richard Montgomery Simmons b. 1/27/1834, d. 7/11/1836.
            d) Martha Simmons 1. 11/26/1836, d. 1/18/1923, md. 12/24/1857 to Edward K. Tisdale of New Orleans.
            e) George Boardman Simmons b. 4/29/1839, d. CSA as member of Quitman's Guards--wounded in Seven Days Battle near Richmond, Va., and d. 30 days later.

f) Reddick Fulton Simmons b. 2/18/1841, d. 12/25/1883, md. Cordelia Dickey, widow of ____ Raborn. Family moved to Catahoula Parish, La.
g) Marcus Aurelius Simmons b. 3/15/1843, d. 10/25/1919, md. 10/10/1865 to Cordelia Varnado.
h) Columbus Waldon Simmons b. 1/7/1845, d. 6/29/1917, md. Sarah McQueen.
i) Robert L. Simmons b. 9/10/1847, d. 2/27/1939, md. 8/31/1871 to Sarah Louise Fortenberry.

For a more detailed account for the family of Mary Ann Sibley Simmons see: Hansford L. Simmons, Bala Chitto Simmons Family: Desdendants of Richard and Ann Tyler Simmons (McComb, Miss.: 1965).

d) Sarah Albritton d. April 1816, md. in Bullock County, Ga., 12/27/1808 to David Mizell and had only three children: John David, Elvira, and Avarilla Mizell.

e) James Albritton md. in Bullock Co., Ga., 11/11/1801 to Laney Kent.

f) Elizabeth Albritton md. Laban Kent and was still living in Georgia at the time of Richard's death in Louisiana.

g) John Albritton

h) Avarillah Albritton md. Robert Sibley

i) Richard Albritton b. ca. 1788, d. 8/13/1876 in Pike County, Miss.; md. in Bullock Co., Ga., to Nancy Richardson b. ca. 1792 on 12/14/1809. (This Richard has often been confused with his father in Georgia. It is claimed that Mary Lanier Albritton d. after 1800 and that Richard Sr. md. Nancy Richardson. But this is not true. At Richard Sr.'s death in 1817, his wife was Ann ____, but her maiden name is unknown. Ann might have been a "nickname" for one Margaret Kent, who married a Richard Albritton in Bullock Co., Ga., on 2/19/1802. Richard Albritton Jr. had issue:
1) Stephen Albritton b. 1812 d. before 1860, a school teacher by profession, md. Mary A. Jones and had
   a) William J. b. 1836
   b) John H. b. 1838
   c) Richard b. 1840
   d) Francis b. 1842
   e) Mary b. 1844
   f) Martha b. 1847
   Stephen lived in Washington Parish at the time of the 1850 Census. Later he moved to Holmesville, Miss., where he supposedly died. Mary was living there with her children in 1860.
2) James Albritton b. 1813/4, md. 1) Sarah Brown 1/19/1836. She was b. 7/22/1817, d. 1/27/1860. They had issue:
   a) Matilda b. 1837
   b) Any b. 1838
   c) Lucy Elizabeth b. 1842
   d) Mary Ann (Nancy) b. 1843,   [See also Albritton Supplement]
   e) Richard A. J. b. 1846
   f) John H. b. 1847
   g) Matthew R. b. 1848
   h) Sarah Jane b. 1850
   i) Frances L. b. 1852
   j) Martha Ann b. 1854
   k) Lilly Julia b. 1857
3) Benjamin Albritton b. ca. 1817
4) Elizabeth Albritton b. 1819
5) Jane Albritton b. 6/27/1821 in La., d. in Pike Co. 11/19/1890. She left a brother and sister living.
6) Henry H. Albritton b. 1830, md. Elizabeth ____ and had issue:
   a) James b. 1859
7) Sarah Albritton b. 1832
8) Frances M. Albritton b. 1834

Son no. 8 on the James Albritton list, John Albritton, migrated to Georgia and lived in Effingham originally, then Screven, Bullock, and possibly Bryan. John's wife was Abby ___. Many of the children often attributed to Richard belonged to this couple. The names of three of his children comes from Folks Huxford's <u>History of Brooks County, Georgia</u>, p. 416.

    a) Thomas Albritton b. ca. 1776, d. ca. 1866, md. 1) ___; 2) Frances or Fanny ___ in Bryan Co., Ga., later lived in Ware Co.
    b) Rev. Matthew Albritton b. ca. 1788 in area of Bullock Co., d. 1850 in Brooks, md. Ann, dau. of James and Diana Bullock, ca. 1805.
    c) Jane Albritton b. ca. 1795, md. John Dean of Laurens Co., Ga., and lived in Brooks County.

John Albritton (g), son of Richard of Ga. and La., b. 12/16/1789, d. 2/28/1819, md. in 1816 to Mary Glover b. 3/2/1800, d. 2/28/1854, dau. of John Glover. Issue:
1) Sarah Albritton b. 3/11/1817, md. 8/10/1835 to Nathan Grantham and moved to Arkansas where they lived at Ozark (in 1880).
2) Richard Glover Albritton b. 4/16/1818, d. 1/9/1897, md. 1) 12/20/1839 to Arlene Yelvington and had 6 children:
    a) Mary Ann b. 1840, md. Abe Kerby
    b) Alzene b. 1841, md. Ike Christmas
    c) Nancy Jane b. 1843, d. 1908, md. James Kinard
    d) Andrew Jackson b. 1844, d. 1938 (?), md. Della Kelly
    e) Sarah Frances b. 1847, d. 1874, md. James Barnet
    f) Abitha Amanda b. 1849, d. 1881, md. Gilliam Barnet
Richard md. 2) 4/24/1851 to Agnes Mullin and had 8 children:
    g) William Robertson b. 2/23/1853, md. 11/22/1871 to Rebecca Cox
    h) John Gabriel b. 1854, md. 1879 to Mary Frances Jefferson
    i) Angeline Rebecca b. 11/30/1856, d. 1883, md. in 1879 to William H. Harrison
    j) Lama Richard b. 1858, d. 1905, md. in 1880 to Emma Fenn
    k) Emma Dorah b. 8/3/1860, d. 1891, md. in 1879 to "Doc" Hill
    l) Agnes Catherine b. 1864, d. 1917, md. in 1883 to William Fenn
    m) Etna Joseph b. 2/2/1867, md. in 1887 to Jennie Tull at Gillsburg, Miss.
    n) Ethel Dupre (called Pet) b. 5/1/1869, md. 4/15/1894 to Lula Ambrose.

Richard Glover Albritton served in the Mexican War as a private in Capt. Robertson's Company, Co. D, 5th Regt., La. Inf. Later he served the Confederacy as 1st Lieut, Co. H., 3rd La. Cavalry.

    After John Albritton's death in 1819, his widow Mary Glover Albritton md. in 1821 to Joseph D. Minton b. 12/11/1895, d. 10/7/1929. This union had four children.

ALFORD

    The Alford family of Pike County, Miss., and its neighboring parishes in Louisiana, had its roots in North Carolina and Virginia. In 1955 Mrs. Duncan Murphey (nee Pearl Alford) of Oakdale, La., had the Alford line accepted in the Colonial Dames of the XVII Century. She was the daughter of Marshal Thomas Alford b. 9/30/1839, d. in Pike Co. in 1904, husband of Charity Ann Self. Marshal Thomas was the son of John Seborn Alford b. 1807, d. in Washington Parish, La., in 1891, and his wife Martha or Peggy Brumfield b. 1818, d. 1885.

    John Seborn, a twin to Seborn John, was the son of Jacob Alford, the subject of this family sketch and the progenitor of many of the Alfords for the area under consideration. This Jacob descended from a John Alford Senior who died in New Kent County, St. Peter's Parish, Virginia, in 1709/1710.

    The Alford family was an ancient line in Virginia. The Minutes of the Council and General Court of Colonial Virginia show that on 4/20/1670 a William Alford was on a jury. Later that same year his name appeared on a certificate of importation in a land quest--a record which implied that he had not been long in the colony--and perhaps came in as an indentured servant since he did not receive land in his own name. If he did, he was soon out of indenture--perhaps had come as a redemptioner (or a person who paid his passage soon after arrival). His name appeared in a legal action (a suit) in 1674 in which he was referred to as "Major" William Alford. But that same year there is the notation that on 3/4/1674/5 "Robert Gilbert being indicted for murthering Lt. Col. Wm. Alford, the Grand Jury brought in their Virdict, billa vera, then a jury of Life and Death was impannelled according to law, who bringing their Verdict, Homecide by misadventure, the said Robt. Gilbert was therefore acquitted by p(ro)clamation." The widow of this Lt. Col. Wm. Alford later married John Hurst.

Since William Alford must have lived near New Kent, he is probably the father of John Alford Senior who lived in St. Peter's Parish in New Kent. This man's name appears frequently on the few remaining records for that area of Virginia.

John Alford, Sr., d. 3/14/1709/10 (according to the St. Peter's Parish Register) and was the possible husband of Frances Alford, who died there on 4/27/1726. [However it must be noted that one of John Alford's granddaughters had that name, and possibly the funeral notice was for this young girl and not an older woman.] John's family probably was as follows (deduced from birth recordings in the St. Peter's Register):
1) James Alford who had children baptized as follows:
   a) James Alford b. 2/7/1713, baptd. 4/12/1713
   b) Warren Alford baptd. 8/28/1715
   c) Julius Alford b. 9/1717
2) Lodowick Alford who had children baptized as follows: (wife Elizabeth)
   a) William b. 7/31/1734
   Elizabeth Alford d. 5/29/1735. Lodowick md. 2) Susannah and had:
   b) Elizabeth Alford b. 12/22/1736, baptd. 2/6/1736
   c) Jacob Alford b. 12/12/1838, baptd. 2/18/1738
3) Goodrich Alford who had a wife named Grace and had children baptized:
   a) Unity Alford b. 12/16/1724
   b) Lucy Alford b. 2/25/1736, baptd. 3/27/1736
   c) Susanna Alford b. 10/15/1739, baptd. 11/18/1739 (She had a mother named Sarah.)
4) John Alford d. 5/2/1726; had children baptized as follows:
   a) Elizabeth Alford b. 7/1/1719
   b) Frances Alford b. 8bre ye 4th, 1717 (8bre probably was October)
   c) Isaac Alford, son of John, departed this life 8/21/1723.
The eldest male members of the family alive by 1735 is proved by the notation of processioners for St. Peter's on 10/5/1735 as follows:
"Petition of William Paisley an Overseer of High Road from Old Church to Mr. Chamberlayne's Ordinary--that he have tithables Lodowick Alford, Goodrich Alford & Julius Alford among others."
These men were to help procession the line for William Paisley's district.
5) Elizabeth Alford (no doubt a dau. of John Alford Sr.) md. 11/3/1698 to Jacob Winfrey and had children baptized as follows:
   a) Jane Winfrey bapt. 12/25/1701
   b) Jacob Winfrey bapts. 5/14/1704
   c) Elinor Winfrey baptd. 6/4/1707
   d) Elizabeth Winfrey baptd. 4/10/1709, d. 8/23/1709
   e) Henry Winfrey baptd. 2/4/1710
   Elizabeth Alford Winfrey probably died 3/27/1714 since there was a recording for an Elizabeth Winfrey on that date.
6) Mary Alford md. 10/21/1711 to Robert Wood

A Grace Alford md. on 2/14/1726/7 to Michael Harfield in St. Peter's. Her father is not known, but she had to be one of the John Alford family.

Alford family entries stopped in the St. Peter's Register in 1739, thus indicating that the family had removed from the parish. It is almost certain that they moved into Edgecomb Precinct, North Carolina.

Lodowick Alford purchased property (100 acres on Elk Marsh, joining Griggs Swamp and Miery Branch) from Henry Dawson on 11/17/1740 (Edgecomb Precinct Deed Book 1, p. 427). Alford lived on that property to which he added other holdings and in 1746 fell into Granville County, N.C., with that county's creation. As evidenced by a deed in the Edgecomb Precinct deeds, Lodowick Alford had a third wife named Sarah at which time he sold land on both sides of March Swamp to Thomas Gardner (1758) as a resident of Granville County (Edge. Prct. Deed Bk. 6, p. 347).

The number of children born to Lodowick (or to the date of his death) is open to conjecture. The son named Jacob was probably the Jacob Alford who migrated to Robeson (originally Bladen) Co., N.C., where he received grants on Gum Swamp as early as 1764. His family will be noted later. However, Jacob's migration to that area probably attracted the younger Jacob, the Jacob of Louisiana, to migrate there a few years later.

Lodowick Alford no doubt had a son named Julius Alford, who was of age or near age by 1754 at which time Lodowick sold some 200 acres (out of a 400-acre grant on both sides of Tarr River) for £ 20 to him. (Granville Co. Deed Bk. B, p. 305-307) It is strange that since Julius was born ca. 1725 that his baptism was not recorded in the St. Peter's Register.

With the exception of Julius Alford, most of the Lodowick Alford family later became residents of Wake County, N.C. Since many early records for Wake were destroyed, the death of Lodowick is obscured. It is known that he was a resident of that county in his last years. This older Lodowick was reputed to have had nineteen children by his three wives. Others believed to be his children were: Benjamin, William, James, Lodowick, Warren, and James. Lodowick Jr. left a will in Franklin Co., N.C., in 1792.

Jacob Alford, son of Lodowick Alford, migrated to Robeson where he left a will dated 7/4/1794 in which he named his children. His wife was Mary Pace. Children:

    a) Warren Alford
    b) Charity Alford
    c) Sion Alford
    d) Elias Alford
    e) James Alford
    f) Lod or Lodowick Alford
    g) Wiley

Witnesses to the will were Duncan McEachern, Sarah Ann McTyer, and Sion Alford.

Julius Alford, son of Lodowick, left a will in old Bute (now Warren Co.) County, N.C., in the 1760's. The exact date or year cannot be read on the original, but the recorded copy states 7/14/1768. At the time of his will, he was a resident of St. John's Parish. His wife was Lucy and he names his children as follows:

    1) John Alford, land on s. side of Crooked Creek & n. side of Ferrills Road
    2) Isaac Alford, land on n. side of Crooked Creek below Ferrills Road to mouth of Wright's branch
    3) Goodrich Alford, land where John Rose now lives--or money from land if Rose wanted to buy (as must have been the case as Julius sold this property to Rose before his death)
    4) Jacob Alford, land on both sides of Tarr River, where i now live--
    5) Job, money and livestock
    6) Patty Alford
    7) Sarah Alford

Executors of the will were his brother Lodowick Alford and his (Lodowick's) son James Alford. Witnesses: James Alford, Thomas Gay, and John Arrendell.

Julius Alford was dead by the time of the November court, 1771. Now it is said that this Julius Alford was the father of Jacob Alford who came to Louisiana. He possibly could be, but it must be noted that the Louisiana Jacob was born either in 1761 or 1766, making him a lad either 2 or 7 years old when his father wrote his will. Did a father leave a mere boy the homeplace and not name a guardian to oversee that property in his will? This compiler has not checked the Bute County minutes to see what the disposition of the property was, or to see if a tutor was named for Jacob. But since Jacob's name does not appear in the Bute or Warren County Deeds-- and if he lived to maturity--he must have migrated to the southern section of North Carolina and lived near his uncle Jacob Alford.

By 1790 there were only two Jacob Alfords on the 1790 Census for North Carolina, one in Robeson and the other in Cumberland. Neither man really has family enumerations which fit the Jacob of Louisiana. However, Jacob Alford in Cumberland Co., N.C., bought 60 acres of land for £ 80 from Henry Stephenson on North River of Cape Fear on corner side of Malcom Bass's Creek. Wits: Nathaniel and Israel Folsom (Cumberland Deed Bk. 14, p. 402). Dated 1/1/1791.

It is possible that Jacob Alford of Louisiana was not counted on the 1790 Census. He could have been moving about that time, and thus missed by all enumerators. This seems probable as the question could be asked--where did Jacob Alford get his wife or wives? The Seaborn family seems to be a group which lived in Virginia. A Benjamin and Martha Seaborn had a daughter Frances christened in the Albemarle Parish Church in Surry/Sussex Counties, Va., on 11/4/1764 (born 9/29/1764). Godparents were William Seaborn, Francis Bond, and Anne Shands. This Frances was about the right age to have been the wife of Jacob Alford of North Carolina and Louisiana. Thus did Jacob go to Virginia to get his bride? Was he travelling to Virginia in 1790?

Since several of the Jacob Alford children claim Georgia as their native state (or at least the state they were from on the 1850 Census), it is obvious that the family sojourned in that state before their removal on west. There was a Jacob Alford (as well as an unaccounted for Ferrell or Terrell) on the 1797-1798 Tax List for Montgomery Co., Ga. This is possibly the Jacob Alford under consideration. This Jacob Alford received a land grant for 450 acres in 1802 (Ga. Grants Bk. DDDDD, p. 572). Between that date and 1806/7 Jacob Alford and his family moved to Louisiana. Thus, if this is the correct line for Jacob Alford's ancestry, it runs as follows:
William Alford d. 1674 and had issue
John Alford Sr. who died in 1709/10 and married Frances by whom he had Lodowick Alford who by his first wife Elizabeth had a son named Julius Alford who died ca. 1771 and by his wife named Alice had a son named Jacob Alford b. in 1761.

Jacob Alford settled a tract of land in the Warnerton area of Washington Parish, Louisiana, by December, 1807. He no doubt arrived in that locality from Georgia (possibly Montgomery County) where he had been for a few years previously. It is again probable that he was the Jacob Alford who lived in Cumberland Co., N.C., at the time of the 1790 Census. At that time he had 2 males under 16 and himself and his wife.

In 1812 in Louisiana, he was listed as a resident of St. Tammany Parish on the tax list for that year. This record indicated that he had nine children in his household (ages not given). By 1820 and the census of that year, he was counted as a resident of the newly-created Washington Parish. Then he had 2 males under 10, 3 males 10 to 16, 3 females under 10, and 1 female 10 to 16 (in addition to himself and his wife). He was dead prior to 1830.

In 1830 Jacob's widow Frankie Seaborn was listed on the census with 1 male 10 to 15, 2 males 20 to 30, and 1 female 10 to 15 (plus herself). However, from all of these numbers (statistics) it is still impossible to create a family for Jacob Alford. There are too many conflicting lists.

From deduction it is possible to arrive at a partially correct list of children for Jacob Alford. Since all lists contain the name Needham, it is obvious there was a son by that name. Thus, the only Needham in the area (and perhaps Louisiana and Mississippi at the time) was Needham J. Alford b. 7/12/1789, d. 9/19/1879 in Limestone County, Texas. It appears that he was the Needham in question. The descendants of this Needham have proof that he was the son of a Jacob Alford who was born in N.C. on 8/15/1761 and died 7/18/1824, about the same time that Jacob Alford of Washington Parish died. However, Needham's mother was Elizabeth Bryant b. 6/20/1765. Thus, if Needham of Texas was the son of Jacob Alford of Washington Parish, it is apparent that Jacob married Elizabeth Bryant first and Frankie Seaborn second. This is highly possible. The ages and skips in births make it appear that Jacob had two wives. In addition to this, it is strongly possible that Jacob's first three children were by Elizabeth Bryant as will be noted by the following list of possible children.

Jacob's children by Elizabeth Bryant:
1) Needham J. Alford b. 7/12/1789, d. 9/19/1869 in Texas, md. 2/18/1815 to Martha Waddell in Franklin Co., Miss.
2) Sarah Alford called Sally b. ca. 1791, d. 186_ at Sun in St. Tammany Parish, La., md. ca. 1820 to Rubin Pierce. There is no proof that Sarah was Jacob's daughter. However, she was an Alford and Rubin had to have married her in either Washington Parish, La., or Pike Co., Miss. Her grandson Rubin Ardo Pierce claimed that Julia Ball Patterson was close kin to his family. Since she was a granddaughter of Edwin Alford, Sally would have been Julia's grand aunt--a fact that she would have known at the time.

3) Edwin Alford b. 11/22/1792, d. 3/10/1878, md. 12/20/1818 in Pike Co. to

Martha Smith b. 3/25/1802, d. 8/8/1861. It is to be noted that Edwin named a son Seaborn--a fact which would make it appear that his mother was Frankie Seaborn--but it must also be noted that Needham J. Alford named his first son Thomas Sebourn. The name Seaborn or Sebourn probably appeared in both families as homage to Frankie Seaborn who must have helped rear both boys.

Jacob probably married Frankie Seaborn a short time after the death of Elizabeth Bryant ca. 1792-1793. Unless there were infants born to the family who died very young, and of whom we have no knowledge, there was a skip in birth years between Edwin and his next brother. Children by Jacob and Frankie Seaborn:

4) Lucy Alford b. ca. 1796/7, d. in Sabine Parish, La., 5/24/1841, md. William Maines.

5) Julius C. Alford b. ca. 1798, d. ca. 1880 (after the census of that year) in Sabine Parish, md. ca. 1828 to Elizabeth Waddell, sister to Needham Alford's wife. All Jacob Alford lists contain the name Julius--this proves, to a degree, that there was a son named Julius. The question is: which Julius? There is the possibility that Julius Harmon Alford b. ca. 1819, who lived in St. Helena (later Tangipahoa Parish) was the correct one. However, he does not fit the 1830 Census enumeration for Frankie Alford's household. She had only the one son 10 to 15 and that was the son Joseph C. Alford listed later. There was the legend in the Julius Alford family (of Tangipahoa Parish) that once Julius left home for a business trip to Osyka, Miss. When he reached his destination, he met Edwin Alford, a long lost brother whom he had not seen for many years. The story is no doubt true, but the kinship between them had to be cousins, not brothers. This Julius was no doubt a brother to Rebecca Alford, who md. Raleigh Hazard in St. Helena Parish in 1826. (She was dead by 1838.) However, Rebecca's marriage record proves that she was the ward of a family who lived in Lawrence Co., Miss., and was therefore not a daughter of Jacob and Frankie Alford.

The Sabine Parish Julius C. Alford, in his early life, was a resident of the Washington Parish area. In 1855 when Holden W. Adams (then a resident of Sabine Parish) applied for bounty land due him by his service in the U.S. militia, War of 1812 (then a resident of Washington Parish on or near Pearl River), Julius C. Alford made a statement that he served in the same company with Adams--as well as with Adams's two brothers Sherrod and Hiram. Thus, this Julius was in the right area at the right time to have been the son of Jacob Alford and Frankie.

6) William Alford b. 1800 md. Eveline Ginn b. 1808 and lived in Police Beat #1 of Pike Co., Miss., in 1850 (and was a near neighbor of Edwin Alford). His name appears on all Alford lists so must have been a son.

7) Children born between 1800 and 1806 are not known. Since the names Nancy (a dau.) and Jacob (a son) appear on most lists, they might have been born in this time span.

8) Seborn (Seaborn) John Alford b. 10/11/1807, d. 2/7/1884 in Pike Co., md. 1) Mary Catherine Felder; 2) Mary S. Kirk, widow of Rev. Daniel Wadsworth. His obituary proves that he was a son of Jacob Alford.

9) John Seborn (Seaborn) Alford b. 10/11/1807 (twin to the above), d. 11/15/1891 in Washington Parish, La., md. Margaret Brumfield b. 2/9/1819, d. 11/15/1891.

10) Joseph C. Alford b. 1816 (not married in 1850), migrated to Sabine Parish where he lived near Julius C. Alford.

11) Martha Alford b. ca. 1819, md. William Stovall b. 1819 and lived in Marion Co., Miss. Proof of her parentage is found in Marion Co. Deed Bk. C, p. 185, where Frankie Alford gives her daughter Martha wife of William Stovall property.

Other Alford lists give Jacob and Frankie two additional sons, namely, Warren and Moses. There was a Moses Alford in Amite Co., Miss., but there is no proof that he fits this family. No record for a Warren Alford exists except for one who lived in Lauderdale Co., Miss. The latter-named Alford was not of this family.

1) Needham J. Alford and Martha Waddell b. 5/15/1796, d. 11/7/1876, dau. of John Waddell and Sarah ___, in Limestone Co., Texas, had:
   a) Thomas Sebourn Alford b. 2/1/1821, md. 11/26/1854, in Sabine Parish, La., to Bersheba C. Moorehead.
   b) Needham Bryant Alford b. 2/25/1826, md. Ruthis ___.
   c) William Theodore Alford b. 2/25/1832, d. 7/8/1905, md. 12/29/1857, to Margaret Maximillion.
   d) Richard Alford.
   e) Jesse Powell Alford d. 8/2/1890, md. 1) 7/24/1849 to Harriett Crawford; 2) 7/28/1886 to Cornelia Crawford.
   f) Jacob L. Alford b. 12/25/1824, md. 8/13/1855 to Sarah Smith.
   g) Noel Waddill Alford b. 12/25/1838, d. 8/7/1915 in Limestone Co., Tx., md. 1) Elizabeth Smith; 2) Mrs. Ann Langston.
   h) John Waddell Alford b. 11/15/1842, md. 12/30/1886 to Ona V. Arnett.
   i) Samantha Alford b. 2/5/1818.
   j) Elizabeth Bryant Alford b. 9/16/1823, md. 8/9/1849 to George W. Morris.
2) Sarah (Sally) Alford md. 1) Rubin Pierce b. ca. 1780, d. ca. 1840, son of John Pierce and Abigail ___, and had issue:
   a) John Quincey Adams Pierce b. 7/3/1825, d. 11/23/1898, md. Lucinda Burnette Morris b. 10/22/1839, d. 12/23/1902.
   b) James Pierce b. 11/14/1827, d. 8/21/1905, md. Alcy Asenath Morris b. 9/5/1831, d. 6/7/1899.
   c) Abigail Pierce b. 6/19/1830, md. 1) Arnold Hightower d. in CSA; 2) Fielding Adams.
   d) Harriet Pierce b. 10/9/1832, d. young.
   Sarah Alford Pierce md. 2) Joseph Letchworth. No issue.
3) Edwin Alford md. Martha Smith and lived in Pike Co., Miss., and had issue:
   a) Warren Alford b. 9/13/1819, md. Celia Ann Lewis. Lived in Washington Parish, La., in older years.
   b) Cynthia Ann Alford b. 12/11/1820, md. Jesse Ball and lived on Magee's Creek above Tylertown, Miss.
   c) Ira Payne Alford b. 1/22/1822, md. Betsey Hope and lived in Washington Parish, La.
   d) William Harmon Alford b. 8/3/1823, moved to Texas; lived at Matagorda at one time.
   e) Jane Alford b. 1825, md. Tyra Tynes.
   f) Lacey Alford b. 9/11/1828, md. James Michael Ball and lived on Pearl River near Balltown, La. Buried at the Pleasant Valley Cemetery.
   g) Dr. Jeptha J. Alford b. 8/2/1830, md. 1) Fanny, dau. of James Roberts and Clarinda Pace of Washington Parish, La.; md. 2) Corinne Edwards. Left one son, Andrew Alford.
   h) Julia Ann Alford b. 8/15/1832, md. John Ratliff McElveen. She died young leaving 1 daughter.
   i) Dr. Seaborn S. "Sebe" Alford b. 8/15/1834, md. Anice Ball and lived on Pearl River at Balltown, near Angie, La.
   j) Newton Alford b. 11/14/1838, md. Mary Brumfield.
   k) Martha Elizabeth Alford b. 8/8/1848, md. J. Alex Brumfield.
   Edwin Alford served as a private on the 12/13th Consolidated La. Militia at the Battle of New Orleans. In 1850 he stated that he was born (or at least came) from Georgia.
4) Lucy Alford md. William Maines, who died in Sabine Parish, La., leaving a will dated 9/15/1849 (probated 11/10/1849) and had issue:
   a) Jacob Maines
   b) ___ Maines, md. Matt Jones
   c) John Maines
   d) Richard Maines
   e) ___ Maines md. Calvin Hughes
   f) Elbert Maines
   g) ___ Maines md. Francis Buvens
   h) Luraney Maines
   i) Williamson O. Maines b. 2/24/1817 in Pike Co., Miss., d. 6/26/1904 in Sabine Parish, La., md. Elizabeth Carter b. 11/15/1822, d. 9/23/1896, dau. of Redmond Carter and Nancy Kemp (?).
   j) Leurany Maines
   k) William Seaburn Maines
   l) Noah Maines
5) Julius C. Alford of Sabine Par., md. Elizabeth Waddell and had issue:
   a) Laure Alford b. ca. 1831, md. 3/15/1852 to Claiborn Waldrop.
   b) Nancy Alford b. ca. 1833, md. 11/13/1851 to Joseph E. Varner.

    c) Dicey Alford b. ca. 1835, md. 8/12/1862 to John Varner.
    d) Martha Alford b. ca. 1837 md. Napoleon Waldrop.
    e) Frances (Franky) Alford b. ca. 1840, md. 12/10/1857 to Claiborne P. Waldrop.
    f) William Riley Alford b. 8/14/1842, d. 1/22/1917, md. 1) 9/26/1867 to Isabella E. Presley; 2) Mrs. Ann Dugan Gandy.
    g) Joseph Seaborn Alford b. ca. 1845, d. 12/5/1872 to Mrs. Nancy Dugan Arnette.

6) William Alford md. Eveline Ginn and had issue:
    a) Henderson Alford b. 1828
    b) Sebastian Alford b. 1830
    c) Ramond Alford b. 1833
    d) Clarasy Alford b. 1836
    e) Jesse Alford b. 1839
    f) Milton J. Alford b. 1842
    g) Calpernia Alford b. 1843
    h) Jackson Alford b. 1845
    i) Needham W. Alford b. 1848

8) Seborn (Seaborn) John Alford md. 1) Mary Catherine Felder and had issue:
    a) Leander Alford b. 1833
    b) Martha R. Alford b. 1835
    c) John Wesley Alford b. 6/25/1836, d. 11/27/1879 in Denton Co., Tex. He and his family migrated there from Miss. only two years before.
    d) Sophia E. Alford b. 1842
    e) Simon B. Alford b. 1846
    Seaborn John md. 2) Mary S. Kirk, widow of Rev. Daniel Wadsworth and had:
    f)
    g)
    h)
    i)
    j)
    k)

9) John Seaborn (Seborn) Alford md. Margaret Brumfield. This union lived in Washington Parish, La., and supposedly had 18 children:
    a) Esther Alford b. 1838 md. ___ Stringfield
    b) Thomas M. Alford b. 1838
    c) Emily S. Alford b. 1841
    d) Sarah E. Alford b. 1842
    e) Seaborn Lochran Alford b. 5/19/1844, d. 11/22/1919, md. Laura Malissa Angeline Ellzey
    f) Martha Alford b. 1845
    g) Willis Alford b. 5/30/1847, d. 12/20/1891, md. Claretta B. ___
    h) Isaac Alford b. 1849
    i) John G. Alford b. 1851, md. Maranda Hobs
    j) Mary Alford b. 1852
    k) Laveta Alford b. 1854
    l) Jesse Alford b. 1855
    m) Hugh Alford b. 5/4/1857, d. 12/5/1923, md. Rose Holliday
    n) Cynthia Alford b. 1859
    o) Hosea Alford
    p) Otis Alford
    q) Luther Alford
    r) Willie J. Alford

11) Martha Alford b. 1819, md. William Stovall b. 1817 and lived in Marion Co., Miss., in 1850 and 1860. Issue:
    a) Mary Stovall b. 1840, md. Jesse Davis
    b) Nancy Stovall b. 1841/2
    c) Emeline Stovall b. 1843
    d) Frances Stovall b. 1845/6
    e) William Stovall b. 1850
    f) Myra Stovall b. 1853
    g) Warren Stovall b. 1857

ALLEN/ALLMAND

Felix Allen and his first wife Catherine Williamson migrated into Pike Co., Miss., from Tennessee and settled on the Bogue Chitto below Silver Creek Baptist Church. This union had twin daughters b. in 1817 named Catherine and Elizabeth Ann. Conerly in his original study stated that Felix Allen's first wife was a Williams and that the twins were Catherine and Olivia which was in error.

Elizabeth Ann Allen b. 1817 in Tenn. (probably Nashville), d. in New Orleans, La., in November, 1863, md. Charles Claiborne Harris Allmand b. 1807 in Tenn., d. in 1855 in New Orleans. He was a lumber merchant in the firm of McGuire and Allmand. He drowned in February, 1855, off Pleasident Island (near the Rigolettes in Lake Ponchartrain) attempting to board a mail boat. The wheel of this vessel struck the skiff in which he was standing, thus throwing him into the water. His body was recovered the following March. The issue of Elizabeth Ann and Charles C. H. Allmand:

1) William Allmand b. 1836 in Mississippi.
2) Sarah Allmand b. 1838 in Miss., d. 1925; md. 1) ___ Summers, 2) ___ Swingle by whom she had 3 children (two died in infancy).
3) Henry Allmand b. 1840 in Miss., d. Aug., 1863, in New Orleans, unmarried.
4) Anne Allmand b. 1842 in Miss., d. ca. 1870 in New Orleans, md. Morgan Brown (one child survived her).
5) Isaiah Allmand b. 3/27/1847 in Covington, La., d. 12/13/1927 in Magnolia, Miss., md. Melissa Ann Whitehead Allen (widow).
6) Allice Allmand b. 1852 in New Orleans, d. 1864 (lived with her sister Sarah after her mother's death).
7) Mary Jane Allmand b. 1853, d. 1929 in New Orleans, md. Peter Belotte.

[Note: The death notice for Allice asked that Tennessee and Delaware papers please copy, thus indicating relatives then living in both states.]

BACOT

The Bacot family which enjoyed such prominence in Pike Co., Miss., in the nineteenth century descended from a noted Huguenot family which arrived in Charles Towne in the South Carolina colony after the revocation of the Edict of Nantes in 1685. Much of the following data has been abstracted from South Carolina Legal Records by the compiler, but a noted and more detailed account can be found on this family in the Transactions of the Huguenot Society of South Carolina Nos. 77 and 78. Two different articles appeared in these publications authored by Mrs. Edmond Allan (Martha Bailey) Burns of Charleston, S.C.

The Bacot family originated (or first accounted for) in Tours, south France, in the sixteenth century. One Francois Bacot md. either Marthe Daleu or Anne Moulu and had been born ca. 1560. Francois fathered Pierre, a Calvinist or Huguenot, in 1597, who in turn married in Tours on 2/21/1637 to Jeanne Moreau and had issue:
1) Pierre Bacot "maitre Ourier en soye" b. at Tours on 12/25/1637 (see later).
2) Esaye Bacot b. 1/30/1639 in Tours, md. 1/12/1670 to Marguerite Baudoin.
3) Jeanne Bacot b. in Tours 2/19/1640, md. 8/31/1679 to Hector Foucault.
4) Marthe Bacot b. 9/1/1641 in Tours, md. 2/9/1669 to Rene Gilles. Pierre Bacot or Peter Bacot, the master silk worker, md. in Tours on 6/6/1666 to Jacquine Menessier, alias Mercier, b. 4/4/1649 in Tours, dau. of Abraham Menessier and Jacquine Phelypau, alias Selipeaux. While in Tours they had:
   a) Pierre Gilles b. in Tours 11/22/1668, d. 10/11/1670
   b) Abraham Gilles b. 1/12/1670
   c) Pierre Gilles b. at Tours on 11/15/1671 (see later)
   d) Rene Gilles b. in Tours 2/15/1673, d. 8/21/1677
   e) Daniel Gilles b. in Tours 9/30/1674
   f) David Gilles b. 11/14/1676, d. in Tours in 1756, md. Magdeleine Villiers

After the Revocation of the Edict of Nantes, Pierre Bacot and family, especially he and his wife and two sons, Pierre and Daniel, escaped from France (probably sailed from LaRochelle) for South Carolina and were in Charleston before 1694. In America

Pierre obtained at least two Royal grants--one in 1696 and another in 1699 in St. Andrew's Parish, lands which became known as the Middleton Place near Charleston. Pierre d. there on 9/6/1702. His widow Jacquine d. at the same place on 8/11/1709. After the death of the parents, Pierre II, or Peter, and Daniel left Charleston and settled in the Goose Creek (only 20 miles from the capital) in what is today called Ladson's Station. Pierre II remained, but Daniel left the colony for England.

Pierre Bacot II md. 1) Marianne, widow of Jacque DuGue, dau. of Abraham Fleur de la Plaine--a wife who d. prior to 1716 without giving him issue. Pierre md. 2) in 1716 to Marie or Mary Peronneau born "en voyage" to America in 1685, dau. of Samuel Peronneau. She d. ca. 1773. Pierre wrote his will, calling himself a planter, on 2/3/1729/30 (and died that year) in which he named his children:
1) Samuel Bacot
2) Pierre Bacot III
3) Mary Bacot
4) Elizabeth Bacot

In this will Pierre mentioned his sister-in-law Elizabeth Perroneau and his God-daughter, dau. of his sister Elizabeth, named Elizabeth Bonohost. The executors of the will were his wife, Gideon Frutharode and Tobias Fitch (a kinsman).

Samuel Bacot, son of Pierre II, was b. ca. 1716 in Charleston, md. 4/14/1741 in Christ Church Parish to Rebecca, dau. of Elias Foissin. Elias d. in Charleston in 1739 but was a wealthy planter of Georgetown District. His wife had been Louise Frisselle. Rebecca Foissin Bacot d. before 4/26/1768 and not long afterwards her husband Samuel migrated to the Pee Dee of Darkington Dist., S.C., where he d. ca. 1771 (or shortly thereafter). Samuel's sister Mary d. unmarried in 1806, and Elizabeth md. Charles Dewar, a prominent merchant of Charleston. Pierre, son of Pierre, md. 11/11/1764 to Elizabeth Harramond in Charleston and left a large family.

Samuel Bacot (as above) b. 1716, d. after 1771. Left issue:
1) Samuel Bacot, Jr., b. 3/3/1745, d. 1795 (and a noted patriot of the American Revolution), md. 7/13/1769 to Sarah Margaret Allston b. 12/1/1748, d. in 1797, dau. of Peter Allston, Sr., and Sarah ___ (probably Torquet).
2) Elizabeth Bacot b. ca. 1746, md. William Gause b. 1745. Both died in 1801 and left a large family.
3) Mary Bacot b. 1747, d. 1795, md. 7/13/1769 to Peter Alston, Jr., and lived in Darlington Dist., S.C., and in N.C.
4) Susannah Bacot b. 1754, md. Edward Wingate of Prince George's Parish, Craven County.
5) Peter Bacot b. 1754, d. 8/12/1821, unmarried.

Samuel Bacot, Jr. or II, and Sarah Margaret Allston had issue:
1) Rebecca Foissin Bacot b. 2/14/1774, md. either a Powers or Powell Love.
2) Labon Bacot b. 4/13/1776 in Darlinton Dist., S.C., d. 4/6/1848 in Pike Co., Miss., md. 1) 1797 to Mary Letman; 2) in Apr., 1822 to Margaret Love. Labon Bacob in company with the Robert and Dixon families left S.C. for Miss. See below.
3) Samuel Bacot III b. 6/2/1778, d. 10/19/1833, md. 1) Marcey McCall; 2) Emelie Leslie (or Laslie) b. 10/12/1797, d. 6/20/1869.
4) Cyrus Bacot b. 4/22/1780, md. Elizabeth, dau. of Mark Holloway and Mary Westfield.
5) Maria Allston Bacot b. 3/30/1783, d. 12/10/1847, md. 10/23/1801 to Matthew Brunson.
6) Peter Hannibal Bacot b. 12/9/1795, md. in 1808 to Hannah Mason of Va.

Labon Bacot was in Mississippi prior to 1807 as he was listed on the 1807 Census for Amite County. He and his first wife Mary Letman had issue as follows:
1) Samuel Bacot
2) Susanna Bacot
3) Elizabeth Bacot
4) Maria Louisa Bacot
5) Mary Lucinda or Louisiana Bacot b. 1800, md. in 1825 to Robert Potter Wingate. They had at least one dau. Salome Elizabeth b. 11/16/1840, d. 7/13/1909, md. 12/20/1859 in Newton Co., Tx., to Wiley Mangrum Harper.

After Mary Letman's death ca. 1812 in Miss., Laban Bacot md. 2) Margaret Love by whom he had issue:
6) Lorinda Bacot md. Joe Tuff Martin

7) Robert Bacot who md. Satine May
8) Levi Bacot md. Ann, dau. of James Roberts of Washington Parish, La.
9) William Bacot
10) Adam Bacot b. 1/14/1834, d. 1/4/1900, md. Rebecca Sibley and had at least one son named Eugene H. Bacot b. 3/7/1859, d. 9/12/1952, md. 2/1888 to Margaret Foxworth.
11) Julia Bacot
12) Rachel Bacot died young

BICKHAM

The following are corrections and addenda of the Bickham family as mentioned in this volume, supplied by Mr. Bickham Christian of 644 Herndon Avenue, Shreveport, Louisiana:

Page 90: "Major Benjamin Bickham." Benjamin Bickham was never a Major. He arrived in the Mississippi Territory in 1798 from Georgia. He came from the area of Burke and Jackson Counties. Mr. Conerly was probably referring to Major Thomas Bickham who married Mary Curry, daughter of Jacob Curry.

Jacob Curry was from South Carolina and died in Amite County. He was a Revolutionary veteran having served in South Carolina and Georgia.

Thomas Bickham with his four brothers Abner, John, William, and Benjamin were all in Louisiana/Mississippi area by 1799.

Page 151: Lewis Champness Bickham was the son of James Salisbury Bickham and the grandson of the above Maj. Thomas Bickham. James Salisbury Bickham died in New Orleans on the 23rd of March, 1843. He was a representative from Washington Parish to the State Legislature at this time. He was also the sheriff of Washington Parish during the 1830 decade.

Lewis (Louis) Champness Bickham's mother was Elizabeth Culp Curry Terry, daughter of Champness and Hannah Terry.

The complete family group of James Salisbury and Elizabeth Culp Curry Terry Bickham were: (All of the following children lived in Holmesville, Mississippi, with their widowed mother.)
1) Benjamin Franklin Bickham b. 1828, d. 1872, md. Lou Harper.
2) Mary Fletcher Bickham b. 1829, d. 1860, md. Daniel Hillary Quinn.
3) Lewis Champness Bickham b. 1834, d. 1882, md. Adeline Lindsey.
4) Hannah L. Bickham b. 1836, d. 1894, md. Ritchie Robertson.
5) Thomas Benton Chism Bickham b. 1839, d. 1860, not married.
6) Alexander Mouton Bickham b. 1842, d. 1886, md. Katherine Huldah DeLoache.
7) Sarah Bickham b. 1831, md. 1st Willis Germany, a Methodist preacher; and 2nd B. A. Bridges.

BULLOCK

Joel Bullock and Rhoda Davis had the following children: Hugh, Richard, Thomas, Quinney, William, Davis, Samuel C. and Lemuel T. (twins), Simeon, Bedia, Aida, and Joseph R. The Louisa listed by Conerly as a daughter (p. 68) was in actuality a dau. of Joel's son Hugh.

Hugh Bullock did not marry Caroline Smith as reported by Conerly on p. 69, but married Caroline Brumfield, dau. of Isaac Brumfield of York Co., S.C. Isaac Brumfield left the Pike Co. area for St. Tammany Parish, La., where he died between 1810 and 1816. His widow named Elizabeth md. 2) Seymour Robertson in St. Tammany Parish and migrated on to Corpus Christi, Texas.

Hugh and Caroline Brumfield Bullock were parents of seven children: Cynthia Ellen, Louisa, Joel J., Davis Isaac, Alexander A., Jim Jordan, and Jesse Leonard.

[Corrections by Mrs. R. Chester Upton (Marie Luter), Jackson, Miss.]

BURKHALTER

Henry T. Burkhalter d. in Franklinton, La., in Aug., 1884, in his 70th year. He was the son of Daniel Burkhalter. Henry md. Theresa Luter, sister to Joseph Luter, who md. Eliza Burkhalter. Henry and Theresa had three known children:

1) Mary Ann Burkhalter md. John C. Foil of Washington Parish, La.
2) Emily Burkhalter md. John R. Wood of Washington Parish, La.
3) Henry S. Burkhalter, a sheriff of Washington Parish when accidentally killed in the 1890's; md. 1) Sele Lucas, and 2) Maria Lucas (Sele's sister).

Elizabeth Burkhalter and Joseph Luter had 10 children as follows: William Daniel, John J., Mary Ann, Jesse Crawford, Sarah Caroline, Therese Elizabeth, James Monroe, Thomas Jefferson, Louisa Matilda, and Jacob Westley. Most of these are buried at China Grove.

On pages 153-154 of Conerly's volume, a "fandango" is mentioned. This entertainment was held in the home of Eliza Burkhalter and Joseph Luter. Eliza's younger sister Louisa was the "star" performer.

[Mrs. R. Chester Upton, Jackson, Miss., is in the process of preparing the genealogy of this family--a volume which should be ready for distribution by 1979.]

CARTER

Isaac Carter was born in Cumberland County, North Carolina, in 1764; married in Orangeburg District, South Carolina, in 1780; and died in Pike County, Mississippi, Mar. 24, 1834. He is buried on Rocky Creek near Chatawa, Mississippi.

On Feb. 5, 1777, he joined the Revolutionary Army in N.C. and was in the army until Jan., 1780. Then, presumably, he was in Orangeburgh Dist., S.C., until 7/1/1781 when he re-enlisted. After discharge on 7/1/1782 he was again a resident of Cumberland Co., N.C., and remained there until summer, 1785. From 1785 until 1810 he resided in Orangeburgh Dist., S.D. In the spring, 1810, he moved by covered wagon caravan to Pike Co., Miss., having come from the Wateree River, through Georgia, and settled on the east side of Rocky Creek, Pike Co., Miss.

Isaac Carter married Ann Elizabeth (Nancy) Young, supposedly "Dutch, short, dumpy, jolly, adept, etc." She spoke Dutch and was born in Orangeburgh Dist., S.C. She died after Isaac, having spent her last years with her son Israel. Their issue:

1) William Carter b. 1781, Orangeburgh Dist., S.C., on Wateree R.
2) Hardy Carter b. 1784, N.C., Cumberland Co.
3) John Carter b. 1787, S.C.
4) Mary (Polly) Carter b. 1789, S.C.
5) Allen Carter b. 1793, S.C.
6) Redmond Carter b. 1795 (see Kemp record)
7) Burrell Carter b. 6/3/1796, S.C.
8) Elizabeth (Betsey) Carter b. 1799, S.C.
9) Derrell Carter b. 1802, S.C.
10) Harville Carter b. 1/21/1805, S.C.
11) Israel Carter b. 12/15/1807, S.C.

All these children were well educated Latin scholars, classical students. Harville in particular was musically talented.

Isaac Carter's war record: Volunteer, N.C. Regt., Col. Hogan, Capt. John Welch's Co., 2/5/1777--to winter after, then transferred to Cpt. Robt. Fenner's Co., Col. Sylvanus Harney's Regt. In Battles of Brandywine, Germantown, Monmouth, and discharged Lockhart's Folly, 30 miles south of Wilmington, N.C., about 1/1780. From 7/1/1781 to 7/1/1782 he served in Capt. Dennis Porterfield's Co. of N.C. Militia, a "balloted substitute." Wounded in arm at Eutaw Springs. Discharged at Bacon's Bridge, S.C.

Family data:
1) William Carter md. Hannah Cole at Liberty, Miss. He was 20 yrs old when he came to Miss. from S.C. with father. His war record: War of 1812: 1st Lieut. in Cpt. Henry Quin's Co., 13th Regt. (Nixon's) Miss. Served from 1/6/1815 to 2/5/1815. Enlisted at Magnolia, Miss. His brother Hardy Carter served as a private in the same company.

Issue of William and Hannah:
a) Isaac Carter md. Margaret Holden
b) Artabanus Carter md. Widow Self, no issue; d. 1858
c) Marion Carter md. Julia Holden
d) Harmon Carter md. Martha Estes, 1 son died young
e) Peter Horry Carter, youngest member of family, d. in CSA, Va.
f) Mahala Carter md. Jacob Leonard Amacker
g) Emily Carter md. B. D. Owens
h) Caroline Carter md. 1) Locke Martin; 2) Judge Robert Rutland
i) Mary Carter md. Wm. Cook
j) Jinsy Carter md. Jesse Morris. No issue.

4) Mary Carter md. Ashford Addison, editor of the Greensburg Imperial at one time.

7) Burrell Carter md. Judith Taylor, widow of Robert White and the mother of Caroline Virginia White, called Callie. Burrell was b. 6/3/1796 and d. 8/28/1860, at Darlington, La. He served in the War of 1812. He resided at Darlington's Plantation, Chipola, La., and was buried on Darling's Cr. as was Judith and daughter Malitta Ann Quin. Judith was b. 11/3/1796 and d. 5/2/1883. Issue:
a) Capt. William A. Carter md. Elizabeth Doughty
b) Malitta Ann Carter md. Peter Quin of Liberty, Miss.
c) Walton H. Carter
d) Wilford M. Carter md. Julie Ann Taylor, a niece of Judith and dau. of David Taylor.
e) Dr. Wellington W. Carter md. Mary Doughty, sister of Elizabeth
f) Sereptha Carter
g) Nancy Carter md. Alex S. Doughty, brother of Doughty sisters
h) Elizabeth Carter md. Dr. J. A. Anderson, Shreveport, La.
i) Angeline Carter md. Thaddeus Robinson

8) Elizabeth Carter md. John Houston of Red River Plantation. Issue:
a) John Houston, d. in CSA
b) Lily Houston
c) Nancy Houston
d) Willie Houston
e) Eugene Houston
f) James Houston
g) Joe (daughter) Houston

9) Derrell Carter md. Sereptha Taylor, sister of Judith Taylor Carter. They lived near Minden, La., and had issue:
a) John J. Carter b. 1832, d. 1927
b) Hardy Carter
c) Isaac Carter

10) Harville (Harvil) Carter b. 1805, d. 11/2/1865, St. Cloud, La., md. Caroline Virginia White, dau. of Robert White and Judith Taylor, and granddaughter of Nimrod White. Her father died in 1816 in St. Tammany Parish, La., and her brother David died young. She was b. in 1812 and d. in 1897 at Jackson, La. Issue:
a) Marcus Tallious Carter b. 2/27/1828 in Pike Co., Miss., d. in Livingston Parish, La., 4/7/1884; md. 9/25/1855 to Amanda Richardson b. 2/15/1829,

dau. of George Richardson and Margaret Eliza ___. Issue:
   1) Tullia Carter b. 11/4/1856, d. 12/24/1884
   2) Lillie Carter b. 10/9/1858
   3) Ralph Turner Carter b. 11/3/1860, d. 7/16/1888
   4) Earl George Carter b. 8/22/1862
   5) Zoa Carter b. 4/4/1865
   6) Tullius Colmer Carter b. 4/14/1867
b) Hannibal Carter b. 2/27/1829 in Pike Co., Miss., d. 1/28/1904, in Franklinton, La. (buried at Ellis Cemetery), md. 2/19/1856 to Missouri Lenora Pettitt d. 12/23/1856, aged 16 yrs, 2 mos., 6 days; md. 2) Mellissa Bernard. Issue:
   1) Prentiss Bernard Carter b. 12/18/1856
c) Robert G. or S. Carter b. 8/27/1831, d. 1/1889; md. Elisa Bernard, sister to Mellissa. Issue:
   1) Haley Carter
   2) Alice Carter
   3) Walter Lee Carter
   4) ___ Carter md. Dave Rawlins
d) Infant died young
e) Infant daughter
f) Haley Montgomery Carter b. 4/13/1837, d. either in St. Helena Parish, La., or in Texas; md. Louisiana T. Carter, dau. of Capt. Billy A. Carter.
g) Addie M. Carter md. Selas (Sellers?) Norwood of E. Feliciana Parish, La. No issue.
h) Lilah Virginia Carter md. Samuel Cothran Schwing of E. Feliciana Parish. Some issue:
   1) Ada Schwing
   2) Carrie Schwing
   3) Willie Schwing
   4) Carter Schwing
i) Dewitt Carter b. 1845, d. 11/7/1925 at the home of his sister Lilah V. Schwing in Jackson, La. He was a student at old Centenary College in his young life.

11) Israel Carter b. 12/15/1807 in S.C., d. 7/22/1878 in Sunny Hill, La. (buried in the Carter Cemetery); md. 1) Maria Felder b. 1806 in S.C. Issue:
   a) Fenderland (Finland) Carter b. 1829
   b) Isaac Carter b. 1831
   c) Augustus Carter b. 1833, d. CSA
   d) Elizabeth Carter b. 1841, md. Harvil W. Easley
   e) Laban (Labron) Carter b. 6/11/1837, d. 7/18/1891, md. in 1866 to Fanny Powell b. 2/5/1850 in Amite Co., Miss., d. in Washington Parish, La., 2/1917. Issue:
      1) John Carter b. 11/5/1867, d. 3/22/1844, md. Louise Brumfield, 1864-1943.
      2) Elijah Augustus Carter b. 1/11/1869, d. 12/14/1931; md. Ora Kemp.
      3) Israel W. Carter b. 5/22/1871, d. 4/15/1944, md. Mary Crowe, 1876-1958.
      4) Felden (Felder?) Carter
      5) Cornie C. Carter b. 5/27/1874, d. 8/15/1946, md. Vol. Simmons.
      6) Burley Carter b. 3/6/1879, d. 3/1888, buried in the old Carter/Parker Cemetery at Sunny Hill, La.
      7) Infant
   f) Brazella Carter b. 1844, md. ___ McCreary
   g) Eveline Carter b. 1847, md. Joseph Addison.

Israel Carter md. 2) 4/29/1863 to Elizabeth Turner b. 5/5/1834, d. 5/4/1916, dau. of Philip Turner and Mary Roberts. Issue:
   h) Mary Augusta Carter b. 11/25/1864, d. 9/14/1869.
   i) Joseph W. Carter b. 7/16/1866, d. 7/2/1932, md. on 3/3/1889 to Mary Ann Maranda Richardson b. 12/15/1868, d. 7/15/1955, dau. of Hardy Richardson and Martha Roberts (nee Warren).
   j) Martena Carter b. 2/24/1868, md. William "Uncle Billy" Bickham.
   k) Cora Arlena Carter b. 3/4/1870, d. 3/12/1939, md. William Wilks Parker.
   l) Aria (Ara) Carmadia Carter b. 7/4/1872, d. 1942, md. George Parker. No issue.
   m) Lola Mary (Mae) Carter b. 8/8/1874, md. Jake Woods. Buried in Amite, La.

CONERLY-CONNERLEY

The major portion of the Conerly material was contributed by Mrs. Alma Marcus Conerly in honor of her husband W. K. (Ted) Conerly and her children: (1) Mrs. Wilma Lou Conerly Sanders, and (2) Jerry Marcus Conerly; and her grandchildren: (1) Mrs. Dana Corinne Sanders Queenan, and (2) Thomas Walter Sanders, Jr. (Kip); (3) Leslie Maret Sanders; and (4) Andrea Michelle (Andy) Conerly.

The Conerly-Connerley family of Mississippi and Louisiana descends from John Conerly of Johnston County, North Carolina, who wrote his will on October 17, 1751. This document named his wife Keziah and his brother Rich Jones and Stephen Herring, a brother-in-law. To his two sons William and Cullen he willed 300 acres in Duplin County, North Carolina. John Connerly also mentioned his daughter Patience. Anthony Herring, a brother-in-law was to serve as the executor of the will. Elizabeth and Griffen Jones acted as witnesses to the instrument. John Connerly died prior to the March Court, 1752, for Johnston County.

Keziah Connerly, before marriage, was Keziah Herring, daughter of Samuel Herring of Johnston County. The latter wrote his will on 10/22/1750 and named therin his three sons--Anthony (Antony), Stephen, and Michael (to whom he willed the "plantation whereon I now live." He mentioned only one daughter by name, Barthena Herring, but he did mention his son-in-law John Connerley. Antony Herring was to be the executor. The witnesses to the will were Antony and Joseph Herring. Samuel Herring died prior to the December Court, 1750, for Johnston County. (The Connerly and Herring Wills are deposited in the North Carolina Department of Archives and History, Raleigh.)

William Conerly, the probable son of the above-named John and Keziah Connerly, probably moved to Craven County, N.C. He left a will in that county dated 3/31/1807, and was dead by the December Court, as an inventory was taken at that time. His wife Margaret died in Craven County in 1817 as the inventory of her estate carried the date March 1818. The children named in the William Conerly will were:
1) John Conerly
2) William Conerly
3) Nancy Conerly
4) Cullen Conerly
5) Charity Conerly
6) Polly Conerly
7) Nelly Conerly
8) Susannah Conerly
9) Elizabeth Conerly
10) Margaret Conerly
11) Thomas Reives Conerly

William Conerly named his wife Margaret and John Jackson as the executors of his will in 1807.

Cullen Conerly, son of John & Keziah Conerly, lived in Duplin, probably on the land left him by his father's will. He was quite active in that county until his death. He dated his will in Duplin County, November 11, 1811, and was dead by January 7, 1812--when the will received probate. John and Luke Conerly, his sons, were executors of the will. Cullen's wife Lettitia Ward d. August 26, 1846. The Wilmington Journal on September 4, 1846, mentioned her death and stated that she was in her 97th or 98th year. The Raleigh Register of September 22, 1846, reported her death and stated that she was 110 years old. The will of Cullen Conerly mentioned the following children:
1) John Conerly
2) Owen Conerly
3) William Conerly
4) Luke Conerly
5) Polly Conerly Guy
6) Tibitha Conerly Lanee (Lawes?)
7) Frances Conerly Duncan
8) Susan Conerly Page
9) Chelly Conerly Blount
10) Betsy Conerly

A number of Cullen and Lettitia Conerly's children and grandchildren migrated to Mississippi and Louisiana ca. 1820.

1) John Conerly b. ca. 1774, md. 11/1805 (bond dated Nov. 4) to Susannah Newton in Duplin Co., N.C. One John left a will in Duplin dated 6/13/1839 in which he named a son John. He possibly had given other children their share and, therefore, did not mention them in his will. The possible family for John and Susannah:
   a) John Conerly, Jr., md. 9/23/1834 in Duplin Co., N.C., to Ann J. Kornegay.
   b) Cananiza Conerly b. ca. 1813, d. in Washington Parish, La., in extreme old age; md. in Duplin Co., N.C., in 1832 to Zachariah Kornegay b. ca. 1807. Counted on the 1850 Census in Marion Co., Miss. Issue:
      1) Abram Kornegay b. 1836
      2) S___ A___ Kornegay b. 1842
      3) L. W. Kornegay b. 1846
      4) Elvina Kornegay b. 2/27/1847, d. 2/1889, md. in 1863 to W. W. Rester.
   c) William Conerly settled in Pike Co., Miss.
   d) Major Owen Conerly b. 7/3/1815, d. 10/8/1889, md. on 12/15/1842 to Susan A. Tynes b. 11/11/1825, d. 7/28/1891 and had issue:
      1) Fleming "Flem" Tynes Conerly b. 10/3/1843, d. 5/13/1910, buried at China Grove; md. Sarah Hammonds b. 5/27/1848, d. 6/7/1871.
      2) Elizabeth Conerly b. 12/28/1854, d. 3/29/1888.
      3) Isaac N. Conerly md. Sarah Harvey.
      4) Julius C. Conerly md. Hester Catherine Sumrall b. 4/25/1850, d. 2/23/1921.
      5) Franklin Sands Conerly b. 5/22/1849, d. 2/26/1926, md. on 12/31/1878 to Josephine Sumrall b. 4/25/1849, d. 7/4/1920.
      6) Julia B. Conerly md. Dawson Powell.
      7) William T. "Bill" Conerly b. 12/23/1852, d. 2/22/1906, md. Abigail Reagan b. 4/12/1862, d. 11/9/1945, buried at China Grove.
      8) Cullen M. Conerly md. Ellen Brumfield.
      9) Randolph Conerly b. 3/21/1858, d. 12/19/1891, md. Nelly Reagan.
      10) Mary Jane Conerly b. 5/29/1857, d. 1/30/1910, md. W. S. Yates.
      11) Luke Owen Conerly b. 4/17/1860, d. 1/7/1896, md. ___ Forbes.
      12) Adaline (Addie) Conerly md. Dawson Brumfield.
      13) Rufus Conerly md. Mundy Williams.
      14) Richard Conerly md. Mattie Riley.
      15) Monro Conerly
      Additional possible children for this family are:
      16) Sarah Conerly b. 11/25/1846, d. 3/22/1922, buried China Grove.
      17) George Conerly md. Lucy Graham.

2) Owen Conerly, Sr., b. 8/27/1777, in Duplin Co., N.C., d. 12/18/1848 in Pike Co., Miss. (possibly buried at China Grove); md. on 1/14/1808, to widow Mary Wilkinson Russell b. 12/18/1791, in Duplin Co., N.C., d. 8/24/1860 at Holmesville, Miss., dau. of William Wilkinson and Elizabeth Jackson. Issue:
   a) Cullen Conerly b. 10/13/1808 in Duplin Co., N.C., d. 6/1856 in Miss., md. 10/7/1829 in Marion Co., Miss., to Levisa Lewis b. 1808, dau. of Martin and Nancy Lewis of Marion Co. Issue:
      1) Owen Lewis Conerly b. 9/15/1830, d. 11/30/1864 CSA, md. 11/4/1852 to Saleta Azalena Paine Warner b. 1830, d. 1917, and had issue:
         a) Alexander Bryon Conerly b. 1853, d. 1901, md. Dessie Peavy in Tex.
         b) Thomas Wilfred Conerly b. 1855, d. 1917, md. Addie Norris, in Tex.
         c) Levisa Jane Conerly b. 1857, d. 1920, md. Eddie Elias Brooks.
         d) Salena Rebecca Conerly b. 1859, d. 1964 (age 105), md. Joseph Mayberry Cocke in Texas.
         e) Samuel Roland Conerly b. 1860, d. 1873.
         f) Owen Monroe Conerly b. 1862, d. 1944, in California.
      2) John M. Conerly b. 10/17/1831, d. 10/28/1923, md. Lucinda Lampton b. b. 1/24/1834, d. 1/29/1885 and had:
         a) William Franklin Conerly b. 1853, d. 1908, md. Susanna Wiltshire.
         b) Nancy Elizabeth Conerly b. 12/28/1854, d. 3/27/1888, md. J. Wes Holmes.
         c) Leona Josephine Conerly b. 12/28/1856, d. 3/27/1945, md. Gholson Gilbert Ginn.
         d) Eugene Josephine Conerly b. 1858, d. 1908, md. Flora Stringer.
         e) Henry Pascal Conerly b. 1860, d. 1945, md. Martina Statham.
         f) Ida Eugenia Conerly b. 1864, d. 1891, md. William W. Pope.
         g) Berkley Sherwood Conerly b. 1866, d. 1868.
         h) Lillie Olivia Conerly b. 1868, d. 1956, md. Luther Reagan.
         i) John Lampton Conerly b. 1867, d. 1953, md. Kittie Ratliff.
         j) Albert Baxter Conerly b. 1871, d. 1939, md. 1) Maggie Ratliff; 2)

Lula King.
3) William M. Conerly b. 7/30/1833 in Pike Co., d. 11/23/1901 at Hornbeck, La., md. Jane Ann Harvey b. 11/20/1838, d. 9/5/1892 in Vermillion Parish, La. Issue:
   a) Cullen William Conerly b. 3/9/1856, d. 12/10/1912, md. 2/12/1880 to Mary Dixie Simmons b. 9/24/1861, d. 6/10/1895.
   b) Sarah Elizabeth Conerly b. 4/30/1858, d. 2/16/1891 in Vermillion Parish, La.; md. Edward Smiley.
   c) Mary Nancy Conerly b. 6/24/1860, d. 5/30/1861.
4) Mary Ann Conerly b. 10/10/1835, d. 12/11/1884 in Simpson Co., Miss., md. John Calquhoun and had 12 children, 7 sons and 5 daughters, all of Simpson Co., Miss.
5) Nancy Rebecca Conerly b. ca. 1840, md. Loftin Calquhoun.
6) Catherine L. Conerly b. 1842, md. W. H. H. Brumfield.
7) Jabez Newton Conerly b. 1847, d. 12/24/1898 at Spring Creek, La., md. Henrietta Angeline Brumfield, dau. of Isaac and Elizabeth Holmes Brumfield, b. 1846, d. 1906 near Spring Cr., and had issue:
   a) Lizzie Conerly b. 8/26/1869, d. 4/1/1901, md. ca. 1899 to James A. Dixon b. 12/16/1861, d. 1/14/1902 and had issue:
      1) James Van Dixon b. 3/12/1901, md. 1) ___ ; 2) ___ ; 3) on 6/5/1935 to Mary F. McKinstry b. 12/13/1921, and had: George Michael Dixon b. 12/15/1940.
      James md. 4) 6/27/1953 to Beatrice Massey b. 10/24/1906.
   b) Thomas Bryon Conerly b. 3/31/1874 at Columbia, Miss., d. 9/3/1965, buried at Spring Creek; md. 1) 9/1892 to Nettie Frances McDaniel b. 1874, d. 1901; 2) in 1902 to Arie Varnado b. 1878, d. 1919; 3) 12/1922 to Martha McDaniel b. 1884, d. 1963. Issue by 1st wife:
      1) Claude Iddo Conerly b. 11/6/1893, d. 7/1/1818 (WWI at Camp Beauregard). Not married.
      2) Herman Elias Conerly b. 3/1/1897, md. 12/22/1933 to Thelma Kennedy by 6/27/1905.
      3) Jabe T. Conerly b. 1898, d. 1901.
      4) Angie H. Conerly b. 1900, d. 1901.
      Issue by 2nd wife:
      5) Donald Wentz Conerly b. 10/16/1905, d. 3/1/1963 (merchant at Osyka, Miss.); md. 7/15/1939 to Doris McDaniel b. 11/19/1908 and had issue: Karen Elizabeth who md. John David Singleton and Donald Vincent Conerly.
      6) Uldric Earl Conerly b. 1/10/1906, md. ca. 1928 to Hazel Louise ___ b. 5/11/1911 and had: Wallace Jack b. 12/2/1930; Bobby Bryon b. 3/25/1932 md. Mattie Pruitt; and Patricia Ann b. 12/3/1933 md. ___ Bennett.
      7) Thyra Evelyn Conerly b. 6/23/1909, md. 8/31/1931 to Peter Joseph Tafaro b. 4/6/1908 and had: Joseph Thomas b. 1943 and Sharon Dee b. 1946.
      8) Loyd Conerly b. 11/20/1911, md. 11/9/1940 to Wilkie Stringfield b. 7/7/1917 and had Barbara Kay b. 1946.
      9) Maxwell Roysdon Conerly b. 11/6/1913, md. ca. 1940 to Ana (Anna?) Allene "Sally" Hullett b. 7/30/1923 and had: Connie Maxine Conerly b. 1942 who md. Frank Lane.
      10) Dorothy "Dot" Southerland Conerly b. 7/6/1925, md. 1) 4/9/1933 to Oswald Wentz Young b. 10/24/1909 and had: John Oswald b. 5/28/1934, md. Shirley Stratton; Arie Lou b. 8/21/1936, md. in 1954 to Walter Dewey Craft.
   c) Cullen Conerly b. 1876, d. 1908 near Spring Creek, not married.
   d) Watt Smiley Conerly b. 1/28/1880, d. 12/23/1960, buried at Spring Creek, md. 3/7/1901 to Corine Frances McDaniel.
      1) Myrtis Elizabeth Conerly b. 10/27/1902, md. 9/24/1936 to Lewis Diehl b. 11/30/1890, d. 5/29/1956. No issue.
      2) Owen Watt Conerly b. 8/21/1904, md. 9/25/1936 to Lillie Reed b. 10/2/1911 and had issue: Frances Elizabeth b. 9/25/1938 md. in 1962 to John Heffner; Smiley Eugene b. 3/27/1941; and Michael Lamar b. 8/25/1943.
      3) Lila Juanita Conerly b. 1/10/1908, md. 1) Frank Wilton McDaniel b. 5/2/1894, d. 1/18/1947; 2) in 1952 to William A. Peters b. 10/2/1882, d. 6/12/1952--a man who taught school for 45 years (principal for 13). Juanita taught at the Spring Creek School for 34 of her 36 years as a teacher.
      4) Jabe Thomas Conerly b. 3/19/1910, md. ca. 1934 to Myrtle Strick-

             land b. 5/7/1908 and had issue: Steve Garland b. 9/16/1936 md.
             Imogene Louise Brown; and Lanny Pat b. 2/15/1941, md. in 1960
             to Joyce Rushing.
          5) Thelma Louise Conerly b. 4/27/1912, d. 10/6/1912.
          6) Wesley Smiley Conerly b. 10/21/1918, md. 12/3/1940 to Elizabeth
             Sullivan b. 12/6/1920 and had issue: Delores Kay b. 9/5/1941
             md. Kenyon Lewis; Glenda Iris b. 11/9/1942, md. in 1962 to Henry
             Brock; and Donna b. 4/20/1950.
          7) Willie Pearl Conerly b. 3/3/1921, md. 7/1/1948 to M. DeWitt
             Pipkin b. 9/20/1920 and had: Larry Joe b. 1949; and Conerly
             "Conny" DeWitt b. in 1957.
       e) Owen Columbus "Doc" Conerly b. 4/1885, d. 4/7/1922 in Osyka, Miss.,
          md. ca. 1908 to Fannie Thompson b. 12/23/1890, d. 8/1952 (buried
          at Osyka) and had issue:
          1) Selma Gertrude Conerly b. 7/27/1910, md. 11/27/1934 to Price
             A. Adams b. 7/10/1907 and had issue: Sandra Ione b. 8/14/1939
             md. in 1949 to William Brant b. 1933.
          2) James Edward Conerly b. 12/15/1912, md. 3/14/1937 to Evelyn
             "Dutch" Varnado b. 10/20/1913 and had issue: Lelia Scott b.
             1941, md. Harold J. Prange; Carol Frances b. 1945; Jane Evelyn
             and her twin James Edward b. 1951.
    8) Eliza Jane Conerly b. 1845, md. James Ward.
    9) Martha Lenore (Leona?) Conerly b. 9/18/1858, d. 2/28/1916, md. Needham Holmes b. 10/6/1844, d. 9/30/1919 and had issue:
       a) Nancy Letica Holmes b. 1874.
       b) Jabus Newton Holmes b. 1876, d. 1949
       c) Emily Levida Holmes b. 1879, d. 1967
       d) Jane Elizabeth Holmes b. 1881, d. 1967
       e) Benjamin Cullen Holmes b. 1883, d. 1943
       f) Jesse Olen Holmes b. 1886, d. 1919
       g) Flora Rebecca Holmes b. 1889, d. 1906
       h) James Taylor Holmes b. 1892
       i) Alton Eugene Holmes b. 1900, d. 1942
   10) James T. Conerly b. 1849
b) William Wilkinson Conerly b. 8/11/1810 in Duplin Co., N.C., d. 11/19/1879
   in Pike Co., Miss.; md. 1) on 2/15/1832 to Caroline Starnes d. 1851 in
   Sabine Parish, La., dau. of Moses Starnes of Marion Co. Issue:
    1) James Rayford Conerly b. 11/2/1835, d. 4/9/1911, md. on 1/16/1861 to
       Mary Elizabeth Harvey b. 12/27/1840, d. 6/2/1927. Issue:
       a) Mark Russell Conerly b. 1864, d. 1935, md. Elizabeth May.
       b) Mary Jane Conerly b. 1866, died young.
       c) William Harris (Harrison) Conerly b. 1868, md. Gertrude Willis.
       d) Ida Liddy Conerly md. William Brock and lived in Akron, Ohio.
       e) Jesse Monroe Conerly md. 1) Lottie Brumfield; 2) India Cherry.
       f) Ada Lucy Conerly md. Jefferson Causey and lived at Gloster, Miss.
       g) Needham Eugene Conerly md. Ada Ellzey.
       h) Cora Conerly
       i) James Cullen Conerly b. 1881, md. Alyce Corine McDaniel.
    2) Mark Russell Conerly b. 1838, d. 1890, md. Sophronia Tyler b. 1846,
       d. 1885 (buried in the Founder's Cemetery, Tylertown, Miss.)
    3) John Conerly
    4) William Conerly
    William Wilkinson Conerly md. 2) in 1853 to Margaret O. Connally b.
    1/6/1811, d. 6/5/1878 (Founder's Cemetery) and had issue:
    5) Lula R. Conerly b. 9/10/1855, d. 4/18/1917, md. T. W. Holmes.
c) John R. Conerly b. 7/7/1812 in Duplin Co., N.C., d. 9/27/1853 in Sabine
   Parish (now Vernon), La., buried in the Holly Grove Cemetery near
   Anacoco; md. Elizabeth Henrietta Tynes b. 4/28/1813, in Miss., d. 10/14/
   1895, dau. of Fleming Tynes and Jane Warren. Issue:
    1) Mary Jane Conerly b. 12/14/1834, in Marion Co., Miss., d. 12/30/1920,
       md. on 7/27/1852 in Sabine Parish, La., to William Fletcher Sandel
       b. 11/19/1827, d. 1/25/1902 in Natchitoches Parish and buried in the
       Prospect Cemetery. They had 5 children:
       a) Winifred Elizabeth Sandel b. 10/1/1853, d. 6/24/1933, md. 10/13/
          1875 to Francis Marion Dowden b. 2/24/1850, d. 7/13/1926 in Sabine
          Parish and buried in Prospect Cemetery.
       b) John Monroe Sandel b. 11/27/1855 (56?), d. 9/17/1933, md. Laura
          Jane Lee b. 9/8/1867, d. 4/2/1956.
       c) William Wesley Sandel b. 10/25/1856, d. 1/12/1902.

d) Susan Catherine Sandel b. 1/11/1862, d. 7/11/1941 in Vernon Parish,
      La.; md. ___ Miller; 2) Joseph Pantalion b. 1850, d. 1897.
   d) James Fletcher Sandel b. 9/2/1870, d. 2/16/1957, md. 1) Mary Emma
      Butler; 2) Susan Lourena Thompson.
2) William Luke Conerly b. 12/14/1834 in Marion Co., Miss., d. as a
   soldier in the Confederate Army (Pvt. Co. E, 11th Battn., La. Inf.)
   near Marksville, La., between April and December, 1863; md. Virginia
   Elizabeth German b. 12/5/1838, d. 11/7/1870 (Holly Grove Cemetery);
   md. 12/12/1856 in Sabine Parish. Issue:
   a) Emaline Elemmie Conerly b. 1/1/1858, d. 3/6/1882, md. Wiley Lee.
   b) Mary Jane Conerly b. ca. 1862, md. Young Palmer.
   c) Wilmuth Octavia Conerly b. 12/18/1863, d. 7/27/1954, md. George W.
      Hughes b. 1/22/1861, d. 5/29/1909.
3) Harriett Rebecca Conerly b. 4/27/1836, in Marion Co., Miss., d. 7/9/
   1916; md. 1) 4/6/1854 in Sabine Parish to James S. Moss b. in Ala.,
   d. 2/1860 in Sabine Parish; md. 2) in 1860 to Charles Henry Mitchell
   b. 9/26/1839 in Adair Co., Ky.; served in the army and was wounded at
   the Battle of Mansfield, d. from wound on 4/26/1864. Issue:
   a) Susan Elizabeth Mitchell b. 1/4/1862, d. in Texas; md. ___ Hughes.
   b) Laura Jane Mitchell b. 7/20/1864, md. ___ McElveen.
   Harriett Rebecca Conerly Moss Mitchell md. 3) 4/17/1867 in Sabine
   Parish to William James Dowden b. 12/1/1842, d. 1/1/1928. Issue:
   c) James Cullen Dowden b. 8/22/1868, d. 1/16/1869.
   d) William Wilkerson Dowden b. 11/29/1869, d. 9/2/1872.
   e) Malissia Caroline Dowden b. 4/8/1871, d. 9/21/1872.
   f) Francis Asbury Dowden b. 6/2/1873, d. 8/9/1965, md. 12/4/1895 to
      Elizabeth E. Self b. 6/28/1878 in Limestone Co., Texas, d. 2/11/
      1945 in Caddo Parish (buried in Holly Grove Cemetery).
4) Malissa Conerly b. 1838/39 in Miss., d. 8/12/1868; md. 11/9/1856 to
   James Miers Franklin b. 9/14/1836, d. 2/3/1907. (She is buried in
   Holly Grove and he at the Fort Jesup Cemetery. Supposedly, she died
   from a wasp sting and was the first person interred at Holly Grove.)
   Issue:
   a) Dr. Raleigh Franklin b. 9/6/1857, d. 3/19/1905, buried at Fort
      Jesup; md. 5/11/1880 to Florence Broom.
5) Susan Conerly b. 3/2/1841, in Marion Co., Miss., d. 3/5/1921; md.
   10/21/1858 to George W. House b. 11/9/1833 in Jones Co., Tex.; died
   as Confederate soldier in Ark. in the closing months of the war.
   Issue:
   a) Hattie A. House b. 11/4/1859, d. 3/9/1939, md. 12/5/1880 to Wayne
      Theodore German b. 11/29/1857, d. 12/11/1927.
   b) Elizabeth House b. 9/18/1861, d. 2/26/1939, md. 1/18/1881 to Henry
      Solomon Beckcom b. 2/4/1860, d. 2/7/1934 in Shreveport, La. (buried
      at Holly Grove).
   Susan Conerly House md. 2) on 7/6/1865 to Reverend John Franklin b.
   11/12/1845, d. 11/4/1925, and had issue:
   c) Dr. William Thomas Franklin b. 8/18/1866, d. 4/21/1942, md. 1)
      Sarah A. Bray b. 5/16/1869, d. 2/1/1902; md. 2) Flora S. Franklin
      b. 8/27/1883, d. 3/16/1926; md. 3) Mrs. Eleanor Murphey.
   d) Mirah A. Franklin b. 8/15/1868, d. 10/18/1876.
   e) John Coleman Franklin b. 5/18/1870, d. 10/9/1872.
   f) Nannie Jane Franklin b. 8/10/1872, d. 5/4/1939, md. Joseph
      Augustus Brown b. 1/15/1869, d. 10/4/1958.
   g) Josephine Franklin b. 8/26/1875, d. 11/21/1939, md. Benjamin Frank-
      lin Koonce b. 7/24/1860, d. 11/6/1924.
   h) J. Warren Franklin b. 1/12/1877, d. 7/3/1897.
   i) Mary Elnora Franklin b. 11/12/1879, d. 9/2/1884.
   j) Edgar Franklin b. 3/14/1881, d. 12/28/1881.
   k) Lillie Virginia Franklin b. 11/28/1883, d. 6/11/1965, md. 4/12/1904
      to Dempsey Finley Turner b. 12/6/1880, d. 6/19/1938.
6) Cullen Fleming Conerly (CSA) b. 12/29/1842 in Marion Co., Miss., d.
   11/13/1887 (was sheriff of Vernon Parish when he died); md. 3/3/1870
   to Mary Jane Koonce b. 8/17/1846 in Bienville Parish, d. 1/20/1904 in
   Vernon. Issue:
   a) Harriett E. Conerly b. 12/20/1870, d. 4/27/1884.
   b) Phillip Owen Conerly b. 4/1/1872, d. 2/7/1872.
   c) John Marvin Conerly b. 3/5/1874, d. 3/19/1939, md. 3/11/1896 to
      Lillie May Kay b. 12/27/1872, d. 11/1/1948.
   d) William Wilkerson Conerly b. 3/4/1877, d. 7/11/1944 in Shreveport

(buried at Holly Grove), md. 9/10/1902 to Geneva Angeline Bivens b. 9/11/1880 in Newton Co., Tex., d. 5/16/1967 at Port Arthur, Tex. (buried at Holly Grove Cemetery). [This is the parents of the husband of the compiler.]
- e) Dr. Cullen Clarence Conerly b. 6/9/1879, d. 12/1/1935, md. 1) Bell Franklin b. 9/4/1882, d. 9/21/1916; md. 2) 3/21/1917 to Josephine Cora Bivens b. 10/9/1878, d. 5/22/1959.
- f) Lenora Theodocia Conerly b. 2/9/1882, md. 7/29/1902 to William David Dixon b. 6/15/1875, d. 12/25/1966.
- g) Grover Cleveland Conerly b. 12/14/1884, d. 11/20/1956, md. 2/17/1910 to Malissia Dixon b. 3/7/1890, d. 1/9/1972.
- h) Laura Fleming Conerly b. 6/21/1888, d. 2/11/1906, md. Edward Ellzey.

7) James Wilkerson Conerly b. 11/23/1847, in Marion Co., Miss., d. 11/18/1925; md. 1) 1/5/1871 in Sabine Parish to Laura Virginia Conerly b. 11/15/1851 in Simpson Co., Miss., d. 6/5/1881. Issue:
- a) Thomas Warren Conerly b. 10/14/1871, d. 9/9/1946 (Prospect Cem.), md. 8/22/1894 to Cora Elizabeth Lee b. 9/15/1877, d. 8/2/1844.
- b) Mary E. Conerly b. 8/2/1873, d. 2/1/1887 (Prospect Cemetery).
- c) John Wright Conerly b. 7/4/1877, d. 5/29/1943 in Nacogdoches, Tex. (Prospect Cemetery); md. 2/2/1898 to Jane Lee b. 10/3/1881, d. 12/20/1940 in Flora, La. (Prospect Cemetery).
- d) Sarah Jane Conerly b. 10/25/1878, d. 3/1881.

James Wilkerson Conerly md. 2) 3/23/1882 to Mary Eliza Bush b. 10/12/1861, d. 3/7/1926 and had issue:
- e) William Cullen Conerly b. 1/1/1884, d. 5/26/1969, md. 1) Mattie Talbert; 2) Emma Self Rayburn on 2/27/1944. She d. 5/5/1973 (buried at Self Cemetery near Hornbeck, La.).
- f) Luther Wilkerson Conerly b. 8/6/1887, d. 11/2/1938, md. 2/21/1917 to Maggie C. Self b. 8/17/1895.
- g) Owen Dudley Conerly b. 1/22/1889, d. 1/7/1956, md. 12/9/1911 to Maggie Elizabeth Graham Killet b. 1/14/1881, d. 12/9/1973 in Beaumont, Tex. (Prospect Cemetery).
- h) Richie Lee Conerly b. 2/7/1892, d. 8/22/1922 in Newton Co., Tex., md. 9/4/1919 to Charles Franklin Cummings b. 6/22/1875 in Ga., d. 9/14/1949.
- i) Robert J. Conerly b. 7/7/1894, d. 8/6/1894.
- j) Ruth Genella Conerly b. 8/5/1899, d. 3/12/1915.

8) Murphey Conerly b. ca. 1846, d. before 1860.
9) Martha Elizabeth Conerly b. 12/10/1848 in Marion Co., Miss., d. 7/1/1936 (Prospect Cemetery); md. ca. 1862 to Lorenzo Dow Williams b. 4/5/1839 in Lauderdale Co., Miss., d. 1899.
10) Owen Conerly b. ca. 1849, died before 1860.
11) Jesse Warren Conerly b. 10/4/1851 in Sabine Parish, La., d. 7/7/1870. Elizabeth Tynes, widow of John R. Conerly, md. 2) Absalom Wright on 9/20/1855.

d) Eliza Conerly, dau. of Owen and Mary Conerly, b. 8/5/1814 in Duplin Co., N.C., d. 5/17/1838, md. 10/14/1830 to Jesse Ball and had issue:
1) William Ball md. Nancy Fortenberry and had issue:
- a) James Ball md. Mary Jane Rankin and had 4 children.
- b) Arthur Ball md. Irma Garrett and had 2 children.
- c) Jesse Ball died as a young man.

2) Rebecca Ball md. Jesse Warren and had issue:
- a) Mary Warren md. Thomas Johnson
- b) Emily Warren md. John Black
- c) Effie Warren died young
- d) James Warren died young

3) Needham Ball md. Cynthia Bracy and had issue:
- a) Eliza Ball md. Rayford Turnage
- b) Emily Ball md. Thomas Pittman
- c) Kitura Ball md. William Forbes
- d) Blant Ball md. Birdie Poole
- e) Walter Ball md. Roxie Mullins
- f) William Ball md. Laura Mullins
- g) Mary Ball md. Walter Whittum (?)
- h) Carrie Ball md. Charlie Corley
- i) Myra Ball md. Albert Cooper
- j) Iddo Ball md. Nettie ___
- k) Wilmuth Ball md. Harrison Fletcher Ford

4) Newton Ball md. Lizzie Tyler and had issue:
   a) James Ball md. Amelia Paul
   b) Jeffie Ball died young
   c) Jesse Ball md. Lovie Brumfield and had 6 children
   d) Needham Ball md. ___ McDonald
   e) Sophia Ball md. Willie Stephens
   f) Effie Ball
   g) Robert Ball md. Hattie Walker
   h) Minnie Ball
   i) Alma Ball md. S. D. Green
   j) Fannie Ball md. Leslie Alford
   k) Thaddaeus Ball
   l) Walter Ball
   m) Emma Ball
   n) Bennie Ball
e) Owen Conerly, Jr., b. 9/30/1817, d. 6/9/1860 and was buried at Holmesville, Miss., md. in 1838 to Ann Louise Stephens b. 1822 (buried in Summit, Miss.) and had issue:
1) Chauncey Conerly b. 1839
2) Luke Ward Conerly b. 2/3/1841, d. 1922 (buried in the old Soldiers Cemetery, Beauvoir, Miss.), md. 11/12/1867 to Emma Eoline Quin b. 2/17/1852 and had 14 children:
   a) Courtney Lula Conerly b. 7/29/1868, d. 1901, md. Campbell Jones and had 2 children: Campbell, Jr., and Welda.
   b) Robert Luckett Conerly b. 11/8/1869, died young.
   c) Murray Quin Conerly b. 12/5/1871, md. Pauline Crone and had 3 children: Amelia Emma, Luke William and Philomina Ernesin.
   d) Minneola Conerly b. 1/14/1873, died young
   e) Luke M. Conerly b. 8/14/1874, d. 10/14/1903, md. 8/10/1901 to Jennie Melicon.
   f) Emma Louise Conerly b. 1/22/1876, died young.
   g) Sargent Prentiss Conerly b. 6/17/1878, md. Allie Alexander and had 2 daus.: Hazel and Elouise.
   h) Mollie Conerly b. 10/21/1880, died young.
   i) Preston Johnson Conerly b. 2/5/1882, md. Mamie Jackson (E. Baton Rouge Parish), no issue; md. 2) Ethel Bush of Harrison Co., Miss., in 1911 and had 10 children:
   Emma Louise Conerly md. Edward Roebuck
   Mamie Lee Conerly md. Chesley Hulon
   Preston J. Conerly md. Shirley Jennings
   Willie Herman Conerly md. Mildred Davis
   Lonnie (Lannie) Samuel Conerly b. and d. 1922, twin to Walter
   Walter Daniel Conerly md. Magaline Summer
   Marjorie Hansel Conerly b. and d. 1926
   Joanne Conerly md. James Eugene Westbrook
   James Howard Conerly md. Joyce Neel Dings
   Ruby Eoline Conerly md. Edward S. Ballard
   j) Ada Lee Conerly b. 7/24/1884, d. 1964, md. James W. Hamilton (Cove, Ark.) and had issue: Robert, May, Waldo, Essmal, and Albert who died young.
   k) Ida May Conerly, twin to Ada Lee) md. George W. Campbell of New York and had: Edith Rosalie, George Edwin, Bobby, Gene, and Paul.
   l) Clara Eola Conerly b. 7/15/1886, md. Alfred Saucier of Harrison Co., Miss., and had: Alfred Jr., Ruby May md. William S. Thompson, Jr., Ellis, Emma, Percy, Clarence b. 1919, and Hazel (a twin born dead).
   m) Elma Eoline Conerly b. 9/21/1888, md. Irvin Hill of Okolona, Miss., and had issue: Marguerite, Eola, Eric Irvin, Thelma Gladys, Earl Donaldson (killed in WWII, 1/31/1943).
   n) Son, unnamed, b. and d. 10/20/1890.
3) Mary Ann Conerly b. 1843
4) Robert J. Conerly b. 1845, died young
5) Buston R. Conerly b. 1847
6) Owen Conerly b. 1849
7) Thomas Conerly
8) Samuel L. Conerly
9) Edward S. Conerly
[Two daughters given on some lists of children are Lula and Cecelia. This may be in error.]

f) Emily Conerly b. 6/7/1819 in Duplin Co., N.C., d. 3/30/1878, md. Daniel Ball and had issue:
   1) Edward Ball md. Maggie Powell and had 6 children.
   2) James Ball md. 1) Kate Reagan, and 2) Mollie ___. He had 4 children by his first wife and 2 by the second.
   3) Monroe Ball md. Ella Duncan.
   4) Samuel Ball md. Nancy Pittman and had 12 children.
   5) Catherine Ball md. Morgan Wood.
   6) Philonia Rebecca Ball md. Nelson Monroe Fortenberry and had 13 children.
   7) Lizzie Ball md. 1) Joe Pittman; 2) Nathan Lott. She had 2 children by the first husband and 6 by the second.
   8) Jeanette Ball md. Henry Pittman and had 4 children.
   9) Frances Ball md. Joab Foxworth and had 12 children.
   10) Daniel Warren Ball md. Ava J. Floyd and had children.
   11) Robert Ball died young. (I have no record of these.)
   12) Iddo Ball died young. (No record of these.)
g) Luke Conerly, son of Owen and Mary, b. 2/18/1821, d. 11/4/1833.
h) Rebecca Ann Conerly b. 9/16/1823, d. 1/2/1827.
i) Catherine Conerly b. 3/13/1826, d. 8/15/1832.
j) Mary Jane Conerly b. 10/13/1828, d. 4/10/1879 (buried at China Grove), md. 1) Jabez Lewis; 2) 9/28/1848 to Benjamin Lampton b. 2/18/1825, d. 7/9/1885. Issue:
   1) Walter Monroe Lampton b. 1850, d. 1930, md. 1) Lucy Barton; 2) Lucy Brumfield.
   2) Lucius Lafayette Lampton b. 1852, d. 1924, md. Mary Babington.
   3) Iddo Wilkinson Lampton b. 1856 d. 1913, md. Victoria Babington.
   4) Mollie Lampton b. 1858, d. 1887, md. J. Wes Sandifer.
   5) William Edward Lampton b. 1861, d. 1950, md. Lou Baylis.
   6) Cora Lampton b. 1865, d. 1912, not married.
   7) Thad B. Lampton b. 1867, d. 1938, md. Mamie Terrell.
   8) Lelia Lampton b. 1868, d. 1898, not married.
k) James Conerly b. 2/7/1831, d. 12/25/1887 (Founder's Cemetery), md. on 10/20/1852 to May Lampkin and had 6 children, one of whom was:
   1) Mary Narcissa Conerly b. 5/1859, d. 10/19/1860.
l) Melissa Conerly b. 2/27/1834, d. 10/19/1837.
m) Susan Conerly b. 5/30/1826, d. 10/17/1837.

3) William Conerly d. prior to 1848 in Marion Co., Miss.; md. 1) in 1814 in Duplin Co., N.C., to Sarah Brown b. 1799, living in Washington Parish, La., in 1860. They had issue:
   a) Amanda Conerly b. 1816, md. John Pigott Stogner b. 1817, a noted chairmaker.
   b) Stephen Conerly b. 1826, md. Ascenith ___ and lived in Washington Parish, La., in 1860.
   c) Sarah T. Conerly b. 1828, md. in 1847 in Marion Co., Miss., to James McNabb.
   d) Elizabeth (Betsey) Jane Conerly b. 1833, d. 3/12/1910 in Washington Parish, md. ___ Hodge (possibly George W.).
   e) Mary Ann Conerly b. ca. 1836, md. ___ Breland and had a son George. She is possibly the Mary Breland who was a deaconess in the Crain's Cr. Baptist Church and who died 2/15/1907.
William Conerly apparently divorced Sarah ca. 1835/6 and md. 2) in 1835 in Marion Co., Miss., Eliza Cameron b. ca. 1819/20. She was living next to Sarah Conerly in Washington Parish in 1860. Issue:
   f) Melissa Conerly b. 1839.
   g) William James Conerly b. 1842.
   h) Caroline Conerly b. 1837.
   i) John (called Jacky in 1850 and Jackson in 1860) Conerly b. 1843.
   j) Winny (called Sarah in 1860) Conerly b. 1845.

5) Mary (Polly) Conerly, dau. of Cullen Conerly and Lettetia Ward, b. ca. 1779, md. 1) William Bennett by whom she had issue:
   a) Litha Bennett
   b) John Bennett.
Mary (Polly) Conerly Bennett md. 2) Jesse Guy, who d. in Marion Co., Miss., before 1850 leaving issue:
   c) William Guy b. 4/7/1813, d. 4/16/1885, md. Sallie Magee b. 8/3/1812, d. 4/1/1885 and had issue:

1) Alex Guy b. ca. 1838
2) M. A. R. Guy b. 1839 (dau.)
3) J. W. Guy b. 1841 (son)
4) William J. Guy b. 1842
5) S. A. E. Guy b. 1843 (dau.)
6) M. E. Guy b. 1844 (dau.)
7) C. L. Guy b. 1847 (son)
8) M. E. Guy b. 1848 (dau.)
9) George W. Guy b. 3/26/1852, d. 8/7/1922, md. 1/8/1874 to Victoria Greer b. 10/22/1857, d. 9/11/1920. They had issue:
   a) William Lewis Guy b. 10/22/1874, d. 6/3/1931, md. in 1892 to Emma Brister.
   b) George Monroe Guy b. 2/8/1876, d. 7/5/1951, md. 11/8/1894 to Annie Armstrong.
   c) Rosa Guy b. 7/15/1878, d. 6/22/1948, md. 11/25/1896 to Willie Andrews.
   d) DeWitt Guy b. 2/15/1880, d. 11/5/1930, md. Ethel Smith.
   e) John Wesley Guy b. 11/26/1882, d. 4/27/1952, md. 2/14/1901, to Della Dunaway.
   f) Griffin Guy b. 3/8/1884, md. 2/24/1909 to Mamie McEwen.
   g) Percy R. Guy b. 11/28/1886, d. 9/21/1949, md. 1914 to Christine Boyd.
   h) Chancey Wade Guy b. 11/22/1888, d. 7/2/1935, md. 1/10/1913 to Lelia Adams.
   i) Betty Lura Guy b. 11/22/1888 (twin to Chancey), d. 6/11/1968, md. Sim Cothern.
   j) Lela Mae Guy b. 8/8/1890, d. 2/1/1932, md. Hughey Greer.
   k) Beler Guy b. 11/16/1892, d. 10/30/1923, md. in 1913 to Temie Moore.
   l) Leslie Guy b. 9/19/1897, d. 10/4/1949, md. in 1917 to Florence Bushings.
   m) Edwene Guy b. 10/21/1899, d. 2/11/1955, md. in 1913 to Dock Ham.
10) James Monroe Guy md. Julia, dau. of Ansel Prewett, and had:
    a) William Guy, died young.
    b) Vince Wroten Guy md. Katherine Wright.
    c) Nellie Guy md. Robert S. Brent.
    d) Emile Guy, died young.
    e) Ruth Guy md. Charlie Hennington of Crystal Springs, Miss.
    f) Boyd Felder Guy md. Maude (Mande?) Hughes.
    g) Cecil Lamar Guy md. Hazel Ware.
11) Louis Guy md. Sally Martin and had a dau.:
    a) Mary Eleanor Guy md. Lee Quin.
12) Jeff Guy.

In September, 1851, Iven M. (Ivenell?) Fortenberry and William Guy ordered Henry Cook, guardian to Lewis Guy; Susan Hines, wife of Enock Hines; Mary Thomas, wife of Matthew Thomas of Washington Parish, La.; and Rebecca Morris, wife of William Morris of Holmes Co., Miss., into the Marion County Court to answer why the accounts for the Jesse Guy Estate cannot be accepted. This gives other heirs of Jesse Guy, and possibly children of Mary Conerly Guy.

   d) Susan (Susannah) Guy md. 1/28/1824 Enoch Hines and lived in Washington Parish. Issue:
      1) Henry Hines b. 1837 md. Susan ___.
      2) Felix Hines b. 1840.
      3) Frances Hines b. 1846.
   e) Rebecca Guy md. 2/8/1825 to William Morris.
   f) Mary Guy b. ca. 1817, md. Matthew Thomas b. ca. 1817 and had issue:
      1) Jesse Thomas b. 1842
      2) Oliver P. Thomas b. 1844
      3) Elizabeth Thomas b. 1846
      4) Mary Thomas b. 1851
      5) Henry Thomas b. 1856
   g) Lewis Guy b. 5/9/1839, d. 11/6/1915, buried in Crystal Springs, Miss., Cemetery.

7) Frances (Fanny) Conerly b. ca. 1783, dau. of Cullen and Lettitia, md. 1) Cullen Duncan who d. in Duplin Co., N.C.; md. 2) Elijah Turnage. She had three children by Cullen named James, Cullen, and Jane [This may be wrong. In the Court Minutes for Duplin Co., the third Monday in January 1815, John

Conerly received the appointment as guardian (by posting a $1000 bond) to the orphan minors of Jacob Duncan decd, to wit: James, Cullen, Susan, and Luke. Since the names James and Cullen are the same as the list found in Mississippi, it may be the same family.]
   a) James P. Duncan b. 10/6/1805, d. 3/29/1885, md. 3/30/1831, in Marion Co., Miss., to Winney Carmen and had issue: (James is buried in the Isaac Duncan Cemetery near Salem in Walthall Co., Miss.)
      1) Eliza Ann Duncan b. 1832
      2) Frances Duncan b. 1833
      3) Isaac Duncan b. 12/14/1834, d. 5/8/1880 CSA
      4) Talitha H. Duncan b. 1836, md. Thomas H. Holmes
      5) Emily Duncan b. 1838
      6) Chelly Duncan b. 1839
      7) Susan Duncan b. 1841
      8) Melissa Duncan b. 1842
      9) Rebecca Duncan b. 1843
      10) John W. Duncan b. 1845
      11) Needham L. Duncan b. 1846
      12) Hugh J. Duncan b. 1849
      13) Charlotte Duncan b. ca. 1850
   b) Cullen Duncan b. 1808, lived in Washington Parish, La., md. Mary ___ b. 1810 and had issue:
      1) Benjamin J. Duncan b. 1835, md. in 1870 to Nancy, dau. of Nathan and Mary Blackwell b. 1828, d. 3/14/1896.
      2) Robert Duncan b. 1841, md. Susan Knight
      3) William Duncan b. 1843
      4) Walton Duncan b. 1846
      5) Martin Duncan b. 1848
      6) Frances Duncan b. 1850
   c) Jane Duncan (?) md. William Walker.

8) Susan Conerly md. in 1808 in Duplin Co., N.C., to Joseph Page.

CONEY

The Coney family of Pike Co., Miss., possibly had its origins in a Jeremiah Cony (Coney) and his wife Mary who were dealing in real estate in Edgecomb Co., N.C., in the 1770's. This Jeremiah possibly died ca. 1782, as Mary soon after obtained a land grant in her name. Children for this couple, if any, are not known by this compiler.

The name Jeremiah is very common in the Coney family in Georgia and Mississippi, thus the line possibly descends from the above-mentioned man in N.C. The 1805 Tax List for Montgomery Co., Ga., shows an Aquila Coney (with 2 slaves) and a Jeremiah. This Aquila had two draws in the 1805 Lottery in Washington Co., Ga., but did not get land. This is probably the same Aquila Coney who had a daughter Elizabeth who married John Ellzey in St. Tammany Parish, La., in 1823.

Prior to removal to the west, Aquila Coney had gotten land in Laurens Co., Ga., which he sold on 4/11/1818 to William Coney (Laurens Deed Bk. F, p. 82). William sold this same piece of land on 10/8/1818 to William Albritton (Deed Bk. F, p. 249). Aquila and William were probably brothers.

Since there was a Jeremiah (b. 1772, d. 1845/46 in Pulaski Co., Ga.) and Joel (b. 1786, d. 2/1853 in Laurens Co., Ga.) in Laurens Co. at the same that Aquila and William were there, it is possible that all were brothers.

William Coney d. 1848 with a wife Rachel arrived in the area of Pike County, Miss., prior to 1820 with at least four sons, namely: Jeremiah, Joel Jackson, William and Lewis. Almost all of these Coney men died before 1850. Coney descendants:

1) Jeremiah Coney b. 1806, d. 1868, md. Emily Quin and had issue:
   a) Franklin Coney
   b) William Coney
   c) Van Crawford Coney d. 6/26/1901, aged 60 years, 7 mos., 16 days; md.

    P___ A___ Dickey on 3/21/1867.
- d) Luke J. Coney
- e) Joel R. Coney
- f) Mary E. Coney
- g) Sarah K. Coney
- h) Caroline A. Coney
- i) Jane Coney
- j) Jerzine Coney

2) Joel Jackson Coney b. 9/22/1813, d. 10/27/1859, md. 9/20/1838 to Emmaline Morgan b. 10/21/1820, d. 5/17/1884 and had:
- a) Jasper Coney
- b) Lorraine Coney
- c) Charles Coney
- d) Rachel Coney
- e) Nancy Josephine (called Jodie) Coney b. 3/1/1847, d. 5/7/1925, md. 7/10/1865 to Major Alexis Pierre LeBlanc (12th Miss., CSA), b. 4/29/1841, d. 3/9/1899, who had at least 1 dau., Estelle Carrie LeBlanc.
- f) William L. Coney d. ca. 1909

3) William Coney II b. 1804, d. 1842, md. Eliza Morgan and had issue:
- a) Morgan Coney
- b) Green Coney
- c) Daniel Coney
- d) Ann Coney
- e) Eva Coney
- f) Rosaline Coney b. 1/10/1839, d. 2/28/1889, md. 12/26/1855 to Clinton Martin.

4) Lewis Coney b. 7/31/1813, d. 3/4/1841, md. 4/2/1834 (or 35) to Isabel (Isabella) N. Kaigler b. 2/18/1817 and had issue:
- a) David Aquila Coney b. Friday 12/18/1835, d. 11/24/1924 (buried at Johnston's Station, Miss.), md. Mary Jane Walker b. 3/18/1835, d. 2/2/1923 and had:
  1) Lucy Coney b. 1/13/1859, d. 3/11/1921 in McComb, Miss.; md. ___ Ellzey.
  2) Louis Coney b. 10/1/1861.
  3) John Thomas Coney b. 7/22/1864, d. 12/30/1937 (buried Amite, La.).
  4) David Cicero Coney b. 4/13/1867, d. 4/15/1947 (buried Jackson, Miss.).
  5) Leon Josephus Coney b. 9/5/1869, d. 10/2/1966.
  6) Henry Eugene Coney b. 7/21/1875, d. 7/24/1952 (buried Johnston's Station), md. Essie Mae Akers.
  7) Lena Mae Coney b. 11/21/1877, d. 4/10/1868, md. ___ Dunn.
  8) Morgan Jefferson Coney killed when 19 yrs. old on ICRR.
  9) Jerry Coney.
- b) Lewis Newsom Coney b. 7/31/1837, d. 7/31/1861 at CSA camp, Corinth, Miss.
- c) John Hancock Coney b. 6/13/1839 (twin).
- d) William Jefferson Coney b. 6/13/1839, d. in Confederate hospital at Columbus, Miss., 7/10/1862; md. Selena Elizabeth Huffman.

Isabel Kaigler Coney md. 2) Hiram M. Norman and had issue:
- e) Josephus Norman b. 8/3/1843.
- f) Ann K. Norman b. 4/7/1845
- g) W. G. Norman b. 5/6/1847
- h) Thomas L. Norman b. 11/6/1849
- i) Barnes W. Norman b. 4/19/1853
- j) M. D. Norman b. 12/30/1856
- k) H. H. Norman b. 5/29/1858

Isabel died at the home of her son-in-law B. S. Alford 9/2/1895. She had lost four sons in the Confederate Army and two sons at home.

    Data on Lewis Coney was supplied from the family Bible of Lewis Coney owned by Mrs. Boyd Edwards, Jackson, Miss., and other material from Mrs. Gordon Willoughby (Norma Gene Coney) of Summit, Miss. Mrs. R. Chester Upton of Jackson, Miss., is preparing a detailed genealogy of the family.

CRAWFORD

The Crawford family of Pike/Walthall Counties, Miss., descend from a William Crawford who made a deed of gift to his wife Martha and her children Thomas, Nelly, Patience, Selete, and Jesse on 3/9/1796 in Effingham Co., Ga. (Effingham Co., Ga., Deed Bk. A-B, p. 274). This William was apparently dead prior to 7/3/1798 when a Mrs. Martha Crawford md. Richard Touchstone in Effingham.

In a Bible owned by Mrs. Bessie Waters of Sylvania, Ga., in 1953, the following list of children was found:
1) Sarah Crawford b. 11/14/1775
2) Thomas Crawford b. 2/18/1784
3) Elender Crawford b. 5/1/1786
4) Patience Crawford b. 9/6/1782
5) Selete Crawford b. 10/19/1781
6) Jesse Crawford b. 2/4/1795

Of these children, Patience possibly married Luke Wilson of Effingham on 3/8/1806, and Eleanor married Benjamin Alexander in Effingham on 2/11/1808. Jesse Crawford migrated on to Marion Co., Miss., ca. 1820 where he later married.

William Crawford, who d. ca. 1796/7, was a resident of Effingham as early as 1787 when he obtained a land grant. It is believed that he was the son of an older Thomas Crawford--possibly the Thomas Crawford who obtained a 100-acre land grant in St. Matthews Parish, Ga. (later called Effingham). This Thomas petitioned for and obtained his grant ca. 1770/1771. About the same time a Carter Crawford obtained a grant in the same general area and claimed to be formerly of South Carolina. If there was a kinship between these Crawfords, both possibly came into Georgia via South Carolina, although it is claimed that Thomas Crawford hailed from Virginia.

Jesse Crawford b. 2/4/1795, son of William and Martha, appeared in Marion Co. ca. 1820 (as stated) where he married 1) Flora Graham, dau. of Dougal or Dougald Graham and Flora Scruggs. Flora died ca. 1836/8 leaving Jesse his first eight children. During his married life with Flora, Jesse joined the Antioch Baptist Church near Cheraw, Miss., in Marion Co. in November, 1824. On 7/16/1826 he became a deacon in the church, and on 3/28/1828 he was licensed to preach by the congregation. He was recognized as an ordained minister of the gospel on 10/17/1828.

From 1831-1835 he represented the Antioch Church at the annual meetings of the Pearl River Baptist Association. Thereafter, he became the pastor of the Silver Creek Baptist Church in Pike County. He was a noted orator and sought as a preacher for the remainder of his life. He died 3/11/1869 in Pike County.

Jesse married 2) on 6/3/1839 to Hettie H. Clark Lee by whom he had at least three more children. After Hettie's death in 11/1848, Jesse md. 3) 6/2/1851 to Terry Ginn Magee, widow of Benjamin Magee. No issue. It is said that Jesse md. 4) Caroline Rials in 1859.

The Rev. Jesse Crawford's children:
1) Josiah A. Crawford b. 1841, d. 10/24/1895 (buried in Hollywood Cemetery, McComb), md. 1) Tabitha Hogan; 2) Sallie Breeland b. 1827, d. 7/16/1893.

2) William H. Crawford b. 1816, md. Sarah Ann ___ b. 1822, migrated to Rusk Co., Texas.

3) Thomas Bailey Crawford b. 10/17/1819, d. 5/10/1900, CSA (buried in Crawford Cemetery), md. Mary Lewis.

4) Benjamin Alexander Crawford b. 1825, d. 5/3/1890, a Baptist Minister (buried in Carter's Creek Baptist Church Cemetery), md. Nancy Cook.

5) Albert L. Crawford b. 1827.

6) Charles Felder Crawford b. 9/20/1831, d. 9/25/1886, a noted Baptist preacher in his own right--served as pastor of Beulah Church in Louisiana for a number of years; md. Frances L. Douglas.

7) Hasseltine Crawford b. 1834, d. 9/20/1858, md. 1/20/1853 to John H. Simmons.

8) Andrew Crawford

On 2/2/1829 Jesse Crawford officiated at the marriage of Henry Monroe Lee and Hettie, dau. of James Clark. Ten years later he married Hettie, then a widow, by whom he had issue:

9) Sophronia (Fronie) E. Crawford b. 10/27/1840, d. 9/22/1915, md. Calvin E. Simmons b. 1/23/1833, d. 10/5/19__.

10) Jesse D. Crawford

11) James Howell Crawford b. 11/16/1845, d. 5/5/1929, md. Elizabeth Minerva Sandifer b. 3/1/1845, d. 9/13/1906. He was the father of Dr. B. L. Crawford who in turn fathered Drs. Everette, Walter, and Ben Crawford of Tylertown, Miss.

12) Martha A. Crawford b. 1842, d. 3/14/1930, md. Benjamin Franklin Branch.

DILLON

Richard Dillon, according to his Revolutionary War Pension file, was born on October 7, 1745, in Norfolk, Virginia. Family tradition claims that he was a native of Ireland. However, since Norfolk was a well established port town in the colonial era, it is possible that his family had just migrated there from the old country (Ireland).

As a young child, Richard was taken by his parents James Theopilious and Mary Dillon to Bertie County, N.C. James Theopilious must have died prior to 1759 as on January 23 of that year Richard Dillon was ordered "bound as an apprentice to Christopher Harrison until about the age of twenty-one years . . . to be taught the business of a Cooper . . . ." (Bertie Co. Court Minutes, Vol. 1761-1769--earlier dates recorded in volume also.) He must have been free from his indenture or apprenticeship by 1768.

By 1776 Richard Dillon married Ann or Annys Morris of an old Bertie County family and immediately thereafter bought land from Jeremiah Lester and William Meredith. These land transfers came at the time the country was thrown into the revolution.

With the starting of the war, Richard Dillon enlisted in the patriot militia near Edenton, N.C., under Captain John Faulk. He saw service at the "Northwest River Bridge" under the command of Colonel Bluntin Maginnis and General Gregory Cloissant. After a three-month tour of duty, he returned to his family.

In 1781 he again saw service as an enlistee on the vessel "Greyhound," a privateersman commanded by Samuel Butler. With the capture of that vessel, he was made a prisoner on the English frigate "Baloosa" which carried 36 guns and was commanded by a Captain Kennedy, a Scotsman. After a nine-month imprisonment, he again returned to Bertie County.

Shortly before the taking of the 1790 Census for North Carolina, Dillon and his family migrated southward to Barnwell County (District), S.C., where he lived until 3/20/1897. Upon his departure for the west, or Amite Co., Miss., he left two of his older sons in South Carolina--sons who probably joined him in Mississippi at a later date.

By 1810 Dillon was a resident of Amite County (listed in the 1810 Census for that year). In that same year he obtained a land grant in Marion County in a portion of the county that later became Pike County. This was probably the land that became known as "Dillon's Bridge."

Richard Dillon lived in Pike County until his death which supposedly occurred on his 89th birthdate in 1833. The Jackson (Mississippi) newspaper, the **Mississippian**, carried a notice of his estate in the 1/24/1834 issue. Willis Dillon and Laurence

Dillon were named as the executors of the estate.

The known children of Richard and Annys Morris Dillon:
1) Lawrence Dillon   5) Willis Dillon
2) JoAnna Dillon   6) Mary Dillon
3) Nancy Ann Dillon   7) Theophilius Dillon
4) Clarkson Dillon   8) Clara Dillon

1) Lawrence Dillon was a resident of the Mississippi Territory prior to 1816 and on the 1820 Census for Pike Co., Miss., with a family. Issue not known.

2) JoAnna Dillon b. 8/22/1778, md. 12/16/1798 to Jeremiah Smith b. 12/23/1773, son, supposedly, of an older Jeremiah Smith, and settled near Dillontown, Pike Co., Miss. Issue:
   a) Hollander Smith b. 7/8/1800.
   b) Martha Smith b. 3/25/1802, d. 8/8/1861, md. in 1818 to Edwin Alford b. 1792. See family under Alford.
   c) Eli Smith b. 1/21/1804, d. 8/2/1838, md. 1) Orpha Roberts; 2) Ann Crews.
   d) Jane Smith b. 10/9/1805, d. 1846, md. 12/25/1825 to Thomas Coulter Warner.
   e) Edwin Smith b. 6/3/1807
   f) Wyatt Smith b. 8/31/1809, md. 1) Libbey ___ ; 2) Eusaba Fortinberry.
   g) Calvin Smith b. 9/22/1812, md. 1) Sarah Brumfield, 2) Ann Crews, widow of Eli Smith.
   h) Eliza Smith b. 2/14/1811, d. 4/6/1837.
   i) Lidda (or Lidya or Liddy) Smith b. 4/6/1810, md. Harris Harvey.
   j) Mehala Smith b. 7/15/1816.
   k) Jeremiah Smith b. 1821, d. 5/13/1894, md. 7/15/1841, to Pernecia (Pernesa) Smith b. 9/26/1820, d. 4/4/1887.
   l) Milevey Smith b. 4/13/1818.
   m) Jo Anna Smith b. 10/5/1819.

3) Nancy Ann Dillon b. 10/26/1779, d. 5/28/1869, md. John Stallings who d. 9/23/1851. Stallings was reputedly of Indian descent. Issue:
   a) James Stallings b. 5/21/1814, d. 6/23/1896, md. 9/6/1832 to Sarah Pearson b. 7/21/1813, d. 11/5/1878 and had issue:
      1) Winney Stallings b. 7/5/1833, md. 11/20/1850 to Eli Brock.
      2) Mary Jane Stallings b. 10/24/1835, d. 2/15/1859.
      3) Eliza Jane Stallings b. 2/18/1838, d. 2/1/1871.
      4) John Everett Stallings b. 6/15/1840, d. ___ ; md. 12/22/1859 to Frances A. Ginn.
      5) Margaret Stallings b. 11/7/1848, d. 7/21/1868, md. 12/19/1865 to W. C. Holmes.
      6) Ann Stallings b. 2/26/1845, d. 5/27/1869.
      7) James Harvey Stallings b. 3/18/1847, d. 10/25/1854.
      8) Jessey Stallings b. 2/5/1849, md. 12/3/1868 to Harriet C. Graves.
      9) Joseph Stallings b. 6/27/1851.
      10) Richard Willis Stallings b. 11/12/1854, d. 5/14/1927, md. 11/19/1874 to Zonetta Smith.
   b) Winney Stallings b. 2/21/1817, md. John Williams and had issue:
      1) Nancy Williams b. 10/18/1835, d. 5/28/1882, md. W. J. Holmes.
      2) Samuel L. Williams b. 5/4/1837.
      3) Sarah E. Williams b. 9/30/1839.
      4) Lucinda L. Williams b. 12/24/1841.
      5) John H. Williams b. 3/24/1844.
      6) Ansaleme (?) D. Williams b. 1/14/1847.
      7) Mary J. Williams b. 12/16/1850.
4) Clarkson Dillon b. ca. 1785, md. Sarah ___ of S.C. Clarkston served in the famed Battle of New Orleans in the War of 1812 as a member of the 13th Miss. Inf. Known issue:
   a) Thomas Everett Dillon b. ca. 1806. This man has always been listed as a son of Richard Dillon Sr. However, it is most probable that he was a son of Clarkston as listed, a fact based on the point that he named one of his older sons Clarkson or Clarkston. Thomas Everett md. Elizabeth ___ b. 1806 in S.C. and had issue:
      1) Ancel Green Dillon b. 1834 md. Sophronia A. Morgan.
      2) Clarkson Dillon b. 1835 md. Elvira or Elvina Magee b. 1839.
      3) Martha Dillon md. (probably) 1) Blount; 2) Smith
      4) Chauncey Dillon b. 1842, md. 1) ___ Parsons, 2) Ensie or Ampsey Elvira Johnson.

    5) Sally Dillon b. 1846, md. ___ O'Brien.
    6) Mary Dillon b. 1849.
  b) Richard Dillon b. 1813, md. Catherine, dau. of Ephraim Rushing, widow of
     Henry Magee.
  c) James Dillon b. 1823.
  d) Adaline Dillon b. 1829, md. in 1854 to John P. Jones b. 1829 in Franklin
     Co., Miss.
  e) Mary Dillon b. 1831.
  [The census figures for 1820 and others indicate that there were at least
  five other children.]

5) Willis D. Dillon b. 12/31/1787, md. Mary ___ b. 1783 in S.C. Willis was a
   trumpeteer in the 13th Miss. Regt., War of 1812. Possible issue:
   a) Magdaline Dillon b. 1828
   b) John Irvin Dillon b. 1830
   c) James T. Dillon md. Elizabeth Brock and had issue: Rempsi, Uriah, Laborn,
      Richard, Mary, and Hester.

6) Mary Dillon b. 1793, d. 7/4/1876, md. 1) Salathial Morris and had issue:
   a) Clara Morris md. ___ Hollingsworth.
   Mary Dillon md. 2) Moses Miller who d. 8/7/1836 and had a son and two
   daus. by him.

7) Theophilous Dillon b. 5/26/1796, d. in Washington Parish, La., a veteran of
   the War of 1812, md. 1) in St. Tammany Parish, La., in 1817 to Peggy Pearson,
   probable dau. of Joel Pearson. She was b. 1808, d. 9/5/1857. Issue:
   a) Joel Pearson Dillon b. 1/30/1825, d. 9/15/1866, md. 2/5/1846 to Hettie
      (Harriet) Lewis b. 1/18/1826 and lived to be 99 yrs. old.
   b) John P. Dillon b. 1824, md. 9/22/1858 in St. Helena Parish, La., to
      Margaret E. Knighton.
   c) Willis R. Dillon b. 1834, d. 10/10/1862 CSA, md. in Amite Co., Miss.,
      on 7/17/1854 to Angeline Gwin d. 8/24/1862.
   d) Leroy L. Dillon
   Theophilous Dillon moved to Washington Parish, La., (where he lived in 1874)
   and md. 2) 11/6/1866 to Lucy King. By her he possibly had:
   e) Consetta Dillon md. James Bolton Morris.

8) Clara Dillon b. 1799, md. George Smith who d. in 1833 but left issue:
   a) William Dorten Smith b. 1/1818, d. 10/1906, md. 11/14/1839 to Lucretia
      Dykes b. 1825 and had issue:
      1) George Smith b. 12/6/1840
      2) Clara Ann Smith b. 1/11/1843
      3) William L. Smith b. 4/6/1847
      4) Henry J. Smith b. 5/24/1847
      5) Jarott R. Smith b. 6/2/1849
      6) Newey Smith b. 1/21/1852, d. 8/9/1854
      7) Isaac Frank Smith b. 5/30/1854
      8) Cinderilla Smith b. 7/12/1856
      9) Jasper D. Smith b. 12/17/1858, d. 12/20/1928, md. 5/27/1896 to Minnie
         Lou Brumfield
      10) Nancy C. Smith b. 9/5/1860
      11) Lucretia Smith b. 2/18/1863
      12) Murrey Smith b. 5/3/1866, md. 7/23/1890 to Ada Simmons
      13) Wright Smith b. 11/1/1871, d. 3/18/1873
   b) Jared D. Smith b. 1821
   c) Dr. Newell C. Smith b. 1822, d. 1895, md. Melissa A. Smith b. 1835
   d) Seleta Smith b. 1825
   e) Jasper R. Smith b. 1828, md. Mary Holmes
   f) Pernissa Smith b. 9/26/1820, d. 4/4/1887, md. 7/15/1841 to Jeremiah Smith
   g) Nancy A. Smith b. 1830, md. Densmore W. Smith
   h) Eliza A. Smith b. 1833, md. Densmore Smith, son of Daniel and Kitty
      Magee Smith

ELLIS

The Ellis family of Pike County migrated into Pike County from Columbia County, Georgia. The progenitors were Stephen Ellis and Hannah Lowery. This union had at least seven children: Daniel, John, Owen, Lowery, George, Avis wife of 1st Jacob Curry and 2nd Even Whittington; and Elizabeth Ellis.

John Ellis d. prior to 1840, married 11/5/1793 to Sarah Johnson (b. 5/17/1776, d. 1847) in Columbia County, Georgia. This union lived in Pike County in 1816 and 1820. They moved into Washington Parish after the latter date. In 1832 John Ellis migrated to Texas and entered claim with Austin's Colony. He did not take his family. On 4/28/1833 he wrote a forlorn letter to his wife Sarah. He mentioned the "United States" and returning home. This letter is still in an excellent state of preservation.

This union had nine children: Stephen Ellis md. Mary Magee; Samuel Ellis, not married; Olivia Ellis md. ___ Graves and migrated to Texas; William Ellis lived near Utica, Miss.; Ellen Ellis md. 1) ___ Slocumb and 2) ___ Daniel; Margaret Ellis md. Jarage Slocumb; Sarah Ellis md. Garland Hart; Nancy Ellis md. Benjamin Bickham; and Ezekiel Parke Ellis md. Tabitha Warner, dau. of Col. Thomas C. Warner and Tabitha Cargill.

George Ellis married Elizabeth Warren. This union also lived in Pike County. They had 12 children: Lott Warren Ellis b. 9/11/1799, d. 7/30/1857; Reuben Ellis; Richmond Ellis; Solomon Ellis; Washington Ellis; George Ellis b. 10/7/1807, d. 11/9/1885; Willis Ellis b. 6/29/1820, d. 9/27/1858; Louisa Ellis; Mary Ellis; Susan Ellis; Lourancy Ellis; and John Ellis.

Lott Warren Ellis, son of George, married Anna Roberts b. 6/24/1801, d. 6/8/1863. This union had fifteen children: George Ellis b. 12/12/1821, d. 7/30/1857 (killed in the Battle of the Wilderness); Caroline Elizabeth Ellis b. 8/4/1828, d. 12/30/1858; Warren M. Ellis b. 1824; Susan Ellis b. 3/28/1828, d. 8/28/1845, md. W. B. Vaughan; Thomas B. Ellis b. 4/30/1830, d. 8/22/1840; Washington Ellis b. 4/11/1832, d. 5/16/1849; Nancy Holliday Ellis b. 1834; Rhoda Roberts Ellis b. 1838; John Ellis b. 1840; Mary Ellis; Anna Ellis; Lott Ellis; Benjamin Franklin Ellis b. 1846; Isaac Newton Ellis b. 1/1849, d. 11/30/1939, md. Georgia Stapleton. [Only 14 of these children are listed.]

Isaac Newton Ellis and wife Georgia Stapleton had 11 children: Kate, Anna, Frederick Warren, Mary, Caroline, Hal Roberts, Isaac Newton, Francis, Hilda, Nell, and William Carroll Ellis.

[The foregoing dates of the births and deaths of the George Ellis family were taken from the tombstones of the Ellis family buried in Pine Bluff Baptist Church Cemetery near Dentville, Copiah County, Mississippi. Isaac Newton Ellis is buried in Hazelhurst, Miss. This research was done by Miss Nell Ellis of Hazelhurst.]

McCARTY

Daniel McCarty appeared in Lincoln (now called Tyron) County, N.C., in the late 1750's. He dealt extensively in land until ca. 1780. He wrote his will in Lincoln Co. on 8/14/1782--an instrument which was probated in Richmond County, Ga., a few years later. His will named the following family:
- Wife: Agness
- Sons: John, Jacob, David and Cornelius
- Daus: Jemimah wife of Hugh Blair (who was to inherit the slave woman Sarah. Sarah was to descend to Jemimah's son Hugh upon her death. Ann Bennett (husband not named)
- Sons-in-law: David Tomlinson (who was to get 300 acres on Little River in Georgia; Samuel Johnston; John Kelly (land where McCarty then lived--with furniture

Grandson: David Kelly who was to inherit the slave named
Dublin
This will also denoted that John, Jacob, Ann Bennett, Samuel Johnston, David Tomlinson and John Kelly were to share equally in the estate of Cornelius McCarty, decd., who had lived on St. Helena Island (spelled Santilina in the will) of South Carolina. David and Cornelius had received their shares as they were awarded only 5 shillings each. William, Robert and Amelia (Emelia) Crawford witnessed the will.

A check of the Lincoln/Tyron County, N.C., deeds did not reveal anything about the ancestry of Daniel or Agness McCarty. One deed, however, related that the Cornelius McCarty, decd, of St. Helena in South Carolina, was a brother to Daniel in Lincoln County.

Prior to the McCarty family's residency in Lincoln County, they probably lived in Granville County, N.C. There are deeds in Daniel's name there. As early as 1757 Samuel Johnson sold land to Daniel McCarty in that county.

There is the possibility that the McCarty family originated in Stafford County, Virginia. Using the family name Cornelius as a clue, it can be suspected that they were kinsmen of a Cornelius McCarty who left a will in Stafford County, Virginia, in 1755.

JOHNSON--JOHNSTON

Samuel Johnston, named as a son-in-law of Daniel McCarty, married Olive or Ollie McCarty. Samuel, who had lived in Lincoln Co., N.C., before moving to Richmond County, Ga., left a will in the latter-named county on 10/12/1787. He died between that date and 7/16/1788 when the will was presented to the court for probate. Samuel named in his will the following heirs:
Daus: Olley, Nelly, Sarah, and Maggy
Sons: Alexander, Cornelius, Daniel, Jacob and John
He devised to each of his children an equal share in the estate due him from Cornelius McCarty, decd. Wife: Olley. Witnesses to the will were John Kelly, David Tomlinson, and Henry Massey.

1) Alexander Johnston served in the American Revolution with the patriots under Captain John Moore.
2) Cornelius Johnston
3) Daniel Johnston d. in 1788--left a will in which he named his wife Verlinda. She is probably the Verlinda Johnston who md. on 6/23/1789 to David Elam.
4) Jacob Johnston
5) John Johnston
6) Olley Johnston md. Thomas Whittington
7) Nelly Johnston md. Ayres Holliday b. ca. 1774--lived in Washington Parish, La., moved to Copiah Co., Miss., and back to Washington Parish where he died. Issue:
    a) Elizabeth Holliday d. 1841, md. in Copiah Co., Miss., to Thomas Millsaps on 9/15/1825 and had 5 children: Martha; Uriah; Mary; Sarah; and Thomas J.
    b) John Johnson Holliday md. 12/8/1825 to Mary M. Ainsworth in Copiah Co.
    c) Thomas Holliday
8) Sarah Johnston md. 11/5/1793 to John Ellis in Columbia Co., Ga. (See family under Ellis.)
9) Maggie or Margery Johnston md. possibly John Walker.

Proof of the marriage of the Johnston children by 1791 can be found in Columbia County, Ga., Deed Book B, p. 113: 10/22/1791: Alexander Johnson & others to Robert Allen--Thomas Whittington and Olly Whittington of Columbia Co.; also Alexander Johnson, Ayres Holliday; John Walker; Cornelius Johnson; Jacob Johnson; John Johnson; Salley Johnson; Majory Johnson of Wilkes Co., to Robert Allen of Columbia Co., for 150 £ sterling, 2 tracts on White Oak Creek granted to Richard Castleberry by patent on 6/29/1785; and another granted to Jacob Castleberry. (Total sale of 200 acres) Wits: Mary Golsy, Margt. Golsy. Recorded 5/2/1793.

ELLZEY

In the early 1900's when Luke W. Conerly was gathering data for his proposed history of Pike County, Miss., it is regretable that he set down such a few facts for the future. Such is the case with the Ellzey family. He, no doubt, knew family members of the older family that came to Mississippi. These hardy people would have known their ancestry and recited it, but he failed to question them thoroughly and record what they said.

Conerly made the statement in his book that Louis Ellzey (actually should have been spelled Lewis) was a "full-fledged Englishman of the noted Ellzey Craig, a mountain point in England," and that Louis's wife was a "full-blooded German" named Eve Shafer or Shaver (who d. 8/8/1852). Thus with this brief notation it is now impossible to ascertain if Ellzey came directly from England to America or if he was a Virginian who came to Mississippi via South Carolina.

In 1800 Lewis Ellzey was a resident of Fairfield Co., S.C., (named spelled on the report as Elzy or Elsy). His household had 3 males under 10 years old, and two girls--one under 10 and another 10-16. The older males or sons would have been the three sons that came to and remained in Pike County, Miss. By 1810 Lewis Ellzey had a fourth male counted in his household--this possibly could have been a son named James, as a man of that name did reside in the early or formative years of Pike County's existance. Of Lewis Ellzey's daughters, only Nancy is known.

Most genealogists who have worked on the Ellzey line contend that Lewis Ellzey hailed from Virginia (as substantiated by the 1880 Census) and that he was born ca. 1770. There is little doubt that he was a descendant of the Ellzey family of Fairfax County, Virginia.

In 1785 in Fairfax Co., Va., two Lewis Ellzeys were listed on the tax list for that year. One had 7 whites and 1 slave in John Gibson's district. The other lived in William Payne's district and had 8 white souls, 1 dwelling, and 12 other buildings.

Neither Lewis Ellzey of the 1785 tax list could have been the Lewis who came to Mississippi if the last-named Lewis was b. ca. 1770. But there is the strong possibility that one of the two Lewis's listed was the grandfather of the Lewis under consideration. It has been claimed that the father of the Mississippi Lewis was one Thomasin Ellzey of Fairfax, but this is not possible. Thomasin Ellzey died in Fairfax ca. 1830 intestate (Fairfax Will Bk. Q--1830-1832 for inventory of estate), supposedly leaving no forced heirs. Thus the father's name for Lewis is still open to conjecture. But his line of descent has to be as follows:

Thomas Ellzey appeared in Essex County, Va., by 1700, where he obtained land. By 1723 he was a resident of Stafford Co., Va., as he was counted on the Quit Rent Roll for that year with 518 acres. (There was also a John Ellzey on the same roll with 150 acres.) Thomas Ellzey, presumably, fathered Lewis Ellzey who md. before 1726 to Elizabeth, the only dau. of Giles and Ann Waugh Travers, the then widow of John Cave.

Lewis and Elizabeth moved to Fairfax Co., Va., from Stafford Co., ca. 1730 (see George H. S. King, The Register of Overwharton Parish, Stafford County, Va., 1723-1758). This Lewis Ellzey gave a deposition before the Fairfax Co. Court on 4/16/1743 in which he stated that he was then about 41 years old, a statement which placed his birth year at about 1702.

Lewis Ellzey had his first children by Elizabeth Travers Cave, and after her death he md. Mary ___ and had at least 3 children. These forced heirs, collectively, were named in his will dated 10/1/1786 and probated 12/19/1786. His children (according to the will were):
    1) William Ellzey who received land in Loudoun Co., Va. (he left a will there in 1795)
    2) Elizabeth Ellzey who md. William Hancock
    3) Mary Ellzey who md. William West
    4) Sarah Ellzey who md. William Turner
    5) Stacy Ellzey who md. 1) Burgess Berkley and 2) Benjamin Grayson
    6) Thomasin Ellzey

7) Sybill Ellzey md. ___ Beck (actually Beckwith)
8) Grandson Lewis Ellzey
William Ellzey was to serve as the executor of the will.

Mary Ellzey, Lewis's widow, wrote her will on 12/27/1788--a will not probated until the 1790's. In this instrument she named her three children: Thomasin, Sarah Turner, and Sybil Beckwith. Thomasin was to have been the executor of this will. The witnesses were Richard Ratliff, George Sumners, Bennett Hill and R. Wheeler.

The grandson Lewis, named in the Lewis Ellzey Will of 1786, possibly could have been the Lewis Ellzey of Pike County, Miss. If so, there was a John Ellzey who died in Fairfax ca. 1775--or about the time that Lewis would have been a minor of a few years in age. The deceased John would not have been named in Lewis's will, but his heir would have been--this grandson Lewis.

Lewis Ellzey left Virginia for S.C. in the 1790's and appeared in Fairfield County, S.C., as previously noted. He married Eva Shaffer (Shafer or Shaver) in that state and had his family. After the birth of Nancy in 1802, the Ellzey family left for the west and settled eventually in Pike County, Miss. His family was as follows:
1) William Ellzey b. 5/1/1791, d. 1/1866, md. 7/27/1815 to Easter "Essie" Sibley, dau. of John Sibley, Jr., and Elizabeth Cassel. Essie was b. 8/5/1795, d. 11/1/1866 and had issue:
   a) Martha Ann Ellzey b. 1816, md. Ransom Magee
   b) Thomas Ellzey b. 1818, died young
   c) Mary (Polly) Ellzey b. 1820 md. Solomon Obed Magee
   d) John H. Ellzey b. 1822, md. Mary Jane Sibley
   e) James Ellzey b. 1824, died young
   f) William "Dutch Bill" Ellzey b. 1825, md. Madaline, dau. of Joseph B. May
   g) Esther Ellzey b. 1828, md. Jesse Brent
   h) Caroline Ellzey b. 1830, md. S. A. Matthews
   i) Nancy Ellzey b. 1832, md. Dr. D. H. Quin
   j) Angeline Ellzey b. 1834, md. John E. Keegan
   k) Iverson DeWitt Ellzey b. 1836, md. 3/1/1855 at Holmesville to Amanda Barr
   l) Emmeline "Emma" Ellzey b. 1839, died young

2) John Ellzey b. 11/10/1796, d. 10/18/1880, md. 7/18/1823 in St. Tammany Parish, La., to Elizabeth Coney, dau. of Aquila Coney, b. 4/24/1808, d. 3/19/1858. Issue:
   a) William Shaffer Ellzey b. 8/4/1824, md. 1/20/1842 to 1) Winneyfred Sibley and 2) Adeline Dendy
   b) Mary N. Ellzey b. 12/25/1825
   c) Benjamin Franklin Ellzey b. 9/10/1827, md. 9/2/1852 to 1) Sarah Elizabeth Holmes, 2) Emily Holmes
   d) John S. Ellzey b. 3/13/1829, md. Sarintha Smith
   e) Eliza J. Ellzey b. 9/5/1830, md. 8/15/1850 to Burrell Fortenberry
   f) Lewis N. Ellzey b. 2/12/1832, md. 9/1/1853 to Mary Ann Holmes
   g) Jackson J. Ellzey b. 12/8/1833, d. CSA
   h) James W. Ellzey b. 8/9/1835, md. 9/18/1856 to Nancy Catherine James
   i) Thomas J. Ellzey b. 4/19/1837
   j) Wesley W. Ellzey b. 2/1/1839
   k) Rachel A. Ellzey b. 12/23/1840, md. 1) Wm. Smith, 2) Barney Schillings
   l) Lemuel Neut Ellzey b. 11/1/1842, not married.
   m) Laura A. Ellzey b. 4/25/1844, md. 4/25/1861 to Seaborn Lockran Alford (1844-1919)
   n) Eveline Elizabeth Ellzey b. 2/6/1846, md. Rev. Esco M. Schillings
   o) Jesse C. Ellzey b. 4/15/1848, md. Sarah Alford
   p) Sarah W. Ellzey b. 9/13/1851, md. Cicero Walker
   After the death of Elizabeth Coney, John md. 2) on 1/5/1860 to Indiana Hall by whom he had:
   q) Mary Eve Mollie Ellzey b. 1865, d. 1943.
   r) Daniel Julius Ellzey md. 1) Fannie Courtney Lee, 2) Julia Ida Simmons
   s) Infant 1863-1868

3) Thomas Ellzey b. 7/15/1800, d. 10/3/1847, md. 4/17/1825 to Mary Quin b. 3/22/1800 and had 14 children:
   a) Ross Alanson Ellzey b. 6/30/1826, d. 2/1907, md. 9/2/1852 Amanda, dau. of James and Mary Booker of Clinton, La.
   b) Mary E. Ellzey b. 9/10/1827, d. 10/29/1908, md. 10/26/1848 to Joseph O'Mara.

c) Rankin C. Ellzey b. 11/10/1828, d. 3/4/1912, md. 12/21/1853 to Mary L. Thompson.
d) Wesley James Ellzey b. 5/28/1830, d. 5/1/1918, md. 2/12/1856 to Margaret dau. of Isaac and Elizabeth Holmes Brumfield.
e) Harriet A. Ellzey b. 8/28/1831, d. 9/14/1920, md. 12/23/1850 to Morgan J. Coney.
f) Hugh F. Ellzey b. 5/10/1833, d. 10/19/1844.
g) Carolina Ellzey b. 8/28/1834, md. Dr. James H. DeLaney.
h) Sarah E. Ellzey b. 4/24/1836, md. Samuel McNulty of Amite Co.
i) Nancy Katura Ellzey b. 12/10/1837, d. 11/3/1859.
j) Thomas W. Ellzey b. 7/13/1839, d. 12/2/1859.
k) Josephine M. Ellzey b. 12/22/1841, d. 1866, md. in 1865 to Elisha C. Andrews. No issue.
l) George W. Ellzey b. 1/28, d. 1/30/1843.
m) Joan Virginia Ellzey b. 3/10/1844, d. 5/7/1919 in McComb, md. 11/8/1865 to Simeon R. Ratliff.
n) Courtney Amelia (Amella) Ellzey b. 2/17/1846, d. 9/15/1938, md. 1/26/1870 to William H. Badon (1846-1917).

[See: The Family History of Peter Quin, compiled by Mrs. Madge Quin Fugler, 1922, revised and edited by Jerome C. Hafter 1963-1964, for a more complete family data on the family of Thomas Ellzey.]

4) James Ellzey (possibly)

5) Nancy Ellzey b. 1802

FELDEREN--FELDER

In 1735 a group of German-speaking Swiss arrived from the old country and settled in the Orangeburgh Township (upper Edisto River) of South Carolina. Among this group appeared ___ Felderen and his wife Ursula. They obtained land in the area about the time of the senior Felderen's death. Then in 1739, between the months of August and October, Ursula also died.

On August 30, 1739, Widow Ursula Felderen made her will (written in German) in which she left land purchased from "Gelser" to her son John Henry Felderen or Felder. The executor of the will was to have been Henry Wurzer. Witnesses to the document were Henry Wurtz, George Giesendanner, Jacob Christaller, and Michell Christopher Rowe. However, before this instrument received probate on October 10, 1739, it was translated into the "English tongue" from the German. (S.C. Will Book 1736-1740, p. 404)

The son John Henry Felderen (or Felder when translated into English) was not yet nineteen when his mother died, a fact mentioned in her will. Thus when he married Mary Elizabeth Shaumloffel on December 15, 1747, in Orangeburg by the old minister (probably Lutheran) John Giessendanner, Henry was about 21 years old.

In his married life with Mary Elizabeth, he became a man of substance--buying and selling property in Orangeburg, and by 1775, a short time before the eruption of the American Revolution, he was one of the Justices of the Quorum. This man became the progenitor of the Felder Family who eventually migrated to Mississippi.

The Giessendanner Register (a record of birth, death, and marriages as kept by the old preachers Giessendanner in Orangeburgh) gives the births of at least six of the Felder children born in Orangeburgh and baptized in the Orangeburgh Church.
1) a son born 9/8/1748, baptd. 9/25/1748 with Jacob Giessendanner, Jacob Lovisia Horger sponsors
2) John born 12/12/1751, baptd. 1/1/1752; Suceptrs were: Jacob Romph, Jacob Giessendanner, and Ann Margaret wife of Jacob Strowman (probably the infants aunt--his mother's sister who md. Strauman on 7/18/1748).
3) Frederick born 9/1/1753 with susceptrs.: Frederick Huber, Nicholas Shuler, and Barbara wife of John Jennings.
4) Samuel born 6/5/1755 with susceptrs. Samuel Suther, John Inabnet and Anne wife of Henry Richenbacher.
5) Abraham born 3/28/1757 with susceptrs.: Abraham Yessenhoot, Bernard

Lebeender and Margaret wife of John Inabnet.
6) Peter born 4/2/1759 with susceptrs.: John and Barbara Giessendanner and Jacob Giessendanner.

Of this group of six sons (the older was probably Henry II) all served with distinction in the American Revolution. In addition to the six listed, there was supposedly another son named Jacob, the probable son of Henry Felder by his second wife. Thus, Mary Elizabeth Schaumloffel (Shaumloffel) probably died ca. 1760 after Peter's birth.

Henry Felder (often referred to as Hans Henry Felder) had one dau. by his first wife:
7) Mary Elizabeth
Henry md. 2) Catherine Snell in 1763 by whom he had:
8) Ann Margaret wife of John Hartzag (or Hartzog)
9) Rachall wife of ___ Summers
10) Catherine wife of John Walker
11) ___ wife of George Hartzag
12) David md. 1) Esther Addison and 2) Elizabeth Guess

Of Henry's first family, Henry md. Margaret Staudenmire; Frederick md. Catherine Harger; Samuel md. 1) Mary Myer, 2) Ann Harger; and Abraham md. 1) Mary Erlinger (?) and 2) Elizabeth Whitmore.

A. S. Salley, Jr., in his book entitled <u>History of Orangeburgh County</u>, (South Carolina), related the following:

> The traditions of the Felder family say that Captain Felder had his seven sons Henry, Jacob, John, Frederick, Samuel, Abraham, and Peter, in his company. It is said that John was killed during the war. He was captured with his step-mother's brother, Snell, and while the British soldiers were at dinner on the banks of the Congaree River, they attempted to escape. Snell escaped into the woods, but John jumped into the river and swam across while his hands were tied, the guard shooting at him all the while, but after he reached the opposite bank a bullet struck him in a vital place and killed him on the spot. And, strange to say, he was killed by his own gun in the hands of the guard.

Salley also related that a Col. Paul S. Felder had told that the latter had once met a Mr. Rice who served with Captain Felder and was present in his company when they defeated a group of Tories at "Holman's Bridge over the South Edisto River in Orangeburgh District."

The Felder family suffered materially during the war. In September of 1778 Henry Felder's home was burned, supposedly by the Tories. The same disaster befell him near the end of the war and in that burning, the senior Felder, too lost his life.

Salley printed from a work by Judge O'Neall on the South Carolina Bench and Bar the following about Capt. Henry Felder:
> This gentle man was a very active partisan in the Revolution. He brought his love of liberty from his native canton, and like Tell, of his fatherland, he was willing to peril all, rather than to submit to tyranny. He guided General Sumpter in his approach to Orangeburgh, and bore a part in the capture of that post.

Continuing, O'Neall stated:
> At or about the close of the war, the Tories surrounded his house: the gallant Swiss, by the aid of his wife and servants, who loaded his gun while he fired, killed more than twenty of his foes. His house was at last fired, and he was thus forced to fly. In attempting to escape, he was shot, and killed.

Salley, after relating what O'Neall had reported, cited from the family tradition as passed down by the Col. Paul S. Felder, who had heard the story from his father and other family members, and an old black servant who as a young man had been an eye witness to the tragic scene.

One day Capt. Felder received a message from Samuel Rowe, a good Whig friend, that the Tories intended to attack his home the next day. With his sons, and his overseer whose name was Fry he defended his house, defeated the Tories, and drove them off. As soon as they had left he sent his sons through a bypath to waylay and ambush them, but before reaching the ambush the enemy returned to the siege and, setting fire to a load of hay that was under a shed near the house, they thereby set the house on fire. Capt. Felder put on some of his wife's clothes and attempted to escape but was recognized by his boots as he jumped the yard fence and was filled with bullets. He continued his flight for several hundred yards, however, and dropped from exhaustion and loss of blood just as he reached the woods. The same Negro above mentioned was cutting wood nearby and went to his master's assistance. He was not yet dead and, help being procured, he was taken to a place of safety where he lived a day or two before he died.

In the fight he is said to have killed about twenty of the Tories with the assistance of Fry, his wife and servants loading the guns while he and Fry shot.

There are two old cannons used as corner posts in Orangeburg that are said to have been used by him on the occasion of the siege of Orangeburgh by Sumter. However that may be, one of the guns has cut on it, "H. Felder 1781" and the other has cut on it the mark HF.

After the death of the father, his son Henry Felder commanded the company. After the war this company formed a part of the district militia.

Peter Felder, Sr., was born in Orangeburgh Dist., S.C., 4/2/1759, and died in Pike Co., Miss., in the 1820's. He married ca. 1780 to Elizabeth [Long or Lowe?]. He served with distinction in the patriot army in a unit commanded by his father Capt. Henry Felder.

After the turn of the century, Peter Felder and his family migrated to Mississippi, settling first in Amite County, but he lived his last years in Pike. His family is as follows:

1) Gabriel Felder b. ca. 1780/1782 (no doubt the first born) lived in Amite County where he was active in the 1820's into the 1830's. The 1820 census shows him with three sons [1 in the age bracket 16-18 and 2 in the bracket 16-26].

2) Mary Felder md. on 1/24/1802 to Henry Dickerson and had issue:
   a) Levica Dickerson b. 8/5/1805
   b) Martin Dickerson b. 1/28/1808, d. 1/26/1870
   c) Priscilla Dickerson b. 10/2/1815
   d) Samantha Dickerson b. 4/10/1817
   e) William Dickerson b. 4/13/1820, d. 12/26/1849, md. 12/23/1841 to Vienna Hucabee
   f) Jane Elizabeth Dickerson b. 8/26/1823, md. 1/2/1845 to James Hucabee
   g) Elizabeth Dickerson b. 9/29/1825

3) Peter Felder b. ca. 1787, d. in the 1840's in Pike Co., Miss., md. in Marion Co. 5/31/1813 to Lydia Lowe. In 1820 he had 2 sons under 10 and a dau. under 10.

4) Daughter--perhaps Jane, who md. ___ Sibley

The above children would make up Peter Felder's family as denoted on the 1790 Census.

5) John Felder b. 5/27/1793, d. 12/20/1875 in Pike Co., md. three times. See family which follows.

6) Nancy Felder b. in the early 1790's, md. in Marion Co., Miss., on 7/31/1813 to David Winborne. This union had at least a son named Harvey b. in 1814 who md. Temperance Brister. The Amite Co. Census for 1820 shows them with 2 sons and 2 daus. under 10.

7) Charles Felder b. ca. 1795, md. Sarah ___. See family which follows.

8) Keziah Felder b. ca. 1796, d. near Hattiesburg, Miss., 9/29/1886, md. 5/20/1818 in Pike Co. to Jabez Rawls d. 7/22/1834 in Marion Co., Miss. See family which follows.

9) Daniel Felder b. ca. 1799, lived in Marion Co., Miss., in 1850, md. 1)

_____; md. 2) Narcissa ___. See some family data following.

10) David Felder b. in Orangeburgh Dist. in the 1790's (although not listed as a son of Peter Felder, it is most probable that he was), md. in Amite Co., Miss., 6/17/1819 to Jane McMorris b. 9/4/1795, d. 11/9/1882 in Livingston Parish, La. David also died in Livingston Parish 10/1/1841 or 1842. See family data following.

11) Maria Felder b. 1806 in South Carolina (given on some lists as a dau. of Peter Felder), md. Israel Carter b. 1807. See family under Carter.

12) Isaac Felder b. 1/9/1800, d. 9/9/1853. He was living in Pike Co., Miss., in 1850.

- - - - - - - - - - -

5) John Felder was born in old Orangeburg Dist., S.C., on May 7 (or 27), 1793, migrated from that state to Mississippi to an area not too far from Magnolia in 1810. He and his brothers brought the stock (mainly horses) overland, while his father and mother came by boat. After arriving in Mississippi, he left the stock near Magnolia and went on to Natchez where the old couple was to have landed. Upon his arrival, he was much distressed not to find his parents there--a delay caused by the slowness of the vessel on which they were passengers. After a week's wait, the boat arrived and the Felders enjoyed a reunion. They travelled on to Magnolia and established a permanent homesite.

The next year, on John's birthday, he went through a conversion experience with the Methodists at a camp meeting held about where Magnolia sits today. From that date until his death, he was a strong and devout Methodist and thereby established a strong Methodist family thereafter.

John Felder married three times. At age 19 he married Elizabeth Sandell b. 6/17/1794, d. 5/18/1848, in Amite County on 10/15/1812. The next year his first daughter was born on 9/23/1813 and received the name Caroline. She was the only child when he saw service in the American forces at the famed Battle of New Orleans. He served as a private in Captain H. Quin's unit of the Mississippi Militia (enlisting supposedly in New Orleans if the enlistment date is correct on 1/6/1815). He was mustered out on 2/5/1815. His brief service enabled him to draw a United States Government pension in his twilight years.

After John's return from New Orleans, he and Elizabeth sired an additional half-dozen children before she died at an early age. Almost immediately thereafter, John married a second time to widow Patience Simmons nee Allen b. 1809 by whom he had one child.

About 1830 John moved his family to land on the Topisaw--a location where he spent the last 45 years of his life. While there he married a third time to the widow Martha Stanfill (Stanfield) nee Douglas by whom he had no children. Martha survived him.

John died on the Topisaw on December 20, 1875. His noted life received attention from the old Methodist minister for the region J. W. Sandell in two different obituary notices published in the New Orleans Christian Advocate, the Methodist organ.

His issue:
1) Mary Catherine Felder b. 9/13/1813, d. 11/23/1860, md. 12/29/1831 in Pike Co., Miss., to Rev. Seaborn John Alford. See family under Alford.

2) Wyatt Wesley Felder b. 5/16/1815, d. 5/16/1877, at the Topisaw, md. 1) Cynthia Isabel Hope b. 5/31/1821, d. 2/17/1848, leaving six children. Wyatt md. 2) Sarah Curtiss, widow of Ira Felder, b. 8/23/1816, d. 7/3/1883, by whom he had 3 sons and 1 dau. Wyatt Felder was a great Methodist and was one of the founders of the old Topisaw Camp Meeting in the late 1840's. This camp ground was one of the oldest, if not the oldest, of the kind in south Mississippi. His family:
a) Jane Felder b. ca. 1835
b) Peter James Felder b. 7/8/1836, d. 2/27/1862
c) Charlotte A. Felder b. 2/6/1840, d. 12/16/1891, md. 1) ___ Rollins;

md. 2) W. N. Brown
   d) May (or Mary) Felder b. 1841
   e) Courtney A. Felder b. 6/1/1842, d. 8/9/1881, md. 12/13/1866 to Jackson Williams
   f) John Smith Felder b. 6/17/1845, d. 11/18/1932, md. Julia Huffman, 1846-1919
   Children by 2nd wife:
   g) Zebulon Pipkin Felder b. ca. 1849/50, d. 8/23/1877, leaving a wife and 2 daus.
   h) William Pinckney Felder b. 11/8/1851, d. 7/8/1883
   i) Wade Hampton Felder b. 7/13/1854, d. 8/19/1921
   j) Sarah (?) J. Felder b. ca. 1856

3) Elizabeth Griffin Felder b. 2/2/1818, d. 9/10/1846.

4) Gabriel Nally Felder b. 3/25/1850, d. 9/1/1901, md. 12/1/1842 to Frances (Fanny) Hodges and had issue:
   a) Mary A. (or C.) Felder b. 1845
   b) Ira L. (called John D. on one census) b. 2/17/1847, d. 10/23/1925, md. Isabella T. ___, 1861-1908
   c) William L. Felder b. 1/29/1849, d. 10/3/1924, md. 12/27/1875 to Belle Byrd 1856-1918
   d) James E. Felder b. 1852
   e) G. M. Felder (a son) b. 1856
   f) Ella Felder md. 1/22/1885 to Gabriel Godbold

5) Levi Darius Felder b. 9/22/1827, d. 4/24/1900, md. 9/16/1847 to Martha M. Williams b. 1/18/1831, d. 2/3/1904. Issue:
   a) Abie Elizabeth Felder b. 5/31/1849, d. 8/17/1898, md. on 1/10/1867 to George W. Huffman b. 1836, d. 1904.
   b) Mary A. Felder b. 1851
   c) Amanda Jane Felder b. 10/3/1853, d. 9/22/1877, md. 12/1871 to William Mathew Tyler
   d) Sophia R. Felder b. 8/5/1855, d. 4/20/1932, md. D. C. Greer
   e) John Byrd Felder b. 4/20/1858, d. 6/19/1919, md. Dolly Jane Greer b. 1861, d. 1894. Issue:
      1) Clifton Lee Felder b. 10/10/1879, d. 10/5/1883
      2) Dora Mabel Felder b. 5/15/1881, d. 7/3/1882
   f) Jordon Monroe Felder b. 2/14/1873, d. 6/16/1875

6) Robert Henry Felder b. 10/9/1824, d. 5/10/1918, md. 6/19/1863 to Elizabeth Thompson b. 7/13/1838, d. 8/24/1916. Issue:
   a) Lula S. Felder b. 9/12/1867, d. 12/16/1890.

7) Simeon Noble Felder b. 2/23/1827, d. 9/1917, md. Mrs. Mary Buie and had issue:
   a) William L. Felder b. 1858
   b) Lucy S. Felder b. 1859
   c) Frances S. Felder b. 2/27/1864, d. 10/4/1868

8) Minerva Felder b. 6/6/1848, d. 1924, md. 1/12/1871 to Monroe McEwen b. 8/12/1845, d. 7/23/1906, and left issue:
   a) George Clifton McEwen b. 11/6/1871, d. 8/11/1954, md. Sarah Barnes
   b) Mary S. McEwen b. 7/26/1873, d. 1/3/1935
   c) _____
   d) _____
   e) James Monroe McEwen b. 10/19/1879, d. 5/16/1884
   f) Chauncy C. McEwen b. 9/6/1882, d. 2/9/1959

- - - - - - - - - - -

8) Keziah Felder b. 1795 (or 1798) in S.C., d. 9/29/1886, md. 5/20/1818 in Pike Co., Miss., to Jabez Rawls d. 7/22/1834 and had issue:
   a) Allen B. F. Rawls b. 1820, md. 2/3/1844 to Obedience Pope and had:
      1) John Rawls b. 1847
      2) James Rawls b. 1849 (Benjamin)
      3) Harriett Rawls b. 1851
      4) Luther Rawls b. 1854
      5) Sarah Rawls b. 1856

      6) Harris Rawls b. 1860
- b) Caroline Eveline Rawls b. 1826, md. 1/25/1848 to William J. Adams b. 1815 and had a son:
  1) James E. Adams b. 1849
- c) James Rawls, Jr., b. 1826 (possibly a twin to Caroline), md. 8/31/1854 to Sarah J. Barnes
- d) Susannah Rawls
- e) William E. Rawls b. 1829, md. Elizabeth ___. Issue:
  1) Elizabeth Rawls b. 1855
  2) Jesse Rawls b. 1857
  3) Kisiah Rawls b. 1859
- f) Thomas Rawls b. 1831
- g) Harriet E. R. Rawls b. 1837

- - - - - - - - - -

9) Daniel Felder b. ca. 1800 in S.C., md. 1) _____ ; md. 2) Narcissa ___ b. 1809. Issue:
- a) Henry H. Felder b. 1823, md. Anne Burk 9/24/1842 in Marion Co., Miss. Issue:
  1) Emily Felder b. 1845
  2) Daniel Felder b. 1846
  3) Martha Felder b. 1850
- b) _____
- c) _____
- d) John Felder b. 1829
- e) Daniel Felder, Jr., b. 1821
- f) _____
- g) Nancy Felder b. 1836
- h) James Felder b. 1838
- i) Franklin Felder b. 1840
- j) David Felder b. 1842
- k) Harriet Felder b. 1846
- l) Tabor Felder b. 1850

Daniel probably was the father of Louisa Jane Felder who md. on 11/3/1842 to William Wallis and of Rebecca J. Felder who md. on 5/20/1847 to John Raney. Daniel had married a first time as he had a daughter on the 1820 Census. This must have been Elizabeth Felder who md. Noah Standford on 6/22/1837.

1850 Census: 339/344 N. Standford   36 m Tanner   Ga.
                                    E   35 f   Miss.
                                    Mary   12   La.
                                    Nancy   11   La.
                                    Harriett   9   La.
                                    Green   7   Miss.
                                    Sarah   5   Miss.
                                    Frank   2   Miss.

- - - - - - - - - -

DAVID FELDER OF PIKE CO., MISS.

AND LIVINGSTON PARISH, LA.

    David Felder born in Orangeburgh Dist., S.C., d. in Livingston Parish, La., on October 1, 1841 (or 42) married in Amite Co., Miss., on June 17, 1819, to Jane McMorris b. in S.C. on Sept. 4, 1795, d. in Port Vincent, La., at the home of her son Rufus K. Felder on Nov. 9, 1882. Her husband and his family lived in Pike Co., Miss., up to approximately 1830 when they moved to Louisiana. He was a veteran of the War of 1812, having served as an Ensign in Capt. Barnett's Miss. Militia. He enlisted on 9/25/1814 and was discharged on 3/22/1815. His widow drew a pension on his war service in late life.

10) David Felder and wife Jane McMorris had issue:
- a) Rufus Knight Felder b. 4/18/1820, d. 7/15/1894 at Port Vincent, md.

on 12/8/1855 to Sarah A. Singletary b. 11/14/1824, d. 1/5/1916. They are buried at the Felder Cemetery, Gray's Creek Baptist Church about 9-10 miles south of Denham Springs, La., on Hwy to Port Vincent. Issue:
   1) Newton Felder b. 9/2/1855 (?), d. 4/17/1942
   2) Charlie Felder b. 8/4/1858, d. 1/30/1943
   3) Olive Felder (middle name Elizabeth) b. 10/4/1860, d. 8/4/1935
   4) Alfred R. Felder
   5) Edgar Felder
   6) Emma I. Felder b. 5/25/1868, d. of meningitis on 1/26/1884
   7) Gertrude Felder
b) Otis H. Felder b. in 1822 in Pike Co., Miss., CSA, md. Rachel ___ and had issue:
   1) David Watson Felder b. 6/26/1851, d. 6/15/1944, md. 1) on 5/14/1874 to Jennie Kirby b. 9/15/1857, d. 5/21/1882; md. 2) on 4/11/1883 to Jane C. Miller b. 9/29/1856, d. 3/31/1939. Issue:
      a) Edna Grace Felder b. 9/6/1875, md. Robert L. Fridge
      b) Palmira Elazine Felder b. 4/21/1878, md. John E. Montgomery
      c) Otis Dorace Felder b. 9/12/1881, md. Maud Cannon
      d) Rachael Caroline Felder b. 1/18/1884, md. Rufus Alford Felder
      e) Charles Dennis Felder b. 3/14/1886, md. Myrtle King
      f) Winnie Laurine Felder b. 1/30/1888, md. Oliver Montgomery
      g) Jesse Milton Felder b. 7/14/1889, d. 1/1973, md. Ina Octavia Harris
      h) Edwin Gates b. 3/15/1891, md. Mabyn Browning
   2) Otis Felder b. 1856
   3) Winnefred Felder b. 1853
   4) James Felder b. 1859
c) Louisa Felder b. 5/24/1824 in Pike Co., Miss., d. 4/26/1880, md. on 2/11/1851 to William Jefferson Gates who died in 1855. Issue:
   1) Rufus J. Gates b. 11/26/1851, d. 10/19/1890, md. Mary Louise Spiller.
   2) Almyra (Palmyra) Gates b. 1854, d. 2/4/1884, md. ___ Brannon.
d) Jesse T. Felder b. 7/15/1827, d. 7/6/1883, CSA, md. North Ann West b. 1835, and had issue:
   1) Jane Felder
   2) George Felder b. 2/16/1855, d. 11/2/1916, md. 12/1884 to Iowa Carruth.
   3) Louisa Felder
   4) Zella Felder b. 1860
   5) Jesse T. Felder b. 1863
   6) Benjamin B. Felder b. 1873
   7) D. William Felder b. 12/30/1864, d. 9/27/1876
   8) Robert E. Felder b. 9/6/1869, d. 1/27/1874
   9) Anna Felder b. 1867
e) Baxter Felder b. 1836, md. Adeline Cockerham b. 1844 and had issue:
   1) Lenora J. Felder b. 1861, md. Gus King
   2) Julius Edward Felder b. 1866
   3) Ida B. Felder b. 9/10/1870, d. 7/11/1964, md. 4/1/1891 to George Oliver Hood b. 10/28/1866, d. 12/8/1967 (buried in Felder Cemetery). Issue:
      a) Iris Hood b. 1892, md. Fenimore Bond
      b) Addie Hood b. 1893, md. Percy Vincent
      c) Joe Hood b. 1895, md. Lavina Cambes
      d) Jesse Hood b. 1897, md. Anna Moore
      e) Clyde Hood b. 1897, md. Oma Tyler
      f) Ulyse Hood b. 1901, d. 1924, buried Felder Cemetery.
      g) Georgia Hood b. 1903, md. Joe Henderson
      h) Mamie Ethel Hood b. 1906, md. Morris E. May
      i) Elva Hood b. 1909, md. Alton Watt
      j) Elmo Hood b. 1911, md. Lelia Bourgeois
      k) Gladys Hood b. 1914, md. George Forbes
   4) Henry D. Felder b. 1872
   5) Loula B. Felder b. 1874
   6) Otis L. Felder b. 1878
   7) Bernice Felder b. 5/1880, md. Joseph Scivilque
f-i) Names unknown, all died young

HOLMES

Elisha Holmes and his wife Sarah, called Sally, Stovall settled in Pike County on Collins Creek after their arrival in the area from Morgan County, Georgia. This family had not long been residents of the latter-named area before their departure for the young state of Mississippi. In February, 1817, Elisha transacted several deeds in Morgan County--deeds in which he sold what estate he had in Georgia. On February 2 he sold 202½ acres lying on Indian Creek in the 15th Dist. of Baldwin County for $1500 to William Faine (Morgan Co. Deed Bk. F, p. 330); and on the 11th of the same month, while a resident of Morgan County, sold property (as will be mentioned hereafter) in Lincoln County.

Prior to their residence in Morgan County, Elisha and his family lived in Lincoln where they had lived from the time of creation of the political and geographic entity. Most of Elisha's children were born in that area.

While a resident of Lincoln County (after having spent, perhaps, many of his younger years in Wilkes County, the parent of Lincoln), he served on occasional juries such as in April, 1802, and October, 1804. And in his religious life, he was associated with the Baptists and for a time was a member of the Goshen Baptist Church. Religion was not his forte, for as the church minute books reveal, he was brought before the church in July, 1806, for using improper language and by August, 1806, was expelled altogether for his "indifference towards the church." Many of the Stovalls, his wife's people, held membership in the same congregation.

Elisha's origin prior to his appearance in Lincoln County, Georgia, is obscure. It has been a common belief by many of his descendants that he was of Irish descent and that he was the son of a James or Jim Holmes who came directly from Ireland to Virginia. However, there is no proof to back up that contention.

However, in Lincoln County, Georgia, it appears from the extant records that he was closely associated and must have been closely related to a John Holmes, Senior, for whom Elisha served as administrator on a 1794 Tax List. He was perhaps an agent for an absent John only, as John was then a resident of old Wilkes County. In addition to that mention, two deeds recorded in Lincoln also point to a strong relationship--deeds executed in 1811 and 1812. [See Lincoln Co. Deed Bk. H (1812-1816), p. 87/88 and 11/12.] On December 28, 1811, Elisha sold John Holmes (then claiming Lincoln County residency) for $500 a tract of land on Soap Creek. This deed was witnessed by William Mays, John Hardy, and R. Rensom (?). Five months later John Holmes, Sr., and Margaret his wife sold Elisha some 100 acres on the same creek for $300-- John then was in Wilkes, so this is probably John the father and a John the son. The 100 acres transferred by John to Elisha in 1812 was no doubt the 100 acres that Benjamin Holmes of Wilkes sold to John on Jan. 24, 1792, land which bounded Paschal's line (Wilkes County Deed Bk. H-H, p. 366).

The Benjamin Holmes (son or brother of John, Sr.?) had a wife named Elizabeth who must have been the daughter of Philip Thomas, who left a will in Wilkes County in 1786. This Philip named a daughter Elizabeth in that will. Thereafter, Elizabeth probably died comparatively young, and Benjamin married Mary ___ with whom he was living in the 1815 period. By her Benjamin fathered Elizabeth, William, Mary, Thomas, Rebecca, and Jonathan--most of whom were minors at the time of his death.

In addition to the above, an examination of the 1791 Tax List for Wilkes County illustrates that two different John Holmes (plus the Benjamin previously listed) resided in the county. One was the John Holmes who left a will there in 1802 and is not to be confused with the John Holmes, Sr., who was possibly the father of Elisha Holmes.

The John Holmes, Senior, under study died in Lincoln County around 1807, and one Thomas Trammel got possession of some of his estate. Lincoln Deed Book I reveals that this Trammel sold Hannah Holmes (the then widow of John) 50 acres of land in Lincoln for $60, land on which the said Hannah lived and land which belonged to the John Holmes Estate. James Olive and H. Holmes witnessed the transaction.

It is impossible to explain who this Hannah was, but if the John Holmes of Lincoln was the John Holmes, Sr., of Wilkes, he had married a second or third wife.

Irrespective of that, it is most probable that Elisha settled with the administrators of the John Holmes estate prior to his removal into Morgan County. Since there does not appear to be a transference of land, he must have received his share in other forms--cash, livestock or household goods.

After Elisha became a resident of Morgan County, he sold the 100 acres that he had acquired from John Holmes, Sr., on February 11, 1817 to Absalom Tanksley for $400--$100 more than he paid for it (Lincoln County Deed Bk. K, p. 895). It was after that transaction that he set out for Mississippi.

Although circumstantial evidence seems to indicate that Elisha was the son of John Holmes, Sr., it cannot be stated so emphatically. This is only given as clues as to which family he probably belonged. He was, no doubt, related to Benjamin Holmes and possibly to a Joseph Holmes, who served as witnesses to some Holmes transactions in Wilkes and Lincoln Counties.

The widow Hannah Holmes became the administrator of the John Holmes Estate, ca. 1815, and was so acting through 1817. References to that estate (which does not mention heirs) can be found in Lincoln County Minute Book N (C-1). The only Holmes in addition to herself was an Ikabod (Ichabod) Holmes who acted as agent. The latter was selling and buying back land from the John Holmes Estate as late as 1823. He, at that time, still professed to be a resident of Wilkes County.

In Mississippi Elisha Holmes followed the profession of a blacksmith and did well with it. He reared a large family--all of whom were respected within the community. As time advanced his old home became located near the present town of Tylertown. For a time some residents believed that the old county seat of Pike, Holmesville, had been named in his honor, but that is not so.

The exact date of Elisha's birth (according to one record 7/6/1773 in Ireland) or death is not to be found. He died before 1850, but his widow Sally was alive at the time and related that she was in her 70th year, or born ca. 1780 (12/28/1777 in Granville Co., N.C.). The issue of Elisha Holmes and Sally Stovall:

1) Josiah Holmes (named for his grandfather Stovall) b. in 1798 in Lincoln Co., Ga., md. 10/1821 in Marion Co., Miss., to Agnes Sumrall b. 1798. Issue:
   a) Elijah Holmes who migrated to Texas after the Civil War.
   b) Jefferson Davis Holmes md. Amanda Fortson.
   c) Sarah Holmes b. 11/12/1824, d. 10/17/1916, md. Skinner Boone b. 1816, d. 1876.
   d) Susan Holmes md. Benjamin Bryant Washington Lee.
   e) William Graham Holmes b. 1842.
   f) James Prior Holmes b. 1837, died young.
   g) Henry Holmes died young.
   h) Mary Ann Holmes died young.
   Josiah Holmes md. 2) 9/7/1859 to Louisa Willoughby and had an additional set of 5 children:
   i) Stephen T. Holmes b. 9/5/1863, d. 1941, md. in 1891 to Sarah Ann Rowley.
   j) John Collins Holmes d. when 12.
   k) Wallace Holmes d. at age 12.
   l) Francis Holmes died young.
   m) Ernest Holmes md. 1) Elizabeth (Lizzie) Bearden; 2) Elizabeth Beecher.

2) Benjamin Holmes b. 1801 in Georgia, md. 4/1825 in Marion Co., Miss., to Mary Sumrall b. 1808. This union lived on the E. side of Magee's Creek, 2 miles north of old China Grove Church and community. There he ran a foundry and manufactured plantation bells. Issue:
   a) David (Dave) Holmes md. ca. 1850 to Rosanna Bullock by whom he had John A. Holmes b. 11/10/1851; and Emma. Dave md. 2) Jane Lewis b. 4/16/1832, d. 5/9/1909.
   b) Capt. John Holmes of the Quitman Guards, CSA, b. 1831, d. 1907 in Picayune, Miss., md. Alvira Sparkman who d. 9/28/1898, leaving issue: Dr. Bennie Holmes who d. 9/20/1898; Johnie who md. Homer Stevens; and Daisy who md. C. W. Morris of Fernwood, Miss.
   c) Elizabeth (Betsy) Holmes b. 1833, md. Frank Kaigler, who after Betsy's death md. her sister Emily.
   d) Mary Ann Holmes b. 1834, md. Louis Ellzey and had a son, John I.
   e) Emily Holmes b. 1836, md. Frank Keigler.

    f) Benjamin Holmes b. 1838, d. 1881, md. on 1/17/1866 to Lizzie Smith b. 1847, d. 1922, and had issue:
      1) Richard A. Holmes md. Mrs. Maggie Auston Busch
      2) Bennie M. Holmes md. 1) Helen Nas; 2) Maude Morgan
      3) Annie Bell Holmes md. J. I. Cain of McComb, Miss.
      4) Edgar Holmes died at 2 yrs. of age
      5) John T. Holmes b. 7/18/1875, d. 12/24/1917 in McComb, md. Etta Gardner
      6) James Monroe Holmes d. 1904, md. in 1903 to Pinkey, dau. of Elias Newman
      7) Lewis Benton Holmes md. Stella Teagarden
      8) Bessie Holmes md. A. A. Huckabee
    g) Raiford Holmes b. 1840, d. CSA, 1864
    h) Jesse Holmes b. 1841, died young
    i) Elisha Holmes b. 1842, md. 1) Winnie Pearson and had issue:
      1) James Holmes md. Rosa Magee
      2) John T. Holmes md. Rosa Frances Stewart
      3) Ira Holmes md. 1) Laura Turnage; 2) Lula Holmes
      4) Fred L. Holmes md. 1) Ella Duncan; 2) Ethel Patterson.
    Elisha Holmes md. 2) Frances Turnage and had issue:
      5) Seaborn (Seab) Holmes md. Lula Duncan
      6) Charley Holmes md. Della Sandford
      7) Gene Holmes md. Manson Holmes
      8) Hattie Holmes md. Lloyd Duncan
    j) Needham Holmes b. 1844, md. Martha Conerly
    k) James Holmes b. 1846, md. Sarah Kaigler
    l) Eliza Jane Holmes b. 1848, md. James Kaigler
    m) Calvin Holmes md. Mary Brewer and had issue:
      1) Lizzie Holmes b. 1876, d. 1939, md. 1) Joe Smith; 2) Leon Gatlin
      2) Lillie Holmes md. John O'Quin
      3) Lula Holmes md. Will Lang of New Orleans
      4) Dixie Holmes md. Herbert East
      5) Emmett Holmes md. Lizzie Wells
      6) Icie Holmes b. 1883, d. 1947, md. Tom Jones
      7) Bennie Holmes md. Mamie Davis
      8) Stella Holmes md. 1) George Scarborough; 2) Judge Rufus Trahan of Osyka
      9) Carrie Holmes md. 1) Walter Wroten; 2) ___ Lenhart
    n) Allen Holmes died young
    o) William Holmes died young
    p) Josiah Holmes died young

3) James Holmes b. ca. 1800 in Georgia, md. Nancy Shirley and had issue:
    a) Elisha Holmes
    b) David Stovall Holmes b. 2/10/1826, d. 5/4/1917 at Lake, Miss., md. 9/14/1848 to Mary Louise Henderson b. 9/28/1828, d. 9/16/1906.
    c) William Holmes d. 4/1862 at the Battle of Shiloh, CSA

4) Elisha Holmes, Jr., b. ca. 1803 in Georgia, md. Mary Roberts b. 1808 and lived on Varnel Creek. Issue:
    a) Thomas H. Holmes b. 4/1832, d. 1/1905, md. Telitha Duncan b. 4/1836, d. 6/1923 and had issue:
      1) Mary Jane Holmes md. Robert Johnson
      2) Mellissa Holmes md. Henry Forbes
      3) Sally Holmes md. Ben Duncan
      4) John T. Holmes b. 12/31/1861, md. 12/20/1882 to Mindana Cothern (of Carter's Creek) and had issue: Eula Holmes md. Mose Crawford of Meridian, Miss.
      5) Minnie Holmes md. Louis Ainsworth of Meridian
      6) Lettie Holmes md. Jesse Howell of Jayess, Miss.
      7) Victor Holmes md. Edna Ginn of Jayess
      8) Kerschell Holmes md. Bertha Jones of Jayess
      9) Herbert Holmes md. Alvie Blackwell of Jayess
    b) Polly Ann Holmes md. John Walters. He and a son died in the Civil War.
    c) Ellen or Eleanor Holmes b. 1843, md. Jesse Yawn
    d) Emily Holmes b. 1838, md. John Grimesley
    e) Harriet Holmes b. 1847, md. Alexander Breland
    f) Sarah Holmes md. George Gartman of McComb
    g) Elizabeth Holmes md. Dave Gartman of McComb

h) Needham Holmes b. 1850, md. Delilah Bearden
5) John Coleman Holmes md. Mary Ann Foil and had issue:
   a) W. Jack Holmes b. 1/19/1832, d. 1/4/1913, md. 6/9/1863 to Nancy Stallings d. 5/28/1882, and had issue:
      1) Dort Holmes b. 1870, d. 1939, md. Janie E. Brock
      2) Jane Holmes md. Daniel R. Smith
      3) Sallie Holmes md. G. W. Hinson
      4) Walter Wilton Holmes b. 6/18/1871, md. 4/7/1896 to Ella Eaton
      5) Sam Holmes died when about 10 years old
      6) Janette Holmes md. 1) Thad Harvey; 2) John Ratliff
      7) Joan Holmes d. in infancy
      8) P. Burk Holmes md. Emma Wilson
      9) Martha Lena Holmes md. Wayne Harvey
   b) Sarah Holmes md. Burton Morris and had:
      1) John Sim Morris b. 10/23/1849, d. 1936
      2) William (Billy) Morris b. 2/6/1854
      3) Victoria Morris md. Hillery Thornhill
      4) Lizzie Morris
      5) Chinck (?) Morris md. Price Lewis
   c) Jane Holmes md. Causeby Conerly and had issue:
      1) Mollie Conerly
      2) John Price Conerly b. 2/10/1854
   d) Francis Marion Holmes d. 9/10/1867 or 9/16/1870 (?), md. Lou Hill. They had issue:
      1) Andrew Holmes
      2) John Coleman Holmes md. Miss Fridge and lived in St. Helena Par., La.
      3) Crawford Holmes
      4) Polly Holmes
   e) Serena Holmes md. Gale Johnson
   f) Elisha Crawford Holmes b. 6/16/1839, d. 6/22/1917, md. 1) Margaret Stallings b. 1844, d. 1868, and had issue:
      1) Jesse Longino Holmes
      Elisha md. 2) Lucretia Ginn and had:
      2) Madison Holmes md. Hattie Ratliff
      3) Dean Crawford Holmes d. 5/5/1936, md. Nellie Kprnrumpf
      4) Yates L. Holmes md. 1) Minnie Lenoir; 2) Maud Andrews
      5) Maggie Holmes md. John A. Packwood
      6) Murn (?) Holmes
      7) Elisha Holmes
      8) Katie Holmes md. John Robinson
      9) Grover Holmes md. Burdette Carter and 2) ____
      10) J. L. Holmes
      11) Moyes Holmes md. 1904 to Annie G. Pugh
   g) Cynthia Holmes md. Van Arnold
   h) Newton Holmes md. Eliza Hancock
   i) John T. L. Holmes d. 8/28/1882 near Greensburg, md. Sarah Yarborough
   j) Samantha Holmes died young
   k) Ransom Coleman Holmes b. 3/10/1852, d. 11/11/1923, md. 11/1879 to Lula Julia Everette, and had issue:
      1) Myrtle Holmes b. 1888, md. 5/14/1905 to Sam Montgomery
      2) Bessie Amanda Holmes b. 3/19/1882, md. 3/27/1902 to Claude L. Fenn
      3) Florence Ladora Holmes b. 8/7/1885, md. 12/24/1901 to L. W. McManuel
      4) Velma Holmes b. 10/6/1889, d. 9/27/1938, md. 1) Owen Marsalis; 2) Angelo M. Uli; 3) ___ Guy
      5) Willie Pearl Holmes b. 9/18/1884
      6) Clifton Leon Holmes b. 10/1/1896, md. 12/27/1922 to Reta Babin
      7) Alton Holmes b. 1/23/1899, md. 12/6/1938 to Pauline Mae Roberts
      8) Roy Holmes b. 3/18/1902, md. 3/30/1925 to Thelma Muirhead
      9) John Herbert Holmes b. 4/12/1887, d. 12/13/1904, buried in the Hollywood Cemetery, McComb, Miss.
   l) Francis Edwin Holmes b. 12/22/1866, d. 7/22/1867
   m) T. N. Holmes d. 3/10/1873

William Stovall Holmes
and Jane Perkins Foil Holmes

6) William Stovall Holmes b. in Lincoln Co., Ga., 11/12/1806, d. at the home of his son Wm. Dawson Holmes near Tylertown on 12/20/1876, md. 9/29/1831 to Jane Perkins Foil b. 1/6/1815, d. 6/23/1874. This old couple lies buried in the Jesse Brumfield Cemetery 3 miles E. of Tylertown, Miss.

According to notes on the Holmes family made by Katie Lea Jones, wife of W. F. Holmes, now deceased, but then a resident of McComb, Miss., in the 1930's, Mrs. Arvie Brock, a daughter of the old couple, once told her that the Holmes and Foil families came to Mississippi together in the same caravan, that often many families banded together for the trek across country for security--especially against possible Indian attack.

According to "Aunt" Arvie Brock, Jane Perkins Foil, daughter of William Foil, was just old and large enough to ride horseback to their new home. She often rode behind William Holmes and could not have guessed at that time that they would one day marry. But on the trip the horse she and William rode "shied," jumped to one side and threw Jane to the ground, but the animal stepped over her and she was not hurt in the episode.

Also, according to Katie Holmes's notes, a grandson of William and Jane, William Franklin Holmes, told her that after the marriage of his grandparents they accumulated some wealth, a large amount in the pre-Civil War days, and that they were slave owners. In their many enterprises, William ran or operated a cotton-gin run by horse power. William Holmes, a grandson, and Sallie, a granddaughter, drove the horses that went round and round and produced the power. In addition to a gin, William S. Holmes owned the first molasses mill in that part of old Pike County (later Walthall), and by its very creaking as the horses made it operate (especially the presser) people gathered for miles around to get a sample of the cane juice that came forth. The molasses which was cooked from that juice was always clean and of best quality. William had no formal education, but was a self taught man and was exceptionally talented in mathematics.

William and Jane's family were Baptist. He joined the Union Baptist Church the second Sunday in June, 1851, and Jane became a member of the same church in 1855 where both retained membership until death. William had complete faculties until about six years prior to his death when he contracted palsey, but his faith never faltered until the end.

The children of William S. and Jane Foil Holmes:
  a) Jefferson Frank Holmes b. 2/28/1833, d. 6/6/1904, md. on 6/7/1859 to Sarah Lenora Bickham b. 4/23/1842, d. 12/30/1904 (only a few months after her husband), the dau. of Thomas Bickham and Elizabeth Magee. Frank and Sarah had thirteen children:
    1) Thomas William Holmes b. 5/20/1860, d. 9/13/1949, md. 12/22/1882 to Lula R. Conerly b. 1855, d. 1917, and had 7 children.
    2) Jane Elizabeth Holmes (Lizzie) b. 4/29/1861, d. 7/3/1928, md. Bouie Smith
    3) Mary Ida Holmes b. 4/24/1874, d. 5/7/1912, md. 8/1889 to Franklin Davis, son of Zaborn Davis, b. 1/25/1864
    4) Jasper Franklin Holmes b. 4/8/1866, d. 2/27/1933, md. Jessie Ida Ligon, widow of John Foster Godbold
    5) Martha (Mattie) Louise Holmes b. 11/14/1870, d. 3/6/1915, md. 1884/5 to Jeremiah Jackson Simmons b. 11/4/1868, d. 5/27/1927
    6) Amanda Una Holmes b. 7/11/1872, d. 1926, md. Thad Pigott
    7) Benjamin Oscar Holmes b. 5/26/1874, d. 6/8/1923, md. 1) 4/1895 to Maggie E. Pounds b. 1877, d. 1901; 2) 2/18/1922 to Annie Edna Simmons.

8) Ada Lucretia Holmes b. 4/28/1876, d. 1955, md. Will Andrews
   9) James Wesley Holmes b. 3/18/1878, d. 2/21/1954, md. 11/20/1899 to Emma
      Hobgood b. 1882, d. 1963
  10) Marcus Lafayette Holmes b. 5/5/1880, d. 8/31/1954, md. 10/3/1907 to
      Murtie Adaline Lee b. 5/3/1882
  11) Rufus Edgar Holmes b. 5/22/1882, d. 7/5/1956, md. 12/14/1905 to Lou
      Reeves b. 1887, d. 1969
  12) Ethel L. Holmes b. 1/18/1884, md. Estes Pigott
  13) Sidney Dolphus Holmes b. 2/12/1887, d. 2/16/1958, md. 1) Maggie Eaton;
      2) on 5/20/1921 to Sallie Pittman b. 3/14/1885
b) William Dawson Holmes b. 2/12/1835, d. 6/7/1919, md. 12/12/1851 to Dorcas
   Catherine Lewis b. 6/22/1834, d. 3/28/1922, dau. of Joseph Lewis and Sarah
   Morris. They had 6 children:
   1) William Franklin Holmes b. 5/31/1854, d. 11/29/1939, md. 12/11/1882 to
      1) Bobbie Lea b. 1855, d. 1902; md. 2) 12/25/1901 to Katie L. Jones b.
      4/12/1874, d. 12/12/1952
   2) Sarah Jane Holmes b. 1/12/1858, d. 7/29/1940, md. 12/17/1873 to Kenzie
      Monroe Johnson b. 1854
   3) Angeline Elizabeth (Lizzie) Holmes b. 4/14/1861, d. 4/30/1949, md. 1/18/
      1882 to Newton Fortenberry b. 1859
   4) Laura Holmes b. 4/23/1865, md. 1/22/1891 to Dudley Fortenberry b. 1867,
      d. 1937 at Baytown, Texas
   5) Hilborn B. Holmes b. 6/14/1869, md. 1/13/1891 to Evie Mixon b. 1872
   6) James Marshall Holmes b. 7/3/1872, d. 4/1/1962, md. 1) 4/6/1898 to
      Leota Thomas b. 1882, d. 1914; md. 2) 1/3/1915 to Mrs. Addie Rheams
      Brill
c) Mary Holmes b. 12/20/1836, d. 6/12/1882, md. 1) 2/5/1857 to Jasper Smith
   and had issue:
   1) Eugene Smith md. 1) Ella Brock; 2) Johnie Wilson
   2) Preston Alonzo Smith md. Fannie Brock
   Mary married 2) John Ratliff McElveen b. 1828, d. 2/2/1903 and had issue:
   3) DeWitt McElveen d. 7/10/1940, md. Mollie Brock b. 1871, d. 1924
   4) Ophelia McElveen md. Dr. Henry F. Hart
   5) Ira McElveen d. 9/12/1930 at Rochester, Miss., md. Mrs. ___ Hall
d) Ruth Holmes b. 8/5/1838, d. 12/3/1919, md. 1) 2/1867 to Charles H.
   Stateham b. 1838, d. 1896 and had issue:
   1) John Stateham md. Myra Lewis
   2) Martia Stateham md. Pascal Conerly
   3) Walter Stateham b. 7/11-12/28/1869
   Ruth married 2) John Conerly b. ca. 1821, d. 10/29/1913. No issue.
e) Angeline Holmes b. 4/18/1840, d. 10/28/1841
f) Laura Drucilla Holmes b. 2/9/1842, d. 3/11/1895, md. Daniel Cornelius
   Warner b. 1/1/1833, d. 1907, and had issue:
   1) William Coulter Warner b. 7/27/1865, d. 1/31/1943, md. 6/1887 to Leta
      Graves b. 1867, d. 1951
   2) Daniel Densmore Warner b. 3/13/1867, d. 9/16/1867
   3) Virgel Cornelius Warner b. 1/22/1869, d. 10/3/1934, md. Permelia Burch
      b. 1871, d. 1943
   4) Laura Jane Warner b. 3/8/1871, d. 3/31/1939, md. on 5/12/1897 to Jeptha
      Martin Alford b. 1862, d. 1948
   5) Tabitha Arvazine Warner b. 3/9/1875, d. 3/30/1930, md. 6/11/1911 to
      Frederick Ellis Alford
   6) Saleta Lenor Warner b. 10/10/1875, not married
   7) Hettie Zonetta Warner b. 11/17/1880, md. 2/12/1905 to Willis Richard
      Pirtman b. 12/3/1878. [See more complete record on this family in
      <u>Kinsmen All</u>, Descendants of Wettenhall Warner and Related Families, by
      E. Russ Williams, Jr.]
g) Jasper Newton Holmes b. 2/2/1844, d. 6/27/1914, md. 3/15/1864 to Armetha'
   Smith b. 1837, d. 6/28/1912. They had issue:
   1) Lucius Holmes d. 4/8/1911, md. 7/10/1889 to Laura Andrews
   2) Dora Holmes b. 1864, d. 1924, md. Jesse W. Ball
   3) Catherine Rosetta Holmes b. 1872, d. 1879
   4) Rosa Holmes b. 8/20/1874, d. 2/8/1902, md. 2/10/1891 to Needham Packwood
   5) Madison Hilborn Holmes b. 3/16/1868, d. 11/12/1916, md. Mary Holmes
   6) Bessie Pauline Holmes b. 1/4/1880, d. 9/15/1881
h) James Monroe Holmes b. 4/24/1845, d. 2/10/1876, md. 1/17/1866 to Fannie
   Smith b. 1849 in Amite Co., Miss., d. 12/11/1939. They had issue:
   1) James Monroe Holmes, Jr., b. and d. 7/26/1867

2) Annie Holmes b. 6/7/1868, d. ___, md. 1) 7/7/1887 to Frank McL'Wrath
      (?) b. 1864, d. 1896, buried in McComb; md. 2) George Bickham; md.
      3) L. B. Burnham
   3) Elizabeth (Lizzie) Holmes b. 4/30/1873, d. 6/21/1908, md. 8/1897 to
      T. J. Gordon and had issue: Fannie Iona and Lewis Monroe
   4) Dixie Holmes b. 6/30/1871
 i) Sarah Jane Holmes b. 3/17/1847, d. 9/2/1849
 j) John Wesley Holmes b. 2/28/1849, d. 9/24/1916, md. 1) 12/19/1867 to
    Dorcas Amanda Bickham b. 1/30/1852, d. 8/7/1880 and had issue:
    1) DeWitt Ernest Holmes b. 10/21/1861, md. 1) Martha Simmons b. 1868, d.
       1900, md. 2) Narcissus Fortenberry
    2) Una Holmes b. 4/30/1870, d. 3/5/1912, md. Rodney Quin
    3) Enos Holmes b. 4/24/1871, md. Delia Stogner
    4) Thomas Carroll Holmes b. 5/3/1873, md. 1) Pinkey Broom; 2) Katie ___.
    John Wesley Holmes md. 2) 2/8/1881 to Elizabeth Conerly b. 1854, d.
    1888, and had issue:
    5) Byron Holmes b. 3/12/1883, md. Dixie Smith
    6) Victor Monroe Holmes b. 2/18/1886, md. 1) Reta Smith b. 1886, d.
       1924; md. 2) Miss ___ Newman
    7) Ruby Bonner Holmes b. 10/21/1884, md. E. L. Magee
    John Wesley Holmes md. 3) 5/22/1888 to Mary E. Pope b. 8/17/1865 and
    had issue:
    8) Edgar Virgil Holmes b. 9/23/1890, md. Susie Mae Brewer
    9) Other (Otha?) Wesley Holmes b. 1891, d. 1892
   10) Ottis Ott Holmes b. 1/16/1893, md. Una Smith
   11) Ollie Edwin Holmes b. 9/25/1895
   12) Lexie Lelia Holmes b. 11/20/1901, md. ___ Smith
 k) Sophronia Holmes b. 7/23/1852, md. 12/16/1869 to Richmond Brock and
    had issue:
    1) William Valentine Brock b. 4/15/1871, md. 1) Samantha Smith; 2)
       Ida Conerly
    2) Ida Brock b. 12/24/1872
    3) Janie Brock
    Sophronia md. 2) W. Cornelius Blackwell and had issue:
    4) Benjamin M. Blackwell b. 11/9/1879, md. Fannie Hilburn
    5) J. L. Blackwell b. 2/2/1880, md. Janie Rimes
    6) J. Edgar Blackwell b. 10/15/1881, md. Maggie Lambert
    7) Sam Sidney Blackwell b. 9/1883
    8) A. C. Blackwell b. 3/28/1885, md. Mary Andrews
    9) Myrtis Blackwell b. 6/1887, md. Will Ball
 l) Armetha Martina Holmes b. 11/16/1853, d. 3/6/1908 at Mt. Herman, La.,
    md. 12/21/1872 to Dr. James (Jim) Brock d. 12/20/1916 and had issue:
    1) Valentine Brock md. Henri McClendon
    2) Una Brock md. William Banister
    3) Jasper Brock md. 1) Beulah Bailey; 2) ___
    4) Victoria Brock md. Dr. Andrew J. Fortenberry
    5) Dr. Lucius William Brock md. Miss Dannie Tate
    6) Ollie Brock md. Bell Conerly and lived in Bogalusa, La.
 m) Susan Arvanzine Holmes b. 6/28/1856, d. 6/7/1954 in McComb, Miss., md.
    on 12/7/1874 to Dr. Jeptha S. Brock d. 10/7/1914 and was buried at
    Brockdale, La. Issue:
    1) Oliver Seymore Brock b. and d. 11/28/1875
    2) Bethany Brock b. 2/10/1877, d. 1937, md. 7/15/1901 to James A.
       McClendon
    3) Dr. Lattimore Brock b. 8/10/1879, d. 4/27/1949, md. 3/11/1903 to
       Lenora Babington
    4) Dora Brock b. 3/10/1882, md. 1) 4/3/1901 to J. H. Hoskins; 2) 5/17/
       1911 to Wm. A. Knight b. 1874, d. 2/16/1940 in Goodman, Miss.
    5) Ross A. Brock b. 6/20/1884, d. 10/10/1906, md. 12/1904 to Mamie Bickham
    6) Edna Brock b. 1/17/1886, d. 2/20/1909, md. 12/25/1909 to Elmer
       Brumfield
    7) Lena Brock b. 1888
    8) DeWitt Talmadge Brock b. 4/6/1890, md. 10/3/1909 to Mary McDougle
    9) Bessie Brock b. 7/23/1893, md. 11/19/1916 to James Robert Thornhill
   10) Dr. Hobson Brock b. 9/22/1898, d. 1961, md. Hazel Packwood
   11) Jewell W. Brock b. 8/23/1896, d. 12/21/1896

7) Elizabeth S. (called Betsey) Holmes b. 2/11/1808, d. 6/25/1898, md. 1/31/

1827 to Isaac Brumfield b. 3/9/1801, d. 2/14/1862, son of John Brumfield and Margaret (Peggy) Kelly. Elizabeth and Isaac are buried near Walker's Bridge on the Bogue Chitto River. Their issue:
a) Lucy Jane Brumfield b. 1830, md. Green B. (Berry?) May
b) Nathaniel G. Brumfield b. 12/26/1831, d. 2/8/1862. In 1860 he was the overseer on the Green B. May plantation.
c) Sarah Ann Margaret Brumfield b. 2/12/1834, d. 1/30/1902, md. 2/12/1856 to Wesley James Ellzey b. 5/28/1830, d. 5/1/1918, buried at Walker's Bridge near her parents. Issue:
   1) Isaac Marshall Ellzey b. 9/9/1857, d. 6/1945, md. 1) Angeline Simmons b. 1865, d. 1938; md. 2) Lelia Longmire
   2) Rankin N. Ellzey b. 1859, md. Hettie M. Alford
   3) Mary E. Ellzey b. 10/31/1860, d. 6/11/1930, md. 1) John W. Bishop b. 1855, d. 1880; md. 2) Daniel Zaborn Magee b. 1863, d. 1934
   4) Victoria Ellzey b. 1863, d. 1953, md. Wesley H. Bullock b. 1858, d. 1928
   5) Sarah M. Ellzey b. 10/14/1865, d. 10/12/1948, md. Jacob Haverson Magee b. 1865, d. 1926
   6) Wesley Harrison Ellzey b. 10/21/1867, d. 6/28/1907, md. in 1890 to Carrie Josephine Thomas b. 1869, d. 1954
   7) Caroline Vertna Ellzey b. 1/6/1870, d. 9/10/1936, md. 11/14/1889 to John Thomas Richmond b. 1867, d. 1945
d) Jesse K. Brumfield b. ca. 1836, md. Elizabeth Jane Harvey and had issue:
   1) Jesse Brumfield b. 1/30/1877, md. 12/6/1903 to Charles Morgan Davis b. 1875, d. 1903
   2) Claude Brumfield md. Fannie Sandifer
   3) Lovie Brumfield b. 7/9/1875, d. 9/1963, md. Dr. Jesse K. Ball
e) Mary (Polly) A. Brumfield b. ca. 1838, md. Edwin May of Johnson's Station.
f) William Henry Harrison Brumfield b. ca. 1840/41, d. 6/22/1931 at Beauvoir Hospital on Gulf Coast at age 90; md. Catherine (Kitty) Conerly on 8/6/1863. They were married for 67 years.
g) Elizabeth Brumfield b. 11/18/1842, d. 2/25/1862.
h) Henrietta Angeline Brumfield b. 1846, d. 1906, md. ca. 1868 to Jabez Newton Conerly b. 1847, d. 12/24/1898 near Spring Creek, La., and had issue:
   1) Lizzie Conerly b. 8/26/1869, d. 4/1/1901, md. ca. 1899 to James A. Dixon b. 12/16/1861, d. 1/14/1902
   2) Thomas Byron Conerly b. 3/31/1874 at Columbia, Miss., d. 9/3/1965 at Spring Creek; md. 1) Nettie Frances McDaniel b. 1874, d. 1901; 2) Arie Varnado in 1902. She was b. 1878 and d. 1919. He md. 3) 12/1922 to Bertha McDaniel.

Isaac Brumfield and Elizabeth Holmes Brumfield

   3) Cullen Conerly (named for his grandfather Conerly) b. 1876, d. 1908, not married.
   4) Watt Smiley Conerly b. 1/28/1880, d. 12/23/1960, buried at Spring Creek; md. 3/7/1901 to Corine Frances McDaniel b. 9/25/1879, d. 6/24/1947
   5) Owen Columbus "Doc" Conerly b. 4/1885, d. 4/7/1922 at Osyka, md. 1908 to Fannie Thompson b. 12/23/1890, d. 8/1952, buried at Osyka.

8) Berry Ann Holmes (a son) b. ca. 1809 in Ga., d. ca. 1860, not married.

9) Jesse Holmes (dates unknown) md. 5/8/1845 to Nancy Sumrall and had several children, all of whom died young. Jesse md. 2) Melissa Duncan and had:
a) Cancy Holmes md. Mece Carter and lived near Brockdale, La.
b) George Holmes

10) Virginia (called Jenny and Jane) Holmes b. ca. 1797 in Ga. (and one of the

older children), md. 1/25/1818 to Willis Brumfield b. ca. 1794, d. 10/16/1833. He served as a corporal in the 12/23th Consolidated Regt. La. Inf. at the famed Battle of New Orleans in January, 1815. They lived in Washington Parish, La., at the time of Willis's death in 1833. Issue:
a) Margaret Brumfield b. 2/9/1819, d. 9/8/1885, md. John Seaborn Alford (See family under Alford)
b) John Griffin Brumfield b. 1820, d. 9/1849 (age 27 of pneumonia), md. Louisa Bullock, dau. of Hugh and Carolina Brumfield Bullock and had:
   1) Cynthia Jane Brumfield b. and d. in 1849
   2) John G. Brumfield b. 2/16/1850, d. 4/27/1936, not married
c) Elisha Brumfield b. 5/23/1822, d. 1860, md. 1/15/1845 to Salena Arvozena Jane Warner b. 8/14/1829, d. 6/9/1911. They had issue:
   1) Mary Jane Goodridge Brumfield b. 1846, d. 1884, md. 1) Tom Hinson, 2) Wm. Chalender
   2) Nancy Louisa Brumfield b. 6/2/1848, d. 1/12/1918, not married
d) Sarah Brumfield b. 4/9/1824, md. ca. 1843 to Calvin Smith, son of Jeremiah Smith and JoAnne Holly (?). Calvin was b. 9/22/1812. Issue:
   1) Jeremiah Smith b. 1844
   2) Margaret (Martha?) E. Smith b. 1845
   3) Emily M. Smith b. 1847
   4) Cynthia A. Smith b. 1848
   5) Wyatt R. Smith b. 1849
   6) Cecelia Smith (Sintha) b. 1853
   7) Caroline J. Smith b. 1856
   8) John W. Smith b. 1858
   9) Jackson C. Smith b. 1859
   10) Jessie Smith b. 1860
   11) Davis E. Smith b. 1862 in La.
   12) George N. Smith b. 1863
   13) Sarah L. Smith b. 1866
e) Isaac Nelson Brumfield b. 11/10/1823, d. 10/6/1909 in Pike Co. (now Walthall), md. Sarah JoAnn Smith, dau. of Eli Smith and Ann Crews, b. 11/23/1836, d. 8/1/1929, buried Foil Cemetery, Walthall Co., Miss. They had issue:
   1) James Monroe Brumfield b. 12/24/1854, d. 11/22/1896, md. 1) Cynthia Shivers; 2) ___
   2) Jesse Eli Brumfield b. 6/29/1857, d. 5/12/1952, buried at China Grove, md. Mary (Mollie) Ellzey b. 1858, d. 1929. They had 12 children.
   3) Lenora Elizabeth Brumfield b. 1/29/1860, md. Louis Rowell
   4) Margaret Jane Brumfield b. 4/13/1862, d. 2/20/1937, md. 3/11/1878 to Samuel Matthew Foil b. 1848, d. 1926
   5) Lucy Ann Brumfield b. 6/18/1864, d. 8/25/1934, md. Walter Monroe "Buddy" Foil b. 1860, d. 1947
   6) Richard Silman Brumfield b. 3/31/1867, d. 8/17/1949, md. 1/29/1902 to Nora Fitzpatrick b. 1/20/1882, d. 4/13/1969
   7) Joseph Davis Brumfield b. 12/20/1869, md. Annie Quinn
   8) Alexander Griffin Brumfield b. 4/12/1873, d. 9/29/1963, md. Netie Aramanthia Conerly
   9) Samuel Omelia Brumfield b. 1/15/1876, d. 3/13/1963, buried Foil Cemetery near Salem, Walthall Co.; md. 1) Liza McKenzie, 2) Lestie Smith, 3) Edith Pigott
   10) Lottie Irene Brumfield b. 4/6/1879, d. 10/16/1908, md. 2/23/1906 to Jesse Monroe Conerly
f) Josiah Brumfield b. 3/2/1827, in Washington Parish, La., d. 8/4/1897, md. Margaret Burch and had issue:
   1) Pamela Jane Brumfield b. 11/27/1853, d. 2/12/1925, md. Jason Whittington
   2) John Wesley Brumfield b. 4/20/1857, d. 4/17/1940, md. Laura Fatima "Timey" Burkhalter
   3) Melissa Brumfield b. ca. 1859, died young
   4) Uriah Brumfield b. ca. 1861, md. Lucy Rebecca Bickham, widow of Alexander Haverson Brock
   5) Willis Dawston Brumfield b. 7/3/1863, d. 6/30/1947, md. 1) Eliza Alice Simmons b. 1870, d. 1905, md. 2) Mrs. Alice Lenore Brock Pierce
   6) Elisha Thomas Brumfield b. 11/19/1865, d. 11/15/1952, md. Courtney Smith, dau. of Tom Smith and Thissa Ann Magee
   7) Josiah Brumfield b. ca. 1867, md. Maggie Crowe and lived in Washington Par., La.
   8) Margaret Amanda Brumfield b. 5/21/1870, d. 9/17/1946, md. Jeptha J.

Miller b. 1857, d. 1932
9) Isaac Richard Brumfield d. 1954 in Abbeville, La.
g) William Brumfield b. 1/5/1829 (possibly), md. Sarah Lewis and was buried at Beulah Baptist Church, Tangipahoa Par., La.
h) Axa (?) Jane Brumfield b. 5/2/1831 (could be the one called Nanny), not married.
i) Charles Dawson Brumfield b. 3/27/1832
j) Willis Nathaniel Brumfield b. 3/31/1834 in Washington Par., La., d. 12/21/1895 in Pike Co., Miss., md. Nancy E. Haley b. 1/15/1837, d. 12/27/1910. Issue:
  1) Priscilla Jane Brumfield b. 1857
  2) Mary Ellen Brumfield b. 10/25/1858
  3) M. Dawson Brumfield b. 11/2/1860
  4) Josiah Brumfield b. 1863
  5) William Isaac Brumfield b. 1/22/1864
  6) Sarah Brumfield b. 9/16/1866
  7) Willis Easley Brumfield b. 6/21/1867
  8) John E. Brumfield b. 2/29/1870
  9) Charles Brumfield b. 2/17/1874
  10) Henry J. Brumfield b. 1/13/1875
  11) Jesse Davis Brumfield b. 2/5/1877
  12) Effie Brumfield b. 10/11/1878
Virginia or Jane Holmes, widow of Willis Brumfield, md., after the latter's death, on 8/24/1844 to Nazareth (Nisra) Faust b. ca. 1810 (and many years his wife's junior). No known issue.

11) Cynthia Holmes b. 1804, d. 7/10/1884, md. 11/23/1823 in Pike Co., Miss., to Davis Brumfield b. 1795 in S.C., d. 4/23/1863, son of John Brumfield and Margaret Kelly (buried in the Davis Brumfield Cemetery near Tylertown but no markers). Issue:
a) Elijah Brumfield b. ca. 1826 in La.
b) John Brumfield b. 11/8/1830, d. 3/25/1896, md. 1) Mary Josephine James b. 1836, d. 1879, and had 10 children:
  1) James Wesley Brumfield b. 10/18/1855, md. Mary Jane Allen (buried at Lexie, Miss.)
  2) William T. Brumfield b. 7/30/1857, d. 3/7/1941, md. Laura Ophelia Rushing b. 1874, d. 1954
  3) Davis Alexander Brumfield b. 1/13/1860, d. 8/22/1929, md. Millie Ann Lucinda Rushing
  4) Myra M. Brumfield b. 1/17/1862, md. James Sims
  5) John Brumfield b. 5/15/1864, d. 8/23/1915, md. Serena Rushing
  6) Monroe H. Brumfield b. 10/25/1866, d. 1936, md. Leola Rushing
  7) Syntha Rosaline Brumfield b. 3/6/1869, md. James Wm. Griffin (buried in Magnolia)
  8) Emma Brumfield b. 7/5/1871, md. George Stewart (buried at China Grove)
  9) Chester C. Brumfield b. 1/25/1874, d. 7/28/1935, md. 1) Selina Morris, 2) Lilly C. Johnson
  10) Cora B. Brumfield b. 8/30/1877, d. 4/19/1963, md. Claude E. Johnson
John Brumfield md. 2) on 10/21/1881 to Angeline Bullock and had issue:
  11) Leslie Brumfield b. 7/27/1882, md. 1) Florence Magee, 2) Lezzie Bunnings
c) William Brumfield b. ca. 1833
d) Emily Brumfield b. 2/6/1835, d. 7/23/1914, md. Jordon Ginn, son of Huriah and Salena Ann Smith Ginn, b. 1830, d. 1914. Issue:
  1) Margaret E. Ginn b. ca. 1854, md. Charlie McManus
  2) Huey Ginn b. ca. 1856, md. in 1882 to Victoria Lewis b. 1857, d. 1927, and had 8 daughters
  3) Sarah Corene Ginn b. 12/25/1857, d. 4/11/1912, md. John Sims Morris
  4) Cynthia Talitha Ginn b. 1860, d. 1913, md. Jim W. Allen. No issue.
  5) Eliza Ginn b. 10/8/1865, d. 11/19/1952, md. Jesse O. Spence b. 1873, d. 1940
  6) Quitman Davis Ginn b. 1869, d. 3/15/1956, md. Mrs. Mollie Regan Conerly
  7) Jordan J. Ginn, not married
  8) Georgia Ann Ginn b. 1/15/1874, d. 5/1958, md. 1) Louis Rowell, md. 2) Joe Cothern
  9) Lafayette "Doc" Ginn b. 5/11/1877, md. Eugenia Graham b. 1882, d. 1956

[For a complete history of the Ginn family see: Ginns & Their Kin by Marie Luter Upton.]
e) Eveline Brumfield b. 8/8/1837, d. 1/20/1922 (buried at New Zion), md.
1) 10/20/1853 to Zabon F. Davis b. 10/27/1833, d. 4/18/1863. Issue:
  1) James Rayford Davis md. Susan Fortenberry
  2) Cynthia Davis b. 1/25/1860, d. 11/1940, md. Thomas Pigott b. 1857, d. 1929
  3) Franklin Davis b. 1/25/1863, d. 1/11/1934, md. Ida Holmes
  4) Angeline Davis md. Charles Magee
[See this family more complete in Luter, Davis and Allied Families by Marie Luter Upton.]
Eveline Brumfield Davis md. 2) Sam Pinkerton.
f) Angeline Brumfield b. 8/8/1837 (said to have been a twin to Eveline), d. 7/8/1866, md. on 5/19/1857 to Joel J. Bullock b. 2/4/1834. Issue:
  1) Emma Elizabeth Bullock b. 11/5/1859, d. 9/23/1873
  2) Myra Ophelia Bullock b. 7/18/1861, d. 3/13/1944, md. 10/5/1884 to V. Jones Greer.
[See this family more complete in Bullock, Twigs and Branches by Marie Luter Upton.]
g) Elisha Kelly Brumfield b. 12/1/1840, d. 11/25/1911 (buried at New Zion), md. 1) Lamenda Smith, dau. of Jarred Smith, and had 3 children:
  1) George W. Brumfield b. 1869, d. 1887
  2) Ida Brumfield b. 3/26/1871, md. Marcus Graves
  3) Emma Narcissa Brumfield b. 1874, d. 1876
  Elisha md. 2) Nancy Fortenberry, widow of William Willis, and had issue:
  4) Kelly Calvin Brumfield b. 7/13/1878, d. 12/23/1959, md. Louisa Magee
  5) Cynthia Louisa Brumfield b. 1/28/1879, md. Herbert Davis
  Elisha md. 3) Sarah Corinne Simmons, dau. of James Jackson Simmons, b. 5/11/1853, d. 9/14/1928, and had an additional 6 children:
  6) Addie Angeline Brumfield b. 4/16/1883, md. Robert Monroe Fortenberry
  7) Ella Edith Brumfield b. 4/16/1886, d. 8/26/1941, md. Jesse L. Simmons
  8) Lucy Leota Brumfield b. 12/11/1887, md. Walter Lewis
  9) Sarah L. O. Brumfield b. 7/14/1890, d. 1/1/1937, md. Luther Alford
  10) Albert Davis Brumfield b. 4/27/1892, md. Ellis Blackwell
  11) Annie Lee Brumfield b. 8/3/1894, md. Eudean Blackwell.
h) Isaac Preston Brumfield b. 3/5/1843, d. 10/26/1921, md. George Ann McClendon b. 1853, d. 1931 and had issue:
  1) Mattie Estell Brumfield b. 9/7/1872, md. 12/16/1891 to Charles E. Pigott b. 1866, d. 1902
  2) William Preston Brumfield b. 4/27/1874, md. Beulah Pigott
  3) Fred Lafayette Brumfield b. 1/1/1876, md. Alice Caldwell
  4) Minnie Louise Brumfield b. 7/26/1878, md. J. Dort Smith
  5) Dudley Clarence Brumfield b. 11/20/1881, md. 1) Frances McCain, md. 2) Montoria Pittman
  6) Florence Caturah Brumfield b. 11/5/1883, md. William Patton
i) Jesse E. Brumfield b. 3/4/1845, d. 12/6/1918 (buried at old Jap Holmes place out from Tylertown), md. Clara Cumire, dau. of Winston Smith, in 1873. She was b. 1855, d. 1931. They had issue:
  1) Eliza L. Brumfield b. 9/9/1875, d. 1/25/1943, md. Felder Fortenberry b. 1869, d. 1951
  2) William Davis Brumfield b. 7/5/1878, d. 12/14/1941, md. Sarah Fortenberry
  3) Zonetta E. Brumfield b. 1/6/1880, d. 2/27/1949, md. John Brumfield
  4) Linnie Brumfield b. 9/9/1881, d. 10/24/1971, md. 1) James Stallings, 3) Willie Alford
  5) Eula Brumfield b. 1/23/1885, d. 11/28/1959, md. Henry Ginn
  6) Leslie Brumfield b. 4/16/1887, d. 9/3/1903, not married
  7) Beulah Brumfield b. 6/20/1889, d. 3/25/1947, md. Freddie Fortenberry
  8) Fannie Brumfield b. 11/5/1891, d. 4/23/1954, md. 1) Marshall Reagan, 2) Herman Myers
  9) Willis R. Brumfield b. 1/28/1894, d. 4/28/1868, md. Ollis Blackwell
  10) Jesse Lee Brumfield b. 5/19/1896, d. 12/24/1868, md. George Kaigler
  11) Ellis Brumfield b. 6/25/1899, md. Nellie May Pittman
j) Louisa Brumfield b. ca. 1847, md. William M. Parker and had issue:
  1) Miley Parker md. 1) Monroe Boyd, 2) Billy J. Pigott
  2) Sarah Victoria Parker b. 11/19/1868, d. 3/20/1960, md. Dewitt David Ginn
k) Cynthia Brumfield b. 10/11/1850, d. 8/28/1889 (not given on list of

children by Katie Holmes, but added by deduction by Alma Dell Magee Clawson). She md. Tommy Pigott and had issue:
1) Martha Pigott md. Clint Stogner
2) Eva Pigott md. Esley Stogner
3) Lena Pigott md. ___ Strickland
4) Sarah Pigott md. Archie Mitchell
5) Elinore Pigott
6) Mary Pigott
7) Georgia Pigott md. Otis Alford
8) John Pigott
9) Jesse Pigott
l) James Brumfield killed in an accident while riding a horse. He is a possible son of Cynthia Holmes Brumfield. He md. Sarah Ann Breland and had issue:
1) Nancy Jane Brumfield md. Joseph Stephtoe Pigott
m) Davis Brumfield

[For a complete picture of the Brumfield Family see: Fields of Broom: John Brumfield and Margaret Kelly, Their Ancestors and Descendants, by Alma Dell Magee Clawson, 4636 Rosalia Drive, New Orleans, LA 70127.]

KEMP

The 1816 Census of Pike County lists one Brandford Kemp. It is believed that Brandford (Bradford) Kemp was then a resident in St. Tammany Parish, Louisiana. They settled on the dry prong of Little Silver Creek in 1812. They purchased property from William G. and Martha Wheat in that year. The Wheats then removed to Hancock County, Mississippi. Depositions on this differ.

In one deposition now in the Louisiana State Land Office, William Pace, a Justice of the Peace during this period, stated that Bradford Kemp moved from the state of Mississippi to the waters of Silver Creek, now the parish of Washington, Louisiana, in 1816. The document was dated 2nd day of June, 1824.

Bradford was enumerated on the 1820 Census of Washington Parish. He was listed as J. Kemp. He had been known as John in Georgia before his removal to Mississippi.

Circa 1830, Bradford Kemp served Washington Parish as a Justice of the peace. His signature was found on many documents of this period in the State Land Office.

This compiler has been unable to determine the ancestry of Bradford Kemp. Some genealogists of the present generation state that he is the son of Thomas Camp and Nancy Tarpley. Thomas Camp died in the area that is now Walton County, Georgia. Thomas Kemp, son of Bradford, the only living son in 1880, stated on that census that his father was born in South Carolina. It had been a legend in the family that he was from Scotland. Bradford's older children were born in Georgia.

The family of Bradford Kemp and Drusilla Campbell (?):
1) Nancy Kemp b. 10/30/1797 in Ga., or S.C., md. by 1825 to Redmond Carter b. 1795 in Ga. (according to 1850 Census). Carter had md. 1) in 5/1818 St. Tammany Parish, La., to Patience Pace. Nancy and Redmond d. in Sabine Parish. Issue:
a) William Redmond Carter b. ca. 1825, md. 7/10/1845 to Eliza Jane Moore
b) D. R. Carter b. ca. 1826
c) Bradford Carter b. 8/3/1832, d. 12/27/1899, md. 10/1/1857 to Sarah Ann Loving in Sabine Parish, La., b. 7/24/1837, d. 10/9/1865. Issue:
1) Sarah Elizabeth Carter b. 9/1/1864, d. 2/19/1926, md. 7/24/1881 to Acey Jefferson Stroud b. 4/26/1856, d. 1/25/1898 in Sabine Parish, La. (buried Beulah Cemetery in Many Valley)
2) Benjamin Bradford Carter b. 1/21/1860, d. 3/20/1906, md. 12/11/1880 to Della Russell
3) William Kemp Carter b. 4/25/1862, d. 12/28/1871
d) James Carter b. ca. 1843
e) Patience Carter b. 1844, d. 9/1849
Bradford Carter and wife were buried in the Carter Burial Ground, Carter House, Sabine Parish, La.

2) John Taylor Kemp b. in Ga. or S.C., d. at Sunny Hill, La., 4/17/1877, md. ca. 1837 to Mary Roberts, widow of Phillip Turner b. in N.C. 9/16/1804, d. 5/10/1874. Issue:
   a) Isaac Kemp b. 7/3/1838, d. 7/14/1886 in Sunny Hill, La., CSA, md. on 12/30/1865 to Samantha Ann Davis b. 12/25/1844, d. 12/24/1936. Issue:
      1) John Morgan Kemp b. 10/21/1866, d. 1944 (buried at Mt. Pisgah Baptist Church, Washington Par., La.), md. 12/21/1894 to Rose Westmoreland d. 1944
      2) Ida O. Kemp b. 4/1/1868, d. 8/31/1916, md. 2/2/1885 to Charlie E. Bickham
      3) Alice A. Kemp b. 3/9/1870, md. 4/18/1888 to J. D. Carson
      4) Etta M. Kemp b. 7/27/1872, d. 7/30/1873
      5) Andrew D. Kemp b. 5/27/1874, md. 1) 12/27/1899 to Emma Magee 1879-1923, 2) Mary Wood
      6) Lula A. Kemp b. 9/29/1876, md. 12/31/1896 to G. W. Smith
      7) Luther E. Kemp b. 7/12/1879, d. 9/6/1891
      8) Minnie Estelle Kemp b. 11/4/1881, d. 1/23/1946, md. 1/24/1900 to Samuel Warren Wilkes b. 3/30/1875, d. 3/31/1950
      9) Ella Beel Kemp b. 3/16/1884, md. 10/11/1905, to M. A. Smith
   b) Thomas Kemp b. 6/10/1840, d. 7/21/1861 at muster for CSA service--had he lived he would have been a private in Co. I, 9th La. Inf. He was buried at old Kemp Cemetery, Sunny Hill, La.
   c) Joseph Kemp b. 4/21/1842 in Sunny Hill, d. 7/2/1919 in Walnut Springs, Texas, md. 1/1875 to Leila Delamore Stamps b. 1856, d. 1928. Issue:
      1) John Franklin Kemp b. 12/15/1876, d. 12/18/1947, md. Augusta Harslock
      2) Mary (Mae) Kemp b. 12/16/1878, md. 10/15/1902 to Robert Emmette Martin b. 1871, d. 1942, lived at Palestine, Texas
      3) Annie Jeff Kemp b. 5/26/1880, d. 1882
      4) Joseph Israel Kemp b. 2/25/1882, d. 1952 in Waco, Tex., md. Pearl Hampton
      5) Albert Edward Kemp b. 12/7/1886, d. 4/13/1891
      6) Threat Isaac Kemp b. 9/27/1890, d. 1919 while a student at Naval Academy, Annapolis, Md.
      7) Dennis Edwin Kemp b. 9/23/1888, d. 2/16/1954, md. 10/18/1918 to Vera Annapolis Barry b. 10/12/1893
      8) Fannie Belle Kemp b. 11/19/1875, d. 6/7/1905, md. Alonzo Sheppard
   d) Drusilla Kemp b. 6/6/1844, d. 10/28/1926, md. 12/12/1865 to Charles Bluford Seale b. 5/13/1839, d. 8/3/1927 (buried on old home place on Silver Creek between Mt. Herman and Clifton, La.). Issue:
      1) Lizzie I. Seale b. 10/26/1867, d. 7/5/1908, md. J. M. White
      2) Ella (Mary Ella) Seale b. 8/3/1870, d. 12/31/1900, md. J. Leon Sharp
      3) Charles Rudolph Seale b. 3/20/1874, d. 1941
      4) F. A. Seale b. 10/17/1879
      5) Allie C. Seale b. 7/24/1882, d. in California in 1970's
      6) Arthur M. Seale b. 10/28/1885
   e) Celia Kemp b. 11/25/1846, d. 1942, md. for a short time to ___ Gill. No issue. Buried Carter Cemetery, Sunny Hill, La.

3) Elihu Kemp b. 7/28/1801, d. after 1860 (on Census that year). Not married.

4) Mary Kemp b. 8/8/1805, md. Alfred L. Watkins. In Washington Parish, La., as late as 1838 when Bradford Kemp died. By 1840 Census in Natchitoches Par. Census: 1 male between 30-40; 2 f 10-15; and 1 f 30-40

5) William Kemp b. 12/29/1807, d. in old age in Marion Co., Miss., md. ___ and had issue:
   a) Martha (called Patsey) Kemp

6) Caroline Matilda Kemp b. 11/1809 at Sunny Hill, d. 2/29/1865 in Sabine Par., La., md. 3/23/1843 to Nicholas Jack b. 10/7/1816, d. 4/27/1875 in Pineland, Tex. Issue:
   a) Andrew Franklin Jack b. 12/17/1854, d. 10/11/1878
   b) Martha Eveline Jack b. 6/15/1845, d. 4/16/1881, md. 12/3/1871 to George W. Whitehead
   c) Amelia Elizabeth Jack b. 2/22/1847, d. 1/7/1938, md. James Amberson Cooper
   d) Mary Drusilla Jack b. 2/1849, md. 1877 to Louis A. Jordan
   e) Nicholas Warren Jack b. 11/1/1851, d. 2/23/1889

7) Thomas Kemp b. 6/8/1812, d. 1886 in Sunny Hill, La., md. ca. 1838 to Sidney Turner b. 5/11/1822, d. 1/26/1900, dau. of Phillip Turner and Mary Roberts. Issue:
   a) Mary Jane Kemp b. 2/21/1839, d. after Civil War.
   b) Elijah Kemp b. 6/8/1840, md. in 1872 to Lacy Alford, dau. of ___ Alford and ___ Lewis. Issue:
      1) Wyatt Kemp b. 11/12/1872, md. Martha Brady
      2) Emma Kemp b. 5/24/1874, not married
      3) Rosa Kemp b. 2/6/1876, md. T___ Dodd
      4) Carry (Carrie or Carey?) Kemp b. 8/22/1878, md. Fannie Griffith
      5) Anne Cirdelia Kemp b. 5/28/1880, md. Yearli Batton
      6) Alice Ophelia Kemp b. 5/28/1880, md. Buck Barton
      7) Joel D. Kemp b. 9/13/1882, md. Irene Terrell (Turell?)
      8) Ivy Kemp b. 4/24/1885, md. Callie Terrell (Turell?)
      9) Eley Kemp b. 4/24/1885, d. 1886
      10) Clara L. Kemp b. 5/10/1887, md. George Carter
      11) Robert L. Kemp b. 2/22/1889
   c) Thomas Green Kemp b. 12/25/1841, d. CSA, md. Nancy Strickland and had issue:
      1) William Wesley Kemp b. ca. 1873 (or 1871?)
      2) George W. Kemp b. 4/3/1873, md. 11/10/1901 to Lucy Lillian Toney b. 8/27/1879
      3) Clancy V. Kemp b. ca. 1877
      4) Charles D. Kemp
      5) Ella D. Kemp
      6) Cauley Kemp d. in his 90's in Bogalusa, La. He was a retired RR worker.
      7) Mary Kemp
      8) Ben Kemp
   d) Fanny Eveline Kemp b. 4/10/1846, d. 12/17/1932, md. G. W. Pierce (buried at Pleasant Hill Church, Sunny Hill, La. Issue:
      1) Rosa Lee Pierce b. 10/17/1877, d. 4/6/1964, md. William H. Pettit
   e) Harriet Kemp b. 5/2/1848, d. 1923/4 in New Orleans
   f) John Kemp b. 3/7/1854, died as a young boy
   g) James Kemp b. 3/7/1854, d. 1942, md. 1/30/1879 at the home of Hines Newsom in Tangipahoa Par., La., to Alice Carpenter Newsom b. 1857, d. 3/8/1892. James is buried in Hayes Creek Church Cemetery; Alice, in the old Beulah Church Cemetery. Issue:
      1) Sidney Ann Kemp b. 11/27/1879, died young
      2) Flossy Leander Kemp b. 11/10/1881, d. 12/1964, md. Charlie Rogers
      3) Maggie Lorraine Kemp b. 2/21/1883, md. Alonzo Calvin Smith b. 4/3/1872, d. 9/17/1950
      4) Melissa Ophelia Kemp b. 1/14/1885, md. Alcus Jerry Smith b. 1881, d. 1928
      5) Ruby Coteel Kemp b. 6/16/1887, d. 3/24/1897
      6) Thomas Burlin Kemp b. 7/16/1889, d. 1890
      7) Frances Ellen Kemp b. 3/15/1891, md. Oscar A. Foil b. 11/9/1884, d. 5/22/1954
   h) Samuel Kemp b. 7/7/1856, d. 7/8/1940, md. 12/12/1879 to Clara Duval (Della) Newsom b. 8/2/1865, d. 6/21/1936. Issue:
      1) Quency Edward Kemp b. 5/5/1881, d. 12/20/1955, md. 1) Dicey Bambert, 2) Ally Easterling
      2) Ora Victoria Kemp b. 10/3/1883, d. 1969, md. 11/11/1900 to Elijah Augustus Carter b. 1869, d. 1931
      3) Milton Jones Kemp b. 4/5/1888, d. 1977, md. 1) 4/4/1907 to Lien Schillings, 2) Maud Blackwell
      4) Lillie Belle Kemp b. 6/22/1888, d. 1952, md. T. C. Rhodus
      5) Riplon Waller Kemp b. 7/9/1890, d. 11/1976, md. 1910 to Mattie Brock.
      6) Una Eva Kemp b. 6/26/1895, md. in 1913 to Oscar Denton Morris
      7) Elva Finley Kemp b. 12/16/1900, d. 11/2/1913
      8) Velma Ozy Kemp b. 1/19/1907, md. 4/22/1922 to Ernest Russ Williams
   i) Sidney Ann Kemp b. 12/24/1858, d. after 1870 while still young
   j) Ann (Aner) Clarinda Kemp b. 5/26/1861, md. J. F. Westrope and had:
      1) Mae Westrope md. ___ Stuart
      2) Della Westrope b. 7/20/1888, md. Jesse Hutchinson of Kentwood, La.
      3) Gettie Westrope b. 4/24/1892, md. 11/23/1909 to T. R. Strickland
      4) Steletta Westrope b. 4/15/1894, md. Leo Hartmen of Monroe, La.
   k) Philip Bradford Kemp b. 12/11/1864, d. 3/14/1954, md. on 10/7/1891 to Sarah Ella Breland b. 9/4/1868, d. 10/11/1903. Issue:

1) Owen Sylvester Kemp b. 2/14/1893, d. 12/12/1951, md. Lucy Alford
2) Myrtie Mae Kemp b. 5/6/1894, not married
3) Artie Virginia Kemp b. 9/6/1895, d. 1/21/1915
4) Alta Eugenia Kemp b. 9/7/1897, d. 3/24/1968, md. 12/24/1929 to Fred E. Compton
5) Winnie Edwena Kemp b. 2/14/1899, md. David Caldwell Brumfield
6) Homer Bryan Kemp b. 2/27/1902, md. 3/7/1942 to Lillie Keaton
7) Sidney Granberry Kemp b. 10/8/1903, md. 3/3/1929 to Bevie Gerald
1) Hosea Kemp b. 5/18/1868, d. in Texas, md. and had issue:
   1) Wyman Kemp

8) Drusilla Kemp b. in 1814--went west to live with her sisters, supposedly never married.

LEE

There were several Lee families in the area of Marion and Pike Counties, Mississippi, which seem to have little, if any, kinship. The line under consideration stems from one John Lee who appeared in old Chowan Precinct, North Carolina, ca. 1694.

John Lee, as proved by a subsequent deed, was dead in Bertie Co., N.C., by 1739--where he left a will which did not survive. His children (John's) are proved as follows:
1) Chowan Deed Bk. G, p. 354--Joshua Lee sold to Samuel Lee for 30 barrells of lawful tarr, land beginning on the land that was Godfrey Lee's . . . being part of a patent formerly granted to John Lee on 4/7/1694. Wits: Simon Pope, Arthur Lee, and Joshua Lee. Regt. 1/25/1755
2) Chowan Deed Bk. G, p. 356--8/8/1754, Chowan Co., N.C., William Lee of Bertie Co., sells to Samuel Lee, son & heir of Godfrey Lee of North Hampton Co., N.C., for 20 £s lawful money of Va., 100 acres in Chowan Co. on NS of Cypress Swamp, beginning at the mouth of Plumb Tree Branch being part of a tract granted to John Lee. Wits: Anne A. Lee, Sampson Pope, Franc^s Lee.

Thus, John Lee had at least two sons, Joshua and William, and was possibly the father of the other Lee men in that area such as Godfrey, Richard, Arthur, and Francis.

Further evidence that Joshua Lee was the son of John came in a Bertie Co., N.C., deed (Bk. E, p. 522) in which Joshua and his wife Mary ___ sell to William Battle of Chowan on 8/22/1739, for 40 £s, 150 acres on NS of Indian Creek Swamp "to the former Virginia line" . . . part of a patent granted John Lee decd. and given by the said John Lee in his last will and Testament to Joshua Lee his son. Wit: Henry Gray, Elisha Williams, jurat, & James Gray. Prvd. Nov. Ct., 1739.

Joshua Lee, b. ca. 1710, md. Mary ___ and was a resident of Edgecombe Precinct (later county) about 1740 and died there ca. 1774 at which time he left a will. Abstract of will: (Edgecombe Wills, VI, p. 75, folio 3) Dated 3/29/1767, died before 4/1774 when will was probated. Children: 1) John Lee--five shillings; 2) Joshua Lee--five shillings; 3) Sarah--five shillings; 4) Elizabeth--five shillings; 5) Ann--five shillings; 6) Nancy--five shillings; 7) Mary. Grandchildren: Ann Watson--a cow, calf, and a yearling heifer. Wife (as of 1767) Eleanor. Wits: Benjamin Brand, Charles Lee, and David Lee.

Of Joshua's children, John left a will in Robecon Co., N.C., in 1792 in which he named a wife Rebecca and the following children: Shadrack, Mary Rozar (mother of Rebecca Rozar), Jerina Jackson, Rebecca Kinlaw, and Elizabeth Bullard (mother of Shadrack). Wits. were: Ralph Regan, Olive Regan, Margaret Sims.

Joshua Lee II, son of Joshua I, b. ca. 1720, d. ca. 1800, md. Mary ___ and had nine children:
1) Jesse Lee I (as proved by a deed of gift in Edgecombe Co., N.C.) b. ca. 1740, d. ca. 1816 in Robeson Co., N.C., md. 1) Miriam Baggett, 2) Treacy ___.
2) Joshua Lee III
3) Stephen Lee (possibly)
4) Abraham Lee (as proved by a deed of gift in Duplin Co., N.C., in 1774)
5) ___ Lee md. ___ Nance (probably Daniel Nance)

6) Benjamin Lee
7) Joseph Lee
8) James Lee
9) Everitt Lee

At the time of Joshua Lee's deed of gift to Jesse in Edgecombe (Edgecombe Co. Deed Bk. 1, p. 224), Joshua claimed to be a resident of Duplin County. The land in question was 100 acres on Contentnea Creek, part of a 600-acre grant to Joshua Lee in 1760, adjoining Jacob Barnes. Wits. were Jacob & William Barnes. The deed was dated 3/19/1762.

Shortly after the above deed, the Lees moved to Bladen County, N.C., ca. 1780 where they remained until the creation of Robeson. Thus, Jesse was listed as a resident of both counties. He was an extensive land dealer and after the turn of the century was a merchant in Lumberton. In 1806 Jesse made his will, a will not probated until 1816 (the presumed year of his death). This will named:
1) Jesse Lee II b. 11/10/1768 (in Edgecombe), d. in Marion Co., Miss., 7/30/1859, md. 1) ca. 1795 to Nancy Lewis b. 2/17/1778, d. in Pike Co., Miss., ca. 1838; md. 2) Jane Graham
2) Elizabeth Lee md. Daniel Drinkwater and had 2 children: John and Keziah
3) Obedience Lee md. ___ Sterling
4) Sarah Lee md. ___ Pope
5) Keziah Lee md. Willis Loe and had a large family--migrated to Mississippi
6) Benjamin Lee b. ca. 1771, d. in Marion Co., Miss., in 1828
7) Rosy Lee (not mentioned in will--probably by 2nd wife)

Numerous members of Jesse Lee's family migrated to Mississippi after Jesse Lee I died in 1816. The family of Jesse Lee II is as follows:
1) Ann Lee b. 12/20/1797, d. 12/28/1856, md. 11/15/1821 to Coleman Nichols
2) Asa Lee b. 1/3/1799 in Robeson Co., N.C., md. 6/9/1824 in Marion Co., Miss., to Martha Ann Applewhite b. 3/17/1804. This family moved from Marion Co., Miss., to Carroll County. Issue:
   a) Benjamin Franklin Lee b. 3/4/1825, d. 10/19/1860, md. 3/11/1846 (or 3/4/1846?) in Copiah Co., Miss., to Nancy Emeline Causey b. 10/12/1830. They had issue:
     1) Jesse Asa Lee b. 1/1847, d. 1847
     2) Sarah Luvinia Ann Lee b. 5/5/1848, d. 10/1853
     3) William Causey Lee b. 12/31/1850, d. 5/12/1867
     4) Martha Jane Lee b. 1/5/1853
     5) DeWitt Clinton Lee b. 11/1854, d. 7/29/1855
     6) Jesse Walter Lee b. 9/11/1856
     7) Benjamin Franklin Lee b. 11/10/1858, md. 9/30/1883 to Fannie Roberts
     8) Mary E. Lee b. 6/6/1861
     9) Hettie Lee (possibly a dau. since her marriage to James M. West 7/21/1867 is recorded in the Benjamin Franklin Lee Bible. Two of their children were: John Franklin b. 5/10/1868 and William Causey b. 5/11/1868
   b) Martha Lee md. John Goss
   c) Eliza Lee md. Cias Rayborn
   d) Elisha Lee, not married, CSA--killed at the Battle of Gettysburg
   e) John Henry Lee md. 12/18/1860 to Susan Harbin
   f) Dewitt Lee md. Lou Shaw
   g) Mary Lee md. ___ Burson
   h) Asa Lee md. Mary Woodell
3) Sallie Lee b. 10/9/1801, died young
4) Benjamin Lee b. 2/28/1804, died young
5) Henry Monroe Lee b. 1/4/1807 in Robeson Co., N.C., d. 4/11/1835 in Carroll Co., Miss., md. 2/2/1829 to Hettie H. Clark, dau. of James Clark, b. between 1810 and 1815 in Marion Co., Miss., d. 4/25/1848 in Pike Co., Miss. Issue:
   a) Benjamin Bryan Washington Lee b. 11/18/1829 in Carroll Co., d. in Marion Co., in 1906, md. Susan Holmes, dau. of Josiah, b. 8/1833, d. 11/8/1916. They had issue:
     1) Lucy Ann Agness Lee md. 12/24/1874 to Walter Julius Cowart
     2) Simon Henry Lee b. 10/8/1856, d. 3/15/1932, md. 1) 9/25/1879 to Ada Adelia Magee b. 3/5/1859, d. 11/30/1905 in Columbia, Miss. Issue:
       a) Stella Wilmuth Lee b. 10/8/1880, 12/13/1963
       b) Myrtie Adeline Lee b. 5/3/1882, d. 3/6/1976, md. 10/3/1907 in Columbia, Miss., to Marcus Lafayette Holmes (1880-1954) and had: Robert Sidney Wendell Holmes, Ada Lee Holmes O'Quin, Jessie Merle Holmes Dale, Ruth Holmes McHaney, Hazel Virginia Holmes Barnes,

Marcus Lafayette Holmes, Linda Elizabeth Holmes and Patty Louise Holmes Puchacz
c) Susie B. Lee b. 6/21/1884, d. 11/21/1958
d) Nettie May Lee b. 1/1/1886, d. 1/1/1886
e) John Walter Lee b. 3/1/1887, d. 12/1963
f) Beatrice Sarah Lee b. 6/27/1889, d. 2/20/1956
g) Mattie Belle Lee b. 5/17/1891, d. 12/21/1920
h) Ella Lee b. 1/21/1893, d. 11/1919
i) Lottie Lee b. 12/9/1895, d. 4/30/1965
j) Jewell Lee b. 12/3/1897, d. 10/1925
k) Robert Edward Lee b. 2/7/1900, d. 7/28/1975
Simon Henry md. 2) Missouria Elmina Forbes b. 2/18/1869, d. 6/11/1915, and had issue:
1) Aileen Lee b. 5/25/1909
Simon Henry md. 3) Narsie Hammond b. 5/11/1886, d. 12/25/1867. They md. on 11/5/1913 and had:
m) Henry Benjamin Lee b. 5/20/1915
n) Doris Lee b. 4/10/1917
o) Frank Marion Lee b. 9/20/1919
p) Dimple Jane Lee b. 3/14/1921

[Much of the family data on the family of Jesse Lee II, especially the section on Henry Monroe Lee, was supplied by Mrs. Roy O'Quin, nee Ada Lee Holmes of Tylertown, Mississippi.]

b) Charlotte Katurah (Lottie) Lee md. Raiford Smith
c) Francis Marion Lee b. 4/26/1832, d. 1/14/1904 in Pike Co., md. 6/11/1857 to Mary Ann Sandifer, dau. of John J. and Nancy Caro Morgan. She was b. 4/1/1839, d. 3/18/1925 (buried in Magnolia, Miss.). They had issue:
1) Nancy Elizabeth Lee died young
2) Henry Monroe Lee md. Lizzie Brumfield
3) Fannie Courtney Lee md. Daniel Julius Ellzey
4) John Jesse (Professor) Lee md. Alice Brumfield
5) Sarah Elizabeth Lee md. John J. Brumfield
6) George Washington Lee md. 1) Bell White, 2) Pinkey Meyer
7) Francis Marion (twin to George E.) Lee, died young
8) Mary Jane (Mollie) Lee md. Thomas James Mitchell
9) Albert Sidney Lee, M.D., md. Mary Musick
10) Robert Eugene Lee md. Jess Emma Brumfield
11) Joseph E. Lee never married
[Note: Francis Marion Lee served in the War Between the States with the Holmesville Guards.]
6) Maesy (Molsie) Lee b. 2/14/1810 in Robeson Co., N.C., md. 1) 11/30/1829 in Marion Co., Miss., to Elisha Applewhite, 2) Andrew Lawrence
7) Obedience Lee b. 8/23/1812 in Robeson Co., N.C., md. 1) 12/17/1828 in Marion Co., Miss., to John Applewhite Jr., md. 2) 10/29/1835 to Hugh Fortenberry
8) Nancy Lee b. 2/10/1815, md. 12/24/1836 to Jacob Pope, Jr., b. 1809 in Mississippi
9) Eliza Lee b. 9/20/1816, md. 1/14/1836 to Eldridge R. Applewhite

Kesiah (Keziah) Lee, dau. of Jesse Lee I, must have pre-deceased her husband Willis Loe (Lowe) who died in Marion Co., Miss., ca. 1829. He left a will (a document which did not name Felix Loe as named in the will of Jesse Lee I) in which he named children:
1) David Loe
2) Willis Loe b. ca. 1804 in N.C., md. Treacy ___ b. ca. 1815 and had (according to the 1850 Census for Marion Co.):
   a) Joseph Loe b. 1834
   b) Nancy Loe b. 1834
   c) Sarah Ann (only S. A. on census) Loe b. 1836
   d) J. W. Loe b. 1840
   e) C___ Loe (dau.) b. 1838
   f) Felix Loe b. 1842
   g) Benjamin Loe b. 1844
   h) Augustus Loe b. 1846
   i) Josephine Loe b. 1849
3) Thomas Loe
4) Benjamin Loe (possibly B. L. Loe on 1850 Marion Co. Census) b. 1816

5) Joseph Stephens Loe
6) Sarah Ann Loe md. ___ Mayer (Myers)
7) Elizabeth Loe md. ___ Grimsby (Grimsley?)
8) Martha Loe md. ___ Herring

NEWSOM

Frederick Newsom was listed as an early settler in Pike County. Very little data has survived on this man. He came to Mississippi from Warren County, Georgia. Prior to 1802 he had married Elizabeth May. In Deed Book B, page 129, of Warren County, Georgia, the following is recorded:

Joseph May of Washington County, Georgia, gives to daughter Elizabeth Newsom 2 Negro boys, Charles & Jacob. Elizabeth was the wife of Frederick Newsom. Witnesses were Isaac Hurt and Joeday Newsom.

Frederick Newsom was the son of Solomon Newsom b. 1745 in Virginia, d. 1804 in Warren County. His mother was Elizabeth. He was a brother to John, Joeday, Solomon, David, Peter, Asa, William, and Nathaniel.

Frederick Newsom received a passport to travel through the Creek Indian Nation on December 21, 1806 (Ga. Passports, p. 18). He first settled on land located on Beaver Creek, December 3, 1807, in Amite, Co., Miss. This settlement of land was for 320 acres.

He claimed property in St. Tammany Parish as well as the above mentioned land. He lost this claim in 1811 for it was sold at sheriff's sale during that year (Conveyance Book 1, St. Tammany Parish, La.).

In Marriage Book A, p. 130, Marion Co., Miss., the marriage of Polly Newsom is listed: James Reed and Polly Newsom--Bondsman: Stephen Ellis; Nov. 27, 1816--Frederick Newsom, father of Polly, consented.

Frederick was counted on the 1810 Census of Amite County, Mississippi. At that time there were 1 free white male over 21, 2 free white males under 21, 1 free white female over 21, 3 free white females under 21.

Frederick was counted on the 1816 Census of Pike County, Miss. The probable children are:

1. Joseph Newsom b. 1795 md. Lavinia Lea (1850 Census for Pike)
Joseph Newsom	55 M	Farmer 1000	Georgia
Lavinia	43 f		Miss.
William W.	25 m		Miss.
Augustus R.	18 m		Miss.
Balis P.	16 m		Miss.
Thaden W.	14 m		Miss.
Martha E.	11 f		Miss.
Mary J.	7 f		Miss.
Ann C.	5 f		Miss.
Emily F.	1 f		Miss.

2. Mary Newsom b. 1787 md. James Reed (1850 Census for Pike)
Mary Reed	43 f	Miss.
Elizabeth	30 f	"
Eleazer	28 m	"
Joseph	26 m	"
Wm.	10 m	"
Lurany	18 f	"
Eliza	21 f	"
Mary	4 f	"
James Page	10 m	"
Larany "	9 f	"

3. William S. Newsom b. 1810 md. Sarah L. ___ (1850 Census of Pike)
William S. Newsom	40 M	Farmer	Miss.
Sarah L.	39 f		"

Edwin	19 m	farmhand	Miss.
Caramelia	15 f		"
Mary	14 f		"
Joseph T.	14 m		"
James W.	10 m		"
John W.	8 m		"
Sarah B.	6 m		"
Nathaniel M.	4 m		"
Daniel T.	2 m		"
Francis J.	6/12 f		"

4. Daughter, name unknown
5. Daughter, name unknown

Elizabeth Newsom was enumerated on the 1850 Census of Pike County, household #376:

Elizabeth Newsom	77 f		S. Carolina
Nancy L. Payne	28 f		Miss.
Thos. "	5 m		"
Mandany "	3 f		"

Under all probability this was the widow of Frederick Newsom. This would have placed her birth year in or near 1773.

In Box 43, pkg. no. 1787, Edgefield Co., S.C., Sarah Newsom, widow of John Newsom, applied for letters of administration for the goods and chattels, rights and credits of his estate, Sept. 23, 1803. On Sept. 23, 1803, Sarah Newsom, Fedrick Newsom, Abraham Richardson and Joseph Day gave bond in the sum of $2000 for Sarah to administer the estate.

The John Newsom mentioned in the paragraph above was a brother to Frederick Newsom. Deed Book B, p. 63, Warren County, Ga., states that Solomon Newsom, Sr., and his sons John and Solomon Newsom sell to David Neal 400 acres granted to Solomon Newsom, Sr., in 1785, then located in Wilkes County. The land was across Little Rocky Comfort Creek. Witnesses were Joeday Newsom, Joel Neal and James McCormick.

John Newsom died in 1803, married Sarah ___ in Warren County, Ga. This union had only two children, Keziah and Moses Newsom.

1) Kesiah Newsom b. 1792, d. 1880, md. 3/12/1812 in Marion County to Samuel Varnado b. 1793. This union lived in Pike County and had at least ten children:
   a) Howell Varnado b. 1820
   b) Charles Varnado b. 1822
   c) Archibald Varnado b. 1824
   d) Newton B. Varnado b. 6/26/1827
   e) Dr. George Washington Varnado b. 2/6/1828
   f) Sophronia Varnado
   g) Meridith Varnado
   h) Sarah Varnado
   i) Matilda Varnado
   j) David Varnado
2) Moses Newsom b. 1794, d. 2/17/1824, md. 3/8/1821 to Martha Singleton b. 8/27/1804, d. 1/15/1864. She was the dau. of Etheldred Singleton and Rhoda Holly of South Carolina. Etheldred was the son of Robert Singleton. Moses was a veteran of the War of 1812, serving as a private in the 12th/13th Consolidated La. Mil. This union lived in St. Helena Par., La., now Tangipahoa. They had 8 children:
   a) Maston Smith Newsom b. 8/22/1822
   b) Berlin Childress Newsom b. 5/24/1824
   c) Kesiah Newsom b. 6/7/1826
   d) Leah Keep Newsom b. 8/17/1832
   e) Rhoda Newsom b. 3/10/1830
   f) Thomas Ripley Newsom b. 10/17/1833
   g) Sarah Newsom b. 8/2/1837
   h) Martha Newsom b. 8/10/1840

Berlin Childress Newsom d. July 13, 1866. He served in the Confederate Cavalry. He married in 1848 to Ann Catherine Tate, dau. of Jesse Tate and Nancy Jackson. This union lived at Tangipahoa. After Berlin's early death, Ann operated a mercantile store in Tangipahoa. Her personal estate was valued at $20,000 on the

1870 Census. This was great wealth for the years after the war. This union had:
   1) Martha (Mattie)Newsom b. 1849, md. J. F. Tull
   2) Hinds Scott Newsom b. 1855, md. Keziah ___
   3) Leah Newsom md. Alfonso Kase
   4) Alice Carpenter Newsom b. 1857, md. James Kemp, son of Thomas
   5) Ida Belle Newsom b. 7/16/1859, md. ___ Sanders
   6) Clara Duval (Della) Newsom b. 8/2/1865, md. Samuel Kemp, son of Thomas and brother to James above.

Sarah Harp Newsom married 2nd James Hughes. He died in St. Helena Parish in 1821. Sarah died in St. Helena in 1854. It is not known how many Hughes children she had.

PIERCE

John Pierce b. 1742, d. 1841, married Abagail ___. The first-known residence of John Pierce and family was in Washington Parish, Louisiana. He purchased the claim of Malcolm Monroe, Jr., on a spring on Pushapattappa Creek prior to 1812. He was enumerated on the 1820 Census of Washington Parish. At that time there was a son 10-16 years; 3 sons 26-45; and he and his wife were over 45 years.

The known family of John Pierce and his wife Abagail:
1) Reuben Pierce b. 1780, d. 1841, married Sarah (Sally) Alford b. 1791
2) Augustus Pierce d. prior to 1850, md. Smithie Thigpen b. 1803, d. 1885. This union lived on the John Pierce place named above. Issue:
   a) Charlotte Pierce b. 1828
   b) Jane Pierce b. 7/1832, d. 2/22/1890
   c) John P. Pierce b. 1834, md. Samantha Blackwell
   d) Cordelia Pierce b. 1838
   e) Eliza Pierce md. ___ Hardy. They had 1 dau., Mary Anne Hardy.
   f) Julia Ann Pierce b. 1846, d. 1916, md. John Strahan
   g) George Washington Pierce b. 5/8/1845, d. 1/12/1924, md. Sarah Ann Rester b. 3/15/1847, d. 5/15/1920
3) Aaron Pierce md. Elizabeth Adams
4) Jesse Pierce b. 1819 (?), md. 1) Elmiry Rogers, 2) Melissa Jenkins. (Buried in the old Hunt Cemetery in the Oak Grove settlement, Washington Parish, La.)
5) Israel Pierce b. 1805, d. ___, md. Jane Rester, widow of Travis Thigpen. (Buried in the Mt. Olive Cemetery near Varnado, La.)

John Pierce was listed as a pensioner on the 1840 Census of Washington Parish, La. He was listed as 98 years old at that time. He was living with his son Augustus (Gus) Pierce. It is presumed that he was buried on the Pushapatappa at his death.

John Pierce and family were members of New Zion Baptist Church in 1823 and 1824. It is not known if they removed to Pike County or if they traveled there for the weekend meetings from their home on the creek named above. By 1830 they were living in Hinds County, Miss. They belonged to the Palestine Church in that county.

This compiler has not been able to establish a Revolutionary record for this John Pierce. To date, the state or country of his origin has not been determined.

POUND/POUNDS

The Pound/Pounds family that lived in Hinds, Copiah, Lawrence, and Marion Counties in Mississippi, as well as Washington and St. Tammany Parishes in Louisiana, were all related and, no doubt, spring from the same South Carolina stem. The Daniel Pound who lived and married in Pike County came to that area from Tennessee but was probably related, distantly, to the people of the same name who had settled in close proximity years before his arrival.

The Pound family is not prolific in South Carolina, as in 1800 only two of the name were enumerated on the census for the state, namely, Peter in Orangeburg and John in Greenville. However, in 1790 there was a John Pound and according to the census figures not the same as the John in Greenville ten years later who lived with a family in Prince George Parish, Georgetown Dist., S.C. Since this family did not appear on the 1800 Census (even though there is the possibility he moved on west), there is the possibility that he died leaving a widow who remarried--and was thus unidentifiable at a later date.

However, in 1810 two Pounds men, presumably brothers, re-appear in what was part of old Prince George Parish, then Marion Co., S.C., named Isom (Isham) and Joseph. There is little doubt that this is the Isom who later moved to Marion Co., Miss., then St. Tammany Par., La., then to Hinds Co., Miss., and back to St. Tammany Parish after 1835. Most of the older children for this Isom declared to have been born in S.C.

The possible family for John Pounds of old Prince George Parish:
1) Isom Pounds b. ca. 1775, d. in 1856 in La.; md. Margaret Parker d. ca. 1861 in Liberty Co., Texas
2) Joseph Pounds b. ca. 1777 in S.C., living in Washington Par., La., in 1820--later went to Lawrence Co., Miss., where he died ca. 1838
3) William Pounds who appeared on the 1820 Census for Washington Parish, La., later migrated with Isom Pounds to Hinds Co., Miss. He disappeared thereafter, but supposedly had a small family.
4) ___ Pounds, a dau., who probably md. Moses Smith and possibly the Moses Smith who appeared on the 1820 Census for Amite Co., Miss.
5) ___ Pounds, a dau., who possibly md. a Lewis since a Lewis witnessed most Pounds deeds in Marion County, S.C.

The Moses Smith mentioned above had to be closely associated with the Pounds family. If he did not marry a sister to the Pounds men, he possibly married their widowed mother--and thus was the step-father to the men Joseph and Isom Pounds. A deed recorded in Marion Co., S.C., Bk. I, p. 239, states that Moses Smith sold to Isom Pounds (spelled Isham in the body of the instrument) for $80, 80 acres where Isham Pounds lived on Gully Branch, ½ of a tract granted to Smith, it being the S. part of sd. tract [which was] to be divided between Isham and Joseph Pounds. It was dated May 11, 1810, witnessed by Joseph Pounds and Jane Harrelson. This Jane Harrelson witnessed two such deeds for the Pounds men.

1) Isom or Isham Pounds b. 1775 in S.C. (75 yrs. old in 1850 Census for St. Tammany Par., La.), d. in 1856 in La. or Liberty Co., Tex.; md. 1802/3 in S.C. to Margaret Parker b. 1786 in S.C., d. 1860 in Liberty Co., Tex., while living with her dau. Minerva Pounds Keller. Issue:
   a) Mary (Polly) Ann Pounds b. 1/16/1804, d. 1854, md. in 1824 in Marion Co., Miss., to Nathaniel Pigott b. 10/21/1796, d. on Poole's Bluff, S. of Bogalusa, La., ca. 1842 from diptheria. Issue:
      1) Nathaniel Pigott b. 3/17/1825, md. Permelia Thigpen Rester
      2) John B. Pigott b. 12/16/1826, md. 5/13/1853 to Frances Rester
      3) Martha Ellen Pigott b. 1829, md. Robert Turnage
      4) Thomas E. Pigott md. Mary Stogner
      5) Eliza Pigott
      6) William J. Pigott b. 5/22/1836
      7) Seaborn Pigott b. 12/24/1838
      8) Margaret Pigott b. 7/30/1842, md. ___ Stogner
   b) A son b. prior to 1810, possibly named Theodore as a man of this name witnessed the marriage of Isom Johnson Pounds in St. Tammany Par., La., 1838.
   c) A dau., name unknown, b. prior to 1810
   d) Margaret L. Pounds b. 1813, md. in Hinds Co., Miss., in 1831, to William Collins b. 1806, lived in St. Tammany Parish in 1850. Issue:
      1) M. L. Collins (dau.) b. 1835, md. ___ Seals
      2) S. J. Collins (son) b. 1836
      3) W. N. Collins (son) b. 1839
      4) M. M. Collins (dau.) b. 1841
      5) J. C. Collins (son) b. 1843
      6) Thomas L. Collins b. 1845
      7) G. E. Collins (dau.) b. 1849
   e) John J. Pounds b. 1814 (or 1824--ages varied on census), d. 1871, md. in Marion Co., Miss., in 1842 to Mary Hennessey b. ca. 1827, lived with family of Isaac Henessey in Washington Par., La., in 1850. Issue:

1) George Washington Pounds b. 1844
2) Dau. Pounds b. 1848 (not named by time of 1850 Census)
f) Isom Johnson Pounds b. 6/10/1815 in S.C., d. 12/26/1875 in Washington Par., La., md. 5/9/1838 to Sarah Matilda Keller b. 6/23/1825 in Marion Co., Miss., d. 3/17/1898 in Lee's Creek, La., the dau. of Henry Keller and Sophia Page. He was a Baptist minister for most of his life. Issue:
   1) Helen Pounds b. 10/18/1844, d. 2/19/1919, md. 11/12/1865 to Martin G. Williams 1838-1911, CSA, and had issue:
      a) Abner Carter Williams (A.C.) b. 9/27/1867, d. 1939, md. 1) Eliza Stewart 1872-1890, 2) Celia Adams 1870-1950
      b) William Johnson Williams (B.J.) b. 2/13/1868, d. 11/1/1931, md. Mary Stewart 1869-1950
      c) Evander Mortimer Williams b. 3/9/1870, d. 7/31/1938, md. 1) Ida Byrd d. 1892, 2) Isabel Cooper 1873-1940
      d) Herdenia Dee Williams b. 1/14/1871, d. 10/19/1954, md. John Mason 1865-1949
      e) Martin Julius (Jules) Williams b. 6/11/1872, d. 6/19/1935, md. Laura Pierce 1876-1935
      f) Walter Ernest Williams b. 6/12/1877, md. 1) Burnette Cooper, 2) Allie Miller b. 1898
      g) Robert Lee Williams b. 9/13/1881, d. 4/1965, md. 1) Florie Rester 1884-1931, 2) Nellie Cooper Paul 1885-1965
      h) John Dutsch Williams b. 4/25/1885, d. 4/1/1950, md. Mary Vera Stewart b. 1900
      i) Belton Betterly Williams b. 6/13/1890, d. 2/17/1968, md. 1) Annie Angeline Mabury d. 1939, 2) Nancy Amacker Seal
      j) Lillie Mae Williams b. 4/22/1888, d. 1968, md. Robert Adams 1887-1952
   2) Miriam Pounds b. 10/31/1846, d. 9/19/1921, md. 11/1/1866 to Stephen R. Poole 1837-1908. No issue.
   3) Sarah Pounds b. 11/29/1848, d. 6/26/1928, md. Andrew J. Seals 1848-1928 and had issue:
      a) Jesse Pierce Seals b. 10/6/1880, md. ___ Jenkins
      b) Filer Seals b. 9/13/1884
   4) Joseph Leon Pounds b. 2/27/1852, d. 8/25/1915, md. Bernette Pierce 1857-1926. Issue:
      a) Inez Pounds b. 1883, d. 1949, md. 1) Charles Davidson, 2) J. B. Chandler
      b) Idalia Pounds b. 1898, md. James Irwin Waller and lived in Nashville, Tenn.
   5) Sophia Pounds b. 4/4/1854, d. in Texas, md. 12/7/1876 to Monroe Jenkins and migrated to Colorado City, Texas. They had issue:
      a) Carlus E. Jenkins b. 8/29/1877
      b) Edna R. Jenkins b. 2/11/1879
      c) Bertha E. Jenkins b. 7/2/1881
      d) Infant, unnamed, born and died 1883
      e) R. S. Jenkins b. 2/1885
   6) Elizabeth "Lizzie" Pounds b. 9/19/1856, d. 1942, md. 1) D. R. Karr, 2) John Jenkins
   7) Linnie Pounds b. 4/27/1859, d. 11/18/1944, md. 12/18/1876 to C. William Magee and had issue:
      a) Gordon Edgar Magee b. 12/24/1878, d. 2/1963, md. Florence Talley
      b) Whit Morris Magee b. 9/4/1882, d. 12/21/1932, md. Mary Jane Talley
      c) Sally Magee b. 3/30/1887, md. Edgar Mizell 1878-1956
      d) Phillip Magee b. 1888, md. 1) Anna Talley, 2) Salena King
      e) Klea Magee b. 1889, md. James F. Jones b. 1888
      f) Alex Johnson Magee b. 6/17/1891, md. Iona Talley
      g) David Magee b. 5/26/1894, md. Nancy Jeanette King b. 1895
      h) Wilson Magee b. 3/8/1896, md. Lula D. King b. 1894
   8) Catherine "Cathie" Pounds b. 7/9/1861, d. 5/21/1904, md. 1/9/1879 to Israel Magee 1861-1942. They had issue:
      a) Ida C. Magee b. 11/11/1880, d. 1/16/1881
      b) Lula Mabel Magee b. 5/3/1882, md. Warren Edgar Byrd 1878-1943
      c) Charles Y. Magee b. 3/17/1884, md. Fannie Josephine Schillings
      d) Stephen Ellis Magee b. 3/1886, md. 1) Leona Talley 1885-1917, 2) Florence Magee Barner 1871-
      e) Henry Elton Magee b. 11/13/1888, d. 11/2/1949 to Bertha Celestine Talley b. 189_

   f) Delos Johnson Magee b. 4/16/1890, md. Sarah Mildred Burkhalter
    b. 1906
   g) Robert Samuel Magee b. 1/31/1892, md. Floyd Ball
  9) Isabella Pounds b. 8/30/1865, d. 9/23/1947, in California, md. 1/3/
   ____ to James Andrew Page and had issue:
   a) Alexander Leak Page b. 9/4/1887, d. 12/4/1938
   b) Kirby Page b. 9/7/1890, in Tyler Co., Tex., lived in LaHabra,
    Calif.; md. Mary Alma Folse
   c) Perry Leon Page b. 7/31/1894
   d) Bessie Page b. 5/16/1898, d. 3/19/1900
 g) Joseph E. Pounds b. 1818, d. 1882 in Marion Co., Miss., also a Baptist
  minister, md. in 1838 in St. Tammany Parish to Elizabeth Keller, sister
  to Sarah Matilda Keller. Issue:
  1) Margaret C. Pounds b. 4/4/1839, md. 10/11/1855 to John Lott
  2) Sophia Ardell Pounds b. 11/14/1841, md. 4/6/1865 to Morris M.
   Williams
  3) Johnson Bruce Pounds b. 3/20/1844, a Baptist minister, md. 12/15/1864
   to Mary E. Pittman
  4) Joseph L. Pounds b. 4/22/1846, md. 11/29/1866 to Martha V. Pittman
  5) Henry Bonaparte Pounds b. 3/4/1849, md. Jane____
  6) Sarah E. Pounds b. 1/11/1857 (8?), md. ____ Lott
 h) Minerva Pounds b. 1825, d. 1902/04, md. in 1849 to William Keller and
  migrated to Liberty, Texas. Issue:
  1) John Henry George Keller
  2) Joseph Isom Keller
  3) Rose Ann Keller
  4) Feliciann Aseneth Keller b. 3/25/1852, d. 8/3/1937, md. in 1868 to
   Francis Marion Green
  5) Louisiann Keller
  6) Margarett Ann Keller
 i) Elizabeth Ann Pounds md. in 1848 to Alexander Davis
 j) Robert M. Pounds b. 1828, d. 1863 while a soldier of the Confederacy
 k) Andrew Jackson Pounds b. 1832, md. 1/4/1853 to Lucinda Smith b. 1831.
  Issue:
  1) George M. Pounds b. 1855
  2) Rose Ann Pounds b. 1859

2) Joseph Pounds b. ca. 1777, d. in Lawrence Co., Miss., in July, 1838, md.
 ____. He was in Washington Par., La., in 1820; moved to Miss. ca. 1830.
 Issue:
 a) Mary Ann Pounds b. 1810 in S.C., md. 1) ____ Harcel, md. 2) in 1/1830
  to Robert Underwood b. in Ireland in 1810. Issue:
  1) John A. Underwood b. 1831
  2) Ellenora Underwood b. 1834
  3) Cressey (Theresa) Underwood b. 1836
  4) J. William W. Underwood b. 1838
  5) Robert D. Underwood b. 1841
  6) Sarah S. Underwood b. 1844
  This family lived in Copiah Co. in 1850.
 b) William Pounds, of age at the time of his father's death. No record.
 c) Theresa Pounds (Cressy) b. 1819 in S.C., md. Alfred Sartin b. 1819.
  Issue:
  1) Samuel Sartin b. 1841
  2) John G. Sartin b. 1843
  3) Minerva R. Sartin b. 1847
  This family lived in Copiah Co. in 1850
 d) Samuel Pounds, of age in 1838. He is possibly the Samuel Pounds on
  the 1850 Census for Titus Co., Tex.:

Samuel Pouns	33	Merchant	b. in Miss.
Amanda	"	26		"
Louisa		5		Texas
Isaac		2		"
Baby		3/12 (Sept. 1850)		"

 e) Daniel Pounds b. 1824 in La., lived in Lawrence Co. in 1850
 f) Julia Pounds b. 1830 in La., md. in Lawrence Co., 1846, to John May,
  Jr. Lived in Lawrence Co. in 1850
 g) Prudence Pounds
 h) Emeline Pounds
 i) Sarah Pounds

The Keller (Kellar) brothers and sisters, who married the Pounds brothers and sisters had migrated into Marion County, Mississippi, from Orangeburg Co., S.C., in the 1820's with their parents Philip and Lydia Keller. Shortly thereafter, they moved further south to St. Tammany Parish, Louisiana, where Philip Keller, the father, died on April 9, 1834. Lid'ye (as spelled on one record) died about the same time. Her maiden name was never discovered, but she was probably a Singletary. Philip and Lydia's children:

1) John Keller b. 1795 in S.C., d. in St. Tammany Parish, md. Hannah Browning b. 1790--left issue.
2) Henry Keller b. 5/9/1796 in Orangeburg, d. 1/31/1889 in Silsbee, Texas (buried in the Knipple Cemetery), md. 5/5/1818 in Marion County, Miss., to Sophia b. 1/2/1863 in St. Tammany Parish, dau. of Thomas and Elizabeth Page (probably of Lawrence Co., Miss.). Issue:
   a) John Keller b. 2/15/1822, d. 9/2/1886, md. Martha E. Seals
   b) William Keller b. 7/24/1827, d. 11/28/1905, md. Minerva Pounds
   c) Elizabeth Keller b. 4/14/1819, d. 8/30/1873, md. Joseph Edward Pounds
   d) Sarah Matilda Keller b. 6/23/1825, d. 3/17/1898, md. Isam (Isham) Pounds.
   e) Martha Ann Keller b. 5/24/1848, d. 2/6/1910, md. John Brown
   f) Henry K. Keller b. 8/17/1832, d. 9/3/1890, md. Susan Jane Brown
   g) Catherine Keller md. John Joyner
   h) Rachel P. Keller md. Thomas Seals
3) Susan or Susannah Eveline Keller b. 1811, md. Caswell Joyner b. 1808, d. 1868. Lived in Hancock Co., Miss.
4) Philip Keller b. 1819, md. Margaret Ruddock d. 1886. Lived in Covington, La.

Philip Keller who died in St. Tammany in 1834 arrived in South Carolina in 1766 at the age of two years. He, with his mother Anna Margaret aged 28 and an older brother John aged 8, came on the ship named the Belfast Packet. His father Daniel Keller had arrived in the South Carolina colony prior to October, 1766, on the ship Britannia which had embarked several months before from Amsterdam. Being Protestant and upon accepting an invitation to Protestants from the South Carolina General Assembly in 1761, Daniel had come to America. The S.C. Assembly had awarded Daniel 250 acres for his family on 10/17/1766--land which was later surveyed in the German settlement in Orangeburgh District.

In Orangeburgh Daniel Keller and his two sons John and John Philip (and Jacob of the same area was possibly a son) belonged to the Calvinistic Church on Fourhole Swamp which went by the name of the Calvinistic Church of St. John on the Fourhole.

At the onset of the American Revolution, Daniel Keller must have been too old for the militia, but he submitted a bill to the assembly for supplies used by the Continental and Militia in 1781 and 1782 in the amount of two shillings eight pence (for forage) [S.C. Rev. War Accts AA 4194]. Several other receipts for supplies (additional fodder and flour) were also included in his account. One voucher had been signed by Samuel Felder (mentioned elsewhere in this compilation) for 150# flour dated 5/6/1781.

Daniel Keller's account was still being paid by the assembly in 1787. In addition to this account, others for the family were as follows: John Keller had seen service (78 days) with General Francis Marion, the Swamp Fox, in 1782. When he signed the account, Keller spelled his name Johannas, Account #AA 4197. On 10/25/1787, John Keller completed this account by accepting 200 acres of land for Philip Keller.

Philip Keller also served as a private in General Marion's Brigade (34 days) in 1782. His account was still to be satisfied (yearly interest paid) as late as Mar. 13, 1788.

In a review of the Keller land grants, the one for his original survey, surveyed on 2/4/1767 (granted the preceding 10/17/1766) fell in St. Matthew's Parish, Berkley County, and was bounded on the northwest by Maria Bushee and the east by Cathrina Margaret Simerins (?) (all other sides vacant). Four Hole Creek ran through his grant. Daniel got a second pre-Revolutionary War grant on 11/7/1770, for fifty acres adjoining his original concession. It was bounded by Mary Bouse, John Myers, Sr., and Jacob Whitman. Two years later, Daniel got a third grant in the same general area for 150 acres with all sides vacant.

For the membership of the Calvinistic Church of St. John on the Fourhole, see Paul Quattlebaum, "German Protestants in South Carolina in 1788--a Petition for the Incorporation of their Churches," Journal of South Carolina History, Vol. VLVII, No. 4, p. 198.

DANIEL W. POUNDS

Family 663 of the 1850 Census for Pike Co., Miss., was Julia A. Pound aged 49, native of Virginia, and her dau. Flurana aged 31 years, also from Virginia. Julia Ann Pounds was nee Clayton, widow of Daniel W. Pounds as mentioned by Conerly in his Pike Co. History. Julia and Daniel had issue:
1) Daniel M. Pounds d. 1905, md. Jane Olivia Leggett, dau. of B. W. Leggett, and had the following children:
   a) Julia Elizabeth Pounds b. 10/31/1856, d. 8/3/1886, md. 1/1876 to D. Monroe Simmons
   b) Carrie Pounds d. 7/4/1898, aged 24 years, 5 mos., 9 days
   c) Maggie Pounds b. 7/3/1876, d. 5/3/1901, md. 1/7/1895 to Oscar Holmes
2) Virginia Ann Pounds md. J. F. Shoup
3) Rachel Pounds md. Joseph M. Lewis

REGAN

The Regan family of Marion and Pike Counties, Miss., descends from a Joseph Regan who left a will in Bladen Co., N.C., dated 1/4/1773. This Joseph left a wife named Anna and three sons, namely, Ralph, John, and Richard. Not long after, these three sons gave their mother a ½ interest in a 300-acre tract of land in Bladen Co.--land which later fell into Robeson Co. with the entity's creation.

Anna Regan was a widow in Robeson Co. on the 1790 Census. She had at that time four slaves. The three sons lived nearby. Ralph was counted with 3 males over 16 yrs. old, 1 male under 16, 6 females and 4 slaves. John Regan had 3 males over 16, 1 male under 16, 3 females and 13 slaves. Richard had 1 male over 16, 1 under 16, and 5 females and 7 slaves.

Anna Regan left a will in 1796 (according to Fred Olds' will abstracts, which cannot be depended upon) in which she named: Richard, Sarah, Nancy, Martha, Mary, Elizabeth, Spann, William, John Jr., Ralph, Sarah Hawthorne, Olive Powers, Olivia Ezzell, and Nancy Andrews or Andress. Many of those named were her grandchildren.

Ralph Regan predeceased his mother and wrote his will in 1795. He named: Joseph, Samuel, Daniel, Richard, Millie, Sarah, Nancy, Martha, and Olive Powers.

Joseph and Anna's son John was b. ca. 1746, was a patriot (and possibly a soldier) of the American Revolution, d. ca. 1814. He md. Mrs. Ala Bennet Brown and had issue:
1) Elizabeth Regan md. prior to 1807 to John Pope. (John in 1807 made a deed of gift to John Jr. in Robeson Co., N.C.) Elizabeth md. 2) ___ Funchess
2) Ralph Regan md. Phoebe White
3) John Regan, Jr., md. Sarah ___
4) Nancy Regan md. Joseph Andress
5) Joseph Regan
6) Neill Regan md. Nancy Musselwhite (?)

All children listed for John plus those counted for Ralph leaves several named not accounted for in Anna Regan's will. The remaining children named in that document must have been Richard's children.

John Regan, Jr., md. Sarah ___ and migrated to Marion County, Miss., where he became a noted local Methodist preacher. In the late 1820's he gave each of his children the property that he wished them to have. His children were:
   a) Joseph Regan, who left a will in Marion Co., Miss., in 1831 in which he named his brothers and sisters. He probably never married.
   b) Stephen A. Regan b. ca. 1800 in N.C., d. before 1860 in Marion Co., Miss., md. 1/1818 to Elizabeth Applewhite, dau. of John Applewhite.

They had issue:
1) William Spann Regan b. ca. 1831, md. Sarah Ann ___
2) Joseph R. Regan b. 1838, md. Eliza Magee
3) Thomas G. Regan b. 1842
4) Ralph Regan (see obit. in this compilation)
5) John S. Reagan
6) Sarah Ann Regan md. 9/24/1840 to Thomas R. E. Warner
7) Mary Jane Regan md. 2/24/1842 to Morris Smith
8) Nancy P. Regan md. 4/4/1850 to Joseph H. Loe
9) Rebecca Regan (possibly)
10) Harriet Malisa C. Regan b. 1840, md. 1/17/1856 to Soloman E. Causey
  c) Mary Ann Regan md. 4/12/1817 to James Applewhite (possibly moved to Hinds Co., Miss.) She had at least:
    1) John R. Applewhite
  d) Nancy P. Regan b. 1805, md. 1/13/1820 to John Pittman and had at least:
    1) K. T. Pittman b. 1822
    2) Joseph A. Pittman b. 1823
  e) William S. Regan b. 1803 in N.C., lived in Marion Co., Miss., md. 3/3/1823 to Catherine Pittman and had issue:
    1) Robert Regan b. 1824
    2) Rufus Regan b. 1827
    3) J. W. Regan b. 1829
    4) E___ (dau.) Regan b. 1832
    5) Sarah Jane Regan b. 1834
    6) S___ (son) Regan b. 1836
    7) William P. Regan b. 1837
    8) M. A. Regan b. 1839
    9) W. A. Regan b. 1841
    10) Nancy Regan b. 1844

RHODUS

William Rhodus, who appeared as a resident of Pike County on the Bogue Chitto River by 1825 had the birthdate 3/14/1781. On the 1850 Census the Rhodus family claimed to be from South Carolina. Thus, William Rhodus could have been the son of Widow Elizabeth Rhodus of Sumter (Sumpter) Co., S.C., in 1800. This woman appeared on the report with a son in the age bracket 16 to 26--or the range of William Rhodus of Pike Co. This Elizabeth is no doubt the same woman who had a Revolutionary War Claim in South Carolina. Since a Solomon Rhodus got land grants after the Revolution, he is possibly of this same family and possibly William's father.

William Rhodus md. 3/28/1820 to Elizabeth Bond b. 4/21/1804 and had issue:
1) Mary Ann Rhodus b. 7/29/1823, md. 6/13/___ to Michael Cook
2) Jane Rhodus b. 4/16/1825, md. 2/3/1843 to James Sandford (Sandifer) b. 5/3/1825, d. 7/15/1896, and had issue:
  a) Emily Sandifer d. 4/1/1884, md. Peter Sandifer and lived near Tylertown.
  b) Hansford Sandifer, died young
  c) Child, died young
3) William Wesley Rhodus b. 12/15/1827, md. 11/30/1848 to Elizabeth Ann Mixon
4) Isaac Rhodus b. 2/18/1830, md. 1/16/1851 to Mary M. Sandgord or Sandifer. Issue:
  a) Mary Elizabeth Rhodus b. ca. 1851, d. 1924, md. Judson A. Varnado b. 1850, d. 1920 and had issue:
    1) W. Ivey Varnado b. 1/23/1876, d. 9/18/1914, md. Alice May and lived at Spring Creek, La.
    2) Allie Varnado b. 1871, d. 1949, md. T. Jeff Simmons of Spring Creek
    3) Anna Varnado b. 3/40/1881, d. 3/15/1915, md. Franklin Willis Simmons
    4) Luther Sidney Varnado md. 10/3/1906 to Ada Smith of Warnerton, La.
  b) Nancy Edora (Queeny) Rhodus b. 12/15/1853, d. 10/24/1921, md. 12/12/1872 to Iley Arthur Varnado b. 10/29/1854, d. 11/30/1939 and had:
    1) Wright Varnado b. 1/5/1874, d. 4/16/1850, buried at Osyka. He md. Jenny Varnado.
    2) Fred E. Varnado b. 10/1876, buried at Mt. Zion; md. 12/10/1900 to

           Agness Simmons
        3) Cassie Varnado b. 10/8/1878, md. 9/16/1912 to John P. Wolfe
        4) Clara Varnado b. 1883, d. 1903
        5) Oliver Thomas Varnado b. 7/27/1889, d. 11/10/1946, md. 2/11/1908 to
           Eula May Wiltshire b. 1889, d. 1954
        6) Ethel Varnado b. 3/15/1894, d. 9/7/1928
     c) William Leander (Dock) Rhodus b. 2/29/1856, d. 4/21/1940, md. 1) 12/12/
        1872 to Nancy Jane Dykes b. 7/11/1859, d. 8/13/1891, buried at Mt. Zion;
        md. 2) Georgia Ann Sanders b. 1869, d. 1954, buried at E. Fork Church,
        La. Issue by 1st wife:
        1) Alice Waldeen Rhodus b. 2/7/1879, md. Joe Tig Carter b. 1853, d.
           1932. They had 12 children.
        2) William Floyd Rhodus b. 1880, d. 1883
        3) Lucy Rhodus b. and d. 1883
        4) Isaac Arthur Rhodus b. 6/15/1884, d. 1/20/1946, md. Lelia J. Sandifer
        5) Mary Lena Rhodus b. 10/20/1886, md. John Lea of New Orleans
        Children by 2nd wife:
        6) Edith Rhodus b. and d. 1894
        7) Eula Elaine Rhodus b. 10/2/1897, md. 12/25/1919 to James Calloway
           Strickland of Roseland, La.
        8) Rudel Rosa Rhodus b. 10/15/1899, md. 10/28/1927 to Otto Otis Goings
           of Mt. Herman, La.
        9) Henry Morris Rhodus b. 9/23/1901, md. 8/3/1929 to Iva Mary Bullock
       10) Willie Georgia Rhodus b. 10/28/1903, md. 1) Wallace E. Hodges; 2)
           Willie J. Holmes
     d) Ella D. Rhodus b. 9/1/1866, d. 3/12/1920, md. Fred Tate and lived near
        Sun, La. Their children:
        1) Linnie Tate md. Rainer Emmett Wells
        2) Carrie Tate md. Oliver Spike
        3) Hughey Tate
        4) Ewell Tate
        5) Roy Tate
  5) Willis Rhodus b. 2/17/1832
  6) John James Rhodus b. 4/2/1834
  7) Linda Ann Rhodus md. 7/15/1855 to Jackson Simmons
  8) Thomas Cemore Rhodus b. 3/28/1839, d. 11/15/1888, md. 6/27/1876 to Elizabeth
     M. Hughes b. 1/13/1839, d. 7/11/1894 and had issue:
     a) Una Mae Rhodus b. 4/18/1877
     b) Thomas Cemore Rhodus, Jr., b. 3/20/1879, md. Lillie Belle Kemp
  9) Zachariah Reeves Rhodus b. 4/14/1842, md. Letitia Ann Addison b. 5/15/1845
     and had issue:
     a) Hiram W. Rhodus b. 7/26/1866, d. 4/9/1942, buried at Mt. Zion; md.
        Montorio Berry.
     b) Mary Rhodus b. 12/17/1866, md. Robert DeWitt Dickey and had 5 children.
     c) Zidelia Elizabeth Rhodus b. 8/3/1869, d. 8/25/1950, md. Raleigh D.
        McDaniel b. 1960, d. 1937
     d) Florence Rhodus b. 10/18/1872, d. 4/2/1940, md. Seaborn H. Dickey of
        Osyka b. 1869, d. 1951
     Zachariah Reeves (called Reeves) md. 2) Eliza Schillings by whom he had
     a child who died young.

TATE

The Tate family of the area under consideration descends from the Tate (Taite) family which first appeared in the area of New Kent County, Virginia, ca. 1680. A James Tate who was an extensive land holder of that area had several of his children baptized at the old St. Peter's Church as follows:
   1) Ann baptd. 8/29/1689, d. 11/3/1702
   2) Robert bapt. 2/27/1691, born 2/27/1691
   3) Mary baptd. 4/20/1694
   4) James baptd. 11/11/1698
   5) Ufan (dau.) baptd. 1/5/1700, d. 4/13/1703
   6) William baptd. 4/12/1702

The last named child, William Tate (or Taite as then spelled), migrated westward after reaching maturity and left a will in Lunenburg County in 1751. He was a parishioner of old Bristol Parish Church but was in Cumberland Parish when he made his will. His will related that he left a wife named Sarah and the following children:

1) James
2) Thomas
3) Samuel
4) Jesse
5) William
6) Mary
7) Sarah
8) Elizabeth
9) Lucy

Some of these children were baptized in old Bristol, and thus the recordings of their births are found there. Nathan b. 4/23/1736 was dead before his father wrote his will. William was b. 8/26/1738, Samuel b. 11/3/1741, and Lucy or Lucia b. 2/19/1733.

Of the children of William Tate, most migrated into Johnston County, N.C., and from there toward Spartanburg in South Carolina.

1) James Tate d. in Anderson Co., S.C., and left a will there in which he named:
   a) Robert
   b) Samuel died in Ga.
   c) William
   d) Ann Tate Burton
   e) Margaret Tate Speake
   f) Elizabeth, wife of Farlar Thompson

2) Thomas Tate (born probably before the family moved to Lunenburg Co. or into the parish of Bristol in what was then Brunswick) b. ca. 1725 in perhaps old Prince George Co., md. Elizabeth ___ and moved in the 1760's to Johnston Co., N.C., where he died in July, 1781. His will was supposedly destroyed by a son-in-law. His children were:
   a) John Tate b. ca. 1751, who did not receive anything from his father's estate, d. after 1809. Family to follow.
   b) Susannah Tate b. ca. 1753, md. Rev. Joseph Camp
   c) Mary Tate md. Moses Kemp (Camp)
   d) James Tate b. 1760, md. Mary McDaniel
   e) Nathaniel Tate b. 1762
   f) Henry Tate b. ca. 1764
   Elizabeth was still living in the area of Spartanburgh (dealing in property in York, etc.) as late as August, 1800. Union Co., S.C., Deed Bk. G, p. 19: Elizabeth Tate, relict of Thomas Tate, decd., then of the Greenville Dist., assigned her interest to 500 acres of land on Broad River to her sons James, Nathaniel, and Henry for $100 on 8/9/1800. She, no doubt, did this in obeying her deceased husband's will that these three share equally in his remaining estate.

3) Samuel Tate--untraced by this compiler

4) William Tate left a will in Spartanburg dated 2/7/1792 in which he named his children:
   a) William Tate md. Molly ___, d. in Union Co., 1832
   b) Jesse Tate
   c) James Tate
   d) Sarah, possibly wife of Samuel Clark
   e) Elizabeth Tate Macomson, later md. ___ Arnold
   f) Lucy Tate Lefever
   g) Mary Tate Bridges
   h) Delilah Tate md. Abner McAfee of Lincoln Co., N.C.

5) Jesse Tate was probably the Jesse who dealt in land in Spartanburg and surrounding counties but left a will in Rutherford Co., N.C., naming his wife Mary and the following children:
   a) Samuel Tate
   b) Reuben Tate
   c) James Tate
   d) Randall Tate
   e) Kessey or Kesiah
   f) Patsey
   g) Nancy Tate Arnold
   h) Fanny Tate wife of Peter Willis

i) Sarah Tate wife of John Hester
   j) Susannah Tate McCraw
   k) Mary Tate McCraw
   6-9) Daughters not traced by this compiler

John Tate, probable son of Thomas and Elizabeth Tate, appeared in the Spartanburg District, S.C., shortly after the American Revolution. Prior to his removal from North Carolina (Johnston County), he had married Nancy ___ by whom he had eight children to grow to maturity.

Records on John Tate in South Carolina are scarce, but it is to be deduced that he was the John Tate on the 1790 Census for Spartanburg who had the 2 sons under 16 and 1 daughter. By 1800 he had five sons (3 under 10 and 1 in the 10-16 bracket) and 2 daughters under 10. He was in the age category over 45 years--which meant that he had been born prior to 1755. Nancy was listed in the 26 to 45 age column.

Only two deed records were identified as being executed by John in Spartanburg--both deeds of sale. Deed Book O, p. 142, cites that he sold 555 acres in Spartanburg to Daniel McKee for $500, land on Arnold's Creek, waters of the Enoree River. The 555 acres had been part of a 572-acre grant to John Tate Senior. This deed specified that it was land "whereon John Tate Senr. and Noah Westmoreland formerly lived." It was dated Oct. 8, 1809, and was witnessed by H. M. Harrison and Richard Sowell.

The second deed, executed Oct. 14, 1809, or a week later, John Tate sold for $200 to Samuel Jones 200 acres on the Enoree River, land bounded on property of Thomas Westmoreland (Noah Westmoreland's brother). Deed was recorded June 28, 1813.

There was no other record for John Tate in Spartanburg after 1809. Thus, he and his family moved west towards Louisiana. It cannot be determined if John came on or if he deserted his wife and family a short time later.

Long before 1820 Widow Nancy Tate and her large family were in St. Helena Parish, La. Her sons petitioned for and received public land. She did, too, supposedly was awarded a claim, but later lost this to Dr. Robert Yair. The property in question consisted of the land where Kentwood, La., is now located.

Nancy lived on in Louisiana (a near neighbor to her in-law Noah Westmoreland) until her death 11/3/1833. The Tate children:
1) Elizabeth or Betsey Tate b. ca. 1775 (perhaps not a daughter to Nancy, but a step-daughter), md. ca. 1800 to Lenoir (Lenoah) Westmoreland. She was dead long before 1850.
2) John Tate b. ca. 1783, d. 4/2 or 21/1854, md. 8/3/1806 to Martha (Mary on one record) Otaly (probably Otier).
3) Harvey Tate b. ca. 1786, d. 5/20/1871, md. in 1824 in St. Helena Parish to Elizabeth Breed, widow of Thomas Quillon, and mother of Avery Breed Quillon by that 1st marriage.
4) Mary Tate b. 1786 (twin to Harvey), md. 1) Isaac Lindsey who d. 4/1833; md. 2) Nehemiah Newman.
5) James Tate b. 1790, d. in Marion Co., Miss., in 1860, md. in 1809 to Abigail Holden.
6) Jesse Tate b. ca. 1792, d. after 2/1849 (but before 1850), md. 11/1820 to Nancy Jackson, dau. of James and Ann Sibley Jackson.
7) Charles Tate b. ca. 1795, md. Mary Miller b. 1794. In 1850 they were living in Pike Co., Miss.
8) Catherine Tate b. ca. 1799/1800, md. 1/1821 in Amite Co., Miss., to Robert Willey. She died ca. 1825.

Descendants of the 8 Tate children:
1) Elizabeth or Betsey Tate, the oldest Tate child, b. between 1775 and 1780, md. before 1800 to Lenoir Westmoreland b. between 1775 and 1780. Lenoir (called Noah) was named for the Lenoir family of Virginia and was the son of Ann Lenoir b. in Va. in 1731, d. in S.C. in 1825, and her husband John Westmoreland. He was a brother of the Thomas Westmoreland who lived in Spartanburg and of the John Westmoreland, Jr., who lived in the Greensville Dist., S.C., in 1819. In a letter from John Westmoreland, Jr., to his uncle William Lenoir (then in North Carolina) dated in 1819, he mentioned that his brother Lenoir was living in "Florida."

The names of all children born to Betsey Tate and Lenoir Westmoreland cannot be realized, but the following is a partial listing.
a) William Westmoreland
b) Nancy (Ann) Westmoreland md. 7/1819 in St. Helena Par. to Benjamin Fortner
c) John Westmoreland b. 1805, md. 1) ___; 2) Cynthia ___, lived in Washington Par., La., and had issue:
   1) William Westmoreland b. 1833
   2) George Westmoreland b. 1835
   3) Sarah Westmoreland b. 1843
   4) Rachael Westmoreland b. 1845
   5) James Westmoreland b. 1841
   6) Louise Westmoreland b. 1847
d) Catherine Westmoreland b. 1806, md. 2/15/1827 to Jacob Dykes and had (partial list):
   1) Jehu Dykes b. 1834
   2) Nathaniel Dykes b. 1837
   3) Jane L. Dykes b. 1842
e) Sarah Westmoreland b. 1815, md. 12/22/1835 to Thomas Jennings and had:
   1) Pernitian (?) Jennings b. 1836
   2) John Jennings b. 1838, md. Elizabeth Kent 12/29/1864
   3) Augustine Jennings b. 1840, md. Mary Jones on 7/25/1862
   4) Amanda Jennings b. 1844
   5) Elizabeth Jennings b. 1844 (twin?)
   6) Catherine Jennings b. 1846
   7) Jesse F. Jennings b. 1847, md. Nancy Purvis 5/17/1873
   8) Nancy Jennings b. 1849, md. John G. Matthews 7/9/1869
f) Elizabeth Westmoreland b. 1809, md. 1) Sheriff Hicks; 2) David Taylor d. in 1853. Issue:
   1) Nimrod A. Taylor b. 1835, md. Martha Brown on 3/16/1854
   2) James Monroe Taylor b. 1838, d. of typhoid in CSA
g) Levunza Westmoreland b. 1818, md. William McNabb and had:
   1) Seaborn McNabb b. 1838
   2) Newton McNabb b. 1840
   3) Rebecca McNabb b. 1842
   4) John G. McNabb b. 1844
   5) James McNabb b. 1846
   6) Rhoda McNabb b. 1848
   7) Jesse McNabb b. 1849
h) Jesse Westmoreland b. 1821, md. Nancy Cutrer and had:
   1) Elizabeth Westmoreland b. 1840
   2) Necia A. Westmoreland b. 7/17/1867, d. 2/5/1885, md. 12/12/1884 to J. B. Dees. No issue.
   3) Others
i) West Westmoreland md. Mary Johnson 10/27/1830

2) John Tate b. ca. 1783, d. 4/1854, md. 8/3/1806 to Martha (Mary) Otaly (Otier?) b. 1787, d. 12/1852. John was a veteran of the War of 1812. They settled a claim near Kentwood, La. Issue:
   a) Nancy Tate b. 5/8/1807, d. 8/1844, md. 9/18/1828 to Henry Carter of Mississippi
   b) James Tate b. 3/18/1809, d. 10/4/1855, md. 3/9/1836 to Tennessee Lee b. ca. 1815/16, d. 2/17/1859. Issue:
      1) Martha Ann Elizabeth Tate b. 1/20/1837, md. 6/19/1856 to Emanuel Cutrer and had issue:
         a) Josie Texas Cutrer
         b) Deanie Cutrer md. 1) R. W. Easley; 2) ___ Schillings; 3) Thompson. She had by 1st husband: Johnnie, Blanche, Emma, and Maude.
         c) Johnny Tate Cutrer
         d) Joseph Cutrer md. Corcus (?) Wells
         e) Frederick Cutrer
         f) Samuel Cutrer
         g) Cora Cutrer (twin to Samuel) who md. in 1892 to Pascal Deas
      2) Ann Cassander Tate b. 3/6/1839, d. 7/10/1847
      3) Nicholas Baylies Tate b. 12/19/1839, md. Julia Wade
      4) Thomas Scott Tate b. Fri., 5/15/1843, d. age 45
      5) Jesse Naul Tate b. 3/11/1845, md. 1/5/1865 to Martha E. Wall. Issue:
         a) Nicholas W. Tate b. 1/23/1866
         b) Rhodie Missouri Tate b. 5/4/1867

c) Estelle J. Tate b. 6/18/1870
   d) Lady Tennessee Tate b. 10/16/1871
   e) James H. Tate b. 4/14/1873
   f) William Benjamin Tate b. 7/3/1875
   Jesse Naul Tate md. 2) 6/10/1880 to Lizzie J. Carruth
  6) James Tate b. 3/4/1847, d. 10/4/1855
  7) Letha Ann Tate b. 3/22/1849, md. Doc, son of Charles Tate Smith
  8) Josephine Tate b. 6/9/1852, md. George, brother of Doc Smith
  9) Franklin M. Tate b. 2/23/1854, d. 10/13/1857
 10) Julyann Tate b. 2/17/1856, md. Eskie (?) Ott
c) Thomas Tate b. 7/31/1812, d. 5/15/1831
d) Harvey Tate b. 4/13/1814, d. ___, md. 6/18/1835 to Belinda ___. Issue:
  1) Mary Tate b. 1836
  2) James Tate b. 1839
  3) Nancy Tate b. 1842
  4) Delphine Tate b. 1844
  5) Dallas Tate b. 1846
  6) Sarah Tate b. 1847
e) Obediah Tate b. 8/27/1816, d. 6/27/1875, md. 6/23/1834 to Nancy Dykes
   and had issue:
  1) Florence E. Tate
  2) Charles W. Tate
  3) Obediah Tate
  4) Louis J. Tate
  5) Emma G. Tate
  6) Cora Tate
  7) Frederick E. Tate
f) Charles Tate b. 6/10/1818, md. Malinda Betilda Bates d. 1853, dau. of
   John and Elizabeth Bates, and had issue:
  1) John Tate b. 1838
  2) Jesse C. Tate b. 8/9/1839, d. 6/23/1915, md. 11/21/1859 to Malica
     Ann Gordon b. 10/14/1844, d. 7/7/1894 and had:
     a) Charles Tate 1860-1862
     b) Lillian Drucilla Tate b. 9/9/1863, d. 5/12/1938
     c) Prudence Missouri Tate b. 1/1/1866
     d) Marsha Parilee Tate b. 2/24/1868, d. 11/22/1951
     e) Georgiana Corrinth Tate b. 4/31/1870, d. 7/23/1951
     f) Van Ghylotia Tate b. 8/31/1872
     g) Rebecca Elizabeth Tate b. 5/18/1874, d. 5/5/1894, md. ___
        Kinchen
     h) Oby Nickles Tate b. 11/5/1876
  3) Martha Tate b. 1841
  4) Poke Tate b. 1845
  5) Alexander Tate b. 1848
  6) Obediah Tate
g) Mary Ann Tate b. 7/8/1820
h) Eleanor Caroline Tate b. 11/25/1822, d. 1853, md. 1/1/1836 to Avery
   Breed Quillen and had:
  1) Nancy Quillen md. Lafayette Draughan and had: Rosella, Francis,
     and Louisa, who md. Lewis Smith and had: Ella, Clinton, Willis, and
     Charles Smith.
i) Louisa Tate b. 12/5/1828, d. 9/13/1830
j) Mosilie (Moselle) M. Tate b. 2/15/1831, d. 4/29/1892, md. Kenion
   Thompson of Washington Parish. Issue:
  1) Minerva Thompson b. 1854
  2) Alexandria Thompson b. 1855
  3) Thomas Thompson b. 1858
  4) Obediah Thompson b. 1858 (twin?)
k) Elizabeth Tate b. 9/23/1835 (or 9/27/1934?), d. 1876, md. 12/23/1852
   to Jefferson C. Waller and had issue:
  1) John Tate Waller b. 4/28/1854
  2) Ivy F. Waller b. 8/3/1856
  3) Martin P. Waller b. 9/22/1858, d. 10/11/1878
  4) Ripley B. Waller b. 9/12/1862, d. 12/3/1885
  5) Charles F. Waller b. 7/6/1863
  6) Benson B. Waller b. 9/6/1865, d. 10/23/1895
  7) Joseph Waller b. 7/7/1867, d. 12/16/1894
  8) Obediah C. Waller b. 11/2/1869
  9) Elva Waller b. 8/19/1872, d. 1/7/1887 (?)

10) Dora Waller b. 3/2/1874
   1) Nicholas W. Tate b. 1/10/1837

3) Harvey Tate b. 1786, d. 5/20/1871, md. Elizabeth Breed in 1924, dau. of
   John and Lucy Breed. Elizabeth d. prior to 10/1855. Harvey Tate served
   at the Battle of New Orleans, War of 1812, Bounty claim: 18,527. (The
   succession of Elizabeth Breed Quillon Tate stated that she and Harvey Tate
   md. 2/15/1826.) Issue:
   a) Washington Tate b. 1826, died unmarried
   b) Lafayette Tate b. 1839, md. 11/8/1854 to Sarah Ann Cutrer. (This was
      probably the Lanfry W. Tate on the 1860 Census for Washington Parish.)
      Issue:
      1) Clarinda Tate b. 1856
      2) Mary J. Tate b. 1858
      3) George W. Tate b. 1860
   c) Jackson Tate b. 1834
   d) Mary Jane Tate b. 1836, md. in 1855 to Charles B. Wall
   e) Clarinda Tate b. 1838, md. Hampton Wall
   f) Morgan Tate b. 1840
   g) Rachel Tate b. 1855 in Pike Co., Miss., md. Beverly Taylor and had:
      1) William Taylor
      2) Julia Ann Taylor, wife of Newton Q. Easley
      3) Washington J. Taylor

4) Mary Tate b. 1786, md. 1) Isaac Lindsey who died in 4/1833, a veteran of
   the War of 1812, Pension #74,565. Mary and Isaac md. in St. Helena Par.
   4/14/1816 by John R. Salisbury, Parish Judge. She md. 2) Nehemiah Newman.
   Issue:
   a) Matilda Lindsey md. Jameson Carter
   b) Malinda Lindsey md. Jerry (Jeremiah?) Thompson
   c) Lucinda Lindsey md. Samuel Newman
   d) Mary Lindsey md. John Brabham
   e) William T. Lindsey b. 1825, md. Elizabeth Day 9/14/1848 and moved
      to Amite Co., Miss., in 1851. Issue: Nathaniel; Mary Ann, wife of
      Hampton McGuirt; John; Martha Ann; Isaac; William; Mosella; and
      Cinderella
   f) Harvey Lindsey b. 1831

5) James Tate b. 1790, d. 1860 in Marion Co., Miss., md. in 1809 to Abigail
   Holden. James was a veteran of the War of 1812--Blwt No. 23,856. This
   union had at least 8 children:
   a) Louisa Tate md. R. P. Evans
   b) Lydia Tate b. 1812, md. James R. Amacker b. 1812 and had:
      1) J. J. Amacker b. 1835
      2) E. Amacker b. 1839
      3) William Amacker b. 1842
      4) M. Amacker b. 1844
      5) W. B. Amacker b. 1846
      6) A. N. Amacker b. 1848
   c) Susannah Tate b. 1820, md. Pierson Holden b. 1819 and had:
      1) Willis Holden b. 1846
      2) Lydia Holden b. 1846
      3) Abagail Holden b. 1849
      4) Angeline Holden b. 1851
      5) Susannah Holden b. 1854
   d) Thomas W. A. J. Tate b. 1828, d. 1904, md. Mary Matilda Byrd
   e) Eastman R. Tate b. 1836, d. 1897, md. in 1855 to Martha Ann Wheat and
      had issue:
      1) Everett Tate b. 1856
      2) Joseph Tate b. 1859
   f) Ascenith M. M. Tate b. 1839, md. 1/26/1864 to Thomas P. Fornea
   g) Nancy Tate md. 11/5/1840 to William Smith
   h)
[Louise Tate above md. 1) Willis Bonner; 2) Patterson Bass; and 3) R. P. Evans,
Marion Co. Deed Bk. C, p. 378.]

6) Jesse Tate b. ca. 1792, d. after 2/1849, was a merchant in Greensburg,
   La., at the time of his death. He md. 11/13/1833 to Nancy Jackson, d.
   prior to 1833, dau. of James Jackson and Ann Sibley. For a short time in

the 1840's, Jesse was married to widow Rebecca Robinson Ricks of Washington Parish. Issue:
a) Wilson Tate (lived in E. Feliciana Parish), md. Mary Ann Gordon and had at least:
   1) Nancy Tate b. 8/14/1843
   2) Leatha Ann Tate b. 3/1/1845
b) Catherine Ann (went by Ann) Tate b. ca. 1825, d. early in 1877, md. ca. 1848 to Burlin Childress Newsom of Tangipahoa. Issue:
   1) Martha called Mattie Newsom b. 1849, d. 1881, md. J. F. Tull
   2) Leah Newsom md. Alonzo Kase of New Orleans
   3) Hinds Scott Newsom b. 1855, d. in Texas, md. Kesiah ___
   4) Ida Belle Newsom b. 1864, d. 1900, md. Henry J. Sanders
   5) Alice Carpenter Newsom b. 1859, d. 1892, md. James Kemp
   6) Clara Duval Newsom b. 1865, d. 1935, md. Samuel Kemp
   7) Son died young, name unknown

7) Charles Tate b. 1795, md. Mary Miller b. 1794 and had issue:
   a) Warren Tate b. 1830, md. 3/6/1854 to Ann Kirkland
   b) Louisa Tate b. 1833
   c) Joseph Tate b. 1836
   d) John Guy Tate
   e) Other children died young

8) Catherine Tate b. ca. 1800, d. ca. 1825, md. on 1/25/1821 in Amite Co., Miss., to Robert Willey. They supposedly lived on the Louisiana/Mississippi line. Names of a number of children are not known. Only known heir was Lewis or Louis Willey, who in 1850 was living with his first cousin Lydia Tate, wife of James Amacker, in Marion County, Miss. This is perhaps the same Lewis Willey who appeared on the 1860 Census for Washington Parish with wife named Matilda. The Census is as follows:

77/73	Lewis Willey	38	m	Farmer	La.
	Matilda	25	f		"
	Martha	7	f		"
	William A.	5	m		"
	Stephen R.	4	m		"
	Nancy A.	2	f		"
	Warren	5/12	m		"
	Elciby	23	f		"

Elciby or Elcaba and Lewis were sister and brother--but were half kin no doubt. Robert Willey or John as his name was supposedly md. 2) Jane Jenkins b. ca. 1798 (census) or 1802 (tombstone). Jane was probably the mother of Elcaba and Susan who married James A. Erwin.

TATE

A second Tate family which had family members living in Pike County, Miss., is that of Thomas Edward Tate, the Probate Judge of Pike County in 1869. Data on this family has been supplied by Mrs. Horace W. Fletcher (Myrtle Tate Simmons) of Magnolia, Miss. This material came from her files and from data gathered by the late Col. W. E. Lessard.

Thomas Edward Tate descended from Joseph Tate b. 1746, d. 10/28/1821 in Warren Co., Ohio, and his wife Elizabeth Pattison who d. after 1821. This union had children, namely: Robert, James, Margaret, Thomas, Hugh, William and John. This Joseph Tate (father) was a Revolutionary soldier.

Of James Tate's sons James and Thomas, the latter with his family migrated to Covington, La., from Clarksburg, Va. ca. 1814. James Tate d. in Texas after 1821, but had married in St. Tammany Par., La., in 1817 to Ann Collins, widow of Thomas Wharton Collins, and had a daughter Ann Tate b. 1819 who died young in Texas. Before James removed to Texas, he served as the parish judge for St. Tammany Parish from 1812-1819.

Thomas Tate, brother of James and son of Joseph, b. 1775, d. in Covington 7/23/1838, md. 1) 6/19/1806 to Ingaba d'Evecmon at Little Yough Gladis, Md. She was

born 1790, d. 10/1814 on the north shore of Lake Pontchartrain. Her parents were Peter d'Evecmon and Hannah Sinnex. Thomas and Ingaba had children born at Clarksburg, Va.:
1) Maris Louisa Tate b. 9/10/1810, died young
2) Hugh D. Tate b. 5/8/1812, d. 2/4/1860 in Covington, La., md. 12/15/1835 to Catherine Ann McNeil b. 10/1/1810 in Robeson Co., N.C., d. 12/15/1874, buried in the Ellis Cemetery in Amite, La. She was the dau. of John C. McNeil and Catherine Taylor. Issue:
  a) Thomas d'Evecmon Tate
  b) John McNeil Tate b. 1838, d. 1936, md. 1869 to Martha A. Kemp Womack, 1838-1918
  c) Catherine Ingaba b. 1839 in Covington, md. 1) 1863 to William H. Dunnica d. in Civil War; 2) 1868 to Wilber Hoag Webber b. 1840
  d) James Finley Tate
  e) Mary (Maida) Tate 1843-1904
  f) Flora T. Tate b. 1846 in Texas, md. ___ Conner
  g) Hugh d'Evecmon Tate, Jr., 1848-1925
  h) Harriet C. Tate b. 1852, md. Thomas Benton Kemp
3) Margaret Ann Tate b. 6/20/1813, d. 6/7/1887 at Mt. Herman, La., md. 12/11/1828 to Charles Ott b. 1799 in S.C., d. 1867 at Mt. Herman. Issue:
  a) Frances Ott b. 1829, d. 1906 at Johnson Station, Miss., md. 1/11/1860 to James English. No descendants.
  b) Samuel Edward Ott b. 1830, d. 1922 (buried at Osyka, Miss.), md. in 1848 to Esther Addison
  c) Lumanda Louise Ott b. 1832-1834, buried Ott Cemetery, Mt. Herman, La.
  d) Charlotte Ingaba Ott b. 1834, d. 1897, md. 12/4/1854 to Virgil Varnado and lived in Mt. Herman.
  e) Alfred Hugh Ott b. 1836, d. 1838
  f) Sarepta Ann Ott b. 1838, d. 1921, not married
  g) Mary Amanda Ott b. 1840, d. 1913, buried at Mt. Herman, md. in 1866 to Lorenzo Dow Snell
  h) Emma America Ott b. 1843, d. 1905, md. in 1861 to Joseph Porter and lived at Mt. Herman
  i) David Jackson Ott b. 1845, d. 1905, buried in Ott Cemetery, Mt. Herman, md. in 1879 to Rosa Ella Virginia Powell
  j) Charles de Vecmon Ott b. 1848, d. 1915, md. 4/26/1880 to Martha Tynes and lived in Mt. Herman
  k) Walter Thomas Ott b. 1850, d. 1948, md. 2/14/1877 to Leah Magee and lived on part of old Jacob Ott estate
  l) Elbert Weston Ott b. 1855, d. 1924, md. 12/24/1885 to Martha Estelle Leggett. They lived on the Charles Ott place.
  m) Adolphus Everett Ott b. 1858, d. 1924, buried at Peoria, Miss., md. Barilla Dampiere

[For a more detailed account for the Ott family, see Ruth Ott Wallis, Descendants of Jacob Ott of South Carolina and Louisiana (Bogalusa, La.: privately published, 1967 (?)]

Thomas Tate md. 2) 2/14/1821 to Margaret Edwards, widow of Jacques Lorrins, dau. of Morgan Edwards and Margaret Smith of New York. Margaret Smith was the dau. of Maurice Smith, an earlier settler ca. 1780 to Louisiana. Margaret Edwards Tate was b. 1789, d. 11/6/1864 in Washington Parish. Issue:
4) Thomas Edward Tate b. 2/16/1821 in Covington, d. 11/21/1914 at Gretna Farm E. of Osyka, Miss., md. 1) 1/5/1845 to Mary Vernon Cutrer b. 8/7/1825, d. 8/11/1892, dau. of Lewis B. Cutrer and Nancy Ricks.

Thomas Edward moved to Pike Co., Miss., in 1847 and lived on Gretna Farm on Fox Chase Road. He kept a detailed account of all operations which included farming, a sawmill, a grist mill and cotton gin; discount and brokerage business plus an ox-cart freight line to Lake Pontchartrain. (These detailed diaries and account books are in the possession of one of his descendants, Marie Williamson.) In addition, Thomas Edward was a poet of local renown, an area newspaper writer, participated in debates, and occasionally filled a church pulpit. In April, 1869, he received the appointment as the Probate Judge for Pike County and in 1874-1875 held the position of Superintendent of Education for the county. He and his wife are buried in a family plot at their old home. From Thomas and Mary (plus family members from the families of Daniel, Hugh D., Margaret Tate Ott and Ener Tate Brumfield), five generations of Tate descendants have lived in Pike County and nearby areas.

Issue of Thomas Edward Tate and Mary Vernon Cutrer:
a) Rosa Elizabeth Tate 1847-1935, md. 1867 to Cyrus Sullivan Simmons 1840-1920, son of William Simmons and Nancy Hope
b) William Edward Tate b. and d. in 1850
c) Frances Mary Tate 1852-1881, md. 1871 to Walter Edwin Tynes 1848-1929, son of Tyra Jennings Tynes and Jane Alford
d) Walter Scott Tate 1855-1931, md. 1) 2/8/1877 to Rebecca Courtney Brumfield 1857-1912, dau. of Charlotte Ott and Elijah Brumfield; md. 2) Bessie Simmons 1886-1945, dau. of Charles A. Simmons and Annie McDaniel.
e) Margaret Luna Tate 1867-1893, md. 1887 to James E. Lea

5) Ener E. Tate b. 1824, md. in 1839 to Alex C. Brumfield b. 1811 and had:
a) Daniel E. Brumfield 1840-1928, md. Sarah E. Brown 1847-1907
b) Thomas Brumfield 1842-1930, md. Nancy Eliza McClendon 1849-1934
c) George Alex Brumfield 1844-1877, md. Jane L. Roberts 1846-1912
d) Mary Ann Margaret Brumfield 1846-1914 (known as Mallie), md. Julius Newton Alford 1838-1916
e) Jesse Brumfield b. 1848, md. 1) Jenny Longmire; 2) Martha E. Alford
f) Emma Brumfield 1853-1873, unmarried
g) Others

6) Charlotte Mary Tate b. 1826, d. 1905, md. 1) William Sidney Lenear of Osyka, Miss.; 2) 1859 to Henry D. Berry b. 1825, S.C. Issue:
a) Ida Ana Lenear 1864-1910, not married
b) Minnie Ella Lenear 1860-1884, md. John A. Magee
c) Mary Alice Lenear 1867-1957, md. Farrar Carruth 1879-1959

7) Daniel Edward Tate b. 8/25/1831, d. 3/2/1877, in Washington Par. (near Mt. Herman), md. 1) 1865 to Caroline Collins, 2) 7/21/1868 to Margaret Jane Dyson b. 12/15/1844, d. 6/22/1930, dau. of George W. Dyson and Bethana Magee. They had issue:
a) George Murray Tate 1869-1933, md. Clothide Alford, dau. of Jess Alford and Philone Carson, b. 1875, d. 1963
b) Georgia Tate 1871-1948, md. George Walter Parker
c) Thomas Roland Tate md. Lonie McElvin
d) Margaret Bethany Tate 1873-1878
e) Eva Etna Tate 1875-1878
f) Dannie E. Tate 1877-1882
Daniel was a successful farmer in his lifetime. After his death, his widow married Leslie Parker.

TYLER

Abden Tyler b. ca. 1790 in South Carolina settled in Pike Co., Miss., as early as 1819. He was probably the son of an earlier Abdon (spelled Abdan and Abden) Tyler who first acquired 350 acres in Colleton District, S.C., on 2/23/1773. This older Abdon Tyler received grants later in Orange (Orangeburgh) in June, 1784; December 30, 1785; and June 30, 1788.

It is thought that Abdon (Abden) and the many South Carolina Tylers were descendants of John Tyler, son of the immigrant Henry Tyler of Virginia, who had two additional sons named Henry and Daniel. Henry II was the ancestor of President John Tyler of Virginia. Daniel Tyler was "carried off by the Turks" and after seven years declared legally dead and his estate divided between his brothers. (The names Henry, John, and Daniel appear in many branches of the Tyler family.)

John Tyler, son of Henry I, moved from Virginia to Albemarle, N.C. His known sons were John, Jacob, Moses, Absalom, "Shorty," Richard and possibly Kelly and Thomas. (The name William appeared quite often in the Tyler line--President Tyler had a brother named William.) Absalom, son of John I possibly migrated on to South Carolina, as a Tyler of that name obtained 100 acres in Colleton on 6/13/1775. The

N.C. Absalom had a son named Aaron who served in the American Revolution.

The subject of this sketch, Abdon Tyler (the second of the name) married before his removal to Pike Co. to Cassandra (Cassy or Kassy) ___ about 1813. She may have been an Ellis, as the couple named their first-born son Ellis. She was b. in S.C. in 1785. This Abden and Cassandra Tyler had issue:
1) Ellis Tyler b. ca. 1814, md. Martha M. ___
2) Margaret Tyler b. ca. 1817, md. William Riley Tyler, son of Moses Tyler b. 1780 in S.C.
3) Marthena Tyler b. between 1818 and 1821, md. 1) Aaron Tyler, son of Moses; 2) Joseph Sandifer
4) James W. Tyler b. 1822, md. Ackland Ann Sandifer (?)
5) Henry Milton Tyler b. 1825, md. Sarah ___
6) Eliza Tyler b. ca. 1828, md. Joseph McMillan
7) Zachariah Milford Tyler b. 1828 (?), d. 1852/3
8) Meredith (Meridy) Tyler b. ca. 1838, d. 4/24/1859

In 1819 Abden Tyler was appointed a Constable for Pike Co. by the Governor of Miss. (Governor's Papers, Ser. E., Vol. 3--June 1, 1819-Jan. 4, 1820). Upon the basis of area dignitaries, he was confirmed in the position as appears in the Register of County Appointments 1818-1824, Ser. F, Vol. A, to serve in 1820. His position with his peers in Pike Co. demonstrates that he was well known and considered a responsible man. Not long after this tenure, Abden Tyler moved his family to Copiah Co., Miss., where his name appears on the 1827 Tax Roll. In the 1830's several Tylers patented land in Copiah County as follows:
    Henry Tyler, 12/20/1833
    Moses Tyler and his son Allen,11/15/1834
    Abden Tyler and Ellis Tyler, 1/7/1835
    Aaron Tyler, son of Moses Tyler, 10/26/1835
    Daniel Tyler, 10/26/1835
    (William) Riley Tyler, 10/30/1835
    Marthena Tyler's 2nd husband Joseph Sandifer in 1835/6
Abden Tyler lived his remaining years in the Copiah/Hinds County areas.

[Contributed by Mrs. Bruce H. (Trudi C.) Nicholson, Jackson, Mississippi]

VAUGHN

The following is an abstract of an original deed found for Josiah Vaughan of Pike County. It is presently owned by Mr. ___ Parker, Lacombe, La.:

State of Missippi./Pike County/ Josiah Vaughan and Aby F. Vaughan--in consideration of one hundred and fifty Dollars--have granted, bargained, sold and by these presents do bargain. Sell and convey jnto Mr. Isreal Carter of sd. county the following described tract of land viz: North West quarter of the North East quarter of Section No. Seven in Township No. One of Range No. Seven East, containing forty acres more or less; also twelve acres of the South East quarter of Section No. Six of Range No. Seven East lying in the South West corner of said quarter and the said twelve acres up to the function of Isreal Branch. Seventeenth day of December, eighteen hundred and forty five. Signed by:
                      Josiah Vaughn (L.S.)
                      Aby Jane Vaughn

Inside the deed:

Josiah Vaughn acknowledges that he signed sealed and delivered the within deed to land on the day and year therein written--Also his wife Aby J. Vaughn being privately examined separate from her husband acknowledges that she signed sealed and delivered the deed to land on the day and year therein written as her own act. Before John W. Miller, J.P.

On cover:

I, Leonard Magee, Clerk of the Probate Court of said county, do hereby certify that the within Deed was received in my office for record on the 22nd day of December, 1845, and the same has been recorded in Book G, page 8 of the Records of Deeds of my said office. Given under my hand and seal of Office this 9th day of January A.D., 1846. L. Magee, Clerk

MORGAN

[The following data was contributed by the late Doris Varnado Green of Magnolia and Natchez, Mississippi.]

David Morgan, an early Pike Co. resident, came first to Amite Co., where he is shown in the 1810 Census with 1 male over 21; 2 males under 21; 1 female over 21; 2 females under 21; a total of 6 white persons and 3 slaves. His land in Amite Co. was assigned to Peter Quin 7/18/1817, it being S½ of S. 20, T-3, R-7E.

According to the pension application of Mary for service in the War of 1812, he and Mary Andrews were married 3/31/1806, Franklin Co., Ga., by J.P.

The 1816 Census of Pike Co. shows him residing in Pike Co. with 8 members of his family. His estate was administered in Pike Co., 10/1839 with William Coney as administrator.

David Morgan volunteered in 1812, Marion Co., Mississippi Territory, served in Capt. John Bond's Co. under Col. George Nixon and Maj. McGuffy as a private in mounted light horse company. Mary was granted 160 acres of land by act of 3/3/1855 for War of 1812 Miss. service, Blwt. 68916-160-55. Granted 6/1857 by warrant #6816.

Mary Andrews Morgan d. 10/11/1868, according to minutes of Silver Creek Baptist Church and is buried in what is known as the Magee Cemetery, now in Walthall Co., near Nesa on the McComb-Tylertown highway.

Their known children were:
1) Eliza Morgan md. William Coney
2) Benjamin Morgan md. Louisa C. Payne
3) Laura Morgan md. Marion Banton
4) Nancy Caro Morgan md. John J. Sandifer
5) Emaline Morgan md. Joel Jackson Coney
6) Mary Morgan md. Jack Craft
7) Minerva Morgan md. 1) Mr. Adams; 2) John Smith. No issue.
8) William Morgan md. Angeline Sanders

SANDIFER

[The following was contributed by the late Doris Varnado Green of Magnolia and Natchez, Mississippi.]

John J. Sandifer resided near Mesa in what is now Walthall Co. but at the time was Pike Co. He died ca. 1860 and is buried at his old home place, the cemetery now called Magee Cemetery. Many members of his family including his wife Nancy Caro Morgan and his mother Mary are buried there.

His children were:
1) William J. Sandifer
2) Mary Ann (Polly) Sandifer md. John Manning
3) Rhoda Elizabeth Sandifer md. John Manning
4) Sarah E. Sandifer md. Malachi Olaf Andrews
5) Elizabeth Minerva Sandifer md. 1) Jesse Ball; 2) Howell Crawford
6) Margaret Courtney Sandifer md. Gholston Ginn
7) David N. Sandifer
8) James M. Sandifer md. Arkansas Rushing
9) John Wesley Sandifer md. Mollie Lampton

VARNADO

Samuel Varnado, Sr., b. 2/15/1754, Orangeburgh Dist., S.C., son of Leonard Varnado and Sarrah Hutto, came to Mississippi in 1809 and settled on the Mississippi-Louisiana line near Osyka, Pike Co., Miss. He had 14 children by his two marriages, and all but two resided in this area. The children by his first wife, all born in South Carolina, were:
1) Leonard Varnado md. four times. His children were by his 1st wife Rachel Schilling.
2) Elizabeth Varnado md. Leonard Vincent Reeves in S.C.
3) Arcadia Varnado md. James Daugharty
4) Sarah Varnado md. John J. Amacker
5) Mary Varnado md. David Hurlong
6) Isham Varnado md. Drusilla Gill
7) Moses Varnado md. 2) Mrs. Nancy Ward Thompson
8) Nathaniel Varnado md. Ann T. Jones and resided in Ga.
9) Samuel Varnado, Jr., md. Keziah Newsom
10) George Varnado md. Prudence Luce Cory

The children by his 2nd wife were all born in Mississippi:
11) William Pearl Varnado md. Rebecca Thompson
12) Clarissa Varnado md. Henry Strickland
13) Rachel Varnado md. Joseph Cutrer
14) Nancy Varnado md. Warren Ricks

Samuel Varnado, Jr., b. 1793, Orangeburg, S.C., d. 9/26/1874, Pike Co., Miss.; md. 3/8/1814 to Keziah Newsom, who was b. 1792 and d. 6/1/1881 near Osyka, Pike Co. They had 13 children:
1) Matilda Varnado md. Jeremiah Strickland
2) David Varnado md. Catherine Hartley
3) Howell Varnado md. Asenith Davis
4) Charles Varnado md. Rebecca Jane Davis
5) Archibald Varnado md. Penelope Sibley, dau. of Rev. Wm. L. Sibley, a pioneer Baptist minister responsible for the formation of many of the early Baptist churches in the area.
6) Newton B. Varnado md. Isabell Simmons
7) George W. Varnado md. Lucy Jane Amacker
8) Meredith Varnado md. Mary Lillard
9) Sophronia Varnado md. Solomon Simmons
10) Sarah Varnado md. John Prescott; md. 2) Joe Noble
11) Oliver Varnado, died young
12) Franklin Varnado, died young
13) Samuel Varnado, died young

ALBRITTON SUPPLEMENT

James Albritton md. Sarah Brown and had 11 children. He md. after her death Martha C. Hart in 1863. She was b. 10/26/1824, d. 5/30/1886, and was buried at Mt. Pleasant Church, Norfield, Miss.

Record of children of James Albritton and wife Sarah Brown [taken from the record in the Bible of James Albritton]:

a) Matilda Albritton b. 6/20/1837, md. Thomas Dickerson 1/12/1858

b) Nancy E. Albritton b. 12/1/1838, md. James A. Moak 12/1859

c) Lavina Elizabeth Albritton b. 6/22/1842, md. Robert Johnson

d) Mary Ann Albritton b. 10/12/1843, d. 2/16/1918, md. W. J. Dickerson b. 2/29/1848, d. 12/17/1916
[Above buried at Montgomery Church, Lincoln County]

e) Richard A. J. Albritton b. 3/22/1845, md. 1) Elizabeth M. Hart 1/2/1869; md. 2) Nancy Mary Roberts

f) John H. Albritton b. 11/5/1846, d. 11/17/1919, md. Delilia Prestridge b. 1/2/1854, d. 10/18/1930
[Above buried at Montgomery Church, Lincoln County]

g) Matthew R. Albritton b. 12/7/1848, d. 1876, md. Mary Prestridge b. 1855, d. 1891
[Above buried in Moak-Sasser Cemetery near old Sasser's Mill in Lincoln County]

h) Sarah J. Albritton b. 8/2/1851, md. F. B. Erwin b. 1828, d. 1896

i) Francis L. Albritton b. 2/16/1854, md. J. R. Roberts

j) Margaret M. Albritton b. 10/7/1855, d. 9/30/1864

k) Lorinda J. Albritton b. 2/27/1857, md. Seaph Roberts

Children of Richard A. J. Albritton (from 1880 Census):

    James L. Albritton age 10
    Mary C. Albritton age 8
    Richard Albritton age 5
    Edward Albritton age 2

Children of John H. Albritton as follows:

    John L. Albritton b. 6/14/1872, d. 6/10/1956
    James S. Albritton b. 3/10/1874, d. 2/1938
    Avis Albritton b. 5/8/1877, d. 3/10/1947
    Benjamin P. Albritton b. 1/15/1881, d. 4/17/1961
    Bertha J. Albritton b. 9/8/1882, d. 8/7/1976
    Henry H. Albritton b. 11/6/1893, d. 12/12/1966
    Myrtis Albritton b. 11/29/1890, d. 3/27/1975

The above Albritton Supplement was submitted by O. O. Albritton, McComb, Mississippi.

ELLZEY SUPPLEMENT

Rankin C. Ellzey b. 11/10/1828, d. 3/4/1912, md. Mary L. Thompson, dau. of Hugh Thompson, b. 10/7/1833, d. 8/5/1911. They md. 12/21/1853. They were buried at Holmesville, Miss. Issue:

1) Hugh Nelson Ellzey b. 9/22/1856, d. 6/2/1930, md. Lucy Coney, dau. of David Coney and Mary Jane Walker. She was b. 11/12/1859, d. 3/11/1921. They were buried at Hollywood Cemetery, McComb, Miss. Issue:
   a) Leon Frank Ellzey b. 11/14/1879, d. 8/29/1961, buried in Hollywood Cemetery, McComb.
   b) Maggie May Ellzey b. 3/17/1881, d. 9/26/1965, buried Hollywood Cemetery, McComb.
   c) Julia Ellzey b. 2/7/1883, d. 3/14/1968, buried in Hollywood Cemetery, McComb.
   d) Edward C. Ellzey b. 12/14/1885, d. 5/13/1963, buried at Felders Camp Ground.
   e) Rosa Amanda Ellzey b. 11/26/1888, d. 12/9/1976, buried at Felders Camp Ground.

2) Clifton Ross Ellzey b. 1/8/1862, d. 11/2/1930, buried at Holmesville, md. 1) Florence Tynes, dau. of Thomas Fleming Tynes and Eliza Ann Terrell. She was b. 8/23/1865, d. 3/15/1889, and was buried at Auburn, Miss. They had issue:
   a) Clyde C. Ellzey b. 11/23/1884, d. 3/8/1901, buried at Holmesville.
   b) Hugh S. Ellzey b. 2/14/1886, d. 8/14/1889, buried at Auburn, Miss.
   c) George Clifton Ellzey b. 9/26/1887, d. 3/29/1912, buried at Holmesville.
   d) Ray Ellzey b. 3/2/1889, d. 1/1962
   Clifton Ross Ellzey md. 2) Ada Tynes, sister of Florence, b. 5/16/1867, d. 9/18/1942, buried at Holmesville. They had issue:
   e) Fredy Ellzey b. 10/28/1895, d. 10/4/1900, buried at Holmesville.
   f) Lee Ellzey, buried in Texas.
   g) Frank Ellzey b. 2/2/1898, d. 12/31/1949, buried at Jackson, Miss.
   h) Bobby Ellzey died young, buried at Holmesville.
   i) Thad F. Ellzey b. 2/5/1899, d. 12/14/1937, buried Hollywood Cemetery, McComb.
   j) Dolph Thompson Ellzey b. 4/2/1901, d. 2/1/1977, buried at Holmesville.
   k) Roy Ellzey b. 9/7/1903, d. 4/21/1965, buried at Magnolia, Miss.
   l) Otelia Ellzey b. 3/21/1906.

Hugh Nelson and Clifton Ross Ellzey bought joining farms on Bogue Chitto River between Holmesville and Quins Bridge around the turn of the century. Hugh sold out before 1920, but Clifton's is still in his family.

The above Ellzey Supplement was submitted by O. O. Albritton, McComb, Mississippi.

INDEX

Prepared by Miss May Davis, Bogaulua, Louisiana

Adams, John 26
Adonis, Evelyn French 288
  Lucy Whitmore 288
  J. Q. 288
Aikin, I. 27
Alcus, Louis 152
Alford, Edwin 36
  John 83
  Martha Smith 36
  Seaborn 41
  William C. 123
Allen, Catherine 100
  Chastine 90,100
  Felix 102
  Gabriel 14,15,24,25,100
  William M. 100
Alston, Margaret 47
Anderson, Mr. 46
Anding, I. H. 351
Andrews, Burrell 92
  Charlie Lee 93
  Elisha 40,77,93
  Elizabeth 93
  Felix 92,93
  J. 46
  James 92,93
  Jackson 93
  John Warren 93
  Martha 93
  Minerva 92
  Rachel 96
  Rhoda 93
  Sarah Jane 92
  Thomas J. 93
  Thompson 92
  W. 46
  Wilkes 93
Andrews, William 92
  William Pinkney 93
  Zebulon P. 93
Applewhite, Isaac 296
  John 12
Arthur, John 127
  Thomas 56
Atkinson, Emily 207
  James 152

Babbington, Ellen Ellis 60
  Robert 60
Bacot, Adam 47
  Elizabeth 47
  Julia 47
  Laban 25,32,44,47,48,136
  Levi 40,48,136
  Lorinda 50
  Maria Louisa 47
  Mary Lucinda 47
  Rachel 47
  Robert 47,92,136,151,153
  Samuel 47
  Susan 47
  William 47
Badon, Henry 40,92,128
  Margaret 92
  William 41
Bagley, Benjamin 19,24
  William 97
Bain, S. McNeil 112,127
  William J. 120,127
Baird, Mary 52
Ball, Daniel 74
  Jesse 68,74
  Louisa 68
  Needham L. 68,74
  Newton 74,83
  Rebecca 74
  Sampson 224
  William 74

Ballance, James 290
Ballard, Louis 99
Bancroft, Charles 90,110,
    112
  Joseph 90
Banner, Asan 139
Bardwell, Polly 86
Barnes, Allen 207
  G. L. 87
  Harris 207
  John 37,42,58,79,87
  L. T. 207
  Margaret 37,39,78
  Mary Virginia 207
  Miss 99
  Nancy 42
  Pinkney 42,79
  W. Clinton 42,79,160
Barnett, James 89
  Thomas 89
Barr, Amanda 41,128
  Annor 41,77
  Caroline 41,66
  James A. 41
  Joseph 41,88,351
  Thaddeus 41,99
  Thomas M. 41,351
  William A. 41,128,137
Barr, R. Wesley 41
Barrett, Miss 77
Barron, Jesse 100
  Lucinda 156
Bass, Ellen 29
Bateman, Gabriel 60
  Hugh 60
  Jason 97
Batson, Thomas 97
Baxter, Elizabeth 50
Bearden, Angeline 77,79,
    115
  Delilah 79,280
  Jackson 39,79
  Jeremiah 27,79
  Mrs. ----- 78
  Nancy 42,79
Beasley, ----- 95
Benjamin, Judah P. 124
Bickham, A. M. 224
  Alexander Moulton 117,
    160
  Benton 117,118,151
  Benjamin (Dr.) 117,151
  Eliza 122
  Hannah 117
  Louis C. 110,117,118,151
  Louisa J. 100
  Mary 117
  Sarah 117
  Thomas 117,151
Bickham Family 61
Bishop, A. S. 89
  John 153
  Johnnie 117
  Josh 117,153
  Nancy 117
  Sissie 117
Black, John 106
Blunt, ----- 76
Bonaparte, Napoleon 55
Bond, Betsy 100
  Henry 97,99
  John 106
  Liddie 100
  Milton Napoleon 100
  Preston 99
  Rebecca 99
  Thomas 99
  William 97
Bonner, Asen 139

Bonney, C. D. 290
  Flora A. 290
  Harriet 288
  H. S. 123,128,288
  Joel 288
  Martha Elizabeth 288
  Mary Louise 288
  Nancy Floyd 288
  Nelson P. 289
  Perez 288
  R. M. 290
  Samuel 288
  William 288
Booker, Amanda 40
  James 40
  Mary 40
Boone, Frederick 66
  John 39,66
  Nannie 43
  Richard 66
  Skinner 43,66
  William 78,122
Booth, Dr. ----- 78,122
Bougue Chitto Guards 190
Bracey, Cynthia 68
  Harrison 67,68
  Lucy 68
  Margaret 68,96
  Mary 68
  Rebecca 68
  Sarah 68
  Washington 68
Brandon, Gerard C. 107
Branton, Marion 86
Breland, Leroy 37
  Liddy 82
Brent, Captain ----- 160
  C. 24
  Fanny 98
  Jacob 44
  Jane 98
  John 44,98,99,115
  Julia 98
  Michael 35
  Mike 44
  Miss ----- 44,115
  Preston 98,137
  Rifles 197
  Thomas 93
  William 44,98
Bridges, Frank 100
  H. F. 53
  Hugh 160
  James 160
  Linas 100
  Nancy 100
  Robert 116
  Walter 134
Briley, Ben 44
Brock, Eli 81
Brown, Anne 50
  Matthew 86
Brumfield, A. J. 130
  Alexander 105
  Angeline 105
  Benjamin 105
  Charles 105
  David 66,105
  George 123
  Harrison 105
  Henry S. 16,17,22,23,
    24,105,151
  Isaac 40,66,105,151
  James 105
  Jesse 105,151
  Joe 90
  John 90,105,151
  Joseph W. 105
  Leah E. 105

171

Brumfield continued
 Luch 105
 Margaret 40
 Mary 105
 Nathaniel 105
 Sarah 77,105
 W. H. H. 84
 Willis 66,105
Brunette, Birkett Thompson 152
 Frank 152
 Rene H. 152
 William M. 152
Bryant, Miss ----- 94
Buckley, James M. 78
Buckner, H. S. 125
Bullock, David 46,68,69
 Delia 68
 Eptha 68
 Governor of Georgia 69
 Hugh 68,69
 James M. 78
 Joel 68
 John Thomas 69
 Joseph 68,69
 Lemuel 68,69
 Louisa 68
 Quinney 68,69
 Richard 68,69
 Rhoda 68
 Samuel 68
 Silas 97
 Simeon 68,69,86
 Thomas 68,69
 William 14,46,68,69
Burke, Glendy 124
 J. D. 289,290,291
Burkhalter, Cynthia 66
 Daniel 65,66,69
 Eliza 66
 Flem 115,154
 Henry 66,69
 John 66
 Louisa 66,155
 Mary 66
 Mary Palmore 65,66
 William 66
Burns, David 77
 Luther 77
Burris, James M. 61
 Selena 96
Burton, Elbert 106
Busby, William 97
Butler, Isopline 96
Byars, Phillip 346

Cage, William 106
Cain, General William 100, 145
Campbell, Colonel 43
 Felix 153
 William S. 125
Cappell, Henry C. 290
Carmack, H. C. 124
Carmon, Winnie 66
Carr, Mary 83
 William 153
Carroll, General 16
Carruth, Edward 134
 Robert M. 53
Carter, Charles 75
 John 3,99
 R. S. 95
Cassedy, Hiram 120
Catchings, Benjamin 52
 Charles 52
 Florence 52
 John 52
 Jonathan 24
 Joseph 24,54
 Phillip 24
 Sally 52
 Seamore 52,53

Catchings continued
 Silas 42,52
 T. C. 52
 Thomas 52
 Wm. Love 52,86
Cato, George 106
Causey, Frank 52
 Solomon 25
Claiborne, W. C. C. 26
Clarke, Charles 251
 Dr. 156
 George 124,156
 James 125
 W. D. 155
Clayton, Julia Ann 106
Clemens, Samuel 90
Clendenon, Miss 52
Cleveland, Colonel 43
 David 24,25,46,47,107
Clowers, Mary 70
Coates, Dr. 127
Coffee, General 60
 John W. 56
Coker, Chadrack 107
Cole, Dr. 77
 Pink 46
Collins, Ailsey 84,85,263
 Caroline Victoria 84
 Chauncey 84,85,131,263
 Frederick W. 84,110,262, 263,297,298,302
 George H. 84
 Julia M. 84
 Seth W. 84
 Warren 84
 Wesley 84
Colouhoun, John 83,89
 Loflin 84
Conerly, Mrs. A. L. 112
 Bexton 89,230
 Catheryn 63,83
 Cecelia 89
 Chauncey Porter 89,140, 202
 Conerlys 76
 Conerly & Felder 137
 Conerly's Post Office 81
 Crosby 74
 Cullen 58,59,63,73,81, 83,113
 Edward S. 89
 Eliza 59,74,83
 Emily 63,74
 Fanny 42,76
 George 74
 Jabe 105
 Jack 74
 James 63,73,74,89
 John M. 73,74,83,90
 Letticia 58
 Luke W. 22,55,58,63,69, 76,78,89,95,130,280, 290
 Lula 74,89
 Margaret 74
 Mark 74,83
 Mary Ann (Polly) 89,139
 Mary Jane 63,74,82,90
 Melissa 63
 Owen 35,55,58,59,63,73, 74,76,78,83,86,88,89, 95,116,121,127,130,139
 Polly 76,78,83
 Price 74
 Rebecca 63,74
 Samuel L. 89
 Susan 63
 Thomas B. 89
 Thomas J. 63,72
 William 59,63,73,74,83, 110,129,132
Coney, Ann 129
 Aquila 39,129,156,198
 Caroline A. 129

Coney continued
 Charles J. 129
 Daniel 129
 Emiline 156
 Eva 129
 Elizabeth 39
 Franklin 129
 Green 129
 Jackson 129,137,156
 Jerzine 129
 Jane 129
 Jasper 129,156
 Jeremiah 37,100,129,133
 Joel R. 129
 John H. 129,156,173
 Josephine 129
 Loraine 129
 Louis 129,156,175
 Luke J. 129
 Mary E. 129
 Morgan 40,129
 Rachel 129,137,139
 Rosa 129
 Sarah K. 129
 Van C. 129
 William 129
 William J. 129
 William L. 129
Conklinton, Mary 86
Connally, Crosby 86
 George 86
 Jackson 86
 Mary 83
 Price 83,86
 Rebecca 86
 Thomas J. 86
Conway, Peter 124
Cooper, Fleet T. 289,297
 Narcissa 92
 Quince 78
Corker, Mary 83,86
Corley, Charity Eleanor 37
 Jeremiah 37
Cothern, Elijah 44,99
 John 43,44,99
 Joseph 44,99
 William 44,98,99
Cowart, Dr. ----- 130
 Newton 69
Craft, Frederick 97
 Hugh 68,78
 Jack 68,78
 James 59,78
 John 78
 Major 78
 Seleta 78
 Sidney 78
Crawford, Ben 96
 Jesse 45,97
Crimson, J. B. 150
Crockett, Dave 60
 Houston 60
Crooker, John A. 289,297
Curlette, ----- 288
Cutrer, Isaac W. 296

Dahlgreen, General C. 191
 Rifles 191
Daughdrill, Clarissa 92
David, Mrs. 207
Davidson, John 127
Davies, Hosey 69,130
 Nancy Ann 69
 Rhoda 68
Davis, Charles E. 101
 Lucinda 156
 Pres. Jefferson 90
 Richard 107
Davy, Pilla Experience 289
Dawson, Mary 54,73,77
Day, Jesse 59
 Noah 59

172

Deer, Kitty 37,100
  Joe 75
  Mila 79
  Nancy 79
Denman, J. 46
  Sarah 44
  William 44
DeTrobrand, Colonel 291
Dick, Isaac Charles 51,52
  Jacob 51
Dickerson, Samantha 100
Dickey, Howell 155
Dickson, David 31,107
  James C. 27
  William 27,41,106,107
Dillon, Annie 44
  Clarkston 82,87
  Clara 87
  Eveline 87
  Lawrence 82,87
  Nancy 81
  Richard 82,87
  Sally 87
  Theopholis 82,87
  Willis 82,87
Dixie Guards 207
Dixon, David 25
  J. C. 107
Donahoe, Tom 123
Drake, Miss Ann 52
Drew, Charlie 152
Duffy, Maggie 52
Duncan, Cullen 42,76
  James 43,66,76
  Jane 42
  Telitha 66
Dunaway, Catherine 44,99
  Jonathan 44,99
Dunn, Hollis 350
  Norma 350,353

Elliott, Catherine 122
  Owen 59,78
  Wiley 41,66
Ellis, Ellen 60
  E. John 61
  Ezekiel Parke 59,61
  Gabriella 60
  George 59,60
  John 59,61
  Reuben 59
  Sarah 59,61
  Stephen 59,60,61,85
  Thomas Cargill Warner 61,150
  William 59
Ellzey, Caroline 40,128
  Courtney 40
  Daniel 39
  Dewitt 41,128
  Emma 128,139
  Frank 39
  Harriet 40
  Indiana Hall 39
  Jackson 40,41
  James 39
  Joan 40,68
  John 39
  Josephine 40
  Lenoir Angeline 75,128
  Louis 40,75
  Mary 40,41
  Nancy 128
  Nannie 137
  Rankin C. 40
  Rosa A. 40,124,136
  Thomas 39,40,41,115,128
  Wesley 40,105
  William 39,92,124,128, 136,137
Eschelman, Colonel 142
Estess, John 43
  Ezra 46

Evans, W. G. 85

Fairchild, Loflin 97
Farmer, Franklin P. 348
  Ida M. 348
  Henry Clay 348
  Zachary T. 348
Felder, Camp Meeting 106
  Charles 107
  Elizabeth G. 41
  Felder ----- 137
  Gabriel Nally 41
  John 25
  Levi D. 41,42,117
  Mary 41
  Peter 14,41,27,37
  Rebecca 99
  Robert Henry 41,42,110, 111,297,298
  Simeon Noble 41
  Wyatt Wesley 41
Ferguson, General 43
  James A. 57
  James M. 153
Fields, Jeremiah 89
Finch, James 119,238
  John 119
  Joseph 119
  Milus 118
  Thomas 119
  William 118
Finny, Bell 80
Fisher, Christian 123
Fitzpatrick, Elizabeth 66
Foil, Jane 66
  Polly Ann 66
  William 66
Ford, Dave 77
  Jacob 12
  John 85
Forest, David 18,46,87
  Hettie 18
  Mary 18
  Richard 18
Forshey, Cecelia 56,112
  Florence 56
  William 55
Forsyth, A. W. 288
Fort, Gregg 230
Fortinberry, Eusaba 39
  G. C. 39
  W. J. 39,45
  William 39
  Willis J. 339
Fournieque, Alexis A. 290
Frances, Henry 123,288

Galloway, Bishop 273
  Charles 273
Gard, Samuel T. 112
Gardner, Sally 96
Garland, Baldwin 153
  Bettie 153
  David 153
  Harold 153
  Lizzie 153
  Mollie 153
  Sidney 153
  William H. 124,151,153, 289,297
Garner, Calvin 43
  Harper 42
  James 42
  Thomas 100
  Vincent 25,46,107
  William 35
Garrard, Louis F. 35
Gartman, Bartholomew 75
  Caroline 75
  Cynthia 75
  David 67,75
  Ellen 75

Gartman continued
  George 67,75
  John 75
  Josiah 75
  Katie 75
  Mary 75,86
  Perry 75
Gates, Garner 93
  Keziah 25
  Nancy 44,99
  Mary 71
  Sarah 42
  Vincent 25,46,107
Gatlin, B. 46
  Ebenezer 46
  Edward 46
  Elizabeth 46
  James 46
  John B. 46
  Julia 46
  Mary 46
  Nathaniel 46
  T. 46
  Thomas 46
  William 46
  Zebulon B. 46
George III of England 54
Germany, Dr. ----- 46,117
Gibson, Cornelius C. 290
  Gilbert 95
  Major 288
  Ralph 153
Gilchrist, Susan 54
Gill, Miss 94
Ginn, Mr. ----- 68
  Hugh 69
Gillis, Miss Orrie 127
Glass, Elizabeth 49,50
Goff, Jemime 105
Gooch, Mary 75
Googe, Mary 81
Gordon, John 63
Goslin, Jane 41
Gracey, George T. 136
Graham, Elizabeth 100
  Mary 102
Graves, Benjamin 129
  Liddy 69
  Mary 112,127
Gray, Catherine 96
  Cicero 96
  Eviline 96
  Isaiah 96
  Lemuel 96
  Margeman 96
  Margaret 96
  Selena 96
  Sherod 68,95,96
  Sophia 96
  Thaddeus 96
  Tamentha 95,96
Grouche, Alex 18
Grubbs, Benjamin 75
  Frank 17,18
  Gilbert 75
  Henry 75
  Peter 75
  William 75
Guinea, Thomas 27,99
Guinn, Ellen 96
Gulledge, Rachel 93
Guy, ----- 76
  Chelly 76
  William 76,117,128

Hall, Amelia 18
  Armistead 87
  Barsheba 87
  Ezekiel 87
  Gracia 87
  Harriet 87
  Jane 87
  Lucinda 106

Hall continued
  Nancy B. 87
  Patsy 87
  William 87
Hamilton, Hans 24,95
  John P. 106
  Mary 95
  Nancy 78
  R. 46
  Rachel 79
Hardley, R. 15,24,25
Harris, Buckner 27
  J. H. 94
  Sally 155
  Wiley P. 25,27,78,107
Harrison, J. P. 124
  William Henry 68
Hart, Bertha 116
  Garland 81
  Hannah 116
  Isaiah 95
  Jakie 115
  James 95
  Jacob 137
  John 94,95
  Joseph 95,115
  Mary 116
  Mike 116
  Pincers Morris 116
  R. T. 95
  Sally 94
  Sarah 116
Hartwell, Family 61
  Benjamin C. 99,128
Harvey, Daniel 42,70
  Doc 70
  Evan 70,71
  Harris 70,83,105,130
  Jack 70
  Jesse 70,86
  Michael 12,42,69,70,71
  Mike 70
  Pearl 70,130
  Polly 69
  Ray 96
  Ruth 42,71
  Sarah 83
  Thomas 70,86
Head, James W. 111
  Mrs. W. T. 289
Herrington, Esther 50,51
  Joseph 50
Hewes, Margaret Thomas 55
Hickenbottom, Miss -----
  52
  Nelly 80
Hilborn, Ben 115
  Pauline 115
Hiller, Abraham 111
  Hatch 152
Hillier, Abraham 131
  Albert 131
  Annie 131
  Ellie 131
  Jones 131
Hines, David 97
Hogg, Nancy 41
Holiday, Mary 52
Holmes, Andrew Hunter 14
  Benjamin 66,67,130
  Betsy (Elizabeth) 66,
    67,105
  Berry 66
  Coleman 66
  Cynthia 66,105
  David 47,67,107
  E. C. 81
  Elisha 66,67,75,105
  Ellen 66
  Emily 67
  Harriet 67
  Jackson 68
  James 66,67
  Jenny 66

Holmes continued
  Jeremiah 66
  Jesse 66
  John 130,137,350
  Joseah 66
  Mary 87
  Mary Ann 67,84
  Needham 67,84
  Polly 66
  Sarah 67,75
  William 66,87
  W. J. 81
Holmesville Guards 201
Holmesville Home Owners
  118
Hoover, Christian 41,95,
  99,113,128,207
  Eliza 99
  Julia 99
  Kit 207
  Martha 46,345
  Nancy 99
  Sarah 99
  Thomas 99,120
  William 41,99,345
Hope, James 41
  Nancy 41
Houston, Maggie 85
  Sam 85
Hucabee, Ann 155
  John 96
Huey, John C. 55
  William 77
Huff, D. M. 291
Huffman, John 127,208
  Mary 44
Hurst, David W. 120,284,
  296

Iles, William 97
Impson, Benjamin 60,61
Irwin, Alla 280

Jackson, Andrew 16,60,61,
  76,83
Jacobs, Walter 97
Jacobowsky, John D. 115,
  128,137
  Susan 115
Johnson, E. 46
  Plummer 104
Jones, B. 47
  Benjamin 58,69
  Maggie 51
  Margaret 101
  Michael 94
  Mike 66,69
  William 96,126
Jonte, Susanne 51

Kaigler, Andrew 98,153,
  205,210
  Frank 98
  George 98
  Isabell 129
  Jane 98
  John 24,98,205
  Julia 98
  Rebecca 98
  William 66
  Willie 98
Keegan, John 128
Keen, Jacob 25
Kellogg, William Pitt 62,
  291
Kelly, Margaret 105
Kenna, ----- 125
  James 54
Kenner, Minor 125
Kershaw, Family 59
King, A. 46

King continued
  Jesse 105
  John 93
Kirby, John H. 86
Kirkland, Dud 55
  Joe 55,73
  Obed 14
Kline, Cathorine 100
  Grocery 115
  Olivia 100
  Westley 100,105
Ku Klux Klan 248

Lamkin, Keziah 76
  John S. 120,291,296
  John T. 75,120,127,284
  Mary 74
  Sampson L. 75,106,110
  Samuel R. 180
  William 75,160
Lampton, Benjamin 75,81,
  82,83,90
  Cora 90
  Edward 90
  Elizabeth 90
  Family 61
  Frank 90
  Iddo W. 90
  James 90
  Jane 83
  Lucius 90
  Lucy 90
  Mollie 90
  Sarah 90
  Thadeus 90
  Walter M. 90
  William 75,90
Laney, James H. 40
Laurence, John 86,127
Lavison, Mrs. E. E. 289
Lazar, Abraham 87
Lawn, Ann 54,73
  Bexton 54,73,77
  Betsy 54
  Catherine 54
  Eliza 54,73,77
  Henry 54
  Mary 54
  Robert 54
  Susan 54
  William 54
Lea, James 126
  Major 27
  Robert 101
Leake, Walter 107
Lee, Charlie 290
  Mr. 39
  Surrender 225
Leggett, B. W. 95,105
  Jane Olivia 106
  John G. 105
  L. 46
  Virginia Ann 106
  William 105
Leland, Dr. 100
  Frank 66
Lenoir, Hope 92
Letman, Mary 47
Lewis, Alexander 130
  Alice 77
  Abigail 91
  Barney 76,91,92,115,288
  Benjamin 130
  Bryant 116,128
  Cathorine 130
  Celia Ann 91,130
  Elizabeth 91
  Giles 77,129
  H. B. 122
  Henry 76,91,92
  Ida 77
  Joseph M. 106,130,339
  Jabez 74,82,92

Lewis continued
  James W. 91
  Jane 100
  John 130
  Josiah 92
  Lemuel 76,91,130
  Levisa 73,74
  Little Joe 339
  Malinda 130
  Margaret 130
  Martha 90,130
  Martin 73,76,91,92
  Mary Jane 91
  Mira 75
  Nancy 92,122
  Patsy 76
  Quinney 76,90,100,130
  Rosa 130
  Samuel 92
  Sarah 130
  Silas 92
  Susan 130
  William Bryant 76,91
Lighenstein, Hyman 116
  Isaac 116,152
  Meyer 116
  Simon 116
Ligon, Buxton 77
  Charles A. 77
  Elizabeth Ann 77
  John 77
  Lemuel 77
  Levisa 83
  Martha 77
  Mary 77
  Robert 76,77,79,115,284
  Susan 77
  William B. 41,55,62,73,
    76,77,130
Lightfoot, Hannah 54
Lilly, Jennie 53
Lindsey, Jinnie 151
  Margaret 116,151
  R. B. 116,151
Lott, Julia 205
Lotterhos, Henry 123
Love, Elizabeth 53
  Margaret M. 47
  Robert 46,52,105
  William 24,105
Lowry, Family 59
Luckett, Robert L. 291
Luter, Joseph 66,73,153
  Lizzie 77

Magee, Angeline 69,264
  Calvin 76
  Catherine Naomi 69
  Courtney 280
  Dickey 49
  Elbert 66
  Fleet 88
  Henry 88
  Hezekiah 60
  Jeremiah 49,264
  John 12,25,60,69,96
  Josiah 49
  Judge T. A. 130
  Mary 60,130
  Sarah 122
  Sire 49,264
  William 60,203
  William Levi 177
  William Willis 49,66
Magnolia City Officers 302
  Settlers 156
Mahier, Mrs. A. T. 18
  Etta 18
Mallett, Joe 296
Manning, John 79
  Joseph M. 79
  Mellie 79
  Mosea Moak 79

Manning continued
  Westley J. 79
Marshall, Ada 44,53
  Mrs. 35
  Tom 127
Martin, Eliza R. 50
  Jack 50
  James B. 50
  Joseph T. 49,50,98
  Josiah 24,49,50
  Matthew 131
  Rachel 131
  Wiley 86
  William G. 50
Matthews, La. 127
  Mamie 350
  Sam A. 54,110,128,140,
    224,350
Maxwell, Annie 92
May, E. D. 92
  Edwin 105
  Dudley 99
  Green B. 105
  Joda 92
  Jared B. 92
  James 59
  Joseph 59,92,128
  Mabaline 92
  Obed 92
  Richard B. 290
  Robert 92
  Satina 92
  William M. (Dr.) 78,92,
    123
McAlpin, Dr. 76
  Mark 76
  Patrick 76,90,130
McCarley, George 115
  John 115
  Mr. 115
McClendon, Miss 117
  Stephen 117
McDowell, Colonel 43
McEnery, Governor John 291
McCullough, Alexander 35,
    42
  Benjamin 42
  Jasper 35,42,46
  Melinda 35,42
  Olive 35,42
  Sarah 35,42
  William 35,42
  Winston 35,42
McEwen, Archie 42
  James 42
  Matthew 27,41,42,79
McGehee, Elizabeth 105
  John G. 105
  Julia 100
  Olivia 100,105
  Virginia Ann 105
  W. Frank 350
  William 105
McGowan, Colonel 67,68
  Elijah 67,68
  Elizabeth 68
McGraw, David 14,24,46
  Miss 92
  Zachariah 59
McKitrick, Mary 55
  Mr. 55
McLain, Frank A. 107,110
McMillan, District Atty.
    120
McMorris, Alex 44,50,51
  Esther Ann 51
  Nancy 51
  Richard 51
McNabb, George 86,107
  James Y. 24,25,31,107
  John 50
  Sally 72,186
McNair, E. 110
  Judge 120

McNair continued
  Rifles 193
McNulty, J. 46
  Michael 46,47,130
  Samuel 40,47
  W. 46,47
McQueen, Dr. 78,131
Melland, Eliza 41
  Joseph 41
Mercer, Asa 107
Merchant, John 59
Meredith, Martha 95
Miller, Ebenezer 156
  Joseph H. 156
Millerd, William 68
Millsaps, T. J. 60
  William 60
Minton, William J. 31
Miskell, R. H. 117
Mississippi Regiment 201
Mitchell, Algenon 131
  Marmaduke 131
Moise, E. W. 125
Montgomery, R. W. 124
Moore, John H. 125
  Martha Cathorine 100,280
Morgan, Benjamin 85,86
  David 24
  Eliza 129
  Emiline 129,137
  Miss 69
Morris, J. A. 84
  Nathan 97
Mosely, Sally J. 77
Mullens, Willis 100
Mulligan, Widow 16
Mundalow, Henry 71
Murphy, Captain 128
  Miss 129
Murray, Miss 100,280
Muse, Annie 99
  Mellie 77
  Miss 99

Nash, Company 200
  Erasmus 156
  Newton 155
Nelson, James W. 115,123,
    128,147
Nails, Mary Newland 99,207
Nall, Winnie 52
Newman, Carroll 120
  Family 99
Newton, Isaac 76
Nicholson, George 54,100,
    115,117,123,137
Nixon, Colonel 37
Noland, Mary Levisa 98
Norman, Sarah 44
  T. 48
Norrell, Ettie 51
Norwood, H. H. 291

O'Brien, J. Daniel 86
  James G. 87
  William Thomas 87
O'Callahan, Mrs. 153
O'Mara, Joseph 41
Oppeiner, Caroline 131
O'Quin, Daniel 75,87
  David 87
  Ezekiel 75
  John 75
  Nellie 75
  Rachel 87
Orr, William 27
O'Shea, Thomas 22,24
Otkin, Charles H. 242,279
Owens, Jacob 12,25,81,87
  Jennings 86
  Jemima 347

Packingham, General 16
Packwood, Dudley W. 121
  Joseph 122
  S. E. 109,122
Page, Elijah 153
  Joe 121,123,153,288
Palmore, Mary 65,66,69
Parker, Joseph 79
  Nancy 79
  Sarah 79
  William 79
Payne, Albert G. C. 86
  Alice 86
  Ann 86
  Doctor 78
  J. B. 86
  L. C. 86
  Louisa J. 86
  Mary A. C. 86
  Morgana 86
  Nelson R. 86
  R. A. 86
  S. C. 86
  Thomas W. 86
  William 86
Peabody, School 278,279
  George 278
Pearson, Mary 50
  Lizzie 93
  Nancy Woodward 56
  Sally 81
Penn Family 88
Perryman, Anthony 24,106, 280
Peyton, Colonel 78
Pezant, E. H. 117
Pigott, E. 129
  Ella 129
Pike County 27,28,29,30, 31,107,299,302
Poindexter, George 107
Porter, Charles K. 55
Pound, Daniel M. 106
  Daniel Walker 106
  Eliza Jane 106
  Rachel F. 106
  Thomas W. 106
  Virginia 106
Powell, Wesley 155
  William 51
Preston, Isaac T. 124
Prewitt, Ann Elizabeth 156
  Ansel H. 111,155
  Elisha 155
  James Smiley 155
  Martha 87
  Martha Ann 155
  Naomi Evilene 156
  Sarah Ann 155
  William Harrison 155
Purser, Brittain B. 347
Pushmataha 60

Quinn, Alice Cornelia 77
  Amanda 100
  Arthur 100
  Courtney 100
  Cynthia 100
  Daniel 37,39,100
  Dave Ford 77
  D. H. 128
  Dewitt Clinton 100
  Elizabeth Hugh 100,101
  Emily 100,129,183
  Emma Eoline 280
  Frank M. 37,57,100
  George 77,280
  H. M. 74
  Henry 25,95,100,280
  Hillary 102,117,123
  Hugh Murray 120,151,280
  Ina 280
  Irvin 71,77,100,155

Quinn continued
  James B. 102
  Joe 160
  Josephus 77,100,128
  John Legon 77
  John Schilling 77
  Katy 128
  Laura Virginia 77,86
  Lemuel Grocey 77
  Lemuel Jackson 77,100,134
  Lucy Marcella 77
  Lula 280
  Lucius M. 56,118,280
  Martha 16,77
  Martha Eliza 77
  Mary Arvazena 77
  Mary 39,40,100
  Minerva 100
  Mollie 83
  Nancy Bridges 77
  Nannie 139
  Peter 16,24,25,27,37,39, 47,95,96,100,102,280
  Rachel 172
  Richard 95,100,102,118
  Rodney 37,100
  Sarah 77
  Selena 95,100
  Susan 77
  Wallace W. 280
  William Monroe 102,118, 136
Quitman Guards 137,172
  General John A. 137

Raborn, Julia Ann 155
  Polly 182
Ragland, Henry 24
  Raiford, Ballard 122
  Needham B. 63,88,95,122, 130
  William 43
Rainey, Charlie 43
Randolph, Family 59
Ratliff, Calvin 68
  Franklin 68
  Green 68
  Richard 58,67,68,79
  Robert 68
  Simeon R. 40,68
  Slaves 79
  Warren 68,202
Ravencraft, William 71
Reagan, John 69
  Ralph 91
  Stephen 61,130
Reddy, Jack 66
Redmond, Jesse 126
Red Shirt (Zowaves) 186
Reed, James 59
  William 59
Reeves, Alfred 44
  Elijah 45
  Jane 45
  Jesse 45
  John 44
  Lazarus 44
  Leah 45
  Lenora 45
  Mary 45
  Warren 45
  William E. 45
  Zachariah 44
Reynolds Family 153
Rhodes Cavalry 209
Richmond, Dilla 57,120
  Mr. 57,120
  Reddick 57,120
Ritch, Mary S. 85
  Thomas L. 85
Roark, Mike 114,134
Robb, James 124,125
Roberts, Ann 136

Roberts continued
  David 66
  Frank 134
  James 128,134
  Mary 66
  Martin P. 39
  Tom 134
Roland, Hon. Dunbar 253
Roosevelt, Captain 69
  Theodore 69
Root, George W. 352
Rowan, Charles H. 280
Runnels, Harmon 106
Rushing, Ephriam 41,81,88
  Katie 87
  Mr. 73
  Wiley 71,72
  Claiborne 66
  William 43
Ryals, C. 47
Rymes, Nancy 41
  William 41

Saddler, Isaac 99
Sandell, Camp Meeting 106
  Catherine Nobles 36
  Daniel 36
  Elizabeth 41
  Gabriel 37
  Henry 36
  John Westley 37
  Martha 37
  Mary Ann 37
  Monroe 37
  Samuel Murray 37
  Walter 37
Sandifer, Bertha 87
  Elizabeth 75,79
  Jackson 75
  John 75
  Mary 86
  Peter 63,75,80
  Robert 75
  William 75,86
Sargent, Winthrop 26
Sartin, Alfred 39
  ----- 76
  Amanda 39
  Emily 39
  Helen 39,66
  James 39
  John 39,78
  Joseph 39
  Leander 39,66
  Major 39,49,58
  Wesley 86
  Widow 39
  William 39,78
Schmidt, Jacob 56,68,69
Schilling, John 77
Sessions, Narcissa 76
Secession Convention 148
Sevier, Colonel 43
Shirley, Nancy 66
Shaffer, Eve 40
Shamwell, Miss Alice 152
Shelby, Colonel 43
Shontell, Minnie 77
S---p, J. T. 106
Sibley, Esther 128
  William 39,128
Simmo, I. M. 46
Simmons, Calvin 41,81
  Cyrus 41
  George 41
  Holly 41
  Jackson 41
  James 81
  L. A. 61
  Mary 105,106
  Mason 41
  Narcissa 41
  Richard 41

Simmons continued
  Solomon 41
  William 41
  Willis 41,97
Singletary, Joe 320
Smith, Caroline 69
  Charles 80
  Daniel 69,88
  Densmore 88
  Doit 88
  Eli 36
  Elias 75,80
  Eliza 88
  George 82,83,88,177,178
  Jacob 59,68,69
  James 53
  Jasper 87
  Jeremiah 36,88
  Jerre 71
  Jerry 68,69
  Joan 68,69
  John 24,53,69
  Joseph 80,96,112,130
  Liddy 71
  Luther 42
  Margaret 53
  Mary Elizabeth 264
  Melissa 88
  Melonie 71
  Monroe 75
  N. C. 88
  Nancy 88
  Narcissa 53,83
  Permissa 88
  Pharo 80
  Salena 69
  Sarah 52,53,69
  Wild Bill 98
  Willie 51
  William 69,264
  Wyatt 36,39
  Zachariah 80
Snead, John 75
  Keziah 75
Song of Bonnie Blue Flag 147
Soldiers Friend Society 186
Soule, Mr. 153
Sparkman, A. P. 57,110, 297
  Alvira 57
  Cynthia Adaline 57
  Martha E. 57,120
  Reddick T. 27,56,79,107
  Thomas Wiley 57
  Victoria 57
  William 57,153
Spencer, George 99
Spinks, Brothers 63,64
Sprink, Eliza 101
Stallings, Eliza 81
  James 81
  Jane 81
  Jeff 81
  John 80,81
  Margaret 81
  Nancy 81
  Willie 81
  Winnie 81
Statham, J. B. 54
  Jimmerson 54
  R. Y. 57
Stephens, Ann Louise 55, 73
  Cathorine 55
  Cecelia 55
  Samuel James 55,73
Stephenson, William 125
Stockdale, Thomas R. 112, 120,127,140,151
  Cavalry 203
Stockstill, Joshua 97
Stogner, John 72

Stovall, Charles Green 68, 106
  Drury 58,66,67,68
  Felix Crawford 68
  Henry 58,66,67
  John Lewis 68
  Mary 66,67
  Ralph 58,66,67,72,88,89, 121
  Sally 66,67
  Thomas Peter 68
  William 68
Stuart, George 130
  Oscar J. E. 120
  Sam 77
Summers, Emma 89
Summit Home Militia 210
Summit Settlers 152
Sumrall, Agnes 66
  Margaret 129
  Mary J. 129
  Nancy 66
  Nannie 280
Sykes, Family 61

Tate, Daniel 84
  T. E. 280
Taylor, John 35
Thigpen, Widow 93
Thomas, Baxter 51
  Jesse 40
  Mary M. 51
  Wesley A. 51
  Wesley H. 51,153
Thompson, Alexander 345
  Amelia 345
  D. W. 345
  Ebilene 78
  Hardy 42,46,51
  Hugh 40
  Jefferson 345
  John 46,97
  J. P. Street 345
  Martha S. J. 99,345
  Mary 40
  Parham 78
  Parish 48,59,78
  Reel 96
  Robert 345
  Sarah 44
  Susan Jane 152
  Virginia 345
  William 345
Thornhill, Brian 83
  E. T. 24
  Elisha 17,72,83
  Elizabeth 66
  Evan J. 66
  Hillary B. 83
  Hiram 66
  Isham 83
  J. 83
  James 83
  Joe M. 66
  John 66,83
  Joseph 25,58,66
  Liddy 66
  Lucella 66
  Mary Ann 83
  Millie Ann 83
  Polly 66
  Susan 83
  Thornhills 64,82
  William 18,66,82,83
Tillman, Elizabeth 131
  Lucy 131
  Mary 131
Tony, ----- 75
Townsend, W. H. 290
Travis, John Quincy 181
Tucker, Family 265,297
Turnage, Elijah 42,76
  Teletha 128

Turnipseed, ----- 44
  Berkley 44
  Clifton 44
  Harris 44
  Laura 44
  Widow 134
Tupple, Mary Bradley 131
Twist, ----- 115
Tyler, Fannie 83
  Lizzie 83
  Sarah 83
  Sofrona 83
  W. G. 83,88
  William 74,113
Tynes, Elizabeth 74
  Susan 73

Ulmer, David 131

Vannison, Judge 120
Varnado, Isham E. 126
  Louis H. 126
Vaughn, David 156
  Elizabeth 155
  Polly Ann 155
Vaught, Mary E. 57,297
  Major W. W. 57,131,297
Vincent, Professor 112

Waddell, John 289
Wade, Bob 120
Wadsworth, Sally 60
  William 60
Waggoner, Family 122
  Louis 292
Walker, Augustus Sarah 42
  Annie 43
  Barbara 43
  Cornelius 43
  Daniel 42,106
  Elisha 42
  Elizabeth 42
Walker, Family 99
  John 42,71,72,93
  Jeremiah 42
  Levisa 43
  Margaret 43
  Martha 42,43
  Mary 42,93
  Pollie 43
  Rhoda 43,44
  S. Cicero 35,351
  Sarah Jane 43
  Wesley 43
  William 42,71
  Zebiah 42
Wallace, Jesse 100,123
Ward, Ruhamie 43
Ware, Hyram 91
Warner, John D. 112
  Miss 61
  Taletha 83
  Thomas Cargill 61
Warren, John 12,35,72,92
  Priscilla 35,44
  Sally 35,42
Weathersby, H. E. 120,139, 142,150
  Hatton 96
Wells, Eleazor 44
  Elizabeth 44,46
  George 99
  James 44
  Nannie 99
  Nathaniel 43,44,46,107
  Rebecca 98
  Rhoda 44
  Rosalba 46
  Thomas 43
White League 290
White, J. J. 131
  Thonly L. 54

White, ----- 105
Whitehurst, William 94
Whitworth, Samuel 42
Whitfield, Albert Hall 274
Wicker, Fanny 139
Wiggins, Malissa Ellis 60
  Rev. David M. 60
Wilkinson, Cathorine 76
  Elizabeth 58
  Mary 58,59,76
  Rebecca 58,59,76
  William 58
Williams, Cathorine 100
  Giles 129
  Hezekiah 99
  John 81
  Jeremiah 24
  Madge 85
  Moses 85
  Mary 129
  Nelly 280
  N. 46
  Parham 41,115,128
  R. 46

Williams Continued
  R. 46
  Robert 26
  Sally 129
  Western 85
  William 45
  Colonel 43
Whorton, Dr. Vincent Jones 101
  Wiley H. 101
  William Monroe 101
Wilson, Mary 92,100
Wiltz, Louis A. 291
Winborne, David 25,41,130
  Mary 130
Winston, Colonel 43
Womack, Dorothy Pryder 345
Woodriffs 76
  Amelia 84,85,263
  Elias 85,263
  Eliza 84,85
  Lucetta 85
  Mary 84,85
  Seth 84,85
  William 84,85

Woods, General 78
Weatherford, Lane 89
Wright, Demise 122
  Lucy 67,68
  Luke 22

Yarborough, Rebecca 120, 129
  Jabez 129
Young, Charles B. 111
Youngblood, Benjamin 58, 90,151
  ----- 76
  Hannah 105
  Joseph 122,151
  Mary 122

Zachary, Cornelius 156
  Zeigler, William 117

Abby, Edward 14
Abney, R. R. 68
Adams, Anderson 31
  Anna 31
  Bedy 31
  C. W. 31
  Caroline Rawls 129
  Celia 152
  Elizabeth 150
  Fielding 97
  James E. 129
  John 4,5
  Lelia 113
  Price A. 108
  Col. R. L. 39
  Robert 152
  William 31,129
Addison, Ashford 103
  Bledso 62
  Catherine 9
  Esther 164
  Felix 25
  Hanceford 25
  Hiram 1,19,25,31,45
  Joseph 104
  Julia 62
  Letitia Ann 157
  Rebecca 25
  Richard M. 52
  Sarah M. 35
  Zillia Ann Mullins 52
Aills, James W. 25
Ainsworth, Louis 133
  Minnie Holmes 133
Akers, Essie Mae 115
  Mrs. S. 61
Akin, Isham 13,19
  John 1,13,19,25
  Rev. John 84
  Susan Garlington 84
  William 84
Albritton, Abitha Amanda 92
  Adam 90
  Agnes 89
  Agnes Catherine 92
  Algene 92
  Amy 89
  Andrew Jackson 92
  Angeline Rebecca 92
  Avarillah 91
  Avis 169
  Benjamin 89,91
  Benjamin P. 169
  Bertha J. 169
  Charles 89
  Edward 89,169
  Elizabeth 89,90,91
  Ethel Dupre 92
  Etna Joseph 92
  Frances 50
  Francis 89,91
  Francis L. 91,169
  Francis M. 91
  George 89,90
  Henry 90
  Henry H. 91,169
  James 31,89,90,91,92,169
  James L. 169
  James S. 169
  Jane 50,91,92
  John 89,90,91,92
  John Gabriel 92
  John H. 91,169
  John L. 169
  Julia 52
  Lama Richard 92
  Lanier 90
  Lavina Elizabeth 169
  Lilly Julia 91
  Lorinda J. 169

Part 2

Albritton continued
  Lucy Elizabeth 91
  Luke 90
  Margaret M. 169
  Martha 91
  Martha Ann 91
  Mary 90,91
  Mary Ann 91,92,169
  Mary C. 169
  Matilda 91,169
  Matthew 58,89,90,92
  Matthew R. 91,169
  Myrtis 169
  Nancy 90
  Nancy E. 169
  Nancy Jane 92
  O. O. 169
  Ophelia 63
  Peter 89,90
  Peter, Jr. 90
  R. 51
  Ralph 89
  Richard 4,25,31,89,90,91,92,169
  Richard A. J. 91,169
  Richard Glover 92
  Sarah 56,91,92
  Sarah Francis 92
  Sarah J. 169
  Sarah Jane 91
  Stephen 91
  Thomas 89,90,92
  Webster 63
  William 90
  William J. 91
  William Robertson 92
Albro, Samuel 37
Alexander, Allie 111
  Amanda 58
  Bethany 44
  Courtney 61
  David 25
  Isaac 1,10
  Lura 62
  Robert G. 31
Alford, Anice Ball 97
  Ann 83
  B. S. 115
  Bersheba Moorehead 97
  Betsey Hope 97
  Calpernia 98
  Celia Lewis 83
  Charity 94
  Charity Ann Self 92
  Clarasy 98
  Clothide 165
  Cynthia 98
  Edwin 4,14,19,25,31,95,118
  Elias 94
  Elizabeth 93
  Elizabeth Bryant 95
  Elizabeth Ginn 98
  Elizabeth Waddell 97
  Emily S. 98
  Emma B. 78
  Eveline Ginn 96
  Frances 93
  Frankie Seaborn 95,96
  Frederick Ellis 136
  Georgia Pigott 142
  Goodrich 93,94
  Grace 93
  Harriet Crawford 97
  Henderson 54,98
  Hosea 98
  Hugh 98
  Ira 31
  Ira Payne 97
  Isaac 93,94,98
  Isabella Presley 98
  Mrs. J. B. 62

Alford continued
  Jackson 98
  Jacob 92,93,94,95,96
  Jacob L. 97
  James 92,93,94
  Jane 165
  Dr. Jeptha J. 97
  Jeptha Martin 136
  Jess 165
  Jesse 98
  Jesse Powell 97
  Job 94
  John 92,93,95
  John G. 98
  John Sebourn 96,98,139
  John Wesley 70,98
  Joseph C. 96
  Joseph Seaborn 98
  Julius 92,93,94
  Julius C. 96,97
  Julius Newton 165
  Lacy 144
  Laura Elizey 123
  Laura Warner 136
  Laveta 98
  Leander 98
  Lena 78
  Leslie 111
  Lodowick 92,93,94,95
  Lucy 93,145
  Luther 98,141
  Margaret Brumfield 96,98,139
  Margaret Maximillion 97
  Marshall Thomas 92,98
  Martha 98
  Martha A. 75
  Martha E. 165
  Martha R. 98
  Martha Smith 95,97,118
  Martha Waddell 95,97
  Mary 98
  Mary Brumfield 97
  Mary Felder 96,98,127
  Mary L. Stafford 86
  Mary S. Kirk 76,96,98
  Milton J. 98
  Moses 96
  Rev. N. E. 83,86
  Needham Bryant 97
  Needham J. 95,97
  Needham W. 98
  Newton 97
  Noel W. 97
  Ollie W. 63
  Ona Arnett 97
  Oscar 62
  Otis 98,142
  Patty 94
  Ramond 98
  Richard 97
  Samantha 97
  Sarah 94,150
  Sarah Brumfield 141
  Sarah E. 98
  Sarah Smith 97
  Seabourn (Seaborn) 25,31,65,70,74,76
  Seaborn Lochran 98,123
  Seaborn S. (Dr.) 97
  Sebastian 98
  Simon E. 98
  Sion 94
  Sophia E. 65,98
  Susannah 93
  Tabitha Warner 136
  Thomas Sebourn 95,97
  Unity 93
  Warren 31,92,94,96,97
  Warren Jackson 83
  William 25,31,92,93,95,96,98

Alford continued
　William C. 31
　William Harmon 97
　William Riley 98
　William Theodore 97
　Willie 141
　Willie J. 98
　Willis 98
Alfred, Hester 63
Allday, Daniel 19
Alldridge, Isham 10
Allen, Ann 15
　Barnabas 1,8,11
　Caroline 55
　Catherine 99
　Catherine O. 36,66
　Catherine Williamson 99
　Chestain 31
　Cynthia Ginn 141
　Elizabeth Ann 99
　Ella L. 61
　Felix 19,31,99
　Gabriel 8
　Garret 1,15
　Jim W. 140
　Patience 5
Allgood, Wiet (Wyatt) 1
Allmand, Allice 99
　Anne 99
　Charles C. H. 99
　Henry 99
　Isaiah 99
　Malissa 62,99
　Mary Jane 99
　Sarah 99
　William 99
Allston, Peter 100
　Peter, Jr. 100
　Sarah Margaret 100
Alvarez, Ben F. 63
Amacker, A. N. 162
　E. 162
　J. J. 162
　Jacob L. 103
　James 163
　James R. 162
　John J. 168
　Lucy Jane 168
　M. 162
　W. B. 162
　William 162
Ambrose, Lula 92
Ammond, Frank 19
　Michael 19
Ammons, Jno. 11,19
　Michl. 13,19
Anders, James, Jr. 9
　Michael 78
Anderson, Arthur 31
　Dr. J. A. 103
　Thomas 31
　W. C. 40
Andress, Joseph 155
Andrews, Ada Holmes 136
　August 51
　Burrell 31
　Elisha C. 124
　Hudson 25
　James 1,13,19,25
　James, Jr. 11
　John 31
　Josephine M. 124
　Maggie 36
　Malachi Olaf 167
　Mary 167
　Mary A. Clark 51
　Micajah 4,19
　Nancy 155
　Robert 63
　Sophronia 61
　Thompson 25
　Will 136
　William 1,14,19,25
　Williamson 25,31

Andrews continued
　Willie 113
Applewhite, Dr. E. L. 79
　Eldridge 147
　Elisha 147
　Elizabeth 155
　J. A. (Rev.) 68
　James 156
　James (Rev.) 68
　John 155
　John Jr. 147
　John R. 156
　Martha Ann 146
　Marvin 79
　Mary Ann 68
　Prudence 82
　Stephen 1,4
　Thomas 82
Ard, Thomas 1
Arlidge, Jno. 13
Armstead, Mary E. 73
Armstrong, Abner 1
　Annie 113
　Canty (or Lanty) 19,25
　Jesse 1
　John O. 80
　Jonathan 1
　Mattie Regina 80
Arnold, Ashley 19
　Cynthia Holmes 134
　James 19
　Nancy Tate 158
　Van 134
　William 19
Arrendell, John 94
Arthur, Barnes 14,19
　Thomas 8,14
Ashton, Henry 1
Askue, Henry 1
Atkins, John 8
Atkinson, Jesse W. 39
　Myra C. 39
Atwood, Abr. 13
Austin, William G. 68

Babington, Mary 112
　Victoria 112
Bacot, Adam 60,101
　Ann Roberts 101
　Anna M. 40
　Cyrus 100
　Elizabeth 100
　Esaye 99
　Eugene H. 101
　Francois 99
　Jeanne 99
　Jesse 39
　Julia 101
　Laban 1,7,8,13,19,25,31,
    43,100
　Levi 101
　Lorinda 100
　Maria Allston 100
　Maria Louise 100
　Martha 99
　Mary 100
　Mary Lucinda 100
　Peter H. 100
　Pierre (3) 99,100
　Rachel 101
　Rebecca F. 100
　Samuel (4) 19,25,100
　Susannah 100
　William (Dr.) 39,101
Badon, Courtney Ellzey 124
　Henry 25,31
　Henry B. 88
　Madeline May 88
　William H. 124
Baggett, Miriam 145
Bagley, Benjamin 9,13,19
　William 1,4

Bailey, Abr. 19
　James 1
　Thomas 1
Baker, Kate 77
　W. F. 71
Bales, Martha 63
　Nellie 81
　Noel 31
　J. W. 63
Ball, Alma 111
　Arthur 110
　Bennie 111
　Blant 110
　Carrie 110
　Catherine 112
　Cynthia Alford 97
　D. N. 79,81
　Daniel 31,112
　Daniel Warren 112
　Dora Holmes 136
　Edward 112
　Effie 111
　Eliza 110
　Elizabeth 66
　Emily 110
　Emma 111
　Fannie 111
　Floyd 153
　Frances 112
　Iddo 110,112
　James 110,111,112
　James Michael 97
　Jeanette 112
　Jeffie 111
　Jesse 25,97,110,111,167
　Jesse W. 136
　Kitura 110
　Liberty B. 31
　Lacey Alford 97
　Lizzie 112
　Mrs. M. E. Tyler 81
　Mary 110
　Minnie 111
　Monroe 112
　Myra 110
　Myrtis Blackwell 137
　Nancy 18
　Needham 110,111
　Newton 111
　Philonia Rebecca 112
　Rebecca 110
　Robert 111,112
　Sampson E. 1
　Samuel 112
　Sophia 111
　Thaddaeus 111
　Walter 110,111
　Will 137
　William 110
　Wilmuth 110
Ballard, Elizabeth 53
　James 9,14,19
　John 9,14
　Kittwood King 71
　Lewis 1,19,24
　Nathan 1,20,25
　Reuben 1,19,25,31
Bambert, Dicy 144
Banister, Aaron 52
　Una Brock 137
　William 137
Banks, Levi 1
Bankston, J. J. 31
　John 6,19,25
　Sarah 15
Banton, Marion 167
Barbar, Samuel 9
　William 10
Barkeley, Nancy 16
Barker, John B. 19
　Nancy 16
　Samuel 13,19
Barksdale, Abner 13,19,25
　Collier 1

Barksdale continued
  Fleury S. 31
  William F. 9,13,19,25,31
Barlow, Samuel C. 13
Barner, Florence Magee 152
Barnes, C. C. 76
  Charlie C. 85
  Harris 74
  James Allen 74
  Kate Long 82
  Mrs. M. E. Ford 75
  Mary A. 74
  Mary Hennington 82
  Mary Spears 74
  Mary V. 75
  Missie King 82
  Richard Flower's 75
  Thomas 19
  W. W. 80
  William 9,12,74
  Willis 82
Barnet, Gilliam 92
  James 92
  Mark 4
  P. 5
Barr, Amanda S.P.P. 65
  Mrs. Mart A. 66
  Mollie W. 66
  R. W. 66
  R. Wesley 36
Barrett, Claude F. 40
  George 1
Barron, Ageselous 19
  Daves 14,19
  Edward 19
  Ella 54
  John 31
  Luna 62
  Samuel 15
  Victoria 49
  W. W. 54
  William 49
Barry, Vera A. 143
Barton, Buck 144
  C. (Est.) 19
  Lucy 112
  Robert 19
  Sarah 19
Bass, Patterson 162
Bates, Elizabeth 161
  John 161
  Malinda B. 161
  William 25
Batson, Betsey 14
  Eli 8
  James 1,8,14
  Peter 1,8,14,19
  Seth 1
  Thomas 1,8,14
Battard (Ballard?), Lewis 13
Battles, H. A. 38
Batton, Yearli 144
Baudoin, Marguerite 99
Baugh, Mrs. E. M. 61
Baylis, Lon 112
Beam, C. W. 82,83
  Charles Walton 84
  Fannie Sample 84
  Mollie Carruth 83,84
Beard, Aaron 11,19,31
  Elisha 62
  Ellen 18
  J. A. 61
  Jane 49
  John 31
  Keziah 16,54
  Louise 61
  Rebecca 61
  Thezia 16
  William 1,8,14
Bearden, A. J. 31
  Catherine 62
  Emily 61

Bearden continued
  James 62
  Jeremiah 25,65
  Joseph 62
  Lula 62
  William 19
  Jerem 12,19
Beasley, Cornelius 25
  James 14
  John 14
  William 1
Bechcom, Henry S. 109
Beck, Sybill Ellzey 123
Beesley, John 19
Beeson, Rev. B. A. 80
  Evaline Collins 80
  Uriah 19
Bell, Ann Catherine 20
  Eleazer 9,12
  Thomas 1,8,14,19
Belotte, Peter 99
Bend, Robt. 15
Bennett, Ann McCarty 120, 121
  Elisha C. 79
  John 16,19,112
  Litha 112
  William 112
Berkley, Burgess 122
Bernard, Elisa 104
  Louisa 18
  Mellissa 104
Berry, Henry D. 165
  James 1
  Seborn 31
Berryhill, Robert 19
Bethea, Mary LeGette 80
  Rev. R. C. 80
Bickham, Abner 101
  Alexander Mouton 101
  Benjamin 101,120
  Benj. Franklin 101
  Charlie E. 143
  George 137
  Hannah L. 101
  James A. 39
  James Salisbury 101
  John 101
  Lewis C. 39,101
  Maggie A. 39
  Mary Fletcher 101
  Nancy Ellis 120
  Sarah 101
  Thomas 4,101,135
  Thomas Benton C. 101
  William 5,101,104
Bigner, John 19,31
  Margaret 57
  William 57
Biles, William 25
Bingham, Hugh 31
Bird, Bartlet 19
Bishop, Holloway 25,31
  John W. 43,138
  Mary Ellzey 138
Bivens, Geneva Angeline 110
  Josephine Cora 110
Bixler, William 54
Black, John 19,110
  William 82
Blackbourn, Jesse 20
Blackwell, A. C. 137
  Benjamin M. 137
  Eudean 141
  Fannie Hilburn 137
  J. Edgar 137
  J. L. 137
  Jane 17
  Janie Rimes 137
  Maggie Lambert 137
  Mary Andrews 137
  Maud 144
  Nancy 114

Blackwell continued
  Nathan 114
  Sam Sidney 137
  Samantha 150
  Vina 17
  W. Cornelius 138
Blair, Hugh 120
  Jemimah McCarty 120
Blount, Chelly Conerly 105
  Mary V. 62
Blue, Angus 1
  Daniel 1
Blunt, Granberry 17,18
  Mary 18
Boggs, Frank 62
Bohannon, Wiley 1
Boid, Isaac 19
  James 19
  John 19
Boit, Shadr. 19
Bolling, Mary A. 62
Bond, Elizabeth 156
  Fenimore 130
  Gideon 1,8,14,19
  Henry 1,8,14,19,25
  Henry, Jr. 31
  Hugh Sr. 31
  Iris Hood 130
  James 1
  John 1,6,8,14
  John Sr. 8
  Peter 31
  Preston 19,25,31
  Robert 1,8,19,25
  William 1,8
Bonner, Willis 162
Bonney, Henry 31
  Peris 25,31,86
  William 31
Booker, H. J. 31
  Jackson 25
  James 123
Boone, Daniel 83
  Dela Williams 83
  Emmett 83
  Frederic 25
  J. F. 83
  Sarah 12
  Sarah Holmes 132
  Skinner 31,132
  V. V. 83
  William 12
Booty, C. B. 31
  J. E. 62
  Marshal 62
Boston, John 82
  Mattie Dunman 82
Bosworth, N. W. 26
Botton, Uriah 25
Boutewell, Elisa 6
  James A. 25,31
  Lanson 19
  Thomas 12
Bowman, Claiborne 85
  Elizabeth 52
  Elizabeth S. H. 85
  Jesse 31
  Leroy 11,25,31
  R. J. 86
  Richardson 9,12,19,25,85
  Uriah 25
  William 11
  Willis 53
Boyd, Capt. A. A. 87
  Miss A. A. 57
  Andrew 10,11,25
  Asa 50
  Mrs. C. A. 87
  Christine 113
  Courtney 61
  Courtney Ann 63
  Eliza 44
  F. Marion 64

Boyd continued
  Henry 31
  Hester 63
  Isaac 25
  J. M. 64
  Jackson 31
  James 13,25
  Lewis B. 47
  Martha C. 47
  Miley Parker 141
  Monroe 141
  Nancy 44
  S. C. 63
  Samuel 10
  Simeon 25,31
  W. W. 64
  William 31
  Willie 62
Boyet, Anderson 31
  Shadrack 25
Brabbam, John 162
Bracy, Cynthia 110
Braddy, William 1,19,25
Bradham, Minerva 54
  Wilson 54
  Zaceriah 31
Bradshaw, Thos. 13
Brady, Martha 144
Branan, Jno. P. 25
Branch, Benjamin Franklin 117
  H. M. 59
  Martha Ann 18
  Sarah 59
Bray, Sarah A. 109
Breed, Elizabeth 159,162
  John 162
  Lucy 162
Breedeland, Abraham 9
Breland, Alexander 133
  Christina 62
  David 10,12
  Elizabeth 16,62
  Francis 16
  George 112
  Harriet Holmes 133
  Hillery 1,12,20
  J. Abr. 12
  James 16,25,31
  James M. 20
  James R. 12
  John 20
  John R. 4,17,31
  Mary 17
  Mary Conerly 112
  Sarah Ella 144
  Thomas 31
Brent, Sister A. S. 61
  Charnel 1
  Esther Ellzey 123
  Jesse 31,123
  Joe Lee 39
  John (2) 1,9,11,19,25,31
  John A. 31
  Meredith 1,11,19
  Mollie 70
  Preston 39
  Robert S. 113
  Thomas 1,19,25,31
  William 31
Brese, Fredr. 19
Brewer, D. B. 59
  Rachel A. 64
  Ruby 63
Bridgeport, Miss 39
Bridges, A. F. 31
  B. F. 101
  Berry R. 19
  E. V. 84
  Eliza 66
  Ephr. 11,19
  H. F. 74
  H. O. 66

Bridges continued
  Hugh Franklin 77
  James J. 20,25
  John 19
  L. H. 31
  Martha 74
  Mary Tate 158
  Moses 11,19
  Peter Q. 19
  Richard R. 19
  Sampson 1
  William 19
Bright, Caleb 10
  Jane 11
Briley, Abr. 11
Brister, Emma 113
  Hocketta 19
  John 1
  Thompson 11,19,25
  William 25,31
Britt, Sarah M. 79
Brock, Alexander H. 139
  Armetha Holmes 137
  Arvie Holmes 134,137
  Bell Conerly 137
  Beulah Bailey 137
  Clarence 62
  Dannie Tate 137
  DeWitt Talmadge 137
  Eli 118
  Eli P. 25
  Hazel Packwood 137
  Henri McClendon 137
  Hobson (Dr.) 137
  Ida 137
  Ida Conerly 138
  James 25,31
  James (Dr.) 137
  Jane 137
  Jasper 137
  Jeptha S. (Dr.) 137
  Lattimore (Dr.) 137
  Lenora Babington 137
  Lucius William (Dr.) 137
  Mamie Bickham 137
  Mary McDougle 137
  Mattie 144
  Ollie 137
  R. A. 137
  Richmond 137
  Samantha Smith 137
  Sophronia Holmes 137
  Valentine 137
  William 108
  William Sr. 55
  William Valentine 137
  Winney Stallings 119
Broderick, M. H. 71
Brooks, Eddie Elias 106
  Emily 37
Bronson, Roche Irene 79
Broom, Florence 109
Brown, A. N. 85
  Ala Bennett (Mrs.) 155
  Angie 41
  Ann 64
  Arch. 19
  Birthmella Mack 85
  Charlotte Felder 51,78,120
  Cintha 60
  Daniel 1
  Elbert 84
  Filona Branch 85
  Frank 61
  Franklin 58
  E. G. 31
  Fannie J. 54
  Hugh 19,25,31
  Huldy 54
  Ideller 58
  J. I. 60
  J. L. 72
  James L. 81

Brown continued
  Jane 31
  John 1,9,14,19,154
  John P. 31
  Joseph 9
  Joseph Augustus 109
  Katie 59
  Margaret E. 66
  Marian Grubbs 87
  Morgan 99
  Martha 160
  Moses 1
  Robert 1,19,24
  Rosie 81
  Sarah 91,112,169
  Sarah E. 165
  Susan Jane 154
  Susannah 16
  T. T. 31
  Thomas Jefferson 87
  W. M. 72
  Wiley 64,66
  William 25,51,61,78
Browning, Hannah 154
Brownlee, Belle A. 40
Bruce, Elizabeth 6
Brumfield, Albert Davis 141
  Alex C. 165
  Alexander Griffin 139
  Alice 147
  Alice Brock Pierce 139
  Andrew Jackson 75,86
  Angeline Bullock 140
  Arkansas 62
  Axa Jane 140
  Beulah Pigott 141
  Caroline 101,102
  Catherine Conerly 138
  Charles 140
  Charles Dawson 140
  Chester C. 140
  Clara Smith 141
  Claude 138
  Courtney Smith 139
  Cynthia 141
  Cynthia Holmes 140
  Daniel 165
  David Caldwell 145
  Davis 4,24,31,140
  Davis Alexander 140
  Dawson 106
  Dudley Clarence 141
  Edith Pigott 139
  Edna Brock 137
  Effie 140
  Elijah 140,165
  Elisha 139
  Elisha Kelly 141
  Elisha Thomas 139
  Eliza Simmons 139
  Elizabeth 138
  Elizabeth S. 137
  Ellen 106
  Ellis 141
  Ellis Blackwell 141
  Elmer 137
  Emma 165
  Fannie Sandifer 138
  Florence Magee 140
  Frances McCain 141
  Fred Lafayette 141
  George Alex 165
  George Ann McClendon 141
  George W. 141
  Henrietta Angeline 107
  Henry J. 140
  Henry S. 41
  Isaac 31,101,107,138
  Isaac Nelson 139
  Isaac Preston 141
  Isaac Richard 140
  J. W. 64

Brumfield continued
　Jackson 44
　James 25,31,142
　James Wesley 140
　Jess Emma 147
　Jesse 25,31,138,165
　Jesse Davis 140
　Jesse E. 141
　Jesse Eli 139
　John 138,140
　John E. 140
　John G. 31,139
　John Griffin 139
　John J. 147
　John Wesley 139
　Joseph Davis 139
　Josiah 139,140
　Kelly Calvin 141
　Lamenda Smith 140
　Laura Burkhalter 139
　Laura Rushing 140
　Leslie 140
　Lestie Smith 139
　Lizzie 147
　Lizzie Bunnings 140
　Lilly Johnson 140
　Liza McKenzie 139
　Lois 62
　Lottie 108
　Louisa Bullock 139
　Louisa Magee 141
　Lovie 111
　Lucy 112
　Lucy R. Bickham 139
　M. Dawson 140
　Maggie Crowe 139
　Margaret Burch 139
　Margaret Kelly 138
　Martha Lewis 86
　Mary Allen 140
　Mary Ann Margaret 165
　Mary Ellen 140
　Mary Ellzey 139
　Mary James 140
　Millie Rushing 140
　Monroe H. 140
　Montoria Pittman 141
　Myra M. 140
　Nancy 18
　Nancy Fortenberry 141
　Nancy Louise 139
　Nathaniel G. 138
　Nellie Pittman 141
　Netie Conerly 139
　Nora Fitzpatrick 139
　Ollis Blackwell 141
　Priscilla Jane 140
　Rebecca Courtney 165
　Richard Silman 139
　Salena A. J. Warner 139
　Salena Morris 140
　Samuel O. 139
　Sarah 140
　Sarah Fortenberry 141
　Sarah Jo Ann Smith 139
　Sarah Lewis 140
　Sarah C. Simmons 141
　Serana Rushing 140
　Thomas 84,165
　Uriah 139
　Virginia Holmes 138,139
　William 84,140
　William Davis 141
　William Henry H. 138
　William Isaac 140
　William Preston 141
　William T. 140
　Willis N. 18,139
　Willis Dawston 139
　Willis Easley 140
　Willis Nathaniel 140
　Willis R. 141
　Zonetta 141
Brunson, Matthew 100

Byan, Joseph 69
　Redic 69
Bryley, Abraham 8
Buckaloo, John 1
　Richard 1
Buckhalter, Daniel 19
Buckley, James 1
　James (Capt.) 73
Buford, Byrd 19
　Param 19
Bullard, Elizabeth 145
Bullin, William 1
Bullock, Aida 101
　Alexander 102
　Alice 64
　Angeline Brumfield 141
　Ann 92
　B. W. 57
　Bedia 101
　Caroline 17
　Cynthia 102
　David 1,8,19,25
　Davis 101,102
　Edward 13,19,25,31
　Eliza 18
　Eliza R. 54
　Ellen 102
　Hugh 17,101,102,139
　Iva Mary 157
　J. L. W. 31
　James 1,92
　Jim Jordan 102
　Jerry J. 66
　Jesse L. 102
　Joel 16,101,102
　Joel J. 141
　Joseph J. 54
　Joseph R. 101
　L. T. 62
　Lemuel 14,101
　Luiza 31,102
　Pernecia 18
　Pernus 87
　Quinny 25,101
　Richard 101
　Samuel C. 101
　Silas 1,8
　Simeon 101
　Thomas 101
　Victoria Ellzey 138
　Wesley H. 138
　William 9,11,101
　William (Est.) 25
　William O. 66
　Zechariah 25,31
Burch, Edward 31
Burford, David 11,19
Burge, Nathaniel 1
　Washington 1
Burkhalter, Daniel 25,102
　Emily 102
　Henry S. 102
　Henry T. 25,31,102
　J. F. 62
　Maria Lucas 102
　Mary Anne 102
　Sarah Mildred 153
　Sela Lucas 102
　Theresa Luter 102
　W. J. 31
Burnes, Thos. 20
Burney, Mark 25
Burnham, L. B. 137
Burns, John 31
　Reason 1
Burron, Saml. 19
Burton, Ann Tate 158
　Caleb 13
　Elbert 14
　Mariah M. 5
　Sandra 14
　Thomas 19
Busby, Ezekiel 31,57
　Lourene 63

Busby continued
　Wm. Thompson 48
Bush, Mary Eliza 110
Bushings, Florence 113
Butler, D. P. 79
　John D. 31
　Luke 1
　Margarett Thompson 87
　Mary Emma 108
Buvens, Francis 97
Byerly, George 25
Byrd, Ida 152
　Isabella 68
　Mary Matilda 162
　Waren Edgar 152

Cagle, John 1
Cain, Annie Holmes 133
　J. I. 133
　Mrs. J. I. 61
Calbert, Richmond 1
Calhoun, Lucious 78
Calquhoun, John 107
　Loftin 107
Cameron, Eliza 112
Cammel, Jas. 13
Camp, Joseph 158
　Nancy Tarpley 138
　Thomas 138
Campbell, George W. 111
Canady, Nathen 1
Carmen, Winney 114
Carnes, Johnson 26
Carpenter, John 1
　William 1
Carr, James 12,20
　John 9
　John Peter 71
　Maranda A. R. 71
　Richard 12
　William 20
Carrie, Mary 20
Carroll, John 26,31
Carruth, Alexander 83
　Emma Beam 82
　Farrar 165
　J. A. 82
　John 26,69
　Lizzie J. 161
　Robert A. 31
　Samuel E. 76
Carsey, Susie 63
Carson, Elizabeth 17
　J. D. 143
　John, Jr. 1
　John, Sr. 1
　John W. 31
　Margaret 17
　Philone 165
　Samuel 31
Cartaian, Mrs. Elizabeth 63
Carter, Addie M. 104
　Alice 104
　Allen 1,10,13,20,26,31,102
　Angeline 103,104
　Aria 104
　Artabanus 103
　Augustus 104
　Benjamin Bradford 142
　Bennett 26,31
　Betsey 16,102
　Billy A. (Capt.) 104
　Bradford 142
　Brazella 104
　Burley 104
　Burrell 1,14,20,26,31,102,103
　Cora Arlena 104
　Cornie C. 104
　D. R. 142
　Della Russell 142

Carter continued
  Derrell 14,20,26,31,102,
    103
  DeWitt 104
  Earl G. 104
  Elijah A. 104,144
  Eliza Moore 142
  Elizabeth 16,102,103,
    104
  Emily 103
  Felden 104
  Finland 104
  George 1,144
  Haley 104
  Haley M. 104
  Hannibal 104
  Hardy 1,14,26,102,103
  Harmon 103
  Harvel 20,26,31,102,103
  Henry 31,160
  Isaac 8,14,26,102,103
  Israel 20,26,102,104,
    127
  Israel W. 104
  James 142
  Jameson 162
  Jinsy 103
  Joe Tig 157
  John 31,102,104
  John J. 103
  Jonathan 8,20
  Joseph W. 104
  Laban 104
  Lilah V. 106
  Lillie 104
  Lola Mary 104
  Louisiana 104
  Mahala 103
  Malitta A. 103
  Marcus E. 1
  Marcus T. 103
  Marion 103
  Martena 104
  Mary 16,102,103
  Mary Augusta 104
  Michael 1
  Minton M. 31
  Mollie 83
  Moses 26
  Nancy 20,26
  Nancy Kemp 97,142
  Nehemiah 11
  Peter H. 103
  Prentiss B. 104
  Ralph T. 104
  Redmond 97,102,142
  Richard 20
  Robert 104
  Samuel 8,14,20
  Sarah Loving 142
  Selean 17
  Sereptha 103
  Torrent 31
  Tullia 104
  Tullius 104
  Walter Lee 104
  Walton H. 103
  Wellington (Dr.) 103
  Wilford M. 103
  William 1,8,11,14,16,
    20,31,102,103
  Wm. A. (Capt.) 103
  William Kemp 142
  William Redmond 142
  Zoa 104
Caruth, John 31
  Samuel 31
Cary, J. C. 37
Cason, Mrs. M. E. 71
Cast, C. A. 51
  Norman 51
Castello, Julia Wallace 75
Caster, William 20

Castleberry, Jacob 121
  Richard 121
Catching, Emma A. Smith 72
  J. Noel 72
  Jonathan 10,15,20,26
  Joseph 1,8,15,20,26,31
  Joseph B. (Dr.) 74
  Martha Bridge 77
  Mary 16
  Philip 1,8,15,20
  S. M. 26,31
  Wm. 20
Cater, George 55
  Jno. 11
Cates, Eza. 20
Causey, Elizabeth 50
  J. M. 40
  Jefferson 108
  Jonus 17,20,26
  Lucy Conerly 82
  Margaret 59
  Nancy Emeline 146
  Seretta 17
  Solomon 9,20
  Solomon E. 156
  Virginia L. 54
  W. S. 59
Cawley (Cawsey), Jacob 9
  Jas. 20
  Jeremiah 9
  Jonas 12
  Lobn (Soin?) 12
  Mary 31
  Phillip 20
  Seth 9
Certain, see Sertain
Chamberlain, James 12
Champlin, V. W. 45
Chandler, J. B. 152
  Jno. 20
  William 11,20
Chapman, Jno. 13
Cherry, India 108
Chesnut, David 1,10
Christmas, Ike 92
  Julia Thompson 87
Clark, Aran 26
  B. F. 57
  Benj. 20
  Elisha R. 86
  Elizabeth 49
  Emma 63
  Henry 13,20,26
  Hettie H. 146
  James 117,146
  John 13
  Joseph 31
  Martha 51
  Mary 13,56,61
  Moses 13,20,26,31
  Nicholas 13
  P. C. 35
  Samuel 158
  Susanna 26
  T. J. 63
  Ulysses 26
  William 13,51
  William, Jr. 13
  Willis 20,26,31,49,51,59
  Wilson 13
Clawson, Alma Dell M. 142
Clayton, Julia Ann 155
Clement, Godfrey 20,26
Cleveland, David 1,10,13,
    16,20,26
  Grace 16
  John 20
Clower, Daniel 1,9,12
  John 1
Clowers, Michael 26
Cloy, Mary Ann 79
Coats, Pollard 1,12,20
  Polydore 9
Cocke, Joseph M. 106

Coghlin, A. J. 62
  Jackson 31
Coker, Caleb 20
  Eli 20
  James 31
Cole, Hannah 103
  Mark 8,14,20
Collins, Ann 163
  Burton 20
  Caroline 165
  Chancy 31
  G. E. 151
  Hannah 9
  J. C. 151
  John 5,20
  Joshua 1
  M. L. 151
  M. M. 151
  Moses 1,7,8,12,20
  Miss P. G. 78
  S. J. 151
  Seaborn 1,12,20
  Thomas L. 151
  Thomas Wharton 163
  W. N. 151
  William 151
Colquhone, John 74
  Mary Ann 74
Colston, Saml. 20
Combs, Miss A. A. 77
Compton, Fred E. 145
Conerly, Ada Lee 111
  Ada Lucy 108
  Adeline 106
  Albert Baxter 106
  Aletha Owen 87
  Alexander B. 106
  Alma Marcus 105
  Amanda 112
  Andrea M. 105
  Angie H. 107
  Arie Lou 107
  Baxter 87
  Berkley 106
  Betsey 105
  Buston R. 111
  C. W. 70
  Cananiza 106
  Caroline 112
  Caroline Starnes 70
  Catherine 112
  Causeby 134
  Cecelia 111
  Charity 105
  Chauncey 111
  Clara Eola 111
  Claude Iddo 107
  Cora 108
  Corine McDaniel 138
  Courtney Lula 111
  Cullen 31,105,106,107,
    112,113,138
  Cullen Clarence (Dr.)
    110
  Cullen F. 67,76
  Cullen Fleming 109
  Cullen M. 106
  Cullen Wm. 107
  Davie Edna 78
  Donald W. 107
  Dorothy S. 107
  Edward S. 111
  Eliza 110
  Eliza Jane 108
  Elizabeth 105,106
  Elizabeth Jane 112
  Elma Eoline 111
  Emaline E. 109
  Emily 112
  Emma Louise 111
  Eugene 75
  Eugene Josephine 106
  Fannie Thompson 138
  Fleming 106

Conerly continued
Frances 113
Franklin S. 106
George 106
Grover Cleveland 110
Harriet E. 67,109
Harriett Rebecca 109
Henrietta Brumfield 138
Henry Pascal 106
Herman E. 107
Ida E. 106
Ida Liddy 108
Ida May 111
Isaac N. 106
J. R. 82
J. W. 71
Jabe Thomas 107
Jabez N. 107,138
Jackson 112
James 112
James B. 76
Jas. Cullen 108
James Edward 108
James Rayford 108
James T. 108
James Wilkerson 110
Jane Holmes 134
Jerry Marcus 105
Jesse Monroe 108,139
Jesse Warren 110
John 105,106,108
John, Jr. 106
John Lampton 106
John M. 76,106
John Marvin 109
John Price 134
John R. 31,76,108,110
John Wright 110
Julia B. 106
Julius C. 106
Kesiah 105
Laura Fleming 110
Laura Virginia 110
Lenora Theodocia 110
Leona J. 106
Lettitia Ward 105
Levisa J. 106
Lila Juanita 107
Lillie Olivia 106
Lizzie 107,138
Lottie 63
Lottie Brumfield 139
Loyd 107
Luke 112
Luke (Rev.) 65,105
Luke M. 111
Luke Owen 106
Luke Ward 111
Lula 111
Lula R. 108
Luther Wilkinson 110
M. H. (Bro.) 87
Maggie Ratliff 87
Malissa 109
Margaret 105
Margaret O. 70,108
Mark Russell 108
Martha Elizabeth 110
Martha Lenore 108
Martia Stateham 136
Mary 112
Mary Ann 107,111,112
Mary E. 110
Mary Jane 106,108,109,
  112
Mary Nancy 107
Mary Wilkinson 106
Maxwell R. 107
Melissa 112
Minneola 111
Mollie 111,134
Monroe 106
Murphy 110
Murray Quin 111

Conerly continued
Myrtis Elizabeth 107
Nancy 105
Nancy E. 106
Nancy Rebecca 107
Needham E. 108
Nellie 105
Nettie McDaniel 138
Owen 26,65,70,105,106,
  110,111,112
Owen, Jr. 31,111
Owen (Major) 106
Owen Columbus 108,138
Owen Dudley 110
Owen Lewis 106
Owen Monroe 106
Owen Watt 107
Pascal 136
Patience 105
Phillip Owen 109
Polly 105
Preston Johnson 111
Price 70
Randolph 106
Rebecca Ann 111
Richard 106
Richie Lee 110
Robert J. 110,111
Robert Luckett 111
Rufus 106
Ruth Genella 110
Salena R. 106
Samuel L. 111
Samuel R. 106
Sarah 106
Sarah Elizabeth 107
Sarah J. 112
Sargent Prentiss 111
Selma Gertrude 108
Stephen 112
Susan 109,112,116
Susannah 105
Susannah Newton 106
T. S. (Dr.) 78
Thelma Louise 108
Thomas 111
Thomas B. 71
Thomas Bryon 107,138
Thos. Reives 105
Thos. Warren 110
Thos. Wilfred 106
Thyra E. 107
Uldric Earl 107
Virginia 71
W. K. 105
W. W. 70
Watt Smiley 107,138
Wesley Smiley 108
William 70,105,106,112
William Cullen 110
William Franklin 106
William Harrison 108
William James 112
William Luke 109
William M. 107
Willie Pearl 108
William T. 106
William Wilkinson 108,109
Wilmuth O. 109
Winney 112
Coney, Acquilla 14,114,123
Ann 115
Bessie 40
Caroline A. 115
Charles 115
Clara Jane 54
Daniel 115
David 170
David Cicero 115
Eliza 31
Elizabeth 114,123
Elizabeth Huffman 87
Emeline 41,45
Emily 60

Coney continued
Eva 115
Franklin 114
Green 115
Harriett Ellzey 124
Henry Eugene 115
J. J. 31
Jackson 41
Jane 115
Jasper 115
Jeremiah 26,31,114
Jerry 115
Jerzine 115
Joel Jackson 26,114,115,
  167
Joel R. 115
John E. 72
John Hancock 115
John Thomas 115
Lena Mae 115
Leon Josephus 115
Lewis 114,115
Lewis Newsom 115
Lorraine 115
Louis 115
Lucy 170
Luke J. 115
Marshall W. 54
Mary E. 115
Morgan 115
Morgan J. 42,124
Morgan Jefferson 115
Nancy Josephine 115
Nancy Langston 72
Rachel 20,114,115
Rosaline 48,115
Sarah K. 115
Seth J. 62
Van 40
Van Crawford 60,114
W. D. 61
W. L. 63
William 20,26,48,114,
  167
William II 115
William J. 87
William Jefferson 115
William L. 115
Conn, Richard 10
Virgil 61
Connally, Mary L. 79
Cook, C. R. 63
Dan 47
Drury 85
Drury, Sr. 26
Elbert 26,31
Eliza 48
Green 1
Green B. 1,9
Henry 113
L. D. 45
Matthew 1,9,12,20,26
Mattie 61
Michael 26,156
P. A. 45
Rosalie J. 67
Taylor 31
Thos. 15,20,31
Thos. (Est.) 26
William 12,103
Coon, David 58
James 26
Jacob 10,13,20,26
Luis 31
Martha 63
Samuel 31
Sarah 61
Sophrona 61
Thomas 31
Cooper, Albert 110
Burnette 152
Charles 26
Hambleton 1
Isabel 152

Cooper continued
  James Anderson 143
  John 1
  Joseph 1
  William 1,9,26
  William G. 13
Coore, John 1
Copes, Eveline Rebecca 38
  Henry S. 38
  Mary 78
Coppedge, Charles C. 84
Corby, Austin 26
Corley, Charlie 110
  Elizabeth 26
  Epsa Ann 90
  Jacob 14,20
  Jeremiah 70
  Jerome 14,20
  Wyeth 31
Cory, Prudence Luce 168
Cossey, Solomon 1
Costley, Jas. 63
Cothin, Asea 1
  William 11,20
Cothern, Clarenda 47
  Elijah 47
  Ellie 56
  Joe 140
  John 47,61
  Lottie 62
  Minda 44
  Pearley 46
  Sim 113
Cotton, Emma C. 37
  J. W. 64
Courtney, Robert 31
Cowart, Dr. E. 80
  Richard O. 18
  Walter Julius 146
Crawford, William 1
Craft, Bethany 73
  Frederick 8
  Jack 167
  James 8,14,20,26,31
  John 11,20
  John, Jr. 20
  Jesse 1,20
  Major 12,20
  Russell 26
  Saml. 20
  Walter D. 107
Crain, Cordelia 17
Crawford, A. W. 40
  Albert L. 116
  Andrew 117
  B. A. 59
  B. L. (Dr.) 117
  Ben 117
  Benjamin Alex. 116
  Carter 116
  Charles Felder 116
  Elender 116
  Elizabeth Sandifer 117
  Eula Holmes 133
  Everett 117
  Frances Douglas 116
  Francis William 69
  H. H. 69
  Hasseltine 117
  Hettie Lee 116
  Howell 167
  James C. 67,69
  James Howell 117
  Jesse 31,116,117
  Jesse D. 117
  Josiah A. 116
  Martha A. 117
  Mary Lewis 116
  Minerva 62
  Patience 116
  Sallie Breeland 116
  Sarah 116
  Sarah M. Hall 67
  Selete 116

Crawford continued
  Sophronia 117
  Tabitha Hogan 116
  Thomas 31,116
  Thomas Bailey 116
  Walter 117
  William 116
  William H. 116
Creed, Thos. 20
Creel, Robert 85
Crews, Thos. 11
Crittenden, Elizabeth 61
Crofford, Dock 70
Crouswell, William 20
Crow, John 14
  Martin 13
  Mary 104
Crum, John 14
Cummings, Charles Franklin 110
Cunningham, A. P. 26,31
  Elijah 5
  James E. 26
Cupsted, Samuel 13,20,26
Curleit, George W. 36
Currell, Abr. J. 20
Curry, Elizabeth Culp 101
  Jacob 101,120
  Mary 101
Curtis, Annie 64
  Emma 72
  Jacob 42
  Mamie Stella 58
  Martha A. 48
  Richard 26
  Sarah 69
  T. M. 66
  Thos. C. 40
Cutrer & Allman 31
Cutrer, Catherine 26,31
  Clifton 31
  Cora 160
  Deanie 160
  Emanuel 160
  Frederick 160
  J. D. 62
  Jane R. 61
  Jennie 63
  John 1,8,14
  Johnny Tate 160
  Joseph 26,31,160,168
  Josie Texas 160
  Lewis B. 164
  Mary Vernon 164,165
  Nancy 160
  Samuel 160
  Sarah 62
  Sarah Ann 162

Dallas, Stephen T. 12
Dampiere, Barilla 164
Danaway, Joseph 1
Daniel, Ellen Ellis 120
  Florence M. 64
  Richard 26,32
Danning, William 13
Daugherty, Enous 9,14,26
  James 14,168
David, Daniel 10,11
Davidson, Charles 152
  Richard 12
  W. D. 40
Davis, Adarren 17
  Alexander 153
  Allen 26
  Asenith 168
  Benjamin 31
  Charles 39
  Charles B. 17
  Charles Morgan 138
  Cynthia Brumfield 141
  D. B. 31
  Daniel 20

Davis continued
  Emily S. 17
  Eveline Brumfield 141
  Franklin 135
  Henry 20
  Herbert 141
  James R. 62
  Jane 18
  Jesse 98
  Jesse Brumfield 138
  Jesse E. 31
  John 8,20,32
  Martha Ann 77
  Mary Holmes 135
  Narcissa 18
  Norris 64
  Paul 26
  Rebecca 26
  Rebecca Jane 168
  Rhoda 101
  Samantha Ann 143
  Samuel 1,12,20,31
  Sileta 18
  Steph. T. 20
  William A. 31
  William L. 18
  Zabon F. 141
  Zaborn 135
  Zacheus 1,15,20
Davison, Samuel 32
Dawdle, James 9
Day, David 32
  David M. 5
  Elizabeth 162
  James 1,9,12
  Jesse 5
  Joseph 149
Dear, H. M. 82
  Hardy 77
  Virginia Coffman 82
Deas, Pascal 160
Deaton, George 38
Deer, Ann 32
  John 1,32
  Joseph 32
Dees, J. B. 160
DeLaney, Carolina Ellzey 124
  James 20
  James H. (Dr.) 124
  Margaret 4
DeLaughter, Benj. 26,32
  Brother 45
  James 32
  Nancy 17
DeLoache, Katherine H. 101
Denham, Thos. 20
Denman, Joel 1,9,11
  Thomas 1,15
Dent, James 35
d'Evecmon, Ingaba 163
  Peter 164
Dickenson, Jno. 13,14
  Mary Felder 126
Dickerson, Caleb 1
  Elizabeth 126
  Fanny 63
  Henry 14,20,126
  James 20,26
  Jeto 20
  John 1,9
  Jno., Jr. 14
  Levica 126
  Martin 20,26,31,126
  Martin, Jr. 26,32
  Owen 20,26,31
  Priscilla 126
  Samantha 126
  Thomas 1,20,169
  Vienna Hucabee 126
  W. J. 169
  William 32,126
Dickey, Mrs. A. E. 66
  Cordelia 91

186

Dickey continued
  George W. 31
  Miss P. A. 60
  Robert DeWitt 157
  Mrs. S. E. 63
  Seaborn H. 157
  Wm. L. 63
Dicks Children 37
Dickson, C. T. 31
  David 13
  David, Jr. 1
  James C. 13
  William 15,20
Diehl, Lewis 107
Dillon, Adaline 119
  Angeline Gwin 119
  Ancel Green 118
  Ann (Est.) 26
  Ann Morris 117,118
  Annie Clark 86
  Catherine Rushing 119
  Chauncey 118
  Clara 117,119
  Clarkson 1,9,15,26,31,
    118
  Consetta 119
  Elvira Magee 118
  Eusie E. Johnson 118
  Everett 26,31
  Harriet 17
  Hester 119
  Hettie Lewis 119
  James 119
  James T. 32,119
  James Theopilious 117
  Jane 79
  Jo Anna 117
  Joel Pearson 119
  John 86
  John Irving 119
  John P. 119
  John T. 32
  Labon (Laborn) 119
  Laurence 9,15,20,26,
    117,118
  Leroy 32,119
  Lucy King 119
  Magdaline 119
  Margaret Knighton 119
  Martha 118
  Mary 17,117,119
  Nancy 117
  Peggy Pearson 119
  Ransom 32
  Rempsi 119
  Richard 9,15,20,117,
    118,119
  Sally 119
  Samantha 18
  Sophronia Morgan 118
  Theophilus 1,5,15,20,
    26,32,118,119
  Thomas Everett 118
  Uriah 119
  Willis D. 1,15,20,26,
    32,117,118
  Willis R. 119
Dismukes, Jno. 13,20
Dixon, George M. 107
  James A. 107
  James Van 107
  Malissa 110
  Wm. David 110
Dodd, T. 144
Doddle, James 1
Donaho, Aquila 20
  Lucy 13
  William 13,20
Doolin, C. 24
Doughty, Alex S. 103
  Elizabeth 12,103
  Mary 103
Douglas, Lee H. D. 68
  Martha 5

Douglas continued
  Newton 68
  Robertson B. 68
Dougless, Edward 32
Dowden, Francis Asbury 109
  Francis M. 108
  Jas. Cullen 109
  Malissia C. 109
  Wm. James 109
  Wm. Wilkerson 109
Downer, Mrs. C. M. 65
  Rev. Robert B. 65
Downing, Alice Maria T. 72
  Wm. W. 72
Drake, Britain 1
Draughan, Francis 161
  Lafayette 161
  Louisa 161
  Rosella 161
  W. W. 36
Drees, Barnet 14
Drinkwater, Daniel 146
  John 146
  Keziah 146
Dukes, Jeptha 1
Dunahoo, Daniel 1,8
  Hiram 32
  John 1,9
  William 1,9,10
Dunaway, Annis J. 46
  Betsey 49
  Della 113
  Fielding 26,31,46,55
  George 11,26,31
  Jesse F. 46
  Jonathan 11
  Joseph 10,11,20
  O. S. 63
  Pearl 26,31
  Permelia 44
  Richmond 26,31,49
  Viola 62
Duncan, Ben 133
  Benjamin J. 114
  Charlotte 114
  Chelly 114
  Cullen 113,114
  Eliza Ann 114
  Ella 112
  Emily 114
  Frances 114
  Frances Conerly 105
  Hattie Holmes 133
  Hugh 114
  Isaac 114
  James 113,114
  James P. 114
  Jane 113,114
  John W. 114
  Lloyd 133
  Luke 114
  Martin 114
  Martin P. 18
  Melissa 114
  Needham L. 114
  Rebecca 114
  Robert 114
  Sally Holmes 133
  Susan 114
  Talitha H. 114
  Walton 114
  William 114
Bunkin, Benj. 18
  Sarah M. 18
Dunkley, Richard 1
Dunn, John 1
Durham, Seab. J. 20
Dykes, Abel 14
  Angeline 61
  Jacob 160
  Jane L. 160
  John 160
  Jordan 57
  Lemuel 57

Dykes continued
  Lizzie 64
  Nancy 161
  Nancy Jane 157
  Nathaniel 160
  Oveta 57
  William 20
Dyson, George W. 165
  Margaret Jane 165

Eager, Robert 5
Earle, John 32
  William 13
Easley, Harvil M. 104
  Newton Q. 162
  R. W. 160
East, Dixie Holmes 133
  Herbert 133
Easterling, Ally 144
  Andrew 37
Eaton, Carrie 62
  Mattie Stoks 60
  Rube 60
Eddens, Benj. 20
Edmondson, Amos 1
Edwards, Mrs. Boyd 115
  David 46
  James 49
  Jesse 13,26
  Joseph 5
  Margaret 164
  Mary 52
  Mary A. 59
  Matthew 26,32
  Morgan 164
Elam, David 121
Elliott, Barnet 32
  Elizabeth 65
  Michael 20,26
  Robert 12,32
  S. T. 78
  Samuel 1
  Sarah 12
  William 1,9,21,26
Ellis, Anna 120
  Anna Roberts 120
  Avis 120
  Benj. Franklin 120
  Caroline 120
  Caroline Elizabeth 120
  Daniel 120
  Elizabeth 120
  Elizabeth Warren 120
  Ezekiel Parke 120
  Francis 120
  Frederick Warren 120
  George 1,8,11,75,120
  Hal Roberts 120
  Hannah Lowery 120
  Hilda 120
  Isaac Newton 120
  James 11
  John 120,121
  Jake 120
  Lott Warren 120
  Louisa 120
  Lourancy 120
  Lowry 20,120
  Mary 120
  Mary Magee 120
  Nell 120
  Owen 1,9,12,20,120
  Reuben 120
  Richmond 120
  Samuel 120
  Sarah Johnson 120,121
  Solomon 120
  Stephen 1,20,66,120
  Susan 120
  Tabitha Warner 120
  Thomas B. 120
  Warren M. 120
  Washington 120

Ellis continued
  William 1,9,12,120
  William Carroll 120
  Willis 120
Ellzey, Ada 108
  Adonia 57
  Amanda Booker 123
  Angeline Simmons 138
  B. F. 35,62
  Benjamin Franklin 123
  Bobby 170
  Caroline 123
  Caroline A. 65
  Carrie Thomas 138
  Clifton Ross 170
  Clyde C. 170
  Daniel Julius 123,147
  DeWitt 65,123
  Dolph Thompson 170
  Easter Sibley 123
  Edward 110
  Edward C. 170
  Elizabeth 122
  Elizabeth Coney 123
  Emily 63
  Emily Holmes 123
  Emmeline 123
  Eva Shaffer 122
  Frank 170
  Fredy 170
  George Clifton 170
  George W. 124
  Hettie Alford 138
  Hettie F. 35
  Hugh 170
  Hugh F. 124
  Hugh Nelson 170
  Indiana Hall 123
  Isaac Marshall 138
  Jackson J. 123
  James 32,122,123,124
  James W. 123
  Jesse C. 123
  John 21,26,32,58,114,
    123
  John H. 32,123
  John I. 132
  John S. 123
  Julia 170
  Julia Simmons 123
  Lee 170
  Lelia Longmire 138
  Lemuel 123
  Leon Frank 170
  Lewis 14,20,122,123
  Lizzie Lamkin 84
  Louis 132
  Lucy Coney 115
  Madaline May 123
  Maggie May 170
  Margaret 61
  Margaret Brumfield 124
  Martha Ann 123
  Mary 63,122,123
  Mary Holmes 132
  Mary Mollie 123
  Mary N. 123
  Mary Quin 123
  Mary Sibley 123
  Mary Thompson 124
  Nancy 122,123
  Nancy James 123
  Nancy Katura 124
  Oscar J. L. 45
  Otelia 170
  R. A. 84
  Rankin C. 124,170
  Rankin N. 138
  Ray 170
  Ross Alanson 123
  Rosa Amanda 170
  Roy 170
  Sarah 122,123
  Sarah Alford 123

Ellzey continued
  Sarah Brumfield 139
  Sarah Holmes 123
  Sarintha 62
  Stacey 122
  Thad F. 170
  Thos. 20,26,122,123
  Thomas J. 123
  Thomas W. 124
  Thomasin 122,123
  W. F. 40
  W. H. 62
  Wesley Harrison 138
  Wesley James 124,138
  Wesley W. 123
  William 15,20,21,26,32,
    122,123
  William G. 88
  William S. 123
Emmis, Dora 56
English, James 164
Eppes, Ballard 20
Epps, B. F. 26
Equen, Annette 74
Erlinger, Mary 125
Erwin, F. B. 56,169
  James A. 163
  Mary 18
  Nettie 64
Estess, Dicy 5
  Elisha 32
  Ezra 13,26,32
  John D. 26,32
  William 20,26,32
Esthers, Ephraim 10
Evans, J. P. 40
  R. P. 162
Everett, Annie 50
  Jno. 21
  Martha 49
  T. J. 50
  Thomas 50
Ezel, Benjamin 13
  Benj. (Est.) 26
  Lewis 20
  Olivia 155

Fairchilds, John 1
  Loftin 9,15,21
  Robert 8,15
Fan, Green 21
Fant, Annis 75
  Joe Van 82
  Samuel A. 75
Farie (Faris), Danl. 21
Faris (Farris), Elbert 32
  William 8
Farmer, William 32
  William M. 65
Fatheree, Hilliard 1
  Levi 1
Faulk, Lucy 17
Faust, Jacob 26
  John 32
  N. 32
  Nazareth 140
  William 15,32
Felder, Abraham 124,125
  Adeline Cockerham 130
  Alfred R. 130
  Amanda J. 69
  Anna 130
  Anne Burk 129
  Baxter 130
  Benjamin B. 130
  Byrd 73
  C. C. 56
  Catherine Snell 125
  Charles 126
  Charles Dennis 130
  Charlie 130
  Charlotte A. 127
  Clara Williams 84

Felder continued
  Clifton Lee 73,128
  Columbus 56
  Cynthia Hope 127
  D. William 130
  Daniel 14,126,129
  David 5,32,71,125,127,
    129
  David Watson 130
  Dolly Greer 128
  Dora Mabel 73,128
  Edgar 130
  Edwin Gates 130
  Elizabeth 21,128
  Elizabeth Long (Lowe)
    126
  Elizabeth Sandell 127
  Elizabeth Thompson 128
  Ella 75
  Emily 129
  Emma 73
  Emma I. 130
  Esther A. 125
  Eula 77
  Frances Hodges 128
  Frances S. 128
  Franklin 129
  Frederick 124,125
  G. M. 128
  Gabriel 32,126,128
  George 77,130
  Gertrude 130
  Harriet 129
  Henry 125,129
  Henry D. 130
  Ina O. Harris 130
  Iowa Carruth 130
  Ira 73,81,127
  Ira L. 128
  Isaac 21,26,32,127
  J. J. 32
  Jacob 125
  James 130
  James E. 128
  Jane 21,127,130
  Jane McMorris 73,127,129
  Jane Miller 130
  Jennie Kirby 130
  Jesse Milton 130
  Jesse T. 130
  John 1,5,10,14,21,26,32,
    68,124,126,127,129
  John Byrd 128
  John Henry 84,124
  John Smith 128
  Jordon Monroe 128
  Julia Huffman 128
  Julius Edward 130
  Kate 77
  Keziah 6,126,128
  Lenora J. 130
  Levi 69,82,84
  Levi D. 86,128
  Lewis Raynor 88
  Louisa 130
  Loula B. 130
  Lucy S. 128
  Lula S. 77,128
  Mabyn Browning 130
  Maria 21,104,127
  Martha Williams 86,128
  Mary 128
  Mary Buie 128
  Mary C. 74,127,128
  Mary Elizabeth 125
  Mary Shaumloffel 124,
    125
  Maud Cannon 130
  Myrtle King 130
  Nancy 129
  Newton 130
  Olive 130
  Otis 130
  Otis Dorace 130

Felder continued
  Otis H. 130
  Otis L. 130
  Patience Allen 127
  Paul S. 125
  Peter 8,14,21,68,125,
    126
  Peter, Jr. 8,14,26,32,
    126
  Peter James 127
  R. H. 77
  Rachel 130
  Robert E. 130
  Robert Henry 128
  Rozilla 43
  Rufus Alford 130
  Rufus K. 73,80,129
  Samuel 124,125,154
  Sarah Curtis 73,127
  Sarah J. 128
  Sarah Singletary 130
  Simeon Noble 128
  Tabor 129
  Telitha 56
  Ursula 124
  Virginia H. Kirk 81
  W. H. 88
  Wade Hampton 128
  William I. 68
  William L. 128
  William Pinckney 128
  Winnifred 130
  Wyatt 32
  Wyatt Wesley 69,71,73,
    78,127
  Zebulon P. 69,128
  Zella 120
Fenn, Bessie Holmes 134
  Claude L. 134
  Gabriel H. 32
  William 92
Fergerson (Ferguson),
    Aaron 1
  Eli 1
  Moses 1
  Mrs. Pinkey 36
  Samuel 14
  Wallace B. 87
  William 36
  William B. 71
Fielder, William 1
Finch, Joel 56
  Mary Williams 56
  Sidney 65
  Susan 63
Finley (Findley),
    Elizabeth 10
  Richard 14,21,26
Fisher, John 21
  Lou 37
Fitzgerald, Rebecca 46
Fitzpatrick, Mr. 36
Fletcher, James 21,32
Flippin, Merrit 1
Flowers, Henry 32
  John H. 32
Floyd, Ava J. 112
Flynn, Ann E. 80
Foil, Lucy Brumfield 139
  Margaret Brumfield 139
  Oscar A. 144
  Samuel Matthew 139
  Walter Monroe 139
  William 32,135
Foissin, Elias 100
  Rebecca 100
Folse, Mary Alma 153
Folsom, Israel 94
  Nathaniel 94
Foot, Minnie E. 78
Forbes, George 130
  Gladys Hood 130
  Henry 133
  Mellissa Holmes 133

Forbes continued
  Missouria E. 147
  William 110
Ford, D. C. 81
  David 1
  Dr. J. D. 39
  Rev. John 86
  Harrison Fletcher 110
  Martha 88
  Martha Ball 88
  Mattie Ligon 81
  Olive H. Foxworth 83
  Preserved 1
  W. A. 88
  W. F. 83
Forgy (Forgey), Jos. 21
  William 10,13,21
Fornea, Thomas P. 162
Forrest, Bishop M. 52
  J. M. 63
  Mary 52
  Richd. 21,26
Fortenberry, Adarren 17
  Addie Brumfield 141
  Dr. Andrew J. 137
  Angeline Holmes 136
  Benjamin C. 44
  Beulah Brumfield 141
  Burl 58
  Burrel 32,123
  Calvin 26,32
  Dudley 136
  Eliza Brumfield 141
  Eliza Jane Ellzey 58
  Elizabeth 18
  Emily 17
  Felder 141
  Fleet 62
  Freddie 141
  G. C. 26,32,45
  George W. 17
  Hannah 16
  Hugh 147
  Isabella 17
  Ivin M. 17,113
  James Felder 52,55
  Josephine 63
  Laura Holmes 136
  Louis 61
  Lula Schilling 52
  Maria 45
  Mary 17
  Nancy 110
  Nelson Monroe 112
  Newton 136
  Norcecy 17
  Olivia 17
  Robert Monroe 141
  Rosa E. 44
  Sallie 45
  Sarah Louise 91
  Victoria Brock 137
  Violette 16
  W. Frank 45
  Willis 17
  William 12,16,26,32
Fortier, Benjamin 160
Foster, Isaac 9,15
Foucault, Hextor 99
Fountain, J. B. 81
Fowler, Jno. 15
Foxworth, Harriet 77
  Joab 112
  Margaret 101
  Nancy 65
  Samuel G. 65
  Stephen 1
Francis, Thos. 21
Franklin, Bell 110
  Edgar 109
  Elizabeth 86
  Flora 109
  Rev. J. M. 87
  J. Warren 109

Franklin continued
  James M. 109
  Rev. John 109
  John Coleman 109
  Josephine 109
  Lillie Virginia 109
  Malissa Conerly 87
  Martha Davis 82
  Mary Elnora 109
  Mirah A. 109
  Nannie Jane 109
  Dr. Raleigh 109
  T. J. 86
  Thomas 77,82
  Wm. Thomas (Dr.) 109
Fredericks, C. S. 36
  Victoria 36
Freeman, C. B. 51
Frick, Adrian 21,26,32
Fridge, Edna Felder 130
  Robert L. 130
Frith, Mrs. A. 62
  Sallie 38
Frost, Dr. Ebenezer 37
Fugler, Madge Quin 124
Futch, Polly 17

Gale, Josiah 21
Galland, A. 32
  Thomas 10
Galvant, Chas. 63
Gannir, Vincent 8
Garber, Ledford 32
  Vincent 21
Gardner, Sylvester 38
Garner, Elizabeth 27,32
  Francis E. 62
  John 26,32
  Vincent 13
  William 10
Garrell, Horatio 1
Garrett, Irma 110
  Jos. 21
Gartman, Dave 133
  Elizabeth Holmes 133
  George 133
  Sarah Holmes 133
Gates, Almyra 130
  Elizabeth 16,21
  Jesse 27
  John G. 6
  Joseph 21,26
  Louise Felder 71,130
  Rufus J. 130
  William 10,11
  Wm. Jefferson 130
Gatlin, Alfred 32
  Amanda A. 36
  Angeline M. 52
  Charlie 68
  E. A. (Capt.) 36
  Edward 8,13,21
  Edward (est.) 27
  James 26,32,79
  James S. (Col.) 71,76,
    81
  John 27,81
  John B. 40,68
  Katherine 32
  Leon 133
  Lizzie Holmes 133
  Lula 75
  Martha E. 65
  Martha Hoover 79
  Mollie 40
  N. W. 81
  R. E. (Dr.) 61
  Rosalba 71
  Rosalvia Wells 79
  Thos. 13
  William 32
  Willie 78
  Z. B. 78

Gatlin continued
  Zebulon Butler 79
Gause, William 100
Gay, Jerden 18
  Thomas 94
Geiger, Elizabeth Bush 84
  Lewis 84
Gennison, C. A. (Miss) 35
Gerald, Bevie 145
  E. W. 72
German, Virginia E. 109
  Wayne T. 109
Germany, Ella Ethel 68
  Julia 70
  Martha Gatlin 76
  William 79
  Willie Laurie 79
  Willis 101
  Willie H. (Rev.) 65,75,76
  Zebbie Lee 79
Gibson, C. C. 35,38,40,71,78
  Della Estella 38
  Ellen 37
  Harriet Bonney 86
  Hattie 81
  Jacob 21,27
  James 10,12
  Joseph 21
  Nancy 35,38
  P. L. (Dr.) 38
  W. H. 26,38
Giessendanner, Barbara 125
  Jacob 124
  John 124,125
Gilchrist, David 32
Gill, Drucilla 168
  J. B. 62
  Reubin 27,32
  T. E. (Mrs.) 61
  T. N. 64
Gillapsy, J. R. 38
Gilles, Abraham 99
  Daniel 99
  David 99
  Pierre 99
  Rene 99
Ginn, Dewitt David 141
  Elizabeth 12
  Emily Brumfield 140
  Eugenia Braham 140
  Eula Brumfield 141
  Gholson G. 106,167
  Henry 141
  Huey 140
  Jeptha 1
  Jesse 26,32
  Jordon 140
  Jordon J. 140
  Lafayette 140
  Mollie Regan C. 140
  Penelope 12,21,27
  Quitman Davis 140
  Sarah Parker 141
  Sebastian 27,32
  Seleman 32
  Victoria Lewis 140
Gipson, Gilbert 32
  James 1
  William 1,32
Girtman, Bartholomew 5,9
  David 26,32
  George D. 32
  John 32
Givens, Roberta 62
Glann, Alexander 27
Glass, David 21
  Elizabeth 13
Glover, John 92
  Peter 10,11,21
  Peter (est.) 27

Godbold, Ella Felder 128
  Gabriel 75,128
  Gabriel P. 67
  Irvin 81
  John F. 75
  Levi R. 87
  P. B. 79
  Rowan P. 77
  Sarah Rawls 87
Godwin, William K. 27
Goff, John 4
  Nathaniel 1,8,14
Goflin, Jackson 26
Goings, Otto Otis 157
Goldman, Henry 10,13
  Henry (Est.) 26,27,32
Golifer, ----- 21
Golman (Goldman), Bedley 1,10,13
  William 1,10
  Young 1,10,11
Goodwin, Benjamin 32
Goolin, Martha 32
Gordon, David 21
  Elizabeth Holmes 137
  James 9,13,21
  John 10,21
  Malica Ann 161
  Mary Ann 163
  Nancy 27
  Robert 21
  T. J. 137
  W. 22
  William 27
Gorman, Mrs. E. A. More 78
  M. D. K. 78
Goslin, Martha 32
Goss, John 146
Goygle, Elizabeth 4
Graham, Dougal 116
  James 5
  Jane 146
  William 1
Grant, Thomas 16
Grantham, Daniel 1
  Matthew 1
  Nathan 92
Graves, Daniel 15,21,26,32
  Ida Brumfield 141
  Isaac 1
  James 1
  John 1
  Marcus 141
  Nathaniel 18
  Olivia Ellis 120
  Richard 12
  Sarah 32
Gray, Jas. 20
  Joseph E. 67
  Mesamin 32
  Robert 9
  Ruffin A. 66
  Sherod 15,26,32
Grayson, Benjamin 122
Green, A. R. 26
  Beams 32
  Doris Varnado 167
  Elizabeth 18
  Equilla 32
  Francis Marion 153
  Jeptha 9
  Leonard 1
  John 1,32
  Mary 18
  S. D. 111
  Susanna 17
  William 9,11,27,32
Greer (Grier), Amos 11,21
  D. C. 128
  Ephraim 26
  Fred. 63
  Hughey 113
  Inez 64
  Jesse 11,21,27,32,61

Greer continued
  Jesse, Jr. 26,32
  John 21,27
  John A. 56
  Marguerite Jones 56
  Moses 21
  Myra Bullock 141
  Sarah 61
  Smith 27
  Sophia Felder 128
  V. Jones 141
  Victoria 113
  Wallace 63
Griffin, James Wm. 140
  Robert 14
  Synthia Brumfield 140
Griffith, Fannie 144
Grimesby, Emily Holmes 133
Grimesley, John 133
Grubs, Gilbert 27,32
  Mary 21
  Meredith 27
Grunewall, Renzo 38
Guin, Mary 51
Guinea, Thomas 26,32
Gulledge, Elizabeth 63
  Jane 16
  Martha 16
  Martha Jane 61
  Mary 44
  Patsey 49
  Thomas 11,16,21,27,32
  William 16,21,27,43
  Willins 32
Gunnell, Savilla 57
Gunnells, Esther 62
Guy, Alex 113
  Beler 113
  Betty Lura 113
  Boyd Felder 113
  C. L. 113
  Cecil Lamar 113
  Chancey Wade 113
  DeWitt 113
  Edwene 113
  Emile 113
  George M. 113
  George W. 113
  Griffen 113
  J. W. 113
  James Monroe 113
  Jeff 113
  Jesse 112,113
  John Wesley 113
  Lela Mae 113
  Leslie 113
  Louis 66,113
  Miss M. A. R. 113
  Miss M. E. 113
  Mary 113
  Mary Eleanor 113
  Monroe 39
  Nellie 113
  Percy R. 113
  Polly Conerly 105
  Rebecca 113
  Rosa 113
  Ruth 113
  Miss S. A. E. 113
  Vince W. 113
  William 112,113
  William J. 113
  William Lewis 113
Gwin, John 27

Hackett, Mrs. A. J. 63
Hafter, Jerome C. 124
Hagg, Rhoda McKelvin 62
Hailey, Mrs. 61
Hains, Noble W. 1
Hale, Francis 16
  Henry 10,15

Hale continued
  Joel 32
  Peggy 12
Haley, Golda 64
  Sarah E. 61
Hall, Armstead 12,21,27,
    32
  Clark 9
  Ezekiel B. 32
  Hugh 27,32
  James 32
  John 67
  John J. 32
  Leml. T. B. 11
  Lucinda 48
  Mary E. 36,66
  Useba Jane 36,66
  Wiley W. 48
  William 21,27,32
  William M. 27
  Wyatt 1
Hallman, Thomas 27
Ham, Doc 113
Hambleton, Gemimi 17
  Thomas 1
Hamilton, Alexander 27
  Elizabeth 11,21
  Hans 9,10,11,16
  Isaah 8
  James R. 27
  James W. 111
  Jemima 27
  John 21,27
  Judith 11,16,21,27
  Mary 27
  Rachel 11
  Thomas 10,21
  V. F. 27
Hamlet, George C. 12
Hammond, Narsie 147
Hammons, A. B. 48
  Mary 48
Hampton, John 27,32
  Pearl 143
  Wesley 27,32
  William 13,21
Hancock, William 122
Hannan, Charles 35
Harbin, Susan 146
Hardy, Mary Anna 150
Harger, Ann 125
Harkness, Robert 49
Harless, Teletha 27
Harper, Absolom 10,12
  Alexander 10,11,21,32
  Elmore 27
  Edwin 32
  Jesse 10,11,21,27,32
  Laban B. 74
  Lewis 21
  Lou 101
  Seab. 21
  Wiley M. 100
  Winafred 74
Harrell, Bernettie 54
  James P. 68
  Kearney 68
  W. J. 54
Harrelson, Jane 151
Harris, Buckner 13
  Charles 21
  Earley 14
  Wiley 12,21
Harrison, Rebecca 63
  William H. 92
Harslock, Augusta 143
Hart (Heart), Daniel 32
  Elizabeth M. 169
  G. W. 56
  Garland 120
  Henry F. (Dr.) 136
  Isaiah 27
  J. E. 51
  J. L. 60

Hart continued
  James 21,27,32
  James M. 32
  Janie 60
  John 21
  John B. 27
  Joseph 21,27,32
  Josiah 21
  M. J. 59
  Martha C. 169
  Mary 21
  Ophelia McElveen 136
  Sarah Ellis 120
  Thomas A. 72
  Trusie 63
  Washington 59
Hartley, Catherine 168
Hartmen, Leo 144
Hartzog, Ann M. F. 125
  C. C. 74
  George 125
  John 125
Harvey, D. L. 27
  Daniel 27
  Evin 9
  Harris 27,32
  Jane Ann 107
  Janette Holmes 134
  John, Jr. 2
  John W. 2
  Martha Holmes 134
  Mary Elizabeth 108
  Michael 9,12.21,32
  Nehemiah 2
  T. C. 78
  Thad 134
  Thomas 2
  Thos. C. 21
  Thomas P. 2
  Thomas, Sr. 2
  Wayne 134
Harville, Edward 2
Hather, Isaac A. 32
Hathorn, N. L. 66
Havers, E. P. 77
Hawthorne, Sarah 155
Hayes, Rebekah 85
  W. C. 85
Hayman, John T. 85
  Miss R. J. 72
  William M. 80
Haynes, Delia 66
Hays, R. H. 64
Hayworth, J. H. 32
Hazewood, Benjamin 21
Heard, Thomas 2,8,15,21
Helton, John 2
Hemphill, Mrs. N. R. 63
Henderson, D. C. 27
  Georgia Hood 130
  Joe 130
  John, Jr. 39
  Kate E. 39
  Martha Ford 86
Hennessey, Isaac 151
  Mary 151
Hennington, Charlie 113
  L. F. 70
Henson, Jno., Sr. 21
Herreld, Benjamin 32
Herring, Anthony 105
  Joseph 105
  Michael 105
  Samuel 105
  Stephen 105
  Susanna 27
Herrington, Hardy 2
  James 21,52
  Thomas 2
  William 21
Hester, John 159
Hickman, Aaron 21,27,32
  Henry 27
  John 10,11

Hicks, Sheriff 160
Higgenbothom, Henry 21
  Nelson 14
  Robert 14,21
  Saml. 13
  Sol. 21
Hightower, Abigail P. 97
  Arnold 97
Hill, Mrs. A. S. 35
  Doc 92
  Hardy 2
  Irvin 111
Hiller, Daniel 38
Hilton, John 9
Hines, David 8,14
  Enoch 113
  Felix 113
  Frances 113
  Henry 113
  Jane Fletcher 84
  Susan Guy 113
  W. B. 84
Hinson, G. W. 134
  Isabella 47
  Isham B. 32
  John 8,14
  Mary Brumfield 139
  Nancy 27
  Sallie Holmes 134
  William 27
Hobgood, Gracy 18
Hodges, Mrs. C. R. 63
  Clarenda 57
  Drury 11,21,27
  Edmond 11,21,27,32
  Elizabeth 52
  George W. 112
  I. R. 61
  Jesse 12,21
  John C. 32
  Martha 64
  Sidney 11
  William 11,21,27
Hog, John 10
Hoke, Andrew J. 41
  F. M. 40
  Lizzie J. 40
Holden, Abigail 158,162
  Angeline 162
  Julia 103
  Lydia 162
  Margaret 103
  Pierson 162
  Susannah 162
  Willis 162
Holland, Martin 11
Holliday (Holiday), Ayres
    121
  Elizabeth 121
  John 86
  John Johnson 121
  Mary Ainsworth 121
  Nelly Johnston 121
  Thomas 121
Hollingsworth, Isaac 2
Hollis, Silas 13
Holloway, Caroline Frances
    74
  Elizabeth 100
  Mark 100
  William B. 74
Holly, Rhoda 149
Holman, Samuel 14
Holmes, Ada Lee 146
  Addie Rheams 136
  Agnes Sumrall 132
  Allen 133
  Alton 134
  Alton Eugene 108
  Alvie Blackwell 133
  Alvira Sparkman 132
  Amanda Fortson 132
  Andrew 134
  Annie 55

Holmes continued
  Annie Pugh 134
  Annie Simmons 135
  Armetha Smith 136
  B. F. (Dr.) 64
  B. Oscar 60
  Benjamin 21,27,32,131,
    132,133
  Benjamin Cullen 108
  Benjamin Oscar 135
  Bennie 133
  Bennie F. 63,132
  Bennie M. 133
  Berry Ann 138
  Bertha Jones 133
  Burdette Carter 134
  Byron 137
  Calvin 133
  Cancy 138
  Catherine Rosetta 136
  Charlie 133
  Clifton Leon 134
  Crawford 134
  Cynthia 4
  David 132
  David Stovall 133
  Dean Crawford 134
  Delia Stogner 137
  Delilah Bearden 134
  Della Sandford 133
  DeWitt Ernest 137
  Dixie 137
  Dixie Smith 137
  Dorcas Bickham 137
  Dorcas Lewis 136
  Dort 134
  Edgar 133
  Edgar Virgil 137
  Edna Ginn 133
  Elijah 132
  Elisha 12,21,27,32,131,
    132,133,134
  Elisha, Jr. 21,133
  Elisha Crawford 134
  Eliza Hancock 134
  Elizabeth Bearden 132
  Elizabeth Beecher 132
  Elizabeth Conerly 137
  Ella Duncan 133
  Ella Eaton 134
  Emily Levida 108
  Emma 132
  Emma Hobgood 136
  Emma Wilson 134
  Emmett 133
  Enos 137
  Ernest 132
  Ethel Patterson 133
  Etta Gardnes 133
  Evie Mixon 136
  Fannie Smith 136
  Flora Rebecca 108
  Francis 132
  Francis Edwin 134
  Francis Marion 134
  Francis Turnage 133
  Fred L. 133
  Gene 133
  George 138
  Grover 136
  Hannah 131
  Hattie Ratliff 134
  Hazel Virginia 146
  Helen Nash 133
  Henry 132
  Herbert 133
  Hilborn B. 136
  Ichabod 132
  Ira 133
  Isaac 124
  J. F. 79
  J. L. 134
  J. T. L. 68
  J. Wes. 106

Holmes continued
  Jabus N. 108
  James 12,131,133
  James Marshall 136
  James Monroe 133,136
  James Monroe, Jr. 136
  James Prior 132
  James T. 108
  James Wesley (?)
  Jane Elizabeth 108
  Jane Lewis 132
  Jane Perkins 43,135
  Janie Brock 134
  Jasper Franklin 135
  Jasper Newton 136
  Jefferson Davis 132
  Jefferson Frank 135
  Jesse 133,138
  Jesse Longino 134
  Jesso O. 108
  Jessie I. 79
  Jessie Ligon 135
  Jessie Merle 146
  Joan 134
  John (Capt.) 132
  John, Sr. 131,132
  John A. 132
  John C. 21,32
  John Coleman 134
  John Collins 132
  John Herbert 134
  John T. 133
  John T. L. 134
  John Wesley 137
  Josiah 132,146
  Katie Jones 136
  Kerschell 133
  Laura Andrews 136
  Laura Turnage 133
  Leota Holmes 136
  Lewis Benton 133
  Liberty 2
  Linda Elizabeth 147
  Lizzie Smith 133
  Lizzie Wells 133
  Lou Hill 134
  Lou Reeves 136
  Louisa Willoughby 132
  Lucious 136
  Lucretia Ginn 134
  Lucy 18
  Lula Conerly 135
  Lula Duncan 133
  Lula Everette 134
  Lula H. 133
  Madison 134
  Madison Hilborn 136
  Maggie A. B. 133
  Maggie Pound 135
  Mamie Davis 133
  Manson H. 133
  Marcus Lafayette 136,
    146,147
  Margaret Stallings 119,
    134
  Martha Conerly 133
  Martha Simmons 137
  Mary Ann 132
  Mary Brewer 133
  Mary Foil 134
  Mary Henderson 133
  Mary Pope 137
  Mary Roberts 133
  Mary Sumrall 132
  Mattie D. 79
  Maud Andrews 134
  Maud Morgan 132
  Mece Carter 138
  Melissa Duncan 138
  Mindana Cothern 13?
  Minnie Lenoir 134
  Moyes 134
  Murtie Lee 136
  Nancy 17

Holmes continued
  Nancy E. Conerly 76
  Nancy Letica 108
  Nancy Shirley 133
  Nancy Stallings 134
  Nancy Sumrall 138
  Nancy Williams 118
  Narcissus Fortenberry
    137
  Needham 63,108,133,134
  Newton 134
  Ollie Edwin 137
  Oscar 155
  Ottis Ott 137
  P. Burk 134
  Patty Louise 147
  Pauline Roberts 134
  Pinkey Broom 137
  Pinkey Newman 133
  Polly 134
  Raiford 133
  Ransom C. 68
  Ransom Coleman 134
  Reta Babin 134
  Reta Smith 137
  Richard A. 133
  Robert S. W. 146
  Rosa Magee 133
  Rosanna Bullock 132
  Roy 134
  Rufus Edgar 136
  Ruth 146
  Sallie Pittman 136
  Sam 134
  Samantha 134
  Sarah Bickham 135
  Sarah Kaigler 133
  Sarah M. 20
  Sarah Rowley 132
  Sarah Stovall 131,132
  Sarah Yarborough 134
  Seaburn 133
  Sidney Dolphus 136
  Stella Teagarden 133
  Stephen T. 132
  Susan 146
  Susie Brewer 137
  T. N. 134
  T. W. 108
  Telitha Duncan 133
  Thelma Muirhead 134
  Thomas Carroll 137
  Thos. H. 114,133
  Thos. William 135
  Una Smith 137
  Victor 133
  Victor Monroe 137
  W. C. 119
  W. J. 118
  W. Jack 134
  Wallace 132
  Walter Wilton 134
  Wesley 76
  William 27,133
  William Dawson 135,136
  William Franklin 135,136
  Wm. Graham 132
  Wm. Stovall 43,135
  Willie Pearl 134
  Winnie Pearson 133
  Yates L. 134
Honea, Wilks 2
Hood, Anna Moore 130
  Clyde 130
  Elmo 130
  George Oliver 130
  Ida Felder 130
  Jesse 130
  Joe 130
  Lavina Cambes 130
  Lelia Bourgeois 130
  Oma Tyler 130
  Reason 21
  Ulyse 130

Hoover, Dr. C. B. 75
  Charles 27
  Christian 2,21,27,32
  Elizabeth 9
  John 2
  Joseph S. 32
Hope, Angeline Smith 57
  Cynthia 69,127
  H. S. 27
  James 8,15,21
  Nancy 165
Hoppman, John 21
Hord, John T. 36
Horger, Jacob 124
Houghman, Daniel 8
House, Elizabeth 109
  George W. 109
  Hattie A. 109
  Henry 21
Houston, Eugene 103
  James 21,27,32,103
  Joe (Mrs.) 103
  John 103
  Lily 103
  Nancy 103
  Willie 103
Howard, Alice Regan 85
  H. P. 27
  P. (Rev.) 86
  Robert 85
  William 11
Howell, Henry 2,21
  Hudson 13
  James 12,21,27
  Jesse 133
  Lettie Holmes 133
  Lewis 10
  Lewis, Jr. 21
  Mary 74
  Samuel 2,14
  Thomas 27
Hubbard, George 83
Huber, Frederick 124
Hubert, David 2
Huckabee, A. A. 133
  Bessie Holmes 133
  James 126
  Jane Dickerson 126
  Jerome 14,21
  John 14,21,27,32
  Martha 57
Hudson, ----- 79
Huff, Stephen 13
Huffman, Abi Felder 82,
    128
  Belle Coney 84
  Daniel 2,27
  George W. 82,128
  Jane 14
  John 27,32,80
  Joseph L. 84
  L. O. (Sister) 70
  Mary Glass 81
  Selena E. 115
Hughes, Abr. 14,21
  Calvin 97
  David 21
  Elizabeth M. 157
  George W. 109
  Hyram 21
  James 21,32,150
  Jefferson 21
  Jos. 14,21
  Martha 17
  Maude 113
Hullett, Ana Allene 107
Hunly, John 2
Hunt, Nancy Ann 78
  W. H. 78
Hurlong, David 168
Hurst, Kaloolah 35
Hutchinson, Jesse 144
Hutto, Sarah 168

Impson, Martha J. 79
Inabnet, John 124,125
  Margaret 125
Ingram, Oliver R. 22
Irby, N. G. 74
Isaac, Elijah 9,13
Isaacks, Elijah 2
  Samuel 2,9
Isle, William 2
Isles, Demsy 2
Isrel, Greenberry 32

Jack, Amelia E. 143
  Andrew Franklin 143
  Martha Eveline 143
  Mary Drusilla 143
  Nicholas 143
  Nicholas Warren 143
Jackson, Alice 61
  Andrew 2
  Ann 15
  D. H. 62
  James 159,162
  Jerina 145
  Mamie 111
  Nancy 149,159,162
Jacob(s), Waller 2,8,14,
    22
James, Angie D. 64
  Bartholomew 9
  Matthew 90
  Peter 12,71
Jefferson, Mary F. 92
Jenkins, Allen 2
  Bertha E. 152
  Carlus E. 152
  Daniel 13
  Davis B. 2
  Edna R. 152
  Elijah 27
  Jane 163
  John 152
  John L. 79
  L. 67
  Mary 85
  Melissa 150
  Monroe 152
  R. S. 152
  William 9,13,22
  William, Jr. 27
Jennings, A. W. 77
  Amanda 160
  Augustine 160
  Barbara 124
  Catherine 160
  Elizabeth 160
  Jesse F. 160
  John 124,160
  Nancy 160
  Pernitian 160
  Thomas 160
John, ----- 2
Johns, John 2
Johnson, Claude E. 140
  Cora Brumfield 140
  George 2,10,27
  George W. 32
  James 27,32
  John 2,10
  Jordan Denson 67
  Julia 75
  Kenzie (Kinza) 32,136
  Mary 160
  Mary Holmes 133
  Monroe 63
  Nathaniel 10
  Nora 62
  Robert 133,169
  Sarah Holmes 134
  Serena Holmes 134
  Thos. 110
Johnston, Alexander 121
  Benton 54

Johnston continued
  Cornelius 121
  Daniel 121
  George 13,21
  J. D. 53
  Jno. 13,21
  Lizzie 57
  Louisa 54
  Maggie 121
  Mary 51
  Nathaniel 13,21
  Nelly 121
  Ollie 121
  Olive (Ollie) M. 121
  Robert 21
  Samuel 120,121
  Tho. 21
  W. C. 57
  W. H. 51
  William 53
Jones, Allbritton 13
  Ann T. 168
  Benjamin 12,21,27,32
  Britain 2,10
  Eliza 18
  Emily 17,48
  Emma Adelaide B. 80
  Harwood 14,22
  Hutson 27
  Icie Holmes 133
  Ida G. 63
  Isham 32
  J. E. 40
  J. J. 38
  J. M. 59
  James 22,27,32
  James F. 152
  James M. 61
  Janie 48
  Jesse T. 76
  John 5,12
  John P. 119
  John Walton 76
  Lewis 2
  Lucy 18
  Mariann 16
  Marsten G. 21
  Mary 17,160
  Mary A. 91
  Mary Ann 17
  Matt 97
  Michael 27,32
  Milton 27,32
  Rich. 105
  Samuel W. 2,9
  Sarah Elizabeth 59
  Siller (Celia) 17
  Susannah 15
  Thomas 2,9,22,27
  Tom 133
  Wiley 27,32
  Wiley, Jr. 32
  William 22
  William C. 2
  William D. 80
  William Hugh 80
  Zebulon P. 6
Jordan (Jourdan), David
    22,27
  Miss L. D. 79
  Louis A. 143
Joyner, Caswell 154
  John 154
  Mrs. M. A. 36
Julian, Renny 21

Kaigler, Eliza H. 133
  Elizabeth Holmes 132
  Emily Holmes 132
  Frank 132
  George 141
  Isabel N. 115
  James 133

193

Kaigler continued
  Jane V. 67
  Jesse Brumfield 141
  John 27
  Wm. W. 32,41
Karr, D. R. 152
Kase, Alonzo 150,163
Kavanaugh, Caroline 61
Kay, Lillie May 109
Kearns, Ella C. 39
Keath, William 27
Keaton, Lillie 145
Keegan, Angeline E. 123
  John E. 123
Keen, Gilbert 22
  Jacob 10
  Josiah 22
  Milton 8
Keevy, Thomas 10
Kellam, Myra P. 85
Keller, Anna Margaret 154
  Catherine 154
  Daniel 154
  Elizabeth 153,154
  Feliciann Asenath 153
  Henry 152,154
  Henry K. 154
  Jacob 154
  John 154
  John Henry G. 153
  John Philip 154
  Johnannas 154
  Joseph Isom 153
  Louisiann 153
  Lydia 154
  Margarett Ann 153
  Martha Ann 154
  Phillip 154
  Rachel P. 154
  Rose Ann 153
  Sarah Matilda 152,154
  Susan 154
  Susannah Eveline 154
  William 153,154
Kellner, Carl Wm. 88
  Wm. 88
Kelly, David 121
  Della 92
  James 22,27
  John 14,120
Kemp, Albert Edward 143
  Alice A. 143
  Alice Ophelia 144
  Alta Eugenia 145
  Andrew 143
  Ann C. 144
  Anne Cirdelia 144
  Annie Jeff 143
  Artie Virginia 145
  Ben 144
  Bradford (Brandford)
    8,142,143
  Caroline Matilda 143
  Carrie 144
  Cauley 144
  Celia 143
  Charles D. 144
  Clancy V. 144
  Clara L. 144
  Dennis Edwin 143
  Drusilla 143,145
  Eley 144
  Elihu 143
  Elijah 144
  Ella Beel 143
  Ella D. 144
  Elva Finley 144
  Emma 144
  Etta M. 143
  Fannie Belle 143
  Fanny Eveline 144
  Flossy Leander 144
  Frances Ellen 144
  George W. 144

Kemp continued
  Harriet 144
  Homer Bryan 145
  Hosea 145
  Ida O. 143
  Isaac 143
  Ivy 144
  James 144,150,163
  Joel D. 144
  John 144
  John Franklin 143
  John Morgan 143
  John Taylor 143
  Joseph 143
  Joseph Israel 143
  Lillie Belle 144,157
  Lula A. 143
  Luther E. 143
  Maggie Lorraine 144
  Martha 143
  Mary 143,144
  Mary Jane 144
  Melissa Ophelia 144
  Milton Jones 144
  Minnie Estelle 143
  Moses 156
  Myrtie Mae 145
  Ora Victoria 144
  Owen Sylvester 145
  Philip Bradford 144
  Quency Edward 144
  Ripley Waller 144
  Robert L. 144
  Rosa 144
  Ruby Coteel 144
  Samuel 144,150,163
  Sidney Ann 144
  Sidney Granberry 145
  Thomas 143,144,150
  Thomas Benton 164
  Thomas Burlin 144
  Thomas Green 144
  Threat Isaac 143
  Una Eva 144
  Velma Ozy 144
  William 143
  William Wesley 144
  Winnie Edwena 145
  Wyatt 144
  Wyman 145
Kenady, Benj. 12,15
  Moor 14
Kendall, Azzle 84
Kendrick, Victory 56
Kennedy, Amon A. 47
  Sister M. J. 62
  N. E. 63
  Robert 55,62
  Zilla A. 55
Kennington, Violette 16
Kenny, John M. 70
Kent, Benj. 14
  Elias D. 22
  Elizabeth 160
  James 27,32
  Jonath. 12,22
  Laban 12,22,90
  Margaret 91
  Uriah 22
Kerby, Abe 92
Kilborn, James 22
Killet, Elizabeth G. 110
Kinard, James 92
Kinchin, Henry 2
  John 2
King, Allen 8,11,22
  Allen (Est.) 27
  Ann 65
  Charles 10,15,32
  David 2,27
  Daniel 22
  Eml. 15
  Evilene Dean 82
  F. M. 32

King continued
  Gus 130
  J. F. 53
  James 2,11,22
  James H. 82
  Jeremiah 27,32
  Jesse 2,8,15,22,27,71
  John 2
  John C. 27
  John F. 2
  Kittwood 71
  Lemuel 9
  Lenora Felder 130
  Lucy 5,16
  Lula D. 152
  Mary Tabor 82
  Matilda 53
  Nancy Jeanette 152
  Salena 152
  Thomas 22
  William 2
  William L. 65
Kinlaw, Rebecca 145
Kinschen, Matthew 2
Kirk, George M. 81
Kirkland, Ann 163
  Joseph A. 27
  Obediah 2,9
Knapp, Cairy 27
Knight, Dorn Brock 137
  Joseph 14
  Susan 114
  Mrs. W. A. 63
  William A. 137
Koil, John 32
Koonce, Ben. Franklin 109
  Mary 76
  Mary Jane 109
Kornegay, Abram 106
  Ann J. 106
  Elvina 106
  L. W. 106
  S. A. 106
  Zachariah 106
Kramer, Eugenia Esker 39
  John B. 39
Kuykendall, Morgan T. 36

Lain, John 27
  John M. 27
  Middleton 27
Lambert, Hiram G. 62
Lamkin(s), John 87
  John S. 4
  John T. 32
  Kezia 67
  Mary 76
  S. L. 67,80
  Sampson L. 84
  Mary 112
  Wm. Griffin 68
Lampton, Benjamin 112
  Cora 112
  Iddo Wilkinson 112
  Lelia 112
  Lucinda 106
  Lucius Lafayette 112
  Lucy 69
  Mollie 112,167
  Thad B. 112
  Walter B. 38
  Walter Monroe 112
  William Edward 112
Land, Annie 58
Lane, John 32
  Joseph 8
  Middleton 32
Lang, J. C. 64
  Lula Holmes 133
  Mary 64
  Sarah 60
  W. P. 60
  Will 133

Lanier, Mary 90
  Robert 32
  Wm. H. 32
Laurence, Delitha 59
  H. B. 27
  Jno. 13,22,28
  Wm. H. 13
Lavisson, Jules 35
Law, Frederick 9
  Lunsford 9
Lawes, Tebitha Conerly 105
Lawrence, Andrew 147
Lazarre, Abraham 32
  Andrew J. 36
Lea, Alexander 2
  Alfred 73
  Barton 22,27,32
  David 32
  James E. 165
  John 157
  Lavinnia 148
  Luke 27
  M. R. 45
  Major 13,22,27
  Noble 27
  Reubin 27,32
  T. W. 62
  Tate 63
  William 28
Leach, Dugall 73
Leaven, Samuel 5
LeBlanc, Maj. Alexis Pierre 115
  Estelle Carrie 115
Lee, Abraham 145
  Aileen 147
  Albert Sidney 147
  Ann 146
  Ann A. 145
  Arthur 145
  Asa 146
  Beatrice Sarah 147
  Benjamin 146
  Benjamin Bryant 132
  Benjamin Bryan W. 146
  Benjamin Franklin 146
  Charlotte Katurah 147
  Cora Elizabeth 110
  Dewitt 146
  DeWitt Clinton 146
  Dimple Jane 147
  Doris 147
  Eleanor 145
  Elisha 146
  Eliza 146,147
  Elizabeth 145,146
  Ella 147
  Everitt 146
  F. M. 64
  Fannie Courtney 123,147
  Frances 145
  Francis Marion 147
  Frank Marion 147
  George Washington 147
  Godfrey 145
  Henry Benjamin 147
  Henry Monroe 146,147
  Hettie 146
  James 2,146
  Jane 110
  Jesse 146
  Jesse Asa 146
  Jesse Walter 146
  Jewell 147
  John 145
  John Henry 146
  John Jesse 147
  John P. 74
  John Walter 147
  Joseph 146
  Joseph E. 147
  Joshua 145
  Keziah 146,147

Lee continued
  Laura Jane 108
  Lottie 147
  Lucy Ann Agness 146
  Maesy 147
  Major 2
  Martha 146
  Martha Jane 146
  Mary 146
  Mary E. 146
  Mary Jane 147
  Mary R. 38
  Mattie Belle 147
  Myrtie Adeline 146
  Nancy 145,147
  Nancy Elizabeth 147
  Nettie May 147
  Noble 65
  Obedience 146,147
  Rebecca 145
  Richard 145
  Robert Edward 147
  Robert Eugene 147
  Rozy 146
  Sallie 146
  Samuel 145
  Sarah 145,146
  Sarah Elizabeth 147
  Sarah L. A. 146
  Shadrack 145
  Simon Henry 146
  Sophronia 65
  Stella Wilmuth 146
  Stephen 145
  Susan Holmes 132
  Susie B. 147
  Tennessee 160
  William 145
  William Causey 146
Lefever, Lucy Tate 158
Legan (Legon), Posey 22
  J. J. 32
  W. B. 28
Legget (Leggit), B. W. 32,155
  Clenth 22
  James 10,22,27
  Jane Olivia 155
  John 32
  John G., Sr. 62,63
  John Goff 90
  Lewellin 8,13
  Martha Estelle 164
  W. P. 27
  William 12,32
Leitch, Effie 73
Leland, L. C. 27
Lemmons, James 2
Lenear, Ida Ann 165
  Mary Alice 165
  Minnie Ella 165
  William Sidney 165
Leney, Rev. James H. 65
Lenoir, Albert 38
  Alice Betha 37
  Ann 159
  Bessie 40
  Francis B. 2
  Mary 83
  Nannie F. 37
  Pinckney 67
  Polly H. 15,22,27
  Robert L. 37
  V. T. 40
  Walter A. 77
  William 27,159
  William H. 40
Leonard, Virginia 72
  William 27
Leslie, Emelie 100
Lessard, Col. W. E. 163
Letchworth, Joseph 97
Letman, Mary 100
Levy, Julia 38

Lewis, Abigail 76
  Alice 69
  Arthur 2
  B. B. 85
  Barney 67,79,80
  Beulah Ball 76,85
  Britton 2
  G. W. 87
  H. P. 71
  J. W. 69
  Henry 22
  Henry Tilman 67
  Hugh 66
  Iddo 77
  Jabez 112
  James 76
  Joseph 9,12,16,17,22,28,136
  Joseph, Jr. 16
  Joseph M. 155
  Miss K. A. 72
  Kesiah Lamkin 80
  Lemuel 76,83,85,86
  Levisa 106
  Lucy Brumfield 141
  Martha Spears 67,68
  Martin 76,106
  Mary 4
  Nancy 146
  Pamela Ann 69
  Price 134
  Q. C. 78
  Q. M. 75
  Quinea 27,67,71,76,80,83,85
  Quinea M. 79
  Rebecca Yarborough 87
  Sampson H. 75
  Samuel 17
  Stephen A. 85
  Susan Warren 76
  Tarner (?) 14
  W. B. 71
  W. Ben 77
  Walter 141
  William 2,12,16,22,28,42
Lezarre, Victoria V. 39
Lieb, Tillie 38
Ligon, Angeline E. 65
  George V. 68
  Jesse 75
  Martha Louise 68
  Mary Louise 67
  R. B. 65
  Robert B. 67
  William 81
Lillard, Mary 168
Linderman, Henry 35
Lindsey, Adeline 101
  Cinderella 162
  Harvey 162
  Isaac 159,162
  John 162
  Lucinda 162
  Malinda 162
  Mary 162
  Mary Ann 162
  Martha Ann 162
  Matilda 162
  Mosella 162
  Nathaniel 162
  William 162
Lish, Amasa 27
Literal (?), John 32
Little, Rolly 13
  Samuel 2
  William 13,32
Loch, Maggie 40
Lockhart, Jacob 14
Loe, Augustus 147
  Benjamin 147
  David 147
  Elizabeth 148

Loe continued
  Felix 147
  Joseph 147
  Joseph Stephens 148
  Martha 148
  Nancy 147
  Sarah Ann 147,148
  Thomas 147
  Willis 146,147
Loftin, Ezekiel 2
  Zachariah 58
Longmire, Jenny 165
Lord, A. Y. 82
Lorrins, Jacques 164
Lott, Abraham 2
  Arthur, Jr. 2
  John 153
  John, Sr. 2
  Luke 2
  Nathan 2,112
  Simon 2
  Solomon 2
  William, Jr. 2
  William, Sr. 2
Lottery, Fritz 48
Love, Franklin 22,27,32
  Jefferson 27
  Margaret 100
  Powell 100
  Robert 2,9,13,27
  William 8,15,22,27
Lovin, Bailey 2
Low(e), Jane 22
  John 2,9,15,22
  L. (Est.) 22
  Lunchford 2,14
Lowery, George W. 66
  Mary Angeline 66
Luis, John 32
  Joseph B. 32
  William 32
Luiza, Hamilton 32
Lumkin, James C. 35
  Hendrick 2
Lumpkins, Hendrick 10
  Hene 14
Lundy, Alfred 32
  Robert 32
  William 22,32
Lute (Luter), Jacob 28,32
  Daniel 102
  Jacob W. 102
  James M. 102
  Jesse C. 102
  John J. 102
  Joseph 28,32,102
  Louisa Matilda 102
  Mary Ann 102
  Sarah C. 102
  Therese E. 102
  Thomas J. 102
  William 102
Luthrell, Jane 13
Lyles, Nancy 62

McAfee, Abner 158
McAffrey, Jno. M. 18
McAlister, Samantha 18
McAnulty, James 2,10,13
  Jas. P. 22
  Michael 28,32
  Robert 2
  William 2,10,13
McCafety, Jno. 11
McCafry, Michael 23
McCall, Marcey 100
McCann, Susan S. 85
McCarty, Agness 120,121
  Cornelius 120,121
  Daniel 120,121
  David 120
  Jacob 120,121
  John 120,121

McClendon, Benson 32
  Bethany Brock 137
  James A. 137
  Jesse 14,22,28
  Joseph 28
  Nancy Eliza 165
  Stephen 32
  Urbin 33
McCluskey, George 39
McClutchie, Will 41
  William G. 74
McCoy, Robert 66
McCraw, Mary Tate 159
  Susannah Tate 159
McCollough, Benj. 22
  Isaac 32
  James 22
McComb, Joseph 32
  Wm. M. 2,13,22,32
McCoy, R. 22
  Robert 33
McCrary, Matthew 2
McCullie, Benjamin 2
  James 2,10
  William 10
McCullough, Arminda M. 64
  Ben 57
  Benj. 11
  James 11
  Jesse 22
  Lonore 63
  William 59
  William, Jr. 11,32
  William, Sr. 11
McCurker, William 35
McDaniel, Alyce Corine 108
  Annie 165
  Calvin 22,28,32
  Corine F. 107
  Daniel 8,14,22,32
  Doris 107
  Frank Wilton 107
  Henry 28
  James 62
  John 2,8,14,28
  Judson 63
  Martha 102
  Mary 158
  Micajah 28,33
  Middleton 22,28
  Nettie F. 107
  P. C. 52
  Raleigh D. 157
  Theodocia 60
  Ubane 28
  Wiley 79
  Winston 60
McDavid, William 11
McDermott, Charles 28
McDonald, Peter 28
  Mrs. S. H. 63
  Zach. 28
McEachern, Duncan 94
McElrath, Frank 55
McElveen, Dewitt 136
  John Ratliff 97,136
  Julia Alford 97
  Katie 62
  Mary 39
  Mollie Brock 136
  S. S. 62
  J. R. 39
McElvin, Elizabeth 6
  Louie 165
  Mathew 10
  Moses 2,8,14,22,28
McElvinn, John 2
  William 6
McEwen, Arch. 22,28,32
  Chauncy C. 128
  G. M. 87
  George Clifton 128
  James Monroe 128

McEwen continued
  James W. 32
  M. R. 86
  Mamie 113
  Mary Lenoir 87
  Mary S. 128
  Matthew 11,22,28,32
  Minerva Felder 86,128
  Monroe 86,128
  Sarah Barnes 128
  Thos. 32
McGaller, Tho. 22
McGehee, Lula 62
  Tenia 73
  W. C. (Dr.) 35
McGowen, Mrs. Elizabeth 69
  Hugh 2
  James 2
  William 2
McGowers, John 28
McGraw, David 9,11,13,22,28
  David G. 22
  David, Sr. 10
  Dempsey 16,28
  Isaac 12
  James 2
  Nathan 16,28
  Nathaniel 13
  Phebe 22
  Uriah 12,28
  Zach. 22,28
McGrew, Dency 33
  Phebe 33
  Wiley 33
  Zaceriah 32
McGruw, Alexander 2
McGuffee, Alfred 2
  John 2
  Wm. 22
McGuirt, Harmpton 162
McKay, Robert 28
McKelvin, Rhoda 62
McKennon, Victoria 62
McKenny, Mettie 63
McKinney, Fannie M. 36
McKinsey, ----- 2
McKinstry, Mary F. 107
McKinzy (McKenzie), Daniel 16,57
  David 12,22
  Israel 17
  John T. 59
  Webster 59
McKisich, Jane 14
McLain, John M. 27
McLean, Charles E. 79
  Clarissa Wildblood 88
  Eliza Jane W. 73
  J. W. 88
  John 73
McL'Wrath, Annie Holmes 137
  Frank 137
McLeod, Norman 23
McManuel, Florence H. 134
  L. W. 134
McManus, Charlie 140
  Margaret G. 140
  Permelia 61
McMillan, Joseph 166
  Laura 39
McMorris, Jane 5,71,73
  Nancy 65
  William 14,22
McMullin, Jas. 15
McNabb, George G. 28
  James 112,160
  James Y. 9,13,22,28
  Jesse 160
  John G. 33,160
  Newton 160
  Rebecca 160
  Rhoda 160

McNabb continued
  Seaborn 160
  William 160
McNeal, Hector 2
McNeil, Catherine Ann 164
  John C. 164
McNiff, Mary 37
McNulty, Hattie 63
  Sadie 77
  Samuel 124
  Sarah Ellzey 124
McQueen, Martha 17
  Samuel 17
McRee, J. J. 74
  Samuel 74
McTyer, Sarah A. 94

Mabury, Annie A. 152
Macomson, Elizabeth 158
Magdalen, Mary 16
Magee, Ada Adelia 146
  Alex Johnson 152
  Andrew G. 80
  Anna 17
  Bethana 165
  Betheny 22
  C. William 152
  Calvin 28,33
  Celia 47,69,76
  Chapman 28,32
  Charles Y. 152
  Clementine 63
  Daniel 2
  Daniel Zaborn 138
  David 72,152
  Delos Johnson 152
  E. (Est.) 22
  E. L. 137
  Elisha 2
  Eliza 156
  Emma 143
  Ester 60
  Fleet 2
  Gatsey 17
  George 2,9
  Gordon Edgar 152
  Henry 2,9,12,22,33
  Henry Elton 152
  Haverson 28,32
  Hezekiah 5
  Ida C. 152
  Israel 152
  J. A. O. 75
  J. J. 87
  Jacob 2,9
  Jacob Haverson 138
  John 2,9,12,33
  John (Est.) 23
  John A. 165
  Klea 152
  Leah 164
  Leah D. 69
  Lem L. 78
  Leonard 17
  Lobn (Soln?) 12
  Louis A. 17
  Lula Mabel 152
  Martha Ann 18
  Mary 17,163
  Minnie Ella Berry 75
  Nehemiah 2,22,28,33,47,76
  Nehemiah, Jr. 32
  Nelson 36,66
  Mrs. O. S. 64
  Obed 32
  Phillip 152
  Pope 33
  Ransom 75,123
  Rebecca 17
  Richd. 23,28
  Robert 2
  Robert Samuel 153

Magee continued
  Rosa Jane 76
  Ruby Holmes 137
  S. O. 43
  Sally 112,152
  Sarah Ellzey 138
  Sire, Jr. 33
  Sire (Sier) 2,12,17,22,28,33
  Solomon 2,9,23
  Solomon Obed 123
  Stephen Ellis 152
  W. C. 78
  Whit Morris 152
  Willis 2,9,12,16,23,28,33,60
  Wilson 152
Magruder, Mrs. C. E. 66
Maines, Elbert 97
  Elizabeth Carter 97
  Jacob 97
  Lucy Alford 96
  Luraney 97
  Noah 97
  Richard 97
  William 96
  William Seaburn 97
  Williamson O. 97
Maish, James D. 37
Majors, Mary L. 74
Makenzie (Makinza), A. 33
  Daniel 9
  David 9
  James 33
  William 32
Manning, John 167
  Melia 32
Manship, Luther 37
Maples, Adaline 50
  John A. P. 5
Marsalis, Ephraim 66
  Letitia 66
  Owen 134
  Velma Holmes 134
Marselas, William 42
Marsh, John H. 9,63
  John K. 16
Marshall, Amanda Black 82
  Dr. C. C. 82
  George B. 59
  L. L. (Col.) 35
  Mary Clay 39
  Matthew 2
Martin, Aaron 2
  Clinton 48,73,115
  Cornelius 2,9
  Derrell 2,13,22
  Elijah 10,13,22
  Eliza R. 67
  Eugenia C. 48
  F. A. 67
  Florence 39,45
  J. L. McNeill 72
  J. T. 39
  J. W. 75
  James 22,28
  James B. 28
  John 13
  John C. 28,33
  John O. 70
  Joe Tuff 100
  Josiah 10,13,22,28,32
  Lorinda 63
  Loyd 67,72
  Mary 33
  Medora A. Huffman 70
  Mollie E. 70
  Nannie 45
  Phillip 22
  Robert Emmette 143
  Rosaline 48
  Sally 113
  Sarah 33,66
  Thomas J. 48

Martin continued
  Wayne 72
  William 2,10,13,22,67,73
  William G. 22,28
Mason, John 152
  Ralph 22
Massey (Masse), Beatrice 107
  Benjamin 2,22
  Calvin 22
  Elisha 22,28
  Pool 22
  Rufus 23
  Uney 28,32
Matthews, J. R. 40
  James 22
  John 2,10,13,33
  John G. 160
  Laura 40
  Meshack 13
  Shadrach 2,13,22
  Silas 2
  William 32
May, A. G. 58
  Alice 156
  Annie 62
  Benjamin 2
  Berry 2,10,22,28
  Dan 56
  Edwin 138
  Elizabeth 61,108,148
  Enos D. 81
  Esaac 64
  Etheldredge 2,22,28,33
  Green 2,12,33
  Green B. 138
  Hiram 28
  J. D. 55
  James 9,22
  Joda 33
  John 2,9,12,22,28,65,153
  John D. 74
  John W. 61
  Joseph 2,9,12,22,23,28,33,148
  Joseph B. 123
  Little B. 12
  Lucy Brumfield 138
  Lula 56
  Mamie Hood 130
  Mary A. 58
  Mary Brumfield 138
  Morris E. 130
  Polly 28
  R. B. 63
  Rachel Collins 81
  Rebecca 33
  Rosa 61
  Willie W. 74
Mayfield, Edmond (John) 5
Mayo, Gardner 90
Megrew, see McGrew
Mellon, William (Est.) 28
Melton, Isaac 14
  Samuel 22
  W. G. 63
Melville, Anthony 38
Menessier, Abraham 99
  Jacquine 99,100
Meng, Henry 28,32
Merchant, Jas. 22
  Jno. 12,22
Mercier, Mrs. V. P. 62
Merrell, Edmund 2
  Joel 10,13
Merret, Joel 2,22,28,32
Merritt, Mary 4
Meyer, Pinkey 147
Michel, Alexander 33
Middleton, Charles 73
  Robert 10

197

Mikell, James 2
  John 2,6
Mikey, Elizabeth J. 35
Miller, A. D. 82
  Alexr. 22,28
  Allie 152
  Asa 22
  Benj. 22
  Brice 8,14,22
  Clara 62
  Fleet M. 33
  Hyram 22
  Jacob 2,10
  Jeptha J. 140
  John 14,33
  Katie 51
  Margaret Brumfield 139
  Mary 159
  Moses 10
  Thompson 12,23
  Thoms J. 33
  Thomson 33
  William 10,22,28,33
Milsaps, Isaac 15,23
  Martha 121
  Mary 121
  Sarah 121
  Thomas 121
  Thomas J. 121
Milton, Isaac 8
  Keen 8
Minor, John 2
Minton, Joseph D. 92
Miskel, R. H. 32
Mitchell, Anizi 18
  Ann 18
  Archie 142
  Charles Henry 109
  Laura Jane 109
  Martin 18
  Sarah Pigott 142
  Susan E. 109
  Thomas James 147
  Warren 18
  Wright 2
Mixon, John 2
  Cornelius 2
  Elizabeth Ann 156
  Milberry 85
  Milliard F. 85
  Obed 33
  Wm. 2
Mizell, Avarilla 91
  David 91
  Edgar 152
  Elvira 91
  John David 91
Moak (Moke), Andrew 2,10,
    13,22,28,32,53
  Catharine 58
  Emanuel 61
  Henry 28,32
  Jacob 28,52
  James A. 61,169
  Joel 61
  John 53
  Labon 48
  M. M. 53,55
  Miss M. S. J. 72
  Matilda A. 50
  Middleton 28,33
  Nancy 53
  Sarah A. 62
  T. A. 44
  Thedius 53
  Viola 63
  W. A. 64
  Zachariah 50,53
Moffat, Henrietta 41
Monk, Sarah 22,28
Monroe, Malcolm 150
Montgomery, David 11
  Elizabeth 61
  Hugh 51

Montgomery continued
  John E. 130
  Myrtle Holmes 134
  Neill 33
  Oliver 130
  Palmira Felder 130
  Sam 134
  Sarah 13
  W. 32
  Winnie Felder 130
Moore, Ann J. 79
  John W. 28,32
  Mary Garner 81
  Nancy 57
  Temie 113
  Thomas G. 81
  William 2
Moran, Frank B. 35
Moreland, T. C. 5
Morgan, Ann 72
  Benj. 14,22,28,167
  David 8,15,22,167
  David B. 5
  Davis 2
  Eliza 167
  Emmaline 115,167
  Isaac 22
  John 28
  John J. 147
  Joseph P. 22,28
  Laura 167
  Mary 167
  Minerva 167
  Nancy Caro 147,167
  William 32,167
Morris, Benj. 14,22,28,33
  Burton 134
  C. W. 132
  Daisy Holmes 132
  Elizabeth B. Alford 97
  George W. 97
  James 33
  James Bolton 119
  Jesse 103
  John Sim 134,140
  Lizzie 134
  Michael 14,22
  Milly 61
  Nathan 9,14,16
  Oscar Denton 144
  R. B. 44
  Sarah Ann 17
  Sarah Ginn (?)
  Sarah Holmes 134,140
  Selathiel 2,10,119
  Simeon 14,22,28,33
  William 113,134
  William B. 33
Morrow, William 10,13
Moses, ----- 2
Moss, James S. 109
Muggah, Katella E. 85
  Capt. Thomas R. 85
Mullen (Mullens, Mullin)
  Gabriel 28,33
  George W. 74
  Isabella 47
  Laura 110
  Laurence 22,28,33
  Nancy 8,14
  Roxie 110
Mullis, Agnes 92
  Willis 22,28
Murphey, Pearl Alford 92
Murr, David 9
Murray, Louisa Sandell 66
  Mattie C. 36
  Rev. Wesley 66
Muse, James H. 76
  Julia A. 76
Musselwhite, Nancy 155
Musick, Mary 147
Myers, David 12

Myers, Herman 141
  Isaac 2
  Myra 125

Nance, Daniel 145
Napp, Cary 23
Naul, Dr. J. W. 64
Neace, John 28
Neal(e), Daniel 33
  James 13,28
  Josiah 28
  Samuel 28
  Thos. 14
  William P. 33
Nease, John 33
Neighbors, John 15
Nelson, Fred 77
Nesom, Miss L. J. 72
Netherlin, Levi 2
  William 2
Nettles, Sarah 4
Newman, Carrol 33
  Elias 133
  Farny (Fanny?) 23
  John 8,22
  Mary 6,11,22
  Mary Mixon 85
  Nehemiah 23,28,159,162
  Samuel 33,162
  Sarah 22
  Smylie 33
  Soloman 23
  Thomas 33
  William 28
Newsom, Alice Carpenter
    144,150,163
  Ann C. 148
  Asa 148
  Augustus R. 148
  Balis P. 148
  Berlin Childress 149,163
  Caramelia 149
  Clara Duval 144,150,163
  Daniel T. 149
  David 148
  Edwin 149
  Elizabeth 28,33,149
  Emily F. 148
  Francis J. 149
  Frederick 9,148,149
  H. Y. 38
  Hines Scott 144,150,163
  Ida Belle 150,163
  Isaac 10
  James W. 149
  Joeday 148
  John 149
  John W. 149
  Joseph 23,28,33,148
  Joseph T. 149
  Keziah 7,149,168
  Lavinia 149
  Leah 150,163
  Leah Keep 149
  Martha 149,150,163
  Martha E. 148
  Mary 6,148,149
  Mary J. 148
  Maston Smith 149
  Moses 149
  Nathaniel 148
  Nathaniel M. 149
  Peter 148
  Polly 148
  Rhoda 149
  Sarah 149
  Sarah B. 149
  Sarah Harp 150
  Sister 66
  Solomon 148,149
  Thaden W. 148
  Thomas Ripley 149
  William 10,28,33,138

Newsom continued
 William S. 148
 William W. 148
Newton, Frances 80
Neyland, Benj. F. 28
 J. L. 28
 Joshua 28
Nichols, Coleman 146
 David 2
 Noah 2
Nicholson, George 33
 Dr. George 40
 Robert 33
Night (Knight), John 9
Nix, Della 72
 Miss Z. L. 76
Nixon, Geo. Henry 2
 Thomas 6
Noble, Joe 168
 Levi 2
 Mark 2
Norman, Ann K.115
 Barnes W. 115
 Miss C. A. 51
 H. H. 115
 Hiram 2,10
 Hiram M. 115
 Hugh M. 48
 James 2,10,11
 Josephus 115
 Lucy 63
 M. D. 115
 Mary 28
 Mattie D. 66
 Presley 10
 Sally 11
 Tho. 11
 Thomas L. 115
 W. G. 115
Norris, Acquilla 2
 Addie 106
 Ezek. 11
Norwood, Sellers 104

Obanion, Dawson 23,28
Odom (Odam, Odum),
 Margaret Ann 28
 Richard 2,9,12,23,28
 Shadr. 23
 William 2,9,12
O'Mara, Adalia V. 73
 C. R. 72
 J. Laney 73
 Joseph 73,123
 Mary Ellzey 123
Oneal, Ransom 2
O'Quin, Charles W. 67
 Danis 23,28,33
 Elender 5
 J. M. 40
 Jehu 12,33
 John 9,12,23
 William J. 36,66
Orr, Mrs. E. E. 35
 William 13
Osteen, Simon 14
Osten, Daniel 23
Otaly, Martha 159,160
 Mary 159
Ott, A. D. 33
 Adolphus Everett 164
 Alfred Hugh 164
 Charles 47,76,164
 Charles deVecmon 164
 Charlotte 165
 Charlotte Ingaba 164
 David 12,23,28
 David Jackson 164
 Elbert Weston 164
 Eskie 161
 Eva America 164
 Frances 164
 Jacob 164

Ott continued
 Jacob M. 44
 Jeptha 33
 John A. 33
 L. W. 45
 Lumanda Louise 164
 Margaret Ann Tate 47,
  76
 Mary Amanda 164
 Mattie 62
 Naomi 46
 Samuel Edward 164
 Sarepta Ann 164
 Walter T. 69
 Walter Thomas 164
Owens, B. D. 103
 Benjamin F. 36
 Jacob 12,23,28,33

Packwood, Catherine S. 35
 J. E. 71
 J. H. 35,38
 John A. 134
 Maggie Holmes 134
 Needham 136
 Rosa Holmes 136
 S. E. 38
 Samuel Franklin 38,71
Paddeford & Catching 33
 T. D. (or O.?) 33
Page, Alexander Leah 153
 Bessie 153
 James 148
 James Andrew 153
 Joseph 114
 Kirby 153
 Miss L. A. 6
 Laramy 148
 Perry Leon 153
 Sophia 152,154
 Susan Conerly 105
 Thomas 154
Pain (Paine), Nelson 23
 Thos. 23
Palmer, Young 109
Pantalion, Joseph 109
Parker, Caroline 58
 George 104
 George Walter 165
 Jno. 23
 Joseph 29
 Leslie 165
 Louisa Brumfield 141
 Margaret 151
 Richard 9
 S. E. 46
 William M. 141
 Wm. Wilkes 104
Parkman, Crenshaw 10,11
Parks, John B. 29
Parnell, Geo. Washington
 72
Parrsons, F. C. 72
Parsons, Francis 23
Passman, Rutha 17
Pate, Judy 59
 Mary 61
Patterson, Julia Ball 95
Pattison, Elizabeth 163
Patton, Florence B. 141
 William 141
Paul, Amelia 111
 Nellie Cooper 152
Payne, Louisa C. 167
 Maudany 149
 Nancy L. 149
 Nelson 28
 Thos. 149
Peak, Elizabeth 72
 Stephen 2
 Stephen (Est.) 23
Pearce, Humphrey 33
 William 28

Pearson, Joel 119
 Malachi 28
 Malikia O. 33
 Reding 33
 William E. 28
 William W. 23,28
Peavy, Dessie 106
Pelatta, Francis 2,12,23
Pendarvis, Even 23
 Mrs. Mahala 61
 Sarah 8,14
 William 14,23,28
Penn, Margaret 11
Penny, Charles 62
Perkins, Samuel 2
Peronneau, Elizabeth 100
 Marie 100
 Samuel 100
Perryman, A. M. (Est.) 29
 Anthony 13
 Flower 16
Persell, S. H. 37
Petelfiles, Francis 11
Peters, Etheldred 29
 William A. 107
Pettitt, Missouri L. 104
 William H. 144
Petty, Presley 2
Phelps, Belmont 37
 I. M. 58
 Sarah 60
Philippe, Alfred 35
Philips, Annie A. 62
Phillips, James 2
 Thompson 2
Pierce, Alcy A. Morris 97
 Abigail 16,97
 Aaron 150
 Augustus 150
 Bernette 152
 Burnette Morris 97
 Charlotte 150
 Cordelia 150
 Edward 18
 Eliza 150
 Elizabeth 18
 G. W. 144
 George Washington 150
 Harriet 97
 Israel 150
 James 97
 Jane 150
 Jesse 150
 John 16,62,97,150
 John P. 150
 John Q. A. 97
 Julia Ann 150
 Laura 152
 P. W. 58
 Reuben 16,95,97,150
 Rubin Ardo 95
 Rosa Lee 144
 Sarah Alford 95,97
Pigott, Amanda Holmes 135
 Billy J. 141
 Charles E. 141
 E. W. 18
 Elinore 142
 Eliza 151
 Estes 136
 Ethel Holmes 136
 Henry 8
 Jesse 142
 John 142
 John B. 151
 Joseph Stephtoe 142
 Malinda 18
 Margaret 151
 Martha Ellen 151
 Mary 142
 Mattie Brumfield 141
 Nancy 17,18
 Nancy Brumfield 142
 Nathaniel 151

Pigott continued
  Rebecca 17
  Seaborn 151
  Thad 135
  Thomas 151
  Thomas, Jr. 17
  Thomas, Sr. 17
  Tommy 141
  William J. 151
Pinkerton, Eveline B. 140
  Sam 141
Pipkin, M. DeWitt 108
Pittman, Catherine 156
  Everit 17,18
  Henry 112
  Hettie Warner 136
  James 28
  Joe 112
  John 156
  Joseph A. 156
  K. T. 156
  Martha V. 153
  Mary E. 153
  Molsey 17
  Nancy 112
  S. E. 61
  Thomas 110
  W. W. 72
  Willie Henry 72
  Willis Richard 136
Pitts, Col. T. T. 37
Platt, Sidney 17
Pleasants, Thomas 5,23
  Washington 2
Plunkett, Dr. J. H. 63
Poindexter, Josie C. 37
  Herbert E. 37
Pollard, Gatney 29
Ponder, Reuben 9,12
Pool(e), Birdie 110
  Malinda 82
  Stephen R. 152
Pope, Bell 62
  Benjamin 2
  Jacob 147
  James 2
  John 155
  Rebecca 18
  Samson 145
  Simon 145
  William W. 106
Porter, Sister E. A. 62
  Emma A. 62
  Horace N. 63
  Joseph 164
Pound(s), Amanda 153
  Andrew Jackson 153
  Carrie 57,155
  Catherine 152
  D. Write 62
  Daniel 150,153
  Daniel M. 46,56,60,62,155
  Daniel W. 155
  Miss E. J. 67
  Edna Sparks 81
  Elizabeth 152
  Elizabeth Ann 153
  Emeline 153
  Flurana 155
  George M. 153
  George Washington 152
  Helen 152
  Henry Bonaparte 153
  Idalia 152
  Inez 152
  Isaac 153
  Isabella 153
  Isam 154
  Isham 151
  Isom 151
  Isom Johnson 151,152
  John 151
  John J. 151

Pound(s) continued
  Johnson Bruce 153
  Joseph 151,153
  Joseph E. 153
  Joseph Edward 154
  Joseph L. 153
  Joseph Leon 152
  Julia 33,46,153
  Julia A. 155
  Julia Elizabeth 155
  Linnie 152
  Louisa 153
  Maggie 155
  Margaret C. 153
  Margaret L. 151
  Mary Ann 151,153
  Minerva 151,153,154
  Miriam 152
  Peter 151
  Prudence 153
  Rachel 155
  Robert M. 153
  Rose Ann 153
  Samuel 153
  Sarah 152,153
  Sophia 152
  Sophia Ardell 153
  Theodore 151
  Theresa 153
  Virginia A. 47
  Virginia Ann 155
  William 151,153
Powell, Dawson 106
  Eliza Morton 81
  Elizabeth 16
  Fanny 104
  Howell 33
  J. M. 39
  J. S. 85
  J. W. 85
  Joseph 33
  Joseph W. 67
  Josiah 13,23,28
  Maggie 112
  Otis Argyle 85
  Rosa Ella Virginia 164
  Starlin 16
  Thomas 28,33,79
  W. L. 81
  William 28
Powers, Olive 155
Prescot, Ephraim 8,14,23,33
  Gusiar (Susan?) 33
  Jesse J. 28
  John 168
  Michael 2,8,14,23
  Nathan 2,8
  Nathaniel 14,23
  Penelope 23
  Willis 2,13,28
  William 28
Prestige, Elijah 45,58
Prestridge, Delilia 169
  Elijah 33
  Elsey 33
  Howell 2,10,13,23
  John 2
  Mary 169
  Robert 2
  Samuel 2,23,33
  Sarah 58
  Simeon 33
Prewit (Prewett, Pruet), A. H. 33
  Ancel 28,113
  Elisha 23,28,33
  Elizabeth 69
  Eva 68
  Harrison 67
  Joe 40
  John 33
  Julia 39,113
  Mary 46

Prewit continued
  Maybell 78
  Polly Ann Vaughan 67
  Smiley 40,69
Price, Alexander 33
  Allen 28
  Celestine 61
  Elizabeth 53
  Emanuel 52,61
  Ester 63
  F. M. 53
  Ida Gill 61
  James 33
  Jesse 53
  Jesse Maxwell 52
  Joseph 23,28,33
  Joseph, Jr. 33
  Lucinthia 50
  Lula 53
  Mary Elizabeth 53
  Mary J. 48
  N. E. 33
  Robert 23,28,33
  S. E. 53
  Stephen 2
  Uriah 33
  W. J. 59
  William 23
  William A. 29
Prichard, William 2,9,12,23,28
Prier, James 33
Pullin, John 2
Purdy, Miss M. A. 71
Purvis, Clemens 33
  Nancy 160

Queen, Jno. 13,23
  Thomas 23
Quillon, Avery Breed 159,161
  Nancy 161
  Thomas 159
Quin, Amanda 87
  Arthur 87
  Arthur G. 29,33
  Dr. D. H. 123
  Daniel 2,9,23,29,33
  Daniel Hillary 101
  Elizabeth 33,78,87
  Emma E. 111
  H. 5
  H. M. 33
  H. Murray 83
  Henry 2,8,23,87
  James B. 29,33
  Judith 23,29
  L. J. 33
  L. M. (Dr.) 64
  L. M. (Mrs.) 36
  Lee 113
  Lizzie 37
  Mary 87
  Minerva 87
  Monroe 33
  Nannie Sumrall 83
  Oscar 62
  Patsey 33
  Peter 87,103,167
  Peter, Jr. 9,23,29,75
  Peter, Sr. 9,13,23
  Peter G. 33
  Richard 15,23,29
  Richard (Est.) 33
  Rodney 137
  Una Holmes 137
  Urvin 33
  Virginia T. 36
  Wallace W. 35

Raby, Gayoso 33

Ragland, Esther 15
  Henry 2,10
Raiborn, James 2
Raiford, Mrs. E. J. 84
  N. B. 33
  William B. 77,84
Ralls, Harris 2
Ramsey, Josiah B. 70
  Thomas Y. 80
  W. M. 83
Raney, John 129
  Rebecca Felder 129
Rankin, George W. 80
  Mary Jane 110
Rasberry, Green 16
  William 12,23
Rask, R. S. 65
Ratliff, James 2
  Joan V. Ellzey 124
  John 134
  Kittie 106
  Maggie 106
  Simeon R. 124
  Richard 12,23,29,33
Rawlins, David 104
Rawls, Allen B. F. 6
  Charles 2
  Elizabeth 129
  Harriet 120
  Harriet E. R. 129
  Harris 29,129
  Jabez 2,6,75,126,128
  James 2,128
  James, Jr. 129
  Jasper 29
  Jasper S. 33
  Jesse 129
  John 128
  Kisiah 129
  Kesiah Felder 75,128
  Luther 128
  Sarah 128
  Sarah Barnes 130
  Susannah 129
  Thomas 129
  W. A. 51
  William E. 6,129
Rayburn (Rayborn), Cias 146
  Emma Self 110
  Fannie 59
  John 33
  Joseph 29,33
  Josephine 64
  Louis 33
  Nancy 35
  Samantha 44
  Susan 63
  Washington 29
Ready, Jno. 23
Reagan (Regan), Abigail 106
  Alif Farrar 78
  Anna 155
  Daniel 155
  E----- 156
  Elizabeth 67,69,155
  Fannie Brumfield 141
  Harriet Malisa C. 156
  J. A. 78
  J. W. 156
  John 155
  John (Rev.) 68
  John, Jr. 155
  John S. 156
  Joseph 69,74,155
  Joseph R. 156
  L. J. (Miss) 72
  Lula 62
  Luther 106
  M. A. 156
  M. E. (Mrs.) 68
  Maggie 112
  Marshall 141

Reagan continued
  Martha 155
  Mary 155
  Mary Ann 156
  Mary E. 53
  Mary Jane 156
  Millie 155
  Nancy 155,156
  Nancy P. 156
  Neill 155
  Nellie 106
  Ralph 76,155,156
  Rebecca 156
  Rebecca Jane 74
  Richard 155
  Robert 156
  Rufus 156
  S----- 156
  Sallie M. 69
  Samuel 155
  Sarah 155
  Sarah Ann 156
  Sarah Jane 156
  Spann 155
  Stephen 76
  Stephen A. 155
  Thomas G. 156
  W. A. 156
  William 155
  William P. 156
  William S. 156
  William Spann 156
Reals, Charles 10
Reams, Alfred 29
  Thomas 29
  Zachariah 29
Read (Reed), Ezekiel 33
  James 2
Reddy, John 29
Redman (Redmon, Redmond),
  D. M. 63
  Jesse 6,23,29
  Wilson 2
  Zachariah 8,14,23
Reed (Reid), Eleazer 148
  Eliza 148
  Elizabeth 148
  James 23,62,148
  Jas. L. 23
  Joseph 33,148
  Lillie 107
  Lurany 148
  Mary 148
  Millie 84
  William 29,148
  William G. 39
Reeves (Reives, Reaves),
  Alfred 2,23,33,43
  Catherine 48
  D. W. 54
  Elijah J. 59
  J. J. 62
  Jesse J. 59
  John 2,6,13,23,29,33,56
  John, Jr. 33
  John Kinzie 54
  Julia Bell 61
  Lazarus 8,13
  Leonard Vincent 168
  M. A. 61
  Margaret F. 59
  Martha 6
  Nancy 52
  Olive 59
  Sophia 62
  Sophronia 58
  Thomas 2,13,23,33
  William 33,52,63
  Zachariah 58
Rehorst, Josephine 40
Reid, Ezekiel 6
  James 6
Rembert, Tery 29

Rencher, Dr. C. R. 82
Reppe, Jno. 23
Rester, Florie 152
  Frances 151
  Jane 150
  Permelia Thigpen 151
  Sarah Ann 150
  W. W. 106
Reuben, Dr. W. H. 61
Rewil (?), Lewis 9
Reynolds, Annie 73
Rhodus, Alice Waldeen 151
  Edith 157
  Elizabeth 156
  Elizabeth Hughes 53
  Eula Elaine 157
  Florence 157
  Henry Morris 157
  Hiram W. 157
  Isaac 62,156
  Isaac Arthur 157
  Jane 156
  Jane A. 56
  John James 157
  L. Ann 63
  Linda Ann 157
  Lucy 157
  Mary 157
  Mary Ann 64,156
  Mary Elizabeth 156
  Mary Lena 157
  Nancy Edora 156
  Nancy Jane 50
  Rudel Rosa 157
  Solomon 156
  T. C. 144
  Thomas 53
  Thomas Cemore 157
  Una Mae 157
  William 23,29,33,156
  William Floyd 157
  William L. 50
  William Leander 157
  William Wesley 156
  Willie Georgia 157
  Willis 157
  Zachariah Reeves 157
  Zidelia Elizabeth 157
Rhymes, Miss T. E. 83
Rice, Joseph 29,33
  Robert J. 40
  T. J. 78
Richardson, Abraham 149
  Amanda 103
  F. S. 37
  George 104
  Hardy 104
  Henry 23
  John 90
  Mrs. M. H. 63
  Mary M. 104
  Nancy 4
  Richard 12
  Sarah 29
Richenbacker, Henry 124
Richmon(d), A. R. 66
  Andrew 2,10,13,23,29,33
  Caroline Ellzey 138
  Emily 62
  James 29,33
  John 15,29,33
  John Thomas 138
  Thomas 10,13,23
  William 23
Ricks, Nancy 164
  Warren 168
Riggins, Jno. 23
Riley, James 29,33
  Polly 8,14
Rimes, Oscar 64
Ripule, Henry J. 33
Rippy, John 29,33
Risher, Eliza M. 80
Rizer, Adam 2

Roark, Joseph 36
Robins (Robbins), E. D. 86
  Jane K. 18
  Orison F. 86
  Mrs. Vernon 62
  W. D. 63
  William 18
Roberds, James 8
Roberson, James 10
  Nancy 8
Roberts, Abraham 61
  Abraham J. 82
  Absolem 16
  Barzilla 33
  Catherine Anders 82
  Celia 47
  Clarinda Pace 97
  David 23,29,33
  E. 23
  E. M. (Miss) 67
  Elijah 14,23,29,33
  Elizabeth 51
  Fannie 146
  George W. 88
  Henry 62
  Isaac 12,23
  J. R. 50,169
  Jackson 33
  James 2,14,23,33,54,97, 101
  James (Rev.) 67
  Jane L. 165
  Janie Guy 88
  Jeptha 29,33
  Joseph 52
  Lightel 29
  Martha 16
  Martin P. 29,33
  Mary 104,143,144
  Mary Ann 68
  Minerva 54
  Moses 29
  Nancy Mary 169
  Samuel 15
  Seaph 169
  Susan E. 78
  Thomas 2,9,15,23
  Wade 61
Robertson, Lucinda 48
  Nathan 2
  Seymour 101
Robinson, Elizabeth 23
  Jas. 15,23
  John 134
  Katie Holmes 134
  Mary 23
  Rebecca 163
  Rosa 62
  Thaddeus 103
Rodgers, Emily 17
  Lucinda L. 17
  Mary 17
Rodrigarz, Jos. 14
Rogers, Charlie 144
  Elmiry 150
  Luranne 4
  William 29,33
Rollin(es), Henry 29
  James 13,23,29,33
  Jeremiah 75
  Julia Elizabeth 52
  Thomas 51,78
Rolls, Harris 23
Rolan, William 10
  Wiley 10
Romph, Jacob 124
Rose, Robert 13
Roset, Jno. G. 23
Ross, Francis 8
  John 2
  Richard 2
Rowell, Abashaba 17
  Frances 17

Rowell continued
  Georgia Ginn 140
  Lenora Brumfield 139
  Lewis 2,29,33
  Louis 139,140
  Pamelia 17
  Sarah 17
  Susan 17
  William 17
Rozar, Mary 145
  Rebecca 145
Ruddock, Margaret 154
Rule, Natn. 23
  Thomas 2,9,12,23
Runnels, Harmon M. 2
  Hiram G. 2
  Howell W. 3
  Picket 36
Rushing, Anna 18
  Arkansas 167
  Claiborne 12,23,29
  Ephraim 17,29,119
  Jacob 50
  John C. 18,33
  Julia E. 17
  Laura 35
  Levie 18
  Lucinthia 50
  Moses E. 1
  Myrtis 62
  Nancy 17,18
  Nowel 17
  William A. 18
Russ, Effie Leach 73
  J. L. 73
  Jasper L. 73
  S. P. 73
Rutland, Asa 3,23
Ryall (Ryals), Bilbra 16
  Brandon 18
  Chas. 23
  Eliz. 13
  Estate 20
  Hardy 16
  Joseph 21
  Martha R. 18
  Mary 17
  Willaby 29,33
Rymes, James 14,23
  Jesse D. 29
  Little John 15
  William 13

Sadler, Isaac 3,8,13
Safford, Judge E. 40
  Hettie Blanche 40
Salley, A. S., Jr. 125
Sample, Dr. John 82
Sandeford, Amos 24
  Jas. 24
  Robert 24
Sandell, Anna Davis 85
  Daniel 3,9,14,23,29,33, 36,70,86
  Darius 29,33,70
  Elenor Corley 70
  Gabriel 33,70
  Henry 9,14,29,33,70
  J. Darius 85
  James Fletcher 109
  James M. 37
  Jeptha Winborne 70
  John Monroe 108
  Martha 70
  Mary 70
  Monroe 70
  Murray 70
  Nelson 70
  Permelia L. Powell 79
  Peter 29,33
  Sarah Martin 70,73
  Susan Catherine 109
  Wesley 70

Sandell continued
  William Fletcher 108
  William N. 35
  William Wesley 108
  Winifred E. 108
Sanderfer, see Sandifer
Sanders, Angeline 167
  Henry J. 163
  Jackson 57
  Leslie Maret 105
  Mollie 63
  Thomas Walter 105
  Travis 3
  Wilma Lou Conerly 105
Sandgord, Mary M. 156
Sandifer, Ackland Ann 166
  Benjamin 45
  D. R. 61
  David N. 167
  Delia E. 56
  Elizabeth Minerva 167
  Emily 156
  Emma Dickey 57
  Georgia Ann 157
  H. W. (Dr.) 57
  Hansford 156
  Hardy 12,33
  J. H. 61
  J. J. 61
  J. T. 41
  J. Wes 112
  James 156
  James Jackson 56
  James M. 167
  John 14,34
  John J. 29,33,167
  John H. 30
  John Wesley 167
  Joseph 11,166
  Lelia J. 157
  Lona 61
  Louminda 61
  Margaret C. 167
  Martha 33
  Mary Ann 147,167
  Peter 12,24,29,34,156
  Peter, Jr. 29
  Rebecca 45
  Rhoda Elizabeth 167
  Robert 29,34
  Sarah E. 167
  Telitha I. 55
  W. E. 63
  William 14,24,30
  William E. 33
  William J. 167
  William N. 29
  William N. (Est.) 33
  William Y. 29,33
Sartin, Alfred 80,153
  Alonzo 76
  John 9,12,24
  John G. 153
  Louisa A. Cowart 80
  Minerva R. 153
  Samuel 153
  Selph 80
Sasser, Frances 55
  Jas. G. H. 33
  Julia 44
Saucier, Alfred 111
Savage, Aley 13
Saville, Aaron 2
Scarborough, Charles 83
  George 133
  Sarah Power 83
  Stella Holmes 133
  Thedras 53
Schilling(s), Barney 123
  E. M. 55
  Eliza 44,157
  Emma A. 63
  Esco M. (Rev.) 123
  Eveline Ellzey 123

Schilling(s) continued
 Fannie Josephine 152
 John B. 60
 Lien 144
 Lizzie 63
 Michael 44
 Quincey C. 55
 Rachel 55,168
 Sarah Jane 52
 Susan R. 60
Schwing, Ava 104
 Carrie 104
 Carter 104
 Willie 104
Scivilque, Bernice P. 130
 Joseph 130
Scott, Burw. 24
 Julia A. 74
Seaborn, Benjamin 95
 Frances 95
Seal(e, s), Allie C. 143
 Almeda L. 69
 Andrew J. 152
 Arthur M. 143
 Barney 29
 Charles Bluford 143
 Charles Rudolph 143
 Daniel 2
 Eli 2,33
 Ella 143
 F. A. 143
 Filer 152
 Jesse Pierce 152
 Jilson Y. 29,33
 Lewis 2
 Littleton 23,29
 Lizzie I. 143
 Martha E. 154
 Nancy Amacker 152
 Thomas 14,154
 William 2
Self, Elijah 23
 Elizabeth 109
 Maggie C. 110
 William 29,33
Sellers, William 8
Selman, W. R. 77
Sertain, Alfred 31
 Jno. 12,29,31
 Major 29
 William 31
Seymour, Sarah A. Talley 75
 William 75
Shadrack, Amanda 49
Sharon, Jno. 13
Sharp, Effie A. 77
 J. Leon 143
Shateris, Judith 47
 Richard 53
Shaves, John 3
Shaw, Fannie W. 73
 Lou 146
Sheppard, Alonzo 143
 William W. 16,24
Sherby (Shirley?), Philip 12
Sherrin, John 9
Ship, John 9
Shirk, Mary 63
Shirley, N. 5
Shoup, J. F. 155
Shoupe, J. T. 33
Shirler, Nicholas 124
Sibley, Ann 159,162
 Elizabeth Cassel 123
 Jane 60
 Jane Felder 126
 John, Jr. 123
 John Coleman 90
 John E. 29,34,44
 John I. 90
 Lizzie 38,71
 Mary 65

Sibley continued
 Mary Ann 90
 Penelope 168
 R. A. 65
 Rebecca 101
 Reddick 90
 Richard 90
 Robert 91
 Robert F. 90
 Sarah 90
 Susan 44
 William 15,23,29,33
 William L. 168
Silman, Abner 11
 Tho. 11
Silmon, Elias 3,8,11
Simmons, Agnes 157
 Ann 14,24
 Barcana Hope 70
 Bessie 165
 Calvin E. 117
 Charles A. 165
 Columbus W. 91
 Cyrus Sullivan 165
 D. Monroe 155
 Dave W. 86
 C. L. 64
 Clara 79
 Clinton 79
 Cyrus 55
 Dixie 70
 Eliza Webb 86
 Ella Brumfield 141
 Emmett F. 62
 Francis 58
 Franklin Willis 156
 G. W. 33
 George 29,33,48
 George Boardman 90
 Hansford L. 91
 Harriet C. W. 77
 Henry 16,29
 Ida I. 109
 Isaac 13
 Isabel 48,58,168
 J. B. 37
 J. E. 46
 J. W. 86
 Jackson 157
 James Jackson 141
 Jane Brock 62
 Jefferson E. 90
 Jeremiah Jackson 135
 Jesse L. 141
 John 3,13,23,24,29,33, 43
 John D. 61
 John H. 117
 John R. 33
 Joseph M. 77
 Josephus 3
 L. W. 62
 Liddia 62
 Louise C. 62
 Lucie 55
 M. H. (Mrs.) 79
 M. M. 64
 Marcus A. 91
 Martha 90
 Martha Holmes 135
 Mary 61,63
 Mary Ann 48
 Mary Dixie 107
 Mary Elizabeth 90
 Mayson (Mason) 29,33
 Mollie H. 79
 Myrtle Tate 163
 Nancy 29,47
 Nancy C. 44
 Oliver 79
 P. X. 62
 Rachel 63
 Ralph 3
 Reddick Fulton 91

Simmons continued
 Reuben 58,61
 Richard Montgomery 90
 Robert L. 91
 Rosa Tate 55
 Sarah 44
 S. O. 63
 Semantha 63
 Solomon 168
 T. C. 76
 T. Jeff 156
 Thomas 29,70,86
 Vol 104
 W. W. 70,86
 William 3,24,29,33,47, 86,165
 William J. 33
 Willis 3,8,15,24,29,33
 Willis, Jr. 29
Simpson, Abel 9
 Samuel 3
Sims, James 140
 Julia 33
 Nathan 10,13,23,33
 Olivia J. Ellis 66
 Robert 3,8,11
Singletary, ----- 154
 Sarah 80
Singleton, Etheldred 149
 Martha 149
 Robert 149
Sinnex, Hannah 164
Sipple, Barbara 36
 Louise 37
Sistrunk, Danl. 11,24
 George W. 77
 Jacob 24
 Jno. 12,24,29,84
Sitmon, Abner 24
Skinnes, W. A. 88
Slade, Ida G. 40
Slaughter, David 3
 John 3
 George 3
 Richard 3
 Robert 3
 William 3
Slocumb, Ellen Ellis 120
 Margaret Ellis 120
Small, Bettie 46
Smiley, Edward 78,107
Smith, Ada 156
 Ada Simmons 119
 Alexander 3
 Alcus Jerry 144
 Alonzo Calvin 144
 Angeline 69
 Ann Crews 118
 B. B. 69
 Bailey 15
 Bouie 135
 Britton 15,24,29,71
 C. F. (Rev.) 79
 Cain 64
 Calvin 18,29,33,118,139
 Caroline 139
 Cathern 17
 Cecelia 139
 Charles 35,161
 Charles Tate 161
 Cinderella 119
 Clara Ann 119
 Clara H. 55
 Clary 30,34
 Clinton 161
 Cynthia 139
 Daniel 15,24,34,119
 Daniel, Jr. 30
 Danil R. 134
 David 10
 Davis E. 139
 Densmore 119
 Densmore W. 119
 DeWitt 62

Smith continued
  Doc 161
  Edwin 118
  Eli 3,29,118,139
  Eliza 118
  Eliza A. 119
  Ella 161
  Ella Brock 136
  Emily M. 18,139
  Ethel 113
  Eugene 136
  Eusaba Fortenberry 118
  Ezekiel 3
  Fannie Brock 136
  G. W. 143
  George 15,18,24,119,
    139,161
  Gideon 9
  Henry 3
  Henry J. 119
  Hollander 118
  Hugh 3,29
  Isaac Frank 119
  Isham 3
  J. Carter 3
  J. Dort 141
  J. W. 18
  Jackson C. 139
  Jacob 29
  James 3
  Jane 118
  Jane Holmes 134,135
  Jared D. 119
  Jarred 141
  Jasper 136
  Jasper R. 119
  Jeremiah 3,8,24,29,33,
    118,119,139
  Jeret 33,119
  Jesse 139
  Jo Anna 118
  Joe 133
  John 3,8,9,15,18,24
  John (Est.) 29,33,167
  John, Jr. 34
  John W. 139
  Johnie Wilson 136
  Joseph 29,33
  Joseph C. 10
  Kitty Magee 119
  Lemuel O. 69
  Levi 3
  Lewis 161
  Lexie Holmes 137
  Lidda (Lidya) 118
  Lizzie Holmes 133
  Lucinda 153
  Lucretia 119
  Lucretia Dykes 119
  Luerisisa (Louisiana?)
    17
  M. A. 143
  Margaret 18,77,139,164
  Martha 4,118,139
  Mary 9,17
  Mary (Est.) 29
  Mary Holmes 119,136
  Maurice 164
  Maxy 77
  Mehala 118
  Milevy 118
  Minnie Brumfield 119,141
  Morris 156
  Moses 151
  Murrey 119
  Nancy 17,119
  Nancy C. 119
  Nellie E. 38
  Newel 33
  Newell C. (Dr.) 119
  Newey 119
  Orpha Roberts 118
  Pernesa 118
  Pernissa 119

Smith continued
  Pleas 24
  Preston Alonzo 136
  R. L. 63
  Rachel Ellzey 123
  Raiford 147
  Richard 9,15,24
  Robert 8
  Sarah 18,139
  Sarah Brumfield 118,139
  Seleta 119
  Sileta M. 18
  Susanna 34
  Tabitha 17
  Thomas 3,29
  Tom 139
  William 3,9,12,18,24,29,
    34,162
  William D. 33
  William Dorten 119
  William L. 119
  Willis 161
  Winston 141
  Wright 119
  Wyatt 29,33,55,71,118,
    139
Snell, Lorenzo Dow 164
  William 29,33
Soan, Henry 29
Solomon, Sister E. D. 62
Sommers, Jno. 23
Somner, Owen 3
Sones, Henry 3
Sorrell, Washington 3
Sparkman, R. T. 33
  N. R. 29
  Reddeck 23
Sparks, Richard 3
  W. F. 81
Speake, Margaret Tate 158
Spears, Edgar 64
  Martha 71
  Philip 67
Spell, Aaron 24,65
  Jemima 65
Spence, Eliza Ginn 140
  Jesse O. 140
Spencer, Amanda Adelaide
    36
  Jno. T. 12
  Robert 5
  William 3,6
Spenks (Spinks), Wm. 23,
    29,34
Spike, Oliver 157
Sprich, Dena 38
Stafford, Abraham 86
  Joshua 78
  Joshua J. 81
Stogner, Henry 90
Stallings, Ann 118
  E. (Est.) 24
  Frances Ginn 118
  Harriet Graves 118
  James 29,33,118,141
  James Harvey 118
  Jessey 118
  John 8,9,15,24,29,33,
    118
  Jno., Jr. 24
  John Everett 118
  Joseph 118
  Linnie Brumfield 141
  Richard Willis 118
  Sarah Pearson 118
  Zonetta Smith 118
Stamps, Leila Delamore
    143
Stanfield, Martha 15
  Miss 5
Stanford, Elizabeth F. 129
  Frank 129
  Green 129
  Harriet 129

Stanford continued
  Mary 129
  Nancy 129
  Noah 129
  Sarah 129
Stanley, Chas. T. 33
  Julia 67
Stapleton, Georgia 120
Starkey, Mary 61
Starnes, Moses 108
Statham (Stateham, State-
    hum)
  Charles H. 136
  Elizabeth 52
  John 136
  John B. 33
  Martina 106
  Myra Lewis 136
  N. E. (Miss) 66
  Ruth Holmes 136
  Sherwood 34
  R. Y. 33
  Walter 136
Staudenmire, Margaret 125
Steen, James 3
  Nathaniel 3
  Robert 3
  William 3
Steinburger, Mrs. C. S. 61
Stephens, Ann Louise 111
  Elisha 33
  Robert 85
  Willie 111
Stephenson, Jno. 23,29
  Simeon 29
  William 29,34,53
Steppe, J. P. 41
  Jessie Lot 41
Sterling, Allen 3
  John, Jr. 3
  John, Sr. 3
  Samuel C. 34
Stevens, A. C. 72
  John C. 72
  Homer 132
  Johnie Holmes 132
Stevenson, John 14
  Susan 68
Stewart, Eliza 152
  Emma Brumfield 140
  George 79,140
  Mary 152
  Samuel 39
  Willena 79
Stigler, Benjamin 3
  George 3
Stinson, Arch. 11
Stockdale, Fannie 61
Stockstill, Joshua 8
Stogner, Clint 142
  Esley 142
  Eva Pigott 142
  Henry 24
  John Pigott 112
  Martha Pigott 142
  Mary 151
Stoker, Elizabeth 90
Stone, Marble 9
  Marvel 3
  Richard 9
Story, Richard 29,45
Stovall, Charles 3
  Emeline 98
  Frances 98
  Gilbert 3
  John 3
  Lewis 3,12,24
  Martha Alford 96
  Mary 98
  Myra 98
  Nancy 98
  Ralph 9,12,24
  Thomas P. 34
  Warren 98

Stovall continued
  William 96
Strahan, John 150
Stratton, Dr. E. P. 36
  Shirley 107
Strawther, John 8
Strickland, Allen 14
  Dorothy 63
  Ella F. 77
  Erastus R. (Rev.) 78
  H. D. 64
  Henry 24,29,168
  James Calloway 157
  Jeremiah 29,33,46,50,
    168
  Jno. 24,29,33
  Lena Pigott 142
  Matilda Varnado 50
  Meredith 29
  Myrtle 107
  Nancy 144
  Noah 24
  R. C. 49
  Robert 3,8,14,24,29
  Sarah Jane 49
  Sophronia 33
  T. R. 144
  William 23,29,33
Strickling, Elizabeth 53
Stringer, Flora 75,106
Stringfield, Esther A. 98
  Mary 5
  Wilkie 107
Strong, David 15
  Jas. 24
  John 3
  Joseph 9,15
  Thomas 3
Strother, Hannah 16,29
  Jemmerson 24
  Jno. 11,24
  L. H. 29
  William S. 29
Stroud, Ace Jefferson 142
  Sarah Carter 142
Strowman, Ann Margaret
  124
  Jacob 124
Suddeth, Charles 33
  Jesse 23,29
  Lewis 29,33
Sullivan, Danl. 12,24
  Elizabeth 108
  Patrick 24
  Reni 27
Summerall, Jesse 3
Sumrall, Hester C. 106
  Josephine 106
Summers, Jacob 8,14
  Rachall Felder 125
Sumner, Buford A. 87
  George C. 69
  John 29,33
  Henry 33
Suther, Samuel 124
Sutphen, May 64
Sutton, Allen 33
  J. M. 61
  William (Est.) 29
Swayze, George 39
  Dr. Yandell 85
Symons, Henry E. 23

Tabor, Isaac 10,24
Tafaro, Peter J. 107
Tait, Eliza Bowman 86
  William 9
Talbert, Mattie 110
  Susie 62
Talbot, Elevia 62
Talley, Anna 152
  Bertha Celestine 152
  David 75

Talley continued
  Florence 152
  Iona 152
  Leona 152
  Mary Jane 152
Tarver, Rev. E. L. 84
  Rev. Elijah 76,77
  James 3
  Jane 77
  Jesse 24
  Wm. Allen 76
Tate, Alexander 161
  Ann 157,163
  Ann Cassander 160
  Ann Catherine 149
  Ascenith M. M. 162
  Carrie 157
  Catherine 159,163
  Catherine Ann 163
  Catherine Ingaba 164
  Charles 24,30,34,159,
    161,163
  Charlotte Mary 165
  Charles W. 161
  Clarinda 162
  Cora 161
  Dallas 161
  Daniel Edward 165
  Dannie E. 165
  Delilah 158
  Delphine 161
  Eastman R. 162
  Eleanor Caroline 161
  Elizabeth 158,159,161
  Emma G. 161
  Ener E. 165
  Estelle J. 161
  Eva Etna 165
  Everett 162
  Ewell 157
  Fanny 158
  Flora T. 164
  Florence E. 161
  Frances Mary 165
  Franklin M. 161
  Fred 157
  Frederick 161
  George Murray 165
  George W. 162
  Georgia 165
  Georgiana Corrinth 161
  Harvey 6,159,161,162
  Henry 158
  Hugh 163
  Hugh D. 164
  Hugh d'Evecmon, Jr. 164
  Hughey 157
  Jackson 162
  James 157,158,159,160,
    161,162,163
  James Finley 164
  James H. 161
  James Naul 161
  Jesse 149,158,159,162
  Jesse C. 161
  Jesse Naul 160
  John 6,158,159,160,161,
    163
  John Guy 163
  John McNeil 164
  Joseph 162,163
  Josephine 161
  Julyann 161
  Kesiah 158
  Lady Tennessee 161
  Lafayette 162
  Lanfry W. 162
  Leatha Ann 161,163
  Lillian Drucilla 161
  Linnie 157
  Louis J. 161
  Louisa 161,162,163
  Lucy 158
  Lydia 162,163

Tate continued
  Margaret 163
  Margaret Ann 164
  Margaret Bethany 165
  Margaret Luna 165
  Maria Louisa 164
  Marsha Parilee 161
  Martha 6,161
  Martha Ann Elizabeth 160
  Mary 157,158,159,160,
    161,162,164
  Mary Ann 161
  Mary J. 162
  Mary Jane 162
  Morgan 162
  Moselle M. 161
  Nancy 159,161,162,163
  Nathaniel 158
  Nicholas Baylies 160
  Nicholas W. 160,162
  Patsey 158
  Predence Missouri 161
  Obediah 161
  Obey Nickles 161
  Poke 161
  Rachel 162
  Randall 158
  Rebecca Elizabeth 161
  Reuben 158
  Rhodie Missouri 160
  Robert 157,163
  Rosa Elizabeth 165
  Roy 157
  Samuel 158
  Sarah 158,159,161
  Susannah 158,162
  T. E. 38
  Thomas 47,158,159,161,
    163,164
  Thomas d'Evecmon 164
  Thomas Edward 163,164,
    165
  Thomas Roland 165
  Thomas Scott 160
  Thomas W. A. J. 162
  Ufan 157
  Van Ghylotia 161
  Walter Scott 165
  Warren 163
  Washington 162
  William 157,158,163
  William Benjamin 161
  William Edward 165
  Wilson 163
Tatum, Stephen 11
Taver, Elijah 34
Taylor, Beverly 162
  Catherine 164
  Daniel 3,11
  Daniel, Jr. 11,24
  Daniel, Sr. 24
  David 6,30,34,160
  Edward 34
  Eva B. 75
  Grant R. 30
  James Monroe 160
  John 3,11,24
  Joseph 24
  Jourdan 34
  Judith 103
  Julie Ann 103,162
  Leonard 17,18
  Nimrod 160
  Sereptha 103
  Thomas S. 75
  Washington J. 162
  William 162
Tedder, Elisha 30
Tegarden, M. Key 71
Tellis, John 3
  Silas 3
Templeton, Matilda 61
Terrell (Terrall), Bird 34
  Callie 144

Terrell continued
  Eliza Ann 170
  Hiram 34,81
  Irene 144
  J. L. 34
  James L. 86
  James Landrum 81
  John G. 34
  Josiah 34
  Josiah Martin 72
  M. W. 86
  Mamie 112
  Mary Sandell 81,86
  Philomon 3
  W. J. 86
  William 34
  Z. T. 63
Terry, Champness 101
Thigpen, James 16
  Smithie 150
  Travis 150
Thomas, Angeline 61
  Benj. 11,24
  Benj., Jr. 11
  Charles 3
  Clara 48
  Daniel 3,10,12,24
  Elizabeth 113,131
  Henry 113
  J. A. 53
  James 3,11
  Jeremiah 9
  Jesse 11,24,30,34,113
  Jesse G. 69
  Jonathan 131
  Malachi 11
  Mary 18,113,131
  Matthew 113
  Nathaniel 24
  Oliver P. 113
  Phillip 131
  Rebecca 131
  Wesley 30,34
  William 131
Thompkins, Thomas 3
Thompson, Alexander 24
  Alexandria 161
  Ann Watson 87
  Archibald 3
  Eliza Jones 83
  Elizabeth 44,158
  Fannie 108
  Farlar 158
  Hardy 65
  Hugh 24,30,170
  James 24
  James (Est.) 30
  Jerry 162
  Jesse, Sr. 3,83
  John 8
  John Harvey 87
  Kenion 161
  Malissa J. 65
  Mary L. 170
  Minerva 161
  Nancy Rembert 83
  Nancy Ward 168
  Narcissa 48
  Obediah 161
  Param 24
  Parris 11,24
  R. H. 87
  Rebecca 168
  Sarah 16,43
  Simeon 3,24
  Steph. 24
  Susan L. 109
  Swan (Swain) 9,11,24,30
  Thomas 9,161
  William 24
Thomson, Hardy 34
  Hugh 34
  Parham 34
  Sarah 36

Thornhill, Bessie Brock 137
  Brian 24
  Caroline 57
  Elisha 24,30,34,62
  Evan 30,34
  H. E. 78
  Hildary 134
  J. P. 57
  J. W. 62
  James Robert 137
  Joseph 9,24,30,34
  Joseph, Jr. 30
  H. E. 51
  Henry H. 34
  Louranie 64
  Mary 7
  Patric 30
  Robert 9,12
  Solomon 30
  Victoria 64
  Victoria Morris 134
  William 3,7,9,12
  William, Jr. 24
Tilley, Drury 3
Tisdale, Edward K. 90
Tolar, Henry 3
Tomlinson, David 120,131
  Jacob 3
Tompkins, Jno. B. 3
Toney, Benjamin 9
  Drury 6
  James 3,12
  Lucy Lillian 144
  Thomas 69
Toomer, David R. 72
  Wiley 72
Toosing, Paul 9
Trahan, Rufus 133
Trask & Fetters 30
Travis, Eustatia 30
  Mamie W. 41
  Mary 74
Traylor, Delia 62
  J. J. 50,54
  Matilda L. 50
  Matthew 3
  Sarah E. 54
  William 3
Trawick, Cornelius 30
Traywick, Goodman 15,24
Trebbles (Tribble),
  Spellsby 10,11,24
Trentham, Mary 10
Trewit, Abi 11
  Abraham 10
Troller, Geo. M. 24
Trotter, Geo. M. 14
Tull, J. F. 150,163
  Jennie 92
  Martha 62
Tullos (Tullis), Abr. 24, 30
  Archd. 12
  James 12
  John 9,12
  Margaret 30
  Robin 24
  Stephen 12,24
  Temple 9,12,24,30
  Temple, Jr. 9,12,24
  Thomas 12,24,30
  William 12
  Wiloby 9,12
Turnage, Barbara 45
  Elijah 113
  Rayford 110
Turner, Balis 24,34
  Dempsey F. 109
  Elizabeth 104
  Jackson 34
  Joseph 13,24
  Mathew 10,13
  Philip 104

Turner continued
  Samuel 10
  Sidney 144
  William 122
  Zadock 14
Turnipseed, B. S. 49,56
  Berkly 81
  Harris 30,34
  Mary 44,56
  Mary Huffman 80
Tyler, Aaron 166
  Abden 24,165,166
  Absalom 165
  Allen 166
  Amanda J. Felder 128
  Cassandra 166
  Daniel 165,166
  Elisha 11
  Eliza 166
  Ellis 166
  Henry 165
  Henry Milton 166
  Jacob 165
  James W. 166
  John 165
  Kelly 165
  Lizzie 111
  Margaret 166
  Marthena 166
  Meredith 166
  Moses 165
  Nancy Sandifer 79
  Richard 165
  Sophronia 108
  William 165
  Wm. Glanville 34,79
  Wm. Matthew 69,128
  Wm. Riley 166
  Zachariah Milford 166
Tyner, Elizabeth 18
Tynes, Ada 170
  Elizabeth 110
  Elizabeth Henrietta 108
  Fleming 3
  Florence 170
  James L. 72,78
  Jane Alford 97
  Martha 164
  Minor 3
  Susan A. 106
  T. E. 38
  T. F. 77
  Thomas Fleming 170
  Tyra 97
  Tyra Jennings 165
  Walter Edwin 165

Uli, Angelo M. 134
Underwood, Cressey 153
  Ellenora 153
  J. William W. 153
  John A. 153
  Robert 153
  Robert D. 153
  Sarah S. 153
Upton, Marie Luter 102
  Mrs. R. Chester 115

Vardaman, Jeremiah 3,10,12
Vardeman, Amiziah 10,12
Varnado, Allie 156
  Anna 156
  Arcadio 168
  Archibald 149,168
  Arie 107
  Cassie 157
  Charles 149,168
  Clara 157
  Clarissa 168
  Cordelia 91
  David 149,168
  Elizabeth 168

Varnado continued
  Emmanuel 30,34,53
  Emanuel D. 44,46
  Ethel 157
  Eugene 39
  Evelyn 108
  Franklin 168
  Fred E. 156
  George W. 149,168
  H. Eugene 45
  H. H. 36
  Hezekiah 37
  Howell 149,168
  Iley Arthur 156
  Isabel Simmons 48
  Isham 34,168
  Isham E. 50,56
  J. Marshal 53
  Jenny 156
  Judson A. 156
  Leonard 3,7,8,14,24,30,
    34,168
  Lewis 30,34
  Luther Sidney 156
  Margaret Hope 50
  Mary 168
  Matilda 46,149,168
  Meredith 149,168
  Mitchell 30
  Moses 3,8,168
  N. B. 58
  Nancy 168
  Nathaniel 168
  Newton B. 48,149,168
  Oliver 168
  Oliver Thomas 157
  Rachel 168
  S. Jane 63
  Samuel 7,24,30,34,168
  Samuel, Jr. 24
  Samuel, Sr. 14,149
  Sarah 46,149,168
  Sophronia 149,168
  Telitha 56
  Virgil 164
  W. Ivey 156
  W. L. 37
  W. N. 49,62
  William 30
  William Pearl 168
  Wright 156
Varner, Dicey Alford 98
  John 98
  Joseph E. 97
  Nancy Alford 98
Vaughan, A. J. 67
  Mrs. A. J. 69
  Aby F. 166
  Aby Jane 72
  D. F. 68
  H. 19
  Hendrick 10
  Josiah 166
  Nichl. 11
  Polly 69
  W. B. 120
Vaught, Harrison Robart 40
  Mary H. 76
  W. C. 40
  W. O. 40
Vawes, Josiah 34
Vinant, Addie Hood 130
  Percy 130
  William 10

Waddell, John 97
Waddle, Jas. 15,24
Wade, Julia 160
Wadley, Jennie Belle 54
Wadsworth, Rev. Daniel
  M. 76,96
  Judge John 76
  Mary S. 74

Wailes, Daniel 35
Wainwright, Dickson 30
  Jno. 24
  Seborn 34
Waldrop, Claiborn 97
  Claiborne P. 98
  Frankie Alford 98
  Laura Alford 97
  Martha Alford 98
  Napoleon 98
Walker, A. S. 64
  Catherine Felder 125
  Charles 3,13
  Cicero 123
  D. C. 62
  Elijah 34
  Emily 62
  Hampton E. 58
  Hattie 111
  Jeremiah 30,34,37,43
  John 10,11,24,30,34,
    121,125
  John A. 61
  John E. 34
  Margery Johnston 121
  Martha 63
  Mary Alice 58
  Mary Jane 170
  N. E. (Mrs.) 61
  Sanders 30
  Sarah 16
  Sarah Ellzey 123
  Thomas 49
  W. R. 58
  William 30,114
  Willie 61
Wall, E. T. 63
  Eugene 61
  Hampton 162
  Martha E. 160
Wallace, Adline 53
  Cleveland 61
  Courtney Marcella 75
  H. A. 50,53
  Jesse (Dr.) 75
  Julia Ann 56
  Oliver 3
  Patrick 30
  Sarah 48
  Thompson 7,24,30
  William 56
Waller, Benson B. 161
  Charles F. 161
  Dora 162
  Elva 161
  Ivey F. 161
  James Irwin 152
  Jefferson C. 161
  John Tate 161
  Joseph 161
  Martin P. 161
  Obediah C. 161
  Ripley B. 161
Walling, James 12
Wallis, John 30
  John C. 34
  Louisa J. Felder 129
  Patrick 34
  Thompson 3,8,14,30
  William 129
  William H. 34
Walls, Ophelia 61
Walshe, Mrs. Josephine 39
Walters, John 133
  Josephine 61
  Polly Ann Holmes 133
Wamble, Frank 37
Ward, James 108
  Lettetia 112,113
Warner, Daniel C. 80,136
  Laura Holmes 80,136
  Leta Graves 136
  Nancy 18
  Permelia Burch 136

Warner continued
  Saleta A. P. 106
  Saleta L. 136
  Tabitha 76
  Thos. C. 30,120
  Thomas Coulter 118
  Thomas G. 59
  Thomas R. E. 156
  Virgil Cornelius 136
  William Coulter 136
Warren, Addie E. 78
  Angeline 7
  Daniel R. 3
  Effie 110
  Emily 110
  G. W. 80
  James 110
  Jesse 110
  Jesse M. 70
  John 3,7,8,11,26,24
  John, Jr. 3
  Joseph 3,77
  Mary 110
  Priscilla 16
  Reuben 30
  Solomon 3
  Thomas 10,11,24,34
  Waterhouse, John I. 3
  Waters, Hester Ann 72
  Sue D. 72
  Urven 34
Watkins, Alfred L. 143
Watson, Ann 145
  Harrison 3
Watt, Alton 130
  Elva Hood 130
  Fannie 38
Weatherby, George W. 3
Weathersby, Dr. Hatten L.
  55
  Hinton C. 60
  Isham 3
  R. D. 63
Webb, Bertha Barnes 84
  Feliciana 62
  J. W. F. (Dr.) 39
  Nancy 17
  Nelson 63
  Olivia J. 59
  S. C. (Dr.) 84
  Sampson C., Jr. 84
  Sarah 17
Webber, Wilber Hoag 164
Weeks, Jas. 14
  John C. 13,14,24
  Wiley 14
  William 14,24
Weidmer, Frank 79
Weirauch, E. P. 38
Welch, Mrs. T. C. 56
Welcher, Duke W. 3
Wells, Corcus 160
  George 30,34
  John 3,10,13,24,30
  Nathaniel 3,8,13,24,30,
    34
  Rainer Emmett 157
West, James M. 146
  John Franklin 146
  Susan 61
  William 122
  William Causey 146
Westfall, Samuel 3
Westfield, Mary 100
Westmoreland, Catherine
  160
  Elizabeth 6,160
  George 160
  James 160
  Jesse 160
  John 159
  John, Jr. 157
  Lenoir 159
  Levunza 160

Westmoreland continued
  Louise 160
  Necia A. 160
  Noah 159
  Nancy 160
  Rachel 160
  Rose 143
  Sarah 160
  Thomas 159
  West 160
  William 160
Westrope, Della 144
  Gettie 144
  J. F. 144
  Mae 144
  Steletta 144
Whaley, George 10,34,49
Whaly, Jane 49
Wheat, Martha Ann 162
  William G. 142
Whitaker, E. Carolina S. 72
White, Bell 147
  Caroline Virginia 103
  Charles 10
  Delia 64
  Edward 14
  Fred. 14,24
  H. S. 34
  Henry H. 36
  J. M. 143
  John 11,34
  Nimrod 103
  Phoebe 155
  Robert 103
  Yancy 63
Whitehead, George W. 143
  Melissa Ann 99
Whitmore, Elizabeth 125
Whittington, Addie Bazzoon 80
  B. F. 80
  Catherine 50
  Evan 12,24,120
  Jason 139
  Joseph 59
  M. A. (Miss) 36
  Moses 34
  N. 50
  Noah 51
  Ollie Johnston 121
  Pamela Brumfield 139
  Seborn 34
  Thomas 45,121
Whorton, Susan 14
Wickes, Adam 24,30,34
  Andrew 24
  Andres (Est.) 30
  Enoch G. 30
Wigley, Jos. 24
  Moreton 30
Wilborne, Ebert 34
Wilcher, Duke 9
Wilkes, Samuel Warren 143
Wilkinson, William 106
Willey, Elciby 163
  John 163
  Lewis 163
  Martha 163
  Matilda 163
  Nancy A. 163
  Robert 159,163
  Stephen R. 163
  Susan 163
  Warren 163
  William A. 163
Williams, Abner Carter 152
  Ansalone D. 118
  Belton Betterly 152
  Cordelia M. 35
  Courtney Felder 71,128
  E. L. (Miss) 72
  E. P. 43

Williams continued
  Elisha 34
  Ernest Russ 144
  Evander Mortimer 152
  Floyd 13
  Henry 30
  Henry P. 69
  Herdenia Dee 152
  Hezekiah 30,34
  J. 65
  J. P. 36
  J. R. 39
  Jackson 71,128
  Jacob 12
  James 34,47,53
  Jas. D. 24
  James H. 85
  John 3,8,13,30,34,118
  John Dutsch 152
  John H. 118
  Judith 53
  Lillie Mae 152
  Lorenzo Dow 110
  Louisiana 43
  Lucinda L. 118
  Martin O. 152
  Martin Julius 152
  May 62,64
  Mary J. 118
  Morris M. 153
  Moses 30
  Mundy 106
  Nehemiah 10,34
  Parham 34
  Polly 76
  R. (Est.) 22
  Reubin 3,10,13
  Robert 12,25,30
  Robert Lee 152
  Robin 24
  S. B. (Capt.) 78
  Samuel 3,8,12,24,30
  Samuel, Jr. 30
  Samuel L. 118
  Sarah E. 118
  Susa (Susannah) 24,30
  Therzah Dale 85
  W. M. 30
  W. W. 62
  Walter Ernest 152
  William 10
  William Johnson 152
  Winney Stallings 118
  Zachariah 10
Williamson, Marie 64
Williford, John 3
Willingham, Tho. 24
Willis, Gertrude 108
  Peter 158
  William 141
Willoughby, Emily F. P. 76
  Norma G. Coney 115
  William 76
Wills, Benj. 24
Wilson, Amanda 36
  Arick 24
  Bruce 34
  Cullen C. 55
  John 11,24
  Joseph B. 65
  Lea 49
  Luke 116
  Napoleon 54
  R. S. 55
  Robert 13,24
  S. M. (Sister) 63
  Saline 47
  Samuel 13,24
  William 13,24
Wiltshire, Chas. 24
  Deek (Duke) 24
  Eula May 157
  Susana 106

Win, Mary 13
Winborne, B. F. 68
  David 24,30,126
  Hubart Ottaman 68
  Jeptha 34
  Jesse F. 34
  Nancy Felder 126
Winboro, H. 34
Winfrey, Eleanor 93
  Elizabeth 93
  Elizabeth Alford 93
  Jacob 93
  Jane 93
  Henry 93
Wingate, Edward 100
  Robert P. 100
  Salome E. 100
Winningham, Joseph 30
Woldredge, William 3
Wolfe, John P. 157
Womack, Abram 4
  Jacob 4
  Martha A. Kemp 164
Womble, B. F. 12(?)
Wood(s), Cordelia 61
  Jake 104
  John 3,10,11,15,24
  John R. 102
  Mary 143
  Mary Alford 93
  Morgan 112
  Robert 93
Woodale, William 10,15,24
Woodall, Isichiah 56
  Mary 56,146
Woodreff, Ailsey 34
Woodruff, Elias 25
Woodrough 30
Woodward, James 30,34
Wooley, A. C. 62
  Annie 63
  Elizabeth 51
  James 51
  Joseph W. 54
  Joshua 24
  Zachie 54
Wordley, Caleb 10
Wordsworth, Rev. Wm. 69
Wright, Absalom 110
  Capt. D. C. 77
  Katherine 113
  M. J. (Mrs.) 77
  Reuben 3
Wroten, Carrie Holmes 133
  DeWitt 87
  Elizabeth Quin 87
  Eloise 87
  John (Rev.) 59
  Kate 87
  Katie 39
  Lever 34
  Maggie 87
  Thomas 11,24,30,34
  V. J. (Dr.) 87
  Vincent (Dr.) 78
  Walter 133
  William 11
  William Monroe 87
Wurzer, Henry 126

Yandell, Dr. Henry 85
Yarborough, Elijah 66
  Jabez 83
  John 66,68
  Rebecca Clark 66
  Susan Lewis 83
  T. 80
Yates, W. S. 106
Yawn, Cullin 30
  Ellen Holmes 133
  Jesse 61,133
  Julia Belle 61
  Mary 61

Yawn continued
  Nicholas 9,25,30
Yeagher, David 30,34
Yelvington, Arlene 92
Yessenhoot, Abraham 124
Yopp, Nicholas 40
Young, Ann Elizabeth 102
  Derrell 13
  Franklin 30,36

Young continued
  Green 3
  Mattie 79
  Oswald W. 107
Youngblood, Adelia V. 73
  Benjamin 3,8
  George Henry 73
  Henry 3,30,73
  W. T. 73

Zachery, Benjamin 8,14
  Berry 30
  G. B. 34
  John 14,34
  Wiley 25
Zeagler, David 25
Zealy, Mrs. T. J. 62